The Study of Folklore

PRENTICE-HALL INTERNATIONAL, INC., *London*
PRENTICE-HALL OF AUSTRALIA, PTY., LTD., *Sydney*
PRENTICE-HALL OF CANADA, LTD., *Toronto*
PRENTICE-HALL OF INDIA (PRIVATE), LTD., *New Delhi*
PRENTICE-HALL OF JAPAN, INC., *Tokyo*

The Study of Folklore

Alan Dundes

*University
of
California
at
Berkeley*

Prentice-Hall, Inc., *Englewood Cliffs, N. J.*

© 1965 by Prentice-Hall, Inc., Englewood Cliffs, N. J.

Library of Congress Catalog Card Number: 65–22195

Printed in the United States of America [85894-C]

Preface

The teaching of folklore is definitely impeded by the extreme diversity of both the materials of folklore and the methods of studying these materials. Folklore's necessary liaisons with departments of literature on the one hand and departments of social science on the other make it difficult to survey the discipline with any degree of detail. What usually happens is that students who take folklore as an English course tend to think of the discipline as an adjunct to the study of literature, whereas students who take folklore as an anthropology course are convinced that folklore is a branch of cultural anthropology. Yet the discipline of folklore is an independent one. Although, like linguistics, it may be taught under the auspices of an English department in one university and an anthropology department in another, it constitutes a field of study of such scope as to require as much effort to master it as any of the other disciplines in the humanities and social sciences.

This anthology contains some of the important essays written on various facets and forms of folklore. Many of the papers were originally published in specialized journals, and consequently, are not readily available. An effort has been made to select representative essays from both the humanistic and the scientific studies of folklore. By this means, it should be possible for students of folklore to see the dimensions of folklore scholarship whether they take folklore as an English course or as an anthropology course. This anthology is not a systematic survey of the various genres or forms of folklore, nor does it provide coverage of the folklore of one culture, e.g., American folklore or Russian folklore. It is, however, designed to show the beginning folklore student something about what folklore is, how it might have originated, what some of its patterns are, how it is transmitted, how it functions, and finally, how folklorists study it.

A. D.

v

Acknowledgments

I thank all the authors, editors, and publishers who were kind enough to give their permission to reprint copyrighted materials. I am especially indebted to Jim Clark of Prentice-Hall who discovered and encouraged the project, to my wife Carolyn who helped me carry it to completion, to Mrs. Jeanne Poyntz Steager for her capable research assistance, and to Professor Francis Lee Utley for a critical reading of the manuscript.

Contents

What Is Folklore ? *1*

Folklore   4
WILLIAM THOMS

Folk Literature: An Operational Definition   7
FRANCIS LEE UTLEY

Folklore and Anthropology   25
WILLIAM R. BASCOM

Folklore and the Student of Literature   34
ARCHER TAYLOR

The Esoteric-Exoteric Factor in Folklore   43
WM. HUGH JANSEN

The Search for Origins *53*

The Eclipse of Solar Mythology   57
RICHARD M. DORSON

The Three Bears   84
E. D. PHILLIPS

Psychoanalysis and Folklore   88
ERNEST JONES

Jack and the Beanstalk   103
HUMPHREY HUMPHREYS

Jack and the Beanstalk   107
WILLIAM H. DESMONDE

Jack and the Beanstalk: An American Version   110
MARTHA WOLFENSTEIN

On the Symbolism of Oedipus   114
WILLIAM A. LESSA

Form in Folklore   *127*

Epic Laws of Folk Narrative   129
AXEL OLRIK

The Hero of Tradition   142
LORD RAGLAN

Recurrent Themes in Myths and Mythmaking   158
CLYDE KLUCKHOHN

Stability of Form in Traditional and Cultivated Music   169
GEORGE HERZOG

Unifying Factors in Folk and Primitive Music   175
BRUNO NETTL

Riddles in Bantu   182
P. D. BEUCHAT

Structural Typology in North American Indian Folktales   206
ALAN DUNDES

The Transmission of Folklore   *217*

Folktale Studies and Philology: Some Points of View   219
C. W. VON SYDOW

Some Experiments on the Reproduction of Folk Stories   243
F. C. BARTLETT

Some Cases of Repeated Reproduction   259
ROBERT H. LOWIE

Yugoslav Epic Folk Poetry   265
ALBERT B. LORD

The Cock and the Mouse   269
FRANK HAMILTON CUSHING

The Functions of Folklore *277*

Four Functions of Folklore   279
WILLIAM R. BASCOM

The Role of Proverbs in a Nigerian Judicial System   299
JOHN C. MESSENGER, JR.

Folksongs as Regulators of Politics   308
BETTY WANG

Changing Agricultural Magic in Southern Illinois:
A Systematic Analysis of Folk-Urban Transition   314
HERBERT PASSIN and JOHN W. BENNETT

The *It* Role in Children's Games   329
PAUL V. GUMP and BRIAN SUTTON-SMITH

Selected Studies of Folklore *337*

Some Notes on the Guessing Game, How Many Horns Has
the Buck?   338
PAUL G. BREWSTER

Tina's Lullaby   369
HUGH TRACEY

Origin and Significance of Pennsylvania Dutch Barn Symbols   373
AUGUST C. MAHR

Something About Simple Simon   400
HARRY B. WEISS

The Star Husband Tale   414
STITH THOMPSON

Suggestions for Further Reading in Folklore *475*

The Study of Folklore

What Is Folklore?

Debates about how folklore should be defined have been waged continuously ever since the word was coined in 1846 by William Thoms. Most definitions concern the "lore," but some concern the "folk." Lore—the materials of folklore rather than the people who use the materials—has been described in terms of origin, form, transmission, and function. However, there has been no widespread agreement among folklorists about what folklore is.

Not only do folklorists in different countries have different concepts of folklore, but also folklorists within one country may have quite diverse views concerning its nature. The twenty-one concise definitions contained in the first volume of the *Standard Dictionary of Folklore, Mythology, and Legend* reflect some of this diversity. Perhaps the most common criterion for definition is the means of the folklore's transmission. Specifically, folklore is said to be or to be *in* "oral tradition."

This criterion, however, leads to several theoretical difficulties. First, in a culture without writing (termed "nonliterate" cultures by anthropologists), almost everything is transmitted orally; and although language, hunting techniques, and marriage rules are passed orally from one generation to another, few folklorists would say that these types of cultural materials are folklore. Also, even in a culture with writing, some orally transmitted information such as how to drive a tractor and how to brush one's teeth is not ordinarily considered to be folklore. The point is that since materials other than folklore are also orally transmitted, the criterion of oral transmission *by itself* is not sufficient to distinguish folklore from non-folklore.

Second, there are some forms of folklore which are manifested and communicated almost exclusively in written as opposed to oral form, such as autograph-book verse, book marginalia, epitaphs, and traditional letters (e.g., chain letters). In actual practice, a professional folklorist does not go so far as to say that a folktale or a ballad is not folklore simply because it has at some time in its life history been transmitted by writing or print. But he would argue that if a folktale or ballad had *never* been in oral tradition, it is not folklore. It might be a literary production based upon a folk model, but this is not the same

1

as the folk model itself. However, the written forms previously mentioned are rarely if ever communicated orally.

The third difficulty with the criterion of oral transmission concerns
those forms of folklore depending upon body movements; that is, there
is some question as to whether folk dances, games, and gestures are
passed on *orally*. A child may acquire these forms by watching and
participating without necessarily being instructed verbally. The same
problem is found in folk art, as traditional symbols, like the swastika,
are not orally transmitted. It would thus appear that folklore is transmitted from individual to individual, often directly by word or act, but
sometimes indirectly, as when a folk artist copies a traditional design
from the finished product of another artist with whom he may have had
little or no personal contact.

Definitions of folklore based upon the folk rather than the lore are
more rare but no more satisfactory. There are still some folklorists who
mistakenly identify the folk with peasant society or rural groups. If one
were to accept this narrow conception of folk, then by definition one
would have to conclude that city dwellers were not folk and hence city
dwellers could have no folklore. An equally fallacious view is that
folklore was produced by a folk in the hoary past and the folklore still
extant today consists solely of fragmentary survivals. According to this
incorrect view, the folk of today produce no new folklore; rather, contemporary folk are forgetting more and more folklore, and soon folklore will have died out completely.

It is possible, however, to define both folk and lore in such a way
than even the beginner can understand what folklore is. The term
"folk" can refer to *any group of people whatsoever* who share at least
one common factor. It does not matter what the linking factor is—it
could be a common occupation, language, or religion—but what is
important is that a group formed for whatever reason will have some
traditions which it calls its own. In theory a group must consist of at
least two persons, but generally most groups consist of many individuals. A member of the group may not know all other members, but
he will probably know the common core of traditions belonging to the
group, traditions which help the group have a sense of group identity.
Thus if the group were composed of lumberjacks or railroadmen, then
the folklore would be lumberjack or railroadman folklore. If the group
were composed of Jews or Negroes, then the folklorist could seek
Jewish or Negro folklore. Even a military unit or a college community
is a folk. In the latter instance, there are many customs (e.g., fraternity
pranks and initiation rituals), stories (e.g., about dumb athletes, absent-
minded professors, and difficult deans), and songs about college life.
Probably the smallest group would be an individual family, whose traditions often include sayings and such items as a family whistle (to call
or locate a family member lost in a crowd). Often competent investigation can show that these individual family traditions (which a family
may insist are its very own, unknown to anyone outside the family) are

found among many families and sometimes even among many peoples of the world. The family tradition for disposing of a child's baby teeth (by means of a good fairy, tooth fairy, or fairy mouse) is an example of an international family custom.

It is because of this kind of definition of folk that the professional folklorist is interested in collecting folklore from Australian aborigines and American Indians on the one hand and from labor unions and American primary school children on the other. Every group has its own folklore. But the question remains, what is folklore?

Although it may not be entirely satisfactory, a definition consisting of an itemized list of the forms of folklore might be the best type for the beginner. Of course, for this definition to be complete, each form would have to be individually defined. Unfortunately, some of the major forms, such as myth and folktale, require almost book-length definitions, but the following list may be of some help. Folklore includes myths, legends, folktales, jokes, proverbs, riddles, chants, charms, blessings, curses, oaths, insults, retorts, taunts, teases, toasts, tongue-twisters, and greeting and leave-taking formulas (e.g., See you later, alligator). It also includes folk costume, folk dance, folk drama (and mime), folk art, folk belief (or superstition), folk medicine, folk instrumental music (e.g., fiddle tunes), folksongs (e.g., lullabies, ballads), folk speech (e.g., slang), folk similes (e.g., as blind as a bat), folk metaphors (e.g., to paint the town red), and names (e.g., nicknames and place names). Folk poetry ranges from oral epics to autograph-book verse, epitaphs, latrinalia (writings on the walls of public bathrooms), limericks, ball-bouncing rhymes, jump-rope rhymes, finger and toe rhymes, dandling rhymes (to bounce children on the knee), counting-out rhymes (to determine who will be "it" in games), and nursery rhymes. The list of folklore forms also contains games; gestures; symbols; prayers (e.g., graces); practical jokes; folk etymologies; food recipes; quilt and embroidery designs; house, barn, and fence types; street vendor's cries; and even the traditional conventional sounds used to summon animals or to give them commands. There are such minor forms as mnemonic devices (e.g., the name Roy G. Biv to remember the colors of the spectrum in order), envelope sealers (e.g., SWAK—Sealed With A Kiss), and the traditional comments made after body emissions (e.g., after burps or sneezes). There are such major forms as festivals and special day (or holiday) customs (e.g., Christmas, Halloween, and birthday).

This list provides a sampling of the forms of folklore. It does not include all the forms. These materials and the study of them are both referred to as folklore. To avoid confusion it might be better to use the term *folklore* for the materials and the term *folkloristics* for the study of the materials. Both the definition of the materials and the discipline should become clearer as the relationships between the study of folklore and the study of literature and anthropology are discussed in the following essays.

Folklore

William Thoms

Although folklore is probably as old as mankind, the term "folklore" is of comparatively recent origin. In 1846 William Thoms, using the name Ambrose Merton, wrote a letter to *The Athenaeum* in which he proposed that a "good Saxon compound, Folklore," be employed in place of such labels as Popular Antiquities and Popular Literature. Noteworthy is Thoms' conception of folklore and his essentially enumerative definition: manners, customs, observances, superstitions, ballads, proverbs, and so forth.

Readers are cautioned against attributing any special significance to the date of Thoms' letter, for the materials of folklore had been studied with rigor long before. An obvious example is the work of the Grimm brothers whose "household tales" first appeared in 1812. During the middle and later portions of the nineteenth century, however, the discipline of folklore as it has developed in the twentieth century began to appear. The increasing awareness of folklore was closely associated with nineteenth-century intellectual currents of romanticism and nationalism. The glorification of the common man included a nostalgic interest in his speech and manners which were believed to be dying out. Thoms' phrases, "neglected custom," "fading legend," and "fragmentary ballad," reflect this view. There is more than a hint of nationalism in the very idea of suggesting that a "good Saxon compound" be used to designate the lore of a people. For an evaluation of Thoms' influence upon the discipline of folklore, see Duncan Emrich, " 'Folklore': William John Thoms," *California Folklore Quarterly,* Vol. 5 (1946), 355–74.

August 12

Your pages have so often given evidence of the interest which you take in what we in England designate as Popular Antiquities, or Popular Literature (though by-the-bye it is more a Lore than a Literature, and would be most

Reprinted from *The Athenaeum,* No. 982 (August 22, 1846), 862–63.

aptly described by a good Saxon compound, Folklore,—*the Lore of the People*)—that I am not without hopes of enlisting your aid in garnering the few ears which are remaining, scattered over that field from which our fore-fathers might have gathered a goodly crop.

No one who has made the manners, customs, observances, superstitions, ballads, proverbs, etc., of the olden time his study, but must have arrived at two conclusions:—the first, how much that is curious and interesting in these matters is now entirely lost—the second, how much may yet be rescued by timely exertion. What Hone endeavoured to do in his "Everyday Book," etc., *The Athenaeum,* by its wider circulation, may accomplish ten times more effectually—gather together the infinite number of minute facts, illustrative of the subject I have mentioned, which are scattered over the memories of its thousands of readers, and preserve them in its pages, until some James Grimm shall arise who shall do for the Mythology of the British Islands the good service which that profound antiquary and philologist has accomplished for the Mythology of Germany. The present century has scarcely produced a more remarkable book, imperfect as its learned author confesses it to be, than the second edition of the *"Deutsche Mythologie:"* and, what is it?—a mass of minute facts, many of which, when separately considered, appear trifling and insignificant,—but, when taken in connection with the system into which his master-mind has woven them, assume a value that he who first recorded them never dreamed of attributing to them.

How many such facts would one word from you evoke, from the north and from the south—from John o'Groat's to the Land's End! How many readers would be glad to show their gratitude for the novelties which you, from week to week, communicate to them, by forwarding to you some record of old Time—some recollection of a now neglected custom—some fading legend, local tradition, or fragmentary ballad!

Nor would such communications be of service to the English antiquary alone. The connection between the *folklore* of England (remember I claim the honor of introducing the epithet Folklore, as Disraeli does of introducing Fatherland, into the literature of this country) and that of Germany is so intimate that such communications will probably serve to enrich some future edition of Grimm's Mythology.

Let me give you an instance of this connection.—In one of the chapters of Grimm, he treats very fully of the parts which the Cuckoo plays in Popular Mythology—of the prophetic character with which it has been invested by the voice of the people; and gives many instances of the practice of deriving predictions from the number of times which its song is heard. He also records a popular notion, "that the Cuckoo never sings till he has thrice eaten his fill of cherries." Now, I have lately been informed of a custom which formerly obtained among children in Yorkshire, that illustrates the fact of a connection between the Cuckoo and the Cherry,—and that, too, in their prophetic attributes. A friend has communicated to me that children in Yorkshire were formerly (and may be still) accustomed to sing round a cherry-tree the following invocation:—

> Cuckoo, Cherry-tree,
> Come down and tell me
> How many years I have to live.

Each child then shook the tree,—and the number of cherries which fell betokened the years of its future life.

The Nursery Rhyme which I have quoted, is, I am aware, well known. But the manner in which it was applied is not recorded by Hone, Brand, or Ellis:[1] and is one of those facts, which, trifling in themselves, become of importance when they form links in a great chain—one of those facts which a word from *The Athenaeum* would gather in abundance for the use of future inquirers into that interesting branch of literary antiquities,—our Folklore.

Ambrose Merton

P.S.—It is only honest that I should tell you I have long been contemplating a work upon our *"Folklore"* (under *that title,* mind Messrs. A, B, and C,—so do not try to forestall me);—and I am personally interested in the success of the experiment which I have, in this letter, albeit imperfectly, urged you to undertake.

---

[1] Thoms refers to William Hone (1780–1842) and his *The Everyday Book and Table Book,* 3 vols. (London, 1831); John Brand (1744–1806) whose *Observations on Popular Antiquities* (London, 1777) was a revision of an earlier work of Henry Bourne (1696–1733)—Bourne's collection was *Antiquitates vulgares; or the Antiquities of the Common People,* and it appeared in 1725; and Henry Ellis (1777–1869) who revised Brand's work and republished *Observations on Popular Antiquities* in 1813. For further examples of the cuckoo custom mentioned by Thoms, see James Hardy, "Popular History of the Cuckoo," *Folklore Record,* Vol. 2 (1879), 47–91; Charles Swainson, *The Folklore and Provincial Names of British Birds* (London, 1886), pp. 115–16; and E. Hoffmann-Krayer and Hanns Bächtold-Stäubli, *Handwörterbuch des deutschen Aberglaubens,* Vol. 5 (Berlin and Leipzig, 1932), 714–16. The latter reference is part of a ten-volume work which is perhaps one of the finest compendiums of superstition and custom ever assembled.—ED. NOTE

Folk Literature:
An Operational Definition

Francis Lee Utley

The reader may wish to refer to the twenty-one definitions of folklore in Maria Leach's *Standard Dictionary of Folklore, Mythology, and Legend* before reading this essay by a leading literary folklorist. Utley, who is a professor of English at Ohio State University, tries to arrive at an operational definition of folk literature. (Folk literature is of course only one part of folklore.) Professor Utley tends to exclude custom and superstition from consideration, although he does so reluctantly. In one sense Utley's definition is completely traditional, as it relies heavily upon the criterion of oral transmission.

This paper will first discuss two ways of defining folklore and folk literature, the authoritative and the theoretical, and then concentrate on one more germane to the purpose of serious students, humanists, and anthropologists, the operational.

I

In seeking a consensus of prior scholars, there is some value in using the semantic approach of Richards and Ogden in their *Meaning of Meaning*.[1] Their technique with abstract words like "meaning" or "beauty" is to list prior definitions by authorities or informed writers and then to isolate or classify the varying and conflicting kernels of signification before, as Ogden and Richards usually do, making up one's own mind. The value of such a method does not consist in a mere statistical show of hands but in the possible isolation of some kind of common agreement which may gain acceptance for a later theoretical or operational definition. For our Richardsian approach we

Reprinted from the *Journal of American Folklore*, Vol. 74 (1961), 193–206, by permission of the author and the American Folklore Society.

[1] New York: Harcourt, Brace & World, Inc., 1927. This paper is a revision of one read at the joint meeting of the American Folklore Society, the Central States Anthropological Association, and the American Musicological Society at Bloomington, Indiana, April 1960. It has benefited from the discussion from the floor and subsequent conversation, especially with D. K. Wilgus.

have the famous twenty-one definitions (all by American scholars) in Maria
Leach's *Dictionary*[2] lying ripe and ready to hand. They are said to be
evidence of the chaos in the minds of practising folklorists about the subject
of their so-called science. Is there, perhaps, a common kernel after all?

I present the abbreviated results of my analysis. In the first place I have
sought for key words which might find their place in an austere common
definition. These words are *oral, transmission, tradition, survival,* and *communal*. Only one, *tradition*, appears unblushingly in thirteen of the twenty-
one. The word *oral* is not itself too common, but its synonyms, "spoken,"
"verbal," "unwritten," "not written," appear explicitly in thirteen and
implicitly once. The others are less common. *Transmission* appears only six
times (twice as "handed down"); since the process of oral transmission is so
central to folklore we may perhaps assume that it is merely a synonym for
tradition. *Survival* and *communal* are more controversial words. In six definitions *survival* as a concept appears in some form—usually as the relatively
colorless or neutral "superstition," or as "preserved" or "fossil."[3] The word
itself is used only twice by a believer in the doctrine (Mish and Potter). But
it or its equivalent is used three additional times by positive opponents of the
doctrine: Botkin, who says revival is as important as survival; Herskovits,
the most outspoken enemy of "survivals"; and Erminie Wheeler-Voegelin,
who speaks of "the outmoded term, superstition."[4] The word *communal* is
used only twice, by Gertrude Kurath ("a communal product") and by
Archer Taylor ("communal recreation").[5] It may be assumed that these two
sound folklorists use it as a sign of a process rather than as a theory of
origins. But the communal theory still apparently remains alive under the
name *group*, which six of the definers use.[6] The terms "collective" and the
"laboring many" used by Botkin, "group," "people," and "general currency"
used by Theodor Gaster, and "racial unconscious" used by Potter reflect
individualistic alignments—Botkin as a collectivist, Gaster as a ritualist, and
Potter as a psychoanalyst or Jungian. No sharp criticism is intended—one
assumes that any of these three might wish to reconsider their views in the
light of ten years' passage of time.

So much for key words; now for content analysis. At least fourteen of the
definers positively agree that folklore includes material from both "primitive"
tribes and from subcultures in civilized society. The point seems implicit in

[2] *Funk & Wagnalls Standard Dictionary of Folklore, Mythology, and Legend,* Vol. 1
(New York, 1949), 398–403.
[3] Balys, Espinosa, Gaster, Kurath, Mish, and Potter. For some very pertinent remarks
on survivals, which he rejects without accepting *in toto* the views of Herskovits and
other anthropologists, see Samuel P. Bayard, "The Materials of Folklore," *Journal of
American Folklore,* Vol. 66 (1953), 1–17.
[4] Barbeau, Botkin, Harmon, and Leach emphasize the living process, whereas Kurath
believes that it has lost its function and that *revival* in folksong is not folklore.
[5] On "communal recreation" see D. K. Wilgus, *Anglo-American Folksong Scholarship
Since 1898* (New Brunswick, N.J.: Rutgers University Press, 1959), p. 284.
[6] Four specifically mention *individual* creators of folklore: Botkin, Harmon, Leach,
and Taylor (the last only to deny authority to individual ascription).

at least six more, which is virtual unanimity.[7] Quite as important are the various materials of folklore: (1) literature and the other arts; (2) beliefs, customs, and rites; (3) crafts like weaving and the mode of stacking hay; and (4) language or folk speech. Eighteen include literature; twelve include beliefs but four explicitly exclude them; five include crafts and four exclude them;[8] and only three, Botkin, Taylor, and Herzog, include language. Since the use of the term *folklore* primarily to mean unwritten literature, with beliefs and crafts relegated to the broader rubric of ethnography, is that advocated by most American anthropologists, it is well to note that eight definers take the "anthropological view."[9] Botkin somewhat capriciously reverses this view with the statement that "in a purely oral culture everything is folklore." Eight believe that methodology rather than content is the essence of the affair,[10] whereas Balys argues that content is more important: "folklore is not a science about a folk, but the traditional folk science and folk poetry."[11]

Three other matters deserve brief mention. The problem of origins, which bulked so large in earlier definitions, has virtually disappeared—it is mentioned even casually only by Gaster, Harmon, Leach, and Potter. The identification of folklore with prejudice or bad science, beloved of editorialists and other unenlightened heirs of the so-called enlightenment, is referred to with qualification by another four, Botkin, Espinosa, Potter, and Harmon. Only three say anything about folklore and the mass media, a problem increasingly of our time though surely present in 1949; this subject is rapidly approaching the dimensions of a separate discipline.[12] Botkin, always the individualist, includes the products of mass culture among those of folklore, but Barbeau

---

[7] Four (Espinosa, Herzog, Kurath, and Luomala) consider folklore in civilized society to be mainly rural. Compare the works of Redfield mentioned in note 40 and Sigurd Erixon, "Ethnologie régionale ou folklore," *Laos,* Vol. 1 (1951), 11.

[8] Literature is included by Balys, Barbeau, Bascom, Espinosa, Gaster, Herskovits, Herzog, Jameson, Kurath, MacEdward Leach, Luomala, Mish, Potter, Smith, Taylor, Thompson, Wheeler-Voegelin, and Waterman (omitted from specific mention but not excluded by Botkin, Foster, and Harmon); beliefs are included by Balys, Barbeau, Espinosa, Gaster, Jameson, Kurath, Leach, Mish, Potter, Smith, Taylor, Thompson and excluded by Foster, Herskovits, Luomala, and Wheeler-Voegelin; crafts are included by Barbeau, Gaster, Mish, Taylor, and Thompson and excluded by Harmon, Herskovits, Herzog, and Wheeler-Voegelin.

[9] Barbeau, Bascom, Herskovits, Herzog, Jameson, Smith, Wheeler-Voegelin, and Waterman.

[10] Espinosa, Foster, Herskovits, Jameson, Potter, Smith, Taylor, and Thompson. Bayard (*op. cit.,* p. 6), who argues in part from this series of definitions, is strongly opposed to methodology as the defining criterion.

[11] Balys like several others is presumably concerned about the ambiguous use of the term *folklore* for both the science and its subject matter.

[12] See, for instance, Bernard Rosenberg and David M. White, *Mass Culture: The Popular Arts in America* (New York: Free Press of Glencoe, Inc., 1957) and various works by Father William Lynch, Marshall McLuhan, Gilbert Seldes, Richard Hoggart, Reuel Denney, and others. For a related problem see Margaret Lantis, "Vernacular Culture," *American Anthropologist,* Vol. 62 (1960), 202–16; and for an early anticipation of the subject, Robert Redfield, *Tepoztlan: A Mexican Village* (Chicago: University of Chicago Press, 1930), pp. 5–9.

and Harmon explicitly reject such products. Barbeau states flatly that folk-lore "is the born opponent of the serial number, the stamped product, and the patented standard," and Harmon remarks that "anything which tends to break down the cohesion of a group—communications, diversity of knowl-edge, specialization, etc.—tends to scatter its folklore."

Thus the statistical weight of authority is for the exclusion of bad science, mass culture, survival, communal, and matters of origin, and for the inclusion of *oral* (*verbal, unwritten*), *tradition* (*transmission*), primitive culture, and the subcultures of civilized society both rural and urban. As for the materials of folklore, art and literature are a clearly unanimous choice, custom and belief win the suffrage of about half of the definers, and crafts and language are generally excluded.[13]

II

Our second approach is the theoretical. Presumably we must accept the common tendency to use the term *folklore* to describe both the subject matter and the method, though we can always be more explicit and say "folklore science" when we mean the latter. We are still at the mercy of those who confuse our scientific interests with our personal beliefs—if Kluckhohn says that witchcraft is effective among the believing Navaho the positivist will accuse him of believing in it himself. There is no way out of this dilemma but continued refinement of the science to the point where the public is educated and no confusion is possible. This may be utopian— probably the insistence on the distinction is the true mark of the serious student.[14] He cannot control the common uses, except by long, patient, and nondoctrinal teaching, and by a rigid exclusion of such meanings as might give him a personal interest in the subject matter beyond that a physician has in disease, an art historian in painting, or a physicist in nuclear fission. The folklorist must control rigidly the printed medium which is his tool of expression in order not to create folklore himself.

---

13 It must be emphasized that this has been a canvass of *American* folklorists and anthropologists. Raffaele Corso, using the European definition of *folkliv* or *Volkskunde* ("science etnographique du vulgaire") as base, would include craft and custom but exclude the ethnography of primitive tribes. See his "La coordination des différents points de vue du folklore," *Laos,* Vol. 1 (1951), 20–27. On the European-American divergence see Bayard, p. 2, and Robert Redfield, *Peasant Society and Culture* (Chicago: University of Chicago Press, 1956), p. 78.

14 For a similar semantic problem see Walter Lippman, *Public Opinion* (New York: Penguin Books, Inc., 1946), p. 61: "Dewey gives an example of how differently an experi-enced layman and a chemist might define the word metal. 'Smoothness, hardness, glossiness, and brilliancy, heavy weight for its size...the serviceable properties of capacity for being hammered and pulled without breaking, of being softened by heat and hardened by cold, of retaining the shape and form given, of resistance to pressure and decay, would probably be included' in the layman's definition. But the chemist would likely as not ignore these esthetic and utilitarian qualities, and define a metal as 'any chemical element that enters into combination with oxygen so as to form a base.'"

Our theoretical approach would be easier if we could accept the American anthropological definition, and define folklore as "art and literature orally transmitted," excluding custom, belief, crafts, and language. In 1953 William Bascom tried this:

> Folklore, to the anthropologist, is a part of culture but not the whole of culture. It includes myths, legends, tales, proverbs, riddles, the texts of ballads and other songs, and other forms of lesser importance, but not folk art, folk dance, folk music, folk costume, folk medicine, folk custom, or folk belief. All of these are unquestionably worthy of study, whether in literate or nonliterate societies. . . . All folklore is orally transmitted, but not all that is orally transmitted is folklore.[15]

In the same year Samuel P. Bayard published what looks like an answer to Bascom,[16] though it is apparent that he had not seen Bascom's article, for his major arguments are directed at the twenty-one definitions we have been analyzing. He considers methodological trends no valid basis of definition and denies that "in theory or operation" traditional belief and custom are to be separated from folk literature. His materials of folklore are "the mythopoeic, philosophic, and esthetic mental world of nonliterate—or formally untrained—or unschooled—or nonlearned—or scientifically uninstructed—or close-to-nature folk everywhere," but they are "not necessarily confined to the uncultured or uninstructed groups of a civilized society." Excluded are linguistics per se, crafts unconnected with ritual, and nontraditional politics. "The primary materials of folklore must be certain categories of creative ideas which have become traditional among the people of any society and which may be recognized as their common property." Such ideas are those relating to the universe; the supernatural; wisdom; heroism, beauty, desirability, and propriety and their opposites. Recognizing that such matters may also be the subject of theology, philosophy, aesthetics, and ethics, he provides an inductive list of a number of typical folkloristic items like "evil eye, sign of the horns, animal helper," or mourning black. Bayard speaks with the conviction of a perceptive fieldworker and student of theory, but inductive lists are pretty much what any lister will make of them. The gravest difficulty with his choice of a definition by content rather than by method or process is that he leaves little creativity for what Robert Redfield would call "the great tradition" as opposed to "the little tradition."[17] Certainly there is contact between the two traditions of the dominant society and the various varieties of "folk," but folklorists cannot abandon the field of traditional morals,

---

[15] "Folklore and Anthropology," *Journal of American Folklore*, Vol. 66 (1953), 283–90; see also "Four Functions of Folklore," *Journal of American Folklore*, Vol. 67 (1954), 333–49. [Both these articles are reprinted in this volume.—ED. NOTE]

[16] "The Materials of Folklore," *Journal of American Folklore*, Vol. 66 (1953), 1–17. Bascom is involved only as being one of the twenty-one definers in Leach's *Dictionary*. I am myself to some extent inculpated by capitulating to the anthropologists in "Anthropology and Folklore's Second Century," *Hoosier Folklore*, Vol. 8 (1949), 69–78.

[17] *Peasant Society and Culture*, p. 78.

cosmology, and aesthetics wholly to the "little tradition." This would be to identify ourselves romantically with our subject matter and to reject our debt to the written culture which has provided us with the techniques by which we study folklore itself.

Bascom accepted Bayard's article as essentially an answer to his own, and in 1955 wrote a gracious retraction, accepting the charge that he had been unfair to non-anthropological definitions.[18] He seems not to have realized how the weight of his fellow twenty-one definers favored his own view. Still seeking for a term to distinguish folktales, proverbs, and riddles from custom, belief, and ritual he coined the phrase "verbal art" for the former group. This leaves music in an undefined region, though Bascom admits that verbal art has its parallel in musical improvisation and perhaps in "traditional, unwritten music." One suspects that the danger of the exclusion of music was a grave concern to Bayard as a devoted student of Pennsylvania hill melodies.[19] Bascom's problem is also clear—whatever the province of folktale or proverb in a folk society, the music of chant and dance is so intimately connected with ritual that it seems to belong to a larger order than "verbal art." Yet, recognizing that scientific categories are always something less than perfect equivalences of the immediate reality, we may say first that analysis of a primitive culture can place music in both the categories of folklore or verbal art and of craft and ritual, and second that music in a Western subculture is essentially transmitted as "verbal art," though it too, as in Jackson's White Spirituals or in the college hymn sung in a football stadium, may have ritualistic overtones. That there is a functional shift of roles between literate and nonliterate societies should not be news to an anthropologist.

I have no quarrel with Bascom, though I think he did, through a courteous desire not to favor anthropology over "humanistic" folklore, abandon the field too quickly to Bayard. At the time I told him privately that "the anthropologist's way of pigeonholing is a satisfactory one," and added that "all a definition can do is help us to work better; nature has no fixed categories unless one is a Platonist."

To get away from inductionist or idealist debates we might touch briefly on one promising theoretical approach, the formal one. We might for the first stage of a testing hypothesis accept the limitation to verbal art and then examine the aesthetic forms themselves. Anything then which has aesthetic form and is man-made—a folksong, a riddle, a proverb, a folktale, or one of Thomas Sebeok's Cheremis charms, will then belong, while anything which lacks it will be alien. Physical artifacts like rugs and pottery perhaps may be excluded on the grounds that they are not verbal art. A belief or superstition, when couched in the finer organization of aesthetic structure, like "Red sky at night, Sailor's delight," can thus find its place in the definition. An interesting

---

[18] "Verbal Art," *Journal of American Folklore,* Vol. 68 (1955), 245–52. See some comments on the difficulties of the term "verbal art" by Marian W. Smith, "The Importance of Folklore Studies to Anthropology," *Folklore,* Vol. 70 (1959), 306–7.

[19] Bayard, *op. cit.,* pp. 4, 11.

formal distinction, for instance, might lie between two kinds of jest, the sophisticated joke with a "punch line" and the narrative jest revolving around action more common in the Aarne-Thompson type index. Perhaps the punch line tells us we have a wholly different genre. In the memory of the sophisticated teller the punch line is the kernel out of which on various occasions the story is constructed, whereas the true folkteller carries his jest as he carries his *Märchen,* in a longer configuration including style and diction and set episode. But if the punch lines are transmitted only orally, as they are with the obscene tale, we may still have our distinction break down. Much more study is needed if a set of formal criteria for folk literature is to be set up which will distinguish new data from sophisticated literature.

Theory, essentially, breaks down on the basis of the difficulty of defining either "folk" or "tradition." Tradition may be to T. S. Eliot literary convention of the most sophisticated type, or it may be Ozark folksong. The only unimpugnable definition of "folk" I know is Redfield's "a group which has folklore and folk songs."[20] We must, therefore, turn away from a priori definitions to a study of operational procedures, which takes account of folk literature and folk art.

III

Bayard recognized the value of an "operational" definition,[21] though his own expansive one might have better suited that term if he had narrowed it to his well-controlled special field of folk music. Despairing of ever defining for certain the larger rubric of folklore, I will now confine myself to the circumscribed area of folk literature, music, and art, to see what assurances it may bring us. We will not arbitrarily exclude custom and belief and craft from the matrix of the aesthetic, but merely say that some of us find it easier to work with the folktale, the ballad, the dance, and the song. Perhaps when the results of the energetic work of Wayland Hand and Newbell Puckett are in we shall know better what to do about the place of "superstition"—up to now the gravest difficulty with that subject has been its lack of accurate documentation. Perhaps we may say that as the function of music shifts from the primitive isolated culture to the civilized subculture, the place of some kinds of culture and belief shifts as well and hence demands special treatment. We can never deny the functioning value of knocking on wood, even though we may hold a different view of why we do so than our ancestors did. Like Sophocles, we have intellectualized and rationalized the *hubris.*

For my own operation I will stand by the very simple statement that folk literature is orally transmitted literature wherever found, among primitive isolates or civilized marginal cultures, urban or rural societies, dominant or subordinate groups. The heuristic value of "orally transmitted," our key phrase, is great. Methodologically, if we are to define a folk category which

---

[20] *Tepoztlan,* p. 2. One could object to the term "folklore" unless one understands it, as Redfield appears to do, in the anthropological sense of literature and art.

[21] *Op. cit.,* p. 7.

stands by itself and has meaning, we must subject every document to the test of authenticity in the matrix of oral process. The definition must be as rigorous as that of the historian, who subjects his charters and annals and memoirs to the most searching textual and contextual criticism. It must be as rigorous as that of the descriptive linguist, who finds that he must continually re-examine language in the light of the most recent techniques of recording, and subject the written records of Gothic and Old English and Sanskrit to the major query—do they tell us what we need to know?

The only trustworthy kind of folk literature is that collected under conditions which give such information about the immediate informant as enables us to check his claim to be a bearer of oral tradition—John Jones, in Elmira County, New York, aged 75, who learned his tale from his grandmother, born in 1830 in Wales or Massachusetts. It is better, of course, to have more than this—the full biography of a Siberian taleteller like Mark Azadovsky's Vinokurova[22] or the Lomaxes' Huddie Ledbetter. But for comparative studies the shorter biography is enough. As we gather folktales for cultural comparison and the construction of a life history we face with each individual item a crucial question. Can we be sure we have a genuine folktale and not one of several things that look, to the unwary, much like it: a literary invention out of whole cloth or a literary retelling by a popularizing writer, a careless collector, an expurgating guardian of the morals of children, an author rewriting for religious, political, or commercial reasons, a genius like Scott or Percy or Mark Twain or Chaucer? There is nothing to tell us but the presence of John Jones aged 75 who learned the tale from his grandmother—the mark that the collector knew the operational problem and tried to meet it. Even if the collector is a popularizer, a writer of juveniles, or a genius, he may be kind enough, if we remain friendly with him, to inform us where in an archive or a private collection the accurate version may be, so that we may push the search back to the source we need. A tale in print or in manuscript may be wholly authentic, but if it is not accompanied by our old friend John Jones it cannot be wholly trusted and must be classified among either the doubtful or the literary versions.

One more problem of rigor. How far can we trust John Jones himself? Who is to say that he did not get the tale or song from print, radio, phonograph record, or even from the collector (as often happens when you join, like fire and tinder, a Child ballad and an untrained fieldworker)? On the whole we will have to trust John Jones, though if the collector has gathered a large enough corpus and a full enough biography from him, we can check any tendency on his part to be fraudulent. Anna Birgitta Rooth, for instance, has recently given me valuable warnings about one garrulous and eager

---

22 *Eine siberische Märchenerzählerin* (Helsinki [FFC 68], 1926). Despite his nineteenth-century antecedents George Lyman Kittredge saw the point of biography in his instructions to John Lomax in 1908, not always heeded. See Wilgus, *op. cit.*, p. 160, and for John Harrington Cox, another major collector who failed in the same ideal, see p. 194.

Lund informant who tended to be too anxious to earn his fee.[23] Ideally, I think, a persistence of some three generations would be attested, though we may have to be content with "he got it from his mother." One is not here concerned with ultimate origins—whether the story comes from Perrault's "Cinderella" or Southey's "Three Bears." Print is a contaminator, a reverser and freezer of versions, but it does not necessarily destroy the oral process, which is a very vigorous kind of growth. A printed version does not impugn the oral process; it only impugns itself. So long as the story has had some oral currency we have a folktale, though a refined criticism will take account of the varying kinds of evidence. Our rigor, using modern and authenticated tales, must face up to the fact that the kind of record we want is not much older than the Grimms.

Now let us consider some of the implications of the view that folk literature is simply "literature transmitted orally." Most of us in America who are not anthropologists studying the American Indian find that a great many of our basic versions are either nineteenth-century American or pre-Basile medieval European documents. One reason we envy the Indianist, and should at times work for practice with his materials, is that in spite of Longfellow and a few careless anthologists, the bulk of his folktales are authentically collected in a genuine cultural context. Of our own early American and medieval documents we must ask whether they are folktales in the strict sense even when they fit the motifs and episodes of a well-known tale type. The answer is usually no—most such tales, whether by Longstreet or Chaucer or an anonymous medieval writer of fabliaux or exempla, are literary versions. We may even generalize to the extent of saying that we *know* no medieval folklore, or no American folklore before the end of the nineteenth century. In Europe, where careful collecting began earlier, we may hark back a century or two, though we must always be on our guard against rewriting. In the Middle East we have vast repositories, like the *Arabian Nights* and the *Midrash Rabbah,* which certainly have some connection with folklore, but which bear always the marks of artistic handling.

Richard Dorson, who in his *American Folklore*[24] must fill out the earlier picture with much material not recorded under perfect conditions, is aware of the problem, though the nature of his book makes it impossible to use the rigor I am urging. He reports a tale, "How Sandusky Was Saved from Famine" from the *Norwalk* (Ohio) *Experiment* for 27 January 1857, credited there not to a folk teller but to the *Buffalo Republic.*[25] Hogs blinded by sand each take the tail of the one ahead into their mouths, and a Sanduskian, seeing the long procession, shoots the leader's tail in two and grasping the remnant leads the rest of the hogs to town like a train of cars to feed his

[23] F. L. Utley, "Some Noah Tales from Sweden," *Humaniora: Essays...Honoring Archer Taylor* (New York: J. J. Augustin, 1960), pp. 258–69.

[24] Chicago: University of Chicago Press, 1959.

[25] Pages 52–53.

fellow-citizens. Dorson authenticates the newspaper version by noting its international occurrence and by citing variants he has collected in northern Michigan and Maine. Now this authentication has to be critically examined. It demonstrates that we have no mere isolated local legend of independent origin and that the newspaper story has some connection with folktale reality. But it does not ensure that the text is not garbled, distorted, or "improved." Dorson shows his awareness of this point a few pages later, where he says that "a folklorist can identify a good many twice-told tales among the thousands of stories in the *Spirit* [*of the Times*] and the [*Yankee*] *Blade*, although he must tread warily, for an observed incident, a created piece, or a traveled folktale is written in the same form and style."[26] One must add that if we are ever to be sure of what is authentic folk form and style, our analytical corpus must be chosen with the care I have been urging.

The same problem arises with medieval "folklore." Despite Wesselski's valiant attempt to track the medieval *Märchen* to its lair, we must concede that all or most of the evidence is of versions which cannot be trusted as clear cases of oral transmission. The perennial problem has been raised once more in a significant article by Roger Loomis,[27] who criticizes certain Arthurian scholars who have drawn doubtful conclusions from the medieval documents. I have argued elsewhere[28] that this criticism is correct, but that the folklorist must go one step farther. He is right in assuming that the present evidence makes it impossible to assign Arthurian motifs to strict folktale sources, and right further in saying that modern Arthurian place-names and legends associated with them are not conclusive, since, like similar echoes of Gargantua in France, there is no assurance that the Arthurian romances or the works of Rabelais are not the sources of the modern legends. The scanty medieval evidence about local legends is worth considering, but it is not conclusive. Our real difficulty is that we have no medieval folklore of any kind with which to check our finding.[29] The strict evidence we seek, parallel to that of modern versions recorded under conditions which authenticated them as truly "literature orally transmitted," is woefully absent. For Arthur and Gargantua, then, the medieval legend is doubtful because of its literary context, and the modern legend (even if carefully recorded) is doubtful because of its possible derivation. We need not, of course, say that medieval Celts or Anglo-Saxons had no folktales, any more than in our insistence in descriptive linguistics upon the strictly administered modern

[26] Page 56. Canons of critical selection are also involved in manuscript songbooks, which are primary but often inaccurate in their musical recording or their strict content and authentication (see Wilgus, *op. cit.,* pp. 154, 168–69).

[27] "Arthurian Tradition and Folklore," *Folklore,* Vol. 59 (1958), 1–25.

[28] F. L. Utley, "Folklore, Myth, and Ritual," *Critical Approaches to Medieval Literature: Selected Papers from the English Institute, 1958–1959,* ed. Dorothy Bethurum (New York: Columbia University Press, 1960), pp. 103–5.

[29] See, for instance, the problem of the medieval carol, often called "popular," but usually written by clerical authors and seldom surviving in oral lore today—Erik Routley, *The English Carols* (London: Herbert Jenkins, Ltd., 1958), pp. 28–29.

record of speech need we assume that the Celts and Anglo-Saxons did not talk to one another. There are plentiful evidences of the existence of oral transmission in the Middle Ages, but few or none of the documents can be trusted without qualification since they all come through a literary screen, most often a Latin one.

What is the advantage of such rigor? Had we not better stay in a realm, however misty, of pleasure and nostalgia and half-truth, and lump together the authenticated folk version and the passably possible literary version? I submit that this has been our stumbling block from the beginning, and the reason for such chaos as there is in our definitions. We cannot generalize about the nature of the folktale unless we have a sharply defined corpus as the basis for remarks on folktale or folksong structure, formula, style, content, context, function, and method of transmission. It may well be that most of the folkloristic heresies which we now decry: solar, Freudian, ritualistic, Benfeyan Indian origins, or even the genetic errors of the Finnish school stem from an uncritical use of documents. Oriental materials, for instance, play a large part in such theoretical constructs, and there are few folklorists in the West who can tell the difference between a literary version and a folk version in the rich and valuable Oriental corpus.[30]

Are we then to ignore the literary versions? Of course not. It is well known that they have much to tell the historian of the folktale; above all, they help him to fix the date of a type or motif. A version of Mak hiding a stolen lamb in his wife's bed and claiming it is a baby is as old as the *Second Shepherd's Play,* written in the early fifteenth century. It is also as new as the late Senator Heflin, who recounted several yarns of the kind during congressional filibusters.[31] Genetically, moreover, a literary version may allow useful observations about derivation and variation from a late medieval form. These uses for date and genesis are confined to content; only with the authentic modern tale can we be sure about folklore style or formula or context. And with genesis we may go too far. The common belief of Hans Naumann, Lord Raglan, and even Francis Child that folklore is aristocratic in origin is based on a careless use of the principle that I have indicated. Most so-called documents before the Grimms are *ipso facto* "literary," since that is the only way they can have come down to us. But the absence of authentic folklore does not argue that the source of the modern tale is always literary or "aristocratic." A conditioned silence of this kind must be assessed in the evidence.

The sources of a modern tale may well be literary in fact; such a conclusion is not always based on the specious nature of the evidence. Boccaccio's "Griselda," for instance, is so far as I can find the ultimate source of all

---

[30] A beginning of the sifting process will be found in Stith Thompson and Jonas Balys, *The Oral Tales of India* (Bloomington: Indiana University Press, 1958).

[31] Robert C. Cosbey, "The Mak Story and Its Folklore Analogues," *Speculum,* Vol. 20 (1945), 310–17.

modern tales on the subject (Motif H461, Type 887);[32] though Boccaccio's version certainly has links with older classifications like Cupid and Psyche and various tales of the Persecuted Wife.[33] But this is only one example; in many cases the apparent derivation of a modern folktale from a medieval literary version is mere illusion based on the medieval silence. The historian knows the problem. We cannot be sure that Chaucer met Petrarch on his trip to Italy, however attractive the hypothesis may be, because the documents never show the two of them together in the same small town at the same date. That does not mean that Chaucer did not meet Petrarch—some of the documents may be lost, and documents are proofs only of the positive fact and never of the negative possibilities. So we must leave the problem in limbo.[34] R. G. Collingwood remarks that the historian's rules of evidence differ from those in a court of law. "For the historian is under no obligation to make up his mind within any stated time. Nothing matters to him except that his decision, when he reaches it, shall be right; which means, for him, that it shall follow inevitably from the evidence."[35] The folklorist must accept his role as historian of the folksong or folktale and not be distracted by the desire to appear sage and significant. By hypothesis, then, oral tales may well have been the source of some parts of Arthurian romance and some parts of Rabelais. But at best the cogent evidence is of analogues, literary parallels, and modern derivatives either of the extant medieval literary versions or of lost medieval literary or folk versions, and there are no sure grounds for final genetic conclusions in any individual case.

When the folklorist uses literary versions, as he must, he should realize that he is not now studying folklore but the relationship of oral and written literature. This is a thoroughly valid interdisciplinary study, but it should not be confused with the strict study of oral literature itself. If the folklorist wishes to be useful to the literary historian or critic, he must first stick to

---

32 These numbers come from two of the standard indexes employed by professional folklorists. Motif H461 refers to Stith Thompson's *Motif-Index of Folk Literature, A Classification of Narrative Elements in Folktales, Ballads, Myths, Fables, Medieval Romances, Exempla, Fabliaux, Jest-Books, and Local Legends*, 2nd ed., 6 vols. (Bloomington, Ind., 1955–1958). H461 is Test of wife's patience. Type 887 refers to Stith Thompson's second revision of Antti Aarne's folktale classification system, *Verzeichnis der Märchentypen*, published in 1910. In Thompson's revision, *The Types of the Folktale: A Classification and Bibliography*, Folklore Fellows Communications No. 184 (Helsinki, 1961), one finds that Tale Type 887 is Griselda. The *Motif-Index* and the Aarne-Thompson tale type index provide both a means of identifying a narrative as traditional and a place where folklorists turn first to find parallels (other versions) of tales they have collected as well as references to scholarly studies of these narratives. For example, following the plot summary of Griselda in the tale type index are references to no less than three monographs written on the tale. For a discussion of the difference between a motif, the smallest element of folk narrative, and a tale type, a whole traditional tale consisting of one or more motifs, see Stith Thompson, *The Folktale* (New York, 1951), pp. 415–27.—Ed. Note

33 Types 712, 881, 900A. See Fred N. Robinson, ed., *The Complete Works of Geoffrey Chaucer*, 2nd ed. (Boston: Houghton Mifflin Company, 1957), pp. 709–10.

34 For references see Robinson, *op. cit.*, p. 709.

35 *The Idea of History* (New York: Oxford University Press, Inc., 1956), p. 268.

his own last. Our literary colleagues are sometimes confused because of a failure to understand the difference between type and motif analysis. The Aarne-Thompson types, though still somewhat limited by the Grimm canon, and occasionally accepting a tale from that canon as a true folktale type because the Grimms put it into their collection, are on the whole authentic in the sense that they are first of all based on a group of international tales, recurring in oral tradition again and again over a reasonable number of national boundaries and possessing some stability in that recurrence. The extant oral tales are available for study as oral tales. The existence of literary versions, original or derivative, is a secondary matter. The *Motif-Index of Folk Literature*, on the other hand, contains many motifs which look like real folk motifs, but which have been attested only in a medieval or later literary version. It is a classifying and finding index, not a mark of authenticity—its subtitle clearly indicates that the "narrative elements" may have come from medieval romance, exempla, fabliaux, and jest-books, as well as from folktales, ballads, myths, fables, or local legends. The problem is even greater with Tom Peete Cross's *Motif-Index of Early Irish Literature*, where the main title indicates that written documents furnish the bulk of the material. In Cross the abbreviation "Beal" for *Béaloideas: The Journal of the Folklore of Ireland Society* can be pretty well trusted since the very purpose of that Society was to produce the kind of authentic records we seek. But most of the other abbreviations are to written material—like "LG" for *Leabar Gabála Erenn*, a learned account of the invasions of Ireland which despite its wondrous bad history is a treasure house of the syncretism of medieval scholars, working at times with oral lore but always with their learned biases showing—the desire to exalt Ireland by reconciling the Bible with Irish legend. When an Arthurian student looks in Cross for parallels, he will find plenty of them, but none of them except the rare modern tales represent oral lore without qualification. The *Types of the Folktale*, in short, is selective and rejective; the *Motif-Index* and its derivatives are inclusive and in need of skilled criticism in their use.

IV

An "operational" definition is one used by a particular type of student for his special problems. Only, perhaps, by combining such definitions by a number of students who follow different paths of investigation could we arrive at a theoretical consensus. My own interest, as should be clear by now, is in the folktale and the ballad, studied comparatively and historically, in their own essence and in their relationship with written literature. The exclusion of culture, belief, and crafts is in part convenience based on the wish to concentrate on well-authenticated and circumscribed material which may lead to results of a certain clarity and acceptance. At least one kind of "humanist," I have argued, finds the anthropological distinction useful.

It is apparent from discussions when I have presented this position that acceptance is not automatic. The student of superstitions (often recorded without context) or of local legends (often subject to the manipulations of the mass media) may well be disturbed. I am especially concerned with the reservations of such active collectors as Samuel Bayard, D. K. Wilgus, Herbert Halpert, or Richard Dorson. The study of living folklore in action can best be made by the fieldworker, whose pragmatic awareness of his informants diminishes much of the cloistered concern as to just who the "folk" may be. They are those from whom one collects live folklore.

From the fieldworker, the historian and synthesizer demands one thing besides an accurate recording—the evidence of tradition as it is reflected in the personality, locale, and antecedents of the informant. My use of the term "folklore document" may lead to some misunderstanding, since the collector instinctively distrusts the printed word. Here I am with him in spirit, for the many so-called documents which record without the signature of authenticity are always dangerous in any attempt to define the field. And the best modern collectors share the role of the historian and comparativist themselves.

A common axiom, that the fieldworker should "collect everything" in the field and sort it out at home, is useful for beginners. It is better to take down a Burl Ives or Pete Seeger imitation along with a genuine traditional ballad, as evidence of repertory, and to establish the critical canon later. But for the practised fieldworker the axiom may be naive as well as time-wasting, since informed collections always involve some interaction between fieldwork and hypothesis. The field, that is, is a testing ground for hypothesis. Carl Voegelin has made us aware of this in phonemic studies, where the lack of symmetry provides clues for further questioning. Marian Smith does the same for anthropology.[36] Even in the act of collection there may be certain restrictions. The obscene must be handled with care, not because of prudery on the part of the fieldworker, but because of the prudery of the informant. We may need a Kinsey to avoid freezing off such persistent questions as freeze the whole interview. On the other hand, failure to ask for some kinds of off-color story may leave a gap in the record.[37] Moreover, without infinite tact, the very act of collecting may disturb the matrix. Tales, being associated with leisure, demand leisure to tell, and if one interferes with the work time of the informant, distortion may result. Perhaps that is why our best tellers are old people—not because folklore is a vanishing phenomenon, but because only the old can respond satisfactorily to the persistent stranger.

Our operational ruling out of custom, belief, and craft is no attack on this kind of matrix. A student of folk literature and art needs much exposure to

36 "Boas's 'Natural History' Approach to Field Method," *The Anthropology of Franz Boas,* ed. Walter Goldschmidt (American Anthropological Association Memoir 89, 1959), pp. 51, 54, 56. The "collect everything" axiom was violated by Boas himself, who had relics of nineteenth-century prudery; see Helen Codere, "The Understanding of the Kwakiutl," *ibid.,* p. 69. One should perhaps modify the maxim to "collect everything, but be critical" (see Wilgus, *op. cit.,* pp. 154–55).
37 Utley, "Some Noah Tales from Sweden," *Humaniora,* p. 269.

ethnological background, though it is ancillary to his main purpose. The collector, even if his major concern is folksong or folktale, may find custom and belief a gift he cannot overlook. One should try to understand why those exponents of culture pattern and fieldwork in depth, the anthropologists, do separate folk literature from the larger context. Concerned as they are with the holistic cultural setting, they realize the advantages for special study of "verbal art," which requires unusual techniques of analysis and of publication. *Dahomean Narrative,* by Melville and Frances Herskovits,[38] is a model of folktale study; its enlightening predecessor was Melville Herskovits's *Dahomey, An Ancient West African Kingdom,*[39] which had already discussed the culture as a whole.

The gravest flaw of the British or American folklorist is his tendency to pick up scraps of knowledge—a few superstitions, a handful of proverbs, a folktale, and a ballad without music. We are still heirs to the British country vicar school, which was convinced that the "vanishing survivals" must be recorded at once—and method be hanged. What is actually needed for Kentucky or upper New York State is the field technique of the anthropologist, who knows how to fill in the total folk culture even when it seems to duplicate the dominant culture. But the very heroic nature of the task has led the anthropologist to favor a division of labor. Collectors of American native white or Negro traditions can learn much from those who have studied the patterns of a Maya town or a Hindu village, but if they are not in some fashion to separate the verbal arts from the rest of the culture in a systematic and informed fashion, they had better turn anthropologist like Redfield and make "holistic community studies" of a peasant culture.[40]

It may be that in studying "preliterate" cultures, subcultures, and dominant cultures we may find that the function of folk literature varies. In the dominant culture folklore, whether revived or surviving, has a nostalgic role (though nostalgia is a function). In the subculture the connection between actual belief in the superstition and its persistence in folk literature is closer. In the true "primitive" culture (though one without acculturation from neighbor or colonial is nowadays hard to find) folk literature is probably a more integral part of the isolated ethnic pattern; it reflects reality and integral wish rather than cultural lag in a way which it cannot in our "alienated" modern societies.

The separation of the study of craft, belief, and custom from the study of

[38] Evanston, Ill.: Northwestern University Press, 1958.
[39] New York, 1938. See *Dahomean Narrative,* p. 8.
[40] *Peasant Society and Culture,* p. 15. For Redfield's various definitions of *folk* and *folklore,* which essentially confine the terms to the preliterate ethnic group and the peasant and deny the existence of much folklore, except that of the Southern Negro, in the United States, see his various books in chronological order: *The Tepoztlan* (1930), pp. 1–10; *The Folk Culture of Yucatan* (Chicago: University of Chicago Press, 1941), p. 338; *The Primitive World and Its Transformations* (Ithaca, N.Y.: Cornell University Press, 1953), pp. xi, 40, 48; *The Little Community* (Uppsala: Almqvist & Wiksell, 1955), pp. 1–4, 7; *Peasant Society and Culture* (1956), pp. 19–20, 26, 70, 84, 87, 91, 131.

folk art should be no deterrent to the collector concerned with a living process. It should be a challenge to him to understand that the whole has its parts, each of which needs special attention. The student of folk literature per se makes his choice because special equipment is always needed to study any kind of literature, because much of the record of folktale and ballad has been crippled by faulty documentation, because the total field of culture demands division of labor as well as interdisciplinary breadth, and because the specialist in literature, written or folk, can never pretend to complete competence in psychology, sociology, anthropology, history, and the other sciences of man, however he may need to call upon their informed practitioners. Hence he demands the right to ultimate definition of his field of operation.

V

A final reason for our narrowed definition is that it gives us some protection against those who, unlike the collectors, often show more enthusiasm than clarity or accuracy. I am not one who enjoys perennial quarrels with the "popularizers" of folklore, or with literary students who mistake our conclusions. Vilification, even of "fake-lore,"[41] is of less value than a defined field and a *telos* for our science.[42] Long before the science existed the popularizers were there, though today they show the peculiar exaggerations of a heavily commercialized civilization. Rabelais and Boccaccio were popularizers, as was Joel Chandler Harris,[43] but all three were also distinguished artists. The problem of the popularizer is fundamentally one of artistic rather than scholarly honesty.

This is not to say that, with some good will, he could not serve us better,

---

[41] "Fake-lore" is a term coined by Richard Dorson intended to refer to and to denigrate the consciously contrived creations of commercial writers who insist upon calling their efforts folklore. Dorson utilizes the common criterion for defining folklore when he argues that fake-lore has never been in oral tradition. See Richard M. Dorson, "Folklore and Fake-Lore," *American Mercury,* Vol. 70 (March 1950), 335–43, for a discussion of the term.—ED. NOTE

[42] Edmund Wilson and Stanley Hyman's strictures on the academic folklorist, who shirks the task of criticism (see Wilgus, *op. cit.,* pp. 221–24), do not seem to me to get at the root of the problem—that authentication must precede criticism if one is talking about folklore proper and not its sophisticated relatives. I have expanded some of these views of the needed *telos* of folklore science in a panel led by Richard Dorson at the Eleventh Newberry Library Conference on American Studies, May 7, 1960. See the report by Jules Zanger, *Newberry Library Bulletin,* Vol. 5 (1961), 227–39.

[43] Harris poses a typical problem. Probably no collection in America *reflects* more genuine American Negro folklore than *The Complete Tales of Uncle Remus* (Boston: Houghton Mifflin Company, 1955), though Harris probably incorporated tales *like* those he heard from his Negro informants which come instead from American Indian and European sources. We would give much to have his field notes, if he ever made them. We must treat his collection as literary, and the individual tale can be authenticated in content only by comparison to collections like those of Dorson and other more recent students of the Negro folktale. What is badly needed is a type and motif index of all American Negro folktales, which would in some measure, though not wholly, solve the problem of Harris' sources.

by giving us a quiet clue to the basic oral version where it reposes in archive or serious collection, as even Botkin's *A Treasury of American Folklore* does on occasion. We should face such anthologies not with wholesale ostracism, but with critical testing of the document, just as we do with Boccaccio or even with the Grimms. Some collections are of course better than others, but even in respected works we must look sharply at each tale.[44] As for rewriting, there is a vast difference between the Percy who doctored *Sir Patrick Spens*,[45] the Chaucer who built Tale Type 1361[46] into a great comic story articulated with motive, texture, wit, and character, and the latest teller of Little Red Riding Hood for children who excludes the violent details of wolf swallowing grandmother and of granddaughter's using the excuse of a call of nature to get out of the wolf's clutches.[47] This problem too is an aesthetic one. The folklorist is in the best position to be a critic of folk literature and of the kinds of literature derived from it, and he has special grounds for judgment, since he knows, or should know, what folklore is. Studying the folksong or folktale is not merely compiling bibliographical notes or typing, motifying, and giving Child numbers.[48] It is a critical task, demanding attention to genesis but not that alone, textual accuracy and a sense of history in the broadest intellectual and cultural sense, and a sense of anthropological pattern and contrast. The folklorist must be a textual, a historical, and a configurational critic; because of these roles he can also aspire to be a literary critic.

---

[44] We need better anthologies, either based wholly on authentic oral material or strictly separating the oral from the literary. There is in print no trustworthy representative anthology of American folktales of either Indian or non-Indian origin. Vance Randolph's excellent Ozark collections have only a touch of the "literary," but they are confined to one region, and hence representative only in content, not in breadth of locale. Thompson's *Tales of the North American Indians* is out of print.

[45] The problem of rewriting among the great early folklorists, like the Serbian Vuk Karadžić, is treated by Maja Bošković-Stulli, "O Narodnoj prici i njezina autentičnom izrazu," *Slovenski etnograf*, Vol. 12 (1959), 107–20.

[46] Tale Type 1361, The Flood, a folktale in which a priest persuades a man to sleep in a hanging tub to escape the coming flood, is the basis of Chaucer's ribald classic, "The Miller's Tale." Oral texts reported include Danish, Dutch, German, Irish, Livonian, Lithuanian, Serbo-Croatian, Russian, Turkish, Spanish-American, and West Indies Negro versions. For a study of the relationship between Chaucer's literary version and the folktale, see Stith Thompson, "The Miller's Tale," in William F. Bryan and Germaine Dempster, eds., *Sources and Analogues of Chaucer's Canterbury Tales* (Chicago, 1941), 106–23.—ED. NOTE

[47] Type 333, The Glutton. See Paul Delarue, *The Borzoi Book of French Folktales*, (New York: Alfred A. Knopf, Inc., 1956), pp. 230–32.

[48] Child numbers refer to the standard collection by Francis James Child, *The English and Scottish Popular Ballads*, 5 vols. in 10 (Boston, 1882–1898). There are 305 ballads in this closed canon, and ballad scholars often refer to versions of any of these ballads by their number in the Child collection. Thus "Barbara Allen" would be Child 84. This mode of reference is analogous to that employed by folktale scholars before the advent of the tale type index in 1910 when they referred to folktales by Grimm numbers, that is, their number in the Grimms' collection. What Utley is saying is that studying a folktale or ballad is not simply giving the appropriate tale type or Child number. Identification is only the first step. Analysis and interpretation are also necessary. —ED. NOTE

If we do our job well we need not worry about those commercial exploiters who say we are pedantic because they fear we may interfere with their public domain; we need concern ourselves little with slanted words from controversies where ignorant armies clash by night. Our reward is in the task itself, as it has always been for the philosopher, the scholar, and the honest artist. We must heed our serious co-workers, since disagreement with them may be the dialectic which brings a better state for all of us. One does not disagree with one's enemies with profit—only with one's friends, for only they talk in a realm of discourse where disagreement is meaningful. We may welcome the enthusiasm of the public for our subject matter, which revives for them half-hidden memories, but we must not let tempting Satan seduce us towards an expansionist inclusion of all documents as though they were of equal merit, a playing down to popular nostalgia or taboo or bias, an acceptance of Paul Bunyan with one hand while we reject him with the other. These temptations can destroy our understanding of the very truth we are after, for to call everything folklore is to leave us no field for research or action. If we speak truth, because we have sought it with all our energy, we will be heeded—by foundations, by publishers, by our friends the popularizers who need our results, and by the students whom we train to carry on the honest quest for "literature orally transmitted."

Folklore and Anthropology

William R. Bascom

In this essay by one of the leading anthropological folklorists, one sees clearly stated the view that folklore belongs to one branch of anthropology, namely, cultural anthropology. Bascom, Professor of Anthropology at the University of California at Berkeley, is well aware of the difficulties of relying upon the criterion of oral transmission. He says, "All folklore is orally transmitted, but not all that is orally transmitted is folklore." However, as Utley pointed out, Bascom tends to limit folklore to what he later termed verbal art, which includes prose narratives (myth, folktale, legend), riddles, and proverbs, but not folk dance, folk medicine, and folk belief (superstition). Bascom goes so far as to say that to the anthropologist, the texts of ballads and other songs are folklore but the music of ballads and other songs is not. Most folklorists would regard this definition of folklore as too narrow. On the other hand, Utley's conception of folk literature is really quite similar to Bascom's notion of verbal art.

The dual affiliations of folklore with the humanities on the one hand and with social science on the other are well recognized. They are reflected in the membership of this society and in its policy of alternating presidencies and meetings between the Modern Language Association and the American Anthropological Association. Although the literary and the anthropological approaches are both clearly essential and complementary, the two groups of folklorists have tended to work independently rather than together on their common area of interest, following their own separate courses without becoming familiar with each other's concepts, methods, and objectives. This intellectual isolationism is by no means universal, but it is common enough to present real difficulties to this society and its journal, and to have been mentioned in three recent presidential addresses.[1] This paper is an attempt

Reprinted from the *Journal of American Folklore,* Vol. 66 (1953), 283–90, by permission of the author and the American Folklore Society.

[1] Melville J. Herskovits, "Folklore After a Hundred Years: A Problem in Redefinition," *Journal of American Folklore,* Vol. 59, No. 232 (1946), 89–100; A. H. Gayton, "Perspectives in Folklore," *Journal of American Folklore,* Vol. 64, No. 252 (1951), 147–50; Francis Lee Utley, "Conflict and Promise in Folklore," *Journal of American Folklore,* Vol. 65, No. 256 (1952), 111–19. My paper was presented at the Sixty-fourth Annual Meeting of The American Folklore Society, held at El Paso, Texas, in December 1952.

to bridge this gap by presenting the anthropological approach to folklore, as I see it; it is my hope that one of you may reciprocate by presenting the viewpoint of the humanities.

Of the four branches of anthropology, cultural anthropology, which is also referred to as social anthropology, ethnology, or ethnography, is most closely associated with folklore. Neither physical anthropology nor prehistory or archeology have any direct relationship to folklore, although the latter may occasionally provide information regarding past developments and population movements which is useful to the folklorist. Linguistics is somewhat more closely related, both because the style of verbal expression of a tale or proverb is influenced by vocabulary and grammatical structure, and because linguists have found folktales and myths convenient devices for collecting linguistic texts, with the result that some of the most carefully recorded and translated American Indian tales have been published by linguists. Folklore, however, falls squarely within the fourth field, cultural anthropology, which is concerned with the study of the customs, traditions, and institutions of living peoples.

When the anthropologist goes to the South Seas or to Africa to study and record the ways of life of a particular people, he describes their techniques of farming, fishing, and hunting; their system of land tenure, inheritance, and other phases of property ownership; their kinship terms and obligations, their institutions of marriage and the family, the other units within their social structure and their functions; their legal and political system; their theology, rituals, magical practices, concepts of the soul and the afterworld, omens, techniques of divination, and other aspects of their religion and world view; their housing, clothing, and bodily decoration; their woodcarving, pottery, metalworking, and other graphic and plastic arts; their music, their dancing, and their drama. Such studies, which we speak of as ethnographies, can give only an incomplete description if they do not also include the folktales, legends, myths, riddles, proverbs, and other forms of folklore employed by the people.

Folklore, to the anthropologist, is one of the important parts that go to make up the culture of any given people. It is important, if only because it is one of the universals; that is, there is no known culture which does not include folklore. No group of people, however remote or however simple their technology, has ever been discovered which does not employ some form of folklore. Because of this, and because the same tales and proverbs may be known to both, folklore is a bridge between literate and nonliterate societies. Although some anthropologists, for one reason or another, devote little attention to folklore, it is obvious that any ethnographic study which does not consider folklore can be only a partial and incomplete description of the culture as a whole. Moreover, since folklore serves to sanction and validate religious, social, political, and economic institutions, and to play an important role as an educative device in their transmission from one generation to another, there can be no thorough analysis of any of these other parts of culture which does not give serious consideration to folklore.

"Culture" is the basic concept in anthropology today. Although it has been variously defined, anthropologists are clearly in general agreement as to what it means. And it has become almost impossible for anthropologists to discuss their subject without employing it. Culture has been referred to as man's "social heritage" and as "the man-made part of the environment." It consists essentially of any form of behavior which is acquired through learning, and which is patterned in conformity with certain approved norms. Under it anthropologists include all the customs, traditions, and institutions of a people, together with their products and techniques of production. A folktale or a proverb is thus clearly a part of culture.

The term culture was introduced into English by Edward Tylor in 1865,[2] and defined in his book *Primitive Culture* in 1871 as "that complex whole which includes knowledge, belief, art, morals, law, custom, and any other capabilities and habits acquired by man as a member of society."[3] In the second edition of the earlier work, Tylor acknowledged that he had drawn largely from the writings of Steinheil and "from the invaluable collection of facts bearing on the history of civilization in the *Allgemeine Cultur-Geschichte der Menschheit* and *Allgemeine Culturwissenschaft,* of the late Dr. Gustav Klemm, of Dresden."[4] Both of Klemm's works use the word *Cultur,* the first appearing in ten volumes published between 1843–1852. In the second, published in two volumes in 1854 and 1855, Klemm refers to *Cultur* as including "customs, information, and skills; domestic and public life in peace and war; religion, science, and art"; and says, "It is manifest in the branch of a tree if deliberately shaped; in the rubbing of sticks to make fire; the cremation of a deceased father's corpse; the decorative painting of one's body; the transmission of past experience to the new generation."[5]

Folklorists need not be reminded of the similarities between these definitions and William John Thoms' reference to "the manners, customs, observances, superstitions, ballads, proverbs, etc., of the olden time" in his letter to *The Athenaeum* in 1846 in which the word folklore was first introduced into English.[6] These similarities have in large part been the root of the argument about the scope of folklore which still plagues us. Although

---

[2] E. B. Tylor, *Researches into the Early History of Mankind and the Development of Civilization* (Boston, 1878, first published in 1865), pp. 3, 4, 150–91.

[3] E. B. Tylor, *Primitive Culture: Researches into the Development of Mythology, Philosophy, Religion, Art, and Custom,* Vol. 1 (London, 1871), 1.

[4] Tylor, *Researches into the Early History of Mankind,* p. 13.

[5] G. Klemm, *Allgemeine Culturwissenschaft* (Leipzig, 1854–1855), Vol. 1, 217; Vol. 2, 37. Translations from Robert H. Lowie, *The History of Ethnological Theory* (New York, 1937), p. 12.

[6] W. J. Thoms ("Ambrose Merton"), "Folklore," *The Athenaeum,* No. 982 (1846), 862–63; Duncan Emrich, " 'Folklore': William John Thoms," *California Folklore Quarterly,* Vol. 5, No. 4 (1946), 355–74. It is noteworthy that although Thoms never gave a strict definition of folklore, this description was repeated word for word in *Notes and Queries,* First Series, Vol. 1 (1850), 223. [This is not surprising in view of the fact that Thoms, founder and editor of *Notes and Queries* also wrote the 1850 item. In *Notes and Queries,* Thoms found a way to collect folklore from readers along the lines he had proposed in his *Athenaeum* letter. The fruits of this early attempt to collect folklore from periodical readers may be seen in *Choice Notes from Notes and Queries: Folklore* (London, 1859).—Ed. Note]

historically the word folklore is nearly twenty years older in English than the word culture, culture has become accepted in the social sciences in the sense that the anthropologists use it, while the argument over folklore continues, even among folklorists.

It would defeat the purpose of this paper to revive this argument by pursuing it, but it is necessary to carry it a bit further in clarifying the anthropological point of view. Folklore, to the anthropologist, is a part of culture but not the whole of culture. It includes myths, legends, tales, proverbs, riddles, the texts of ballads and other songs, and other forms of lesser importance, but not folk art, folk dance, folk music, folk costume, folk medicine, folk custom, or folk belief. All of these are important parts of culture, which must also be a part of any complete ethnography. All are unquestionably worthy of study, whether in literate or nonliterate societies.

In nonliterate societies, which traditionally have been the primary interest of anthropologists, all institutions, traditions, customs, beliefs, attitudes, and crafts are transmitted orally, by verbal instruction and by example. While anthropologists agree that folklore should be defined as dependent upon oral transmission, they do not see this feature as distinguishing folklore from the rest of culture. All folklore is orally transmitted, but not all that is orally transmitted is folklore. Because of their concern with nonliterate societies, anthropologists have not yet had to face squarely one of the current problems in folklore, that of defining the relationship between folklore and literature, or of distinguishing folklore from fake-lore, but it may become prominent as more attention is paid to the problems of acculturation and to the study of the literate societies of Europe, Asia, and America.

The content of culture is analyzed in terms of its aspects or broad component parts, such as technology, economics, social and political organization, religion, and the art. Folklore falls clearly in the last category as a form of aesthetic expression as important as the graphic and plastic arts, music, the dance, or drama. All aspects of culture are interrelated in varying degrees, as folklore is, through its function as a sanction of custom and belief, both religious and secular. Nonetheless this system of classification has proved useful as a basis for cross-cultural comparisons and for the development of specialized concepts and techniques for analysis. The use of the term folklore to include such things as folk arts, folk medicine, folk belief, and folk custom ignores this system of classification, which has proven its usefulness for systematic analysis, and groups together phenomena of different order which require different methods of analysis.

Folklore thus is studied in anthropology because it is a part of culture. It is a part of man's learned traditions and customs, a part of his social heritage. It can be analyzed in the same way as other customs and traditions, in terms of form and function, or of interrelations with other aspects of culture. It presents the same problems of growth and change, and is subject to the same processes of diffusion, invention, acceptance or rejection, and integration. It can be used, like other aspects of culture, for studies of these processes or those of acculturation, patterning, the relation between culture and the environment, or between culture and personality.

The development of any item of folklore is comparable to that of any custom, institution, technique, or art form. It must have been invented at some time, by some individual. It can be assumed that many folktales or proverbs, like many other inventions, were rejected because they either did not fill a recognized or subconscious need, or because they were incompatible with the accepted patterns and traditions of folklore or of culture as a whole. If they were accepted, they depended on retelling, in the same way that all cultural traits in a nonliterate society depend upon restatement and re-enactment. An element of material culture, such as a hoe or bow or mask, has of course a certain independent existence once it has been created, but for the craft itself to continue these items must be made again and again. The nonmaterial elements of culture, however, are entirely comparable in this respect to folktales or proverbs; rituals must be performed, beliefs and attitudes must be expressed, kinship terms must be used, and the privileges and obligations of kinship must be exercised. In the course of this retelling or redoing, change occurs each time new variations are introduced, and again these innovations are subject to acceptance or rejection. As this process continues, each new invention is adapted gradually to the needs of the society and to the pre-existing culture patterns, which may themselves be modified somewhat to conform to the new invention.

In some societies for some forms of folklore, as has been clearly established, the narrator may be expected to modify a well-known tale by the substitution of new characters or incidents in an original way or the introduction of a novel twist to the plot, whereas in the fields of kinship, economics, law, or religion, the emphasis may be upon conformity. However, in this respect folklore does not differ from the graphic and plastic arts, music, or the dance, where creativity on the part of the performer may also be expected. The folk element in folklore, therefore, presents no new or distinctive problems as the anthropologist sees it. However, he prefers to consider the question as one of anonymous rather than collective creativity. As an anthropologist, one may raise the question whether there is any significant difference as far as creativity is concerned between the variants on a particular tale as told by individual narrators among the Zuni or Navajo, for example, and the written variations on the current success story, the mystery, or the boy-meets-girl theme. Viewed broadly, there are the same questions as to who first invented these themes, how they have been reworked in the past, and how the previous variations have influenced the product of any given storyteller or writer. In literature there is the possibility of being able to answer these questions, while in folklore one can never hope to find the answers, but this does not mean that the processes involved are essentially different.

In the same manner, the spread of folktales from one society to another is strictly comparable to the spread of tobacco, a religious ritual or concept, a tool or a technique, or a legal principle. Again there is the question of acceptance or rejection, and if accepted the subsequent modification to fit the new item into the other cultural patterns, a process which anthropologists speak of as integration. There are again the same problems in interpreting the present distribution of a given cultural trait or complex or a given folktale or proverb. Does one explain this in terms of migration as the Grimm brothers believed; in terms of borrowing as the Diffusionists insisted; or in terms of independent invention as the Nature Allegorical school and the Cultural Evolutionists assumed? These same problems have been faced a great many times by anthropologists, and a considerable body of materials bearing on this problem has been assembled. Folklorists could profit considerably from the numerous anthropological discussions of this point and from the various principles such as limited possibilities, contiguous distribution, parallelism, convergence, form, and quantity which have been developed as a basis for choosing between these alternative explanations; they could also profit from an examination of studies such as Spier's analysis of the Plains Indians' Sun Dance or the discussions of the age-area concept and its limitations.[7] These have implications of fundamental importance for those who employ the methods of the Finnish Folklore Fellows.

Moreover, since any cultural law must hold for folklore as well as for the other aspects of culture, the data of folklore can be used to test theories or hypotheses about culture as a whole; and conversely, the accepted theories of culture which have been developed can contribute to the understanding of folklore. It is not surprising, therefore, that many of the schools of anthropological theory are considered as schools of folklore, including the American Anthropologists, the Functionalists, the Diffusionists, and the Cultural Evolutionists.

The theory of cultural evolution, developed by Spencer, Tylor, Morgan, and others, remains another point of disagreement between anthropologists and some other folklorists. Although this theory was accepted almost with-

---

[7] Leslie Spier, *The Sun Dance of the Plains Indians: Its Development and Diffusion,* Anthropological Papers of the American Museum of Natural History, Vol. 16, No. 7 (New York, 1921); Edward Sapir, *Time Perspective in Aboriginal American Culture, A Study in Method,* Canadian Geological Survey, Anthropological Series, Vol. 90, No. 13 (Ottawa, 1916); Clark Wissler, *Man and Culture* (New York, 1923) and *The Relation of Nature to Man in Aboriginal America* (New York, 1926); Roland B. Dixon, *The Building of Cultures* (New York, 1928); W. D. Wallis, *Culture and Progress* (New York, 1930); Margaret T. Hodgen, "Geographical Distribution as a Criterion of Age," *American Anthropologist,* Vol. 44 (1942), 345–68; Melville J. Herskovits, *Man and His Works* (New York, 1948); A. L. Kroeber, *Anthropology,* rev. ed. (New York, 1948). [The age-area concept in very simple terms is the notion that the wider the distribution of a culture trait, the older the trait may be. The principle is employed by practitioners of the so-called Finnish method of studying folklore although the principle is not specifically termed the "age-area" hypothesis. For an example of a Finnish (or historical-geographical) method study, see Stith Thompson's "The Star Husband Tale," in this volume. —ED. NOTE]

out question by the scholars of the latter half of the nineteenth century, and was further developed and elaborated by many of the great anthropologists and folklorists of this period, it was severely criticized by the anthropologists of the twentieth century. Analysis showed that the entire theory rested on several hypotheses which its exponents never succeeded in proving and which, at least in some specific cases, have later been disproved. Since the entire theory stands or falls on these assumptions, it has been rejected by anthropologists and by most social scientists. Nevertheless, one finds some folklorists today defining folklore as survivals from earlier stages of civilization, as "the shadowy remnants of ancient religious rites still incorporated in the lives of illiterates and rustics" or as "a lively fossil which refuses to die."[8] These interpretations derive directly from the theory of cultural evolution which, instead of folklore, has really proved the lively fossil which refuses to die. The theory of cultural evolution was developed primarily by anthropologists; it was criticized primarily by anthropologists; and it has been discarded by anthropologists. It is understandably disturbing to anthropologists to find folklorists, or economists, or anyone else, repeating an anthropological theory which anthropologists themselves have rejected. They would prefer that this argument could be kept a private dispute within the family, and wish that it could be hidden forever in some convenient closet.

Anthropologists have come to the conclusion that the search for ultimate origins, whether by means of the cultural evolutionist approach or the age-area concept, is a hopeless one where historical documents and archeological evidence are lacking. In folklore, where archeology can be of almost no help at all, and where documentation does not yield the answers directly, attempts to reconstruct history on an even more restricted scale can yield results only in terms of probability rather than proven fact, and there is the constant danger of being enticed into the realm of pure speculation for which one can never hope to discover supporting evidence. This conclusion has been reached after many serious attempts to reconstruct history using a wide variety of data, and although anthropologists have not completely abandoned the subject of distribution of specific tales, the questions of diffusion and possible origins is receiving less and less attention and is approached with increasing caution. On the other hand, anthropologists are turning to other problems which are now felt to be of equal or greater importance, and more susceptible to study. The concern with these other problems is another point which differentiates, to a certain extent, the anthropologist from his fellow folklorists.

In line with this thinking, anthropologists would agree that change in folklore can be studied more profitably in process than through reconstructions based on distributions. When Cushing some sixty-five years ago had the foresight to record the Italian tale of "The Cock and the Mouse" as retold

---

[8] Maria Leach, ed., *The Funk and Wagnalls Standard Dictionary of Folklore, Mythology, and Legend,* Vol. 1 (New York, 1949), 401.

by a Zuni informant to whom he himself had recited the tale a year previously, he gave to students of folklore an extremely valuable bit of data. The
comparison of the Italian and Zuni variants spotlights many Zuni stylistic
features and serves not only to show "What transformation the original
underwent in such a brief period, and how well it has been adapted to Zuni
environment and mode of thought, but also to give a glimpse of the Indian
method of folktale making."[9] It is still difficult to see how investigations of
this kind can be pursued systematically and without having to depend upon
fortuitous circumstances, but one wishes that there were many more such
examples for comparison and analysis, for here one can approach the
dynamics of folklore on the solid basis of known and recorded fact, rather
than inference, probability, or speculation.

The problem of the creative role of the narrator is receiving increasing
attention. Through examples such as that of Cushing, through the comparison
of tales, and particularly through the comparison of variants of the same
tale within a given folklore tradition, it is hoped to learn the degree and
kind of freedom permitted to the narrator or expected of him in various
forms of folklore and in various societies. Benedict has made an extremely
enlightening analysis of Zuni folklore along these lines, in which she demonstrates how the interests and experiences of the narrators are reflected in the
tales they tell, and other studies have been published or are in process.[10]

The problem of stylistic features of a body of folklore is regarded as of
primary importance, although the anthropologist feels diffident to approach
it when so many folklorists have been trained in literature and are far better
equipped to attack it, as well as the analysis of tales in terms of plot, incident,
conflict, climax, motivation, and character development. Yet Utley in his
presidential address has said, "Some of the most intelligently critical students
of folk literature have been anthropologists: Gladys Reichard, Franz Boas,
and Paul Radin. I am convinced, for instance, that Radin's *Winnebago
Hero-Cycles* contains a more subtle analysis of the poetic meanings of one
segment of oral literature than anything we MLA-ers have done."[11]

Anthropologists are also concerned with the place of folklore in the daily
round of life, in its social settings, and in the attitudes of native peoples
toward their own folklore. One cannot determine these facts from the texts
of tales alone, nor whether a tale is regarded as historical fact or as fiction,
yet without them one can only speculate as to the nature of folklore and its
full meaning.

They are also concerned with the relationship between folklore and the rest
of culture, from two different points of view. First, there is the extent to

---

9 F. H. Cushing, *Zuni Folk Tales* (New York, 1931), pp. 411–22. [This famous example
is reprinted in this volume.—ED. NOTE]

10 Ruth Benedict, *Zuni Mythology,* 2 vols., Columbia University Contributions to
Anthropology, No. 21 (New York, 1935), Vol. 1, xxxvii–xlii; Gladys A. Reichard, "Indi-
vidualism and Mythological Style," *Journal of American Folklore,* Vol. 57 (1944), 16–25.

11 Utley, *op. cit.,* p. 112.

which folklore reflects culture by incorporating descriptions of rituals, technology, and other cultural details. Second, and of broader significance, there is the fact that characters in folktales and myths may do things which are regarded as shocking in daily life. To cite only one example, Old Man Coyote has intercourse with his mother-in-law, whereas in ordinary life the American Indian who finds amusement in these tales must observe a strict mother-in-law avoidance. From the time of Euhemerus on, folklorists have attempted to explain, or to explain away, the striking divergencies between folklore and actual conduct. Most of these explanations are unacceptable today, but the problem remains with us as one of the most intriguing of all those in folklore, and one which raises important questions about the nature of humor and the psychological implications and the function of folklore.

Finally, anthropologists are becoming increasingly concerned with the functions of folklore—what it does for the people who tell it. In addition to the obvious function of entertainment or amusement, folklore serves to sanction the established beliefs, attitudes, and institutions, both sacred and secular, and it plays a vital role in education in nonliterate societies. It is not possible to present an adequate analysis of this problem here, or even a discussion of the very suggestive data bearing on it which have been accumulated from many different parts of the world. But, in addition to its role in transmitting culture from one generation to another, and to providing ready rationalizations when beliefs or attitudes are called into question, folklore is used in some societies to apply social pressure to those who would deviate from the accepted norms. Moreover, even the function of amusement cannot be accepted today as a complete answer, for it is apparent that beneath a good deal of humor lies a deeper meaning, and that folklore serves as a psychological escape from many repressions, not only sexual, which society imposes upon the individual.

The anthropologist, to speak frankly, often feels that his colleagues in folklore are often so preoccupied with the problem of origins and historical reconstruction that they overlook problems of equal or even greater significance, for which one can hope to find satisfactory solutions. He looks to them for guidance in the literary analysis of folklore, and for cooperation on the problems of style and of the creative role of the narrator. He would welcome their cooperation in recording local attitudes toward folklore and its social contexts, in analyzing the relation of folklore to culture and to conduct, and finally in seeking to define its functions.

In my own view, the most effective way to bridge the gaps between the different groups of folklorists is by a common concern with common problems, rather than by reliance as in the past upon a common interest in a common body of subject matter. In conclusion I wish to assure you that these remarks have not, of course, been based upon any assumption that anthropologists are completely without blame, and for this reason I repeat my initial invitation, that one of you address yourselves to this same topic from the point of view of the humanities.

Folklore and the Student of Literature

Archer Taylor

In this essay by Archer Taylor, Professor of German, Emeritus, of the University of California at Berkeley, an eminent American folklorist of international repute, the complex relationships between the materials of folklore and literature are considered. Taylor's opening paragraph is a remarkably succinct definition of folklore.

Students especially interested in the relationship between folklore and literature should consult the papers contained in "Folklore in Literature: A Symposium," *Journal of American Folklore,* Vol. 70 (1957), 1–24. For anthropological literary studies, see Paul Radin's *Literary Aspects of North American Mythology,* Anthropological Series of the Canada Geological Survey No. 6, Museum Bulletin No. 16 (Ottawa, 1915); and his *The Evolution of an American Indian Prose Epic: A Study in Comparative Literature,* Parts I and II (Basel, 1954, 1956). See also Melville Jacobs, *The Content and Style of an Oral Literature* (Chicago, 1959). In Jacobs' stimulating book and in the sequel volume, *The People Are Coming Soon* (Seattle, Wash., 1960), the telling of a tale is treated as a literary event which can only be understood by comprehending the event in its native setting. This setting Jacobs sets out to reconstruct.

Folklore is the material that is handed on by tradition, either by word of mouth or by custom and practice. It may be folksongs, folktales, riddles, proverbs, or other materials preserved in words. It may be traditional tools and physical objects like fences or knots, hot cross buns, or Easter eggs; traditional ornamentation like the Walls of Troy; or traditional symbols like the swastika. It may be traditional procedures like throwing salt over one's shoulder or knocking on wood. It may be traditional beliefs like the notion that elder is good for ailments of the eye. All of these are folklore.

The literary student deals with an equally wide range of materials. He

Reprinted from *The Pacific Spectator,* Vol. 2 (1948), 216–23, by permission of the author and *The Pacific Spectator.*

includes in his studies much more than the written word that conveys an emotion and is moved by imagination. Nowadays he pays little attention to the spoken word, although it has been a great influence in our own times. He deals with materials in which imagination enters in ways entirely different from that in which it appears in *belles lettres* and oratory. Literary students are now working with the documents of theological interpretation and controversy (one might call sermons literature in the narrower sense), with science, history, dictionaries, bibliographies, and almanacs. Literary study embraces the theological interpretation of the *Divine Comedy* and *Paradise Lost,* the investigation of Shakespeare's knowledge of geography or law, the discussion of the political and economic backgrounds of Renaissance travel and exploration, the description and analysis of the education and reading of Petrarch, Shakespeare, or Voltaire; the use of the historial concept of the frontier to interpret American literature, of the sociological milieu to read aright the novels of Dickens, of biological theory to understand the novels of Zola, or of medical knowledge to discover the ailments that affected the careers of De Quincey or Schiller and, in the specialized form of psycho-analytical research, to discover the secrets hidden from the world in a writer's innermost consciousness. Nor do literary students limit themselves to the contents of books and the lives of the men who wrote them. They search into technological processes. They study the manufacturing of books, the methods of the press, and the practices of the binder. In brief, anything in print is literature, and any intellectual discipline or any technological process may yield information needed to answer a question about it.

I would not imply by these wide definitions of folklore and literature that anything is wrong. Indeed, this wide range, which (perhaps by something that may, not inexactly, be called a *tour de force*) one could extend to make every human interest or activity subsidiary to literary studies, signifies that folklore and literature are true university disciplines.

There is a useful practical aspect in setting up these definitions. We are led to see neglected fields. In folklore, for example, we see how little has been done in the history and description of traditional patterns and designs. We have heard a great deal about the swastika, and a good deal has been written about it.[1] But many another symbol has been neglected. The meaning of an angular figure four used by Renaissance printers is, I think, entirely lost. Gestures are traditional motions of the body; there is scarcely anyone, except

---

[1] The earlier literature was surveyed by Thomas Wilson in his monographic article, "The Swastika," in the *Report of the U.S. National Museum Under the Direction of the Smithsonian Institution for the Year Ending June 30, 1894* (Washington, D. C., 1896), pp. 757–1011. For a sample of the scholarship inspired by German nationalism, see Bartel Bauer, *Hakenkreuz und Mythos* (München, 1934) and the references cited there. For an antidote, see W. Norman Brown, *The Swastika: A Study of the Nazi Claims of Its Aryan Origin* (New York, 1933). The swastika also appears on Pennsylvania Dutch barns and is discussed in Mahr's essay on Pennsylvania Dutch barn symbols in this volume.—Ed. Note

F. C. Hayes at the University of Florida, who has paid any attention to them.[2] Perhaps this neglect arises to some extent from the conditions of our modern life. The movies exhibit a much scantier and much less sophisticated use of gestures than a medieval painting. Many curious details in the history, interpretation, use, and style of gestures call for explanation. What of the Shanghai Gesture of thumb to nose? First, indeed, why does it have this name? How old is it? Where is it known and used? How does it come to have the meaning of an insult?[3] In one region of Italy the idea "Come here!" is expressed by holding the extended hand flat with the palm upwards and beckoning with the four fingers; in another, the hand is held flat as before, but the palm must be held downwards. As a sign of respect, we rise and stand. Yet I read that the witnesses rose when the criminals at Nuremberg were led in for execution. Were the witnesses doing honor to the human being or to the process of law? Setting these questions aside, we note that groveling is also a sign of respect. Here, as so often in folklore, we see contrasts signifying the same thing. The description of gestures, the determination of the times and places in which they have been used, and their interpretation—such are the tasks in folklore.

The use of gestures in a piece of literature is a problem for the literary student. What, for example—I am continuing my illustration of a neglected field of study—has been written on gestures in Shakespeare? I have not tried to answer my own question, but I should not expect to find much. I am not referring to gestures invented by an actor to give life to the text, but to gestures named or very clearly implied by the text itself. Samuel Butler's *Hudibras* abounds in gestures. I quote typical examples:

> This said, he clapt his hand on's sword,
> To shew he meant to keep his word.   [I, ii, 681, 682]

> At this the Knight grew high in wroth,
> And lifting hands and eyes up both,
> Three times he smote on stomach stout.   [I, ii, 737–39]

> It griev'd him to the guts that they. . . .
> Should suffer such inhuman wrong:
> For which he flung down his commission.   [I, ii, 893–98]

---

[2] See Francis Hayes, "Gestures: A Working Bibliography," *Southern Folklore Quarterly,* Vol. 21 (1957), 218–317, for a useful survey of some of the scholarship concerning gestures. Another fine survey of gesture scholarship or "kinesics" may be found in Weston La Barre, "Paralinguistics, Kinesics, and Cultural Anthropology," *Approaches to Semi-otics,* ed. Thomas A. Sebeok et al. (London, 1964), pp. 191–220.—ED. NOTE

[3] Archer Taylor has since studied this gesture himself. He suggests that the curious name may allude to a New Zealand and Australian word "shanghai," which means bean-shooter or slingshot, rather than to the better known verb "to shanghai." Neither explanation is particularly convincing. However, Taylor successfully traces the gesture back to the sixteenth century in Europe, and he finds that it is widely distributed in western Europe and in those areas of the world where European culture has made its influence felt. He feels that this insulting gesture may have developed in part as a parody of the military salute. Those interested in a comprehensive study of a single traditional gesture should consult *The Shanghai Gesture,* Folklore Fellows Communications No. 166 (Helsinki, 1956).—ED. NOTE

I scorn, quoth she, thou coxcomb silly,
Clapping her hand upon her breech,
To shew how much she prized his speech.   [I, iii, 814–17]

Let us approach the problem of literature *and* folklore more closely. I shall now limit myself primarily to folklore expressed in words—that is, to folksongs, folktales, proverbs, riddles, and similar categories. Here we see no fewer than three problems arising from three different kinds of relationships: (1) folklore is, in many cultures, indistinguishable from literature; (2) literature contains elements borrowed from folklore; and (3) writers have imitated folklore.

The identity of folklore and literature is an obvious fact. The Old Testament can be called a book of traditions, and it can be called the literature of the ancient Hebrews. In some instances, the culture of even a modern people consists largely in folklore. The *Kalevala* combines folk songs, with negligible changes, into the classical work of Finnish literature. I have been told by a competent authority that perhaps only two per cent of the verses cannot be proved to be of folk origin. The student of such literatures as the ancient Hebrew and the modern Finnish must employ the techniques of both folklore and literary history.

There arises here a fundamental question that is both important and difficult. Are there significant differences in style or matter between folklore and literature? The similarities can be readily discovered and lead to some interesting generalizations. If we state the theme and the manner of treatment of folktales in a general way, we see that they are identical with some literary themes and manners of treatment. The story of Cinderella tells how the poor and virtuous girl rises from obscurity to marry the prince and live happily ever after. This is the characteristic theme of the subliterary novel and appears again and again in the movies.

If we state the history of a genre of folklore and the history of a genre of literature in general terms, we see that the workers in these two fields are trying to solve similar problems. Compare, as examples, the stories about fools and detectives. We set up definitions of each genre, we endeavor to trace each back to its origins, we discover stylistic variations and variations in subject matter that are to be interpreted historically and evaluated critically. As an example of a stylistic variation, note Graham Greene's ingenious manner of telling the story from the point of view of the culprit and not the detective, and as an example of a variation in subject matter, note the modern restriction of the theme to a murder with the consequent desperate search for new and surprising ways of committing it. We find cultural details that call for interpretation: on the one hand, the ideas of the folk about fools and insanity or the relations of fool-stories to the court fool, and on the other hand, the employment of the devices of modern science in the detective story. Such comparisons are suggested by the similarities of folklore and literature when we conceive these fields of study in general terms.

Perhaps the most interesting and attractive problems in folklore arise when one regards folklore as literature and asks the questions that a literary historian might ask. Take riddles as an example. We are all familiar enough with a vague definition of a riddle as a puzzle.[4] We may take it for granted that the puzzle is stated in words and solved by a word. But, does such a definition include all the puzzles that have been printed in collections of riddles? It does not. There are puzzles expressed in terms of pictures. We call them rebuses. There are puzzles expressed in terms of acts. An example of the latter variety is the game requiring some one to put a light where everyone but himself can see it. He must put it on his head. And we can go still further with the analysis of definitions. Not all pictorial puzzles are of the same kind. Some involve a special interpretation of the pictures: an eye and a tin can represent "I can" and some contain pictures of the actual objects intended in place of the words. The latter variety is most often found in Sunday School readers and the so-called hieroglyphic Bibles. Each of these varieties has its own history. If we turn to riddles expressed in words, we find many varieties that have been recognized and many that have not. We have the simple descriptive riddle like Humpty Dumpty, in which an egg is personified as a man and the personification is then contradicted by saying that the man falls and cannot be put together again. This is something entirely different from Samson's riddle in Judges 14, and both are entirely different from such a question as the Danish "Which would you rather have: seven holes in your head or drink a cup of blood?—There are already seven holes in your head."[5] Like the choice of caskets in *The Merchant of Venice*, the proper choice in such alternatives is the one that is apparently the least attractive. These are by no means all the kinds of puzzles that men have used to confuse and entrap one another. There are arithmetical problems, Biblical questions, genealogical puzzles, and still other questions that can be answered by straining one's wits, and all of them are paralleled by such whimsies or parodies as "Is it right for a man to marry his widow's

---

[4] For a consideration of riddle definitions, see Robert A. Georges and Alan Dundes, "Toward A Structural Definition of the Riddle," *Journal of American Folklore,* Vol. 76 (1963), 111–18.—ED. NOTE

[5] Samson's riddle "Out of the eater came forth meat, and out of the strong came forth sweetness," is an example of what Archer Taylor calls a "neck-riddle." The neck-riddle narrates or refers to a situation or event known only to the poser of the riddle. Frequently the poser has been condemned to death, but he is given an opportunity to save his "neck." If he can ask a riddle which no one can guess, he is permitted to go free. Samson constructed his riddle after seeing a swarm of bees with honey in the carcass of a lion. For a discussion of the neck-riddle, see F. J. Norton, "Prisoner Who Saved His Neck with a Riddle," *Folklore,* Vol. 53 (1942), 27–57. For a comprehensive study of the riddle of the seven holes in the head (eyes, ears, nostrils, and mouth), see William A. Kozumplik, "Seven and Nine Holes in Man," *Southern Folklore Quarterly,* Vol. 5 (1941), 1–24. According to Kozumplik, the Danish version cited by Taylor is representative of a form of widespread Asiatic-European riddles found only in West European folk tradition. He gives Dutch, Flemish, French, Low German, Spanish, Swedish, and Swiss texts in this form. He also suggests that the alternative-question is a type of riddle preferred by children.—ED. NOTE

sister?"[6] If we proceed still further with the description of one of these varieties, we find curious subvarieties that have not been previously identified. There is a widely known riddle of the bed, the door, and the window: "One waits for the day, one waits for the night, and the third says, 'It is always the same for me.'" We can safely say that this represents a special category of the descriptive riddle, for it concerns three objects and not one as in an ordinary riddle, it employs the characteristic device of contrasting the activities of the three objects, and in the threescore and more examples that I have noted it deals with a limited range of themes. In this tripartite riddle we have noted that one of the objects is described by the words that it speaks. There are riddles consisting solely of dialogue:

> Zigzag, where are you going?
> Bald is your head, what is it to you?
> Hair will grow on my head before the straightening of your crooked steps.
> (A hayfield that has been mowed speaks to a winding brook that flows through it.)

This, too, is a special variety of riddle with a history of its own.[7]

I need go no further with this illustration of a stylistic analysis of riddles. The procedure is the same as that of the literary historian who recognizes and discusses the distinction between the Petrarchan and Wordsworthian sonnet, the differences between Shakespeare's use of five acts and Ibsen's use of four. The study of folklore can be an elementary exercise in literary history.

A more difficult problem confronts us when we ask: What are the differences between folklore and literature? An obvious difference is that folklore uses conventional themes and stylistic devices and makes no effort to disguise

---

[6] An example of an arithmetical problem is "If a hen and a half lays an egg and a half in a day and a half, how long will it take a hen to lay a dozen eggs?" A Biblical question is an example of a type of enigma which requires the answerer to possess some special information. In Biblical questions, the special information is detailed knowledge of the Bible. "Who was not born, but nevertheless died?" (Adam.) A relatively simple genealogical puzzle would be "The brother of my father had a brother, but he is not my uncle." (He is the father of the speaker.) There are many other curious sorts of riddles and puzzles. For example, a puzzle parody reported in Wisconsin and dating from the turn of the century asks "How do you make love out of wind?" ("A wind is a breeze; a breeze is a zephyr; a zephyr is a kind of yarn; a yarn is a tale; a tail is an attachment; an attachment is affection; and affection is love.") For a discussion of some of the interesting minor forms of riddles, see Archer Taylor, "The Varieties of Riddles," in *Philologica*: The Malone Anniversary Studies, eds. Thomas A. Kirby and Henry Bosley Woolf (Baltimore, 1949), pp. 1–8; and his earlier article "The Riddle," *California Folklore Quarterly*, Vol. 2 (1943), 129–47. For a sampling of the more common descriptive riddles (including the Humpty Dumpty riddle), see one of the finest and most scholarly collections of riddles ever assembled in any language, Archer Taylor, *English Riddles from Oral Tradition* (Berkeley and Los Angeles, 1951) with its 1749 texts, elaborate notes, bibliography, and index of collections of riddles arranged according to languages.—ED. NOTE

[7] For a detailed consideration of this variety of riddle, see Archer Taylor, "Riddles in Dialogue," *Proceedings of the American Philosophical Society*, Vol. 97 (1953), 61–68. —ED. NOTE

their conventional quality while the literary artist either divests his work of conventional quality by avoiding clichés of either form or matter or, as Housman does, charges them with new content. To make a truly critical analysis of the differences between folk literature and the literature of art requires philosophical criticism of a high quality. Efforts toward solving the problem have been made by comparing Homer and Virgil or by separating folk ballads from the poetry of art.

The second problem involving folklore and literature concerns the identification and interpretation of popular elements in a piece of literature. In this problem folklore is merely another discipline that the literary student should have at his command just as he has a foreign language, history, theology, economics, or psychology. The materials of folklore are already admirably arranged for his use in convenient reference works that guide the searcher to the needed information. Folktales have been collected in great abundance and are adequately indexed. The ease with which one can locate a folk theme contrasts sharply with the difficulty in finding examples of a literary theme. It is much easier to discover what has been said about Cinderella than what has been said about the Noble Savage. There are excellent collections of proverbs and more are in the making. One can find the parallels to one of Shakespeare's proverbs more easily than the parallels to one of his stylistic conventions.[8]

I have already suggested the problem of interpreting the folklore elements in a piece of literature by collecting a few gestures from *Hudibras*. The problem comes up again and again. It may be a question of the borrowing of whole themes, as we see in Longfellow's *Hiawatha*. Here there is a two-fold borrowing: Longfellow chose folk themes current among the American Indians and used the folk technique of the *Kalevala*.[9] Any critical and historical interpretation of a text may call for the use of folklore. The *Nigra sum sed formosa* (I am black but comely) of the "Song of Songs" is not, in many of its uses, a literary echo of Solomon's words but a folk theme found in the "Nutbrown Maid" and the hostility of the "Twa Sisters" in balladry. The use of proverbs in literature is always a challenging subject. In the Middle Ages proverbs were, I believe, more readily present to a writer's mind than they are today. He might have been taught to write by the school exercise of setting a proverb before him. He was then required to invent a situation illustrating the proverb and answer the questions, *"Quis, quid, ubi, quibus auxiliis, cur, quomodo, quando?"*[10] He no doubt

8 For the definitive study of Cinderella, Tale Type 510, see Anna Birgitta Rooth, *The Cinderella Cycle* (Lund, 1951). For Shakespeare's use of traditional proverbs, see Richard Jente, "The Proverbs of Shakespeare with early and contemporary parallels," *Washington University Studies, Humanistic Series,* Vol. 12 (1926), 391–444.—ED. NOTE

9 For an account of this twofold borrowing, see Ernest J. Moyne, *Hiawatha and Kalevala: A Study of the Relationship Between Longfellow's "Indian Edda" and the Finnish Epic,* Folklore Fellows Communications No. 192 (Helsinki, 1963).—ED. NOTE

10 Who, what, where, by what means, for what reason, in what manner, when? —ED. NOTE

compiled a commonplace book and included many proverbs in it. In the Renaissance a writer had Erasmus' *Adagia* at his elbow and was constantly aware of such related forms as the epigram and the emblem.

One can easily trace the history of "To bell the cat" and "The dog in the manger" as either a proverb or a fable.[11] Nevertheless, difficulties arise. Clearly "To earn one's bread by the sweat of one's brow" refers to the curse God laid on Adam, but this particular form of the curse is not found in the King James Version. Nor, I may add, in any other that I have consulted. Its origin is obscure. Freidank, a German versifier of didactic themes in the early thirteenth century, said, "The peacock has the gait of a thief, the voice of the Devil, and the garb of an angel," and an anonymous Englishman of about the same time wrote "For the peacock goeth like a thief," but the import of the allusion is no longer obvious.[12] Superstitions represent perhaps the most difficult variety of folklore to track down. Juliet says:

> It is the lark that sings so out of tune,
> Straining harsh discords and unpleasing sharps.
> Some say the lark makes sweet division;
> This doeth not so, for she divideth us;
> Some say the lark and the loathed toad change eyes.

No commentator that I know explains the allusion in the last line.[13]

We come now to the third problem involving literature and folklore, that is to say, to the intentional literary imitation of folk genres. Such an imitation implies recognition of a difference between folklore and literature. Until a differentiation of folk literature and the literature of art occurred, conscious imitations of folk style and folk matter could not have come into being. The proverb yields perhaps the most curious examples. Almost everyone who has studied proverbs has fallen into the delusion that he could invent proverbs. Sometimes he has been unwise enough to print his inventions, but none of them has ever received popular approval. James Howell, the author of the *Epistolae Ho-Elianae* and the compiler of an important dictionary of proverbs, added to the latter work "Divers centuries of new sayings, which may serve for proverbs to posterity." Not one has continued to live in tradition. Poets have imitated the ballad. Heine wrote the *Lorelei* and Dante Gabriel Rossetti, *Sister Helen*. Their failure to employ some obvious technical details of ballad style raises the question whether they

---

11 For a discussion of proverbs related to fables, see Archer Taylor's standard work, *The Proverb* (Cambridge, Mass., 1931), reprinted (Hatboro, Penn., 1962). For references to narratives related to the specific proverbs cited, see Tale Type 110, Belling the Cat, and Motif W156, The dog in the manger.—ED. NOTE

12 This proverbial description of the peacock may refer to the legend in which the peacock helps the serpent or fallen angel gain access to Paradise, where the evil one succeeds in tempting Adam and Eve. See Reverend S. Baring-Gould, *Legends of the Patriarchs and Prophets* (New York, 1872), pp. 39–43. (I am indebted to Francis Lee Utley for both the identification and the reference.)—ED. NOTE

13 This appears to be Motif A2241.5, Nightingale borrows blindworm's eye, or Tale Type 234, The Nightingale and the Blindworm.—ED. NOTE

perceived these conventions. The imitation of folktales in the eighteenth century and the romantic period as well as George Meredith's *Shaving of Shagpat* exhibits the same curious unawareness of the commonplaces of folklore style. The history of such imitations of folklore belongs to the historian of literature and not the folklorist.

There is, finally, a curious modern variation of this procedure that calls for comment. Instead of writing something in imitation of folklore and wishing it to be accepted as literature, a writer may have the wish that his work may pass as folklore. A large part of the stories about Paul Bunyan are such compositions.[14] They, too, show surprisingly little understanding of the conventional aspects of folk materials.

---

[14] Some professional folklorists are reluctant to consider Paul Bunyan a genuine folk hero inasmuch as few oral narratives of Bunyan's exploits have been collected. Paul Bunyan's fame appears to have been largely the product of an ingenious advertising campaign by the Red River Lumber Company. See Richard M. Dorson, *American Folklore* (Chicago, 1959), pp. 214–26; and Daniel G. Hoffman, *Paul Bunyan, Last of the Frontier Demigods* (Philadelphia, 1952), for extended discussion of the oral versus the literary origins of Paul Bunyan.—ED. NOTE

The Esoteric-Exoteric Factor in Folklore

Wm. Hugh Jansen

In this essay written by Professor Jansen of the University of Kentucky, the importance of the folk rather than the lore is emphasized. Specifically, the significance of folklore to a group vis-à-vis another group is stressed. A group's image of itself and its images of other groups are reflected in its folklore repertoire. An analysis of these images would reveal that the folk had made "national character studies" long before anthropologists and sociologists arrived upon the scene. Names, phrases, rhymes, songs, and jokes which one group uses to characterize specific peoples and places fall under a general category which folklorists call *"blason populaire."* There is no standard English equivalent of this French term, but the sense is roughly "ethnic slur." Sometimes the slur is *intra*group folklore. In Mexican folklore, for example, the inhabitants of Monterrey are reputed to be stingy. ("When someone dies in Monterrey, he is buried only to the waist so the price of a monument is saved.") Sometimes the slur is *inter*group. The Swedes say that "A Norwegian is nothing but a Swede with his brains blown out." (The Norwegians in turn define Swedes as Norwegians with their brains blown out.) The point is that both on an intra- and intergroup level, a given group inevitably has traditional rivals, enemies, and/or scapegoats about whom it has traditions.

The factual validity of a particular *blason populaire* tradition can only be determined by comparing the tradition with empirical ethnographic data. But that the tradition exists at all is of interest. Whether or not Jews really are materialistic and money-minded is one thing, but that there is a traditional folk stereotype is indisputable. Moreover, what the folk say may be an indicator of what the folk think. Whether it's a slogan ("Jesus Saves; Moses Invests") or a joking question referring to a supposed physiognomic feature ("Why do Jews have big noses? Air is free") the mercenary slur is the same. It is perhaps difficult to gauge the actual effect of various *blason populaire* traditions in the formation of deep-seated prejudices; it is sufficient to say that folklore not only acts as a unifying force in terms of one group's

Reprinted from *Fabula: Journal of Folktale Studies,* Vol. 2 (1959), 205–11, by permission of the author and Walter de Gruyter & Co.

identity but also as a divisive force in terms of molding or confirming one group's attitudes toward another group.

All over the world there are specific traditions used by one group in reference to another, and a person who travels might very well profit by discovering another group's folklore about his group. For further examples of these traditions, see Henri Gaidoz and Paul Sèbillot, *Blason Populaire de la France* (Paris, 1884); Archer Taylor, *The Proverb* (Cambridge, Mass., 1931), pp. 97–109; A. A. Roback, *A Dictionary of the International Slurs* (Cambridge, Mass., 1944); and Ed Cray, "Ethnic and Place Names as Derisive Adjectives," *Western Folklore*, Vol. 21 (1962), 27–34.

During the 1957 celebration of the traditional American folk festival, the World Series, a television viewing room was unofficially set up at my home university for the benefit of faculty members who had both untimely classes and a conscience.[1] During the games, the televiewers were about evenly divided between harried professors and members of the Negro janitorial staff of the University, which, incidentally, is going through the throes of integration.

At what some sports writers used to call a crucial moment in one of the later games, Hank Aaron, hero of the Milwaukee Braves, struck out. For the benefit of the Milwaukee partisans present, one of the janitors spoke up, "Don't worry; one of our boys will be up this inning." A disgruntled Yankee rooter, a professor, growled, "So what? Covington hasn't done anything today." The janitor looked puzzled for a moment, then with dawning comprehension said gently, "That's right, but Frank Torre's my boy." Genuinely sensitive to interracial etiquette, the professor had no resort but uncomfortable silence compounded by the defeat of his Yankees. Later, still brooding over the *contretemps,* he told me, "Yes, and I suppose Elston Howard is my boy."[2]

The point of this true episode is, I suppose, apparent even to non-baseball enthusiasts who should not have to be told that Aaron, Covington, Howard, and the janitor are all Negro, while Torre and the professor are white. An aftermath of this same experience bears upon the same point. A month after the World Series, in planning a lecture to be delivered at our Negro state college, I decided to retell the episode to illustrate another point. Worrying about its possible reception, I finally telephoned an understanding member

[1] Except for minor changes this paper was read at the annual meeting of the American Folklore Society, in joint session with the American Anthropological Association, December 29, 1957, in Chicago, Illinois.

[2] For the benefit of non-American readers it should be pointed out that the World Series is the climax of the professional baseball season in the U.S.A. Seven games are played for what is considered to be the championship of the world. The contestants are the two top teams from the two major leagues: in 1957 these were the Braves representing the city of Milwaukee and the Yankees representing New York City. *Integration,* of course, refers to the process of incorporating Negro students into schools from which they were previously excluded.

of the Negro college faculty. Laughing, she assured me that the anecdote was of a particularly acceptable nature, at the same time prefacing her assurance with, "We are a sensitive people." All through that lecture, though, I had the weird sensation of wondering whether I had been told my audience was a sensitive people because it was known that I in my sensitivity expected them to be sensitive.

The point being illustrated is no startlingly new discovery. In its general outlines it affects a hazy assumption underlying, in some part, much of the field and library research conducted both in folklore and in various other sciences bent upon analyzing group cultures. Whenever a field worker sets about recording the songs of the lumberjack or the tales of the Appalachian backwoodsman, whenever the library worker meditates on the nature of the humor of minority groups, such a worker is tacitly assuming that the material being recorded or analyzed has peculiar virtues arising from its existence within a more or less peculiar group. This hazy, tacit assumption may be recognized as a truism, and, as with many truisms, deserves a full, careful definition and a systematic exploration of its actual and potential applicability. In the present instance, however, such definition and exploration could fill a book-length study, and so here we can analyze only one factor in the assumption that folklore takes on peculiar properties from the group within which it is found.

The quality that I have so far avoided naming or defining, I am electing to term the *esoteric-exoteric factor in folklore*. The modification implied by the phrase *in folklore* is essential to the term, particularly in the light of my own ignorance of other fields. It is my belief that, with a possible exception in the case of primitive peoples, folklore is that portion of a group's culture and belief that does not derive from formal, institutionalized educational forces, indeed that frequently exists despite such forces. It is within this context that the words *exoteric* and *esoteric* are intended to be understood in this paper.

To define our esoteric-exoteric factor with a simplified and imaginary example, let us take Group A with a definable, fairly homogeneous culture. If we isolate certain elements in its traditions, we find that Group A considers itself to be, among other things, remarkably chivalrous, particularly adept militarily, and completely self-reliant. Group A also is convinced that Group B considers Group A to be old-fashioned, unprogressive, and intolerant. If, however, we move over to Group B itself, we find that it actually considers A to be impractical, unrealistic, and headstrong. Further, sometimes B may fear that A feels B regards A as being inferior, weak, and treacherous. This last may seem less confusing, if I remind you of the not uncommon statement: "They think that we think that they are inferior." Although Groups A and B are quite imaginary, it would not be difficult to substitute for A and B the names of various nations or regional groups that have a history of uneasy relations with each other: e.g., the North and the South in the United States, to choose, I hope, a tactful example.

To return to A and B, above we have three, occasionally four, concepts of what the peculiar or dominant characteristics of A are. There may quite possibly be not one point common to all four concepts, and I venture that it is impossible for there to be complete coincidence among all four. This, then, is the esoteric-exoteric factor in folklore. The esoteric applies to what one group thinks of itself and what it supposes others think of it. The exoteric is what one group thinks of another and what it thinks that other group thinks it thinks.

It is perfectly possible for the esoteric beliefs of a group to be unconsciously held. On the other hand, depending upon isolation, communication, and the like, it is equally possible for a group to know the exoteric concepts held about it and either to reject those concepts or to recognize them tolerantly. Thus it is that American Negro tales collected from Negroes may be based upon obviously white, i.e., exoteric, concepts of Negro characteristics, and thus it is that some of the most pernicious anti-semitism appears in Yiddish jokes told by Yiddish comics. So, too, traveling salesman stories spread through publishing representatives who, perhaps strangely, may totally fail to identify their occupation with that of a traveling salesman.

The esoteric part of this factor, it would seem, frequently stems from the group sense of belonging and serves to defend and strengthen that sense. Evidence for such an assertion might be found in what the old settler's attitude toward the greenhorn shows about the value of being an old settler; in the very word *greenhorn,* incidentally; in the mountaineer's attitude toward the lowlander; in the traditional pranks played upon apprentices by master craftsmen[3] or—less seriously—in the college fraternities' informal initiation rites. The exoteric aspect of the factor is, at least in part, a product of the same sense of belonging, for it may result from fear of, mystification about, or resentment of the group to which one does not belong. Examples of this might be found in the obviously exoteric beliefs behind the Hugh of Lincoln legend long ago retold by Chaucer[4] in the tales of riotous life within monastery walls still being told by backwoods American Protestants.

---

[3] These initiate's tasks or fools' errands (Motif J2346) often vary with the occupation. A plumber's apprentice might be sent for a left-handed monkeywrench and a novice painter might be told to find a bucket of striped paint. For examples, see Oliver Farrar Emerson, "Beguiling Words," *Dialect Notes,* Vol. 5, Part IV (1921), 93–96; and A. M. Honeyman, "Fools' Errands for Dundee Apprentices," *Folklore,* Vols. 69–70 (1958–1959), 334–36.—ED. NOTE

[4] The story of the murder of a Christian boy by a Jew's daughter is found in both ballad (Child 155) and legend (Motifs V254.7, V361). The plot is the basis of Chaucer's Prioress's tale. (See Carleton F. Brown, "Chaucer's Prioress's Tale and Its Analogues," *Publications of the Modern Language Association,* Vol. 21 [1906], 486–518.) Jansen's example is a good one. Like the migratory legend of the wandering Jew (Tale Type 777, Motif Q502.1), the story supports the anti-semitic attitudes of some Christians toward Jews, attitudes based upon the false premise that Jews, not Romans, murdered Christ. No doubt a Jewish version would be likely to stress the fact that Jesus, a Jew by birth, was crucified by Roman gentiles. The same dichotomy is found in contemporary American sacrilegious jokelore. *Jewish* jokes often emphasize the *Hebraic origin of Christianity* (e.g., Jesus speaks Yiddish in the punch line), whereas *Christian* jokes may be based on the idea that Jesus converted *from Judaism to Christianity.* The historical data is the same for both groups, but the selection of details for emphasis by the two groups is quite different.—ED. NOTE

Sometimes the esoteric aspect arises from the special knowledge of a group and, intentionally or not, aids in preserving that knowledge. This phase of the esoteric is most evident in verbal expressions of folk belief, in proverbs, and proverbial sayings, and is most widely recognized in such groups as the farmers with their weather lore, plant lore, astrological signs, and the like. A simple illustration is the answer that the question "How are you" elicits from the Kentucky mountain farmer: "Two to a hill," he says. He plants his corn in hills, four seeds to the hill. Thus two seedlings to a hill represents fifty per cent germination and his answer means a noncommittal "So-so"—to the group which shares his esoteric knowledge.

A set of general statements about the esoteric-exoteric factor may be set down before we turn to folkloric applications of this theory; these seem fairly self-evident, but each of them could be illustrated at length.

1. Within reason, the smaller the group, the stronger the esoteric element in its folklore.
2. The more distinctive or distinguishable a group, the more likely the occurrence of exoteric folklore about that group.
3. The larger and more self-confident the group, the weaker the esoteric element in its folklore; but
4. there are no indications that great size and self-confidence in a group offer any deterrent to the formulation of exoteric folklore about that group.

On this last point of the relation between the size of a group and the esoteric-exoteric factor in folklore, some very interesting material might be turned up by an historian of American thought. To my layman's eye, it does seem that as America has increased in size and strength during the past century, it has steadily protested less and less that it has had size and power. (How much of America's interpretation of its own national characteristics is a part of its folk culture is certainly a difficult question, but also certainly some of it is.)

But to commence more directly the application of the esoteric-exoteric concept to what is more certainly folklore, I propose that there are three classes of material cutting across the various conventional genres of folklore (narratives, songs, beliefs, proverbs, riddles, etc.) to which the esoteric-exoteric concept particularly applies:

1. *Folklore generally prevalent about a particular group.* Anyone may tell tales about sailors, tales that rely upon beliefs about the nature and morality of the seafaring life. Among the many other materials that fit this category are tales about the mendacity of fishermen, the dedication of doctors, the unprincipled cleverness of lawyers, the lechery of tinkers, and the dishonesty of gypsies.
2. *Folklore prevalent in one particular group about another particular group.* Here belongs the folklore prevalent among doctors about lawyers, within the infantry about the Air Force, among soldiers about sailors, and among Norwegians about Swedes (here may be substituted the names of almost any two adjacent nations or regions).
3. *Folklore prevalent within one group and concerned only with that group.* Such folklore frequently involves a private jargon: stories told by musicians, criminals, drug addicts featuring their own lingo. A few years ago, a group of "reefer" stories was being told by marijuana smokers and their curious

hangers-on, each story having its punch line preceded by the sharp sound of inhalation. Here, too, I think, belongs the very private folklore of teenagers with their current Bloody Marys ("Aside from that, Mrs. Lincoln, what did you think of the performance?") stemming back through the callous jokes of another era ("I haven't had so much fun since we ran Willy through the sausage-grinder") to the boorish jokes even further back ("That wouldn't have happened, Mrs. Astor, if you hadn't stepped between me and the spittoon").[5]

Of these three classes of material, the first is obviously heavily exoteric, since it is about but not by any particular group. In the third, the esoteric predominates since it is known to one group and not concerned with any other group. The second, however, has both elements since it is by one group and about another group. If one is concerned with the fact that only one group knows this folklore, it is to that extent esoteric. If one is concerned with the fact that this folklore is about a group and certainly not accepted by that group, perhaps not even known to that group, it is in that connection exoteric. Naturally there are other materials in which the esoteric-exoteric factor enters, and they should be considered, but this paper is intended to be suggestive, not exhaustive.[6]

In all that has gone before, the word *group* stands out, if by no other virtue, at least by repetition. The last section of this paper concerns that word. What groups have a folklore that might be profitably studied with the esoteric-exoteric dichotomy in mind? What traits give these groups this kind of folklore?

Most folklorists would immediately propose as an answer to the first question: those groups ordinarily designated in folklore handbooks as occupational, professional, and industrial. And this would not be wrong, but not all of such groups would be equally profitable and some groups not usually mentioned in handbooks would be very profitable. Therefore I am categorizing these groups according to the influences (or traits) which render them particularly subject to the esoteric-exoteric factor in folklore.

[5] It would be too tangential to take the space here to point out fully why I believe such humor is esoteric. Basically this humor arises (1) because the adolescent is very purposefully excluded from the humor of adult social situations and (2) because the adolescent fears his own easily aroused sentimentality in what he construes to be an unemotional world.

[6] I am deeply indebted to Prof. Dr. Thelma G. James for the suggestion that much material rich in the esoteric-exoteric association springs from people who, forced by modernization or led by their own desires, have abandoned a group association or have tried to assume membership in another group than their own. Ready examples of this shifting are afforded by, among others, those who have abandoned their religions, who have attempted to disguise their racial or national origins, or whose traditional occupation has been obliterated by progress. Certainly much lore, both exoteric and esoteric, about such individuals exists in the groups with which they were formerly associated. That such lore contains *folk* concepts beyond the four introduced at the beginning of this paper, is a question worth debate.

Basically there seem to be three major facts which may make a group liable to the esoteric-exoteric factor. Most evident of the three is isolation. Many groups are definable simply because they each have their own peculiar types of isolation ranging from obvious geographic separation to other not-so-obvious forms of isolation. Too much, perhaps, has been made of the geographic isolation of the farmer, the frontiersman, the mountaineer, and the woodsman, but clearly this isolation has produced a great deal of exoteric, if not esoteric, folklore. Similarly the miner, the sailor, and the lumberjack are isolated for a significant part of their lives because they work under the ground, in the forests, or on the sea. Forced and constant travel as part of an occupation serves to isolate into separate groups the migrant laborers, railroaders, circus and carnival people, theatrical troupers, professional athletes, and, of course, traveling salesmen. The customary wearing of a uniform sets aside such groups as firemen, soldiers, policemen, clergy, and nurses. The danger of an occupation (frequently proudly realized by the members of that occupation) sets apart such groups as miners, structural steel workers, steeplejacks, and oilfield workers.

A number of other peculiar properties, each the common experience of the members of a single group, effectively isolate those groups. Age isolates the very young, the very old, and the teenager into cultural islands somehow more productive and conservative of private folklore than the other insular generations. Regionalism, of course, separates the Yankee from the Southerner, the Texan from the Midwesterner, and so on. Religions, particularly if they make their constituents conspicuous in costume, language, diet, or the observance of holidays, serve to isolate groups within groups. The custom of speaking a language or dialect different from the prevailing one successfully isolates the speakers. Finally lack of education or the possession of an extremely limited education can also isolate a group.

Of course a single group may be subjected to several different isolating forces: thus, migrant fruit pickers are compelled to travel, they frequently speak a "foreign" language, they may belong to a "peculiar" religion, and their opportunities for education are very much limited. In this instance, four different influences all concentrate to isolate the one group.

Before leaving isolation, I might point out that this influence in favor of the esoteric-exoteric factor might also be described as a failure in or an incapacity for communication; but, however it is described, it exerts the same influence.

Second to isolation as a force subjecting a group to the esoteric-exoteric complex is the possession of a knowledge or training that either is or seems to be peculiar. Such a knowledge is that of the telegrapher, mysterious and incomprehensible to the layman. The awe in which printers were held until recently guaranteed the existence of certain license and of exoteric folklore.

The auctioneer is felt to have not only a private language but a psychic insight into the buyer's frailties. Credit jewelers, who delight in calling themselves "junk jewelers," have an argot that can be used to discuss a product and what the market will bear in the very presence of the unwitting customer. When I tried to record this argot, my intended informant begged me to desist, for he was positive that his colleagues would be able to determine the source of my information. Surely an esoteric folk trait lies here. Other groups who have, or feel they have, or are felt to have, special knowledge include racetrack employees, horse breeders, and undertakers.

The third, and last, quality subjecting a group to the esoteric-exoteric factor appears when one group is considered by others as being particularly admirable, particularly favored, or particularly awesome, The most recent group so considered is composed of atomic scientists, and we have not heard the end of the exoteric folklore on that subject—nor, I suppose, of the esoteric either. Other groups who have occupied, more or less recently, this favored spot include the Air Corps, doctors, lawyers, professors, and the clergy. In some cultures, the professional soldier, the officer caste, the government functionary, and the diplomat are considered peculiarly enviable. Certain groups have rather private concepts of favored other groups: witness the way children look upon soldiers, policemen, firemen, railroad engineers, and cowboys.

While the folklorist should be particularly interested in such groups, he should realize that they are not, and have not been, his exclusive concern. Cultural historians and anthropologists, literary historians and critics, artists and authors, have all at one time or another in some way utilized either the esoteric or the exoteric factor, or both, inherent in such groups as the pioneer, the frontiersman, the trapper, the Indian fighter, the cowboy, the tinker, the tailor, the pack pedlar, the midwife, the witch doctor, the herb doctor, the telegrapher, the Jesuit, the evangelist—to name only those that come to mind at random. Modern popular arts deal much with such concepts. In the comics there are a fairly esoteric treatment of the "fight crowd" and several very exoteric treatments of the Kentucky mountaineer. Dick Tracy of the comics and Joe Friday of TV both utilize the same exoteric concept of the policeman, while no one needs to have pointed out the exoteric nature of the TV's ubiquitous cowboys and marshals.

In summary, these are the points that I hope have been made:

1. There is a generally felt but seldom verbalized recognition of esoteric and exoteric attitudes within groups and toward groups.
2. There is a general assumption that the folklore of a group has certain inherent qualities (perhaps virtues) because it belongs to or has been shaped by that group.
3. Some qualities in a given group's folklore reflect esoteric concepts of itself (how it interprets itself and how it conceives others to interpret it).

4. Some qualities in a group's folklore reflect exoteric concepts about another group (how it interprets that group and how it imagines that group feels it is interpreted).
5. Certain types of folklore material are likely to be rich in the reflection of esoteric-exoteric concepts.
6. Isolation or lack of communication with others, the possession of what is considered peculiar knowledge, and the fact of being held in peculiar respect are all influences apt to render certain groups particularly subject to the appearance of the esoteric-exoteric factor in their folklore.
7. Such groups, already of interest to serious and popular artists and to scholars concerned with group culture, should receive the interest of folklorists and should incite them to pursue further the application and significance of the esoteric-exoteric factor in folklore.[7]

---

[7] Because of pronunciation difficulties, Prof. Dr. Newbell Niles Puckett has suggested, in mock seriousness, that the phrase esoteric-exoteric factor be glamorized by terming it the Es-Ex or simply the S-X factor. In like vein, the author admits to no objections to such nicknames.

The Search for Origins

Even if there were some agreement as to what folklore is, it is unlikely that there would be much accord as to how folklore began. The history of the discipline of folklore is riddled with the remains of elaborate theories explaining how folklore arose. Some of these theories are still championed; others are revived only to serve as straw men to be ritually killed in modern surveys of folklore. An example of the latter is solar mythology, which few, if any, folklorists seriously entertain at the present time.

Two of the characteristics of folklore that most of the theories have attempted to deal with in one way or another are (1) *multiple existence* and (2) *irrationality*. Multiple existence refers to the fact that an item of folklore appears at more than one time and place. For example, the flood myth (Motif A1010) and the obstacle flight (Motif D672), in which fugitives throw objects behind them which magically become obstacles in their pursuer's path, are widely distributed throughout the world. The question posed is: How is it that virtually the same story is told among many different peoples who do not appear to be related?

Several explanations have been offered to explain multiple existence. One is the notion of *polygenesis* (many origins), according to which the same item could have independently originated many times. Frequently polygenesis is associated with the concept of the psychic unity of man. Advocates of this idea contend that man is everywhere psychologically the same. Consequently, his psychological products (including folklore) could be and apparently are the same or similar.

Few anthropologists today accept the ideas of polygenesis and psychic unity as satisfactory explanations of seemingly parallel cultural phenomena. However, in the late nineteenth century, many anthropologists subscribed to these theories. According to one scheme strongly supported in England, all men evolved in one evolutionary path through three absolutely identical stages of savagery, barbarism, and civilization. Savagery was said to be exemplified by Australian aboriginal culture, whereas civilization was symbolized by Victorian England. Since unilinear (one line) evolution meant that all peoples passed or were passing through these three (the European ritual number) stages, it was believed that the ancestors of a nineteenth-century Englishman must have been savages like, in fact exactly like, the Australian aborigines. This supposition was crucial for folklore theory inasmuch as it was also postulated that folklore arose during the stage of savagery. As man evolved, he left his folklore behind him. (In other words, as man evolved, folklore devolved or decayed.) With evolution, only fragments of folklore, called "survivals," remained in civilized times. Unfortunately, these survivals were so fragmentary that they could not be understood. To understand European folklore, which consisted of survivals from the past age of savagery, it was necessary to engage in historical reconstruction, a favorite scholarly pastime of the nineteenth century which was allied to the ideals of romanticism and the worship of the past. The task of historical reconstruction was obviously facilitated by the possibility of examining living savage folklore (e.g., American Indian and Australian materials) which were held to be the precursors of European folklore. The technique of studying a European custom was to seek the fuller form which was presumed to exist in savage cultures (past or present). The theory also explained why folklore in Europe was thought to exist primarily among the peasants. Peasants were considered to be essentially barbarians, one step above savagery but clearly not yet belonging to the last stage of civilization.

The explanation of multiple existence, which is generally accepted by twentieth-century anthropologists and folklorists, is a combination of *monogenesis* (one origin) and *diffusion,* the process by which a cultural trait moves from one individual to another, from one culture to another. According to this view, a particular myth or riddle did not arise through independent invention (polygenesis) in all those places where the myth or riddle is now found. Rather, the item of folklore arose in one place, or perhaps in a very few places, and then spread by diffusion to other places. Diffusionists argue that if an item is complex rather than simple (though the question remains how simple is simple) and if there is continuous distribution of the item in the area intervening between points A and B, the occurrence of the item at A and B is to be attributed to diffusion rather than to independent origin. The diffusion theory does not require the idea of psychic unity. However, an important point, which is usually not explained by diffusionists, is *why* many different cultures should accept the same borrowed myth or riddle.

The presence of apparent irrationality in folklore has posed as much of a problem to folklore theorists as has folklore's multiple existence. There cannot be magic combs which turn into forests and thus impede pursuers. There are no *vagina dentatas* (Motif F547.1.1). There are no magic wands (Motif D1254.1). Since these items are not found in nature, in objective reality, their origin must be related to the origin of human fantasies.

The distinction between historical and psychological origins of folklore is an important one. The historical origin of an item of folklore tells *when* and *where* an item may have arisen and perhaps *how* it has spread. It does not, however, explain *why* the item arose in the first place. In contrast, a proposed psychological origin of an item of folklore may purport to explain why the item came into being, but the how and when of the item's diffusion may be ignored. Different questions are being answered, although the answers are both called origins, and both types of explanations are limited by the amount of data available. Historical records go back only so far in the evolution of man. Without some concrete historical evidence, it is difficult, if not impossible, to provide a plausible explanation for the existence of an item of folklore in a particular place. Psychological explanations are usually based upon speculative assumptions about modern man. But whether or not the human ancestor or ancestors who devised the folktale or game had the same psychological makeup as modern man is hard to prove. This factor, incidentally, is why those favoring psychological explanations of origins tend to assume some sort of psychic unity which would make human psychology through the ages more of a constant than a variable.

Another way of viewing the historical versus the psychological approach to origins is through recourse to a literal-symbolic dichotomy. Those who interpret folklore literally feel that there is historical truth underlying folklore. What appears to be irrationality is simply rationality distorted or history misremembered. According to the literal interpretation, folklore is more fact than fiction. The English folklorists of the late nineteenth century held this position, and thus in their aim of *historical* reconstruction they sought to find the factual truth underlying the folklore fragments of civilization. What appeared to be irrational to a civilized man was no doubt rational to a savage (and by philosophical extension to the child and the poet). Thus folkloristics in the late nineteenth century was regarded as a historical science.

The symbolic approach to folklore depends upon the notion that folklore is more fantasy than fact. It is argued that just as things in dreams may never have occurred in waking reality, so also some folklore may be similar mental phenomena. The most perplexing problem of symbolic studies of folklore is the translation of the symbolic code. Each school of symbolism claims to possess the one and only correct key by whose means the secret message concealed by the code is suddenly brilliantly revealed. Most adherents of symbolic interpretations would tend to make the study of folklore a psychological, not a historical, science. Their explanation of the widespread flood story would not be that there was in fact an actual flood (i.e., a literal reading of the myth), but that perhaps the deluge from which man is created anew is a cosmogonic projection of the process of human birth in which the neonate is delivered from the amniotic flood waters.

Probably the most sensible course of action for the beginner in folklore is to avoid the pitfalls of any of the monolithic origin theories.

Some folklore may have arisen polygenetically; some may have spread by diffusion after originating at one point in space and time. Some folklore reflects history and objective reality; some appears to reflect human fantasy and psychological reality. Each item of folklore studied must be critically examined on an individual basis, according to the evidence available, rather than blindly fitting it into a rigid a priori theoretical frame. This means that the satisfying certainty which comes with fanatic adherence to a monolithic theory may have to be sacrificed. In fact, most folklorists despair of answering the intriguing questions of origins and they have moved on to other important problems, namely, form, function, and transmission, where hypotheses may be tested and where there is more chance for certainty. Nevertheless, there is probably no more fascinating aspect of the study of folklore, albeit fraught with theoretical and methodological peril, than that of the search for origins.

The Eclipse
of Solar Mythology

Richard M. Dorson

Probably no theory concerning the origin of folklore has aroused as much interest both within and without the discipline as that of the solar mythologists. In this illuminating essay by Richard M. Dorson, Professor of Folklore and History at Indiana University, the theory is set in historical perspective. Now part of the history of the development of folklore theory, solar mythology serves to illustrate the thesis that folklore interpretations are often as fantastic and fascinating as the folkloristic materials they claim to explain.

We smile condescendingly today at the solar mythologists. So restrained a scholar as Stith Thompson refers to the extinct school as "absurd," "fantastic," "ridiculous," even dangerous to the sanity of the modern reader.[1] Max Müller and his disciples are chided for not recognizing the inanity of their own theories, and Andrew Lang is lauded for piercing them with ridicule.

Max Müller's sun has indeed set. But was the leading Sanscrit scholar of his day a fool? And why did Lang have to spend a quarter of a century in demolishing ideas so patently absurd? The famous *Chips* now sell at the old-book stalls for ten cents a volume, but they once graced the parlor tables of thoughtful Victorians, and in at least one instance distracted a groom on his honeymoon.[2] Viewed as part of the intellectual growth of the nineteenth

Reprinted from the *Journal of American Folklore,* Vol. 68 (1955), 393–416, by permission of the author and the American Folklore Society.

[1] Stith Thompson, *The Folktale* (New York, 1946), pp. 371–75. The conventional view that Max Müller was a second-rate Victorian, slain by Lang's ethnology, is asserted by Richard Chase, *Quest for Myth* (Baton Rouge, La., 1949), pp. 44–48, 58–65. Chase is unaware of Müller's interest in ethnology, and discusses the theories of myth held by Lang and Müller without any reference to the history of folklore, although they are inseparably connected. His ignorance of folklore leads him into the astonishing statement that Lang failed to show interest in folktales until late in life (pp. 61, 77). To Chase, myth is art, and he judges mythologists by his own prejudices.

[2] Andrew Lang, "Max Müller," *Contemporary Review,* Vol. 78 (1900), 785.

century, solar mythology assumes a more honorable aspect.[3] Its devotees contributed a yeasty ferment to the newly baptized field of folklore and drew the attention of a host of scholars and readers to traditional narratives. Thompson neglects to comment on the intensity and drama of this fray, nor does he indicate that it was a two-way battle, lethal for both combatants. For Müller gave as good as he received, and riddled Lang's own cherished concept of "savage" survivals. Before the smoke had cleared, this acrid debate over the origins of myths had greatly broadened the base of folklore scholarship.

Solar mythology primarily deserves the attention of folklore students for the role it played in the history of our subject. In England, where the leading action took place, the comparative mythologists asserted and defended their position throughout the second half of the nineteenth century. As Lang himself conceded, without their provocation he and his fellow folklorists might never have stirred into existence. One wonders indeed what Lang could have written on folklore without the enticing target of Müller, whose name re-echoes on Lang's pages; if Müller were a dying god, apparently he enjoyed successive rebirths, for the Scot kept slaying him through numerous publications. To unravel this intricate literature of controversy, bursting into many books, dipping frequently into periodical essays and reviews, and spreading across the continent, would require another book. This paper will confine itself to England, and to the two principal protagonists, with some consideration of Müller's chief allies, George W. Cox and Robert Brown, and of two American supporters, Daniel G. Brinton and John Fiske.

The historian of any field of learning would be proud to relate the encounter of two such brilliant luminaries as Andrew Lang and the Right Honorable Friedrich Max Müller. Between them they furnished English gentlemen with a well-stocked library. Coming to England from his native Germany as a youth of twenty-six, eager to translate the Sacred Books of India, Max Müller settled in Oxford and never left. He won a vast audience with limpid essays on such forbidding subjects as the science of language and the religion of India, and became so famous that when he considered leaving Oxford University in 1875 at the invitation of European governments, a special decree at Convocation and a prayerful eulogy from the Dean of Christ Church broke precedent to retain him free from all teaching duties.[4] When Müller died in 1900, Queen Victoria sent his widow a personal telegram of sympathy, and royalty around the world added their condolences.

Andrew Lang, who would survive his adversary twelve years, wrote a

---

[3] For the history of folklore theory, even in England, one must turn to European studies. There is gratifying detail on Müller and Lang in Giuseppe Cocchiara, *Storia del folklore in Europa* (Edizioni Scientifiche Einaudi, 1952), Chap. 16, "Nel 'laboratorio' di Max Müller," pp. 309–24; and Chap. 24, "Il primitivo che è in noi," pp. 461–69. A discussion of "Die Astralmythologie" appears in Åke Ohlmarks, *Heimdalls Horn und Odins Auge:* Erstes Buch (I–II), *Heimdalls und das Horn* (Lund and Copenhagen, 1937), pp. 3–22, but the author fails to distinguish between religion and mythology in discussing Müller and Lang (pp. 6–8). Actually they rather agreed on the origin of religious ideas.

[4] Georgina Max Müller, *The Life and Letters of the Right Honourable Friedrich Max Müller,* 2 vols. (New York, London, and Bombay, 1902), Vol. 2, 7; and Appendix C, "Speech of Dean Liddell," pp. 475–79.

gracious letter to Mrs. Max Müller, and spoke of her husband's "good humour and kindness perhaps unexampled in the controversies of the learned and half-learned."[5] Classical "performer," essayist, historian, poet, critic, anthropologist, sports writer, Lang ranged over so many fields of letters and learning that today a whole battery of specialists deliver lectures at St. Andrews on his contributions to their chosen fields.[6] His fecundity and wit were the despair of his contemporaries, who writhed from his thrusts in the evening papers, the weekly and monthly reviews, and the endless books he wrote, edited, and prefaced.[7]

In 1856 Max Müller published a long essay on comparative mythology which reoriented all previous thinking on the origin of myths. The treatise astonished and delighted philologists, classicists, and literary scholars; John Fiske recalls the excitement that swept him on first reading the "noble essay," and Cox and Lang equally pay it tribute.[8] Only ten years earlier William Thoms had devised the term "folklore" to embrace the study of popular antiquities and had begun comparative annotations of beliefs and tales in *Notes and Queries*. Only five years before had the first book appeared which used "Folklore" in its title.[9] The study of mythology remained in a separate, sterile compartment; even Thomas Keightley, who wrote on both fairy legends and Greek myths, produced only a conventional manual of classical mythology interpreting the Homeric gods and heroes as pretty allegories.[10] Müller now offered a key to the understanding of Aryan traditions, whether myths of the gods, legends of heroes, or tales of the people, through the science of comparative philology and the new revelation of Vedic Sanscrit.

From the appearance of this essay to the last years of his life Müller expanded and championed his method. The *Lectures on the Science of Language, Second Series* (1864) included five chapters relating to solar mythology. Three years later Müller brought together in the second volume of his *Chips from a German Workshop* his occasional "Essays on Mythology, Traditions, and Customs" dating from (and including) his epochal monograph. This volume particularly intrigues the intellectual historian by recording Müller's reactions, in the form of review-essays, to classical folklore works emerging in the 1860's: the tale collections of Callaway, Dasent, and

---

[5] *Ibid.*, Vol. 2, 452.

[6] See *Concerning Andrew Lang*, Being the Andrew Lang Lectures delivered before the University of St. Andrews 1927–1937 (Oxford, 1949).

[7] Roger L. Green has written *Andrew Lang, A Critical Biography*, with a Short-Title Bibliography of the Works of Andrew Lang (Leicester, Eng., 1946).

[8] Fiske, *Myths and Mythmakers* (Boston and New York, 1888), p. 209; Cox, *The Mythology of the Aryan Nations*, 2 vols. (London, 1870), Vol. 1, v–vi; Lang, *Custom and Myth* (London, 1893), p. 58. Müller's essay was first published in *Oxford Essays* (1856) and reprinted in *Chips from a German Workshop*, Vol. 2 (London, 1867), 1–143. It was separately issued as *Comparative Mythology*, an essay edited with additional notes and an introductory preface on solar mythology by A. Smythe Palmer (London, 1909).

[9] Thomas Sternberg, *The Dialect and Folklore of Northamptonshire* (London, Northampton, Oundle, and Brackley, 1851).

[10] Thomas Keightley, *The Mythology of Ancient Greece and Italy* (London, 1831).

Campbell, and the seminal researches of Tylor. A lecture "On the Philosophy of Mythology" formed part of the *Introduction to the Science of Religion* (1873).[11] In his *Lectures on the Origin and Growth of Religion, as Illustrated by the Religions of India* (1878), Müller turned critic, and to the question "Is Fetishism a Primitive Form of Religion?" replied with a strong negative; at the same time he discussed the problem of securing reliable evidence from savages on their beliefs. Here Müller strikes at the anthropological evolutionists. The chapters on "The Lessons of the Veda" and "Vedic Deities" in *India: What Can It Teach Us?* (1882) tentatively apply the solar theory to savages.

He considerably extended his critique of rival methods in his Gifford Lectures for 1888 on *Natural Religion* (1889), in analyzing the three schools of mythology contending in England. In *Physical Religion* (1891), Müller devoted particular attention to Agni, the Vedic god of fire, and demonstrated his religious and mythological components in two chapters, "The Mythological Development of Agni" and "Religion, Myth, and Custom." Again in *Anthropological Religion* (1892), the four-time Gifford lecturer touched on such favorite themes as the unreliability of anthropological evidence and the contradictory reports about savage ideas and ways. Because mythology formed a vital link in his chain of being, along with thought, language, and religion, Müller rarely omitted the solar theory from his general discussions of cultural and religious origins. In these books Müller never mentioned Lang by name, although he referred continually to "ethno-psychological" mythologists who studied the tales of savages without learning their languages. Lang remarked on this omission in his review of a new edition of the *Chips* (1894), a review which finally drew blood and led Müller to produce two thick volumes on *Contributions to the Science of Mythology* (1897).[12] Here he massed the arguments of his lifelong researches for a personal clash with Lang, repeated everything he had previously written, and repeated his repetitions throughout the twin volumes.

Lang was equally voluminous and repetitious. He tells us that, with other undergraduates at Oxford in the 1860's, he read Müller's writings on mythology, without conviction; after graduating in 1868, his reading in the myths of savage races hardened his distrust of Müller into a contrary hypothesis.[13] The first fruits of this thinking appeared in a ground-breaking article, "Mythology and Fairy Tales," published in the *Fortnightly Review*

---

[11] This lecture was reprinted in Müller's *Selected Essays on Language, Mythology, and Religion,* Vol. 1 (London, 1881), along with other folkloristic essays previously published in *Chips,* Vol. 2, and a lecture of 1870, "On the Migration of Fables."

[12] Müller does not identify the review in his several repetitions of Lang's comment in *Contributions to the Science of Mythology,* 2 vols. (London, New York, and Bombay, 1897), Vol. 1, 11, *32*, 184. He does mention Lang, and only with praise, in articles in the *Nineteenth Century* on "The Savage," Vol. 17 (January 1885), 117; and "Solar Myths," Vol. 18 (December 1885), 905.

[13] Andrew Lang, *Modern Mythology* (London, 1897), pp. 3–4.

in 1872. Lang continued to snipe away in the magazines at Müller's solar interpretations[14] until the year 1884, when he unloosed a formidable barrage of more permanent criticism. He gathered together his essays illustrating the anthropological approach and undermining the philological method, in *Custom and Myth,* a popular work which enjoyed frequent reprintings. A major article on "Mythology" in the ninth edition of the *Encyclopaedia Britannica,* subsequently translated into French in book form,[15] closely examined and dissected Müller's theory. A detailed introduction to Margaret Hunt's translation of Grimm's *Household Tales* paid special attention to the hypotheses of Müller's leading disciple, George W. Cox. When Müller wrote three articles in the *Nineteenth Century* in 1885 confidently developing his system, even to bringing non-Aryan myths within the solar formula, Lang entered his objections in the first number for 1886, in a brisk piece on "Myths and Mythologists."[16]

Pushing forward his examination of "savage" myths and tales, Lang produced his most substantial work in the field of mythology and folklore in 1887 with his two-volume study, *Myth, Ritual, and Religion.* Here he amassed world-wide evidence to support his contention that primitive peoples everywhere possessed similar beliefs, tales, and customs, which survived in classic Greek myths and in modern peasant lore. This exposition powerfully influenced the new generation of folklorists who had in 1878 formed a Folk-lore Society and initiated a folklore journal. Following Müller's exhaustive rebuttal in his *Science of Comparative Mythology,* Lang replied the same year (1897) with a point-by-point rejoinder in *Modern Mythology.* Curiously, also in this year, the last and most intense of their public disagreement, Lang visited Müller at Norham Gardens, and subsequently they exchanged cordial letters.[17]

Numerous other figures entered into the mythological controversy before, during, and after the debate just outlined. In a lecture delivered before the

---

[14] For example, "Mr. Max Müller's Philosophy of Mythology," *Fraser's Magazine,* n.s. Vol. 24 (August 1881), 166–87, a detailed criticism of Müller's *Selected Essays;* and "Anthropology and the Vedas," *Folklore Journal,* Vol. 1 (1883), 107–14, which disputes the idea in *Müller's Lectures on India, and what it can teach us* [sic] that the Vedas offer earlier information about mythological origins than do savage beliefs.

[15] *La Mythologie,* traduit de l'anglais par Léon Parmentier, avec une préface par Charles Michel, et des additions de l'auteur (Paris, 1886). The book also included material from *Custom and Myth* and Lang's article on "Prometheus" in the *Encyclopaedia Britannica.* The preface by Parmentier (pp. v-xxxi) contains a useful résumé of the literature on comparative mythology. Lang gives interesting details on hearing Scottish "contes populaires" in his youth, and so being led into comparative folklore, in his preface (pp. xxxv-xli).

[16] Lang, "Myths and Mythologists," *Nineteenth Century,* Vol. 19 (January 1886), 50–65. The force of Lang's rebuttal was diminished by a postscript Müller added to his article on "Solar Myths," *Nineteenth Century,* Vol. 18 (December 1885), 919–22, replying to a criticism of "solarism" by William E. Gladstone in the November issue. Müller denied that he was trying to give *all* mythology a solar origin.

[17] Georgina Max Müller, *Life and Letters,* Vol. 2, 381.

Royal Institution in 1871, Müller rose to a greater heat of anger than he ever displayed against Lang, for the smashing denunciation of comparative mythology uttered in that very room a year before by the Greek scholar, John Stuart Blackie.[18] Both Müller and Cox fought a rearguard action with the Right Honorable William E. Gladstone, who insisted on interpreting Greek myths as a degraded form of Revelation. Robert Brown refuted Lang's refutation of Müller's *Science of Comparative Mythology* with his own book of jibes and sneers, which elicited a smoking retort from Lang. Müller and Lang joined hands in pouncing on the mythological innovations of Herbert Spencer, who ascribed the beginnings of myths to savage worship of ancestors. Then they fell to arguing whether Mannhardt in Germany, Tiele in Holland, Canizzaro or Morselli in Italy, Gaidoz in France, and Horatio Hale in the United States supported the philological or ethnological position. But these sideshows merely heightened interest in the main event.

Max Müller arrived at his solar interpretation of myths through comparative philology. He tells in his autobiography of his exhilaration in turning from classical studies to the novelties of Sanscrit; he heard Klee and Brockhaus at the University of Leipzig in the years 1838 to 1841 with the sense of peering into the dawn of civilization.[19] His fascination for Sanscrit took him to Berlin in 1844 to hear Bopp, a founder of comparative philology, to Paris the next year to collate Sanscrit manuscripts under the direction of Burnouf, and to London in 1846 to seek the patronage of the East India Company in publishing a projected translation of the Rig-Veda. Müller candidly reveals in later life what a priggish bookworm he was when a stripling in Paris, sleeping one night out of three and starving himself to continue his studies, with never a thought for society or gaiety. But at twenty-three he had found his life's work, the study of the ancient literature of India, and his master thesis, that the religion, the thought, the language, and the mythology of the Aryan people could be unveiled from the Vedas.[20]

Both Müller and Lang puzzled over an anomaly no scholar had yet explained, the barbarous elements in Greek myths. How could so civilized a people repeat such degrading stories about their gods? The mystery can be cleared up, Müller reasons, by tracing the names of the Greek deities to their Sanscrit equivalents, and then reading in the Veda, the oldest literary monument of the Aryan peoples, to perceive the true nature of the gods. All the Indo-European peoples belonged to a common Aryan stock; after the migration of the European groups from their Indic homeland, the parent language,

---

[18] See Müller, "On the Philosophy of Mythology," *Selected Essays on Language, Mythology, and Religion* (London, 1881), Vol. 1, 617–23; and Blackie, "On the Scientific Interpretation of Popular Myths with Special Reference to Greek Mythology," *Horae Hellenicae: Essays and Discussions on Some Important Points of Greek Philology and Antiquity* (London, 1874), pp. 167–96.

[19] Müller, *My Autobiography, A Fragment* (New York, 1909), pp. 147–50; and also *Contributions to the Science of Mythology*, Vol. 1, 303.

[20] Chapters 5 and 6 in *My Autobiography* give rich details on Müller's early years in France and England.

and the mythology it related, splintered into various offshoots. A time came when the original meanings of the names of the Vedic gods were forgotten, and survived only in mythical phrases and proverbs of uncertain sense. Stories then developed to explain these phrases. From this "disease of language" myths were born.

Müller postulated a "mythopoeic" age when truly noble conceptions of the Aryan gods first arose. This age occurred, not at the beginning of civilization, but at a stage early enough so that language could not convey abstract notions. Two processes developed to carry the burden of communication: polyonomy, where one word carried many meanings, and homonymy, where one idea became attached to different words. Dyaus, the supreme god, might be understood as sky, sun, air, dawn, light, brightness. Conversely, a number of different words might signify the sun, with its complex of associations. These phenomena of mythopoeic thought and speech thickened the confusion resulting from the "disease of language."

Metaphors thus operated in two ways. The same verb root, for instance "to shine," could form the name of the sun or a term for the brightness of thought. Then again, nouns so formed could be transferred poetically to other objects; the rays of the sun become fingers, clouds are called mountains, the rain clouds are referred to as cows with heavy udders, the lightning receives the appellation arrow or serpent. These metaphorical words are "Appellatives," and form the substance of myths.[21] Müller always stressed that solar interpretation must be based on strict phonetic rules. The "ponderous squibs" that had reduced the nursery song of sixpence, or Napoleon, or a gentleman named Mr. Bright, or Max Müller himself, to solar myths, all went wide of the mark in ridiculing the excesses of comparative mythologists who failed to *identify* similar gods and heroes with etymological proofs.[22]

---

[21] Müller, lecture on "Metaphor," *Lectures on the Science of Language, Delivered at the Royal Institution of Great Britain in February, March, April, and May 1863*, 2nd Ser. (New York, 1869), p. 371.

[22] Müller, *Natural Religion: The Gifford Lectures Delivered before the University of Glasgow in 1888* (London, 1889), p. 487. For these squibs see "The Oxford Solar Myth" by the Rev. R. F. Littledale, in Max Müller, *Comparative Mythology, An Essay,* ed. Abram Smythe Palmer (London and New York, n.d.), pp. xxxi–xlvii, reprinted from *Kottabos,* a magazine of Trinity College, Dublin, No. 5 (1870), which proves Max Müller to be a solar hero; anon., "John Gilpin as a Solar Hero," *Fraser's Magazine,* n.s. Vol. 23 (March 1881), 353–71; E. B. Tylor, *Primitive Culture,* 3rd ed. (London, 1891), Vol. 1, 319–20 (the Song of Sixpence, Cortès, and Julius Caesar are "solarized").
Although the Rev. A. Smythe Palmer reprinted a solar-myth satire along with Max Müller's essay, he himself belongs to the school of solar interpretation. His own "Introductory Preface on Solar Mythology," pp. v–xxix, while deploring the excesses of Cox, completely endorses and supports Müller's "epoch-making" treatise with a barrage of references, from ethnology and poetry, on the primal role of the sun in the mind of man. In his own work, Palmer carries out Müller's methods: *The Samson-Saga and Its Place in Comparative Religion* (London, 1913) analyzes the solar character of Samson; *Folk-Etymology, A Dictionary of Verbal Corruptions or Words Perverted in Form or Meaning, by False Derivation or Mistaken Analogy* (London, 1882) and *The Folk and Their Word-Lore* (London and New York, 1904) both illustrate what Müller called "modern mythology" or contemporary examples of the disease of language.

Clearly, mythopoeic man constructed his pantheon around the sun, the dawn, and the sky. How could it be otherwise? Müller asked. "What we call the Morning, the ancient Aryans called the Sun or the Dawn. . . . What we call Noon, and Evening, and Night, what we call Spring and Winter, what we call Year, and Time, and Life, and Eternity—all this the ancient Aryans called *Sun*. And yet wise people wonder and say, How curious that the ancient Aryans should have had so many solar myths. Why, every time we say 'Good morning,' we commit a solar myth. Every poet who sings about 'the May driving the Winter from the field again' commits a solar myth. Every 'Christmas number' of our newspapers—ringing out the old year and ringing in the new—is brimful of solar myths. Be not afraid of solar myths. . . ."[23]

The major triumph of comparative mythology lay in the equation Dyaus = Zeus, which associated the supreme gods of the Greek and Vedic pantheons. If they were identical, their families of lesser gods and goddesses must equally be kin. Dyaus is the Vedic sky-god, and now the ugly mystery of the Greek myth of Cronus and Zeus is cleared up. Cronus castrated his father, Uranus, at the behest of his mother, Gaea, who was both Uranus's wife and daughter. Cronus then married his own sister and swallowed his children as fast as they were born. But Zeus escaped when his mother substituted for him a stone swaddled like a baby. Then Zeus compelled Cronus to disgorge his brothers and sisters. Scarcely a fitting tale to introduce the beauties of Greek mythology to the younger generation! But now we see plainly that the marriage of Uranus and Gaea represents the union of Heaven and Earth. The paternal cannibalism of Cronus originally signified the heavens devouring and later releasing the clouds, and the act of Zeus depicts the final separation of Heaven and Earth and the commencement of man's history.[24]

In making their equations, Müller and other comparative philologists of

---

[23] Müller, *India: What Can It Teach Us? A Course of Lectures Delivered before the University of Cambridge* (New York, 1883), p. 208. Cf. these similar statements: "I look upon the sunrise and sunset, on the daily return of day and night, on the battle between light and darkness, on the whole solar drama in all its details that is acted every day, every month, every year, in heaven and in earth, as the principal subject of early mythology" (*Lectures on the Science of Language, Second Series,* p. 537). ". . .There was but one name by which they [mythopoeic men] could express love—there was but one similitude for the roseate bloom that betrays the dawn of love—it was the blush of the day, the rising of the sun. 'The sun has risen,' they said, where we say, 'I love'; 'The sun has set,' they said, where we say, 'I have loved' " (*Chips from a German Workshop* [New York, 1872], Vol. 2, 128, from "Comparative Mythology," [1856]). "Was not the Sunrise to him [mythopoeic man] the first wonder, the first beginning of all reflection, all thought, all philosophy? Was it not to him the first revelation, the first beginning of all trust, of all religion?" (*Selected Essays on Language, Mythology, and Religion* [London, 1881], Vol. 1, 599–600). " 'Is everything the Dawn? Is everything the Sun?' This question I had asked myself many times before it was addressed to me by others. . . but I am bound to say that my own researches lead me again and again to the dawn and the sun as the chief burden of the myths of the Aryan race" (*Lectures on the Science of Language, Second Series,* p. 520).

[24] Müller, "Jupiter, the Supreme Aryan God," *Lectures on the Science of Language, Second Series,* pp. 432–80; "The Lesson of Jupiter," *Nineteenth Century,* Vol. 18 (October 1885), 626–50.

his day filled their pages with a series of acrostic puzzles that inevitably arrived, after conjecture, surmise, and supposition, at a predestined goal. For Müller it was the sun, for Kuhn the storm clouds, for Schwartz the wind, for Preller the sky.[25] With increasing acerbity Müller told Lang and all non-Sanscritists to stay out of these arguments,[26] but on occasion he did provide English readers with homely examples of the "forgetfulness of language," which he dubbed "modern mythology." The arms of Oxford, displaying an ox crossing a ford, represented such a popular etymology. Look how "cocoa" has absorbed "cacao," how "God" is associated with "good," how "lark," as sport, suggests the bird. We speak of "swallowing" one's pride, and perhaps an early swallower was named Cronus.[27] One dramatic illustration that Müller offered to clinch his point dealt with the modern myth of the barnacle goose, reported by sailors and travelers who had seen birds hatched from shellfish. Working back in time through his sources, Müller eventually arrived at a twelfth-century Irish version from Giraldus Cambrensis. Then he gives the key. Irish birds would be called Hiberniculae, a name eventually shortened to Berniculae, which easily becomes Bernacula, and is confused with "barn-acles." In this way linguistic confusion creates the myth of birds being born from barnacles. Similarly, speculates Müller, the legend of Dick Whittington and his cat could have arisen from misapprehension of the French *"achat,"* trade, to which Whittington actually owed his wealth, but which in English was rendered "a cat."[28] Unravel this kind of verbal confusion, and the puzzling elements in Greek myths appear as legends springing up around divine names which, before the Aryan separation, signified the sun and the dawn.

Andrew Lang read the classics at Oxford in the years just after the bombshell of Darwin burst over the Western world. The theory of biological evolution led logically into the hypothesis of human evolution, so it seemed in the dazzling researches of Edward B. Tylor, whom Lang always cites with reverence. The major works of Tylor appeared in 1865 and 1871, at the very outset of Lang's career, and set his mind in the path of evolutionary anthropology, with a conviction equal to Müller's faith in comparative

---

[25] Müller himself distinguishes between the "solar" and the "meteorological" theories of comparative mythology, the latter championed by Adalbert Kuhn (*Lectures on the Science of Language, Second Series,* pp. 538–40). He attempted to reconcile them by assigning a common root to the meanings of sun, lightning, and fire (*Physical Religion* [New York, 1891], p. 186). See Lang, "Myths and Mythologists," pp. 52–53, for these disagreements; in *Modern Mythology,* p. 35, he gives a table of varying interpretations of Cronus, and makes the point that these differences were unknown to the English public, familiar only with Müller and not with continental mythologists (pp. 1–2).

[26] For example, *Natural Religion,* p. 449: "...no one who is not an expert has anything to say here." In 1897 Müller wrote Lang personally, "Still less could I understand why you should have attacked me, or rather my masters, without learning Sanscrit..." (*Life and Letters,* Vol. 2, 381).

[27] Müller, *Natural Religion,* p. 441; "Solar Myths," pp. 904–5.

[28] Müller, Lecture XII, "Modern Mythology," *Lectures on the Science of Languages, Second Series,* pp. 556–68.

philology. Confounded, like Müller, by the irrational and brutal aspects of Greek myths, Lang moved naturally from his early Homeric studies into the realm of mythology and folklore. His system began with the premise that the history of mankind followed a uniform development from savagery to civilization, and that relics of primitive belief and custom survived still among the rural peasantry, and among contemporary savages. These relics, or "survivals," could assist in reconstructing the earliest stages of human life and culture, much as the fossil bones of a prehistoric creature could conjure up an extinct species. Previous evidence secured from travelers and missionaries, and new testimony steadily being gathered by conscientious collectors, offered a mass of data on the traditions of savages and peasants. Everywhere the same beliefs, and survivals of beliefs, manifested themselves; primitive man ascribed spirits to the trees, the animals, and the elements, he worshipped the animal protector of his clan, he credited the shaman with powers of transformation. Myths and fairy tales continually reveal the concepts of animism, totemism, fetishism, for they hark back to the stage of culture when men did not sharply distinguish between the human and the natural world. Collections of savage folktales and rural folklore demonstrate the continued credence in metamorphosis and other magic. So there is nothing surprising in the myth of Cronus, which obviously dates from an era of cannibalism. Aryan traditions can only be understood through comparison with non-Aryan myths and legends the world over. We learn about Greek gods from red Indian totems.[29]

No compromise could reconcile two such widely divergent theories, and Lang promptly turned his cunning scalpel into Müller's delicate hypotheses. Again and again he pointed to the disagreements among the experts on the Greek-Vedic equations, the cornerstone of Müller's edifice. Then he asked embarrassing questions. Since all primitive men have myths, why did not myths originate before the Mythopoeic Age? Why would mythopoeic man remember phrases and forget their meanings? Why does Müller devise the cumbersome processes of polyonymy and homonymy to explain a very simple phenomenon, namely, that savages regarded the elements as persons? Lang pointed out possibilities for error within the etymological method: antique legends could gravitate to modern heroes whose names would merely mislead the inquirer; names for elements were often taken by savages (as among the red Indians), and would again produce false scents.[30] Folk etymologies exist, of course, but mainly in connection with *place names*.[31] In any case, how can Comparative Mythology explain the myths of non-Aryan races, lower in culture than the Vedic Aryans, unacquainted with Sanscrit, yet possessing legends similar to those found in India and Greece?

---

[29] See especially "The Method of Folklore" and "The Myth of Cronus" in *Custom and Myth* (London, 1884, and later editions).

[30] Lang, "Mythology," *Encyclopaedia Britannica,* 9th ed. (Chicago, 1895), Vol. 22, 137–41, "The System of Max Müller."

[31] Lang, "Myths and Mythologists," 56n.

Lang never denied the presence of solar myths, and lunar and star myths as well, and offered copious examples in his *Myth, Ritual, and Religion*. They issue, he reiterated, not from any "disease of language" but from the animistic stage of culture, which personalized the elements and accepted metamorphosis. Thus the mythical Zeus has "all the powers of the medicine-man and all the passions of the barbarian."[32] Relentlessly Lang bombarded the solar mythologists with examples from Australia, Africa, North and South America, and the south Pacific islands of savage traditions that resembled those of civilized peoples. The believed tales of primitive culture survive in the myths and *Märchen* of a later day, and account for their odd features. "It is almost as necessary for a young god or hero to slay monsters as for a young lady to be presented at court; and we may hesitate to explain all these legends of an useful feat of courage as nature myths."[33] Where Müller and his followers invariably interpreted the hero vanquishing the dragon as the sun conquering the night, Lang saw an ancient storytelling formula.

Müller never conceded an inch. He stuck fast to his etymologies, and berated Lang for discussing Sanscrit matters on which he was ignorant. However, he dissociated himself from any conclusions not based on the identifications of Greek and Sanscrit proper names, and considered his follower Cox unwary for submitting proofs based solely on analogies.[34] While Lang never learned Sanscrit, his opponent increasingly considered ethnological materials. Further, Müller strongly counterattacked the ethnological position, and criticized the ambiguities and convenient vagueness of such terms as totemism, animism, fetishism, and savages.[35] He disparaged the data obtained from savages by missionaries and travelers as credulous, biased, and colored by public opinion and priestly authority,[36] and demanded that observers master the native languages. (English anthropologists today criticize their American colleagues for not learning languages.) Are all savages alike? he asked, and answered that further study of savage myths and customs would reveal more contradictions than ever the philologists brewed, "with this important difference, that scholars can judge of etymologies by themselves, while many a Baron Munchhausen escapes entirely from our cross-examination."[37] Think what a hodgepodge of creeds and customs a curious Finn would find in

---

32 Lang, *Myth, Ritual, and Religion* (London, New York, Bombay, and Calcutta, 1913), Vol. 2, 193–94.

33 Lang, *Myth, Ritual, and Religion* (London, 1887), Vol. 2, 196.

34 See, e.g., Müller's concluding remarks in his review of Cox's *A Manual of Mythology*, in *Chips from a German Workshop*, Vol. 2, 154–59, where he points out the possibility of ancient myths being transferred to historical heroes; and his expression of misgivings about "The Analogical School," in *Natural Religion*, p. 486.

35 Müller, "The Savage," *Nineteenth Century*, Vol. 17 (January 1885), 109–32; *Contributions to the Science of Mythology*, Vol. 1, 7, 185 et seq.; Appendix III, "On Totems and Their Various Origins," *Anthropological Religion*, pp. 403–10; *Lectures on the Origin and Growth of Religion as Illustrated by the Religions of India* (London, 1878), pp. 52–127.

36 Müller, Appendix V, "On the Untrustworthiness of Anthropological Evidence," *Anthropological Religion*, pp. 413–35.

37 Müller, *Contributions to the Science of Mythology*, Vol. 1, 280.

England, especially if he had to rely on interpreters! Unless the motive is the same in each case, the customs extracted from different cultures are not true analogies.[38]

So Müller anticipated the lethal shafts modern anthropology would direct at comparative ethnologists such as Frazer. For totemism he reserved his choicest barbs. Totems conveniently appeared wherever the ethnologist found some belief or rite involving an animal. Should Müller's friend, Abeken, whose name means small ape, and who displays an ape in his coat of arms, be assigned the ape as his totem? "It is true I never saw him eating an ape, but I feel certain this was not from any regard for his supposed ancestor or totem, but was with him a mere matter of taste."[39] What does animism and totemism explain, in any event? To say that the myth of Daphne can be understood because Samoans and Sarawakians believed women could change into trees is to explain *ignotum per ignotius;* why would they believe such a thing?[40] Müller thus threw back at Lang his charge that philology failed to account for the nasty and senseless stories about Greek gods.

Far from abandoning his philological "fortress," Müller sallied forth to annex folklore territory. The ethno-psychological school shared his objectives, and he would gladly work with them, provided they observed proper scholarly caution and learned languages.[41] Müller stoutly asserted his friendship for ethnology. He spoke warmly of Tylor, whose *Researches into the Early History of Mankind* he reviewed sympathetically, but with the admonition that the comparison of customs should keep within the bounds of comparative languages.[42] Indeed, he quoted "My friend, Mr. Tylor," in support of solar mythology, and for evidence on the unreliability of travelers' reports.[43] Müller himself had strenuously pleaded for the establishment of an archives on "Ethnological Records of the English Colonies," recognizing the great opportunity afforded by the dominions, colonies, and missionary societies of the British Empire, but the project was allowed to languish.[44] He had once compiled a Mohawk grammar, and would certainly learn savage tongues if time permitted.[45] Since life was finite, he must rely on scholarly missionaries who had themselves translated the tales of primitive peoples; and so he consulted closely with Patteson, Codrington, and Gill on Melanesian and Poly-

---

38 *Ibid.,* pp. 277, 290.

39 *Ibid.,* Vol. 2, 600.

40 Müller, *Natural Religion,* p. 441.

41 Müller iterates the necessity to learn languages, and not simply engage in the "pleasant reading" of folklore, obsessively in *Contributions to the Science of Mythology,* Vol. 1, 5, 23–24, 28, 128, 232, 286; Vol. 2, 462, 830–31.

42 Müller, *Chips from a German Workshop,* Vol. 2, "On Manners and Customs," 248–83, esp. 260.

43 Müller, *Contributions to the Science of Mythology,* Vol. 1, 143; *Lectures on the Origin and Growth of Religion,* p. 91.

44 Müller, *Natural Religion,* p. 505.

45 *Ibid.,* p. 515; Müller, *Life and Letters,* Vol. 2, 129; *Anthropological Religion,* pp. 169–71, where Müller gives the fullest details of his contact with an educated Mohawk.

nesian dialects, with Bleek and Hahn on African folklore, and with Horatio Hale on American Indian dialects.[46] He knew the work of Reverend J. S. Whitmee, who hoped to collect "choice myths and songs" that would make possible a comparative study of Polynesian mythology.[47] And he supplied a preface for the book of traditions brought back from the island of Mangaia by the Reverend W. Wyatt Gill, in which he pointed eagerly to this record of mythopoeic men who believe in gods and offer them human sacrifices.[48] In 1891 the Oxford don served as president of the Ethnological Section of the British Association.[49]

The modern reader of Max Müller's mythological theory may find himself astonished at the sophistication of the Sanscrit scholar in matters ethnological. With startling insight he dissected the stereotyped notion of a "savage," to show how the qualities imputed to him applied just as readily to the civilized man. "When we read some of the more recent works on anthropology, the primordial savage seems to be not unlike one of those hideous india-rubber dolls that can be squeezed into every possible shape, and made to utter every possible noise. . . ."[50] Contemporary "savages" have lived as long as civilized races, and are nothing like primitive man. Actually the Andaman Islanders enjoyed a felicitous existence that a European laborer would gladly embrace.[51]

Then, after playfully juxtaposing the contradictory reports about savages, which reveal only the ignorance of the beholders, Müller does an unexpected turnabout. In an article entitled "Solar Myths," he relies exclusively on "scholarlike" ethnologists to support his thesis. Almost in the words of Lang, he speaks about "the surprising coincidence in the folklore, the superstitions and customs of the most remote races," and proceeds to explore this mystery. He finds that among the non-Aryan peoples also, the trail always leads back through the disease of language to a solar myth. Legends of the Polynesian Maui become intelligible when we recognize that his name signifies the sun, or fire, or the day; the Hottentot deity Tsui-goab, now understood as Broken-Knee, originally meant the red dawn or the rising sun; Michabo, the Great Hare of the Algonkins, can be traced back to the god of Light. So, thanks to

---

[46] Müller, "The Savage," p. 117; *Natural Religion,* pp. 515–17; "Mythology among the Hottentots," *Nineteenth Century* (1882), pp. 33–38. For Müller's correspondence with Horatio Hale, president of the American Folklore Society, see *Life and Letters,* Vol. 2, 117–18, 129, 145–46. Thus he writes in 1883, "I am glad to hear of your projects. I feel sure that there is no time to be lost in securing the floating fragments of the great shipwreck of the American languages. When you have stirred up a national interest in it for the North of America, you should try to form a Committee for the South. The Emperor of Brazil would be sure to help, provided the work is done by *real scholars"* (145–46).

[47] Müller, *Lectures on the Origin and Growth of Religion,* pp. 74–75.

[48] William Wyatt Gill, *Myths and Songs from the South Pacific* (London, 1876). In his preface (pp. v-xviii) Müller explicitly rejects any one explanation for mythology, whether fetishism or the disease of language.

[49] Müller, *Contributions to the Science of Mythology,* Vol. 1, 11.

[50] Müller, "The Savage," p. 111.

[51] Müller, "The Andaman Islanders," *Anthropological Religion,* pp. 173–80.

the ethnological school of comparative mythology, the preoccupation of early
man everywhere with the life-giving sun, about which he spun his legends and
riddles and myths, becomes manifest.[52]

In his books, too, Müller compares crude New Zealand origin tales with
Greek myths, and juxtaposes the Polynesian Maui with gods of the Veda, in
the manner of Lang, but in the interests of solarism.[53] The *Kalevala*
fascinated him as much as the Scot, and he corresponded with Krohn about
Finnish folklore.[54] Like the most confirmed ethno-folklorist, he culled myths
from the Eskimos, the Hottentots, and the Estonians, to illustrate the male
and female personifications of sun, moon, and stars already known from his
Aryan examples.[55] He produces superstitious customs of Scottish, Irish, and
German peasants, which acquire a mythological hue.[56] And he makes a
vigorous plea for the methods of comparative folklore in studying mythology,
before Lang had ever published a full-scale attack on his system.[57] Reading
these comments, one recognizes that Lang was often pillorying a straw man—
as Müller protested.[58]

In comparing non-Aryan with Aryan myths, Müller remained ever faithful
to philological principles and the solar viewpoint. If myths had degenerated
into heroic legends, and these into nursery tales, the reflection of the sun still
shone, even in Red Riding Hood and Cinderella, and perhaps could be
retraced etymologically.[59] He praised the ethnological work of Lewis Morgan
and John Wesley Powell in the United States, based entirely on linguistics,
and pointed triumphantly to the etymology for Gitse-Manito whose root, "to
warm," clearly led back to the sun.[60] Müller's own inquiries into Mordvinian
myths, relying on collections made by linguistic scholars, revealed the same

52 Müller, "Solar Myths," pp. 900–22, esp. 902, 906, 919.
53 Müller, *Natural Religion*, p. 516; *India: What Can It Teach Us?* pp. 169–75.
54 Müller, Appendix VIII, "The Kalevala," *Anthropological Religion*, pp. 440–46.
55 Müller, "On the Philosophy of Mythology," *Selected Essays on Language, Mythology, and Religion*, Vol. 1, 609–15. Note, e.g., "Among Finns and Lapps, among Zulus and Maoris, among Khonds and Karens, we sometimes find the most startling analogies..." (p. 615).
56 Müller, Lecture XII, "Religion, Myth, and Custom," *Physical Religion*, pp. 286–93.
57 Müller, *Chips from a German Workshop*, Vol. 5 (New York, 1881), p. 89; "How much the student of Aryan mythology and ethnology may gain for his own progress by allowing himself a wider survey over the traditions and customs of the whole human race, is best known to those who have studied the works of Klemm, Waitz, Bastian, Sir John Lubbock, Mr. Tylor, and Dr. Callaway" (in "On the Philosophy of Mythology," 1871).
58 Lang's comments in *Modern Mythology*, p. xx, alleging prejudice on Müller's part against ethnological collections, are manifestly unfair. The unbiased reader will, I believe, agree with the statements of Müller that he was not an adversary but nearly a collaborator with Lang (*Contributions to the Science of Mythology*, Vol. 1, 11; *Life and Letters*, Vol. 2, 381, where Müller writes Lang, "...I am perfectly certain that some good may be got from the study of savages for the elucidation of Aryan myths. I never could find out why I should be thought to be opposed to Agriology, because I was an aryologist. *L'un n'empêche pas l'autre*," July 8, 1897). Note that Müller, as well as Lang, was a charter member of the Folklore Society in 1878.
59 Müller, "Solar Myths," p. 916.
60 Müller, *Natural Religion*, pp. 508–10 and 511n.

solar origins he had traced for Vedic gods. When Letts spoke of the golden boat that sinks into the sea, or the apple that falls from the tree, they referred unwittingly to the setting sun.[61]

At the end of the long debate, it was Lang who gave ground. *Modern Mythology* finds him curiously on the defensive, qualifying his position on totemism, and admitting the differences between himself and Frazer on totemic survivals. Instead of referring to Samoan "totems," Lang will henceforth speak of Samoan "sacred animals," as more exact, since to prove sacred beasts are totems requires definite evidence.[62] In revising his *Myth, Ritual, and Religion,* in 1899, Lang made such extensive concessions that Hartland, who reviewed the new edition in *Folklore,* the organ of the anthropological school, averred Lang had delivered himself into his opponents' hands.[63] Speculating on religious origins, Lang came to accept, on the basis of anthropological evidence, the same conception of "high gods" and pure spiritual ideas among primitive peoples that Müller supported intuitively and philosophically. Lang challenged Tylor on the animistic origins of religious belief, and ceased to present the upward ascent of man as a clear-cut evolutionary climb.[64] In his new edition he added the sentence, "The lowest savagery scarcely ever, if ever, wholly loses sight of a heavenly father," after the statement, "The most brilliant civilization of the world never expelled the old savage from its myth and ritual." Again, he appends two new sentences to his chapter on "Mexican Divine Myths" to soften the original conclusion that even the Spanish Inquisition advanced over barbarous Mexican ritual. The new ending holds that wild polytheistic myths grow around gods unknown to low savage races, who recognize a "moral primal Being."[65] In asserting the Godliness of early man, Lang elevates the savage mentality, and so injures his thesis that survivals or borrowings from savages explain the irrational elements in myths and fairy tales.

The solar theory was carried to lengths far exceeding the etymological boundaries of Max Müller by his most aggressive disciple, George William Cox. An Oxford graduate, clergyman, self-styled baronet (his claim was posthumously denied), and a popular writer on Greek history and mythology, Cox developed what his master called the "analogical" school of comparative mythology. He presented this viewpoint first in conventional retellings of classical myths, *Tales from Greek Mythology* (1861) and *Tales of the Gods*

---

[61] Müller, *Contributions to the Science of Mythology,* Vol. 1, 235 et seq.; Vol. 2, 433–35.

[62] Lang, *Modern Mythology,* pp. 85, 142–43. Lang writes that he begged Müller not to read the book, and vowed not to criticize his ideas again ("Max Müller," *Contemporary Review,* Vol. 78 [1900], 785).

[63] *Folklore,* Vol. 10 (1899), 346–48. Hartland was then engaged in a dispute with Lang over the nature of Australian aboriginal religious ideas.

[64] See Lang's Preface to the new edition of *Myth, Ritual, and Religion,* 2 vols. (London, New York, Bombay, and Calcutta, 1913), Vol. 1, xvi.

[65] Lang, *Myth, Ritual, and Religion,* 1913 ed., Vol. 2, 105, 298; cf. 1887 ed., Vol. 2, 81, 280.

and Heroes (1862),[66] then in a deceptive *Manual of Mythology* (1867), which by a series of leading questions and loaded answers converted innocent school children to solarism, until finally he engulfed the adult reading public with two large volumes on *The Mythology of the Aryan Nations* (1870) and *An Introduction to the Science of Comparative Mythology and Folklore* (1881). Throughout these writings Cox quotes, cites, and invokes the name of Max Müller on nearly every page, and reduces all Aryan myths, legends, and fairy tales to the contest between sun and night. Müller's "Essay on Comparative Mythology" first charmed him into a field previously "repulsive." Building on that solid foundation he had completely reconstructed the original mythology of India and Greece, through one new insight: the resemblance of all Aryan narratives to each other. Max Müller had demonstrated by etymological proofs the identity of certain Homeric and Vedic gods, and their common origin, through "failure of memory" (which Cox preferred to "disease of language"), in phrases about the sun. Now Sir George will interpret the meaning of myths and legends which defied philological assault, through the comparison of their narrative elements.[67] By this method, the striking fact became apparent that every Greek hero performed the same feats, be he Achilles, Odysseus, Heracles, Theseus, Bellerophon, Appollon, Meleagros, or even Paris. Where his master regarded Paris as the night, Cox saw in him aspects of both night and day; Paris begins his career as a power of darkness, but ends as a solar deity.[68] Continually Cox called attention to the similarities in the legends of heroes, to their spears and arrows and invincible darts which represented the rays of the sun, to their wonderful steeds and magic swords. All their adventures follow the same pattern of a long westward journey filled with labors and struggles, and this is the course of the daily sun. "The story of the sun starting in weakness and ending in victory, waging a long warfare against darkness, clouds, and storms, and scattering them all in the end, is the story of all patient self-sacrifice, of all Christian devotion."[69] The Achilleus is a splendid solar epic, portraying the contest between sun and night, and reaching its climax when Achilles tramples on the blood of his enemies as the glorious sun tramples out the dark clouds.[70]

Sir George of course had no patience with euhemerism. He blasted the article in the eighth edition of the *Encyclopaedia Britannica* asserting the historicity of heroes, and denied all factual basis for the saga of Grettir or

---

66 These are combined in No. 721 of Everyman's Library, *Tales of Ancient Greece* (London and New York, 1915, frequently reprinted), whose introduction has no doubt misled countless younger readers into interpreting all Greek myths as activities of the sun.

67 Cox, *The Mythology of the Aryan Nations*, 2 vols. (London, 1870, reprinted 1882), Vol. 1, v-vii.

68 *Ibid.*, Vol. 1, 21n, 65n; Vol. 2, 75–76.

69 *Ibid.*, Vol. 1, 168; cf. 49, 153, 291, 308, and *A Manual of Mythology, in the Form of Question and Answer*, 1st American ed., from the 2nd London ed. (New York, 1868), pp. 39, 70, 78, 81, 104, 109, 117, 119, 211, for references to parallels between solar heroes; indeed, Cox never introduces a hero without indicating these parallels.

70 Cox, *The Mythology of the Aryan Nations*, Vol. 1, 267.

the cycle of King Arthur, or any other solar hero. Four-fifths of the folklore
of Northern Europe he swept into his solar net. Legends of death are blood-
stained sunsets; stupid demons and ogres are the dark powers who must be
conquered by light-born heroes; the episodes of heroes hidden in caves reflect
the waxing and waning year.[71] Sigurd, William Tell, Roland, the Biblical
David, all tell the same tale (and in his last mythological study Cox
annexed Beowulf and Hamlet).[72] The fairy tales, too, conform to the elemental pattern. All the humble heroes who find riches and conquer dragons,
whether Boots or the frog prince or Cinderella, are solar deities; Hansel and
Gretel are dawn-children, and the ubiquitous gold that rewards the valiant
hero is the golden light of the sun.[73] Under Cox's solar touch black becomes
white, for the name of the horse "Black" can signify light and whiteness,
as befits the steed of a solar hero.[74] Small wonder that Max Müller confessed
dizziness at viewing this solar empire he had innocently opened up.[75]

Certain insights in Cox's work show a growing sophistication toward folklore. His extension of Müller's etymological equations into the area of
structural comparisons was actually moving onto the sounder ground of type
and motif analysis. The great heroes of epic and legend do betray astonishing
resemblances, which have evoked the historical thesis of the Chadwicks,
that comparable periods of cultural history produce an "Heroic Age,"[76] and
the ritual-origins theory popularized by Lord Raglan, who substitutes the
dying and reborn god for the waning and waxing sun. Cox recognized common elements in myths, legends, and *Märchen,* and understood more per-
ceptively than Müller that a cluster of incidents hangs together to form a
folktale complex. He pointed out that Müller had confused a fable in the
Hitopadesa with the Master Thief, and commented, "The possible affinity
of thievish stratagems in all countries can scarcely account for a series of
extraordinary incidents and astounding tricks following each other in the
same order, although utterly different in their outward garb and coloring."[77]
He himself then confused the Master Thief with the legend of Rhampsinitus.[78] To protect his pan-Aryan theory, Cox had to deny the possibility

[71] *Ibid.,* Vol. 1, 135n, 170n, 308, 322–25, 409.

[72] Cox, *An Introduction to the Science of Comparative Mythology and Folklore*
(London, 1881), pp. 307, 309.

[73] Cox, *The Mythology of the Aryan Nations,* Vol. 1, 132n. 159 n. Frequently the fairy-
tale hero wears a "garment of humiliation" representative of the toiling, unrequited sun.

[74] *Ibid.,* p. 247n.

[75] Müller, *Natural Religion,* p. 495.

[76] For this thesis, see H. Munro Chadwick, *The Heroic Age* (Cambridge, Eng., 1912).
For a later, more expanded statement, see H. Munro Chadwick and N. Kershaw Chadwick, *The Growth of Literature,* 3 vols. (Cambridge, Eng., 1932–1940). In terms of the
tripartite unilinear evolutionary scheme, the age was associated with barbarism. See
The Growth of Literature, Vol. 3, p. 728.—ED. NOTE

[77] Cox, *The Mythology of the Aryan Nations,* Vol. 1, 113.

[78] The Master Thief is Type 1525 in Antti Aarne and Stith Thompson, *The Types of
the Folktale* (Helsinki, 1961) ; Rhampsinitus is Type 950. Cox used this supposed tale
for evidence against borrowing; see his "The Migration of Popular Stories," *Fraser's
Magazine,* n.s. Vol. 22 (July 1880), 96–111.

that solar legends spread by borrowing, and obtusely contended that the greater the resemblance, the less the chance for diffusion! He conceived of borrowing in purely literary terms, and argued that a borrowed tale must perfectly match its original. Similar but not identical narratives indicate a common source, in Vedic India.[79] Mythology and folklore converge in Cox's solarism, and he claimed as their only distinction the possibility of subjecting a myth to philological analysis.[80]

In his well-known introduction to the Hunt edition of Grimm's *Household Tales,* Lang dealt at length with the theories of Sir George, and in some perplexity. The edge of his wit was turned by the unpredictable departure of the pupil from his master, for on some points Cox veered so abruptly from Max Müller that he landed squarely in Lang's arms. When Sir George posited an animistic state of savagery conducive to mythmaking, and conceived that animistic ideas grew from savage thought, not from confused language, Lang naturally applauded. The foe of solarism approved the way Cox refused to trace myths merely through names, as Müller demanded, and he supported Cox's view that *Märchen* can be both the remains and the sources of myth.[81]

A mystified Lang could not see how Sir George, quoting Müller chapter and verse, drew inferences congenial to the anthropological viewpoint. Cox should have gone to the evidence about savage customs and ideas, not to the philologists, Lang said, and then his correct inferences might have led to correct conclusions. Unfortunately, those conclusions echoed Müller's, in reading the sun and the clouds and the dew into every myth and tale, and Lang mocked the two solarists impartially when he came to analyze their reconstructions. He laughed polyonymy and the forgetfulness-of-words into the ground, as he attempted by these processes to explain the Jason myth, and then he showed how simply the anthropologists could decipher the story. But Cox never became the *bête noire* to Lang that Müller was, and the Scot may have considered that, born a bit later, Sir George would have found the right tutor.[82]

No adversary in the camp of the comparative mythologists smarted from Lang's barbs with such pain as Robert Brown, Junior, of Barton-on-Humber. Brown labored manfully during the 1870's and '80's to establish the influence of the ancient Semitic cultures on Hellenic religious mythology. Invitingly he wrote, "he who is wearied with the familiar aroma of the Aryan field of

[79] Cox, *The Mythology of the Aryan Nations,* Vol. 1, 145.

[80] Cox, *An Introduction to the Science of Comparative Mythology and Folklore,* p. 7n.

[81] Lang, "Household Tales; Their Origin, Diffusion, and Relation to the Higher Myths," Introduction to *Grimm's Household Tales,* with the author's notes, trans. and ed. Margaret Hunt, 2 vols. (London, 1910), Vol. 1, xxiv-xxv, xxxv, xl.

[82] See Lang's note, *ibid.,* p. xxiv: "When *The Mythology of the Aryan Nations* was written, philologists were inclined to believe that their analysis of language was the true, perhaps the only, key to knowledge of what men had been in the prehistoric past. It is now generally recognized...that the sciences of Anthropology and Archaeology also throw much light on the human past. ..."

research may stimulate and refresh his jaded senses with new perfumes wafted from the shores of the Euphrates and the Nile."[83] As Max Müller sought to draw the Greek pantheon into the folds of Vedic conceptions, so Robert Brown, the Assyriologist and Egyptologist, attempted to clasp Hellas within the orbit of Near Eastern cults and myths. Comparative mythology had launched a powerful pincers movement on classical Greece, from India and from Egypt, which bid fair to rob Athens of most claims to originality. If Müller demanded that mythologists study Sanscrit, and Lang insisted they read ethnology, Brown declared they must acquaint themselves with the latest research on Chaldea, Assyria, Phoenicia, Arabia, Persia, and Egypt. Semitic Asia had contributed at least as many divinities to the Greek pantheon as had Aryan India![84] The extent of these contributions Brown measured in studies of *Poseidon* (1872), *The Great Dionysiac Myth*, 2 vols. (1877–1878), *The Unicorn* (1881), and *The Myth of Kirkê* (1883), and summarized his position, in the face of Lang's taunts, in *Semitic Influence in Hellenic Mythology* (1898).[85]

Although this last work originated as a rebuttal to *Modern Mythology*, Brown by no means slavishly followed Müller and Cox. His Semitic bias naturally led him into differences with the Vedic scholar, whose school he criticized for excessive pan-Aryanism.[86] Cox, rather than Müller, dominates his footnotes, however, and the "Aryo-Semitic" mythologist steadily refers to the interpretations in *The Mythology of the Aryan Nations*, with due respect to its author (who returned the compliments), but with cavils at his neglect of Semitic gods.[87] Brown's thesis compelled him to grant some historical basis to legends, in spite of all the harsh words then accorded euhemerism, for he necessarily supported his arguments with geographical and historical facts of commerce, travel, and migration throughout the Aegean area. Cox and Müller laughed away all history behind myth, secure in the

---

[83] Robert Brown, *The Great Dionysiac Myth*, 2 vols. (London, 1877–1878), Vol. 1, 162.

[84] *Ibid.*, Vol. 1, vi; Vol. 2, 334.

[85] Other relevant publications are *The Religion of Zoroaster* (1879), *The Religion and Mythology of the Aryans of Northern Europe* (1880), *Language, and Theories of Its Origin* (1881), *The Law of Cosmic Order* (1882), *Eridanus, River and Constellation* (1883), *Researches into the Origin of the Primitive Constellations of the Greeks, Phoenicians, and Babylonians* (1899, 1900), *Mr. Gladstone As I Knew Him, And Other Essays* (1902), esp. "Studies in Pausanias," pp. 93–235.

[86] Brown, *The Great Dionysiac Myth*, Vol. 1, 4; "Reply to Prof. Max Müller on 'The Etymology of Dionysus,'" *Academy*, (August 19, 1882), cited in Brown, *The Myth of Kirkê: Including the Visit of Odysseus to the Shades. An Homeric Study* (London, 1883), p. 83n.

[87] For example, Brown, *The Great Dionysiac Myth*, Vol. 2, 139–40 [Theseus and the Minotaur]; Vol. 1, 420–26 [statue of Demeter]; "Poseidonic Theory of Rev. G. W. Cox," *Poseidon: A Link Between Semite, Hamite, and Aryan* (London, 1872), pp. 5–9. In his preface to a new edition of *The Mythology of the Aryan Nations* (1882), Cox pays especial tribute to the researches of Robert Brown. In *The Unicorn: A Mythological Investigation* (London, 1881), p. 73, Brown cites the acceptance of his view of Bakchos-Melqarth by Cox.

one historical point that Aryan peoples emigrated from India and carried their language and myths with them; but Brown had to demonstrate that physical contact, not an ancient linguistic inheritance, gave Greek deities a Semitic gloss. Art and archaeology documented his position, and clothed the bare bones of philology.[88] Therefore, he called into evidence the Egyptian character of a splendid belt worn by Heracles, or the Phoenician skill at packaging reflected in the "curious knot" Circe taught Odysseus how to tie.[89] To show his eclecticism, Brown scoffed at some excesses of the "Natural Phenomena Theory."[90] How could Polyphemus be the eye of the sun, blinded by the solar hero Odysseus, for would the sun blind himself? How could Skeiron, the wind, be first slain and then devoured by a tortoise?[91]

Most of Brown's explications, however, conform to rigid solar orthodoxy. The trip of Odysseus to the underworld represents the span of a day and a night, during which the sun descends beyond the horizon, and all the mythical figures the solar hero meets in the depths are also solar characters: Tityus stretched on the ground attacked by two vultures is the sun besieged by the powers of darkness; Tantalus reaching for water that always recedes is the suffering sun, and so is Sisyphus, trying vainly to push a solar stone over the brow of the hill that is heaven, and so of course is Heracles, drawing his bow in the midst of the dead. Thus the dead sun suffers every night.[92] Throughout the massive data on Dionysus the solar character of the complex divinity predominates. One myth associated with his name has a lion chase a leopard into a cave; the leopard emerges from another entrance, re-enters the cave and devours the lion, who has been caught fast, from behind. Here the lion is the flaming sun, and the cave and the leopard are both the dark night; night mounts into heaven behind the hidden sun and gnaws him to death—although he will be reborn at the East portal next morning.[93] No narrow solar mythologist, Brown displayed lunar and stellar sympathies, and analyzed the Unicorn as "the wild, white, fierce, chaste Moon," and Circe as the moon-goddess beloved by the solar Heracles. Medusa is the "Serpentine-full-moon, the victim of the solar Perseus," and her petrifying stare signifies the moon-glare of a soundless night.[94]

On every occasion Brown reasserted the Semitic provenience of gods and myths found in Greece. After following the trail of Dionysus through the poets and dramatists and cults, in gems and vases and epithets, Brown placed

88 Brown, *The Great Dionysiac Myth*, Vol. 2, 140, 213; *Semitic Influence in Hellenic Mythology, with Special Reference to the Recent Mythological Works of the Rt. Hon. Prof. F. Max Müller and Mr. Andrew Lang* (London, Edinburgh, Oxford, 1898), p. 202.

89 Brown, *The Myth of Kirkê*, pp. 163, 92.

90 Brown, *The Great Dionysiac Myth*, Vol. 1, 229, "...one key will never open all locks"; *Poseidon*, pp. 79–80.

91 Brown, *Poseidon*, pp. 39–40; *The Great Dionysiac Myth*, Vol. 1, 229.

92 Brown, *The Myth of Kirkê*, pp. 157–62.

93 Brown, *The Great Dionysiac Myth*, Vol. 2, 9–11; also "The Contest between the Lion and the Leopard," *The Unicorn*, pp. 73–78. In *The Myth of Kirkê*, Brown resolves two variants of the death of Odysseus as the same solar myth, by making a ray-fish the young sun that drops on the bald head of Odysseus, the old sun (p. 23).

94 Brown, *The Unicorn*, p. 1; *The Myth of Kirkê*, pp. 47, 53.

the origin of the vast complex in Chaldea. "Here, then, is Dumuzi-Tammuz on Assyrian and Kaldean ground, side by side, and in truth identical with Dian-nisi-Dionysus, the judge-of-men, the ruling, judging, sinking, life-giving, all-sustaining Sun, diurnal and nocturnal. . . ."[95] As the myth traveled westward across the Aegean, Hellenic culture softened some of its wilder orgiastic features, although traces remained in the Eleusinian mysteries. The sea-god Poseidon also originated in Chaldea, and entered Greece through Phoenicia and Libya; he resembles the Biblical Noah and the Chaldean Oannês, a creature that rose out of the sea and instructed men in the arts and letters.[96] An Egyptian papyrus of the twelfth dynasty first presents in mythical form the great solar voyage across heaven as the tale of an archaic sea captain who visited the land of shadows.[97] From such data, Brown felt justified in capping the debate between Lang and Müller with the formation of the new Aryo-Semitic school of comparative mythology.[98]

Lacking the sparkle of Lang and the limpid style of Müller, Brown appears at a disadvantage when he comes fuming into the controversy. His antiquarian volumes are filled with rejoinders to dead authorities, classical quotations, genealogical tables of deities, philological equations, and the accumulation of recondite evidence more or less germane to the inquiry. In *Semitic Influence in Hellenic Mythology* Brown tried to match Lang at his own game of taunt and gibe, not without some trepidation in tackling an opponent who might have given pause to Heracles himself. Brown and Müller both complained that Lang's numerous journalistic outlets, daily, weekly, and monthly, gave him opportunity to throw up an artificial cloud of scorn over solar mythology.[99] Now the Egyptologist bitterly accused Lang of misrepresenting himself, Müller, and Cox; he pointed to the world-wide evidence for solar myths (which Lang never denied), and attacked the theory of totemism and survivals on the grounds that Hellenic constellation names and legends derive from the advanced civilization of the Phoenicians.[100] If philologists disagree, one can still be right; and they do agree on the general outlines of the Natural Phenomena Theory. The intense pique of Brown emerges on nearly every page, and produces a curious appendix, entitled "Professor Aguchekikos On Totemism," intended as a *jeu d'esprit* paraphrasing the anti-solar arguments of Lang himself. The satire purports to be a review written in A.D. 4886 of a learned study on *Anglican Totemism in the Victorian Epoch,* which infers the prevalence of totemism from the animal names of clans, such as the Bulls and the Bears, who once struggled in a "stock exchange," and from such archaic expressions as calling a man "a snake in the grass."[101]

---

95 Brown, *The Great Dionysiac Myth,* Vol. 2, 332.
96 Brown, *Poseidon,* pp. 2, 110–16.
97 Brown, *The Myth of Kirkê,* pp. 101, 167.
98 Brown, *Semitic Influence in Hellenic Mythology,* p. ix.
99 *Ibid.,* pp. 23–24; cf. *Müller, Contributions to the Science of Comparative Mythology,* Vol. 1, vii.
100 Brown, *Semitic Influence in Hellenic Mythology,* pp. 29–31, 54–66.
101 *Ibid.,* pp. 205–15.

Although Lang flicked Robert Brown with the same whip he used on all his adversaries, including his friends, on this victim he drew the most blood. Brown refers furiously to an anonymous review of *The Myth of Kirkê* in the *Saturday Review,* obviously by Lang, where the Scot had ridiculed the solar theory, saying that Robinson Crusoe, like Odysseus, lived in a cave, and so must be the sun. A debate ensued in the *Academy,* in which "according to general opinion the brilliant journalist came off but second best."[102] In *Custom and Myth* Lang called the views elaborated by Brown in *The Law of Cosmic Order,* that the Accadians named the stars after celestial myths, "far-fetched and unconvincing." Even granting that the Greeks obtained their star names from Chaldea, did the Eskimos and Melanesians name stars after Accadian fancies? The Accadians too must have inherited beliefs from a savage past, which they used in naming the constellations.[103] In another chapter Lang dealt with Brown's analysis of the magic herb moly, given Odysseus to ward off the spells of Circe. Brown construed moly as originally a star, known to the ancient Accadians, that guarded a solar hero; Lang thought it simply a magical herb of the kind everywhere credited by savages. He quotes Brown in the *Academy* for January 3, 1885, as contending that "if Odysseus and Kirkê were sun and moon here is a good starting point for the theory that the moly was stellar." Then he inserted the lance. "This reminds one of the preacher who demonstrated the existence of the Trinity thus: 'For is there not, my brethren, one sun, and one moon,—and one multitude of stars?' "[104] The Accadian theory, he sighs, is becoming as overdone as the Aryan. In a preface to a new edition of *Custom and Myth* (1898), Lang replied to Brown's attack earlier that year with blistering severity.[105]

A word must be given to the massive two-volume work on *Zoological Mythology, or The Legends of Animals,* by Angelo De Gubernatis, which appeared in 1872. The Italian professor of Sanscrit published this work in English as a tribute, no doubt, to the reputation of Max Müller and the lively interest in England in comparative mythology. Ruefully the author remarked, "It has fallen to me to study the least elevated department of mythology,"[106] the appearance of gods in animal forms, assumed when they

---

102 *Ibid.,* pp. 30–31, 34, 150.

103 Lang, *Custom and Myth* (London, 1893), p. 137.

104 Lang, "Moly and Mandragora," in *Custom and Myth,* p. 155n.

105 This polemical preface appears only in the 1898 ed., and was withdrawn in later reprintings of *Custom and Myth.* It is titled "Apollo, the Mouse, and Mr. Robert Brown, Junior, F.S.A., M.R.S.A.," and occupies pp. i–xix.

106 Gubernatis, *Zoological Mythology, or The Legends of Animals,* 2 vols. (New York and London, 1872), Vol. 2, p. 425. Gubernatis also compiled a mythological herbarium, *La Mythologie des Plantes, ou Les Légendes du Règne Végétal,* 2 vols. (Paris, 1878), in dictionary form; the first volume treats mythical heroes and phenomena with plant associations (the sun is like a tree); the second considers plants as they appear in myths. Gubernatis diverges from Müller on "Bernacles," which he traces to a bird-producing tree in India (Vol. 1, 65–70).

broke a taboo, or served a term of punishment. A vast body of popular lore now described the actions of Aryan gods in animal disguises, where formerly they had appeared as celestial phenomena. Beginning with myths about the sacred bull and cows of the Rig-Vedas, who represent the sun-god Indras and the clouds, Gubernatis moved to Slavonic and other European parallel tales, and then systematically considered further beasts recurring in *Märchen*, in the usual solar terms. The soul of the ass is the sun; the whale is the night; the peacock is the starry sky; the crab is the moon; birds of prey are lightning and thunderbolts; the serpent-devil is the power of darkness.[107] In "Jack and the Beanstalk," Jack's mother is the blind cow, that is, the darkened aurora; she scatters beans, and the bean of abundance, which is the moon, grows up to the sky; this Jack climbs to the wealth of the morning light.[108] Gubernatis necessarily brought many folktales within his net, and recognized some kinships; for instance, he discerned the tale type of the man or animal trapped by putting his hands or paws in the cleft of a tree trunk,[109] and he uncovered the legend of the peasant who overheard the talking bulls on Christmas Eve prophesy his own death.[110]

The mythological disputants of the period continually refer to this zoological compendium. Brown praised Gubernatis for recognizing the solar character of the hog,[111] and Lang scoffed at him for interpreting the cat as the moon and the mouse as the shadows of night. How, when the moon-cat is away, can there be any light to make playful mice-shadows?[112] Even the sympathetic reviewer in *The Scotsman* complained that this overdose of celestial interpretations was blunting his confidence in comparative mythology.[113]

The solar theory found strong support across the Atlantic in the ethnologist Daniel Brinton, who wrote widely on American Indian culture and language. In *The Myths of the New World* (1868), a work reprinted for the remainder of the century, Brinton compared the origin and creation myths and culture-hero legends of North and South American Indian tribes, to ascertain their inner meanings. The tropes of language and the rites of worship offered him

---

[107] Gubernatis, *Zoological Mythology*, Vol. 1, 370; Vol. 2, 181, 322, 337, 356, 390.

[108] *Ibid.*, Vol. 1, 244. Cf. this interpretation with that of the modern psychoanalytical school, which considers "beans" and "stalk" as symbols for the testicles and penis, and sees the tale as a masturbation fantasy (William H. Desmonde, "Jack and the Beanstalk," *American Imago*, Vol. 8 [September 1951], 287–88). [Desmonde's interpretation is reprinted in this volume.—ED. NOTE]

[109] Gubernatis, *Zoological Mythology*, Vol. 2, 113. This is Type 38, Claw in Split Tree.

[110] *Ibid.*, Vol. 1, 258n. Motif B251.1.2.2., Cows speak to one another on Christmas (Stith Thompson, *Motif-Index of Folk-Literature* [Bloomington, Ind., 1955–1958]), is well known, but the death prophecy is not. I heard the full tale from a Mississippi-born Negro.

[111] Brown, *The Myth of Kirkê*, pp. 54–55.

[112] Lang, *Custom and Myth*, p. 117.

[113] Unsigned review, *The Scotsman*, December 26, 1872. The lengthy review omits to mention the phallic as well as solar interpretations rendered by Gubernatis (see, e.g., *Zoological Mythology*, Vol. 2, 9–10), with far more boldness than by squeamish Robert Brown (*The Myth of Kirkê*, p. 23n; *The Great Dionysiac Myth*, Vol. 1, 7n).

clues, and before long he had found the answer. "As the dawn brings light, and with light is associated in every human mind the ideas of knowledge, safety, protection, majesty, divinity, as it dispels the spectres of night, as it defines the cardinal points, and brings forth the sun and the day, it occupied the primitive mind to an extent that can hardly be magnified beyond the truth."[114] Through the confusion of language, early man's reactions to the dawn and the sun became transferred to animals or persons. Thus the Algonkin Michabo or Manabozho, the Great Hare, comes from the root "wab," which means both "rabbit" and "white," and in its latter sense originates the words for the East, dawn, light, day, and morning. All the legends about the Great Hare can easily be translated into solar myths. Michabo is both the spirit of light who dispels the darkness and the lord of the winds. Degrading trickster stories associated with Michabo proceed from late and corrupt versions of an inspiring mythology.[115]

Primeval man worshipped no brutes, but his own dim perception of the One, construed as lightness and whiteness. Hence the first white men were regarded as gods. Brinton was especially struck with the recurrence of the number four in different tribal legends, and interpreted the four demiurgic brothers as the four winds and the four cardinal points. Declaring he was no slavish solar mythologist, Brinton proudly emphasized the attention he gave to the moon, and the space he devoted to gods of thunderstorms and lightning.[116]

Max Müller purred with delight on reading the pages of this unexpected ally across the sea. Still licking his wounds from the thrusts of Lang in 1884, the Oxford professor in his article on "Solar Myths" the next year quoted gleefully long passages from Brinton that illustrated the solar theory. "When copying these lines," he marveled, "I felt almost as if copying what I had written myself," and he was all the more pleased because his own work "could in no way have influenced the conclusions of this eminent American writer."[117] While Brinton quoted from Müller only once, on the Dawn and the Sun,[118] he showed familiarity with the celestial theories of continental writers, and confidently asserted the parallels between Indian and European heavenly deities.[119] Happily Müller underscored Brinton's contention that

[114] Daniel Brinton, *The Myths of the New World: A Treatise on the Symbolism and Mythology of the Red Race of America*, 3rd ed., revised (Philadelphia, 1896), p. 109. In spite of its viewpoint, this edition is very favorably reviewed in *Folklore*, Vol. 8 (1897), 57–59 (unsigned), alongside an equally favorable review of Franz Boas, *Indianische Sagen von der nord-pacifischen Küste Amerikas* (pp. 59–62), the study which upset Brinton's anti-diffusionism. See Robert H. Lowie, *The History of Ethnological Theory* (New York, 1937), p. 146.

[115] Brinton, *The Myths of the New World*, pp. 194–99.

[116] *Ibid.*, pp. 94 et seq., 163, 168, 206, 252.

[117] Müller, "Solar Myths," p. 909.

[118] Brinton, *The Myths of the New World*, p. 198, quoting from Müller, *The Science of Language, Second Series*. Brinton refers to both Müller and Cox in his introduction to *American Hero-Myths: A Study in the Native Religions of the Western Continent* (Philadelphia, 1882), pp. 23, 31n.

[119] Brinton, *The Myths of the New World*, pp. 134, 139.

Indian myths conformed to the world view of early man everywhere, and in the etymology of *"wab"* he saw the Algonkin counterpart of the Sanscrit root *div* or *dyu* that produced Dyaus and Zeus.[120]

Replying in the very next issue of the *Nineteenth Century,* Lang poured his vitriol on the Americanist. When there are twenty known Algonkin totems, why does Brinton single out the hare for his dubious etymology, and ignore the bear, turtle, crane, wolf, coyote, and the others? All we know of early Indian opinion directly contradicts this monotheistic conception of the Great Hare—and supports, of course, totemism.[121] Lang failed to strike at a particularly vulnerable spot in Brinton's argument, his exclusion of the trickster aspect of Manabozho. Another weakness, Brinton's postulate of the psychological unity of mankind, came too close to Lang's own views for exposure, although where Lang saw animism, Brinton perceived sun-worship. Irritatedly Lang concludes, "Obviously there is not much to be learned by trying to follow the curiously devious trail of Dr. Brinton through the forest of mythology.[122]

The well-known American historian and evolutionist, John Fiske, also entered the arena of comparative mythology with one extremely popular book, *Myths and Mythmakers* (1873), which ran through eleven editions in fifteen years. In a manner anticipating the pleasant discursiveness of Andrew Lang's *Custom and Myth,* Fiske rambled through the byways of folklore and mythology, to delineate his thesis from different angles. One essay treats the same topic that Lang considers, the divining rod, but where the Scot sees the rod as evidence of a surviving superstition, the American finds in it a representation of the lightning.[123] Fiske shows a remarkable acquaintance with the literature of both mythology and folklore, and quotes equally from the German philologists, the English solarists, ethnological collectors of primitive tales, including Brinton, and the British county fieldworkers, who rarely appear even in the citations of Lang. *Curious Myths of the Middle Ages,* produced by the unquenchable clergyman, Baring-Gould, especially stimulated his thought.

Fiske begins his essays like an orthodox solar mythologist. He explains away William Tell as a sun myth, views the historical Cyrus and Charlemagne as solar heroes, follows Cox on the dual aspect of Paris embracing both sun and night, and seeks to reconcile the storm myths of Kuhn with the dawn myths of Müller, as two aspects of the same interpretation.[124] The epic of the

---

[120] Müller, "Solar Myths," p. 911; also *Natural Religion,* pp. 512–13.

[121] Lang, "Myths and Mythologists," p. 64; also *Myth, Ritual, and Religion* (London, 1887), Vol. 2, 57–59.

[122] Lang, "Myths and Mythologists," p. 64. Brinton criticized Lang for degrading the savage spiritually—the position Lang later recanted—in *Essays of an Americanist* (Philadelphia, 1890), p. 102.

[123] John Fiske, Chap. 2, "The Descent of Fire," *Myths and Mythmakers: Old Tales and Superstitions Interpreted by Comparative Mythology,* 11th ed. (Boston and New York, 1888), pp. 37–68; and Lang, "The Divining Rod," *Custom and Myth,* pp. 180–96.

[124] Fiske, *Myths and Mythmakers,* p. 123. Cf. Müller, "Reconciliation of the Solar and Meteoric Theories," *Physical Religion,* pp. 186–87.

Iliad and the drama of Hamlet alike derive from primary myths about the sun, although Homer and Shakespeare never suspected the fact.[125]

A strange note nevertheless creeps into this conventional solar analysis. The petulant complaint that Cox overpresses his solar analogies seems but a passing mood, especially when the historian lashes at the euhemerism of Gladstone and Robert Brown.[126] But there is no mistaking Fiske's position by the time the final chapter is reached. For all his delight on first reading Müller's "Essay on Comparative Mythology," he sees carelessness and fallacies in its reasoning. The Sanscrit scholar has pressed the philological method into far greater service than it can render; other disciplines are needed to analyze myths, those of history (i.e., ethnology) and psychology. Müller has inverted the story of man's mythmaking; metaphors came from myths, and not myths from diseased metaphors. A new mythmaking does invent later stories about gods and heroes whose original physical meanings are forgotten, and here lies the difference between the simple nature myths of savages and the more fanciful—and often inconsistent—tales of the Greeks. No confusion of language is involved, but merely the propensity of early man everywhere to build stories from his beliefs. "And in all countries may be found the beliefs that men may be changed into beasts, or plants, or stones; that the sun is in some way tethered or constrained to follow a certain course; that the storm cloud is a ravenous dragon; and that there are talismans which will reveal hidden treasures."[127] In the end Fiske quotes Tylor page after page, draws illustrations from primitive folklore, and postulates fetishism and animism as an early stage in the universal evolution of man. All this he does to refute the narrow philological approach of Müller, and to assert the ubiquity of solar myths from a more scientific point of view! John Fiske proves the reality of the Hegelian synthesis, for in his book the ideas of Lang and Müller intertwine like the rose and the briar.

With the death of Max Müller, in 1900, the cause of solar mythology lost its most lustrous name, and rapidly ebbed. When Lang revised his article on "Mythology" for the eleventh edition of the *Encyclopaedia Britannica* in 1911, he condensed his three columns of criticism on "The System of Max Müller" to a scanty half-column in small type, as a dead issue. Supplanting George W. Cox's *Introduction to the Science of Comparative Mythology and Folklore* came *An Introduction to Folklore* (1895, new ed. 1905), by Marian Roalfe Cox, the disciple of Lang, Clodd, and Nutt, who faithfully follows the anthropological method. In the pamphlet series, "Popular Studies in Mythology, Romance, and Folklore," designed for the general public, Sidney Hartland dealt with the topic *Mythology and Folktales: Their Relation and Interpretation* (1900), and buried the philological mythologists

---

[125] Fiske, *Myths and Mythmakers*, pp. 195–96n.
[126] *Ibid.*, pp. 192–94, 204n, 211.
[127] *Ibid.*, pp. 144–48, 151, 238.

under the anthropological viewpoint. Hartland wrote that Lang had given the coup de grâce to comparative mythology in 1887 with his *Myth, Ritual, and Religion;*[128] but this statement ignores the subsequent writings of Müller and Brown and the modifications Hartland himself pointed out in the revised edition of *Myth, Ritual, and Religion.* The eclipse of the solar theorists came in large part from the organization of the Folklore Society in 1878, and the steady exposition in its journals and memoirs, and in the separate writings of its vigorous and prolific members, of the evolutionary interpretation. No Society of Comparative Mythology was formed.[129]

One leaves a review of the great controversy with considerable respect for its protagonists. Müller emerges with scarcely less honor than Lang; the giants slew each other, although the corpse of cultural evolutionism bled more slowly than the dismembered torso of solarism. A spirit of fire and excitement vanished from the scene when the solar mythologists went under; Lang turned to fencing half-heartedly with his own colleagues, debating with Hartland over primitive religion, with Clodd about psychical research, and with Jacobs on the diffusion of tales, but he never rose to his earlier heights, or sustained so intense a campaign. One generation later when Lang and Hartland and Clodd had passed on, the Folklore Society itself would become an outmoded survival, lacking direction or purpose or audience. But from 1856 to 1900 all England followed the battle between solar mythologists and "savage" folklorists. The new field collections were eagerly scanned upon their appearance, and pressed by the disputants into their respective dialectics. We envy the multiplicity of learned articles and books published, read, and bought in those literate Victorian days. And if we scorn the deluded theories of those embattled scholars,[130] let us remember that they had theories, based in erudition and presented with grace to an intellectually curious public absorbed in the furor concerning the early ideas of man.

---

[128] Sidney Hartland, *Mythology and Folktales: Their Relation and Interpretation,* 2nd ed. (London, 1914), p. 13.

[129] However, in June 1906, a society with that name was formed in Berlin. The Gesellschaft für vergleichende Mythenforschung had its own monograph series, the Mythologische Bibliothek, in which solar, and more often, rival lunar interpretations were forcefully argued. Typical contributions in this series were Ernst Siecke's *Hermes der Mondgott,* Mythologische Bibliothek, Vol. 2, No. 1 (Leipzig, 1908); and Paul Ehrenreich's posthumously published *Die Sonne im Mythos,* Mythologische Bibliothek, Vol. 8, No. 1 (Leipzig, 1915). In an essay outlining the goals of the Society, Heinrich Lessman explained that the comparative mythologists took the position that mythology concerned the activities of celestial bodies and that any narrative which did not was simply not considered to be a myth in the strictest sense of the term. See *Aufgaben und Ziele der vergleichenden Mythenforschung,* Mythologische Bibliothek, Vol. 1, No. 4 (Leipzig, 1908), 31.—ED. NOTE

[130] In a gracious letter to Mrs. Max Müller after her husband's death Lang wrote, "Our little systems have their day, or their hour: as knowledge advances they pass into the history of the efforts of pioneers" (Georgina Max Müller, *Life and Letters,* Vol. 2, 452).

The Three Bears

E. D. Phillips

In contrast to the solar mythological theory of origins, the theory of the ritual origin of folklore continues to be ardently advocated. According to this theory, folklore is made up of survivals, vestigial traces of former rituals. For folklorists who regard all folklore as derived from ritual, the search for origins consists of identifying or reconstructing the ritual underlying a given item of folklore. For example, one suggested ritual origin of the counting-out rhyme which begins "eenie, meenie, miny, moe" is an ancient magic rhyme used in Druid times to choose victims for human sacrifice. Similarly, the children's game of London Bridge is supposed by some to be a survival of the actual custom in which a human victim was sacrificed to the spirit of the stream over which a new bridge had been built. In this illustrative short note on "The Three Bears" by E. D. Phillips, Reader in Greek at the Queen's University of Belfast, the familiar origin of ritual sacrifice is once more proposed.

The ritual approach is especially prominent in studies of mythology, one of the most important branches of folklore research. Myth-ritualists, as they are called, go so far as to define myth as "a narrative associated with a rite" or "the description of a rite." Of course, it is also possible that rituals are derived from myths. In this event, the myth or sacred narrative explaining the present in terms of the archetypal past is presumed to have arisen first. The ritual develops later simply as an enactment or dramatization of the myth. Perhaps the sanest comment on the chicken and egg question of the priority of myth or ritual is Kluckhohn's remark that "the facts do not permit any universal generalizations as to ritual being the 'cause' of myth or vice versa."

Probably the most telling criticism of the ritual approach in terms of origins is that the whole question of the *ultimate* origin of an item of folklore is begged. If a myth does come from ritual, where then does the ritual come from? Ritualists delight in tracing folkloristic items back to ritual, but they usually have little if anything to say about the origin of the ritual.

Reprinted from *Man*, Vol. 54 (1954), 123, by permission of the author and the Royal Anthropological Institute.

For defenses of the ritual approach, see Lord Raglan, "Myth and Ritual," *Journal of American Folklore,* Vol. 68 (1955), 454–61; E. O. James, *Myth and Ritual in the Ancient Near East* (London, 1958); and Lewis Spence, *Myth and Ritual in Dance, Game, and Rhyme* (London, 1947). For a partial survey of ritual studies, see Stanley Edgar Hyman, "The Ritual View of Myth and the Mythic," *Journal of American Folklore,* Vol. 68 (1955), 462–72. For criticisms, see Clyde Kluckhohn, "Myths and Rituals: A General Theory," *Harvard Theological Review,* Vol. 35 (1942), 45–79; and William Bascom, "The Myth-Ritual Theory," *Journal of American Folklore,* Vol. 70 (1957), 103–14.

The purpose of this note is to suggest a remote origin in ritual for some fundamental elements in Southey's famous fairy tale "The Three Bears," first printed in *The Doctor.*[1] These are: that there are three bears, that they live together in a house of their own in a wood, and that they sit at table in due order. Their graded sizes, the more elaborate details of the house, their unwelcome and ill-mannered visitor, the little old woman who used their property without permission, and their stereotyped complaints ("Somebody has been at my porridge," etc.) can be regarded as artistic developments or borrowings from other tales.

The question of Southey's sources for his story has been discussed by Mary I. Shamburger and Vera R. Lachmann.[2] They mention Sneewittchen ("Snow White and the Seven Dwarfs") in Grimm, in which the dwarfs, returning to their little house in the woods and seeing that someone had made himself at home in their absence, ask "Who has eaten from my little plate?" etc., until they finally discover the king's daughter Snow White asleep in the bed of the seventh dwarf. They add that Johannes Bolte[3] notes the resemblance between "The Three Bears" and a Norwegian version of "Snow White," in which a king's daughter comes to a cave inhabited by three bears, who are really Russian princes in disguise, and cast off their bearskins at night. She eats their porridge and finally falls asleep, not on, but under the bed that she had chosen, and is duly discovered.

Southey's wide interests certainly included Scandinavia, and Bolte supposed that he used Scandinavian material. This could be oral, since Southey particularly asked his son-in-law J. W. Warter, chaplain to the British Embassy at Copenhagen, to learn Danish: "Learn all you can by help of eyes and ears about the country and note down all you see and hear." At any rate it is generally admitted that Southey could have got various elements,

---

[1] Robert Southey, *The Doctor,* ed. J. W. Warter (London, 1849), pp. 327–29.

[2] "Southey and The Three Bears," *Journal of American Folklore,* Vol. 59, No. 234, (October-December 1946), 400–403.

[3] J. Bolte and G. Polívka, *Anmerkungen zu den Kinder-und Hausmärchen der Brüder Grimm* (Leipzig, 1913), Vol. 1, pp. 450–64, esp. p. 455.

particularly the three bears, their home, and their food, from northern Europe; and the Norwegian tale makes them Russian princes.[4]

I come now to the accounts of animal cults in Siberia and neighboring regions which first put me in mind of the three bears. A. Alföldi, discussing the beliefs of the peoples who created the Scytho-Siberian animal style,[5] mentions the custom, among the hunting peoples of the forests, and nomads in contact with them, of setting aside skins of the animals particularly hunted for a cult designed to appease their angry ghosts. A woolen embroidery from Noin Ula in the first century A.D. showed three tiger skins used in this way, and three bear skins were the object of a special cult among the Voguls of Western Siberia, as described early in the eighteenth century by the Swedish traveler Philipp Johann von Strahlenberg.[6]

Strahlenberg, after discussing the religious importance of the number three, very much in the manner of a modern anthropologist, describes the offering that he has seen among the Voguls:

> What I have said above of the number Three is farther confirmed by an Offering or Sacrifice, which I have seen performed among the Wogulitzi, a Heathen Nation, on the Borders, between Siberia and Russia, when having killed several Bears in the Woods, they offered Three of them to their Gods, in the following Manner. Their Temple is a very poor Building of Wood. In this they placed a Table, instead of an altar, behind which they set the heads of three Bears, with the skins of them flea'd off and stuff'd, in a Row, one by the other. On each side of them stood a Fellow, with a large and long switch in his hand. All this being in Order, another Fellow came in with an Ax, and made as if he would attack the Bears, while the other pretended to defend them, and, at the same time made an Apology, that it was not their fault that the bears were shot, but that the blame was to be laid on the Arrows and Iron which were made and forged by the Russians. In the mean Time, others were busied about the Temple, in boiling and roasting the Flesh of these Bears. And the Women, to whom a certain portion of the Meat was allotted, made themselves merry when the Ceremony was at an end. To this we may properly add what Loccenius writes of the Hunns, that they chose Three Dogs Heads for the Sign or Token of their Offerings, because the Wogulitzi descended from the Hunns.[7]

The ceremony was to appease the bears' resentment at being killed, even though their flesh was being eaten in the same place. The table, with the bears' stuffed skins and heads placed at it, is a remarkable feature, and suggests that the bears themselves were due to receive offerings placed before them. Unfortunately this is not said. But we have three bears in a house in a wood, seated at table. They are honored with an elaborate ceremony to

---

[4] Herbert G. Wright, "Southey's Relations with Finland and Scandinavia," *Modern Language Review,* Vol. 27 (1932), pp. 149ff.

[5] "Die theriomorphe Weltbetrachtung in den hochasiatischen Kulturen," *Archäeol. Anz.,* Vol. 46 (1931), cols. 393–418; see col. 403.

[6] *An Historico-Geographical Description of the Northern and Eastern Parts of Europe and Asia* (London, 1738).

[7] *Ibid.,* pp. 96f.

avert guilt. It is likely that such a ritual was widespread and very ancient among the peoples of the northern forests as far as Lapland and Norway.

Whether Southey's ill-mannered old woman is more truly traditional than the king's daughter in the Norwegian story (or Goldilocks in versions of "The Three Bears" later than Southey) is not easy to decide. But at least the praise of the three bears in Southey, and the blame on their visitor who behaved so badly, would suit a tradition which was originally sacred. The Norwegian story may also preserve a memory of the ritual wearing of the sacred skins. The behavior of the animals' ghosts, if they were slighted, would have been more alarming than anything the three bears do in Southey, but even with him there is a slight feeling of a ghost story. It would be many centuries since any such ancestral ritual was remembered in Europe in its true nature, which would in any case need to be forgotten before a fairy tale could arise.

Psychoanalysis and Folklore

Ernest Jones

Of all the contemporary theories concerning the origin of folklore, none is more controversial than the one proposed by psychoanalysts. Most professional folklorists, tending as they do toward historical not psychological, literal not symbolic, approaches to folklore, utterly reject the attempted application of psychoanalytic theory to the materials of folklore. Some equate psychoanalytic interpretations with those offered by solar mythologists, claiming that both sets of interpretations are equally absurd.

There is, nevertheless, an important difference between the conjectures of solar mythologists and psychoanalysts. The former sought to project narratives about humans upon the movements of celestial bodies such as the sun. The method was considered to be especially meritorious when the narratives contained overt references to "disagreeable" or "shocking" human activities such as castration and cannibalism. However, to say that an act of cannibalism in a folktale is really the heavens "devouring" the clouds, the sun, or the moon is in fact not explaining but explaining away the allusion to cannibalism. Psychoanalysts, on the other hand, say that folklore itself is a projection of the movements of human, not celestial, bodies. Moreover, psychoanalysts have argued that just as the folk have to project their emotional life into a safe, externalized, socially sanctioned form (e.g., folklore) to provide a needed outlet for dealing with it, so the solar mythologists were similarly unable to face the nature of folklore and had to protect themselves against the sometimes ugly elements by projecting these disturbing features onto a safe, distant, externalized, academically sanctioned form, namely, the sun, moon, and stars. The point is that although both psychoanalytic and solar mythological interpretations may well be wrong in any given instance, they are, from a theoretical perspective, not at all identical and should therefore not be equated.

This essay by Ernest Jones, one of the most adamant and dedicated of Freud's disciples, was originally read to the Jubilee Congress of the

Reprinted from *Jubilee Congress of the Folklore Society: Papers and Transactions* (London, 1930), pp. 220–37, by permission of the Folklore Society.

English Folklore Society in 1928. It had virtually no effect at all upon the direction of English folklore scholarship. However, the possibility of using the collective fantasy materials of folklore as psychological source materials is an interesting one. It was Freud himself who observed in *The Interpretation of Dreams* that the symbols which occurred in the dreams of individuals were to be found in a "more developed condition" in folklore, myths, legends, idiomatic phrases, proverbs, and jokes.

Jones' suggestion that there might be a parallel between ontogenesis (the development of the individual) and phylogenesis (the development of man in general) is thought-provoking if not valid. The question is: Are an adult individual's compulsive ritual acts, such as insisting upon a nightcap or even a glass of warm milk before bed, a "survival" from an earlier evolutionary stage, infancy (during which the infant might have been put to sleep by giving him a bottle of milk), and if so, in what sense are they parallel to folkloristic survivals in civilization, survivals allegedly deriving from the supposed earlier evolutionary stage of savagery? Jones implies that there may be an analogue to the Haeckelian biological principle of ontogeny's recapitulation of phylogeny, but this is highly questionable. On the other hand, folklore is used after all by folk, which means that the psychology of individual humans is relevant to the study of folklore.

Those interested in reading further in psychoanalytic studies of folklore should consult such works as Sigmund Freud and D. E. Oppenheim, *Dreams in Folklore* (New York, 1958); Otto Rank, *Psychoanalytische Beiträge zur Mythenforschung* (Leipzig, 1922); Géza Róheim, *The Gates of the Dream* (New York, 1952); and Paulo de Carvalho Neto, *Folklore y Psicoanalisis* (Buenos Aires, 1956). An excellent survey with bibliography is J. L. Fischer, "The Sociopsychological Analysis of Folktales," *Current Anthropology*, Vol. 4 (1963), 235–95. Other references may be found in Alexander Grinstein, ed., *The Index of Psychoanalytic Writings*, 9 vols. (New York, 1956ff.); and Norman Kiell, ed., *Psychoanalysis, Psychology, and Literature: A Bibliography* (Madison, Wis., 1963).

The very extensive and original contributions that psychoanalysis has made to the science of folklore in the past twenty years have passed almost entirely unnoticed by folklorists. That the present is the first occasion on which the matter has been brought to their direct attention cannot, I think, be the main explanation of this remarkable neglect. I should regard it rather as one more manifestation of the anti-psychological bias that prevails among scholars and men of science. In their laudable endeavour to emerge from the subjective prescientific era they have naturally tended to confound objectivity with the study of the outer world, and to identify contemplation of the mind with subjectivity. This attitude has proved eminently successful insofar as the investigation of physical phenomena that are uninfluenced by mental processes is concerned, or at least the drawbacks attaching to it have hitherto been relatively inconsiderable and are only now beginning to be perceived, but the limitations it imposes on the study of phenomena which are the product of mental processes are so grave as to confine such studies to a preliminary charting out of the ground. This is evident when we consider the material studied in folklore, whether it be customs, beliefs, or folksongs, for without exception it is the product of dynamic mental processes, the response of the folk soul to either outer or inner needs, the expression of various longings, fears, aversions, or desires. Indeed the only reason why what I have just said escapes being a platitude is that in providing explanations for any of this material, folklorists have necessarily forged a psychology of their own or else taken a commonly accepted one for granted. When they explain certain customs as having been motivated by the desire for more food or better crops they are justified in assuming such desires as common human attributes and experience no need to investigate their nature any further; that, they would say, is the business of the psychologist or physiologist. This attitude, however, has many pitfalls, for modern psychology has indubitably shown that the human mind is a far more complex apparatus than is commonly supposed, and that many motives which appear simple enough on the surface prove on examination to have a much more elaborate substructure.

Another consideration comes into play here. Psychology itself has in the past been singularly unhelpful to ancillary sciences such as folklore. What is known as academic psychology—and I am leaving philosophy quite out of account here—has found itself in an unprecedented situation, the nature of which is not at all generally appreciated. In approaching its subject matter it finds insuperable barriers almost at the entry. In investigating the genesis of any given mental processes it has, necessarily, to make halt whenever thoughts are approached which are of too intimate a nature to be disclosed, or else a point is reached when the subject himself is unable to provide any further data—a state of things which we now know to be due to the confines having been reached between the conscious and the unconscious mind. The psychologists had perforce to content themselves with relatively superficial mental processes, such as the data of sense physiology or the rapidity with which various objects could be committed to memory and the like. It was only when the science of clinical psychology was born that a motive, namely, mental suffering, was furnished powerful enough to overcome a person's natural objection to laying bare the secrets of his soul, and it was only when Freud provided the special technique of psychoanalysis for the exploration of the unconscious that it became possible to trace any mental process to its ultimate source. The discoveries thus made have, as is well known, proved to be startlingly revolutionary, and have led to a fundamentally new conception of the mind. This in its turn was bound to have repercussions in all the sciences, including folklore, that are concerned with the products of mental activity. Contributions from this point of view have in fact been made to a number of such sciences, such as anthropology, mythology, philology, pedagogy, and—last but not least—to folklore. It is the object of the present paper to present to you some of the points of view in question, and to illustrate a few of the bearings they have on the study of folklore material.

Perhaps the most important conclusion reached by psychoanalytic work is that what we call our mind, i.e., the mental processes known to consciousness, is only a transformed selection of the whole mind, derived from its deeper and absolutely unconscious layers and modified by contact with the stimuli of the outer world. The deeper unconscious layer, originating in our organic instincts, is mainly composed of wishes which are actively striving for expression. They come into conflict with opposing forces, especially those relating to fear and guilt, the nucleus of what later will become the moral conscience. What is allowed to seek expression by entering consciousness represents a compromise between the two groups; the wishes achieve fulfillment only in a modified and disguised form. In our judgments and beliefs about the outer world far more contributions from the obscure inner world of the mind are to be found than is commonly supposed, and it is particularly with those subjective and less rational contributions to thought and conduct that folklore is concerned. When prominent they often produce a quaint or even comical effect, and elicit the disdain to which folklorists are accustomed in regard to the material of their work, but when traced to their origin they prove not only to have a perfectly intelligible logic of their own, but to be derived from the most fundamental sources of our being.

Psychoanalysis has produced much evidence to show that all our conscious ideas, feelings, interests, and beliefs originate in the unconscious; the conscious mind originates nothing, its functions being confined to criticism, selection, and control. Unconscious impulses may be called primitive both as being earlier in development in time, thus being nearly synonymous with "infantile," and as representing a lower stage in mental evolution, one out of which more highly differentiated forms of mental activity develop. Now these primitive impulses may come to expression in consciousness in, broadly speaking, one of two ways. Normally they undergo a process of transformation and adaptation in accordance with external reality; in this process they become adjusted both to the claims of reality and to the demands of inner conscience (what is nowadays called the "superego"). The other way in which they may come to expression is through the formation of complicated forms of compromise which act in effect as disguises, the impulses themselves remaining in their unaltered form and undergoing none of the transformation characteristic of the first mode. The former thus gives rise to what may be called the normal interests, ideas, and occupations of mankind. It is the second class that is of special interest in the present connection. They represent relics of the primitive mental state, fragments left over in the process of evolution. In the language of folklore they would be termed survivals. The value of them to the psychologist is the direct light they throw on the primitive mind before it has undergone evolution. To the ancillary sciences they are of value because through this knowledge they can be interpreted and thus throw light on the context in which they occur. Now the important point is that the material we have termed survivals is to be met with in very similar form in extremely diverse fields. To give a few examples of this: neurotic symptoms, the field in which these discoveries were first made, are all survivals of this nature, and represent part of the infantile life that has resisted the process of normal growth. The phenomena of dream life, the understanding of which has exercised the imagination of so many generations, have proved to be of the same nature and, as you probably know, the elucidation of them plays an extensive part in the modern treatment of neurotic symptoms, to which they afford a close parallel. To come to our present subject, many savage beliefs and folklore customs can be shown to be closely related, in both form and content, to the other phenomena that I have just classed under the same general heading. They show the same peculiar mental mechanisms characteristic of unconscious products and, what is perhaps even more important, they reveal the same underlying content and are derived from the same sources. This sentence, which contains the gist of my whole thesis, I shall presently have to amplify at some length, for to do so is to discuss the relationship between psychoanalysis and folklore. To put the whole matter in another way, what we maintain is that there is a far-reaching parallelism between survivals of primitive life from the racial past and survivals from the individual past. The practical value of this generalization is that the study of survivals in folklore can be usefully supplemented by the study of survivals in living individuals, where they are far more accessible to direct investigation.

One little point may be mentioned at the outset. As you all know, a controversy has raged for many years among folklorists over the very definition of their subject matter; the question was admirably summed up by our last President, Mr. A. R. Wright, in his valedictory address. The point at issue was whether folklore should be confined to the study of survivals from the past, to phenomena which in the nature of things are approaching exhaustion, or whether it should also include the new manufacture of a certain class of data possessing the same characteristics as the familiar survivals. Mr. Wright quoted the following passages from previous presidential addresses: "But folklore, being what it is, namely, the survival of traditional ideas or practices among a people whose principal members have passed beyond the stages of civilization which those ideas and practices once represented, it is impossible for it to have any development";[1] "One advantage possessed by our inclusive science is that the evidence which it presents is not disturbed by the intrusion

---

[1] G. L. Gomme, *Folklore,* Vol. 4, p. 6.

of unsuspected elements. It is a science of survivals, not of discoveries";[2] and he then proceeded to make a vigorous defence of the opposite point of view. "The old tree of folk thought and practice has life not only in its *surviving* branches, on which there are both withered twigs and fresh buds, but also in new and vigorous shoots which are being put out from the old trunk."[3] Now psychoanalysis would certainly support this more comprehensive view of the subject, the one vigorously defended by Mr. Wright, laying stress, as it does, on the dynamic and spontaneous aspects of these survival products and regarding them as efforts on the part of the unconscious to find expression; it would point out not only that the impulses that generated these products are a permanent part of man and are still as actively at work as ever, but also that the differences between the new products and the old can be shown to be more superficial than essential. Mr. Wright takes as an example of the former the war superstition that to use a match to light three cigarettes portended the death of the third smoker. Folklorists cannot fail to be reminded at once of the great part played in superstition by the idea of death following a third act or process, e.g., a third stroke of apoplexy and so on. Psychoanalysis would go still further, and would be able to correlate the form of this belief with certain unconscious ideas concerning the number three,[4] and it would in practice be able to show that just these unconscious ideas have been operative in the case of any particular person who was seriously influenced by the cigarette superstition. In doing so it would establish a continuity between the old and the new products, and would thus justify the inclusion of both in the same region of scientific study. I might illustrate the same point from another example which will also illuminate the connection between psychoanalytical and folkloristic data. In Sir Laurence Gomme's study of anthropological survivals in these islands he comes to the conclusion that "the whole associated group of customs received adequate explanation only on the theory that it represented the detritus of a once existing totemic system of belief."[5] Now in the psychoanalysis of individuals we have in a number of cases been able to demonstrate that ideas closely parallel to totemistic beliefs had been cherished during infancy, partly consciously, partly unconsciously, and what is even more interesting, that

---

[2] Edward Clodd, *Folklore,* Vol. 6, p. 75.

[3] A. R. Wright, *Folklore,* Vol. 38, p. 24.

[4] Psychoanalysts contend that the number three is symbolically related to the male sexual organ. See Sigmund Freud, *A General Introduction to Psychoanalysis* (Garden City, N.Y., 1953), p. 171. The interesting thing about this phallic interpretation is that right or wrong, it was made by the folk long before Freud. For example, Curt Wachsmuth reports in *Das alte Griechenland im neuen* (Bonn, 1864), p. 80, n. 24, that to the modern Greeks the number three was associated with the *phallus cum testiculis.* For a consideration of the importance of the number three in folklore, see Olrik's law of three in his essay "Epic Laws of Folk Narrative," which appears in this volume.—ED. NOTE

[5] G. L. Gomme, *Folklore as an Historical Science* (1908), p. 276.

survivals of this primitive period had been left in later life in the form of particular neurotic symptoms such as animal phobias. In other words, we have before us in the individuals the whole evolution of beliefs, and customs or rituals based on them, which is parallel to what in the field of folklore has run a course of perhaps thousands of years.

The unconscious mind has a considerable number of characteristics which distinguish it from the conscious mind, and indications of many of these can often be traced in the phenomena that I have here grouped as unconscious survivals. I shall not take up your time by enumerating them here,[6] but should like to mention one or two of them with which you will be specially familiar in the field of folklore. In psychoanalysis we refer to it by the name of "omnipotence of thoughts," implying thereby the unconscious belief that the thoughts, or rather wishes, of the person in question possess a magical power of reaching fruition in the outer world. The elucidation of mental processes of this kind plays a large part in daily psychoanalytic work, and as to folklore I am at a loss to choose an illustration of it, for the vast majority of folkloristic data is based on this principle. Every custom or ritual or formula designed to bring about results in the outer world, preservation from sickness, improvement in the crops, and so on, is based ultimately on the idea that the human mind possesses the power to influence the course of nature in the outer world, a power which religion deputes to Deity and achieves by the more indirect technique of prayer.

The characteristic just mentioned may perhaps be regarded as a special example of a more general one, namely, the disregard of reality. In its extreme form this can attain quite delusional dimensions, and in fact, emerges into consciousness among the insane as actual delusions. Most often, however, the tendency to ignore reality is not absolute, at least in its conscious manifestations. It is this attribute that confers on so much of folklore material its apparent irrationality. I use the word "apparent," for the process in question is not really irrational, once one grants its premises; but the premises are often enough not in accord with the facts of external reality. If, for example, peasants beat a saucepan during an eclipse of the sun, the procedure is not so senseless if one admits the presence of a wolf who is trying to devour their hero. Speaking still more broadly, we are concerned here with the part the imagination plays in the vast majority of folklore phenomena, and psychoanalysis can trace the workings of the imagination back to the internal fantasies that precede interest in the outer world and which take their origin in unconscious interests and impulses. Imagination can, of course, be generated in response to an inner need, i.e., act "spontaneously," or be stirred from without. External influences can do nothing except affect the form assumed by the imaginative act. It is through discounting this consideration that certain members of the "diffusionist" school of anthropology have invented an antinomy between the psychoanalytical and the anthropological points of

6 See Freud, "The Unconscious," *Collected Papers,* Vol. 4, Chap. VI (1925).

view which does not, in my opinion, really exist. The all-embracing explanation they find in demonstrating the spread of a given belief or custom reminds me of the similar attitude in psychopathology of those who are satisfied by ascribing every neurotic symptom to "suggestion" from without, and the criticism one would make is the same in the two cases. With neurotic symptoms one can prove that, where outside suggestion has played a part, it has done so only by stirring internal impulses that were ready enough to be stirred, and that its influence is confined to determining in some degree the form taken by the product of the internal impulse. I am persuaded that much the same must be true of the mass as of the individual, for the forces at work are of the same psychological nature with both. It is not a valid argument against this to point out that the original meaning of a custom is sometimes lost in its new setting, and can be discovered only by tracing historically its spread from its place of origin, or even that the meaning may change as the result of the transplantation. To this I would reply that the "meaning" here referred to is rarely more than the rationalistic façade given by the people to the belief or custom, and that behind this façade and quite unknown to them lies the real deeper motive. If the deeper motivation be investigated it will be found to be very similar in the two cases, i.e., that the belief before and after transplantation is often the expression of the same underlying impulse.

I will now consider one of the most puzzling and important features of unconscious mentation, namely, symbolism. A great part of the confusion on this subject arises simply from the fact that many quite disparate processes are often described by the same term.[7] Metaphors, emblems, similes, and so on, in fact almost any process in which one idea stands for another, have had the name "symbolism" applied to them. In psychoanalysis the word is employed in a much more restricted and defined sense, to designate a peculiar process whereby an idea or process represents an associated one which is in a state of repression in the unconscious mind. The number of possible symbols is countless, whereas the number of ideas in the unconscious that can be symbolized is very limited indeed, only those referring to the immediate blood relatives, various parts of the body, and the phenomena of birth, love, and death. Actually the large majority of symbols represents some half-dozen unconscious ideas. It follows that the interpretation of symbols displays a somewhat depressing monotony, though it is not true to say, as is sometimes done, that it is stereotyped. One is often less depressed than amazed by this monotony, though both emotions are obviously irrelevant to the more important question of the truth of the interpretations, a matter I have not the opportunity to discuss here. I would only point out that the data of folklore are replete with examples of symbolism in the psychoanalytical sense, and that the interpretation of such symbols not only illuminates the inner mean-

---

[7] See "The Theory of Symbolism," Chap. VIII of my *Papers on Psychoanalysis* (1923).

ing of the data but can constantly be confirmed by comparative study of allied material.

In the following example I would call special attention to the fact that a symbol always represents a concrete idea, never a general or abstract one. Let us take for instance the custom of throwing rice at weddings, which used to be general in the days of my youth, but which has now been replaced by the use of confetti. It would doubtless be agreed that the rice in this context represents the idea of fertility, and the act of throwing it the corresponding wish in respect to the bridal couple. Psychoanalysts would say that the rice is an *emblem* of fertility, but a *symbol* of seed; and they would mean by this that investigation of the unconscious would show that it was the idea of seed there from which all the other acts and thoughts proceeded. I have published an exhaustive study[8] of the beliefs and customs surrounding the idea of salt, one which has the same symbolic meaning, and have there discussed the relation of symbolism to superstition.

It will be seen that the unconscious ideas are not only more concrete but also cruder than the ideas represented in metaphorical processes, and this crudity and simplicity of unconscious ideas is a matter on which it is necessary to insist. In the allied, but now obsolescent, custom of throwing an old slipper or shoe after the departing couple, a custom which has more than one meaning in different layers of the mind, one would regard the object thrown as a symbol for the (fruitful) female organ itself, an interpretation that may be supported by quoting the decidedly broad saying that used to accompany it—"May you fit her as well as my foot fits this old shoe"—or by the Bohemian custom of getting hens to lay more eggs by feeding them with peas in a shoe on a holy eventide.[9] To take off the bride's shoe has the same defloration significance as to tear through the bridal wreath or loosen her girdle. Symbols with the same meaning that play a very considerable part in folklore are the cowry shell, the crescent moon, innumerable cups, goblets, caldrons, and caskets, and almost any object with an opening, from door portals and snake-stones to hollow trees or even the opening under a leaning ladder. Perhaps that most familiar example of all is the inverted horseshoe still to be seen over most stable doors. This is the descendant of the actual genital organ of the mare or cow displayed in Eastern countries to ward off the evil eye, just as the Shela-na-gig did that used to be found outside the door of Irish churches. It is the counterpart of the numerous forms of Asherah with its usual accompaniment of male symbols such as the arrow, cross, palm tree, star, etc., facing its concavity.

These few examples alone raise a host of problems. I intend to mention

8 "The Symbolic Significance of Salt in Folklore and Superstition," Chap. IV in my *Essays in Applied Psychoanalysis* (1923). [This superb essay should be required reading for anyone seriously interested in the psychological study of folklore. A more recent reprinting may be found in Jones, *Essays in Applied Psychoanalysis*, Vol. 2: *Essays in Folklore, Anthropology, and Religion* (London, 1951), pp. 22–109.—ED. NOTE]

9 Aigremont, *Fuss- und Schuh-Symbolik und Erotik* (1909), p. 54.

only two of them, and indeed shall have to postpone consideration of these until something has been said about the content of the unconscious. The first problem is, how comes it that the very same symbol can be used now as a sign of bad luck and now as a sign of good luck, and that the ideas symbolized are constantly changing in their relation to good and bad luck? An even prior question is, what is the real meaning of good and bad luck, terms which play such an enormous part in folklore beliefs and customs? The second problem concerns the place occupied by the subject of sexuality. Although no one has suggested that all unconscious symbols are sexual, which would be an entirely false suggestion, we have to face the fact that an astonishing number, certainly the large majority, are of this nature, and we cannot refrain from inquiring into the meaning of this unexpected finding. Now it would be quite wrong to ascribe a merely lascivious motive to the occurrence of sexual symbols, and if this were more generally recognized there would perhaps be less prudishness in dealing seriously with the problem. The circumstances that such symbolism pervades all religions, even the higher ones, should in itself be enough to make us regard the matter more soberly. I hope to show presently that the two questions just raised are intimately connected and that they are concerned with the most fundamental issues of life and death.

I think it is fair to say that the phenomena studied in folklore relate for the most part to simple or even lowly themes. The same is true a fortiori of the unconscious mind. In folklore we have to do with the simple wishes and fears of the people and very little with elaborate philosophical, spiritual, or artistic preoccupations. We find the people concerned with such matters as the preservation of health, the warding off of danger and death, the hopes of fortune, and the desire for happy marriage and the blessing of children. The unconscious is similarly engrossed with such topics and in even more primitive terms. I will illustrate this by laying before you two broad generalizations about its content. The first is that it is mainly concerned with the themes of birth, love, and death. These are the springs of life, and psychoanalysis would go so far as to maintain that all our manifold imaginative interests originate there, and consist only in ramifications of these themes modified by the influence of two other factors, the defensive reactions against certain dangers inherent in them (the moral "superego") and contact with outer reality. These two influences exercise a constantly molding effect on the primitive impulses that are striving for expression in their naked form. They control them, thwart them, select from them, and modify them to such an extent that in the final forms in which they emerge they are mostly transformed or distorted out of recognition. From time to time, of course, they emerge in ruder forms in various contexts. If, for instance, myths and nursery tales were taken seriously and not as a form of entertainment, we should doubtless be horrified at the recurring evidences they present of barbarous and loutish impulses. Sir Laurence Gomme is assuredly right when he says that "it is not accidental but persistent savagery we meet with in the folktale."[10] Further, as might be expected, the orientation of these impulses is decidedly egocentric; the unconscious, like charity, begins at home.

The second generalization about the unconscious is that primarily it recognizes no human beings except the immediate blood relatives: parents, siblings, and children. Attitudes and feelings about other people are all developed by either transforming or directly transferring those belonging to the relatives. This finding has tremendous import, but first I should like to make it a little more intelligible by reminding you of the banal fact that an infant's feelings and reactions are of necessity displayed first in respect to the persons in its immediate environment. The generalization I have just enunciated is by no means identical with this banal fact, though it has much in common with it. It illustrates the genetic aspects of the unconscious, and shows how nearly akin it is to the infantile. The really important feature of it is that since the unconscious is composed of our most primitive impulses, we have to face the conclusion that in that region of the mind the relationship to other members of the family far transcends the conventional ones of piety and affection. It does this in both directions, i.e., it is both more and less affectionate than one would infer from conscious manifestations. By less than affectionate I mean the jealous and hostile attitudes inherent in the family relationship, which regularly culminate in death-wishes. By more than affectionate I mean sexual, and in saying this I reach the hotly contested doctrine of psychoanalysis on the subject of infantile sexuality. This is not the place either to expound or to defend the doctrine, and I can only express my personal conviction of its truth. The only possible alternatives are that psychoanalysts are entirely mistaken in maintaining the existence of infantile sexuality, or on the other hand, that, as they assert, powerful motives of repression are generally operative in leading people to overlook or discount the signs of it that exist all around. Those who have seriously examined the mass of evidence that has been adduced can, I think, hardly remain long in doubt between these two alternatives.

The aspect of this subject that most concerns us here is the relationship of infantile sexuality to other members of the family, the so-called incest trends. According to psychoanalysis every child goes through a period in the first few years of its life where its development is dominated by unconscious conflicts relating to these trends, and very much of its future will depend on how it copes with them. Powerful barriers of fear and guilt are constructed against the forbidden and dangerous trends, and these barriers form the nucleus of what later becomes morality, conscience, and much of religion. I cannot describe here the complicated ways in which the two sets of forces in this conflict result in various compromises, out of which much of our conscious mind emerges; what interests us here is the less satisfactory products of the conflict. By these I mean the relics of the primitive state, what I termed

10 Gomme, *op. cit.*, p. 82.

"survivals" in the earlier part of my paper, and as I then pointed out, they are very nearly synonymous with much of the data investigated by folklorists. The most typical group is that which in its psychological structure can be likened to neurotic symptoms. An example would be the averting of "ill luck" by a magical gesture, incantation, or amulet. There is an interesting group, however, which is intermediate between this one and the quite normal transformation of the primitive impulses into daily activities. This intermediate one may, in a broad sense, be called artistic. The prominent part in it that fantasy plays allies it to the last group, from which it is separated, however, by a certain deference to reality. At the present Congress we have had several attractive presentations on the matter of folksongs and folk dance, but there are two topics even more familiar to us all in this connection. I refer to fairy tales and children's games. It has long been surmised, and in part demonstrated, that both these prerogatives of childhood have more to do with adult life than might at first sight appear. It seems clear, for instance, that the building and defending of castles and the use of bows and arrows must be traditionally handed down from times when these were serious occupations in adult life. In some cases, as in the doctor game[11] and the preoccupation with dolls, the relation to the sexual life of adults is unmistakable, but it will suprise many of you to be told that there is good reason to suppose that sexual elements are to be traced in most of these youthful interests. Symbolism plays an even larger part in the mentality of children than in that of adults, and the actual psychoanalysis of young children has shown that both their spontaneously invented games and the traditional ones they adopt so eagerly are often the symbolic expression of the infantile sexuality I mentioned earlier. The same is true of fairy tales. Let me illustrate this by the familiar example of the frog-prince type of tale,[12] in which the frog through repeated pleadings is gradually admitted to increasing intimacy with the maiden and is finally unspelled on being admitted to her bed. We learn from the sequel that the frog was all the time a prince in disguise, but to this we have to add the fact that the frog is in the unconscious a constant symbol of the male organ when viewed with disgust. So we have to complete the interpretation by saying that the story represents the maiden's gradual overcoming of her aversion to intimacy with this part of the body.

This leads me to say a word about the part played by animals in fantasy, in children's games, in nursery tales, in legends, and last but not least, in dreams. The simple fact that these animals, in spite of their frequently objectionable behavior, surprise us by displaying peculiarly human characteristics should provide a hint to their real meaning. This is no more and no less than that they represent particular human beings, most often the parents, espe-

---

[11] The doctor game consists of one child playing the part of a doctor who examines his patient-playmates. To the child, the doctor is perhaps the one individual who appears to have unlimited access to the body parts of anyone he wishes.—ED. NOTE

[12] This, the first tale in the Grimm's collection, is Aarne-Thompson Tale Type 440, The Frog King or Iron Henry.—ED. NOTE

cially the father, less often brothers or sisters or children. In many fairy tales, e.g., "The Twelve Brothers," "The Seven Ravens," etc. (Grimm), this is explicitly stated, and incidentally, we get a hint of the motives behind such transformations, since it is clear that in these instances the father has cast the spell from jealousy of his daughter's fondness for the brothers.[13] It is noteworthy that the father-animal identification is usually much more disguised than the other forms, indicating that the repressed thoughts about the father are in a corresponding state of inhibition. The animals of heraldry, however, might be quoted in this context, for the connection between heraldry and ancestry is evident enough as is that between the worship and taboos about snakes and piety for ancestors. Again, there are the numerous beliefs of tribes and nations being descended from particular animals, as the English are supposed to be from horses. Ancestor worship and the numerous beliefs about ancestors are but a displacement of similar attitudes concerning the father. The animals may of course be actual or imaginary ones, such as unicorns, dragons, etc., and in the latter case indicate a further stage in the disguise of the repressed idea. For the reason of the disguise is certainly repression. If one asks why should not the actual persons intended appear in the story or dream, the answer we get from investigation of the data is always the same, namely, that the theme that has given rise to the fantasy contains elements that are unacceptable to consciousness, and so are allowed to emerge only when they have been changed into an unrecognizable form. The various elements in question fall into two groups, sexual and hostile, a rule to which I know no exception, and the incompatibility of these attitudes with the piety due to one's family is obvious.

These human animals remind us of the other figures of fantasy, giants, dwarfs, fairies, and ghosts, about each of which very much could be said. It is generally recognized by now that the conception of giants, with their clumsy stupidity and their alternation of kindliness and ogerish devouring of children, is a projection of various infantile thoughts about grownups, particularly the parents, and perhaps one might say the same as regards the sexual significance of jesters, and dwarfs, of which Thumbkins and Rumpelstiltskin serve as typical examples. The belief in ghosts is one which has naturally attracted much attention from folklorists, and here again I would suggest that much advantage may accrue from cooperation between their work and that of psychoanalysts. It is surely clear that a limit is soon reached if we confine our investigation of ghosts (and allied spiritistic phenomena) to examination of the purely objective aspects, without taking into account the subjective state of the witnesses. In such studies we cannot distinguish between the parts played by the inner world and the outer world so long as we attend, as is nearly always the case, to the latter only. Psychoanalysis is naturally concerned with the former problem and often enough has to

---

[13] This is Aarne-Thompson Tale Type 451, The Maiden Who Seeks Her Brothers. —ED. NOTE

investigate the fear of ghosts, the proneness to see them, and so on. After unraveling and curing such mental states, it is possible to say something pretty definite about the genesis and meaning of them, and a great deal of evidence has accumulated to show that this is intrinsically connected with unconscious death-wishes relating to one or both of the parents, the strength and ramifications of which are difficult to overestimate.

After making this wide excursion let us return to the two questions I raised earlier in the paper, namely, the problem of luck and the problem of why it is that sexual symbolism occupies such an unexpectedly large part in the unconscious processes from which folklore survivals are derived. Curiously enough, the answer to these questions is substantially the same. Both subjects have to do with certain fears and wishes dating from a particularly difficult phase in development which everyone goes through, which everyone forgets, and of which there is therefore no conscious knowledge. It is perhaps the outstanding discovery attaching to the name of Freud that every young child goes through a stage of intense incestuous attachment which leaves an ineffaceable mark on all its later development. In connection with it two invariable reactions occur, fear and hate, and, soon afterwards, guilt. The dread of punishment, as distinct from the normal fear of punishment or enmity, is in the unconscious always associated with this primary theme, whatever be the context in which it occurs consciously. The sense of sin is born in connection with incest wishes, all sin is apprehended as incest by the unconscious, and therefore all guilt and moral punishment remain throughout life inextricably intertwined with these primary ideas. The very word "incest" is derived from a Sanscrit word signifying "undisciplined," "unpunished." Another remarkable ramification is the way in which the concept of punishment is in the unconscious extended to that of misfortune in general. Here, as in so many other respects, Christian theology follows closely the prototype of the unconscious, for it, too, regards the misfortunes that befall humanity as divine punishment for our sins. The practical corollary from all this is that exactly in proportion to the difficulty an individual has experienced in overcoming this early phase in development will he tend to react to the misfortunes of life as if they were punishments for sin. He will try to ward them off by measures which may be purely magical in nature, or may assume the religious form of penance and propitiation.

The next point is that the punishment for sin is always the same in the unconscious. It appropriately takes the talion form of deprivation of sexual capacity, this being most typically expressed in men as impotence—which is the conscious equivalent of castration in the unconscious—and in women of sterility. Often enough this finds directly conscious expression, as in the endless superstitions and practices to do with fertility and sterility on the one hand, and the manifold dread of what was called the "ligature" on the other hand, the dread which is the secret of the witchcraft epidemic. Usually, however, the dreads and defensive measures are expressed in various symbolic guises that need to be interpreted before their meaning becomes clear. Two vast subjects in this connection are those of ill health and death, which is natural enough when one reflects how largely they bulk among the misfortunes of humanity. Hypochondriacal concern about health and a disproportionate apprehension of death always, as I have expounded elsewhere in a similar connection,[14] prove when investigated to be the manifestations of unconscious guilt with dread of the punishment of impotence.

I come last to what, I think, is the most interesting point of all in this complicated subject. It is that just as the punishment for forbidden sexuality (incest) always takes the talion form of a veto on sexuality, so do the apotropaeic measures designed to ward off evil seek to achieve their aim by means of the same talion, or what might perhaps be here better termed homeopathic, principle. The underlying idea appears to be that if only the person could dare to prove to himself that he could commit incest, symbolically of course, without the dreaded punishment ensuing, that very impunity would be the best reassurance imaginable against his fears. This is the reason why sexual symbolism plays such an astonishing part in the customs and beliefs that make up so much of folklore. As I indicated above, it would be both superficial and erroneous to regard these findings as simply indications of lasciviousness. They are dictated by the desire to free the personality from guilt, from danger from punishment, and from misfortune, and thus to restore the innate faculty of potency and fertility, in short, to ensure happiness. We have here the explanation of how it is that the idea of incest signifies both the maximum of danger and the maximum of security. And that is the reason why the same act, the same object, the same belief can at one moment or in one place represent the idea of good luck and at another that of ill luck.

If this Congress were entirely devoted to the relation of psychoanalysis to folklore, it would be able to deal with only the fringe of such a vast subject. I have singled out, however briefly and inadequately, what I consider to be a few of the most vital points of connection, and will express the hope that future cooperation between workers in what are apparently very different fields will be equally fruitful to both.

---

[14] "Psychoanalysis and Anthropology," *The Journal of the Royal Anthropological Institute,* Vol. 54 (1924).

Jack and the Beanstalk

Humphrey Humphreys

This and the following brief interpretations of the same folktale are intended to demonstrate forcefully the difference between the literal and the symbolic approaches to folklore. In the former, the hypothetical origin of the beanstalk, for example, is said to be an actual beanstalk found in an Asian jungle. In the latter, the suggested phallic symbolic origin of the beanstalk comes from fantasy, not objective reality.

Another reason for presenting these short notes is to illustrate what can happen when non-folklorists attempt to interpret folklore without first investigating the pertinent folklore scholarship. The problem, of course, is that too few workers in other fields realize that there is a discipline of folklore, a discipline which has its own techniques and tools for analysis. It is not merely a matter of properly identifying "Jack and the Beanstalk" as an example of Aarne-Thompson Tale Type 328. It is rather the necessity for knowing first that Tale Type 328 is primarily a European tale with very, very few versions reported from Asia, and second that the particular form—the technical term is sub-type—of the tale in which the magic beanstalk is an introductory episode is charactistic of English and American versions. The beanstalk is *not* found in most European versions of the tale type. The distribution of this element suggests that the beanstalk is a purely local adaptation and that it almost certainly was not present in the older forms of the basic tale type. Information about the distribution of the tale, which might have led Humphreys to reconsider his ingenious hypothesis, could have been obtained by consulting the appropriate section of the voluminous compilation of notes and parallels to the Grimm tales, Johannes Bolte and Georg Polívka, *Anmerkungen zu den Kinder- und Hausmärchen der Brüder Grimm*, 5 vols (Leipzig, 1913–1932); the tale type index; or the commentary on the tale found in Stith Thompson's standard *The Folktale* (New York, 1946).

This familiar English fairy tale, though in its entirety perhaps peculiar to these islands, is a synthesis of a number of themes which separately are found in the folklore of widely scattered peoples. The hen that laid the golden eggs,

Reprinted from *Antiquity*, Vol. 22 (1948), 36–38, by permission of *Antiquity*.

the harp that began to play of itself, a strange world above the sky inhabited by beings of supernatural character, a magic seed that grew into a tree reaching up to heaven, are features in tales told by simple folk literally from China to Peru.[1] Let us consider a little more closely the last two themes.

To primitive minds

> That inverted bowl they call the sky
> Whereunder crawling cooped we live and die

is an object of never-failing mystery and a fertile source of myths. How it is supported and what lies beyond it are questions variously answered, and a difference is discernible between the folklore of peoples whose physical background is tropical forest and of those who live in more open country. In Greece the sky rested on Mount Olympus, and the rebellious Titans piled Pelion on Ossa, one mountain on another, in an effort to reach it; or the sky rested on the shoulders of Mount Atlas in North Africa, imagined as a weary giant. In Japan the sky was thought of as supported on stone pillars. But where the equatorial rainbelt produces jungle the sky is more often depicted as supported by giant trees; such a belief has been reported as current amongst the Caribs of the West Indies, the Indians of Guiana and Central America, the Dyaks of Borneo, and other dwellers in tropical forest.[2]

It is possible also to detect a further difference between the beliefs of North and South. In the North where the contrast between summer and winter is very marked and the winter nights are long, the belief in an underworld of perpetual night, of winter without end, is widespread, and plentiful examples from Classical, Teutonic, and Slavonic mythology will be recalled. In tropical folklore, the abode of beings other than mortal man, whether they be the spirits of the dead, the gods, or other nonhuman creatures, are more commonly considered to be either on the earth or above it. But in all three cases human visits to these normally inaccessible regions are believed to have occurred, and the Jack of our story is akin to Heracles, Orpheus, and True Thomas.[3] It may thus be suspected that our fairy tale, at any rate in respect of this feature of a tree reaching up to a world inhabited by strange beings, had its origin in a distant and very different clime from ours. And the other element

---

[1] The distribution of some of these specific features, for example, the hen that lays golden eggs (cf. Motif B103.2.1, Treasure-laying bird) and the self-playing harp (cf. Motifs D1601.18, Self-playing musical instruments, and D1231, Magic harp) is not nearly as widespread as Humphreys suggests.—ED. NOTE

[2] For these and other traditional means of supporting the sky, see the various subdivisions under Motif A665, Support of the sky.—ED. NOTE

[3] For references to the other world, see such motifs as A660, Nature of the upper world; A670, Nature of the lower world; and E481, Land of the dead. For an excellent study of Orpheus' visit to the land of the dead (Motif F81.1) in the New World, see Åke Hultkrantz, *The North American Indian Orpheus Tradition* (Stockholm, 1957). For an account of the enticement of True Thomas into fairyland, see Child ballad 37, Thomas Rhymer, in the first volume of *The English and Scottish Popular Ballads*.—ED. NOTE

we are considering, that of a magic seed growing up almost overnight till it reached the heavens, strengthens this suspicion. The incredible rate of vegetable growth in regions of monsoon or tropical rain has to be seen to be believed; and there must be many English children who, like the writer long years ago, wonder how anything so tenuous and fragile as a beanstalk, fading at the first breath of winter and needing a stick for its support, can be thought of as propping up the palace of a giant. Of all possible stems why a beanstalk?

Now there occurs very widely distributed in tropical forest a giant bean known as *Entada Scandens*. The pods are 2 to 4 feet long, 3 to 4 inches wide and contain about a dozen perfectly round flat beans 1 to 3 inches in diameter and about ½ inch deep. The plant is found growing in the East Indies, the Malay Peninsula, Burma and Northeast India, West Africa, the West Indies and Central America, and though formerly considered to be one species is now subdivided into a number, all however belonging to the same genus. About 30 per cent of the beans have the remarkable power of floating in either fresh or sea water for an indefinite period. Indeed, water-born beans appear to be the principal propagators of the plant, and this buoyancy has brought about their dispersal by ocean currents to many countries in the temperate and even the arctic zones including the shores of these islands. The beans brought to our beaches probably come from the West Indies as part of the Gulf Stream drift. Wherever they have been found their exotic appearance has given rise to a number of quaint beliefs and superstitions; there is record of their being held in high regard as fertility emblems and they have been put to practical use by conversion into snuff boxes.

In the wet warm jungles of their native lands the beans grow up a tree with remarkable rapidity till they reach the level of interlacing boughs, which in tall jungle may be perhaps 30 to 50 feet up. They then spread horizontally, strangle their foster parents, and come to stand as independent trunks, increasing in the course of years to a circumference of several feet, and attaining the hard consistency of mahogany. The dense canopy of their spreading branches and large leaves may extend to over a hundred feet for a single plant and if these are numerous may form an almost unbroken roof reducing sunlight to Stygian gloom and permitting arboreal animals to scamper about unseen by those below. Here if anywhere is an authentic beanstalk not unfit to have formed the main feature in the familiar fable.

Rarely, if ever, in the study of folklore can we go beyond speculation and produce proof of a scientific order, since nearly all written evidence is absent or late. All we can demand is that a hypothesis shall not strain our credulity, and shall be consistent with other evidence in the same field of enquiry. If then our beanstalk really has its roots in a tropical jungle, this is far more likely to have been in India and its eastern neighbors than in the New World whence our *British Entada* beans are derived. There must be few fairy tales that are not pre-Columbian in point of time, and India has an almost unique record in that there the growth and spread of legend has been continuous for thousands of years, whereas in Europe and hither Asia it has been rudely interrupted by the spread of Christianity and Islam. It is moreover generally accepted that there is an oriental ingredient in European folklore; the anthropomorphic animal stories in the Buddhist "Jataka," themselves of Indian origin and much older than Gautama, are paralleled in Europe, the gypsies are considered to have come from India, and there are many other channels along which tales might have traveled thence to these distant shores.

Can we speculate further on the genesis of the giant whose fatal fall from the higher branches was the climax of our tale? In the Spring of 1944 the writer spent some months in the jungle-clad Naga hills near Imphal before the Japanese advanced and occupied the area. We heard, mainly in the early morning and evening, curious and unfamiliar cries traveling along the tree-tops above our leafy canopy which we finally traced to the gibbons, the anthropoid apes of Southeast Asia. Now a gibbon, though smaller than a man, is a giant when compared with the grey langurs and the red Rhesus monkeys which are the common denizens of Indian jungle. Moreover unlike these it readily walks erect, is easily tamed, and has other human attributes: it is a heavy animal and might well sustain injury from a direct fall of 30 or 40 feet. We know that a few inches average advantage in stature or size is enough to earn a race the reputation of being gigantic, for the Gauls appeared so to the Romans and Nordic men to the Mediterranean races. Perhaps then it is permissible to suggest the possibility that the giant who had a great fall may once have been a gibbon whose mysterious cries fertilized the folklore of frightened villagers in east Asiatic jungle clearings.

Jack and the Beanstalk

William H. Desmonde

In this short but wild Freudian interpretation of Tale Type 328, one finds quite a different analysis of the tale content from that offered by solar mythologists (summarized by Dorson in "The Eclipse of Solar Mythology"). However, both solar and psychoanalytic interpretations contrast markedly with the preceding literal reading of the tale.

Some of the common criticisms of Desmonde's and similar analyses of folkloristic materials made by psychoanalysts are as follows. The analysis is usually based upon only one version (and in this case the "version" is from a children's literature anthology, rather than directly from oral tradition). To comparative folklorists who are accustomed to examining hundreds of versions of a folktale or folksong before arriving at even a tentative conclusion, this apparently cavalier approach to folklore goes very much against the grain. How does the analyst know, for example, whether or not the particular version he is using is typical and representative?

The second criticism concerns the matter of proof. How does one demonstrate what Desmonde calls the "fact" that beans are a common symbol for the testicles? Clearly, it is more difficult to document a psychological speculation than some of the historical speculations folklorists are wont to call facts. For example, most folklorists would consider it a fact that the American Negro versions of the deceptive tug-of-war—in which a small animal after challenging two large animals to a tug-of-war arranges it so that they unwittingly pull against each other—must have come from Africa. The motif (K22) is commonly found in African folklore and in New World Negro folklore. It is not reported in Europe. The African origin of this Negro narrative element is the kind of safe speculation that folklorists might be willing to call fact. On the other hand, the "facts" of psychoanalytic interpretations of folklore frequently strike the folklorist as being somewhat arbitrary. Generally, folklorists tend to feel that the Freudian interpretations are

Reprinted from *American Imago,* Vol. 8 (1951), 287–88, by permission of the author and *American Imago.*

read into, not out of, the tales. However, folklorists do very little themselves in the way of psychological analysis of their materials, and most of their criticism is destructive, not constructive.

The following psychoanalytic interpretation of the English folktale is suggested by the fact that the terms "beans" and "stalk" are common symbols for the testicles and penis.[1]

The story relates that Jack and his mother lived together in a small country cottage. Lazy, irresponsible, and pleasure-seeking, the boy was incapable of earning his living, since "his mother had almost never corrected him as he grew up." Jack's mother supported herself and her child by selling her property, until eventually all that remained between them and starvation was their last asset, the cow. However, instead of getting a fair price, Jack traded the cow for some magic beans. Upon his return, Jack's mother burst into tears at his folly, and in exasperation threw the beans out of the window.

Jack awakened the next morning to find a huge beanstalk growing up into the clouds. Climbing to the top, he stepped off into a strange country, where he met a "queer little old lady" with a wand, who told him that his father was imprisoned in a nearby castle by a cannibalistic ogre. Jack stole the giant's treasures, and was finally pursued down the beanstalk by the ogre. Taking a hatchet, he chopped at the root of the beanstalk. "No sooner had he done so, than of a sudden, the whole beanstalk shriveled up and the giant burst like a monstrous bubble."[2]

We may interpret Jack psychoanalytically as an oral dependent. Incapable of competing successfully in the market, he returned home, the tale tells, feeling depressed and inferior, and went to bed without any supper. We may regard the remainder of the story as an incestuous masturbation fantasy or dream, of a regressive nature.[3]

The miraculous stalk growing from the beans is the erect phallus, and the little old lady with the fairy wand is the phallic mother-image. The imprisoned

---

[1] Havelock Ellis, *Studies in the Psychology of Sex,* Vol. 2, Part I (New York: Random House, 1936), 5.

[2] Olive Beaupré Miller, "Jack and the Beanstalk," in *My Bookhouse,* Vol. 2 (Chicago: The Bookhouse for Children Publishers, 1920), 371–85.

[3] Had Desmonde bothered to examine other versions of the tale, he might have found additional evidence. For example, Desmonde might have cited the self-playing harp in support of his suggestion that the tale is a masturbation fantasy. Musical instruments which play by themselves and for that matter all magically self-operating objects (Motif D1600, Automatic object) are considered by psychoanalysts to represent autoeroticism. The slang phrase "to play with oneself" signifying masturbation supports the interpretation. In the English versions, it is touching the harp which, crying "Master, master," wakes the sleeping giant (father).

Another interesting detail is that in the upper world, the giant's friendly wife who mothers Jack decides to hide the boy in her oven. If the psychoanalytic assumption that the oven is a symbol of the womb is valid, then the fact that the giant does not find Jack in his wife's oven might be construed as an Oedipal triumph for the hero.—Ed. Note

father indicates Jack's Oedipal hostility, while the cannibalistic ogre is the same father in a threatening aspect. Treasures are incestuous representations.[4] Pursued by the menacing ogre for his thefts, Jack castrates himself:[5] the beanstalk shrivels at the first touch of the hatchet, and the threatening father-image disappears.

It is instructive to note the parallel between "Jack and the Beanstalk" and the story of Aladdin and his wonderful lamp, which is also a masturbation fantasy, as Jung recognized.[6] Aladdin is, like Jack, a scapegrace and good-for-nothing, who is supported by his mother. He invokes a genie by rubbing the magic lamp, who grants him all of his wishes, i.e., makes him omnipotent. There was only one of Aladdin's wishes which the genie refused—with great anger—to bring the egg of a giant female bird named the Rukh.[7]

We will remember that, in classical antiquity, the word "genii" meant the ghost of the deified paternal ancestor. World-egg cosmogonies are frequent in primitive cultures, and result from a projection of the mother-image into the cosmos.[8]

Both the Aladdin and the Jack and the Beanstalk stories contain the incest motive, it is apparent. The two tales may be connected by cultural diffusion, or may merely have sprung independently from similar psychic tendencies.

---

[4] C. G. Jung, *Psychology of the Unconscious* (New York: Dodd, Mead & Co., 1942), p. 409.

[5] The arbitrary nature of psychoanalytic interpretation is easily demonstrated when one considers an alternative reading of Jack's cutting of the beanstalk. Since the plot concerns Jack's taking things from the giant, it would be equally logical to assume that the stalk belonged to the giant as well, especially since cutting it kills the giant, not Jack. Moreover, if fairy tales are expressions of wishful thinking and wish fulfillment as psychoanalysts claim, why wouldn't Jack want to castrate his father and live happily ever after with his mother? (Note that in some versions of the tale, it is Jack's mother who aids Jack by handing him the necessary hatchet.) Géza Róheim, in *The Gates of the Dream* (New York, 1952), p. 359, states that the beanstalk is *both* Jack's penis and the father's penis! This lack of agreement among psychoanalysts is considered by folklorists to be indisputable evidence of the error of the approach. However, the analysts do agree that the beanstalk is a penis. The question is whose?—ED. NOTE

[6] Jung, *op. cit.,* p. 187.

[7] Richard H. Burton, *The Arabian Nights* (New York: Blue Ribbon Books, Inc., 1932).

[8] For the world-egg cosmogony, see Motif A641, Cosmic egg. For a comprehensive survey of this motif's distribution, see Anna-Britta Hellbom, "The Creation Egg," *Ethnos,* Vol. 28 (1963), 63–105.—ED. NOTE

Jack and the Beanstalk:
An American Version

Martha Wolfenstein

Comparative folklorists tend to present evidence without drawing psychological conclusions, whereas psychoanalysts tend to draw psychological conclusions without presenting evidence. However, psychologist Wolfenstein's short study of Tale Type 328 illustrates the advantages of employing a more eclectic approach to the origins of folklore, an approach which combines the comparative method with psychological interpretation.

Wolfenstein is not only aware of the English and American versions of this tale, but more important, she uses the various differences in detail as a point of departure for an analysis of themes of American culture. Notice that these differences can only be revealed *after* a comparison of the several versions is made. One cannot possibly tell from looking at just one American version of the tale which particular details are peculiarly American and which are not. This is why it is always risky to base an analysis upon a single version of an item of folklore. Whether one agrees with Wolfenstein's interpretation or not, her method of using the comparative method as a prerequisite to psychological speculation is exemplary. Few studies of folklore as source material for an analysis of national character and of cultural penchants are as sound methodologically.

For a further consideration of some of the theoretical difficulties involved in reconciling the comparative method with the psychoanalytic study of folklore, see Alan Dundes, "Earth-Diver: Creation of the Mythopoeic Male," *American Anthropologist,* Vol. 64 (1962), 1032–51, and the ensuing exchanges, *American Anthropologist,* Vol. 65 (1963), 913–21.

I am indebted to Sylvia Brody for her compilation and classification of variants of this story.—M. W.

"Jack and the Beanstalk" is a variant of a widespread folklore theme: the boy who steals the giant's treasure. The occurrence of the beanstalk as the means by which the boy attains his purpose is a distinctive English invention.[1] Tales of English origin have become a part of American folklore. While these tales retain many of their original elements, they have to some extent been transformed. If we take the version of "Jack and the Bean Tree" as told in the mountains of North Carolina and as recorded by Richard Chase, we can see how the English tale has been modified to assume a characteristic American flavor.[2]

The main outline of the plot remains: there is the wonderful beanstalk which Jack climbs, the giant and his wife, the danger of being eaten by the giant, the wife's hiding of Jack, Jack's three thefts of the giant's belongings, the eventual chase, Jack's chopping down of the beanstalk, and the giant's fatal fall. As to the variations, we may note first that the English version begins with the dire poverty of Jack and his mother, the mother's unhappiness, and some reproach against Jack, who is spoiled or lazy or cannot hold a job or who has carelessly exhausted the family substance.[3] This reproach against Jack, who makes his poor mother suffer, is intensified when he makes the apparently foolish bargain with the man who trades him a handful of beans for the cow. The mother is in despair and enraged against Jack, and the boy then frees himself of this burden of guilt by his heroic feats and the gifts which he brings the mother.

In the American tale Jack is a small boy running at his mother's heels while she is trying to clean the house. She sweeps up a big bean and, to keep the boy occupied, tells him to go out and plant it. Next day Jack finds the beanstalk already knee-high, the second day as high as a tree, and the third day grown out of sight. Each time he tells his mother about this remarkable

---

[1] Richard Chase, ed., Notes on parallels to "Jack and the Bean Tree," *The Jack Tales as Told by R. M. Ward* (Boston: Houghton Mifflin Company, 1943), p. 190.

[2] The "Jack tales," which Chase recorded in the 1930's, had been transmitted by oral tradition among the inhabitants of the mountains of western North Carolina, elsewhere in the southern mountains, and in parts of Virginia. Chase's informants acknowledged as the major source of their tales an admired storyteller of their region, Council Harmon, who lived from 1803 to 1896.

[3] Joseph Jacobs' version of "Jack and the Beanstalk," in his *English Fairy Tales,* first published in 1890, is the best known. Jacobs recorded the tale as he recalled having heard it when he was a boy in Australia. The reproach against Jack as a boy who was unable to hold a job appears in this version. Joseph Jacobs, *English Fairy Tales,* 3rd rev. ed. (New York: G. P. Putnam's Sons, 1898). Variants of this theme, in which Jack is described as lazy, a dreamer, spoiled, extravagant, and so on, occur in the following: Hallam Tennyson, *Jack and the Beanstalk, in English Hexameters* (London and New York: The Macmillan Company, 1886); George Cruikshank, *The Cruikshank Fairy Book* (New York: G. P. Putnam's Sons, 1911); Horace E. Scudder, *The Book of Fables and Folk Stories,* new illus. ed. (New York: Houghton Mifflin Company, 1919); Dinah Maria Craik (Mulock), *The Fairy Book* (New York: The Macmillan Company, 1923); Flora Annie Steele (Webster), *English Fairy Tales Retold by Flora Annie Steele* (New York: The Macmillan Company, 1924); Walter De la Mare, *Told Again* (New York: Alfred A. Knopf, Inc., 1927).

growth, and each time she slaps him for telling lies. This is followed by her confirming each time that he has told the truth and making it up to him by giving him something good to eat. Thus, instead of Jack's being in the wrong, he is falsely accused by the mother. This sequence embodies a major theme of American fantasy in which the hero (or heroine), while innocent, may appear guilty and have to clear himself of false suspicions rather than redeem himself from sin. Comparison of American and British films has shown this tendency to substitute conflict between the hero (or heroine) and false accusers for the inner conflict in which the protagonist struggles with self-accusations.[4]

Another aspect of the American version is that of the little boy exhibiting the marvelous growth of his bean tree to his mother. The beanstalk generally may be taken to have a phallic significance: it is a possession of the boy's which has extraordinary erectile powers. In the episode peculiar to the American version, Jack boasts to his mother about the springing-up of his bean tree and gets first a rebuke and then a reward. There is the fantasy here that the mother will welcome and admire the little boy's phallic showing off, that her scolding for it may give way to affectionate acceptance. In the English tale Jack uses the beanstalk to obtain presents for his mother; the American emphasis is more on masculine exhibition.

The things Jack steals from the giant are also different in the American and English versions. Instead of the moneybags and the hen that lays the golden eggs, the American Jack steals a gun and a knife. These are again symbols of masculine prowess, and they are things that the boy can play around with to amuse himself. "Well, he played around with that knife a right smart while." There is not the element of giving something to the mother but of the boy's winning male accouterments for himself. The theme of giving and getting is considerably played down in comparison with the English version. Thus, also, the exchange of the cow for the beans does not occur here. The things the American Jack takes differ in another way from the English Jack's booty. They are not magical sources of supply, like the hen that lays the golden eggs, in relation to which the possessor can assume a passively receptive attitude. They are rather tools with which the owner can, by the active exercise of skill, do something. While a gun and a knife may have associations of magical power for a small boy, as manifestly presented in the story these objects are nonmagical.

The third thing which the American Jack steals is the "coverlid on the old giant's bed [that] had little bells sewed all over it." This jingling coverlid is the equivalent of the harp that plays by itself. Both may stand for the strange sounds which the child hears in the night and which he takes as signs of his father's sexual prowess. The American Jack, in snatching the coverlid off the giant's bed, boldly exposes and mocks his antagonist. There is an

---

[4] Martha Wolfenstein and Nathan Leites, *Movies: A Psychological Study* (New York: The Free Press of Glencoe, Inc., 1950).

analogy here to another of the Jack tales, in which Jack crowns a series of ingenious feats of robbery by stealing the shimmy off the back of the rich man's wife after she has retired for the night.[5] There is an emphasis here on male rivalry, not so much for the woman's favors as to discomfit and outdo a rival of big pretensions.

The English version, with its emphasis on giving and getting, its golden treasures and magical sources of supply, as well as the theme of a boy making things up to a mother whom he has made to suffer, has many more prephallic components than the American one. The latter takes the springing bean tree more as the dominant theme and, in keeping with this, provides other elements of masculine prowess: showing off to mother, getting a gun and a knife. The American tale ends: "And the last time I was down there Jack was gettin' to be a right big boy, and he was doin' well." Thus the concluding image is that of the boy growing to be fine and big, after the model of the springing bean tree.

---

[5] Chase, *op. cit.*, pp. 195–97. [This is Tale Type 1525A, Theft of Dog, Horse, Sheet, or Ring.—ED. NOTE]

On the Symbolism
of Oedipus

William A. Lessa

One of the tales which Professor Lessa collected on Ulithi Atoll seems
to be similar to Tale Type 931, Oedipus. In this tale entitled "Sikhalöl
and His Mother," Lisòr, the wife of a chief, gives birth prematurely to
a son, whom she abandons by setting him adrift on the ocean. Rasim,
who lives on another part of the island, rescues the boy, becomes his
foster father, and brings him up. One day the boy, Sikhalöl, happened
to pass the menstrual house in which his mother was confined. She saw
him and was attracted to him. She invited him to visit her in the
menstrual house. Later Rasim informed Sikhalöl that he was visiting
his own mother. Sikhalöl then told his mother who he was, but she
said she did not care and that they should continue meeting. One day
the chief, Sikhalöl's real father, impatient with his wife's prolonged
stay in the menstrual house, noticed some scratches on the woman's
face, scratches which had been inflicted by Sikhalöl during one of his
visits. He realized that she had a lover. All the men of the village had
to put their fingers next to the woman's face so that the chief could
see if they matched the marks. Finally, Sikhalöl appeared and when
his guilt was clear, the chief began to swing an axe on his son. However, Sikhalöl seized the ax and cut off his father's head. Then he took
his mother away and they lived together from that time on.

The collection of this tale from Ulithi and the discovery that there
were numerous parallels throughout Oceania led Professor Lessa to
survey the various interpretations made of the Oedipus story. The
revision of a paper presented to the American Folklore Society in 1954
appeared as "Oedipus-Type Tales in Oceania," *Journal of American
Folklore,* Vol. 69 (1956), 63–73. This article was expanded into a
section of a comprehensive monograph on Ulithi folk narrative. Lessa,
Professor of Anthropology at the University of California at Los
Angeles, is definitely sceptical of symbolic approaches, and his array
of interpretations of a single tale must give pause to the student of
folklore intrigued with symbolic rather than literal interpretations.

Reprinted from William A. Lessa, *Tales from Ulithi Atoll,* University of California
Publications: Folklore Studies 13 (Berkeley and Los Angeles, 1961), pp. 193–201, by
permission of the author and the University of California Press.

If ever a myth was given symbolic meaning it is the Oedipus tale. Long ago it captured the fancy of scholars and theorists, and today it is still the subject of active interpretations. Probably the story would have been largely ignored if Sophocles had not made it into what has been called the greatest play of classical antiquity. On account of the prestige which he gave it, it has been fashionable to attempt to "discover" what it stands for. Let us turn to some of these attempts.

A naturistic position is taken by Bréal,[1] who explains Oedipus as the personification of Light, and his blinding as the disappearance of the sun at the end of the day. The chief event in the legend is the struggle with the Sphinx, the storm cloud, which is the prototype of mythical monsters. Bréal separates these events in the story from certain of the others, namely, parricide and incest, which he maintains are later additions. This accords with his hypothesis that the elements of legends are not created simultaneously. The essential facts and names of the story of Oedipus, he says, belong to one period, a "naturalistic" one, whereas disposition and moral belong to a later period, a "moralistic" one. The blindness of the hero, which forms a part of the first period, is no longer understood in the second, and so killing the father and marrying the mother are used to explain the punishment. The idea of fatality, familiar to this age, is mixed in with the story. Bréal believes, with Max Müller, that fairy tales are the last residue of the naturalistic religion of a people.

A position similar to this is taken by Constans,[2] who too believes that the moralistic explanation is a secondary development of later times, transforming a primitive solar myth by the addition of new elements brought to the story by tragic poets imbued with the Greeks' forceful concept of fate.

Both Bréal and Constans had reacted to an earlier theory proposed by Comparetti,[3] who was opposed to the idea of naturalistic origins, and unlike his later critics, did not separate the component parts of the story into episodes of varying chronological sequence. Comparetti, a euhemerist, regarded Oedipus as a purely human person and for this reason discounted the episode of the Sphinx as being a later addition. For him the myth is didactic in that it sets forth the horrors of incest.

Returning to the naturists we find one of the most unbridled of them all in the person of Sir George Cox,[4] who gives every element in the mythos a symbolic meaning. The Sphinx is the dark and lowering cloud who strikes terror into the hearts of men and heightens the agonies of a time of drought. Oedipus, the sun, unfolds her dark sayings and drives her from the throne,

---

[1] Michel Bréal, *Mélanges de mythologie et de linguistique* (Paris: Librairie Hachette, 1877), pp. 163–85.

[2] Léopold Eugène Constans, *La Légende d'Oedipe: Etudiée dans l'antiquité, au moyen-âge et dans les temps modernes* (Paris: Maisonneuve, 1880).

[3] Domenico Comparetti, *Edipo e la mitologia comparata* (Pisa: Nistri, 1867).

[4] George W. Cox, *The Mythology of the Aryan Nations*, 2 vols. (London; Longmans, Green & Company, Ltd., 1870).

"just as the cloud, smitten by the sun, breaks into rain, and then vanishes away" (Vol. 1, 222). "The sun appears once more in the blue heaven, in which he sprang into life in the morning; in other words, Oedipus is wedded to his mother Jocasta..." (Vol. 2, 71). When Oedipus tears out his own eyes it is as the light of the setting sun being blotted out by the dark storm cloud. In his last hours before his death he is cheered by the presence of Antigone, "the fair and tender light which sheds its soft hue over the Eastern heaven as the sun sinks in death beneath the western waters" (Vol. 1, 223).

Robert[5] mixes fact and symbolism when he points out that a truly old Oedipus cultus is found in Eteonos. Here Oedipus is a chthonian hero. The earth goddess, Demeter, in whose grave he was buried, was originally his mother. This explains his incest, for whenever the earth is the mother her sons are naturally her husbands also. In fact, says Robert, whenever in myths we encounter the marriage of a mother to her own son we are justified in recognizing his mother as the earth goddess. Oedipus' sufferings are a trait of the "year-god," who is born in the spring but suffers pain or death in the winter. Oedipus' father, too, is a year-god; the old year must be "killed" before the new one can reign. Parricide as well as incest are rooted in nature religion. Only when the god becomes human and Earth becomes a human woman are these deeds considered crimes.

Using a complex "structural" approach to myth analysis, Lévi-Strauss[6] sees the Oedipus tale as being concerned with the problem of autochthony versus bisexual reproduction. It deals with the inability of Greek culture, which held a belief that mankind is autochthonous, to find a satisfactory transition between this theory and the knowledge that human beings are actually born from the union of man and woman. The slaying of the Sphinx has to do with the denial of the autochthonous origin of mankind. But Oedipus' name, "Swellfoot," refers to the persistence of the autochthonous origin of man, because in mythology it is a universal characteristic of men who are born from the earth that at the moment they emerge from the depth they either cannot walk or they do so clumsily. Oedipus' marriage to his mother and his killing of his father refer, respectively, to the attempt to escape autochthony (by overrating blood relations) and to the impossibility of succeeding within it (by underrating blood relations). Despite Lévi-Strauss's effort to free himself of what he calls sophism, one cannot escape the conclusion that he introduces highly subjective interpretations into his method of analysis and that he emerges with something little better than the high-handed interpretations of the naturists.

Marxian dialectics is brought to bear upon the interpretation of Sophocles' *Oedipus* by George Thomson[7] in a book dealing with the growth of slavery

[5] Carl Robert, *Oidipus* (Berlin: Weidmann, 1915), Vol. 1, 44–45.

[6] Claude Lévi-Strauss, "The Structural Study of Myth," *Journal of American Folklore,* Vol. 68, (1955), 428–44.

[7] George D. Thomson, *Studies in Ancient Greek Society* (London: Lawrence & Wishart, 1955), pp. 282–87.

and the origin of science in ancient Greece. The play is a dramatic expression of Heraclitus' law of the interpenetration of opposites—a doctrine that maintains the world is held together by tension and strife rather than by fusion and harmony, as Pythagoras asserted. Oedipus, we learn, "is man, the new man, the individual owner of commodity-producing society," who is caught in the toils of Apollo, the radical leveler who does away with all distinctions. Sophocles' Apollo is thus like Heraclitus' fire. Fire is comparable to Engels' "universal equivalent" because it is involved in a self-regulating cycle of change which maintains the world in being. Oedipus twice became the opposite of what he was—an outcast who became a king, and a king who became an outcast. The Oracle of Apollo brought about his downfall by denouncing him.

The psychoanalysts have made intensive use of the Oedipus story because to them it represents a splendid example of their general assumption that folklore embodies the substitutive gratifications of desires in men which in the distant past were given free rein but in the course of time were surrendered. These desires have never become lost—merely repressed. In the instance in question, the suppressed desires are basically two: to possess the mother and to slay the father. They form what has been called the Oedipus complex, which is one of the basic tenets of psychoanalytic theory. And they find their symbolic expression in Oedipus-type tales. In short, the Oedipus story symbolically portrays the great psychological reality of the Oedipus complex.

In reviewing the depth psychologists' interpretation of the Oedipus tale type we must begin with the theoretical position of Sigmund Freud.[8] This is so well known that a brief outline will serve. The Oedipus legend is the expression of an actual historical incident. Long, long ago there existed a primal horde, in which an old man retained for himself all the females of the group and drove his sons away from their mothers and sisters. Eventually the sons banded together and killed and ate the old man, after which they [nearly] committed incest with their mothers and sisters. Later, in remorse for their act of violence toward their father, they tried to atone through a ritual act of commemoration centering around his image, or totem. The feeling of guilt that they felt at that time has been perpetuated through the ages and exists today in the form of a complex affecting every person in the earlier stages of his lifetime.[9] This complex involves a normal incestuous striving

---

[8] Sigmund Freud, *Totem and Taboo: Resemblances between the Psychic Life of Savages and Neurotics,* authorized English trans. with introduction by A. A. Brill (New York: Moffat, Yard, 1918); Freud, *The Interpretation of Dreams,* authorized trans. A. A. Brill (London: George Allen & Unwin, 1933).

[9] Freud was well aware of the difference between historical and psychological origins. Although he did seek an actual historical origin for a psychological phenomenon, it was with considerable reluctance that he reached the conclusion that the hypothesized primal horde events really occurred. He noted, for example, that neurotics feel guilt for deeds which they did not actually commit. It is psychic realities, not actual ones, which are the bases of neurotics' sense of guilt. If guilt is not dependent upon actual deeds, then the Oedipus complex need not depend upon any historical event. Freud said that his

toward the mother and an ambivalent feeling toward the father, but if these attitudes become fixated, a neurosis develops. For Freud, it would not be surprising to find Oedipus-type stories anywhere in the world. In fact, he would expect them to be present in the folklore of all peoples, because they are symbolic expressions of the most fundamental of all human relationships and conflicts.

Carl Jung[10] adds some innovations of his own to the Freudian scheme. Thus, he greatly desexualizes the libido. The "love" a child first displays is toward his mother, and results from the fact that she provides protection and nourishment. In time this kind of love may come to be sexual; and if, when manifested by a boy toward his mother, we see fit to call it the "Oedipus complex," then we ought to call it the "Electra complex" when it involves a girl's love for her father. The first feelings of jealousy are concerned with food and only later with eroticism. As for the similarities in forms and themes exhibited by myths in various unrelated parts of the world, they are to be explained as expressions of a collective unconscious. As part of his psyche each individual has a component which is, as it were, the repository of the history of mankind's experiences. Within the collective unconscious are "engrams," or imprints, of the past. They are expressed in the form of mythical motifs and primordial images or archetypes. When the "mother" and "father," as well as such other facts ingrained in racial memory as "male," "female," "generation," "growth," and "decay," appear symbolically in our present thinking, it is because of the basic impression they have made on the human race. If we wish to understand the collective unconscious we must enlist the aid of myths. These are valuable for us because in the unconscious we may find greater wisdom and guidance than in the conscious. Thus, incest merely signifies an adult's desire to return to childhood, when he enjoyed protection and freedom under his parents. This line of reasoning would be used by Jung to explain the incest theme in the Oedipus myth. Parricide would enter because of infantile jealousy. The Sikhalöl story would be a symbolic expression of similar primordial images retained in the unconscious.

For Otto Rank[11] the Oedipus saga is interpreted in terms of his theory of

decision concerning whether or not the primal horde sons did in fact kill their father was a difficult one. Reasoning that primitive man, unlike civilized man, is less inhibited, and that therefore wish or thought could more easily become deed, Freud ended *Totem and Taboo* by assuming that "In the beginning was the deed." Although Freud specifically stated that he did not vouch for the certainty of this decision, his attempted conversion of psychology into history evoked the ire of anthropologists.—ED. NOTE

10 Carl Jung, *The Psychology of the Unconscious,* authorized trans. with introduction by Beatrice M. Hinkle (New York: Dodd, Mead & Co., 1927); Jung, *Contributions to Analytical Psychology,* trans. H. G. and Gary F. Baynes (New York: Harcourt, Brace & World, Inc., 1928).

11 Otto Rank, *The Trauma of Birth* (New York: Harcourt, Brace & World, Inc., 1929); Rank, *Modern Education,* trans. Mabel E. Moxon (New York: Alfred A. Knopf, Inc., 1932).

the birth trauma.[12] The story represents Oedipus' effort to solve the mysterious question of the origin and destiny of man by returning to his mother's womb. His blindness represents intrauterine darkness, and his disappearance into the nether world through a cleft in a rock symbolizes his desire to return into mother earth. This interpretation is based on Rank's broader theory that man finds the womb to be free, protective, secure, and altogether pleasurable, and that he spends the rest of his life trying to undo the trauma of birth, which has ushered him into a world of pain and insecurity. Rank accepts Freud's idea of a primeval horde but gives it a new meaning. Here the father opposed his sons' wishes to return to the mother by penetrating her through the act of coition. But the Oedipus complex is not the narrow constellation proposed by Freud. It varies according to the particular family situation, and involves the whole series of relations between a child and parents. Rank's subsequent formulations are linked with a theory of an elemental struggle for self-perpetuation which arises when the individual begins to free himself from the exaggerated biological dependence on the mother. The strife between father and son is a symbolic portrayal of the struggle of the individual ego to preserve its supposed spiritual immortality against the encroachments of a new ideology, the patriarchate, which refuses to deny personal fatherhood. Under the matriarchate, an idea that Rank borrowed from Bachofen, Morgan, and other evolutionists of the last century, the idea of fatherhood is denied and self-perpetuation is permitted. Laius did not want a son, because in having one he would renounce immortality; therefore, he at first practiced continence with Jocasta, and when that did not succeed he tried to destroy the infant son born to him. Oedipus himself also struggles against the implications of patriarchy. He does not want to lose his immortality by becoming a father. His solution is to commit incest with his mother, for in this way he retains his eternal Self and satisfies society's insistence on fatherhood. But this compromise fails. For Rank, the Sikhalól legend would symbolize the conflict in Ulithian culture between matriarchal principles and patriarchal ones, with the hero attempting to achieve the self-perpetuation that goes with the former principles by committing incest with Lisòr.

Erich Fromm[13] reinterprets the Oedipus story by saying that it is a vehicle for expressing not what Freud called the Oedipus complex, which is based on

---

12 For students of folklore, Rank's earlier 1909 interpretation of Oedipus is much more important. In this classic study, the story of Oedipus is seen as a variation of a plot pattern common to many heroes, a pattern which Rank analyzes in the light of Freudian psychology. One can easily see how close the Ulithi tale is to the pattern by consulting Rank's *The Myth of the Birth of the Hero* (New York, 1956) or even the summary of Rank's pattern given in Clyde Kluckhohn's "Recurrent Themes in Myths and Mythmaking," an essay reprinted in the following section of this volume.—ED. NOTE

13 Erich Fromm, "The Oedipus Complex and the Oedipus Myth," in *The Family: Its Function and Destiny,* ed. Ruth N. Anshen, Science of Culture Series, Vol. 5 (New York: Harper & Row, Publishers, 1949).

incestuous striving, but the conflict between father and son over parental authority. The term "Oedipus complex" is therefore a misnomer because Freud applied it to the wrong constellation. In justification of his interpretation Fromm insists one must read the whole of the Sophocles trilogy, which also includes *Oedipus at Colonus* and *Antigone,* for only in this way can one discover the true intent of the author. The theme that runs throughout is not one of sexual rivalry but one of a child's reaction to parental authority. In the first play, Laius is in conflict with Oedipus; in the second, Oedipus with his two sons, Eteocles and Polynices; and in the third, Creon with his son, Haemon. After all, says Fromm, Oedipus did not fall in love with his mother and woo her; she was an unsought prize who came along with the throne he had acquired by ridding Thebes of the Sphinx. Moreover, the incest problem is not present in the two later dramas by Sophocles. Fromm sees the hostility between father and son as in turn expressing the conflict between the patriarchal system and the matriarchal order which it defeated. In support of this position he cites the contentions of Bachofen, Morgan, and Briffault that matriarchal culture preceded and was succeeded by authoritarian, patriarchal principles. In this way he bends the Oedipus story to fit his general theory of freedom. The Ulithian legend would portray the conflict on the atoll between the freedom inherent in matriarchal principles and the restraints threatened by patriarchal ones. Sikhalòl's act of incest is his drive for freedom.

Certain serious misgivings assail us when we examine the delicate symbolic structures erected by psychoanalysts around the Oedipus story. Freud's *Totem and Taboo,* especially, is a work so repugnant to anthropologists that despite its alleged use of anthropological materials its chief value has been said to have been as an irritant stimulating anthropological research to disprove it.[14] Freud's Lamarckian assertion that Oedipal guilt arises from a single historical incident involving an imaginary primeval horde does violence to biological and ethnological fact and theory. Speculations of this sort were already outmoded in 1912, when Freud's book was published. So were such notions as "racial memory" and "group mind," which are indispensable to acceptance of the primeval horde episodes.

Apologists for this fanciful stage in human existence have reformulated it so as to avoid the implication of the inheritance of an acquired memory. Instead of carrying over the engrams of the past into the present via a collective unconscious they assume that the appearance of the experiences of the primeval horde in myths or rituals is the result of the same type of situation actually recurring historically. Thus, Money-Kyrle[15] says what Freud really had in mind was that "all men inherit an innate, not an acquired, dis-

---

[14] Alfred A. Kroeber, "Totem and Taboo: An Ethnologic Psychoanalysis," *American Anthropologist,* Vol. 22 (1920), 48–55; and Kroeber, "Totem and Taboo in Retrospect," *American Journal of Sociology,* Vol. 45 (1939), 446–51. Kroeber has brilliantly expounded the anthropological objections to this book.

[15] Roger E. Money-Kyrle, *The Meaning of Sacrifice* (London: L. and V. Woolf and the Institute of Psychoanalysis, 1930).

position to incest, which under the conditions of almost every type of family organization will bring them inevitably into conflict with their fathers" (p. 192). Yet he accepts the antiquated views of Darwin and Atkinson that parricide was the usual way in which most primeval hordes ended. On what grounds? The very fact, he says, that we have severe taboos against incest and parricide indicates that these acts were stronger in the past. Also, the behavior of the higher apes in killing their old leader is a clue to early human behavior. Especially, however, must we realize that primeval man must have been much more emotional and jealous, and less restrained in his impulses, than modern man.

Róheim[16] offers an interpretation that would allow us to eat our cake and still have it. Most likely, he says, the primeval horde posited by Freud did really exist as an archaic form of human social organization, but myths of the primal horde type may be based not on the unconscious memory of primeval tragedies but may be actual narratives of events in human times (p. 454). In short, the primeval horde is still with us in the ethnological present, and in substantiation of this, Róheim offers some seeming instances of it in Central Australia. His interpretations leave much to be desired.[17]

Sandor Feldman[18] follows Róheim in accepting both the phylogenetic and the ontogenetic viewpoints, but emphasizes that "it is not necessary to refer to former or different cultures of mankind in order to understand the rituals practiced at the present time and in our present culture because as far as instinctual needs are concerned there is no difference between the human being in primeval and in present times" (p. 173). He uses a Jewish boys' game and two Jewish family rituals to illustrate his contention, which necessitates that one accept an appreciable amount of Freudian symbolism.

Some psychoanalysts have not bothered with modifications such as those described above, and implicitly or explicitly continue to use the primeval horde concept. An interesting variation is given by Gregory Zilboorg,[19] who outdoes Freud by going back a step further to a more ancient, pre-Oedipal time when a highly significant episode occurred. The human male, hitherto submissive to the female, now found the strength to assault her, having acquired greater physical talents through the process of selective breeding

16 Géza Róheim, "The Primal Horde and Incest in Central Australia," *Journal of Criminal Psychopathology,* Vol. 3 (1942), 454–60.

17 In fairness to Géza Róheim, who started out as a Hungarian folklorist and who ended up as perhaps the first psychoanalytic anthropologist, it should be pointed out that in a chapter of his book-length treatment of primitive mythology, a chapter devoted to Oedipus, there is no mention of the primal horde. Interestingly enough, Róheim also criticizes some of the same neo-Freudian interpretations that Lessa does. See *The Gates of the Dream* (New York, 1952), pp. 529–44.—ED. NOTE

18 Sandor S. Feldman, "Notes on the 'Primal Horde,'" in *Psychoanalysis and the Social Sciences,* Vol. 1, ed. Géza Róheim (New York: International Universities Press, 1947).

19 "Masculine and Feminine: Some Biological and Cultural Aspects," *Psychiatry,* Vol. 7 (1944), 257–96.

resulting from women choosing their mates. Says Zilboorg, "I have often felt that the concluding words of *Totem and Taboo*—'In the beginning there was the deed'—were even more fittingly applied to the act of primordial rape than to the murder of the father" (p. 282). This act established the supremacy of males over females, and its consequences have carried through, by means of a phylogenetic component, to the present.

The post-Freudians we have been discussing lack a sound grounding in modern anthropology. Despite their protestations to the contrary they retain a sharply ethnocentric outlook, continuing as Freud had done before them to base their views on Euro-American materials and to pay no more than lip service to ethnology. They usually fail to use either cross-cultural information or the comparative approach so essential to the scientific pursuit of generalizations regarding "human nature." When some of them do venture to use data from the non-Western world they often do so uncritically, as in their use of Frazer's works. In the interests of their general viewpoint they force otherwise sound facts into ready-made molds, interpreting them according to rigid principles derived from a study of greatly circumscribed case histories. These facts are almost invariably removed from their contexts by a process of fractionation.

More often, sad to relate, they do not use real anthropological facts at all—preferring philosophy and speculation instead. Their acceptance of an evolutionary sequence of stages which was discredited more than half a century ago is an example of this, for Rank and Fromm lean pitifully on the writings of Bachofen, Morgan, and Briffault. In the instance of Freud there is a certain excusability in conjuring up his fantastic pseudohistory, for he began to formulate his theories at a time when anthropology was still young. But later writers are willing to incorporate evolutionary theories already rejected throughout most of the scientific world when they began their careers. Since the turn of the century, what professional anthropologist of any stature, outside the Soviet Union,[20] has accepted the postulate of primitive promiscuity, followed by a matriarchate, and then a patriarchate?

Another example of the all too frequent tendency to delve into shaky speculation involves Freudian symbolism. This is a subject too vast to belabor here, and ample critiques on the matter have been published, but we may permit ourselves one inquiry: Is Freud's interpretation of the Oedipus story, first propounded in *The Interpretation of Dreams*, the best one?

A. J. Levin,[21] a lawyer well grounded in psychoanalytic doctrines, thinks not. He has dared to challenge this holy of holies and offer his own interpretation. He points out that Freud made a great to-do over the fact that the *Oedipus Rex* of Sophocles had tremendous appeal for the Greeks, as well as

[20] P. Tolstoy, "Morgan and Soviet Anthropological Thought," *American Anthropologist,* Vol. 54 (1952), 8–17.

[21] A. J. Levin, "The Oedipus Myth in History and Psychiatry: A New Interpretation," *Psychiatry,* Vol. 11 (1948), 283–99.

for contemporary Europeans; but Freud was not aware that the appeal was due to reasons other than those which he imagined. Levin presents a good argument for regarding the Oedipus story as a vehicle for expressing infantile resentment against abandonment and the psychological effects of rejection, rather than incest-longings and father-son conflict. For one thing, he says, Freud skims over the fact that when Oedipus was three days old his ankles were riveted together and he was hung upside down to die of exposure. Oedipus (literally, "Swellfoot") remembers this always, complaining bitterly, "Yes, from my cradle that dread brand I bore," and curses the well-intentioned person who saved his life. Moreover, writes Levin, the Greeks had an underlying fear not of incest but of the cruel impulses imparted to a person through infantile experience and the prevailingly cruel attitude toward children. Aristophanes in his comedy *The Frogs* has one of the characters comment on Oedipus to the effect that he was unhappy not because of the events of his manhood but because of sufferings begun from the very moment of birth. Moreover, Aristophanes treats the matter of parricide and incest with levity rather than with the awesomeness that Freud, on account of his personal fear of such things, injected into the myth. Some of the greatest Greek tragedies, including *Medea* and *Agamemnon,* deal largely with cruelty to children. The Greeks frequently resorted to infanticide, such as by exposure and abandonment, because there existed for them a great problem as to what to do with infants. This concern is reflected in Plato's advocacy of the principle that the state should employ stern measures of eugenics and rearing. Freud's unwillingness to give weight to the traumatic effects of exposure are seen in his *Moses and Monotheism,* even though he pays great notice there to exposure as part of the pattern of hero myths. Moses' life, says Levin, can best be seen in terms of abandonment, for the deprivation of mother love leaves serious mental and emotional consequences. Levin also argues that since the Oedipus legend, as told by Sophocles, was only one of many versions, all of them should be taken into account when one makes an interpretation. One variant has Oedipus put into a casket and floated on water. Another has him married to several wives of Laius. The legend is actually a mixture of fact and fancy dating far back in time. Its very variants show it had many contexts and that these do not always support the Freudian explanation.

Another instance of reinterpretation is provided by Devereux[22] in an article entitled "Why Oedipus Killed Laius." Devereux, an acknowledged Freudian, does not abandon the Oedipus complex but he does feel that the homosexual theme is a strong, if not more important, complement of the complex in Greek drama. Freud and others, he says, have tended to minimize the significance of this because of culturally determined blind spots. According to Devereux's argument, which is based on the interpretation of materials usually under-

---

[22] George Devereux, "Why Oedipus Killed Laius: A Note on the Complementary Oedipus Complex in Greek Drama," *International Journal of Psychoanalysis,* Vol. 34 (1953), 132–41.

played or bowdlerized in the literature, the curse placed by King Pelops upon King Laius arose from the homosexual ravishment of the former's son, Chrysippus, by Laius. But Pelops himself had his own passive homosexual conflicts, having been abducted by Poseidon, who took him as his lover to Olympus. Pelops' father was the evil and cannibalistic King Tantalus, whom he regarded with ambivalence, for he not only had a repressed hatred toward him but also an erotic submission to him, as shown in the devout filial piety he manifested toward Tantalus. Laius was not really plagued by Fate but by the consequences of his character structure. The combat on the road with his son Oedipus was a homosexually motivated encounter—a fight over Chrysippus. Oedipus desired to exchange roles with his father, even though he regarded him as a homosexual aggressor. He turned the tables on him by depriving him of his sword (castration) and of his belt (feminization). His true love-hate object was the now feminized homosexual ogre, Laius. His incestuous cohabitation with his mother, Jocasta, may really have been motivated by a certain degree by his desire to gratify indirectly his own sadomasochistic and homosexual wishes, stimulated by his father's behavior. Some sources bring in his incestuous relation with his mother only as an afterthought.

The reader by this time will undoubtedly have noted that much of what has been imputed to the Sophoclean drama could not apply to Oceanic Oedipus-type stories because the latter omit a good deal contained in the former. This is especially true of the Sphinx, to which some psychoanalysts give much attention. In his essay "Oedipus and the Sphinx" Theodor Reik[23] states that the monster is the totemic representation of the father who is killed, and also of the mother, who, as Rank had already suggested in an earlier work, is violated by her son. The duality of the Sphinx is the result of a device that is called "condensation," or the combining of features, even though often contradictory, in order to form a unity. Róheim[24] makes the Sphinx the subject of a whole book.

One notes with approval the growing efforts of psychoanalysts to amend some of the more glaring errors of the past. Alfred Adler[25] deviated strongly from Freud when he proposed the notion that the Oedipus complex arises in those situations where a child has been so "spoiled" by his mother that he is helpless to move out of the family circle; therefore, he returns to her and finds pleasure in possessing and controlling her. His sexual strivings are, to be sure, centered on her, but they are subordinate to the craving to dominate her. Franz Alexander[26] does not feel that we must regard the Oedipus complex

[23] *Dogma and Compulsion: Psychoanalytic Studies of Religion and Myths,* trans. Bernard Miall (New York: International Universities Press, 1951), p. 327.

[24] Géza Róheim, *The Riddle of the Sphinx* (London: Hogarth, 1934).

[25] Alfred Adler, *Social Interest: A Challenge to Mankind,* trans. John Linton and Richard Vaughan (London: Faber & Faber, Ltd., 1938).

[26] Franz Alexander, *Our Age of Unreason: A Study of Irrational Forces in Social Life* (Philadelphia: J. B. Lippincott Co., 1942), pp. 230–32.

as being necessarily omnipresent; in fact, it may even be missing in societies with settings different from ours. The only truly universal characteristic of the infantile situation is the jealousy aspect. He feels that the young child will be hostile and aggressive toward whomever he looks upon as a competitor who enters into the picture while he is in his long early period of dependency on his parents. Karen Horney,[27] making use of anthropology and sociology, does not concede that the Oedipus complex has the paramount importance usually assigned to it. She substitutes the notion of "basic anxiety." In line with her emphasis on cultural conditions, she says that the Oedipus complex is not rooted in the biological makeup but in certain relationships within the family. Moreover, she says, it is not universal. Harry Stack Sullivan[28] places great emphasis on the role of the parents, especially the mother. The child will turn to a parent of opposite sex because that parent treats it with greater consideration than does the other. Fromm[29] removes the sex aspect from the Oedipus complex and imputes the rivalry between father and son to a struggle over authority. He concedes that the Oedipus complex is not ubiquitous.

These retrenchments, to some extent stimulated a quarter of a century ago by the queries that Malinowski raised out of his Trobriand materials, strengthen our confidence in an ultimately valid interpretation by psychoanalysts of the Oedipal situation; but in demolishing some of the earlier concepts they leave the present author with no strong desire to enroll in the ranks of psychiatrically oriented folklorism. It is obvious that the neo-Freudians are valiantly grappling with serious problems interposed by their recognition of cultural dynamics, and that there are as many schools of thought as there are parts to an elephant's body. But if, as it now seems, the Oedipus complex is neither constant in form nor universal, we should expect that where Oedipus-type stories are similar they would be found only in societies whose designs for living are likewise similar.[30]

---

[27] Karen Horney, *New Ways in Psychoanalysis* (New York: W. W. Norton & Company, Inc.).

[28] Patrick Mullahy, *Oedipus: Myth and Complex* (New York: Hermitage, 1948), p. 315.

[29] *Op. cit.*

[30] Lessa goes on to say that this does not appear to be the case. In Ulithi, for example, though there is an Oedipal tale, the design for living (with particular reference to the way in which the family is defined by members of the culture) is not the same as the Euro-American design. Those readers interested in the question of the universality or quasi-universality of the Oedipus complex should see William N. Stephens, *The Oedipus Complex: Cross-Cultural Evidence* (New York, 1962). Of special interest to folklorists is an appendix (pp. 234–43) on the coding and decoding of the content of folklore.—ED. NOTE

Form in Folklore

One of the characteristics of folklore is its great persistence with respect to form. Content may vary, but form is relatively stable. There may be new riddles or new ballads, but the riddle form and the ballad formula remain the same. However, despite the stability of form and the opportunities for its study, the formal composition of an item of folklore has proved much less challenging to folklorists than the task of searching for that item's origin. Thus, much less effort has been expended on formalistic studies than on theories of origin.

A great advantage in studying form is that one's results can be tested and verified empirically. If a folklorist presents an abstract pattern which he claims underlies a great many hero biographies, or a hypothesis that things occur in groups of three in European folklore and in groups of four in most American Indian folklore, these claims and hypotheses can be critically examined by comparing them with concrete data. Either the pattern does apply to the lives of some heroes or it does not; either three is a pattern number in European folklore or it is not. Although the reasons for the existence of these regularities may be a question of origins, the regularities themselves can be described without regard to etiology. It is for this reason that some of those few studies of form which have been attempted are some of the most successful analyses of folklore ever made.

In a way, one would surmise that the study of form is the logical beginning for the study of folklore. After one has delineated the structure of riddles, the patterns of myth, and formal intricacies of folk dance, one should be in a much better position to define these folklore genres, to hypothesize about their origins, and to investigate their function. Formal criteria might also be used to illuminate the complex interrelationship between folklore and literature: To what extent are the formal features of folklore found in sophisticated literature? Can such features be used effectively to differentiate folk and written literature?

Finally, the formalistic approach to folklore may help to reveal features common to many of its disparate genres. Patterns present in folk music may also be found in other forms of folklore. For example, the pattern of departure and return is found in folk music, exemplified by the melodic or harmonic technique of ending where one began: on the initial note or in the initial tonality. The same pattern is manifested in games (by leaving and returning safely to home base), in folk dance (by leaving and returning to initial position), and in folktale (by the hero's leaving on a quest and returning). Also, some of the patterns in folklore may be found in non-folkloristic materials. Folklore, one must remember, is after all just one part of human culture. If there are formal laws which govern it, there is no reason why these same laws could not regulate other aspects of culture. The point is that folklore, because of its excessively rigid adherence to recurring forms and themes, makes excellent source material for those interested in discovering principles controlling human culture generally.

Epic Laws
of Folk Narrative

Axel Olrik

This essay by the distinguished Danish folklorist is one of the basic studies of folklore. Highly regarded by European folklorists, it is not as well known in the United States. The essay is an ambitious attempt to delineate some of the principal laws governing the composition of folk narrative. Unlike origin studies of the same era, its findings have withstood the criticisms of the passing years and they continue to excite each new generation of folklorists.

In reading Olrik's paper, which was originally presented at an interdisciplinary congress in Berlin in 1908, one needs to be aware of his concept of *Sagenwelt* or world of *Sage*. *Sage,* as defined by Olrik, is virtually an all-inclusive term and is meant to incorporate such forms as folktale, myth, legend, and folksong. This definition is important inasmuch as Olrik feels that the "laws" are not limited to just one genre, such as legend, but rather that they are equally applicable to many genres. To Olrik the world of *Sage* is an independent domain, a realm of reality separate from the real world, subject to its own rules and regulations. These *Sagenwelt* rules are such that they take precedence over the everyday rules of objective reality. It is for this reason, he argues, that folklore must be measured by its own laws, not the laws of everyday life. Folklore does not have to obey any laws but its own.

Olrik's conception of these laws is analogous to what anthropologists term a superorganic conception of culture. By superorganic, anthropologists mean that culture is an autonomous abstract process, *sui generis,* which requires no reference to other orders of phenomena for an explanation of its origin, development, and operation. If the organic level includes man, the superorganic is "above" man, and it is independent of and thus not reducible to purely human terms. The rationale is that just as man himself is considered to be more than the sum of inorganic (chemical) elements of which he is composed, so the super-

This article appeared originally as "Epische Gesetze der Volksdichtung," *Zeitschrift für Deutsches Altertum,* Vol. 51 (1909), 1–12. It is reprinted in translation by permission of the *Zeitschrift für Deutsches Altertum und Deutsche Literatur.* I am indebted to Jeanne P. Steager for making a free translation of the article. The editor, however, assumes the final responsibility for the accuracy of the translation.

organic is asumed to be more than the organic elements which underlie it. Superorganicists in anthropology have abstract patterns or principles, such as evolution, governing human behavior and culture.

Because Olrik's epic laws are conceived to be superorganic, they are presented as actively controlling individual narrators. The folk narrator, according to this view, can only blindly obey the epic laws. The superorganic laws are above any individual's control. This kind of thinking, although it apparently makes folklore somewhat akin to a natural science, takes the folk out of folklore. With this approach, it becomes almost irrelevant that folklore is communicated by human individuals to other human individuals. Note that the superorganic concept of folklore is one reason for the traditional folklorists' antipathy to psychological analysis. If folklore can be explained through recourse to reified superorganic laws, that is, without reference to individual men, then clearly there is no need to consider the psychology of individuals to explain what folklore is and does. This is an important theoretical point inasmuch as Olrik was not the only folklorist to advocate superorganic laws. An example is Walter Anderson's law of self-correction (*das Gesetz der Selbst-Berichtigung*), according to which narratives essentially correct themselves and thereby keep their remarkable stability safe from the possible ravages of errors or inadvertent changes introduced by poor raconteurs with faulty memories. Another example is the concept of automigration, according to which tales can move by themselves without people necessarily moving or migrating. (This concept may be illustrated by the children's game in which one individual in a circle whispers something to his neighbor who passes the item on. The item can "move" without the individual transmitters moving.) The important question is whether these laws are completely superorganic or whether they must ultimately be explained in human terms.

Without a doubt, Olrik's essay on epic laws is one of the strongest arguments in favor of a superorganic, formal approach to folklore. His findings need to be tested in areas other than Europe to see which principles apply elsewhere and which do not. An excellent exercise for a student would be to look for "epic laws" in African or Oceanic folklore.

For a more detailed account of Olrik's epic laws, see his *Nogle Grundsaetninger for Sagnforskning* (Copenhagen, 1921). For further discussion of the concept of the superorganic, see A. L. Kroeber's famous paper, "The Superorganic," *American Anthropologist,* Vol. 19 (1917), 162–213. For a critique of the superorganic, see David Bidney, *Theoretical Anthropology* (New York, 1953), pp. 34–39, 327–33. For the law of self-correction, see Walter Anderson, *Kaiser und Abt,* Folklore Fellows Communications No. 42 (Helsinki, 1923), pp. 397–403. For an English summary of the law, see Emma Emily Kiefer, *Albert Wesselski and Recent Folktale Theories,* Indiana University Publications Folklore Series No. 3 (Bloomington, Ind., 1947), pp. 30–33; or Stith Thompson, *The Folktale* (New York, 1946), p. 437. For "automigration," see Kaarle Krohn, *Skandinavisk Mytologi* (Helsinki, 1922), p. 21.

The most recent advances in folklore research have been based mainly on a variety of highly specialized studies. I certainly hope that the number of such specialized studies will increase, but at the same time, it seems to me that we must also pay attention to more general questions. A method of folklore research, a biology of the *Sage,* is what we need.

I have been concerned with such questions for some time now, and I have found capable collaborators in seminars at the University of Copenhagen. I shall not present all of my endeavors in this field at this time; however, a sample of the biological elements might be appropriate.[1]

Anyone who is familiar with folk narrative has observed when he reads the folklore of a faraway people that he feels a sense of recognition even if this folk and its world of traditional narrative were hitherto completely unknown to him.

Two factors are often cited to explain this recognition: (1) the common intellectual character of primitive man, and (2) the primitive mythology and concept of nature which corresponds to this character. But the matter is not so easily settled. For what touches us the most is not the familiar conception of the entire world of narrative so much as the recognition of certain characteristic details. Why, for example, is the youngest brother the luckiest? Why does the creation of the world or of man occur in exactly three stages among various peoples of the Old and New World?

Let us attempt to put together these pervading similarities so that we get not merely a biology of *Märchen,* or just a taxonomy of myth, but rather a systematic science of a more comprehensive category: the *Sage.* This category would include myths, songs, heroic sagas, and local legends. The common rules for the composition of all these *Sage* forms we can then call the *epic laws of folk narrative.* These laws apply to all European folklore and to some extent even beyond that. Against the background of the overwhelming uniformity of these laws, national characteristics seem to be only dialect peculiarities. Even the traditional categories of folk narrative are all governed by these general principles of *Sage* construction. We call these principles "laws" because they limit the freedom of composition of oral literature in a much different and more rigid way than in our written literature.

I shall mention first the law which is certainly best known to you. The *Sage* does not begin with sudden action and does not end abruptly. This is the *Law of Opening (das Gesetz des Einganges)* and the *Law of Closing (das*

---

[1] This essay, in somewhat shorter form, was given as an address to the Historians' Congress in Berlin, in August 1908. I have expressed the same views although with other illustrative examples in *Danske Studier* (1908), pp. 69–89. As an earlier study, a chapter in Gudmund Schütte's book *Oldsagn om Godtjod* (Copenhagen, 1907), pp. 94–117, must be mentioned. From Schütte, I have borrowed the terms *"Toppgewichts"* and *"Achtergewichts ("forvaegt"* and *"bagvaegt")*; see my review, "Episke Love I Gote-Aettens Oldsagn" in *Danske Studier* (1907), pp. 193–201. Recently Astrid Lund has treated the scope of the epic laws in American Indian materials ("Indiansk sagndigtning og de episke love," *Danske Studier* [1908], pp. 175–88). I am indebted to Astrid Lund for *Märchen* materials for the "Law of Closing."

Gesetz des Abschlusses). The *Sage* begins by moving from calm to excitement, and after the concluding event, in which a principal character frequently has a catastrophe, the *Sage* ends by moving from excitement to calm. For example, the epos cannot end with the last breath of Roland. Before ending, it needs to relax the clenched fist of the sword-hand; it needs the burial of the hero, the revenge, the death through grief of the beloved, and the execution of the traitor. A longer narrative needs many such rest-points; a shorter narrative needs only one. Hundreds of folksongs end, not with the death of the lovers, but with the interweaving of the branches of the two roses which grow up out of their graves.[2] In thousands of legends, one finds the revenge of the dead or the punishment of the villain appended to the principal action. Often the ending takes the form of a locally established continuation of the plot: the ghost in the ruined castle, the description of the tumulus, the perennial return of the victim, or the like. The constant reappearance of this element of terminal calm shows that it is based, not just on a manifestation of the inclination of an individual narrator, but on the formal constraint of an epic law.

A colleague in a Copenhagen seminar who wanted to know whether there were any exceptions to this law read through a multitude of Danish *Märchen* all of which ended with the release from an enchantment. Here, more than anywhere else, one would expect to find an abrupt ending; but the *Märchen* never ends with the statement "she was set free." Sometimes, right after the sudden disenchantment, the tale continues with a new, loosely attached episode. Most frequently following the catastrophe or climax, one finds the release of a minor character or the suggestion of future events. And if there are no other possibilities for continuation, then the storyteller always adds a long jesting closing formula in order to quiet the mood. He hangs a fig leaf on the *Märchen*, as it were, in order to cover its nakedness. Thus, the Law of Closing invariably holds for the various forms of *Sage*.

Yet I should not say that there are no exceptions in the world of folk narrative. In Spanish ballads one may encounter the phenomenon of a sudden beginning or sudden end. For example, the captive sits and awaits his death but—in the last line of the song—the king's daughter, his liberator, opens the door. The frequency of such a phenomenon, however, within this essentially literary domain is sufficient to show that here one has a new type of poetic effect which is lacking in true folk poetry, but which is well known in modern literature.

Another important principle of *Sage* composition is the *Law of Repetition (das Gesetz der Widerholung)*. In literature, there are many means of producing emphasis, means other than repetition. For example, the dimensions and significance of something can be depicted by the degree and detail of the description of that particular object or event. In contrast, folk narra-

---

[2] This is Motif E631.0.1, Twining branches grow from graves of lovers.—ED. NOTE.

tive lacks this full-bodied detail, for the most part, and its spare descriptions are all too brief to serve as an effective means of emphasis. For our traditional oral narrative, there is but one alternative: repetition. A youth goes into the giant's field three days in succession and each day he kills a giant. A hero tries three times to ride up the glass mountain. Three would-be lovers are magically rendered immobile in one night by a maiden.[3] Every time that a striking scene occurs in a narrative, and continuity permits, the scene is repeated. This is necessary not only to build tension, but to fill out the body of the narrative. There is intensifying repetition and simple repetition, but the important point is that without repetition, the *Sage* cannot attain its fullest form.

The repetition is almost always tied to the number three. But the number three is also a law in and of itself. That three appears in *Märchen* and myths and even in simple local legends with incredible frequency, you all know; but perhaps it has not been made sufficiently clear to you though that in hundreds of thousands of folk traditions, three is the highest number with which one deals. Seven and twelve and sometimes other numbers occur of course, but they express only a totally abstract quantity. Three is the maximum number of men and objects which occur in traditional narrative. Nothing distinguishes the great bulk of folk narrative from modern literature and from reality as much as does the number three. Such a ruthlessly rigid structuring of life stands apart from all else. When a folklorist comes upon a three, he thinks, as does the Swiss who catches sight of his Alps again, "Now I am home!"

However, the entire world of folk narrative does not obey the *Law of Three (das Gesetz der Dreizahl)*.[4] In the Indic stories, especially the literary tales, the *Law of Four (das Gesetz der Vierzahl)* often replaces it. This is

---

[3] Motif H331.1.1, Suitor contest: riding up glass mountain, appears in Tale Type 530, The Princess on the Glass Mountain; Motif D2006.1.1, Forgotten fiancée reawakens husband's memory by detaining lovers through magic, appears in Tale Type 313, The Girl as Helper in the Hero's Flight.—Ed. Note.

[4] Olrik was not the first to note the frequent occurrence of threefold repetition. Earlier studies include H. Usener, "Dreiheit," *Rheinisches Museum für Philologie,* Vol. 58 (1903), 1–47, 161–208, 321–62; Raimund Müller, "Die zahl 3 in sage, dichtung und kunst," in *XXX Jahresbericht der K.K. Staats-Oberrealschule in Teschen am Schlusse des Schuljahres 1902–1903* (Teschen, Ger., 1903), pp. 1–23. (It is customary in Europe for scholars to write articles in secondary school graduation programs. Many of these, like the Müller study, are very valuable. Unfortunately, they are often hard to find even in the best libraries.) Some of the scholarship concerning the number three since Olrik's paper includes Alfred Lehmann, *Dreiheit und dreifache Wiederholung im Deutschen Volksmärchen* (Leipzig, 1914); Eugene Tavenner, "Three as a Magic Number in Latin Literature," *Transactions of the American Philological Association,* Vol. 47 (1916), 117–43; Emory B. Lease, "The Number Three, Mysterious, Mystic, Magic," *Classical Philology,* Vol. 14 (1919), 56–73; Fritz Göbel, *Formen und formeln der epischen dreiheit in der Griechischen dichtung* (Stuttgart, 1935); and W. Deonna, "Trois, superlatif absolu," *L'Antiquité Classique,* Vol. 23 (1954), 403–28. This partial list shows one problem folklorists often encounter in the course of their research: Important studies of folklore are published in non-folklore journals, and the problem is finding these scattered studies.—Ed. Note.

connected with the religious conceptions of the Indian people. In India, there are also collections of traditional oral tales in which the number three is completely avoided in an attempt to reflect the authentic fullness of life. Here the investigator can see that the three was once present, but that it has been eliminated by the narrator. The number three has been tenaciously retained though, in the great mass of popular tradition—Greek, Celtic, Germanic—in *Märchen*, myth, ritual, and legend, in all that has the appearance of the primitive. The Law of Three extends like a broad swath cut through the world of folk tradition, through the centuries and millennia of human culture. The Semitic, and even more, the Aryan culture, is subject to this dominant force. The beginnings of its rule are, in spite of all the recent excavations and discoveries, lost in the obscurity of prehistory. We can, however, observe the end of its rule where three gradually succumbs to intellectual demands for greater realism.

In Homer, it has lost its power over the characters and it is limited to such minor details as the number of times an action is performed. Hector, followed by Achilles, runs three times around Troy. It is also found in weakened form in our Danish folksongs. In the heroic songs of the elder Edda,[5] the number three is in a way restricted, but it does play a large role in the mythological songs. The Icelandic family sagas go even one step further, and seem quite modern because of their lack of threes. Only one isolated saga from an outlying region of Iceland (Isfirding's *Hawardssaga*) follows the ancient practice. Everywhere in classical antiquity, and especially in the European Middle Ages, one sees how narrative slowly detaches itself from the number three, with a certain inconstancy according to whether one strives for a realistic representation or a fantastic coloring. But the end result is always the loss of the number three.

In true folk narrative, or more precisely, within the realm of narrative which has traditionally been under the influence of the number three, the Law of Three continues its indomitable rule. About 150 to 200 versions of the *Märchen* about the lucky ring lie before us.[6] Without exception, three magic gifts appear therein. Only in one literary version, the Fortunatus tale, are there two.[7] Thus the Law of Three reigns supreme in the purely oral versions.

I shall now turn to other numbers. Two is the maximum number of characters who appear at one time. Three people appearing at the same time, each with his own individual identity and role to play would be a

---

[5] The "elder Edda" is the Poetic Edda. The "younger Edda," written several centuries later in the thirteenth century by Snorri Sturluson, is usually called the Prose Edda.—ED. NOTE.

[6] This is Tale Type 566, The Three Magic Objects and the Wonderful Fruits (Fortunatus).—ED. NOTE.

[7] See Aarne's valuable *Vergleichende Märchenuntersuchungen* (Helsinki, 1907), p. 131. [The correct reference would appear to be Aarne's *Vergleichende Märchenforschungen*, Mémoires de la Société Finno-Ougrienne, Vol. 25 (Helsinki, 1908), pp. 85–97.—ED. NOTE.]

violation of tradition. The *Law of Two to a Scene (das Gesetz der scenischen Zweiheit)* is a strict one. The description of Siegfried's battle with the dragon can serve as an example. Throughout, only two people appear on the stage at one time: Siegfried and Regin, Siegfried and his mother, Siegfried and Odin, Siegfried and Fafnir, Siegfried and the bird, Siegfried and Grani. The Law of Two to a Scene is so rigid that the bird can speak to Siegfried only after Regin has gone to sleep (and this is entirely superfluous in terms of the epic itself).

For the same reason, the princesses of folktales can attend the battle with the dragon only as mute onlookers. The interaction of three or more characters, which is so popular in literary drama, is not allowed in folk narrative.

The Law of Two to a Scene is correlative to the important *Law of Contrast (das Gesetz des Gegensatzes)*. The *Sage* is always polarized.[8] A strong Thor requires a wise Odin or a cunning Loki next to him; a rich Peter Krämer, a poor Paul Schmied; near a grieving woman sits a joyful or comforting one. This very basic opposition is a major rule of epic composition: young and old, large and small, man and monster, good and evil.

The Law of Contrast works from the protagonist of the *Sage* out to the other individuals, whose characteristics and actions are determined by the requirement that they be antithetical to those of the protagonist. An appropriate example is the Danish King Rolf who is so celebrated in our heroic sagas because of his generosity. He thus requires a stingy opponent. However, in this example, the identity of the opponent changes. Now it is a Skoldung: Rörik; now it is a Swede: Adisl.[9] But even if only one such contrasting person is found, this is sufficient to satisfy the demands of narrative composition.

Some types of plot action correspond exactly to the Law of Contrast. (1) The hero meets his death through the murderous act of a villain (Roland, Rustem, Rolf Kraki, Siegfried);[10] (2) the great king has an insignificant and short-reigning successor (Hjarward after Rolf, Hjarni after Frodi, "Shorthair" after Conchobar).[11]

Further, we might observe that whenever two people appear in the same role, both are depicted as being small and weak. In this type of close associa-

---

[8] Olrik has anticipated Claude Lévi-Strauss's structural analysis of myth insofar as Lévi-Strauss sees myth as a logical model in which polarities are mediated. See Claude Lévi-Strauss, "The Structural Study of Myth," *Journal of American Folklore,* Vol. 68 (1955), 428–44.—Ed. Note.

[9] Most of the individual characters and sagas from Danish and Icelandic tradition used by Olrik as illustrative examples in this essay are discussed in his *The Heroic Legends of Denmark* (New York, 1919) to which the interested student may refer.—Ed. Note.

[10] These heroes appear in the *Chanson de Roland,* the *Shahnamah* of Firdausi, *Hrólfssaga Kraka,* and *Volsunga Saga,* respectively.—Ed. Note.

[11] Hjarward and Rolf appear in *Hrólfssaga Kraka;* the account of Hjarni and Frodi may be found in Saxo Grammaticus, Book VI, article 172 of the *Gesta Danorum;* Conchobar and Shorthair are part of the Cuchulain cycle of Celtic tradition.—Ed. Note.

tion, two people can evade the Law of Contrast and become subjugated instead to the *Law of Twins (das Gesetz der Zwillinge)*. The word "twins" must be taken here in the broad sense. It can mean real twins—a sibling pair—or simply two people who appear together in the same role. The persecuted children of Greek and Roman kings are real twins and we might mention Romulus and Remus as the most famous example.[12] Even more common in northern Europe are the king's two children who are pursued or murdered,[13] as in the *Märchen* of Hansel and Gretel.[14] However the law applies even further. Beings of subordinate rank appear in duplicate: two Dioscuri[15] are messengers of Zeus; two ravens or two Valkyries, messengers of Odin. If, however, the twins are elevated to major roles, then they will be subordinated to the Law of Contrast and, accordingly, will be pitted against one another. This may be illustrated by the myths of the Dioscuri. One is bright and one is gloomy; one immortal and the other mortal. They fight over the same woman and eventually kill each other.[16]

Leaving the subject of numbers, I shall mention briefly another law: The *Importance of Initial and Final Position*. Whenever a series of persons or things occurs, then the principal one will come first. Coming last, though, will be the person for whom the particular narrative arouses sympathy. We may designate these relationships with nautical expressions, "the Weight of the Bow" *(das Toppgewicht)* and "the Weight of the Stern" *(das Achtergewicht)*. The center of gravity of the narrative always lies in the *Achtergewicht*. Now that this theorem has been stated, it appears to be self-evident. You all know how much the last attempt of the younger brother in *Märchen* signifies.[17] *Achtergewicht* combined with the Law of Three is

---

12 Other examples include Amphion and Zethos in Thebes, Pelias and Neleus in Mycenae, Leukastos and Parrhasios in Arcadia (Hahn, *Sagwissenschaftliche Studien,* p. 340: 'Arische Aussetzungs- und Rückkehr-Formel'). [For a discussion of this Hahn reference, see the introduction to Raglan's "The Hero of Tradition," the next article in this volume—ED. NOTE.]

13 Hroar and Helgi (*Hrólfssaga*), Hrêdric and Hrêthmund (*Beowulf*), Erp and Eitil (*Atlamál*), Signy's two children (*Volsunga Saga*), Hadding and Guthorm (Saxo I), Regner and Thorald (Saxo II), Roe and Scatus (Saxo II). In terms of the action, the second of the two brothers is most frequently quite unimportant; he is strictly a silent person. "The two Haddings perform together a valiant deed since they are twins and the youngest" (*Hervarar Saga*). For two as the number of insignificant or indifferent things, see the examples from R. M. Meyer, *Die Altgermanische Poesie*, pp. 74f. In a broader sense, the "twin-structuring" is the preference of folk narrative for a pair of brothers as personages of secondary rank. Gunnar and Hogni, but not Sigurd; the two Saxon warriors and the two sons of Frowin against Uffi; Svipdag and Geigad against Starkad. (One exceptional example is Hamdir and Sörli as either historical survivals or perhaps as secondary characters in relation to Svanhild and Jormunrek.)

14 This is Tale Type 327A, Hansel and Gretel.—ED. NOTE.

15 The Dioscuri are Kastor and Polydeukes in Greek mythology, Castor and Pollux in Roman mythology.—ED. NOTE

16 This event does not occur in all accounts. See H. J. Rose, *A Handbook of Greek Mythology* (London, 1958), pp. 230–31.—ED. NOTE

17 See Motif H1242, Youngest brother alone succeeds on quest, and L10, Victorious youngest son.—ED. NOTE

the principal characteristic of folk narrative—it is an epic law. Note that when we find ourselves in a religious context, then *Toppgewicht* rules; then is Odin greater than his two attendants. However, when these figures appear in folk narratives, then they are governed by *Achtergewicht;* then Odin no longer acts as the principal member of the triad. Instead the principal member is—as the last of the three gods—Loki.[18]

Thus I have discussed the more obvious formulas of folk narrative. Still the question is open as to whether one should attempt to reduce all of the remaining essential structure of the tales to set formulas.

I shall mention only in passing the general principle that each attribute of a person and thing must be expressed in actions—otherwise it is nothing.[19]

Modern literature—I use this term in its broadest sense—loves to entangle the various threads of the plot amongst each other. In contrast, folk narrative holds the individual strand fast; folk narrative is always *single-stranded (einsträngig)*. It does not go back in order to fill in missing details. If such previous background information is necessary, then it will be given in dialogue. In the city, the hero of the tale hears of the man-eating dragon who has caused misery throughout the land. Siegfried hears the story of the Rhinegold from Regin. When one finds such phrases as "now the two stories proceed along together" in the Icelandic sagas, then one no longer has folk narrative; one has sophisticated literature.

With its single thread, folk narrative does not know the perspective of painting; it knows only the progressive series of bas-reliefs. Its composition is like that of sculpture and architecture; hence the strict subordination to number and other requirements of symmetry.

How strictly the *patterning (die Schematisierung)* is followed must be astonishing to a person who is not familiar with folk narrative. Two people and situations of the same sort are not as different as possible, but as similar as possible. Three days in succession the youth goes to an unfamiliar field.

---

[18] This is also the case in the myths of Idunn, of Andvari, and in the Faroese *Lokkatáttur*. In the *Voluspa*, however, the divine function present at the creation of man consists of: Odin, Villi, Vé; Hár, Jafnhár, Thrithi, with the last two in each instance being only associates or reflections of the first. [For a recent study of Loki, see folklorist Anna Birgitta Rooth's *Loki in Scandinavian Mythology* (Lund, 1961).—ED. NOTE]

[19] I shall present only a single example here. If one were to begin "There was once a young motherless girl who was unhappy but beautiful and kind...," it would be entirely too complicated a thought for a *Märchen*. It is much better when these ideas are expressed in action and when these actions are all connected: (1) the stepdaughter is sent out to the heath to gather heather and is given only ash-cakes as provisions; (2) she speaks kindly to the little red-capped man who peeks out from the knoll of heather and she gives him some of her ash-cakes; (3) the little man presents her with gifts; pearls fall from her hair when she combs it and gold pieces from her mouth when she opens it. (E. T. Kristensen, *Jyske Folkeminder*, Vol. 5, No. 15.) Thus, her unhappiness, her kindness, and her beauty are conveyed as three phases of the plot. [Olrik cites this version of Tale Type 480, The Spinning-Women by the Spring, from one of the many collections of E. T. Kristensen, who was one of most active collectors of folklore of all time. For an account of the unbelievable industry of Kristensen, see W. A. Craigie, "Evald Tang Kristensen, A Danish Folklorist," *Folklore,* Vol. 9 (1898), 194–224.—ED. NOTE]

Each day he encounters a giant, carries on the same conversation with each one, and kills each one in the same manner.

This rigid stylizing of life has its own peculiar aesthetic value. Everything superfluous is suppressed and only the essential stands out salient and striking.

The *Sage* invariably rises to peaks in the form of one or more major *tableaux scenes (Hauptsituationen plastischer Art)*. In these scenes, the actors draw near to each other: the hero and his horse; the hero and the monster; Thor pulls the World Serpent up to the edge of the boat; the valiant warriors die so near to their king that even in death they protect him; Siegmund carries his dead son himself.

These sculptured situations are based more on fantasy than on reality: the hero's sword is scorched by the dragon's breath; the maiden, standing on the back of a bull or a snake, surveys the scene; from her own breasts the banished queen squeezes milk into the beaks of a swan and a crane.

One notices how the tableaux scenes frequently convey not a sense of the ephemeral but rather a certain quality of persistence through time: Samson among the columns in the hall of the Philistines; Thor with the World Serpent transfixed on a fishhook; Vidarr confronting the vengeance of the Fenris Wolf;[20] Perseus holding out the head of Medusa. These lingering actions—which also play a large role in sculpture—possess the singular power of being able to etch themselves in one's memory.[21]

The *Sage* has its *logic (Logik)*. The themes which are presented must exert an influence upon the plot, and moreover, an influence in proportion to their extent and weight in the narrative. This logic of the *Sage* is not always commensurable with that of the natural world. The tendency toward animism and even more toward miracle and magic constitutes its fundamental law. It is important to realize that above all else, plausibility is always based upon the force of the internal validity of the plot. Plausibility is very rarely measured in terms of external reality.

Unity of plot (die Einheit der Handlung) is standard for the *Sage*. One sees this best when one compares the true *Sage* with literary works. The presence of loose organization and uncertain action in the plot structure is the surest mark of cultivation. For particular cases, however, there are various degrees of unity: in *Märchen*, songs, and local legends, it is strong; in myths and heroic sagas, it is less strong but still obvious.

It thus appears that the actual *epic unity (epische Einheit)* is such that each narrative element works within it so as to create an event, the possibility

---

[20] Vidarr, son of Odin, killed the World Serpent after it had killed Odin. This episode is found in the description of Ragnarök (the destruction of the world) in the Völuspá of the Poetic Edda. For further discussion, see Axel Olrik, *Ragnarök: die Sagen vom Weltuntergang* (Berlin, 1922).—ED. NOTE

[21] For a discussion of this point based upon some experimental evidence, see Walter Anderson, *Ein Volkskundliches Experiment,* Folklore Fellows Communications No. 141 (Helsinki, 1951), pp. 42–43.—ED. NOTE

of which the listener had seen right from the beginning and which he had never lost sight of. As soon as an unborn child is promised to a monster, then everything hinges on the question of how he can escape the monster's power.[22]

On the other hand, there is also an *ideal epic unity (eine ideale Einheit der Handlung)*: several narrative elements are grouped together in order to best illuminate the relationships of the characters. The king's son is liberated through the cleverness of the monster's daughter, but—and this is the next element—he forgets her and must be won by her once more.[23]

The greatest law of folk tradition is *Concentration on a Leading Character (Konzentration um eine Hauptperson)*. When historical events occur in the *Sage*, concentration is the first consideration.

The fates of leading characters sometimes form a loose agglomeration of adventures as in the case of the tales of "Strong John" or "The Youth Who Wanted to Learn What Fear Is."[24] Only the formal single-strandedness and a certain regard for the character hold the pieces together. In general, however, protagonist and plot belong together. Hamlet with his folly and his father-revenge is—in spite of his verbosity—an example of the total concentration on a leading character. It is only his later adventures which fall outside the province of folk tradition and take on the character of a novel.

It is very interesting to see how folk narrative proceeds when the *Sage* recognizes two heroes. One is always the formal protagonist. The *Sage* begins with his story and from all outward appearances he is the principal character. The king's son, not the monster's daughter, is the formal protagonist of the folktale about the forgotten fiancée. Siegfried, not Brynhild, is the most important person in the *Volsunga Saga*. When a man and woman appear together, the man is the most important character. Nevertheless, the actual interest frequently lies with the woman. It is the forgotten fiancée and not the king's son for whom we have greater sympathy; Brynhild has moved the poets of the Edda songs more profoundly than Siegfried has; Aslaug outshines her husband, the Viking king Ragnar.[25] Folk narrative finds even within its constraints of form the ways to freer and more artistic development.

In summary, we find that folk narrative is formally regulated to a far greater degree than one would think. Its formal rules we may call the epic laws. The principal ones which I have discussed here include the Law of Opening and Closing *(das Gesetz des Einganges und des Abschlusses)*, the Law of Repetition *(das Gesetz der Wiederholung)*, the Law of Three *(das Gesetz der Dreizahl)*, the Law of Two to a Scene *(das Gesetz der scenischen Zweiheit)*, the Law of Contrast *(das Gesetz des Gegensatzes)*, the Law of

---

[22] This is Motif S211, Child sold (promised) to devil (ogre.)—ED. NOTE
[23] This is Tale Type 313, The Girl as Helper in the Hero's Flight.—ED. NOTE
[24] These are Tale Types 650A and 326 respectively.—ED. NOTE
[25] For an English translation of the saga of Ragnar Lodbrok, see Margaret Schlauch, *The Saga of the Volsungs*, 2nd ed. (New York, 1949), pp. 183–256.—ED. NOTE

Twins *(das Gesetz der Zwillinge)*, the Importance of Final Position *(das Achtergewicht)*, the Law of the Single Strand *(die Einsträngigkeit)*, the Law of Patterning *(die Schematisierung)*, the Use of Tableaux Scenes *(die Plastik)*, the Logic of the Sage *(die Logik der Sage)*, the Unity of Plot *(die Einheit der Handlung)* (both actual and ideal unity), and the Concentration on a Leading Character *(die Konzentration um die Hauptperson)* (just as much on the actual character who finally has our sympathies as in certain cases on the character who is the object of formal concentration).

What the limits are of these laws, further empirical research must show. I have not concerned myself with problems such as "Gothic-Germanic" or "Aryan"; as "mythical" or "ritual."

I find myself outside the circle of thought of not a few of my colleagues. They will, for example, view these things as religious history. If I speak of the Law of Twins, then they think "myth of the Dioscuri"; if the Law of Three appears, then they think "ritual triad." But why should I seek the explanation in religion? My Law of Twins is applicable not only to the godlike Dioscuri but also to Odin's Valkyries, who are not the objects of ritual worship. It is a principle common to all narrative tradition that only two people appear together; it applies to Agamemnon's heralds as it does to the maidens of our folksongs. Life itself must be sufficient to create these types.

And so also with the Law of Three. It certainly appears in folk narrative as the number of divine forces in such a manner that all which is great exists in threes. It is unnecessary to trace these back to a religious origin because the organization of nature itself brings it forward: animals, birds, fish; earth, sky, sea; earth, heaven, hell—they are all divided into three. And if nothing constrains it, then three appears as the highest number of persons and things. It is a question whether or not religious as well as epic triads depend upon an ancient folk psychology.[26]

---

[26] By arguing that three is in the nature of nature rather than in the nature of culture, Olrik is unable to see that the folk or native category of trebling and tripartition has infiltrated most of our so-called objective analytic schemes. Nature does not come in threes; we in Western civilization *see* nature in threes. (American Indians, in contrast, see nature in fours.)

Not all peoples divide the continuums of time and space into threes: past, present future; length, width, depth. Nor do they eat three meals a day using three basic implements. Nor do they have three names. Neither do they have three levels of education (primary, secondary, and higher) with three advanced degrees: B.A., M.A., and Ph.D. Not all languages distinguish three persons: first, second, and third; and three degrees of comparison: good, better, best.

The analytic schemes of science as well as art are under the influence of the Law of Three. Is there really an outer, inner, and middle ear? Are there really three developmental stages: larva, pupa, and adult? Are there really three states of matter: solid, liquid, and gas (= land, sea, and air)? Are immunization shots or pill dosages really more effective when given in series of three?

Here are new problems to resolve: to pursue each epic law in its full range over all humanity, and by so doing, to explain the significance of these compositional formulas for the development of man.

However, we do not want to only wander far afield in the search for the solution of the greatest and most perplexing problems. We should also apply the epic laws to the materials nearest at hand. From these stable features, we can determine the characteristics of particular peoples, their special types of composition and cultural themes. Our work on individual traditions can properly begin only when we can measure them along these sharp lines. And this is perhaps the best thing about our theories: they compel us to make empirical observations of things.

The science of folklore is no exception. One finds three types of prose narrative: myth, folktale, and legend. Aarne's tale type system divides folktales into animal tales, ordinary tales (*Märchen*), and jests. The influence of the Law of Three on folklore *scholarship* is evident in several of the essays in this volume. See Bartlett's "Some Experiments on the Reproduction of Folk Stories" for an obvious example.—Ed. Note

The Hero of Tradition

Lord Raglan

Like Olrik's article on epic laws, this essay by Fitzroy Richard Somerset, Fourth Baron Raglan, delineating a pattern of twenty-two elements underlying the life stories of a great number of folk heroes, is considered a classic. The essay was originally given as an address to the English Folklore Society in June 1934. In 1936, it was slightly revised to form the core of a book entitled *The Hero: A Study in Tradition, Myth, and Drama.*

Raglan applied the pattern, derived initially from the biography of Oedipus, to the stories of such heroes as Theseus, Moses, and King Arthur. Then each of these heroes was given a score based upon the number of elements he had in his biography. The striking similarity of the biographies of these heroes is demonstrated by the high scores of more than a dozen examples. From this patterned similarity, Raglan concluded that hero cycles lacked historicity. It could not be, reasoned Raglan, that every one of these heroes had lived identical lives. Even if an individual hero was historical, it was clear to Raglan that his life biography was not, it having been molded to fit the hero life-cycle pattern. According to Raglan, the pattern is not historical, but rather a reflection of a birth, initiation, and death ritual, possibly of a royal personage, who was also considered to be the incarnation of a god.

There were, prior to Raglan's study, many earlier attempts to discover the formulaic pattern of hero cycles. In 1864, Johann Georg von Hahn listed some of the various formulas he had noticed in folk narrative. In a way, this list might be considered a precursor of the tale type system developed by Antti Aarne in 1910. One of the formulas, number four, concerned the exposure of the newborn hero. Later, in *Sagwissenschaftliche Studien,* a theoretical work on folk narrative published in 1876, seven years after his death, von Hahn presents in tabular form a detailed outline of what he termed the Aryan Expulsion and Return Formula (*Arische Aussetzungs- und Rückkehr-Formel*). From the biographies of 14 heroes including Oedipus, von Hahn devised a set of

Reprinted from *Folklore,* Vol. 45 (1934), 212–31, by permission of the author and *Folklore.*

16 incidents which he divided into 4 basic groups: birth (1–3), youth (4–9), return (10–13), and additional events (14–16). The incidents are as follows:

1. The hero is of illegitimate birth.
2. His mother is the princess of the country.
3. His father is a god or a foreigner.
4. There are signs warning of his ascendance.
5. For this reason he is abandoned.
6. He is suckled by animals.
7. He is brought up by a childless shepherd couple.
8. He is a high-spirited youth.
9. He seeks service in a foreign country.
10. He returns victorious and goes back to the foreign land.
11. He slays his original persecutors, accedes to rule the country, and sets his mother free.
12. He founds cities.
13. The manner of his death is extraordinary.
14. He is reviled because of incest and he dies young.
15. He dies by an act of revenge at the hands of an insulted servant.
16. He murders his younger brother.

Five years later, in 1881, Alfred Nutt successfully applied von Hahn's scheme with minor modifications to fourteen examples of Celtic hero narratives, including the cycles of Finn, Cuchulain, and Arthur. Nutt, like von Hahn, presented his findings in a tabular fold-out.

Otto Rank's psychoanalytic study, *The Myth of the Birth of the Hero,* appeared in 1909; however, it contained references only to von Hahn's earlier 1864 work. In 1928, a Russian folklorist, Vladimir Propp, published his *Morphology of the Folktale* in which he proposed an analytic plot scheme for Russian fairy tales. (Fairy tales were defined as Aarne-Thompson Tale Types 300–749.) Propp's scheme has thirty-one elements, which he termed functions, and is perhaps the most complete account of the hero's "life history" as it appears in folktales.

There have also been some studies since Raglan's analysis first appeared. In 1949, Joseph Campbell's *The Hero with a Thousand Faces* divided the hero's adventures into the formula: separation, initiation, and return. Campbell, however, does not analyze any one hero's life in its entirety. His pattern is a composite one which draws single incidents from the lives of many heroes. Campbell refers to Rank's study in one footnote, but he does not mention von Hahn, Propp, or Raglan.

A more recent study of the hero pattern is by Dutch folklorist Jan de Vries. De Vries, after referring to von Hahn and Raglan, but not to Rank, Propp, and Campbell, outlines a hero pattern of ten elements: (1) The hero is begotten; (2) He is born; (3) His youth is threatened; (4) He is brought up; (5) He often acquires invulnerability; (6) He fights with the dragon or other monster; (7) He wins a maiden, usually after overcoming great dangers; (8) He makes an expedition to the underworld; (9) He returns to the land from which he was once banished and conquers his enemies; (10) He dies.

The interested reader may wish to compare Raglan's pattern with some of the other hero studies. For von Hahn's early attempt to analyze form, see his *Griechische und albanesische Märchen,* 2 vols. (Leipzig, 1864). The later expulsion and return fold-out faces page 340 in his *Sagwissenschaftliche Studien* (Jena, Ger., 1876). For Nutt's seldom cited study, see "The Aryan Expulsion-and-Return Formula in the Folk and Hero Tales of the Celts," *The Folklore Record,* Vol. 4 (1881), 1–44. (The illustrative table faces page 42.) Rank's *The Myth of the Birth of the Hero* is available in paperback (New York, 1959). Vladimir Propp's *Morfologija skazki* (Leningrad, 1928) was translated into English in 1958. Propp's *Morphology of the Folktale* was issued simultaneously during that year as Publication Ten of the Indiana University Research Center in Anthropology, Folklore, and Linguistics; as Part III of the *International Journal of American Linguistics,* Vol. 24 (1958); and as Volume 9 of the Bibliographical and Special Series of the American Folklore Society. Joseph Campbell's study is also available in paperback, *The Hero with a Thousand Faces* (New York, 1956), as is a translation of De Vries' 1959 study. For the De Vries pattern, see *Heroic Song and Heroic Legend* (London, 1963), pp. 210–26. Since Raglan's book *The Hero* is also in paperback (New York, 1956), the student of folklore can acquire an extensive yet inexpensive collection of hero studies for his personal library. For a valuable critique of the Raglan book, see William Bascom's "The Myth-Ritual Theory," *Journal of American Folklore,* Vol. 70 (1957), 103–14. For a convenient survey of hero pattern studies in which the schemes of von Hahn, Rank, Raglan, Campbell, and Propp are outlined and compared, see Archer Taylor, "The Biographical Pattern in Traditional Narrative," *Journal of the Folklore Institute,* Vol. 1 (1964), 114–29.

Some years ago I had occasion to study the story of Oedipus, and to try to analyze it. I was struck by the fact that a number of the incidents of the story were remarkably similar to incidents in the stories of Theseus and Romulus. I then studied the stories of a number of other Greek traditional heroes and found that when these stories were divided into separate incidents, there were certain types of incidents which ran through all, or most, of the stories.

Whether these parallels have any significance, or whether they are merely accidental coincidences or the kind of things that might happen to any hero, is a question to which we shall come later. My first task is to show that these parallels exist, and for that purpose it is necessary to tabulate and number them. What I have done is to take a dozen heroes whose stories are narrated in sufficient detail to tabulate the incidents in their careers, and to take as typical those incidents which occur in the majority of the stories. Some of these incidents are miraculous, while others might seem insignificant, but everything that seemed to me to be part of the pattern, for I have been convinced that there is a pattern, has been included. Having arrived at this pattern, I then tried it on heroes from outside the classical world, and I hope that the results will seem as striking to you as they have done to me. The pattern is as follows:

Story of the Hero of Tradition

1. His mother is a royal virgin.
2. His father is a king, and
3. Often a near relative of his mother, but
4. The circumstances of his conception are unusual, and
5. He is also reputed to be the son of a god. .
6. At birth an attempt is made, often by his father, to kill him, but
7. He is spirited away, and
8. Reared by foster parents in a far country.
9. We are told nothing of his childhood, but
10. On reaching manhood he returns or goes to his future kingdom.
11. After a victory over the king and/or a giant, dragon, or wild beast,
12. He marries a princess, often the daughter of his predecessor, and
13. Becomes king.
14. For a time he reigns uneventfully, and
15. Prescribes laws, but
16. Later he loses favor with the gods and/or his subjects, and
17. Is driven from the throne and city.
18. He meets with a mysterious death,
19. Often at the top of a hill.
20. His children, if any, do not succeed him.
21. His body is not buried, but nevertheless
22. He has one or more holy sepulchers.

Oedipus

His mother Jocasta is (1) a princess, and his father is (2) King Laius, who has sworn to have no connection with her but (4) does so when drunk, probably (5) in the character of Dionysus. Laius (6) tries to kill him, but (7) he is spirited away, and (8) reared by the king of Corinth. (9) We hear nothing of his childhood, but (10) on reaching manhood he returns to Thebes, gaining (11) victories over his father and the Sphinx. He (12) marries Jocasta and (13) becomes king. (14) For some years he reigns uneventfully, but (16) later comes to be regarded as the cause of a plague, and (17) is deposed and driven into exile. He meets with (18) a mysterious death at (19) a place near Athens called the Steep Pavement. (20) He is succeeded by Creon, by whose means he was deposed, and (21) though the place of his burial is uncertain, he has (22) several holy sepulchers.

He scores twenty points out of twenty-two.

Theseus

His mother, Aethra, is (1) a royal virgin, and his father is (2) King Aegeus, who is induced (4) to have intercourse with her by a trick. He is also (5) reputed to be the son of Poseidon. At birth he is (6) hidden from the Pallantidae, who wish to kill him and (8) reared by his maternal grand-father. We hear (9) nothing of his childhood, but (10) on reaching manhood he proceeds to Athens, (11) killing monsters on the way. He marries (12) two heiress princesses in succession, but (13) succeeds his father, whose death (11) he causes. For a time (14) he reigns peacefully, and (15) pre-scribes laws, but (16) later becomes unpopular, is (17) driven from Athens, and (18) thrown or falls from (19) a high cliff by order of (20) Menestheus, his successor, who is no relation. His burial place is unknown (21), but bones alleged to be his are (22) laid in a holy sepulcher at Athens.

He scores twenty.

Romulus

His mother, Rhea, is (1) a royal virgin, and his father is (2) King Amulius, who is (3) her uncle and (4) visits her in armor. He is also (5) reputed to be the son of Mars. At birth (6) his father tries to kill him, but (7) he is wafted away, and (8) he is brought up by foster parents at a distance. On reaching manhood he (10) returns to his birthplace, and having (11) killed his father and gained a magical victory over his brother, (12) founds Rome and becomes king. His marriage is uncertain, and he is said to have performed some feats after his accession, but he (15) prescribes laws and (16) later becomes unpopular. Leaving the city (17) after his deposition had been decided upon, he was (18) carried to the sky in a chariot of fire. His successor was a stranger (20). His body not having been found (21), he was wor-shipped in a temple.

We can give him seventeen points.

Heracles

His mother, Alcmene, is (1) a royal virgin. Her husband is (2) King Amphitryon, who is (3) her first cousin, but Heracles is reputed to be (5) the son of Zeus, who (4) visited her in the guise of Amphitryon. At his birth (6) Hera tries to kill him. On reaching manhood he (11) performs feats and wins victories, after which he proceeds (10) to Calydon, where he marries (12) the king's daughter and (13) becomes ruler. (14) He remains there quietly for some years, after which an accidental manslaughter compels him (17) to flee from the country. He disappears from a funeral pyre (18), on the top of Mt. Oeta (19). His sons do not succeed him (20). His body is not found (21), and he is worshipped in temples.

He scores seventeen points.

Perseus

His mother, Danae, is (1) a royal virgin, and his father is (5) Zeus, who visits her in a shower of gold. His grandfather (6) tries to kill him at birth, but (7) he is wafted away and (8) reared by the King of Seriphos. We are told (9) nothing of his childhood, but on reaching manhood he overcomes monsters and returns to his birthplace (10), where he kills his father (11) or uncle, marries a princess (12), and (13) becomes king in his place. (14) We hear nothing of his reign, and his end is variously related (18), though in one version he is killed by his successor. His children do not succeed him (20). His burial place is unknown (21), but (22) he is worshipped at shrines.

He scores sixteen points.

Jason

His mother, name uncertain, is (1) a princess, and his father is (2) King Aeson. His uncle Pelias (6) tries to kill him at birth, but (7) he is spirited away, and (8) brought up elsewhere by Chiron. We hear nothing (9) of his childhood, but on reaching manhood he makes a journey in which he (11) wins the Golden Fleece, marries (12) a princess, kills (11) his uncle, and (13) becomes king. He is (17) driven from the throne and city. His death is (18) obscure, and his children (20) do not succeed him. His burial place (21) is unknown, but he has several shrines (22).

He scores fourteen points.

Bellerophon

His mother, Eurymede, is (1) a princess, and his father is (2) King Glaucus, but he is also (5) reputed to be the son of Poseidon. We hear (9) nothing of his childhood, but on reaching manhood he (10) travels to his future kingdom, (11) overcomes a monster, (12) marries the king's daughter, and (13) becomes king. (14) We hear nothing of his reign, but later he (16) becomes hated by the gods, and (17) goes into exile. His fate is (18) obscure, though it includes (19) an attempted ascent to the sky. His children (20) do not succeed him; his burial place (21) is unknown, but (22) he was worshipped at Corinth.

He scores sixteen points.

Pelops

His mother, Dione, is (1) a goddess, and his father is King Tantalus (2), but he is also reputed to be the son of (5) Poseidon. His father (6) kills and cooks him, but the gods restore him to life. We hear nothing (9) of his childhood, but (10) on reaching manhood he journeys to his future kingdom, (11) defeats and kills the king, (12) marries his daughter, and (13) becomes king. We hear (14) very little of his actions when king, except that (15) he regulates the Olympic Games. We are not told (18) about his death, but (20) his children do not succeed him, and (22) he has a holy sepulcher at Olympia.

He scores fourteen points.

Asclepius

His mother, Coronis, is (1) a royal virgin, and his father is (5) Apollo, who (6) nearly kills him at birth. He is (7) spirited away and (8) reared by Chiron at a distance. On reaching manhood (11) he overcomes death, becomes a man of power (13), and (15) prescribes the laws of medicine, but (16) incurs the enmity of Zeus, who (18) destroys him with a flash of lightning. His burial place is unknown (21), but he has a number of alleged tombs (22).

He scores at least twelve points.

Dionysus

His mother, Semele, is (1) a royal virgin, and his father is (5) Zeus, who (3) was Semele's uncle by marriage, and who visits her (4) in a thunderstorm. Hera (6) tries to kill him at birth, but he is (7) miraculously saved and (8) brought up in a remote spot. We hear (9) nothing of his childhood, but on reaching manhood he (10) travels into Asia, (11) gains victories, and becomes a ruler (13). For a time (14) he rules prosperously and prescribes (15) laws of agriculture, etc., but later (17) is carried into exile. He (18) goes down to the dead, but later (19) ascends Olympus. He seems (20) to have no children. He had no burial place (21) but numerous shrines and temples (22).

We can give him nineteen points.

Apollo

His mother, Leto, is (1) a royal virgin, and his father is (5) Zeus, who is (3) her first cousin. At birth he is (6) in danger from Hera, but his mother (7) escapes with him, and (8) he is reared at Delos. We hear nothing (9) of his childhood, but on reaching manhood he (10) goes to Delphi, where he kills the Python (11), becomes king (13), and prescribes (15) the laws of music, etc.

We hear no more, but he has scored eleven points.

Zeus

He is the son of Rhea and Cronus, who are goddess and god (1 and 5) and also brother and sister (3). At birth (6) his father tries to kill him, but (7) he is spirited away and (8) reared in Crete. We hear nothing (9) of his childhood, but on reaching manhood he sets forth (10) for Olympus, (11) defeats the Titans, (12) marries his sister, and (13) becomes king in succession to his father. He reigns supreme (14) and prescribes laws (15). Nevertheless he has a holy sepulcher in Crete (22), and hilltops are particularly sacred to him (19).

He scores fifteen points.

Joseph

His mother, Rachel, is (1) the daughter of a patriarch, and his father, Jacob, is (2) a patriarch and (3) her first cousin. His mother conceives him (4) by eating mandrakes. In his childhood his brothers (6) attempt to kill him, but he is saved by a stratagem (7) and reared (8) in Egypt. On reaching manhood he is the victor in a contest in dream-interpretation and weather forecasting (11), is married to a lady of high rank (12), and becomes (13) ruler of Egypt. He reigns prosperously (14) and prescribes laws (15), but we are told nothing of the latter part of his life.

He has scored twelve points.

Moses

His parents (1 and 2) were of the principal family of the Levites and (3) near relatives. He was also (5) reputed to be the son of Pharaoh's daughter. Pharaoh (6) attempts to kill him at birth, but (7) he is wafted away and (8) reared secretly. We are told (9) nothing of his childhood, but on reaching manhood he kills a man (11) and goes to Midian (10), where (12) he marries the ruler's daughter. Returning to Egypt, he gains (11) a series of magical victories over Pharaoh, after which he becomes a ruler (13). For a time his rule (14) is successful and he prescribes laws (15), but later he loses (16) the favor of Jehovah, is deposed (17) from his leadership, and (18) disappears mysteriously from (19) the top of a mountain. His children (20) do not succeed him. He has no burial place (21), but nevertheless has a holy sepulcher (22).

He scores twenty-one points.

Elijah

After (11) a victory in a rainmaking contest, he becomes a sort of dictator (13). After a period of success (14) there is a plot (16) against him. He flees to Beersheba (17) and later (18) disappears mysteriously. His successor, Elisha, (20) is no relation. Though not buried (21), he has (22) a holy sepulcher.

We do not know the circumstances of his birth, but we can give him nine points.

Sigurd or Siegfried

His mother, Sieglinde, is (1) a princess, and his father (2) King Siegmund, who is her brother (3), and whom she visits (4) in the guise of another woman. On reaching manhood he (11) kills a dragon, (12) marries a princess, and (13) becomes a ruler. For a time (14) he prospers, but later (16) there is a plot against him and he is killed.

He scores nine only, but I believe the whole story is there and has been cut up.

Arthur

His mother, Igraine, is (1) a princess, and her husband is (2) the Duke of Cornwall. He is, however, reputed to be (5) the son of Uther Pendragon, who (4) visited Igraine in the Duke's likeness. At birth he is apparently in no danger, but nevertheless is (7) spirited away and (8) reared in a distant part of the country. We hear (9) nothing of his childhood, but (10) on reaching manhood he travels to London, wins (11) a magical victory, and is (13) chosen king. After other victories he marries Guinevere (12), the heiress of the Round Table. After this he reigns (14) uneventfully but later (17) goes abroad and is (16) dethroned in his absence. (18) He meets with a mysterious death. His children (20) do not succeed him.

He scores sixteen points.

Nyikang

Nyikang is the traditional hero of the Shilluk of the White Nile, and his story conforms in some respects to the type. He is the son of (2) a king and (1) his mother Nyikaia was apparently a crocodile princess.

We hear nothing (9) of his childhood, but on reaching manhood his brother defeats him and threatens his life, whereupon he goes to (10) another country and (12) marries a king's daughter. After (11) a number of victories, magical and actual, he becomes king. For a time he reigns prosperously (14) and (15) prescribes laws, but at last the people began to complain against him (16). Distressed at this (18) he disappears mysteriously. His body was not buried (21), but nevertheless he has (22) a holy sepulcher.

He scores twelve points.[1]

The fact that the life of a hero of tradition can be divided up into a large number of incidents—I have taken twenty-two, but one could easily make it more—has suggested to me that the story of the hero of tradition is the story, not of real incidents in the life of a real man, but of ritual incidents in the career of a ritual personage. It does not necessarily follow from this that none of the heroes whom I have cited had any real existence, but it does, I think, follow that if they really did exist their activities were largely of a ritual character, or else that their stories were altered to make them conform to type.

I shall have something more to say about that later; what I propose to do now is to go through these incidents—what I regard as these typical

---

[1] In the expanded form of this study which appears in his book, *The Hero,* Raglan revised the scores somewhat, and Nyikang has 14 instead of 12 points. With the exception of Moses who dropped from 21 to 20, the other revised scores are all higher: Oedipus, 22 (20); Romulus, 18 (17); Perseus, 18 (16); Jason, 15 (14); Pelops, 14 (13); Siegfried, 11 (9); and Arthur, 19 (16). In addition the lives of three more figures are tabulated: Watu Gunung, a Javanese hero, scores 18; the Celtic hero, Llew Llawgyffes, 17; and Robin Hood, 13.—ED. NOTE

incidents—in the life of the hero of tradition and make some suggestions as to their significance.

The first point to be noted is that the incidents fall definitely into three groups—those connected with the hero's birth, those connected with his accession to the throne, and those connected with his death. They thus correspond, to the three principal *rites de passage*—that is to say, the rites at birth, at initiation, and at death. I shall have more to say on this when we reach point 9; now I will start at the beginning.

The first fact we note is that except in the case of Moses, for whom there were no actual royalties available, the hero is always the son of royal parents; that in nearly every case he is the first child of his mother, and except where his father is a god, of his father; and that with very few exceptions his father never marries twice. There is, of course, nothing very wonderful in all this—many kings have been the eldest child of monogamous parents—but I have laid stress on it because it seems definitely to be part of the pattern. There is a type of folk tale in which the hero, though he wins a princess and a throne, is of humble birth, but I suspect this of being a derived form, in which merely the central group of incidents is narrated, and in which the hero's birth therefore becomes unimportant.

The fact that in many cases the hero's parents are near relatives brings to mind the widespread custom by which kings marry their sisters, and with which I have dealt elsewhere.[2]

The circumstances in which our hero is begotten are very puzzling. When, as in the case of Heracles, a god takes the form of the hero's father, we are reminded that the Pharaoh, on particular occasions, approached his queen in the guise of a god. In our stories, however, the disguises assumed by the god are extremely varied. He may appear as a thunderstorm, a swan, or a shower of gold. We may conclude that the attribution of divine descent to a hero has nothing to do with his heroism, but is associated with the ritual union of a princess to her own husband, disguised as a god. It is not at all clear how a man disguised himself as a shower of gold; one can guess at the explanation, i.e., that in a darkened room the sunlight was allowed to fall on him alone, but this is merely a guess.

We now come to the attempt on the hero's life at birth, which happens in almost every case, and is quite clearly part of the pattern. We are all familiar with such rites as the Phoenician one, by which the eldest son was burned as a sacrifice to Moloch. In our stories, it would seem, a pretense is made of sacrificing the child, and in some cases an animal is sacrificed instead. It is often the father who tries to kill the infant hero, and this fact brings the stories into line with that of Abraham and Isaac. The attempt on the life of Moses, like that on the other heroes, was made at birth, but the story of Abraham and Isaac suggests that at one period the Hebrews performed this rite at puberty. We may note that while a ram was sacrificed in place of

[2] See Lord Raglan, *Jocasta's Crime* (London, 1933).—ED. NOTE

Isaac, Jacob appeared before his father wearing the skin of a kid, and Joseph wore a special garment which was soaked in goat's blood. We may perhaps suppose that a pretense was made of killing the child, which was wrapped in the skin of a sacrificed goat and soaked in its blood. Such a rite accounts for some of our stories, such as that of Pelops, and also for the widespread story of the Faithful Hound.[3] In the case of Romulus, Moses, and Perseus, however, as in the Japanese myth, the infant hero is set afloat. We must suppose that the pretense sacrifice took various forms, but that it was normally the father who performed the rite.

Having suffered a pretense death, our heroes are all removed to a distance and brought up either by another king, or in the cases of Jason and Asclepius, by Chiron. The latter is easy to understand, if we may suppose that Chiron was a title given to a prince's official tutor, but in most cases the foster father is the king of another country or city. This suggests several possibilities. The first is that it was actually the practice for kings to send their sons to be brought up by other kings, as we read of in the story of Hakon Adalstein's fostri. The second, which I have put forward elsewhere,[4] but which I am by no means confident about, is that princes succeeded their fathers-in-law but became their sons by formal adoption. This might necessitate a pretense that they had been removed at birth. The third is the opposite of the second. It is that in theory princes could not succeed their fathers, but in practice did so, but were reared at a distance from the capital and represented to be foreigners. The question requires much more investigation than I have been able to give it.

We next come to point number 9, that we are told nothing of the hero's childhood. This may seen unimportant, since there are, of course, many great men of whose childhood we know nothing. In such cases, however, we equally know nothing of the circumstances of their birth. We may know the place and date, but that is all. With our heroes it is quite different. Their birth is the central feature in a series of highly dramatic incidents, incidents which are related in considerable detail, and such incidents as seldom, if ever, occur in the lives of real people. The most surprising things happen to our hero at birth; the most surprising things happen to him as soon as he reaches manhood, but in the meanwhile nothing happens to him at all. If, as I suppose, our hero is a figure, not of history, but of ritual, this is just what one would expect, since as a general rule children take no part in ritual between the rites at their birth and those at puberty or initiation. The story of the hero of tradition, if I understand it aright, is the story of his ritual progress, and it is therefore appropriate that those parts of his career in which he makes no ritual progress should be left blank. I would compare the blank which

---

[3] This is Tale Type 178, The Faithful Animal Rashly Killed. In the most common form of the tale, Type 178A, Llewellyn and His Dog (The Brahman and the Mongoose), the dog has saved his master's child from a serpent. The father, seeing the animal's bloody mouth, falsely concludes that it has eaten the child and he kills the brave animal.— ED. NOTE

[4] Raglan, *op. cit.*, p. 195.

occurs during his childhood with the blank which usually occurs after his installation as king is complete.

The fact that on reaching manhood the hero sets out forthwith on a journey from the land of his upbringing to the land where he will reign is of course involved in the problem which I have discussed under point 8. It is, however, a remarkable fact that the hero's victories almost always take place either on the journey to which I have alluded or else immediately on arrival at his destination. He makes a definite progress from a foreign country to the throne, and all his feats and victories are connected with that progress.

This brings us to the hero's victories, and I wish to emphasize the point which I have just mentioned, namely, that the victories of the hero of tradition, unlike those of the hero-king of history, always take place before his accession to the throne. Another remarkable fact is that the hero of tradition never wins a battle. It is very rarely that he is represented as having any army at all, and when he has one he never seems to train it or direct it in any way. In history the king as warrior means the king as commander, and this applies to savages as well as to the civilized. When we think of the great victors of history we think of serried ranks, of the Argyraspides, of the Tenth Legion, and so on.[5] But the hero of tradition is never a commander. All his victories, when they are actual fights and not merely magical contests, are single combats against other kings or against giants, dragons, or especially noted wild animals. He never fights with ordinary men, or even with ordinary animals. And the king with whom he fights is the king whom he will succeed; in the case of Oedipus and Romulus his own father, and in other cases his future father-in-law. It is also possible that the giant or monster with whom the hero fights is merely the reigning king in disguise, or in other words that the reigning king had to wear a particular costume or mask in which to defend his title and his life. I will touch on this later, but will first pass on to the magical contest, which seems sometimes to be more important than the actual fight. Oedipus wins his throne by guessing a riddle; Theseus by escaping from a maze. The magical victories of the three Jewish heroes are all connected with rain-making. Joseph successfully prognosticates the weather; Moses is successful in a series of magical contests in which rain-making is included, and Elijah defeats the prophets of Baal in a rain-making contest. Power over the elements is the most unvarying characteristic of the divine king, and it would seem that in many cases the candidate for the throne had to pass in a rain-making test.

Our hero, then, has to qualify for the throne in two ways. He must pass an examination in such subjects as rain-making and riddle-guessing, and he must win a victory over the reigning king. Whether this was a real fight or

---

[5] These allusions refer to a military leader's victory over a large group of men. For example, when the soldiers of the Tenth Legion at Rome demanded to be discharged and paid, Julius Caesar met the legion himself and disbanded it. He addressed them as citizens instead of as soldiers, which so shamed them that they immediately renounced their demands and repledged themselves to follow him. See Section 70 under Julius Caesar in Suetonius' *Lives of the Twelve Caesars.*—ED. NOTE

a mock contest in which the conclusion was foregone we cannot be certain. There have undoubtedly been many cases in which the king was put to death at the end of a fixed term, or when his powers began to wane. There may have been cases in which there was a fair fight with equal weapons between the king and his challenger, but the evidence for them is rather uncertain. What several of the stories suggest is that the old king was ritually killed, and that his successor had to kill an animal—wolf, boar, or snake, into which his spirit was supposed to have entered.

After passing his tests and winning his victories the hero marries the daughter, or widow, of his predecessor and becomes king. It has often been assumed from this that the throne always went in the female line, and that the reigning queen, or heiress princess, as the case might be, could confer it upon her husband simply by marrying him; in other words that any man who managed to marry the queen became king automatically, whatever his antecedents, and that the only way in which any man could lawfully become king was by marrying the queen. Such an assumption is going a great deal beyond the evidence of the stories, which suggest that the new king established his claim to the throne by his pedigree, his upbringing, and his victories. There were, it would seem, recognized qualifications for the kingship, just as there were recognized qualifications for the queenship. We do not know for certain that the new queen was really the old king's daughter, any more than we know for certain that the new king was really the old king's son. There may have been a ceremony of adoption in both cases. Anyhow the fact that our hero marries a princess and at the same time ascends the throne is far from proving that he ascends the throne in virtue of his marriage. It may merely indicate what we know from other sources to be a fact, namely, that a *hieros gamos*[6] normally formed an essential and highly important feature of the coronation or installation ceremony. I know of no case, in any age or in any country, in which a man has become king simply by marrying the queen; he must, so far as I can learn, always first have qualified for the throne, either by birth or by performing some feat or passing some test. Our heroes seem all to have qualified in all these ways. Even today in Europe marriage never confers the right to a throne. Princes or princesses who marry unqualified persons, who contract, that is to say, what are called morganatic marriages, not merely fail to raise their partners to the throne but lose their own right to it. It is difficult to believe that the rules were less strict in ages in which the ritual functions of the king and queen were far more important than they are today. Our hero, then, as part of his installation ritual, marries the daughter, or widow, of his predecessor. And what does he do then? It might be supposed that, having shown himself so brave and enterprising before coming to the throne, he would forthwith embark upon a career of conquest, found an empire and a dynasty, build temples and palaces, possess a large

---

6 This Greek term means a holy or sacred marriage in which usually one or both human actors represent gods. Often the marriage is consummated in a field so that by means of the principle of imitative magic (like produces like), the fecundity inherent in the act of ritual coitus will ensure agricultural fertility.—ED. NOTE

harem, and behave generally as the conquerors of history have behaved, or attempted to behave. The hero of tradition, however, in this as in all other respects, is totally unlike the hero of history.

He never goes to war, never extends the boundaries of his kingdom, never builds anything. In fact he does nothing at all. The only memorial of his reign, apart from the traditional story of the events which begin and end it, is the traditional code of laws which is often attributed to him. As a fact, however, a code of laws is always the product of hundreds or thousands of years of gradual development, and is never in any sense the work of one man. One man, a Justinian or a Napoleon, may cause laws to be codified, or alter their incidence, but it has never been suggested that all, or even any, of the laws in such codes were devised by the monarchs in question. It is well known, in fact, that they were not. On the other hand it has been clearly shown by Sir James Frazer that the Ten Commandments, in their familiar form, could have had nothing to do with Moses, since the original Ten Commandments, whoever first wrote them down, were entirely different.[7] It seems clear, then, that the attribution of laws to a hero of tradition is merely a way of saying that they are very old and sacred. We next come to the important fact that the hero of tradition, unlike the hero of the fairy tale and many heroes of history, ends his career by being deposed, driven from his kingdom, and mysteriously put to death. This happens to the majority of our heroes, and when it does not their end is usually left uncertain. Even in the case of Joseph we are told of nothing that happened between his father's death and his own. We may conclude that deposition and mysterious death is the normal fate of a hero of tradition. There is one very puzzling feature, however, which is that the hero is never actually defeated in a fight. As he has gained the throne by winning a fight, one might expect that he would lose it by losing a fight, but this he never does.

Oedipus kills his father and marries his mother; one might expect that one of his sons, or some other prince, would kill him and marry Jocasta, or if she were too old, Antigone, and become king. Creon, however, who succeeds him, does so by turning the oracle against him, and we find in several other cases that the hero falls out with a god and of course gets the worst of it. Perhaps the explanation is that when he began to grow old, or his tenure of the kingship, which Sir James Frazer puts at eight years in prehistoric Greece, had expired, there was a magical contest in which he was foredoomed to defeat. It is to be noted that the hero's fall from favor is sudden and not gradual; at one moment he is apparently at the height of his power and popularity, and at the next moment both gods and men are against him.

The next point to note is that the heroes I have cited never meet their

---

[7] Sir James George Frazer, celebrated compiler of the twelve-volume classic inventory of magic, custom, and superstition, *The Golden Bough,* also wrote many other works on folklore. One of the most interesting is *Folklore in the Old Testament,* 3 vols. (London, 1918), in which he cites numerous parallels for the Biblical accounts of creation, the flood, and other events. A shorter account of Frazer's discussion of Moses and the several versions of the Decalogue may be found in the abridged one-volume edition (New York, 1923), pp. 360–63.—Ed. Note

fate inside their cities. In many cases they are actually deposed and driven out; in others they have left it on some sacred mission. Then there is the hilltop, which appears in the stories of Oedipus, Theseus, Heracles, Bellerophon, Dionysus, and Moses. Taken in conjunction with the chariot of fire in which Romulus and Elijah disappear, and the lightning flash which kills Asclepius, we may conclude that in the most usual form of the rite the divine king was burned, either alive or dead, on a pyre erected on top of a hill, and that he was believed to ascend to the sky, in some form or other, in the smoke and flame. In that case it is clear that the person or animal defeated and killed by his successor could not have been himself, but must have been an assumed reincarnation.

The fact that the hero is very seldom succeeded by his son might be explained by supposing that the descent went in the female line. In that case he would be succeeded by his daughter, but he is not. If the king reigned for eight or nine years only, and married at his coronation, it would obviously be impossible for his children to succeed him, since they would be too young; but they might succeed his successor, and this is what seems sometimes to have happened. The story of Creon is not easy to follow, but he seems to have preceded and succeeded Oedipus, and also to have succeeded his sons. Perseus is said to have killed and succeeded Proetus, and to have been killed and succeeded by his son. Aegisthus kills and succeeds Agamemnon, and eight years later Orestes kills and succeeds Aegisthus. There are similar incidents in the stories of Theseus and Jason. There were two ruling families at Sparta, each of which found one of the two kings, and it seems possible that in prehistoric times each city had two ruling families which produced a king alternately.

The last point in the hero's career is that although he is usually supposed to have vanished mysteriously, yet nevertheless he has a holy sepulcher, if not several. I have attempted to explain this vanishing as being cremation; but if kings were cremated, they could hardly have a sepulcher or burial place in the usual sense of the term, for we know that in all forms of religion the essential feature of a sepulcher, or shrine, is that it is supposed to contain the bones, or at any rate some of the bones, of the holy person to whom it is dedicated. A great deal has of course been written on the customs of the Greeks with regard to the disposal of the dead and their beliefs as to the other world, but I am here concerned chiefly to consider the existence, or possible existence, of rites in connection with the hero stories, and what they suggest to me, that while ordinary people were buried, the bodies of kings were burned, but not burned thoroughly, so that the bones were left, and could be buried. I believe that this view was put forward, though on different grounds, by Dörpfeld some thirty years ago, though I have not seen what he wrote. Anyhow similar customs are found in various parts of the world.

I have, I hope, now convinced you that the parallels between the stories of the various heroes of tradition are too numerous to be mere coincidences, and that they can be explained as incidents in ritual. Are we to conclude that all these heroes are mythical? In my own opinion most of them at any rate are purely mythical, but I have arrived at this opinion on somewhat different grounds. It by no means necessarily follows from the facts which I have just put before you. When we are told that Alexander the Great was the son of Zeus, who approached his mother in the form of a serpent, we do not conclude that he was mythical, nor when we read in Herodotus that the maternal grandfather of Cyrus ordered him to be killed at birth, do we conclude that Cyrus was mythical. What we conclude, at least I do, is that the pattern career for a hero was generally known, and that either from flattery, or from a genuine belief that the career of a hero must conform to type, mythical incidents were introduced into the story of genuinely historical heroes. It follows from this, however, that the earlier heroes must have been mythical, else the mythical type could not have arisen. The only possible alternative, and one that seems to me highly improbable, is that Oedipus was a really historical character, who killed his father, married his mother, and so on, but did it all as part of a fixed ritual.

As for the Freudian explanation, it is, to say the least, inadequate, since it only takes into account two incidents out of at least twenty-two, and we find that the rest of the story is the same whether the hero marries his mother, his sister, or his first cousin.

The fault to which we are all of us liable, but which I have done my best to avoid, is to concentrate on one particular incident or one particular aspect, and to disregard everything else. This is what has been done by many classical scholars. Brought up on Homer and the Attic dramatists, they tend to concentrate not on what the heroes of tradition are actually alleged to have done, but on the words which the poets have put into their mouths. On these they base character studies of the heroes, oblivious of the fact that the whole art of the great poets lay in putting new words into the mouths of old characters. The fact is, I am afraid, that classical scholars as a whole are romantically rather than scientifically minded. The reading of the *Iliad* or of the *Seven Against Thebes* fills them with emotion, but they are unwilling to admit that it is emotion of exactly the same type as that experienced by the small boy who reads *Treasure Island,* and therefore they conceal it under a veil of pseudohistory. This veil takes the form of a belief in a "Heroic Age," in which, apparently, the principal features of life were single combats, elopements, and dragons. In my view it is just as reasonable to suppose that there was once a "Comic Age," in which life consisted of backchat and disguises, and a "Tragic Age," in which lovers always came to an untimely end. Our knowledge of all three is derived from the poets, and the poets are not interested in historical truth. Very few people are. It is always assumed by historians that people prefer fact to fiction, but they need only go as far as the nearest lending library to find out that there is not the slightest foundation for this assumption. Homer is read, not because his readers are eager for historical accuracy, but because he wrote good stories, and he will still be read when it has come to be generally realized that these stories have not the slightest historical foundation.

Recurrent Themes in Myths
and Mythmaking

Clyde Kluckhohn

In this essay by a distinguished American anthropologist, the question of the distribution of particular forms is examined. Kluckhohn, who at the time of his death in 1960 was Professor of Anthropology at Harvard University, was very much interested in the matter of universals. Through the use of the standard sampling techniques employed by anthropologists engaged in cross-cultural investigations, Professor Kluckhohn was able to make some generalizations about the over-all distribution of many mythological themes. Kluckhohn's willingness to combine the anthropological cross-cultural approach with psychological considerations is not commonly found among those contemporary anthropologists who study folklore.

It is the purpose of this paper to draw together some information on and interpretation of certain features of mythology that are apparently universal or that have such wide distribution in space and time that their generality may be presumed to result from recurrent reactions of the human psyche to situations and stimuli of the same general order. Addressing a group from a wide range of disciplinary affiliations, I shall utilize recent writings that are, as yet, generally familiar only to anthropologists and folklorists. I shall also add a modest effort on my own part to sample independently the distribution of a small number of mythic elements. The result makes no pretensions to completeness or indeed to more than approximate accuracy on the materials surveyed. But even a crude and tentative synthesis may have some interest and provide some stimulation to more comprehensive and precise research.

Literary scholars, psychiatrists, and behavioral scientists have, of course, long recognized that diverse geographical areas and historical epochs have exhibited striking parallels in the themes of myth and folklore. Father-seekers and father-slayers appear again and again. Mother-murder appears in explicit

Reprinted from *Daedalus: Journal of the American Academy of Arts and Sciences,* Vol. 88 (1959), 268–79, by permission of Florence Kluckhohn, the American Academy of Arts and Sciences, and George Braziller, Inc.

and in disguised form.[1] Eliade[2] has dealt with the myth of "the eternal return." Marie Bonaparte[3] has presented evidence that wars give rise to fantasies of patently similar content. Animal stories—at least in the Old World—show likenesses in many details of plot and embellishment: African tales and Reynard the Fox, the Aesop fables, the Panchatantra of India and the Jataka tales of China and India.[4] The Orpheus story has a sizable distribution in the New World.[5]

In considering various parallels, some elementary cautions must perforce be observed. First, levels of abstraction must be kept distinct. It is true, and it is relevant, to say that creation myths are universals or near universals. But this is a far more abstract statement than are generalizations about the frequency of the creation of human beings by mother earth and father sky or by an androgynous deity or from vegetables.[6] Second, mere comparisons on the basis of the presence or absence of a trait are tricky and may well be misleading. Although there are cases where I have as yet no positive evidence for the presence of the incest theme, there is no corpus of mythology that I have searched carefully where this motif does not turn up. Even if, however, incest could be demonstrated as a theme present in all mythologies, there would still be an important difference between mythologies preoccupied with incest and those where it occurs only incidentally and infrequently. Nevertheless, the methodological complications of reliable ratings upon the centrality or strength of a given theme are such that in this paper I must deal almost exclusively with sheer presence or absence.

Most anthropologists today would agree with Lévi-Strauss[7] that throughout the world myths resemble one another to an extraordinary degree; there is, indeed, an "astounding similarity between myths collected in widely different regions." The differences are there too, of course, between cultures and culture areas, even between versions of "the same" myth collected on the same day from two or more individuals of a particular culture. Some myths appear to have a very limited geographical distribution; other themes that have a very wide or perhaps universal distribution are varyingly styled, weighted,

[1] H. A. Bunker, "Mother-Murder in Myth and Legend," *Psychoanalytic Quarterly,* Vol. 13 (1944), 198–207.

[2] Mircea Eliade, *Le mythe de l'éternel retour* (Paris: Gallimard, 1949), Eng. trans. W. R. Trask (New York: Pantheon Books, Inc., 1954), Bollingen Series, 46.

[3] Marie Bonaparte, *Myths of War* (London: Imago Publishing Company, Ltd., 1947).

[4] See M. J. Herskovits and F. S. Herskovits, *Dahomean Narrative* (Evanston, Ill.: Northwestern University Press, 1958), p. 118.

[5] A. H. Gayton, "The Orphic Myth in North America," *Journal of American Folklore,* Vol. 48 (1935), 263–93. [For a more recent survey of the distribution of Orpheus in the New World, see Åke Hultkrantz, *The North American Indian Orpheus Tradition* (Stockholm, 1957).—ED. NOTE]

[6] For some indication of frequency, see Motifs A625, World parents: sky-father and earth-mother as parents of the universe; A12, Hermaphroditic creator; and A1250, Man made from vegetable substance.—ED. NOTE

[7] Claude Lévi-Strauss, "The Structural Study of Myth," *Journal of American Folklore,* Vol. 68 (1955), 428–45.

and combined. These differences are very real and very massive, and there must be no tacit attempt to explain them away. For some purposes of inquiry the focus must be upon questions of emphasis, of inversion of plot, of selective omission and addition, of reinterpretation, of every form of variation. The similarities, however, are also genuine, and it is upon these that I shall concentrate. After all, presumably no two events in the universe are literally identical. But there are formal resemblances at varying levels of abstraction that are interesting and significant.

Let us begin with some broad universals. I have already mentioned the creation myth.[8] This may seem so broad a category as to be empty. Yet Rooth[9] on analyzing three hundred creation myths of the North American Indians finds that most of them fit comfortably into eight types and that seven of these types appear likewise in Eurasia. She interprets the similarities in types and in congruence of detail motifs between North America and Eurasia (and also some between Peru, Meso-America, and the Pacific Islands) as due to historic diffusion. Were this inference to be demonstrated as valid in all respects, there would still remain the fact that these plots and their details had sufficient psychological meaning to be preserved through the centuries.

There are two ways of reasoning that bulk prominently in all mythological systems. These are what Sir James Frazer called the "laws" of sympathetic magic (like causes like) and holophrastic magic (the part stands for the whole).[10] These principles are particularly employed in one content area

---

8 Myths of the creation of the world are infrequent in some areas (e.g., Melanesia and Indonesia). But stories of the creation of mankind appear to be universal. Many themes recur in widely separated areas but do not approach universality: The first parents are sun and moon or earth and sky; the first impregnation comes from the rays of the sun; the first humans are fashioned from earth by a creator or emerge as vegetables from the earth and cannot at first walk straight. Destruction of an old world and creation of a new is likewise a frequently recurring story. [Of these motifs, the most common are T521, Conception from sunlight; A1241, Man made from clay (earth); and A1006, Renewal of world after world calamity.—Ed. Note.]

9 A. B. Rooth, "The Creation Myths of the North American Indians," *Anthropos,* Vol. 52 (1957), 497–508.

10 Frazer's own terminology differs somewhat. He distinguishes two principles of sympathetic magic. The first is *homeopathic magic* which is based on the Law of Similarity (like produces like). The second is *contagious magic* which is based on the Law of Contact or Contagion. In the first case, a model or replica of the object or event desired is made. An example would be *envoûtement,* the practice of doing something to an image, such as sticking a pin through the heart of a doll. Another example is a Japanese belief that one should bring potted plants, not cut flowers, to a patient recuperating in a hospital. Potted plants, of course, are alive, whereas cut flowers will die. In contagious magic, it is assumed that things which have once been in contact with one another will continue ever afterward to act on each other. Thus any material expelled or removed from the body, such as hair, spittle, or clothing, is a potential source of danger should it fall into the hands of an enemy. Another example of contagious magic is the practice of treating a nail or knife, by such means as coating it with grease, rather than the wound caused by it. According to the logic of magic, the nail had to have been in contact with the wounded place, and by treating the cause, one alleviates the effect. It is possible to combine both principles. If one made an effigy (homeopathic) out of

where the record is so full and so exceptionless that we are justified in speaking of genuine cultural universals. No known culture is without myths and tales relating to witchcraft, and the following themes appear always and everywhere:

1. Were-animals who move about at night with miraculous speed, gathering in witches' sabbaths to work evil magic.
2. The notion that illness, emaciation, and eventual death can result from introducing by magical means some sort of noxious substance into the body of the victim.
3. A connection between incest and witchcraft.

So far as I have been able to discover, the only cultural variability here concerns minutiae: details of the magical techniques; which animals are portrayed; what kinds of particles are shot into the victim or what kinds of witchcraft poisons are employed. It is, to be sure, conceivable that once again we are dealing with diffusion: that all known cultures derive eventually from a generalized Paleolithic culture in which these items of witchcraft lore were already evolved. But, again, their persistence cannot be understood except on the hypothesis that these images have a special congeniality for the human mind as a consequence of the relations of children to their parents and other childhood experiences which are universal rather than culture-bound.

While a comprehensive interpretation of any myth or of mythologies must rest upon the way in which themes are combined—upon, as Lévi-Strauss[11] says, "a bundle of features"—nevertheless the mere recurrence of certain motifs in varied areas separated geographically and historically tells us something about the human psyche. It suggests that the interaction of a certain kind of biological apparatus in a certain kind of physical world with some inevitables of the human condition (the helplessness of infants, two parents of different sex, etc.) brings about some regularities in the formation of imaginative productions, of powerful images. I want to consider examples of these, only mentioning some but discussing others at a little greater length. I have selected themes that have been stated by various students of comparative mythology to be nearly universal in distribution.

In most cases we cannot say strictly that these images are universal, either because of incomplete evidence or because of known exceptions, but we can say that some are known from all or almost all of the major culture areas of

the prospective victim's hair (contagious), he would have both homeopathic and contagious magic working for him.

The distinction between the two principles is analogous to the difference between metaphor and simile. Two objects are compared in both metaphor and simile; in metaphor, however, only one object is present and it stands for the other, whereas in simile both objects are present and are linked (in contact) by such a word as "like." The verbal parallel for holophrastic magic mentioned by Kluckhohn might be synecdoche or even metonymy. For a comprehensive consideration of the two principles of sympathetic magic with numerous illustrative examples, see Frazer's *The New Golden Bough*, ed. Theodor H. Gaster (Garden City, N.Y., 1961), pp. 5–21.—Ed. Note

11 *Op. cit.;* also Lévi-Strauss, "Structure et dialectique," in Morris Halle, compiler, *For Roman Jakobson* (The Hague: Mouton, 1957), pp. 289–94.

the world. To avoid egregious sampling errors and generally to make the inquiry more systematic, I have used Murdock's[12] "world ethnographic sample." He presents a carefully selected sample of all the cultures known to history and ethnography, classified into 60 culture areas. Richard Moench and I tried to cover one culture from each of these areas but were able to work through only 50—and this not exhaustively. The 50 are, however, distributed about evenly among Murdock's six major regions (Circum-Mediterranean, Negro Africa, East Eurasia, Insular Pacific, North America, South America). To the extent that time permitted, we used standard monographic sources on the cultures in question (or excerpts from these sources in the Human Relations Area Files at Harvard). We also had recourse to certain compendia: the Hastings *Encyclopaedia of Religion and Ethics, Myths of All Races,*[13] Stith Thompson's *Motif-Index,* and others.

Our results are far from satisfactory, but they do represent a start. On the positive side, they ought to be almost completely trustworthy. That is, where we report, for example, that brother-sister incest is a mythological theme in Micronesia, this can be regarded as established. It is on the negative side that doubt must be raised. For instance, we did not discover an androgynous deity in the mythology of the Warrau. This, unfortunately, does not necessarily mean that no such deity exists in Warrau mythology—only that we discovered no reference in the one original source and in the compilations we checked. Without question, a more intensive search than we were able to conduct would enlarge—we cannot guess by how great a factor—the number of features to be tabulated as "present."

Flood. We found this theme—usually, but not always, treated as a punishment—in 34 of our 50 mythologies.[14] The distribution is not far from equal in five of the six regions, but we encountered only one reference from Negro Africa. There is the possibility that some of these tales take their ultimate source from the mythology of the Near East and, specifically, Jewish-Christian mythology, although many ethnographers are careful to discriminate explicitly between those that may have this derivation and others that seem definitely "aboriginal." Li Hwei[15] has traced 51 flood myths in Formosa, South China,

---

[12] G. P. Murdock, "World Ethnographic Sample," *American Anthropologist,* Vol. 59 (1957), 664–88.

[13] The full reference is *The Mythology of All Races,* 13 vols. (Boston, 1916–1932). This series, edited by Louis H. Gray, includes individual volumes (or parts of a volume) devoted to the mythology of one area. For example, one volume is entitled *North American Indian Mythology* (Vol. 10) and another is *African Mythology* (Vol. 7).—ED. NOTE

[14] There have been quite a number of scholarly monographs written on flood myths. For references, see Motif A1010, Deluge. For the flood as punishment specifically, see A1018, Flood as punishment. The reader should realize that most of the other "themes" discussed by Kluckhohn are motifs, which could be consulted in the *Motif-Index* if more information were desired. Some of the prominent motifs mentioned by Kluckhohn include A1000, World catastrophe; A531, Culture hero (demigod) overcomes monsters; T410, Incest; S73.1, Fratricide; F547.1.1, *Vagina dentata;* and A12, Hermaphroditic creator.—ED. NOTE

[15] See William Bascom, "The Myth-Ritual Theory," *Journal of American Folklore,* Vol. 70 (1957), 103–15.

Southeast Asia, and Malaysia that it hardly seems plausible to attribute to Jewish-Christian sources.[16] At any rate, if one adds earthquakes, famines, plagues, etc., it is likely, on present evidence, that "catastrophe" can be considered as a universal or near-universal theme in mythology.

Slaying of Monsters. This theme appears in 37 of our 50 cultures, and here the distribution approaches equality save for a slightly greater frequency in North America and the Insular Pacific. Not infrequently, the elaboration of the theme has a faintly Oedipal flavor. Thus in Bantu Africa (and beyond) a hero is born to a woman who survives after a monster has eaten her spouse (and everyone else). The son immediately turns into a man, slays a monster or monsters, restores his people—but not his father—and becomes chief.

Incest. This is overtly depicted in 39 mythologies. In 3 cases (Celtic, Greek, and Hindu) mother-son, father-daughter, and brother-sister incest are alluded to; 11 cases mention two forms of incest; the remaining 25 mythologies apparently deal with only a single type. In our sample we encountered only 7 references to mother-son incest (none in Negro Africa and only one in East Eurasia). In other reading we did find an additional 7 reports—one more from East Eurasia but still none from Negro Africa. Brother-sister incest was easily the most popular theme in the sample (28 cases). There are 12 cases of father-daughter incest. In creation stories, the first parents are not infrequently depicted as incestuous, and there are numerous references to the seduction of a mother-in-law by her son-in-law (or vice versa).

Sibling Rivalry. We discovered 32 instances of this theme, which appears from all 6 "continental" regions but—so far as our sample goes—is appreciably more frequent in the Insular Pacific and in Negro Africa. The rivalry between brothers is portrayed far oftener than any other, and usually in the form of fratricide. There were only 4 cases of brother-sister quarrels (one resulting in murder) and only 2 of sister-sister. There are some indications in the data that a larger sample and a finer analysis would reveal some culturally distinctive regularities as regards the age order of siblings depicted as rivalrous. For example, in parts of Negro Africa it appears that it is always two siblings born in immediate sequence who are chosen as protagonists.

Castration. We found only 4 cases where actual castration is mentioned in the myths, and one of these (Trobriand) is self-inflicted castration, ostensibly as a reaction to guilt over adultery. There are in addition 5 cases in which the threat of castration to boys is mentioned in myths as a socialization technique. There are also instances (e.g., Baiga) where there are reports of severed penes and injured testicles. However, if one counts themes of "symbolic castration," then there is an approach toward univer-

---

16 Lord Raglan relates the flood myth to the flooding of rivers and the whole problem of subsistence in newly agricultural civilizations. But it occurs in many nonliterate societies, including some that do not have even incipient agriculture. See Lord Raglan, *The Hero: A Study in Tradition, Myth, and Drama* (New York: Vintage Books [Alfred A. Knopf], 1956); 1st ed. (London: Methuen and Company, 1936).

sality. The subincision rites of the Australian aborigines have been so inter-preted.[17] And in our browsing (beyond our sample) we encountered the *vagina dentata* motif among the following peoples: Arapaho, Bella Bella, Bella Coola, Blackfoot, Comox, Coos, Crow, Dakota, Iroquois, Jicarilla, Kwakiutl, Maidu, Nez Percé, Pawnee, San Carlos Apache, Shoshone, Shuswap, Thompson, Tsimshian, Walapai, Wichita, Ainu, Samoa, Naga, Kiwai Papuan.[18]

Androgynous Deities. From our sample we can document only seven cases (all from Circum-Mediterranean, East Eurasia, and North America). Eliade[19] says that divine bisexuality is not found "in really primitive religions." The numerous examples he gives[20] are all from "advanced" religions, though we could add a few from "primitive" cultures.

Oedipus-Type Myths

Let us now turn to a brief examination of two patterns in which themes are combined. The Oedipus story has long haunted European literature and thought, even if in very recent times the myth of Sisyphus may have replaced that of Oedipus in popularity (see Kafka, Camus, and many others). Jones[21] has tried to show that *Hamlet* is basically an Oedipal plot. Others insist that Great Mother or Mater Dolorosa tales are simply special variants.

At all events, some scholars have regarded the Oedipal tale as prototypical of all human myths. Critical scrutiny of this generalization, and particularly one's conclusions as to the prevalence of Oedipus-type myths outside the areas the story may have reached through historical diffusion, will rest on how much credence one is prepared to give to psychoanalytic interpretations of latent content, on the one hand; and on how many elements of the Greek myth one demands be replicated, on the other. Thus Róheim's[22] contention that certain Navaho myths are Oedipal strikes many as strained. The main

---

[17] For a description and explanation of urethral subincision and other ritual mutila-tions, see Bruno Bettelheim's *Symbolic Wounds: Puberty Rites and the Envious Male,* rev. ed. (New York, 1962).—ED. NOTE

[18] This statement is somewhat misleading as the distribution of this motif is much wider than that indicated by Kluckhohn's list. Parallels cited in one of Stith Thompson's voluminous notes in his *Tales of the North American Indians* (Cambridge, Mass., 1929), p. 309, include more than a dozen additional tribes. See also Verrier Elwin, "The *Vagina Dentata* Legend," *British Journal of Medical Psychology,* Vol. 19 (1941–1943), 439–53; and Robert Gessain, " 'Vagina dentata' dans la clinique et la mythologie," *La Psych-analyse,* Vol. 3 (1957), 247–95.—ED. NOTE

[19] Mircea Eliade, *Birth and Rebirth* (New York: Harper & Row, Publishers, 1958), p. 25.

[20] Mircea Eliade, *Patterns in Comparative Religion* (New York: Sheed & Ward, 1958), pp. 420–25.

[21] Ernest Jones, *Hamlet and Oedipus* (New York: Doubleday Anchor Books, 1954). Published first as an article in the *American Journal of Psychology* in 1910; again in 1923 as Chap. 1 in *Essays in Applied Psychoanalysis;* rev. ed. (London: V. Gollancz; New York: W. W. Norton & Company, Inc., 1949).

[22] Géza Róheim, *Psychoanalysis and Anthropology* (New York: International Univer-sities Press, 1950), pp. 319–47.

emphasis is upon the father killing his own children—even here Róheim must argue that it is the father's *weapon* that is used (by another). And he must contend that the giant who makes amorous advances to the mother and is killed by the sons is a *father substitute*.

Actually, the 48 Oedipal myths in the Euro-Asiatic area analyzed by Rank[23] and Raglan[24] do not show a very striking fit in detail[25] to the Greek myth. In only 4 of these does the hero marry his mother. Indeed, in only 8 others is an incestuous theme of any kind explicitly present. Again, in only 4 of the 48 myths does the hero cause the death of his father. In 9 other cases the hero kills (or is one case is killed by) a close relative (grandfather, uncle, brother, etc.). One can make a good case for "antagonism against close relatives—*usually* of the same sex" as a prominent motif, and a fair case for physical violence against such relatives. But neither parricide nor Raglan's regicide motifs will stand up literally without a great deal of farfetched interpretation.

In a very interesting paper Lessa[26] has suggested that the Oedipus-type story spread by diffusion from the patriarchal Euro-Asiatic societies to Oceanic peoples with whom the situation is very different. He writes:

> ...we find such stories limited to a continuous belt extending from Europe to the Near and Middle East and southeastern Asia, and from there into the islands of the Pacific. It seems to be absent from such vast areas as Africa, China, central Asia, northeastern Asia, North America, South America, and Australia [page 68].

In an examination of several thousand Oceania narratives Lessa found 23 that bore some resemblance to the Oedipus tale. He points out, however, that none meet all three of his major criteria[27] (prophecy, parricide, and incest) or his three minor criteria (succorance from exposure, rearing by another king, fulfillment of prophecy); only a third meet the combination of parricide and incest. Lessa also calls attention to various "substitutions": mother's brother for father, father's sister for mother, father kills son rather than the other way round, incest merely threatened rather than consummated, baby abandoned but without hostility.

Nevertheless, even if one grants Lessa's inference of diffusion (with culturally appropriate substitutions), I do not think one can at present assent to his main argument without exception. Róheim's[28] case for Oedipal pattern in the myths of Australian aborigines, Yurok, Navaho, and others does indeed involve too much reliance upon "unconscious ideas" and "real motifs." And

---

23 Otto Rank, *The Myth of the Birth of the Hero*, trans. F. Robbins and S. E. Jellife (New York: Robert Brunner, 1952); 1st ed., *Der Mythus von der Geburt des Helden* (Leipzig-Wien: F. Deuticke, 1909).

24 *Op. cit.*

25 See Bascom, *op. cit.*

26 William Lessa, "Oedipus-Type Tales in Oceania," *Journal of American Folklore*, Vol. 69 (1956), 63–73.

27 Lessa's criteria are those of the Aarne-Thompson classification of folktales.

28 *Op. cit.*

yet, in my opinion, something remains that cannot altogether be explained away. Lessa asserts flatly that Oedipal tales are absent from Africa, but they are found among the Shilluk;[29] and the Lamba (central Bantu) have a story of a son killing his father, in which there is a fairly overt motif of sexual rivalry for the mother.

Herskovits and Herskovits[30] make two significant points as regards testing generalizing conclusions about the Oedipus myth in cross-cultural perspective. The first (abundantly confirmed by the present small study) is neglect of rivalry between brothers. Then they say:

> In analyzing the motivating forces underlying the myth clusters that fall into the Oedipus category, we must take into account not only the son's jealousy of the father but also the father's fear of being displaced by his son. Parent-child hostilities, that is, are not unidirectional. As manifest in myth, and in the situations of everyday experience, they are an expression of the broader phenomenon of intergenerational competition. These tensions, moreover, begin in infancy in the situation of rivalry between children of the same parents for a single goal, the attention of the mother. This rivalry sets up patterns of interaction that throughout life give rise to attitudes held toward the siblings or sibling substitutes with whom the individual was in competition during infancy, and it is our hypothesis that these attitudes are later projected by the father upon his offspring. In myth, if the psychological interpretation is to be granted validity, we must posit that the threat to the father or father-surrogate is to be seen as a projection of the infantile experience of sibling hostility upon the son. It may be said to be the response to the reactivation of early attitudes toward the mother under the stimulus of anticipated competition for the affection of the wife.

The hypothesis that the main direction of hostility is from father to son received much confirmation from our reading from the following: 14 North American peoples; 4 Circum-Mediterranean peoples; 5 from East Eurasia; 3 from the Insular Pacific; 4 from Africa. These were noted incidentally in searching for material on our selected themes. In many cases the myth states as an explicit motif the father's fear of being killed or displaced by his son. In some instances a prophecy is mentioned. Sometimes the son is expelled by the father rather than killed. An Azande father is depicted as destroying an incestuous son by magic. An Alor father orders his wife to kill the next chief *if* male. There are many variants, but the basic theme is certainly a prevalent one.

The Myth of the Hero

It strikes me that the Oedipal pattern may best be considered as one form of a far more widespread myth, which has been treated by Rank,[31] Raglan,[32]

---

29 Bascom, *op. cit.*, p. 111.
30 *Op. cit.*, p. 94.
31 *Op. cit.*
32 *Op. cit.*

and Campbell.[33] Rank abstracts the following pattern in 34 myths from the Mediterranean basin and western Asia:

> The hero is the child of most distinguished parents; usually the son of a king. His origin is preceded by difficulties, such as continence, or prolonged barrenness or secret intercourse of the parents, due to external prohibition or obstacles. During the pregnancy, or antedating the same, there is a prophecy in the form of a dream or oracle, cautioning against his birth, and usually threatening danger to the father, or his representative. As a rule, he is surrendered to the water, in a box. He is then saved by animals or lowly people (shepherds) and is suckled by a female animal, or by a humble woman. After he is grown up, he finds his distinguished parents in a highly versatile fashion, takes his revenge on his father, on the one hand, and is acknowledged on the other, and finally achieves rank and honors [page 61].

Raglan's first 13 (of 22) points correspond strikingly to this formula. In a world-wide context Campbell develops essentially the same pattern in a more sophisticated form, tied neither to the doctrinaire psychoanalysis of Rank nor to the limited and culture-bound theories of Raglan.

From the reading done by Moench and myself, many details not cited in any of the above three publications could be added: numerous instances of parricide in myth; virgin and other kinds of miraculous birth; newborn child in basket or pot; care of the infant by animals or humble women; and the like. This would, however, be more of the same fragmentary information. Rather, I shall add to the record two recent pertinent studies that are more systematic.

Ishida[34] shows the prevalence in the Far East of all of this "bundle" of themes except prophecy. There are, of course, certain cultural embellishments that are characteristically different, but the plot is patently similar except for the omission of prophecy and the addition of a theme not present in the Rank formula: greater emphasis upon the mother of the hero, and often the worship of her along with her divine son.

But Ishida's research deals with the same continental land mass from which Rank and Raglan draw their data. Let us therefore take an example from the New World, Spencer's[35] analysis of Navaho mythology. The following similarities may be noted:

1. These are also hero stories: adventures and achievements of extraordinary kind (e.g., slaying monsters, overcoming death, controlling the weather).
2. There is often something special about the birth of the hero (occasionally heroine).

---

33 Joseph Campbell, *The Hero with a Thousand Faces* (New York: Meridian Books, 1956); 1st ed. (New York: Pantheon Books, Inc., 1949), Bollingen Series, 17.

34 Eiichiro Ishida, "The Mother-Son Complex in East Asiatic Religion and Folklore," in *Die Wiener Schule der Voelkerkunde, Festschrift zum 25 jährigen Bestand* (Vienna, 1955), pp. 411–19.

35 Katherine Spencer, *Mythology and Values*, Memoir 48 (Philadelphia: American Folklore Society, 1957), esp. pp. 19–73.

3. Help from animals is a frequent motif.
4. A separation from one or both parents at an early age is involved.
5. There is antagonism and violence toward near kin, though mainly toward siblings or father-in-law. This hostility may be channeled in one or both directions. It may be masked but is more often expressed in violent acts.
6. There is eventual return and recognition with honor. The hero's achievements are realized by his immediate family and redound in some way to their benefit and that of the larger group to which the family belongs.

Contrasts between the Old World and New World forms are clearly reflected in content and emphasis. The themes of social hierarchy and of triumph over (specifically) the father are absent in the American Indian version, and the Navaho theme of anxiety over subsistence is absent from the Euro-Asian plot. Yet at a broad psychological level the similarities are also impressive. In both cases we have a form of "family romance": the hero is separated but in the end returns in a high status; prohibitions and portents and animals play a role; there are two features of the Oedipus myth as Lévi-Strauss[36] has "translated" it—"underestimation and overestimation of near kin."

Of constant tendencies in mythmaking, I shall merely remind you of four that are so well documented as to be unarguable, then mention two others:

1. Duplication, triplication, and quadruplication of elements. (Lévi-Strauss[37] suggests that the function of this repetition is to make the structure of the myth apparent.)
2. Reinterpretation of borrowed myths to fit pre-existing cultural emphases.
3. Endless variations upon central themes.
4. Involution-elaboration.

The psychoanalysts have maintained that mythmaking exemplifies a large number of the mechanisms of ego defense. I agree, and have provided examples from Navaho culture.[38] Lévi-Strauss[39] suggests that mythical thought always works from awareness of binary oppositions toward their progressive mediation. That is, the contribution of mythology is that of providing a logical model capable of overcoming contradictions in a people's view of the world and what they have deduced from their experience. This is an engaging idea, but much further empirical work is required to test it.

In conclusion, it may be said that this incomplete and exploratory study adds a small bit of confirmation to the finding of others that there are detectable trends toward regularities both in myths and in mythmaking. At least some themes and the linking of certain features of them, while differently stylized and incorporating varying detailed content according to culture and culture area, represent recurrent fantasies that have held the imaginations of many, if not most, social groups.

---

[36] "The Structural Study of Myth."
[37] *Ibid.*
[38] Clyde Kluckhohn, "Myths and Rituals: A General Theory," *Harvard Theological Review*, Vol. 35 (1942), 45–79.
[39] "The Structural Study of Myth" and "Structure et dialectique."

Stability of Form in Traditional and Cultivated Music

George Herzog

In this essay by one of the foremost authorities on folk and primitive music, the difference between the concept of form as it is found among people with cultivated music and among people with only folk music is considered. The influence of writing upon what were, originally, folk materials is enormous. Writing, and, even more, print, freezes the form and appreciably reduces the possibility of variation.

It is very difficult for those who are accustomed to the fixedness of print to understand the nature of the relationship betwen form and variation in folklore. There are few, if any, differences in the versions of the scores of a Mozart symphony, although as Herzog points out, the way this kind of music is performed is very much subject to variation from one conductor or performer to another. One reason for this variation is that the transcription techniques for performance lag behind the techniques available for transcribing notes and meter, the latter being facilitated by the development of a fixed scale and standard meters. So the manner of performance in art music is just as variable as are both performance *and* text in folk music.

In folklore, one does not have *the* folksong any more than *the* correct way of playing a traditional game or *the* right way of telling a joke. One has only *a* version of a folksong, game, or joke. To the professional folklorist, *the* song, like *the* tale type, is an abstraction or ideal form which is manifested many, many times (i.e., multiple existence) in concrete versions. After many versions of a folksong have been collected, it is then possible to see what the more usual form or forms of the song are. Versions that differ markedly from the normal form are usually termed variants by folklorists. Thus all iterations of an item of folklore are by definition versions. All variants must be versions, but not all versions are variants. The difficulty lies in determining how different a version has to be from the assumed normal form before it can properly be called a variant.

Reprinted from *Papers Read by Members of the American Musicologcial Society at the Annual Meeting,* Washington, D.C., December 29th and 30th, 1938 (n.p., 1940), pp. 69–73, by permission of the author and the *Journal of the American Musicological Society.*

Some of the various reasons for either relative stability of form or relative flexibility of form are mentioned by Herzog. If the songs are religious in nature and are used in effecting cures, or if there is a restrictive time factor in the case of a singer of epic songs, the stability of form and content may be different from that of nonreligious songs or performances from unhurried epic singers. Notice that if one had just the text alone, one could judge the stability, but if one did not know the particular *context* of the text, one might be unable to account for the form and content. One needs to know the answer to such questions as: Why was the song sung? To whom? By whom? In whose presence? Under what (special) conditions? Unlike much folksong scholarship in which texts are treated apart from their contexts, this article by Herzog not only discusses form but relates variation or the lack of it to specific contexts.

In primitive and folk music we do not find form to be the fixed entity which is taken for granted in "our music," the cultivated music of the last few centuries. A musical creation is stable in our modern practice, since it is conceived to remain the same when performed by the same person at different times, or by different performers, or in different periods. The composition has an essential content with which the performer ought not to tamper—nor the editor, if he can help it. This content is laid down in two media. One is that of writing; a piece is to be played the way it is written. The other is that of tradition. Not only do we refrain from changing form, rhythmic pattern, tones and intervals, but also we often adhere faithfully to some of the so-called expressive features. The course of a ritardando or the approximate length of a hold may be almost as time-honored and sacred as an actual tone. Yet there is on the whole more leeway with expressive features, which we somewhat paradoxically consider vital to an effective performance, though otherwise of minor importance.

Traditional singers do not employ writing as a device to fix musical form. Partly as a result, the form itself and many of its constituent elements appear in a state of constant flux and re-creation. This may be observed in a number of ways. It constitutes perhaps the most essential difference between traditional music and the cultivated music that has grown up in our culture and in the Orient.

Songs which are known to have spread through tradition have been recorded frequently in versions that differ from place to place. As a matter of fact, it is rather the exception for regional versions of a folksong to be identical. Uniformity may come about with the decay of the tradition, as in the folk music of most of Western Europe; it may come about when a tune is stamped in an official mold and is constantly referred to that mold: some children's songs that are taught at school, or Yankee Doodle, or the national hymns.

Since family and group traditions migrate with their carriers and can survive within the larger frame of a region or community, songs that have been recorded from different singers in the same locality show variations at times considerable. But variations may also occur when songs are recorded from the same singers at different times. This is especially noticeable where the singer improvises his material. Improvisation in traditional music may have to be defined carefully, however. It does not imply that the singer-composer produces, under the inspiration of the moment, artistic material that is entirely novel.

Some conversations I had with native singers and instrumentalists in Liberia, West Africa, were illuminating in this respect. Some of the singers were semiprofessionals, women specializing in mourning songs of praise for the dead. The content of these songs is not fixed. As a result, when the words were to be written down after the songs had been recorded, the singers found it practically impossible to repeat the words exactly without recourse to having the record played back bit by bit. Yet the singer usually thinks over beforehand what she will sing. She builds up her song by selecting from a number of stock phrases and formulas, musical as well as textual, and weaving them together into a composition fitted to the occasion. In this case social considerations might explain the limited scope of improvisation; the singer must refer in these songs to all women of the clan by name and with a praising epithet. She also enumerates the privileges, titles, possessions of the clan, and is listened to avidly by those not concerned with the emotion or at least with the display of grief.

In instrumental music, however, similar features came to light. Some dances in this region are accompanied by no singing, but by the drumming of an orchestra comprising five or six instruments. There is a leader who performs on one or two drums; the others are considered subordinate, each playing only one rhythm throughout the piece. The leading drummer uses a large number of rhythmic figures with what seems a great deal of abandon and individual freedom. But these figures are drawn from a limited pool. Only certain ones can be used for a given dance, and certain ones are used only for the particular piece. Even the order of the motives is not entirely free. Some are definitely introductory, others final, still others signal to the dancers a shift in the dance movement. Unless all phases of rhythm are coordinated—the rhythm of the dance and of the various drums—the performance is beneath the contempt of the natives. It is taken for granted that if a drummer "spills" his rhythm, the dancers "spill" it too; they are thrown. The leading drummer's play, then, consists of selecting from already available materials a selection that must follow the needs of the dance and the total rhythmic design. While we have few observations of this kind from other areas, those that have been made tend to bear out this supposition.

Somewhat improvisatory in nature is that form of variation which occurs so frequently between the subsequent repetitions of a melody that are necessary for the performance of the song. Folk music and primitive music are characterized by the miniature form. A song or piece seldom extends beyond a musical stanza of three to six lines or phrases. This unit is very rarely rendered just once. It is repeated a number of times, depending on such circumstances as the length of the text, or the average length of uninterrupted dancing which is accompanied by the song. The number of repetitions may be also fixed by tradition; at times it is a sacred or ritualistically preferred number. Among many North American Indians it is four.

Unawareness of those changes which do not depart too radically from the essential patterns of form, melody, and rhythm is no doubt a factor that enters into the various levels of flexibility indicated. Native or folk singers are usually aware of regional differences in performance. A folk singer may know that another person sings a song differently, or has an altogether different tune for it. But the slighter changes between renditions of the same singers on different occasions, or between repetitions during the same performance, are usually unnoticed and even denied. Among primitives there is apt to be less consciousness of changes, not only because they are unacquainted with the technique and concept of writing, but also because they often hold a theory or standard that songs do not and should not change.

In many primitive cultures, songs are thought to have a supernatural origin, or some function connected with the supernatural. Consequently the songs are not to be changed, else the whole effect of an elaborate ritual might be marred or vitiated. Among the Navaho Indians the fact that some ceremonial cures happen to prove ineffective is taken to mean that in the performance of these cures some mistakes must have been made: either in details of the ritual procedure, or in the hundreds of songs which form an essential part of each of these rites.

There may be other ostensible impediments to change, for instance, a proprietary feeling for songs. On the Northwest Coast of this continent, on many islands of the Pacific, and elsewhere, certain types of songs are individual property. That a man owns a song or songs may add considerably to his prestige and social status; it may accompany and validate certain prerogatives. Thus it is important that the identity of the song be preserved. The owner alone may have the right to sing it, and others may share this privilege only after his permission has been granted. With a limitation on the number of performers and performances through which the song can pass, there is naturally less opportunity for change. Experience with traditional music has shown, however, that a proscription of change, for whatever reason, is no guarantee against it. Nor does the lack of special ideas militating against change necessarily make for greater fluidity.

Different phases of music are affected differently by this element of variability. Fluctuations in the placement of tones and intervals have been described frequently, measured more rarely. They are no doubt linked up with the absence, especially among primitives, of rigidly defined tone systems, and with the comparatively tenuous influence of musical instruments with fixed pitches. Changes of rhythm have been studied less carefully in primitive material; in folk music where regional variants have been collected so assiduously, a tune often exhibits 3/4 in one locality and 4/4 in another. Changes in form proper are more easily detected. Some of these may be connected with the mode of performance itself. A primitive song that is repeated a number of times frequently has some special feature attached to the beginning of the first rendition and another feature to the end of the last: very brief introductions and codas which mark off the marginal renditions. These marginal elements are sometimes optional, and vary considerably. Not infrequently they are on the borderline between what could be considered musical matter, and mere calls, shouts, imitations of animal voices, and the like. If the text changes while the melody is repeated, modifications in the melody may naturally occur. Rules for repeating a certain section of the song can cause changes in form also; interestingly enough, wherever such rules exist, there are terms denoting the different sections; otherwise this is a rarity.

There are, finally, cases in which the form in effect is open, its end being somewhat academic. American Indian gambling songs may be cited as an example. In the games for which they are sung, one side hides an object and sings while the other side guesses. The singing goes on uninterrupted until a correct guess has been made whereupon it ceases abruptly, at whatever point the melody happens to be. In the proper setting the song seldom comes to its proper close. That there actually is an ending point may be gleaned from the repetitions, or from a rendition of the song out of context. Another example is represented in the Yugoslav epic folksongs. Many of these poems are tens of thousands of lines long, comparable to the Homeric epics.[1] They are not subdivided into chants or similar units, and complete rendition of some of them would require at least a whole night each. In reality there is little opportunity to perform such a song in full. The performances, nowadays, are in cafés where the singer may continue as long as there are people willing to listen. Any disturbance may call for a precipitate close. Moreover, the traditional manner of singing these songs requires so much physical participation that after a couple of hours the performer is completely exhausted. While a good singer has full control of the entire song—as was obvious when collectors took down songs from dictation or on phonograph records—he must be prepared to make the most cruel cuts so that at short notice he can bring his singing to some point of close if not to the very end of the song.

The impression is forced upon us that the general attitudes, whether conscious or unconscious, are different in traditional music and in cultivated music. Our own attitude has been strongly influenced by a variety of factors, such as our music theory and its connections with science, a well-defined

---

[1] For a brief consideration of this ongoing epic tradition, see Albert Lord's "Yugoslav Epic Folk Poetry" in this volume.—Ed. Note

tone system, our interest in scales, music writing, the great importance of musical instruments with fixed pitches and standard tuning, our custom of singing or playing music in large choral or orchestral groups; the role of specialization, of professionals in music, the position of the artist and the art object in our society, including, last but not least, legal notions about property and copyright. For us it is an obvious matter to think of a piece of music apart from its performance; for a traditional singer it is just as obvious that there is little if any existence to a song apart from its performance. With us the creative process essentially precedes in time the performance which merely reproduces what has been fixed into a form. In traditional music there is room for individual creation also, but much of the creative process consists of re-creating and remolding the music while it is being performed. Our own music of course has at various times utilized a more fluid manner of dealing with form. In the theme with variations, to give just one example, flexibility of musical form was consciously exploited; one may think also of recent popular dance music. All music, however, has its share of fluidity. The essential differences lie in the points at which this quality is permitted to manifest itself.

Unifying Factors in Folk and Primitive Music

Bruno Nettl

In this article by one of the leading American ethnomusicologists, some of the particulars of traditional musical form are treated. The reader will soon see that the technical discussion of folk music requires a special vocabulary. Most of the terms are more fully explained in Bruno Nettl's *An Introduction to Folk Music in the United States,* rev. ed. (Detroit, 1962). Another useful source for the beginner is George Herzog's excellent "Song: Folksong and the Music of Folksong," in Maria Leach, ed., *The Standard Dictionary of Folklore, Mythology, and Legend,* Vol. 2 (New York, 1950), pp. 1032–50. A key bibliographical aid is Jaap Kunst's *Ethnomusicology,* 3rd ed. (The Hague, 1959). For a survey of American folksong research, see Donald K. Wilgus, *Anglo-American Folksong Scholarship Since 1898* (New Brunswick, N.J., 1959).

Folk and primitive music have traditionally been described in terms of several distinct elements of music, such as scale, mode, melodic contour, and meter,[1] but less attention has been paid to the broader techniques and devices in composition. It would seem possible to make some essential distinctions between cultivated and unwritten music on the basis of such techniques and devices, since the processes of composition and transmission themselves are essentially different. Needless to say, it is no more justified to group all folk and primitive music as an integrated unit and to expect a set of universally used musical devices to emerge than it would be to deal with all cultivated musical styles as a single group. Nevertheless, an examination of some of the devices, approached from the point of view of more general aesthetic principles, may yield some characteristics essential to folk and

Reprinted from the *Journal of the American Musicological Society,* Vol. 9 (1956), 196–201, by permission of the author and the American Musicological Society.

[1] This division of music into various distinct elements is the basis of the ethnomusicological method as developed by Hornbostel, Stumpf, Herzog, and others. Its soundness is indicated by the difficulty of diverging from it even in this paper, in which the material is approached from another point of view.

primitive music that, regardless of cultural differences among the various peoples, are based on the conditions and limitations of composing without notation and on the restricting and elaborating tendencies of communal re-creation.

One possible basis of such a discussion is the problem of unity and variety, the balance of factors that tend to hold a composition together for the performer and listener, and those that make a piece interesting through variety. There are some obvious difficulties in using such concepts, e.g., the lack of measuring devices for degrees of unity and the absence of these theoretical notions in the cultures concerned. Differences of opinion among Western scholars as to what features promote unity and variety would seem to make such an approach almost doomed to failure. This paper, nevertheless, attempts to use it in order to try to illuminate some of the musical essentials of ethnomusicological material.

For the composer, this problem is a practical one, since there must be strong unifying elements in the music to enable the performer to remember it.[2] As a result, compared to most European cultivated music, folk and primitive compositions seem to be very closely tied, and variety is often severely limited. Simplicity itself is a unifying factor, and those primitive styles that are the simplest of all (using two-tone scales and short, repeated phrases) are sometimes hard put to create sufficient variety. The word *sufficient* may be criticized here since the variety sufficient for the Western observer is certainly different from that sufficient for the native musician. But a desire for variety in music must nevertheless be present; evidently it accounts for the large degree of variation of the short, simple phrases that make up these simple styles. Thus it might be correct to say that the simpler a musical style is, the more predominant are its unifying elements. After all, the very use of only a few tones, short phrases, or simple and few rhythmic relationships is unifying. The simplicity of style essential in most folk and primitive music tends to confirm the statement that unifying factors are more essential in unwritten traditions than in those with notation. Rather than describing folk and primitive music as essentially simple, we might more properly consider it as essentially unified, since the features underlying both terms may be more the result of a wish for integration than of inability to create more complex structures.

But the cultures under consideration here also tend to develop some special devices to foster unity and variety. A prominent one of these is the relatively frequent use of isorhythmic structure or some modified form of it.[3] Not all cultures use it, but it is widespread throughout a large part of the world, being found in, among other places, Eastern Europe, aboriginal North

---

[2] The idea of creating new material out of already existing songs is perhaps also a factor in the integrated structure of primitive and folk music. See Bruno Nettl, *Music in Primitive Culture* (Cambridge, Mass., 1956), pp. 15–17.

[3] By isorhythmic structure is meant the repetition of a fairly elaborate rhythmic sequence several times (or throughout a composition), each time with different melody. (The editor is indebted to Professor Nettl for his help in writing the editorial footnotes for this article.)—ED. NOTE

America, and Negro Africa. Sometimes isorhythmic structure cannot be ascribed simply to a longing for unity, for it may be due to a repetitive rhythm in a song text or dance. Even so, it usually has a unifying function, balancing the variety provided by the different melodies of the phrases and thus holding the diverging parts together. Extract 1 illustrates isorhythmic structure, modified by a closing formula, in a Comanche Indian Peyote song.

Comanche

EXTRACT 1. D. P. McAllester, *Peyote Music* (New York, 1949), Song No. 16.

The melodic analogue of isorhythmic organization, i.e., repetition of a melodic unit with different rhythm each time, is only rarely encountered in folk and primitive music. A similar phenomenon, however, is melodic sequence, or, in a more generalized sense, transposition of a section to different pitch levels. This is found in almost all cultures, sometimes as a short, incidental bit, sometimes contributing to the structural organization of the whole piece, sometimes even dominating it. It may be exact or approximate transposition;[4] it may be accommodated to the tonal system already established or give rise to the formation of a special scale. Extract 2, a Cheremis song, is based on transposition, the second half being an exact sequence of the first.

Cheremis

EXTRACT 2. N. Suvorin, "Lira Escheremissica" (MS, Helsinki, 1903), Song No. III 7.

---

[4] If the interval sequence of a piece of melody is repeated exactly at different pitch levels, one has what Professor Nettl calls exact transposition. For example, do-re-mi-do is transposed exactly in sol-la-ti-sol. However, much transposition does not reproduce all the intervals exactly. Instead, one may find only an approximation of the melody, perhaps just its general shape and line, repeated at a different pitch level. For example, re-mi-sol-fa is an approximate or inexact transposition of do-re-fa-mi.—ED. NOTE

Since the melodic contours[5] of folk and primitive cultures tend to be somewhat specialized in contrast to the contours of European cultivated music, it is probably fair to consider certain of these specializations as unifying factors. If a contour such as the arc-shaped one of many English ballads is predictable, it can hold the piece together because the listener knows in a general way what to expect. As in the case of transposition and isorhythmic structure, repetition also plays a part here. For example, among some North American Indian groups, the terrace-shaped contour approximately repeats the same material at increasingly lower levels.

Tonality is, of course, a primary unifying factor in European cultivated music. The home key alternates with related ones in order to establish a feeling of integration. In some styles of European music history, tonality means unity par excellence. It may be a unifying factor in folk and primitive music also, but it is used in ways quite different from cultivated music. Modulation in the Western sense is rare, perhaps because of the brevity of the forms.[6] Tonal considerations would usually include some element of repetition, perhaps a repeated or recurring tone, interval, or motif. The hierarchy of tones in frequency and position tends to underscore this unifying force of tonality. In most folk and primitive pieces it is not difficult to distinguish important tones from others, and there is a certain tendency in some styles for the tones in important positions (climax and end of a phrase) to be repeated and thus to reinforce their importance. Repetition is also evident in many scale formations. Duplicated interval configurations, illustrated in Extract 3a, appear frequently, and analogous ones like the one shown in Extract 3b are encountered occasionally. Such repeated or duplicated patterns are evident not only in the abstract scale but in the practical utilization of it as well.

Scales

EXTRACT 3.

---

5 Melodic contour is the concept used to describe the general, over-all movement of melody, disregarding the details and the movement from note to individual note. Thus, the movement in the melody do-sol-do-fa-do could be described as pendulum-like. But do-sol-la-sol-do-re-do-sol-do could also be described by that term, in spite of the stepwise movement from do to re and from sol to la, because only the over-all movement is taken into account in considering melodic contour.—ED. NOTE

6 The reason for this is that modulation, in order to be effective, requires a certain amount of time. Each new tonality must remain long enough so that it becomes established in the listener's mind. Thus with brief forms, modulation is rare, at least in the sense in which it is normally understood in Western musical usage.—ED. NOTE

In polyphony, the unifying tendency of folk and primitive music is especially evident. Here there is perhaps an added incentive, in contrast to monophonic music, because the unwritten, untrained musical culture is faced with a special problem of perception. As it is, two kinds of polyphony predominate. The various voices may either produce the same musical material, or appear in a hierarchical relationship. In the first kind, two voices may perform the same music at different pitch levels, producing parallelism; at different times, producing imitation; or at the same time in slightly different forms, producing heterophony. Unity is obviously fostered by this duplication of material. Even when the voices differ in material and importance, there is rarely the degree of diversity found in European counterpoint. The piece is unified by restricting the accompanying voice to a drone, an ostinato figure, or the simple alternation of a few chords.[7]

In the over-all form of folk and primitive pieces a unifying force greater than that in Western cultivated music can also be observed. Primarily this is due to the large amount of repetition and reversion. This is true in the strophic forms[8] (in which ABBA, ABAC, AABA, and the like are predominant) as well as in the nonstrophic material, which usually consists of the repetition of a single phrase occasionally alternating with contrasting material. The question of developing a theme does not enter here in the usual sense, but variation, condensation, and elaboration do play a part. Repetition has numerous manifestations, ranging from the short, repeated phrases of the simplest styles through the antiphonally performed forms of Negro Africa, to such complex forms as the binary stanzas of the Plains Indians, in which a long section is repeated in truncated fashion in order to present the meaningful text and set it off from the meaningless syllables that dominate the song. Strophic songs tend to show less repetition than others, whose longer and less well-defined organization is evidently in greater need of unifying elements.

Bose[9] and Lach[10] consider repetition an elaborative principle and believe that the basic function of transposition, for example, is not unification but elaboration and variety. This apparent contradiction of the view presented here becomes resolved if we realize that the two principles involved are not only contrasting but also complementary. Transposition has two aspects: it repeats a melody and it also changes it. And this is true of variation of any

---

[7] A drone is the use of a single long tone or two or more simultaneous long tones to accompany a melody. Bagpipe music always has a drone and provides a typical illustration. An ostinato figure is a short melodic figure repeated many times as an accompaniment to a longer, more elaborate melody. The term comes from the Italian word for obstinate.—ED. NOTE

[8] Strophic form is the form of composition consisting of several musical lines or phrases, which are repeated a number of times. Each time, the words are different; that is, there is a new stanza. Most English and American folksongs are cast in strophic forms —ED. NOTE

[9] Fritz Bose, *Musikalische Völkerkunde* (Freiburg, 1953), p. 77.

[10] Robert Lach, "Das Konstruktionsprinzip der Wiederholung," *Sitzungsbericht der Akademie der Wissenschaft Wien* (1925), pp. 201–2.

sort. Whether the repetition with changes is historically the result of a drive toward variety, or whether it is unity that holds an otherwise unbridled tendency to change to a more limited process, is an open question. To speak of cultural processes that seem somehow divorced from the personality of composers and performers may seem meaningless here. But it is not entirely irrelevant in folk and primitive cultures, since the contents of a repertory are not dependent on the work of the composer alone but are also subject to the selection and changes by performer and listener, i.e., the process of communal re-creation, which is essential to this material.[11]

The use of variation is perhaps the greatest single diversifying factor to balance the many unifying elements in folk and primitive music. Varying a portion of music is the basis of many forms and, indeed, almost always accompanies those forms that are primarily repetitive. In some cases, variation is built into the music, so to speak, or incorporated in permanent patterns; in others it may be improvised. Extract 4 illustrates variation in an antiphonally performed piece.

African Negro

EXTRACT 4. R. Brandel, in *Journal of the American Musicological Society,* Vol. 7 (1954), 60.

The unifying factors are often found in complementary distribution. Several of them do not appear together, and especially those in the same aspect of music (melody or rhythm) tend mutually to exclude each other. This already may justify distinguishing them as unifying factors. Since there seems to be some system in their grouped occurrence, it may be correct to suppose that

---

[11] Phillips Barry, "Communal Re-creation," *Bulletin of the Folksong Society of the Northeast,* Vol. 5 (1933), pp. 4–6, proposes this happy term, which very adequately describes the role of the performers and listeners in accepting or rejecting and shaping a piece into variants and thus indicating their share in the creative process.

they belong in some sense to a class of musical elements based on a common function. Thus, for example, an isorhythmic piece is likely to have irregular or changing metric patterns, while a metrically stable piece is rarely isorhythmic, although there are the inevitable exceptions. A melodically unified piece is likely to have complex rhythms, while a piece simple and repetitive in all respects is especially prone to variation. A transposing piece does not often have a very stable tonal center, while a rigidly defined hierarchy of tones is not usually the basis of transposition.

The contrast between European cultivated music and folk and primitive material is partly due to the essentially European phenomenon of thematic development. This process presupposes a hierarchical relationship between the theme itself (primary material) and the development of the theme (secondary material). Such a relationship is rarely, if ever, found in traditional music, perhaps because it requires an essentially intellectual process of composition. There are evidently no distinctions between primary and secondary material, but there are nevertheless some devices similar to development that are incorporated in the variation technique and in the repetitive forms so prevalent in the material. One such device, condensation, is also a unifying factor. Extract 5, a Rumanian Christmas carol, illustrates it. Composed of two parts, the first longer and more elaborate than the second, in which the same material is presented in slightly shorter, more direct form, this song exhibits gradual integration through the elimination of nonessential features.

Rumanian

EXTRACT 5. B. Bartók, *Rumanian Christmas Carols* (New York, n.d.), Song No. 1.

In this sense, it is the opposite of the kind of thematic development that moves from the concise to the elaborate. Elaboration is occasionally also found in folk and primitive music, but the condensation process, since it focuses on the essential musical idea of the piece, seems more characteristic of traditional music. Thus the idea of unity appears to be at all levels an essential in most folk and primitive music, to a degree significantly greater than in European cultivated music.

Riddles in Bantu

P. D. Beuchat

Although this survey of Bantu riddles by Miss Beuchat, who is Lecturer in Bantu Languages at the University of Witwatersrand in Johannesburg, does touch upon function and origin, it is primarily concerned with questions of form. Moreover, it is linguistic, rather than folkloristic, structure that is analyzed.

Folkloristic structure refers to the logical-semantic ordering of folklore content and may, for purposes of analysis, be considered independent of linguistic structure. For example, one type of folkloristic structure found in riddles is a pattern of contradiction in which the second of a pair of elements denies a logical or natural attribute of the first. The contradiction occurs because it is apparently impossible to have "A minus B" where B is a logical or natural attribute of A. An example of this type of riddle in English is "What has eyes and cannot see?" (potato). The second element, "cannot see," denies a natural attribute of the first element, "eyes." The first riddle cited by Miss Beuchat is of this type in that there is a house without a door (egg). Folkloristic structure is not bound by the nature of particular languages, and for this reason, can survive translation from one language to another. In contrast, linguistic structure usually does not survive translation.

Miss Beuchat divides her study of linguistic form into "general structure" and "linguistic structure." Under general structure is subsumed opening formulas and syntactic patterns (e.g., compound sentences). What Miss Beuchat calls linguistic structure is reserved for the microanalysis of syllable counts and rhythm. Most of the features of the linguistic structure of Bantu riddles, features that are the basis of the literary style of the riddles to a great extent, cannot be translated into English. Symmetry of syllable patterns and onomatopoeic ideophones are culture- or rather language-bound and are very much like the features of poetry everywhere. A poem cannot be translated from one language to another and retain its important linguistic

Reprinted from *African Studies*, Vol. 16 (1957), 133–49, by permission of the author and the Witwatersrand University Press.

features. One can write only a new poem, using the poetic features of the new language. From this, one can see that in order to study the style of folkloristic materials, one needs to know the language in which the folklore is related.

The necessity for knowing the language is especially great in fixed-phrase forms of folklore, in which the exact wording is as traditional as the content or message conveyed. Riddles, proverbs, charms, nursery rhymes, and tongue twisters are all examples of fixed-phrase folklore forms. There may be over-all variation with respect to a given riddle or proverb as it is told by different members of the same culture, but one individual person will always recite the riddle or proverb using exactly the same words. An Englishman may say, "A bird in the hand is worth two in the bush." A German may say, "Ein Spatz in der Hand ist besser als eine Taube auf dem Dach." (A sparrow in the hand is better than a dove on the roof.) A Norwegian may say, "En fugl i hånden er bedre enn 10 på taket." (A bird in the hand is better than 10 on the roof.) Here is variation, but each person who utters the proverb will use exactly the same version every time.

This is in contrast to free-phrase folklore forms, in which the wording is not as traditional as the content. Most folktales (with the exception of formula tales, Aarne-Thompson Types 2009–2340) and most superstitions are free phrase. For example, one can say "Don't let a black cat cross your path" or "A black cat means bad luck" or "If a black cat crosses your path, you'll have bad luck" and so forth. The content is fixed, but the wording is not. The distinction between fixed- and free-phrase folklore forms is important for fieldwork inasmuch as it is imperative to obtain fixed-phrase forms in the informant's native language. It is, of course, also desirable to obtain free-phrase forms in the original language, but it is not quite as essential.

Miss Beuchat's study shows just how traditional the wording is in Bantu riddles. Her analysis demonstrates that there is literary art in riddle language even by Western poetic standards. It is only by such linguistic analyses of fixed-phrase folklore forms that one can comprehend and appreciate the subtleties and beauty of the composition of folk materials.

For other analyses of linguistic form in folklore, see William Bascom, "Literary Style in Yoruba Riddles," *Journal of American Folklore,* Vol. 62 (1949), 1–16; Thomas A. Sebeok, "The Texture of a Cheremis Incantation," *Mémoires de la Société Finno-Ougrienne,* Vol. 125 (1962), 523–27; Sebeok, "Sound and Meaning in a Cheremis Folksong Text," in *For Roman Jakobson,* comp. Morris Halle et al. (The Hague, 1956), pp. 430–39; and Thomas A. Sebeok and L. H. Orzack, "The Structure and Content of Cheremis Charms," *Anthropos,* Vol. 48 (1953), 369–88, 760–72. For a consideration of folkloristic structure with special reference to riddles and for further discussion of the distinction between folkloristic and linguistic structure, see Robert A. Georges and Alan Dundes, "Toward A Structural Definition of the Riddle," *Journal of American Folklore,* Vol. 76 (1963), 111–18.

Riddles are part of the culture of a people, and therefore are often surrounded with taboos. There are many riddles in different Bantu languages which are so alike that it is probable that they have a common origin, but this is not always easy to prove. Riddles are educational because of their varied content, but their primary aim is recreational. They refer to nature as a whole, and to the material and spiritual culture of the people. A great variety of structures, both in the "question" part and in the answer of the riddle, including rhythm and balance of forms, are among their characteristic features.

Introduction

1. The riddle combines recreational and educational features to an unusual degree. Young people love riddles for the amusement they provide; old people encourage their use because of their instructive value. These two aspects are reflected (a) in the very varied contents of the riddles, and (b) in their form, which is subtly adapted to the diversity of subjects referred to.

Because of their recreational and educational features, riddles are socially very significant, and therefore it is not surprising to find that among many tribes taboos are associated with their use.

Their great variety of contents and forms and their social importance make of riddles a most interesting and inspiring subject of study. If one compares the riddles found among many Bantu peoples, one is struck by the resemblances often found. Although many riddles have been collected by various authors, little comparative study of their social importance and of their structure and contents has been made so far. It is a comparative study, dealing with these various points, which will be attempted in this paper.

1.1. For the most part, the original orthography has been retained for the various examples of riddles quoted here. However, in the case of some South African languages, e.g., Kgatla (Kxatla), the spelling has been brought into line with present-day prescriptions. In some cases too, where the structures involved were quite clear, some modifications in the word division have been introduced. For typographical reasons also, it has been necessary to substitute β for the w with circumflex of Lamba, Mwera and Makua, and for the special v of Shona, both representing a voiced bilabial fricative; sv and zv for the symbols representing the voiceless and voiced "whistling" fricatives of Shona; and d for the symbol representing the voiced alveolar implosive of Shona.

Full bibliographical details of all the references cited are given in the bibliography at the end of the article.

The Social Setting of the Riddle

2. Few collectors of Bantu riddles have mentioned how and by whom riddles are indulged in as a pastime. This is an unfortunate omission, for much can be learned about the value and purpose of Bantu riddles by observing what section of the community is most interested in them, and

how important a part they play in the life of the people. The following information does throw some light on this question, however.

Doke, in his article "Bantu Wisdom Lore," describes the riddle as a form of entertainment "commonly indulged in around the fire at night, particularly by the young folk of the village."[1] This is too general a statement, for usages determining who makes use of the riddle, and at what particular time of the year or of the day, may vary considerably from tribe to tribe.

2.1. Among the *Kgatla*,

(a) It seems that riddles may be asked throughout the whole year.
(b) The evening is the appropriate time for riddles, and any child heard asking them during the day will be threatened that "a dog will place a calabash of fat on your head and you will (have to) go about with it,"[2] which statement is a common warning given to children. The child may even be sworn at or beaten.
(c) Riddles are indulged in mainly by children or young people.
(d) Two individuals or two teams may ask riddles of each other.

2.2. Nakene mentions that among the *Tlokwa* (Northern Sotho),

(a) Riddles may be asked at any time of the year.
(b) But they are asked only in the evening, mainly indoors, and anyone asking riddles during the daytime is threatened with becoming a fool.
(c) They are never used by the older people, unless an adult joins the young people to teach them how riddles should be asked.
(d) The team system seems to prevail. Nakene does not mention the possibility of only two people quizzing one another.

2.3. Among the *Tsonga-Ronga* tribes,

(a) The asking of riddles is not restricted to any particular time of the year.
(b) But only the evenings are considered suitable for riddles and telling of folktales. Junod mentions the common belief that persons who tell folktales during the day will become bald, but he does not specify what will be the fate of those who ask riddles at that time; possibly the same thing will befall them, as Junod treats those two evening pastimes together.
(c) Riddles are indulged in by young and old people, as an indoor game in winter, and occasionally as an outdoor game when the weather is suitable.
(d) They are mainly asked by competitive teams, although the game may be played by two children.

2.4. Among the *Shona*,

(a) Riddles, like the telling of folktales and the singing of songs, are usually banned "during the months when the crops are ripening and ready for the harvest and for threshing."[3]
(b) Riddle games take place only in the evening and are mainly an indoor form of entertainment.
(c) Children and adults alike entertain themselves by asking riddles.
(d) The games may be played "between two individuals or two sides."

---

1 C. M. Doke, "Bantu Wisdom-Lore," *African Studies*, Vol. 6, No. 3 (1947), 17.
2 I. Schapera, "Kxatla Riddles and Their Significance," *Bantu Studies*, Vol. 6, No. 3 (1932), 215.
3 G. Fortune, "Some Zezuru and Kalanga Riddles," *NADA* Vol. 28 (1951), 30.

2.5. *Lamba:* Doke does not mention if there is any restriction as to when riddles may be asked; he merely states that "playing at riddles *(ukutyoneka)* is a favourite pastime around the evening fire."[4] Children play at this game two at a time according to Doke's description, but there is no indication as to whether adults may participate, or whether team competitions take place.

2.6. Lyndon Harries gives no details of the playing of riddles in *Mwera;*[5] in *Makua,*[6] however, he mentions that

(a) Riddles are asked in the evening only; a person who asks riddles or tells folktales in the daytime would grow horns.
(b) No details are given of participants. Harries' description is of two persons playing the game, and he says nothing about teams.

2.7. Concerning the *Ila,* Smith and Dale mention that the riddles are asked in the evening, but they do not mention seasonal taboos or details of participants (Vol. 2, pp. 324ff.).

2.8. From the title of Comhaire-Sylvain's article "Quelques devinettes des enfants noirs de Léopoldville," it would seem that riddles are mainly the concern of children, although at the end of her article she mentions a riddle with proverbial reference which is used by adults and never by children. She gives no information about the time for riddle games, or the way riddles are asked.

2.9. Among the *Kamba,*

(a) Riddles are asked in the evening mainly. However, it seems that the Kamba do not object to telling riddles during the day, since Lindblom says, "A good many riddles I have also got from my porters while halting on a march."
(b) Children and adults enjoy guessing riddles.
(c) Lindblom gives no indication that riddles may be asked by two teams, rather than by two individuals.

2.10. From this brief survey, it is clear that in most cases riddles are considered mainly as a form of entertainment, and therefore are indulged in in the evenings and during the less busy months of the year. Although it is mostly young people who indulge in this pastime, in some tribes adults may also join in the fun. Either two individuals or two teams may compete in riddle games.

The Function of Riddles

3. It is clear from what has just been said that riddles have a much more restricted role in the people's life than proverbs. Riddles are often the concern of only one section of the community, and their use is usually restricted

---

[4] C. M. Doke, *Lamba Folklore* (New York: American Folklore Society, 1927), p. 549.
[5] L. Harries, "Some Riddles of the Mwera people," *African Studies,* Vol. 6, No. 1 (1947).
[6] L. Harries, "Some Riddles of the Makua people," *African Studies,* Vol. 1, No. 4 (1942), 275.

by certain taboos or traditions, whereas the proverb is a part of everyday speech. It follows that riddles have a more restricted and definite function than proverbs, although like proverbs they are an integral part of the people's culture and traditions. These functions are as follows:

(a) The main function of the riddle is as entertainment, and this is consciously recognized, whereas other functions of riddles are often not recognized at all by the people.
(b) The riddle also acts as an exercise of intellectual skill and quickness of wit; it becomes a test of memory with those riddles whose answers have to be learned by heart to be known.
(c) Nakene[7] points out that many riddles are instructive, as they may mention geographical names or contain reference to historical events. Certainly they develop a sense of observation and often contain elaborate and rich linguistic forms.

Like proverbs, riddles are educational in their content, which is based on experience and observation. The educational value of riddles is a consequence of their cultural content, but their primary purpose is for entertainment.

The Origin of Bantu Riddles

4. Some riddles are widespread throughout the Bantu area, and this immediately raises the question as to whether they have a common origin.[8]

Q. *Ndamanga nyumba yanga yopanda khomo.* A. *Dzira.* (I have built my house without any door. An egg.) [Nyanja][9]

Q. *Nyumba yangu kubwa, haina mlango.* A. *Yayi.* (My house is large, it has no door. An egg.) [Swahili]

Q. *Ntlo yagotlhôka molômo.* A. *Lekgopa.* (A house without a mouth. An egg.) [Tlokwa]

Q. *Mpolêllê dilô, ompolêllê gore ntlo êtshwêu êesenang mojakô keeng?* A. *Kelee.* (Tell me something, tell me what is the white hut which has no door? It is an egg.) [Kgatla]

Q. *Akaŋanda mbuluβulu?* A. *Mbesana: lili-po nemulyaŋgo?* (A little house absolutely entire? An egg: has it any door?) [Lamba]

Q. *Nyama moko asalaki ndako, kasi ezangi porte, ezangi lininisa, yango nini?* A. *Like.* (An animal built a house, but it lacks a door, it lacks windows, what is it? An egg.) [Lingala]

Q. *Ndzinghenile ndlwini yamanana, ndzikume xilo xohava nomu.* A. *Itandza.* (I entered my mother's house, I found something without a mouth. It is an egg.) [Tsonga]

Q. *Wuruwuru kayano.* A. *Nyoce.* (Round with no mouth. An egg.) [Makua]

Q. *Caŋgali nnaŋgo.* A. *Liji.* (It has no door. An egg.) [Mwera]

Q. *Zihari risina musuo.* A. *Zai.* (The huge pot without an opening. An egg.) [Zezuru]

---

[7] G. Nakene, "Tlokwa Riddles," *African Studies*, Vol. 2, No. 3 (1943), 126.

[8] The question of origin is further complicated by the fact that the specific riddle of the egg now cited by Beuchat, as well as a number of the other Bantu riddles mentioned, are found in many other parts of the world. For a discussion of the egg riddle of the house without doors, see Archer Taylor, *English Riddles from Oral Tradition* (Berkeley and Los Angeles, 1951), pp. 473–75.—ED. NOTE

[9] Q = Question; A = Answer. The language of the riddle is given in brackets in each case.

4.1. It is interesting to note the variations between these riddles in the setting of the problem. In the first seven examples, the egg is compared to a house, and then reference is made to its lacking an opening of some sort (mouth, door, window). In Mwera, although the word "house" does not appear in the riddle, it is nevertheless implied. In Makua, the egg is described but not compared to anything, and in Zezuru it is compared to a big pot. Note that in the Tsonga riddle the "house" concept does not refer to the egg itself: the object without a mouth was found *in the house*. Again, in most of these riddles the mouth or opening concept appears in the question part of the riddle. In Lamba, however, it is in the answer that it is referred to, and in the form of a question. This shifting of "elements," common in folktales, is a most interesting feature of riddles which deserves investigation.

4.2. The following four riddles use the same metaphor to describe the mushroom, and it is tempting to suggest for them a common origin. However, the shape of most mushrooms is so similar to that of a hut, that the comparison is an easy and natural one, and it would be unwise to dogmatize about these riddles having a single origin.[10]

> Q. *Ndako moko ezali na likonzi yoko.* A. *Liyebo.* (There is a house with only one pillar. A mushroom.) [Lingala]
> Q. *Nyumba jikuluŋgwa lwici limo-pe.* A. *Uβai.* (A big house, only one supporting post. A mushroom.) [Mwera]
> Q. *Iŋande yemama luhomelo lumo.* A. *Uβahi.* (My mother's house, one supporting post. A mushroom.) [Makonde]
> Q. *Ndamanga nyumba yamzati umodzi.* A. *Boa.* (I have built a house with one center post. A mushroom.) [Nyanja]

In the case of Kgatla and Ganda the comparison used to describe the mushroom is more farfetched, and if, after some investigation, it were found widely spread, one could more readily postulate a single origin for this riddle:

> Q. *Kgaka yaseêma-kankoto, serope kentsêtsênênê.* A. *Keleboa.* (The guineafowl that stands on one leg, its thigh is very tasty. A type of edible mushroom.) [Kgatla]
> Q. *Obunagenzere Buganda, bakamba enkoko yokuguru kumu.* (I went to Buganda and the people gave me a one-legged chicken to eat.) [Ganda]

In the Kgatla riddle is added an explanation about the taste of the guineafowl's leg, which explanation is not essential to the comprehension of the riddle and is somewhat superfluous. However, this provides an important link with the idea of eating in the Ganda version, and suggests that the answer refers to something edible.

4.3. Many more riddles are found in various tribes, and resemble each other so strongly that polygenesis is distinctly doubtful. However, a great many riddles are not related. In his *Lamba Folklore*, p. 549, Doke mentions that many riddles may be found in one village and be totally unknown in

---

10 However, Taylor, p. 469, cites many East European and African texts of this mushroom riddle. The distribution confirms Beuchat's suggestion of a common tradition rather than polygenetic parallelism.—ED. NOTE

the next. Junod seems to imply the same thing when he says of riddles: "Some are the common property of both the Ba-Ronga and Ba-Nkuna; they seem to be very popular throughout the Thonga tribe."[11] Such a statement implies that other riddles occur in one section of the tribe only.

If some resemblance between the riddles is found, it must be remembered that this may be due to the fact that this type of folklore is based very much on observation: such things as fire, the stars, a mealie-cob, etc., retain their general characteristics wherever they are found and can easily give rise to very similar images.

A few other reasons make the task of determining the origin of riddles more difficult than is the case with proverbs; for instance:

(a) Fewer riddles have been recorded than proverbs.
(b) Few, or no riddles are related to folktales, and this eliminates the possibility of tracing the origin or diffusion of a riddle through a folktale (the diffusion of a folktale is easier to trace than that of a short form such as a proverb or a riddle).
(c) Riddles are the result of wit and deliberate invention and therefore are more likely to vary in form than proverbs.

Only a thorough investigation might give some clues as to the origin of some riddles.

Types of Bantu Riddles and Their Form

5. This section will be subdivided into two main parts: 1, *General Structure*, where the various types of riddles and their literary form and structure as a whole will be considered. In Part 2, *Linguistic Structure*, details of word and grammatical forms will be considered.

PART 1: GENERAL STRUCTURE

6. The "Frame" of the Riddle in Bantu

Often riddles are presented within a "frame," or formula, i.e., a specific, stereotyped phrase which is associated with either the question or answer part of the riddle, or both.[12]

In Kgatla the question is framed in the formula *Mpolêllê dilô, ompolêllê gore...keeng?* (Tell me something, tell me what is...?).[13] After the first riddle, the formula is often omitted or only *Mpolêllê* (Tell me) is retained.

Among the Ronga-Tsonga, *Teka, teka, teka, heee...* (Take, take take...) precedes the riddle. *Tseke-tseke, wakutseke...* or simply *Tseke-tseke...* is often heard too.

The Lamba say *Tyo!*, an expression which means "Guess the riddle,"

---

11 H. A. Junod, *The Life of a South African Tribe* (Neuchâtel: Attinger, 1913), Vol. 2, 181.

12 The introductory and/or concluding frame elements are also common in European riddle traditions. For a discussion of these, see the standard treatise on riddle rhetoric, Robert Petsch, *Neue Beiträge zur Kenntnis des Volksrätsels*, Palaestra 4 (Berlin, 1899), pp. 51–65.—ED. NOTE

13 Schapera, *op. cit.*, p. 217.

before each riddle, and the person challenged answers *Ka kesa* (Let it come)
or *Ka muleta* (Bring it).

The Kamba say *Kwata ndai* (Take hold of the riddle) before putting a
riddle to a person, and the opponent answers *Nakwata* (I have caught hold).
Then the first person presents the riddle itself.

In Zezuru there does not seem to be any formula of this type, although the
game is often started when a person challenges another with *Hatitaurirane
zirahwe* (Let us swop riddles). In Kalanga most riddle games are started
with the challenge *Ngailibane* (Let us puzzle with one another).

6.1. In the sources consulted, only in Northern Sotho has a frame for
the answer been found: *Yare*[14] *gokwa, kerialo:...kele bjang?* (On hearing
I say:..., I being how?). The word which constitutes the answer is found in
a possessive construction, as the possessor of *ngwana* (child), e.g.,

> Q. *Sehlaga saMmamašianoka, seôkama bodiba.* A. *Yare gokwa kerialo:
> Ngwana-letswêlê lakgômo, kele bjang?* (Nest of a hamerkop hangs (sus-
> pended) over the deep pool. On hearing I say: Child of the udder of a
> cow, I being how?)

The essential part of the answer here is "the udder of a cow," while the
deep pool over which it hangs is the milkpail. The frame of the answer here
might be more freely translated as "On hearing (your riddle) I say...how
is that for an answer?" The hamerkop (*Scopus umbretta*) builds an
enormous nest in a tree, usually in a branch overhanging water.

7. The "Question" Part of the Riddle

7.1. Interrogative form of the question.

(a) In a very great number of riddles, in the majority perhaps, the question
part of the riddle takes the form of a simple statement, positive or negative.
However, this is not always the case, and therefore Doke's statement
"Though interrogative in intent riddles are never so in form in Bantu,"[15]
and Lindblom's similar remark,[16] are perhaps applicable to many Bantu
languages, but not true of all of them. In Tsonga, Ronga, and Tswana
(Kgatla) it is very common to find an interrogative word in the question.

> Q. *Lexi, nambi waba, ntshonsi wakone wungabonekiki, ntxini?* A. *Imati.* (The
> thing which you can beat without leaving a scar, what is it? Water.)
> [Ronga]
> Q. *Intxini lexi, loko bahlota xone, batekaka khume djatinhonga kambe kuyad-
> laya tibiri?* A. *Inhwala.* (What is the thing which you hunt with ten sticks,
> and which you use only two sticks to kill? A louse.) [Ronga][17]

---

14 Alternatively *Kare....*

15 Doke, *op. cit.,* p. 117.

16 G. Lindblom, "Kamba Riddles, Proverbs, and Songs," *Archives d'Etudes Orientales,*
Vol. 20, No. 28 (1934), 4.

17 This and the preceding riddle have non-African analogues. For the smashed object
which is not broken or cut, see Taylor, p. 508. For the riddle of the louse, see Taylor,
pp. 360–63. It is interesting that there are close Indic parallels, e.g., a Baiga text which
tells how ten men go to beat the bushes while only two men do the killing. The cultural
and historical connections between India and Africa, especially East Africa, can be seen
in folklore parallels. By the same token, some of the riddle texts from Jamaica cited by
Taylor are very probably African transplants. One (Taylor No. 971e) relates how ten

(b) The very formula of the Kgatla riddle, *Mpolêlê dilô, mpolêlê gore...
keeng?* is interrogative in form. Tlokwa also has a few riddles with an
interrogative "question."

Q. *Sekanyanakanyana, mafoko seatsayakae?* A. *Ketaola.* (It is so very small,
whence does it take the words? It is the divining bone.) [Kgatla]

Q. *Kahampa-kahampa katswalêla kae?* A. *Thaba.* (I keep on going along where
shall I bear? A mountain.) [Tlokwa]

(c) Note also the following song-riddle in Makua:

Q. *Neninne? Neninne? Salakela, ikereca inorwa, inokela unatiβira; Kwiria,
Inama yani?* A. *Haβara.* (Who is that? Who is that? *salakela,* the spots are
going, they are going into hiding; It is said, What animal is that? The
leopard.)

7.2. Simple sentence type.

Usually the "question" of the riddle consists of a simple sentence, a mere
statement with some description of the thing to be guessed.

Q. *Kanthu kosagona tulo.* A. *Madzi.* (Something which does not sleep. Water.)
[Nyanja]

Q. *Akanama takakwete mafupa.* A. *Mbomunsundu.* (A little animal without
bones. The leech.) [Lamba][18]

Q. *Diphiri tsêtlhano tsêditsênang mômosimêng ole mongwe.* A. *Kemenwana.*
(Five hyenas which go into the same hole. It is the fingers.) [Kgatla]

Q. *Kuku wangu akazalia miibani.* A. *Nanasi.* (My hen has laid among thorns.
A pineapple.) [Swahili]

7.3. Compound sentence type.

(a) Often the "question" consists of more than one statement.

Q. *Selô semakhuntukhuntu ekete setlaitsidila, pôtô emôgodimo gasônê, mme
dinaka ekete tsapholo.* A. *Kekgopana.* (The crooked thing seems as if it
will stretch itself, a pot is on top of it, and its horns are like those of an
ox. It is a snail.) [Kgatla]

Q. *Nnamba tie liwundi bata.* A. *Liunde nalitaka.* (The glossy starling above,
the owl beneath. Heaven and earth.) [Mwera]

Q. *Uhokala mwiri mmoka, irinta cefe cikitthi, matthakuru meli, irinta pili
cowuma.* A. *Ipuri.* (There is a tree, it has four fresh branches, two leaves,
and two dry branches. A goat.) [Makua]

(b) The second statement is often a further explanation of the first one. In
this type of "question" the subject of both sentences is usually the same.

Q. *Akantu aka fwale'ŋguo ituβile, pakwinjila pamenda, neli kutontola, i?* A.

---

men go to fetch one prisoner, but only two bring him. The point is that if we did not
know that the American Negro originated from Africa, we could have surmised it from
the folklore evidence alone. Although American Negroes did borrow much European
folklore, there are a great number of unmistakable elements of African folklore in the
New World.

Folklore parallels constitute one of the best kinds of data for either forming a hypothesis concerning the possible contact or relationship between two peoples or confirming
such a hypothesis made originally on the basis of archaeological, linguistic, or other
evidence. In theory, the more closely related two peoples are or the more contact these
peoples have had, the more likely it is that they have folklore cognates. For example, the
close parallels in Asian and American Indian folklore, even without the aid of other
kinds of anthropological evidence, point to a common tradition. See Gudmund Hatt,
Asiatic Influences in American Folklore (Copenhagen, 1949).—ED. NOTE

[18] See Taylor, p. 91, for European versions of the leech riddle, some of which are in
the form of compound and complex sentences.—ED. NOTE

Mbecusi. (A little thing that dresses in white calico, when it enters the water, it does not even get wet. Steam.) [Lamba]

Q. *Intxini amixweni xifamba himune wamilenge, ninhlekani xifamba hamimbiri, amadambyeni loko dambu djipelile xifamba himilenge miraru?* A. *Imunhu.* (What is it that walks with four legs in the morning, with two legs at midday, and with three legs in the evening, when the sun has gone down? It is a person.) [Ronga][19]

(c) The second statement, or the third, may be negative.

Q. *Kukuya ndachiyana, ku kuzhoka shichiyene.* A. *Mume.* (Going I found it, returning I found it not. Dew.) [Ila]

Q. *Ngunda gwaŋkuluŋgwa kuuna yalya ŋgagumbala mkono.* A. *Umbo.* (A big field, harvesting the food, it does not fill the hand. The hair of the head.) [Mwera]

Q. *Mpolêllê, bana bankêtê baabina, mmaabô gaabine.* A. *Kedikala tsasetlhare.* (The children of someone are dancing, their mother does not dance. It is the branches of a tree.) [Kgatla]

(d) The Lamba riddle given above, referring to steam, also illustrates a third statement which is negative. No riddle with two negative statements was found, but quite possibly some of this type do exist.

(e) The whole "question" part of the riddle may be a negative statement.

Q. *Nyumba jaŋgu jaŋgali taa.* A. *Likabuli.* (My house has no lamp. The grave.) [Mwera]

Q. *Nanjeŋguli ŋgamoga.* A. *Mbwa.* (Mr. Patch does not cut his hair. A dog.) [Mwera]

Q. *Caŋgaunicila.* A. *Liiko.* (What is not covered. A well.) [Mwera]

(f) The whole statement may be reduplicated.

Q. *Tsheke, tsheke, xo gi, xo gi!* A. *Xirhendzevuti.* (It goes round, it goes round.[20] A circle.) [Tsonga]

Q. *Leno vatshivela ndzilo, leno vatshivela ndzilo.* A. *Leno vaba ngoma, leno vaba ngoma.* (They just kindle a fire, they just kindle a fire. They just beat a drum, they just beat a drum.) [Tsonga] [A mere comparison.]

Q. *Adzoti, adzoti, axaya.* A. *Tiko.* (I tried to do it, I tried to do it, I failed. The back of the head.) [Kalanga] [One cannot see the back of one's own head.]

7.4. The short-story type.

A few riddles have been noticed in the above examples which consist of more than one statement. It is but one step from there to the very lengthy riddles. It is really quite arbitrary to subdivide such riddles into different categories, but this will be done to contrast this type with those discussed under 7.5.

Q. *Eyenga ezali awa, kenda kobenga mokonzi! Obengi mokonzi, yo nainu okumi te, ye asili akomi o mboka.* A. *Mbila.* (There is a feast here, go and call the chief! You call the chief, you have not yet arrived and yet he is already at the village. A cluster of palm fruit.) [Lingala]

Q. *Ndinapita kwa bwenzi langa nandiyalira mphasa, ndisanakhale anakhala ena.* A. *Ncence.* (I went to my friend's [house understood], he spread a mat before me, before I sat others sat. A fly.) [Nyanja]

---

[19] The reference is, of course, to the "four-legged" crawling of a child, walking of an adult, and use of a stick as a "third leg" by an old person. A similar riddle was found for Shona. There exists a common English riddle which is essentially the same as these. [This is the famous riddle of the sphinx. See Taylor, pp. 20–24.—ED. NOTE]

[20] *gi* is an ideophone—denoting the action of going round, turning.

Q. *Weta utthela maβaja. βano urwa maʃeŋgoni, kahokoleeke, inupa imoka uhitthia ilaku yonyocolia, inupa ikwawe uhitthia ilaku wapeiya nimapururu aya. βanoβa uruia iʃima inupa copili, kuwiheria mlopwana ole. Matthapa ombone paβi?* A. *Ilaku yohinyocolia.* (To set out to marry two wives. Now to go to work, when I return, at one house a plucked fowl is killed, at the other house a fowl is cooked with its feathers. Now porridge is stirred in both houses and brought to the husband. Which is the better relish? The unplucked fowl [a symbol of the wife who during a man's absence at work has been faithful to him].) [Makua]

7.5. One-word type.

As opposed to the long explanation, statements of one word only are also found to constitute the "question" part of the riddle.

Q. *Silitha.* A. *Tulo.* (Never ending. Sleep.) [Nyanja]
Q. *Sioneka.* A. *Mphepo.* (Invisible. The wind.) [Nyanja]
Q. *Osawerengeka.* A. *Maudzu.* (Innumerable. The grass.) [Nyanja]
Q. *Caŋgaunicila.* A. *Liiko.* (What is not covered? A well.) [Mwera]

7.6. Phrase type.

Under this heading could be classified all the riddles whose "question" consists of a possessive phrase (two words), or two words linked by a conjunctive formative, or a verb and adverb, etc.

Q. *Kuenda kwaCipegede.* A. *Nguruve.* (The gait of the lumpish, ill-mannered person. The pig.) [Zezuru] (Possessive phrase.)
Q. *Xikhatu xatsuri.* A. *Likulu lamandza.* (The bottom of the mortar. The large side of the egg.) [Tsonga] (Possessive phrase.)
Q. *Kalama nampemba.* A. *Mbeŋguo.* (The watchman and the councilor. Calico.) [Lamba] (Two coordinated nouns.)
Q. *Icilila pamo.* A. *Mbeciwi.* (That which eats in one place only. The door.) [Lamba] (Relative and adverb.)
Q. *Icine camusi.* A. *Mbensima.* (The owner of the village. The porridge.) [Lamba]. (Possessive phrase.)

8. *The Answer to the Riddle*

8.1. For the majority of riddles the answer consists of one word only.

Q. *Shumba mbiri dzakagaririra gomo.* A. *Nzeve.* (Two lions are waiting on the hill. The ears.) [Zezuru]
Q. *Mokonzi moko, akofandaka se o kati ya nzube.* A. *Lolemo.* (A chief who only sits among thorns. The tongue.) [Lingala]
Q. *Malwa ate 'ntse'.* A. *Indlala.* (The one who fights silently. It is hunger.) [Tsonga]
Q. *Ndayaya intite, ibanda diezula buloa.* A. *Mudilo.* (I killed a little bird and the plain filled with blood. The fire. [Ila]
Q. *Nimepanda koonde yangu kubwa, nimevuna, haujaa mkono.* A. *Nyele.* (I sowed my big field and reaped it, and my hand was not full. Hair. [Swahili]
Q. *Ingombe yakesu ikumba butete.* A. *Mbwato.* (Our cow rubs the reeds. A canoe.) [Tonga]

8.2 Many answers consist of two words, nouns usually, often in a copulative construction. This is the case mainly when the question itself describes two things.

Q. *Tshimo êntsho emabêlê-maswêu.* A. *Kelegodimo ledinalêdi.* (A black garden with white corn. It is the sky and the stars.) [Kgatla]

Q. *Icine cimo, utunwa ikumi.* A. *Mbeculu nemisombo.* (Itself one, its mother ten. An anthill and the holes therein.) [Lamba]

Q. *M'nyumba imodzi amao ali ndi azi ndi ana onse amene ali ndi madazi.* A. *Mwezi ndi nyenyezi.* (In one house the mother is bald, and so are all the children. The moon and the stars.) [Nyanja]

Q. *Ala naala utunana.* A. *Nittho niipula.* (This one and this one love each other. The eye and the nose [they are close together].) [Makua]

Q. *Ndakuliba nebudzi lakawa pakati kwamanhaŋga.* A. *Mŋedzi nenyenyedzi.* (I puzzle you with a melon that fell among the pumpkins. The moon and the stars.) [Kalanga]

8.3. In a great number of cases the answer consists of a possessive phrase, i.e., a noun + qualificative, which really is an extended form of type 7.2. above. This also may appear in a copulative construction.

Q. *Akacekulu kalipalawila.* A. *Mbomutondo wabwalwa.* (The gnome that boils over itself. A pot of beer.) [Lamba]

Q. *Fyonsefi fyanji, ne mwine ncile?* A. *Mbamunsisiŋga kuβuluβa.* (All these are mine, I myself go over them. The wasp at the flowers.) [Lamba]

Q. *Ndrapala mhina inama βatthe.* A. *Ifiniŋki yolaku* or *Itthanyaŋgo yolaku.* (Skin on the inside, flesh outside. Gizzard of a fowl.) [Makua]

Q. *Selô sêsesekang setlhôfala môfatsheng.* A. *Keleoto lamotho.* (The thing that is never away from the ground. It is the foot of a person.) [Kgatla]

There are many other examples of riddles the answer of which consists of two words. These may be a noun with its qualificative, as above, or a subject (noun) and verb, etc.

Q. *Tuβuri tuβiri tunoramba kuzara; munopinda βanhu, mombe, mbudzi nezvimŋe.* A. *Tuziso tuβiri.* (Two little holes that refuse to be filled; there enter people, oxen, goats and other things. Two little eyes.) [Zezuru]

Q. *Monse mucalo kali maβeŋga.* A. *Mbemilando munsila.* (Throughout the country there are slices. The fallen trees in the path.) [Lamba]

Q. *Tihuku takaMuzila tocina hiswisuka matsutsu.* A. *Mbita yavila.* (Muzila's hens dance with their tails. The pot is boiling.) [Tsonga]

Q. *Tamba, ndakwira.* A. *Tsaiya iri kuβira.* (Play, I have climbed up. A pot on the boil.) [Zezuru]

Q. *Mvura cena.* A. *Dada jena.* (Clear water. A white duck.) [Zezuru]

8.4. Some cases have been found where the answer consists of one word followed by an explanatory sentence, which can almost be considered as parenthetical, and given to explain a somewhat obscure answer.

Q. *Wonse βaisala, βuliciti bwasyala.* A. *Mbecinu, tacisala-po.* (All have closed, the stamping has remained. The pestle-mortar, it does not close up.) [Lamba]

Q. *Akaŋanda mbuluβulu?* A. *Mbesana, lilipo nemulyaŋgo?* (A little house absolutely entire. An egg, has it any door?) [Lamba]

Q. *Umusitu peulu, umuloŋga pansi?* A. *Mbemfuko, pakuti ubwina pansi, amafuki peulu.* (A swamp-forest above, the stream beneath. A mole, for his tunnel is beneath, the molehill above.) [Lamba]

Q. *Ndapha nyama, pamene ndasenda ndatenga cikopa ndataya; Ndatenga matumba ndataya, ndipo ndadya minofu yokha.* A. *Papaya, Sitidya kungu ndi nthanga.* (I have killed game, when I have skinned it, I have taken the skin and I have thrown it away; I have taken the entrails and thrown them away, and I have eaten only the flesh. Pawpaw, we do not eat the skin and the seeds.) [Nyanja]

8.5 We have seen that with the majority of riddles the answer consists of one word only. With a smaller number it consists of two words, which, however, constitute one semantic unit. But many riddles are to be found which have a whole sentence as answer. These are especially numerous in Tsonga-Ronga, where riddles with a one-word answer are in the minority. In other Bantu languages such riddles are rarer, and Schapera mentions that none were found in Kgatla.

Q. *Kuringe mbhaha, kukokole nkuku.* A. *Namuntlha kuni ntsuvi yobiha, ayikoti kuxa.* (The hen has crowed and the cock has cackled. Today there is such a bad mist that the sun cannot appear.) [Tsonga]

Q. *Lexofa xibohiwile.* A. *Ivele loko ribolela emakhambeni yarona.* (The thing which is dead while still clinging (to the stem). A cob of mealies rotten while still in its leaves on the stem.) [Tsonga]

Q. *Motu abomi nyama, motu akomi na nsima, nyama akomi liboso.* A. *Ntina lokola: okei kokata mbila, mbila ekokwa liboso na mabele, yo na nsima.* (A person kills an animal, the person arrives after, the animal before. I answer: A person cuts a palmfruit cluster, it falls down before, he afterwards.) [Lingala]

The answer, consisting of a whole sentence, can even take the form of a question or a negative statement.

Q. *Syu waβatuka βamama.* A. *Mbomukulu wacilile-po iculu ninani?* ("Syu" has reviled my mother. What big man has ever jumped over an anthill?) [Lamba][21]

Q. *Motu moko akonaki bilanga ya pilipili, mpe ye akoliaka pilipili yango te.* A. *Lokola: Soko oboti mwana ya mwasi, yo moto okokwela ye? Te.* (A man planted fields of chillies, and himself does not eat those chillies. Answer: If you have a daughter, would you marry her, you a man? No.) [Lingala]

Q. *Ndacera msampha wanga kalangali kapita.* A. *Mphepo. Sigwidwa mu msampha.* (I have set my trap—the "kalangali" has already gone. The wind is not caught in a trap.) [Nyanja]

9. General Observations

9.1. Some riddles have several possible answers for the same question.

Q. *Tsheke, tsheke, waku tsheke, hilexiyaa!* A. (i) *Xingwala-ngwandla* or (ii) *Irikarhi.* (Tsheke, tsheke, he said, tsheke, it is yonder there!) (i) That which is doing *ngwala-ngwandla* (the thunder), or (ii) A little zebra [pierced by an arrow].) [Tsonga]

Q. *Ici tacikala kulutende?* A. (i) *Mbenguni,* or (ii) *Mbenama.* (What does not sit on a grass stalk? (i) A honey guide, or (ii) An animal.) [Lamba]

Q. *Cedembo, tamba, ndaβata muswe.* A. (i) *Badza,* or (ii) *Mugoti.* (Play, polecat, I've got hold of your tail. (i) Hoe, or (ii) Porridge-stirring stick.) [Zezuru]

9.2. Some riddles seem to indicate no similarity of idea between the ques-

---

[21] "Herein is a reference to a peculiar custom. Supposing A is beating B, and B pronounces the name of his own father, A will leave off beating B, lest he should get into trouble with the latter's father, on the grounds of having criminally defamed him." Doke, *op. cit.,* p. 567.

tion and the answer, and only similitude of sound is observable. Usually there is great resemblance between the question and answer as far as the structure of the sentences is concerned, and this adds to the effect of balance and alliteration. Such examples perhaps should be treated under a special category, "the jingle."

Q. *Hikumi nkuhlu, uwupfa-wupfa, kakusala huhlu yin'we.* A. *Hikumi mulungu, awondja-wondja, kakusala ndjepfu yin'we.* (We found a *nkuhlu* which ripens, which ripens; only one nut is found. We found a white man, who gets thinner, who gets thinner; nothing is left but a hair of his beard.) [Ronga]

9.3. With many riddles the meaning is obscure and in such cases an explanation of the answer is necessary; in recording riddles, many researchers have failed to record the explanations, considering only the formulas of the answer and of the question. However, among the players of riddle games, the explanation is often given, especially to young children or to persons not initiated in the game. The answers to such obscure riddles are learned by heart by the people of the community.

Q. *Sejêre mahlaka, seaeba-eba.* A. *'Mamolangoane—masiba aeôna ahlôôhông.* (It carries reeds on its head, it rocks, it rocks. The secretary bird—its feathers are on its head.) [Southern Sotho]

In many cases, however, the riddle is so obscure that no meaning can be attached to it.

Q. *Bekhumbi.* A. *Mayo, kufa.* (The people against the wall. Ah! if only I should die.) [Ronga]

PART 2: LINGUISTIC STRUCTURE

10. Special words or grammatical forms are often found in riddles; a few of them are noted here, but many more no doubt remain to be described.

10.1. Frequent use of ideophones in the riddles, in the "question" part mainly, but occasionally in the answer too, has been noted.

Q. *Tsheke, tsheke, 'kotlo'!* A. *Infenhe.* (Tsheke, tsheke, it hides itself! It is the baboon.) [Tsonga]
Q. *Ndzihoxile nseve wuya ku 'dzi.'* A. *Ndzicerile timanga tiya ku 'tshoko.'* (I have thrown an arrow, it has struck deep. I have dug peanuts, they are plentiful.) [Tsonga]
Q. *Xiba 'chuyu.'* A. *Ixidzengwe.* (It does *'chuyu.'* It is the jerboa.) [Tsonga]
Q. *'Unoku buda.'* A. *Luwajo.* (Covering, uncovering. It is the foot.) [Mwera]
Q. *Mpolêllê, 'dompi donkgôtswe'!* A. *Ketlhapi.* (Tell me *'dompi donkgôtswe.'* It is the fish [plunging in the water].) [Kgatla]

10.2. The subject of the verb of the metaphor, or the subject of reference, is often indicated by a noun in the diminutive, occasionally in the augmentative, although there may be no special reference to a small or big object.

Q. *Akalindi inswaswa pa.* A. *Mbameno.* (The little hole full of grass litter. The teeth.) [Lamba]
Q. *Kakomana anoridza tapreta.* A. *Rurimi.* (The little chap who plays the typewriter. The tongue.) [Zezuru]

Q. *Kamba kaŋgu kakasviβa kunze, kukacena pamusuo, kukatsvuka mukati mako.* A. *Huso hutema, mazino macena, mukanwa ͵mutsvukutsvuku.* (My little house is black outside, white at the door, and red within. A black face, white teeth, a red, red mouth.) [Zezuru]

Q. *Akanama kakalukwiso'luβilo, pakusaŋge' nsila yakaβyakwe, kakacileko'-βukali.* A. *Mbomulilo.* (The little animal that comes swiftly, but when it reaches the path of its little mate, it leaves off its fierceness. The fire.) [Lamba]

Q. *Ziβako raβaKuzhoko.* A. *Mazino.* (The huge cave of Mr. Kuzhoko. The teeth.) [Zezuru]

Q. *Makomana akapfeka zvipepe gumi zvakafanana.* A. *Nzara neminwe.* (The big boys have put on ten caps like one another. The nails and fingers.) [Zezuru]

10.3. For the sake of conciseness, words are often compounded in riddles.

Q. *Lendlwini kamamana kupfurha ndzilomungoma.* A. *Lendlwini kamamana valahla munhu wakufa.* (In mother's hut, the firewitchdoctor is burning. In mother's hut, they are burying a dead man.) [Tsonga]

Q. *Ndzihlangene nanhwanyana wakaxikosimananga.* A. *Ndzihlangene nanhlalala-mananga.* (I have met a girl turning her back-on-the-desert [lit. of the nape-desert]. I have met the honey bird of the desert.) [Tsonga]

Q. *Majoê, mabetsa-holê.* A. *Mahlô.* (The stones, the far-throwers. The eyes.) [Southern Sotho]

Q. *Bahlankana ba-kola-tšoêu, baêntsêng mokoloko.* A. *Telegrafi.* (The young men with the white headdresses, who are in a row. Telegraph poles.) [Southern Sotho]

10.4. Reduplication of the whole "question" part of the riddle has been noted already. More common, however, is the reduplication of one word only, or part of a word, in the riddle. This serves as a device to indicate diminution, augmentation or intensification; more often it is merely for the sound effect.

Q. *Tinyeleti madzala-dzala.* A. *Vana vamana un'we vadya hikutovana.* (The stars are far away from each other. The children of a woman eat and pinch one another.) [Tsonga]

Q. *Napite kukajaŋgu boi βala kotimaŋga jika koti koti koti.* A. *Mpuŋga.* (I went to my friend's, all of them bending, bending, bending. Rice.) [Mwera]

10.5. In a great number of riddles the subject of the action of the metaphor is in the first person singular.

Q. *Kahorwa waanlokwaka kahountthelia icuβe yolipa.* A. *Mtthale.* (I went to my friend and a hard piece of sugar cane was broken for me. Bamboo.) [Makua]

Q. *Ndinanto yam ivuza amanzi ngambambo.* A. *Intluzo nxa kuhluzwayo* (I have a thing which oozes water through its ribs. Beer strainer when straining.) [Xhosa]

10.6. In very many riddles there is reference to "my father," "my mother," and other relatives; another word which is often used as subject in the metaphor is "animal." This is just a conventional usage which does not in fact refer at all to any of the relatives mentioned or to any animal.

Q. *Mwasi na tata akamati libumu na mokongo.* A. *Mpende.* (The wife of my father carries her belly on her back. The calf of the leg.) [Lingala]

Q. *Bandeko babale bakotambola ndenge yoko.* A. *Makolo.* (Two brothers who walk in the same way. The legs.) [Lingala]

Q. *M'nyumba yamai alipo munthu waalamba ambiri.* A. *Mtolo wa nzama.* (In the house of my mother there is a person of many belts. A bundle of *nzama* beans.) [Nyanja]

Q. *Mombe yaɓaɓa waŋgu yawira mudziβa; ndasara, ndaɓata muswe.* A. *Mukombe muciroŋgo.* (My father's ox fell into the pool; I remained and held its tail. The water ladle in the pot.) [Zezuru]

Q. *Nyama yoko enene, ekoliaka mikolo minso pe ekotondakate.* A. *Mabele.* (The big animal, it eats always and is not yet full. The earth [swallowing water, corpses, seeds, etc.].) [Lingala]

10.7. In riddles are to be found many archaic words and structures no longer used in everyday speech. These, to be understood by children, have to be explained to them by older playmates or by adults. Riddles are rich in colorful idioms, many of which reflect some aspect of the people's spiritual or material culture.

Q. *Akauβi kujaŋgala-jaŋgala-pe, aimba citamile-pe mbo mbo mbo.* A. *Litende lyaukana.* (Mr. Leopard just trotting along, Mr. Lion just sits doing nothing. A pot of beer.) [Mwera][22]

Q. *Naŋkwakwa kulya likonde mcilo-li mbanda.* A. *Lijela.* (A lizard eating the bush, the tail is in a hole. A hoe.) [Mwera][23]

Nakene mentions that in Tlokwa such words as *nkekenene* (round), *sedibêlô* (a calabash for fat), *medupi* (rain that falls continually), and many other words which are found in riddles are never used in ordinary speech.[24]

Rhythm of the Riddles

11. Endemann, in his article "Rätsel der Sotho," describes a type of riddle in which the question and the answer, he says, are set in verse, the governing element of which is rhythm based on stress or beat.[25]

Q.   *Monna êmohubêtswana*
            Kamohwêtsa aduste.
            Ahlôka le-"êšêê morêna."
            (A little reddish man,
            I found him seated,
            He even lacked [to say] "Greetings Sir.")
A.   *Yare gokwa kerialô:*
            Ngwana-seolo,

---

[22] Instead of *citamile, citemi* could be used. In fact, "in ordinary speech, the form -*temi* is generally employed." Harries, *op. cit.,* p. 32.

[23] "*mcilo-li,* coalescence of final vowel *a* with initial *u* in form with the defective verb, *mcila-uli.* The only example of such coalescence observed." Harries, *op. cit.,* p. 33.

[24] Nakene, *op. cit.,* p. 127.

[25] "Der 'Aufgeber' des Rätsels (*monyeli*) stellt seine Rätselfrage (*nyeli* oder *thai*) in einer vom Rhythmus der Starktöne beherrschten Strophe, und der Löser des Rätsels (*monyeloli*) antwortet in einer Strophe, deren Rhythmus sich dem der Frage anpasst." See Charles Endemann, "Rätsel des Sotho," *Zeitschrift für Eingeborenen-Sprachen,* Vol. 18 (1927–1928), 55.

Kele bjang?
(On hearing I say/said:
Child of antheap,
I being how?)

This type of riddle does not seem to differ radically from the general type of riddles, except for the way in which the author has set it. Many riddles are found in which rhythm is a salient feature, and they could easily be set in the same form as those mentioned by Endemann. In many, however, the answer would not form verse, as it consists of one or two words only.

11.1. In these riddles where rhythm is a prominent feature, the same types of syllable patterns are observable as in Bantu proverbs.[26] The pattern and resulting balance may be found in the "question" part of the riddle, or in the riddle as a whole.

Q. *Inama ikani inociβa ukura, yonnuwaka kinociβa tthotthoni, uβeŋgia.* A. *Ncuwa.* (A very small animal which is tasty to eat, when it grows up it is not tasty any more, it is harmful. The sun.) [Makua] Pattern: [3.3.4.3, 5.4.3.4].

Q. *Xikhatu xatshuri.* A. *Likhula lamandza.* (The bottom of the mortar. The large end of the egg.) [Tsonga] Pattern: [3.3., 3.3].

Q. *Lendlwini kamamana kupfurha ndzilomungoma.* A. *Lendlwini kamamana valahla munhu wakufa.* (In mother's hut, the firewitchdoctor is burning. In mother's hut, they are burying a dead man.) [Tsonga.] Pattern: [3.4.3.2.3, 3.4.3.2.3.].

11.2. Such rhythm is achieved by a balanced number of syllables. But often the balance of recurring words, or of words with opposite meaning, or parallelism in the words as regards the parts of speech to which they belong, are factors producing rhythm.

Q. *Swipeni swimbirhi aswiyiveki* [noun, adjective, verb]. A. *Tihosi timbirhi atiluveki* [noun, adjective, verb]. (One cannot steal two steenbucks. One does not pay tax to two chiefs.) [Tsonga] Pattern: [3.3.5, 3.3.5].

Q. *Iciseβa mukati, iminefu posonde* [noun, adverb, noun, adverb; adverbs opposite in meaning]. A. *Mbetaβa.* (Skin within, flesh without. A maize cob) [Lamba] Pattern: [4.3, 4.3].

Q. *Oweta kunyaraka oheta, oheta kunyaraka oweta.* A. *Nyoce.* (The walker gives birth to the nonwalker, the nonwalker to the walker. An egg.) [Makua] Pattern: [3.4.3, 3.4.3].

Q. *Mvura cena.* A. *Dada jena.* (Clean water. A white duck.) [Zezuru] Pattern: [2.2, 2.2].

Q. *Atende kwenda mwacupi, acupi kwenda mwatende.* A. *Nomelo naciŋwelo.* (*Atende* goes into *acupi*, *acupi* goes into *atende*. The ladle and a small calabash.) [Mwera] Pattern: [3.2.3, 3.2.3].

Content of Bantu Riddles

12. From the various examples set in the preceding pages, it can be seen that riddles deal mainly with the material world surrounding the people. In

---

[26] See, for example, C. L. S. Nyembezi, *Zulu Proverbs* (Johannesburg: Witwatersrand University Press, 1954).

the riddles is described nature as a whole, particularly numerous being the riddles which refer to natural phenomena, and fauna and flora, from insects and grass to trees and elephants. Riddles also commonly describe material objects in the culture of the people.

Being more or less accurate, complete or suggestive descriptions of the world and its phenomena, riddles are a good reflection of the reactions of people to things, or their interest therein. Such things include:

(a) Natural phenomena, e.g., water, fire, lightning, thunder, etc.;
(b) Animals, plants, and occupations related to these;
(c) Their own bodies, which have retained the people's attention, and given rise to numerous riddles.

In addition to these, many riddles contain precise references to the way of life of the people, and aspects of their abstract culture.

12.1. Some riddles refer to some customs, and only a knowledge of the customs of the people enables one to understand and solve the riddle.

Q. *Kapaya wakifwile, umusowa kosyala mumuβa?* A. *Mba pakufwe'nseβula, βalafunde' ciseβa, nekufukutilako umuβa.* (The puku ram died, the cry remained in the bellows. When a puku dies, they skin it, and use it to blow the bellows with.) [Lamba]

Q. *Fiêla-fiêla, Nkoko atsoalê.* A. *Litaola (liafiêlloa).* (Sweep, Sweep, so that Nkoko should bring forth his children. The divining bones [one cleans (a patch on the ground) for them, i.e., before they are cast].) [Southern Sotho]

Q. *Mvana natu dzakatarisana.* A. *Mapfiwa.* (Three women who have borne a child facing each other. Hearthstones. [*Mvana*, a woman who has borne a child. Children are born when a family is set up. Only married women have hearthstones.]) [Karanga]

See also last riddle of paragraph 11.2.

12.2. Many riddles refer to the habits of the people in their daily life, or picture (often with much humor) their faults and reactions.

Q. *Mpolêllê, ditshipa tsêpêdi tsêekare gê dilwa tsaseka tsakgaoganngwa.* A. *Kebanyadi.* (Tell me, two genet cats which when they fight should not be separated. It is a married couple.) [Kgatla]

Q. *Daidza amai, hosha yakura.* A. *Hari iri kuβira.* (Call mother, the fever has gone. A pot on the boil.) [Kalanga]

Q. *Ndakuliba ndaŋkonde kutonaka.* A. *Hazvadzi.* (I puzzle you with a *mukonde* tree [in] being just pretty. The sister—however pretty she may be, one cannot marry her.) [Kalanga]

Q. *Twana tutema twakaita muduŋgwe.* A. *Hari parukuβa.* (The little black children have formed a line. Pots on the shelf.) [Zezuru]

Q. *M! m! m! m!* A. *Mbomukulu pakuteŋga.* (Oh! Oh! Oh! Oh! An adult when he grumbles.) [Lamba]

12.3. Occasionally one finds a riddle which expresses some profound human truth, e.g.,

Q. *Icitoŋkala mumasala.* A. *Mbomutima.* (That which digs about in the deserted village. The heart—which always turns to think of the past.) [Lamba]

12.4. Riddles often reveal the artistic sense of the people. Examples have already been noted where rhythm, or balance of words and concepts, is an important factor. The richness of the metaphors found in riddles to describe various circumstances of life and the contents of the universe is in itself a reflection of the lively imagination, acute observation and artistic sense of the people.

Q. *Ezalaki motu moko na mboka na biso, lokola na Leo II, soko bazali kobola mbonda na ye kuna na Leo I, azali kobina na mboka.* A. *Lokola: mopepe na bula ezali musika, matiti ezali motu akobina.* (There was a man in our village, let us suppose that it is Leo II, who, as people were beating his drum over there at Leo I, was dancing in the village. Answer: The wind and the rain are the music, the grass is the man who dances.) [Leo I and Leo II are parts of Léopoldville, Leo II being further than Leo I.] [Lingala]

Q. *Vakomana voku bvidza kuruka sero.* A. *Nyuchi.* (Boys who know how to make winnowing baskets. Bees. [The holes in the honeycomb are likened to the plaiting of the winnowing basket. Bees are small, so are boys.]) [Karanga]

Q. *Cinhu caŋgu cakatsvuka pasi, cakasvipa pakati, cakacena pamusoro.* A. *Moto mutsvukupasi, hari nhema pakati, sadza rejena pamusoro.* (My thing is red below, black in the middle, and white on top. Red fire beneath, black pot between, white porridge on top.) [Zezuru]

12.5. Many riddles exhibit highly poetical forms, but many others by their realism would surprise or shock any person lacking a sense of humor. Some cannot be recorded here because of their vividness of imagery, but here are a few which show that the people retain their sense of observation in any circumstance.

Q. *Khadi ya sigwemugwemu.* A. *U dya ngutu nyadiso-wee.* (A pot breaking on all sides. A man eating more than his fill.) [Chopi]

Q. *Intxini lexi loko bahlota xone, batakala khume dzatinhonga, kambe kuyadlaya tibiri?* A. *Inhwala.* (What is the thing which you hunt with ten sticks, and which you use only two sticks to kill? A louse.) [Ronga]

Q. *Mombe yaɓaɓa waŋgu inoura yirwa paruware.* A. *Inda.* (My father's ox is killed on the flat rock [i.e., thumbnail]. A louse.) [Zezuru]

Q. *Iyopwe yaamwene kimalia utinta.* A. *Mamila.* (The cooking pot of the chief never finishes being scooped out of. Nasal mucus.) [Makua]

12.6. Riddles, like other aspects of Bantu culture, have been affected by foreign influences, mainly European. This is seen in the use of foreign words, or when the riddle itself describes some object or custom which is typically European in origin. Images or words of foreign origin are also used in riddles which otherwise seem to be quite old and certainly are typically Bantu in underlying significance.

Q. *Mpolêlê, monna yôoapêreng ferofero baki.* A. *Kekhudu.* (Tell me, the man who wears a multicolored jacket. It is a tortoise.) [Kgatla]

Q. *Mpolêlê, phôlôgôlô êeareng gê egôtlhôla entshe dijô kaserota.* A. *Ke'plane'.* (Tell me, the animal which when it coughs sends out food through the hump. It is the carpenter's plane.) [Kgatla]

Q. *Matombo aɓaɓa waŋgu mamŋe anama ɓuri, mamŋe haana.* A. *Makoɓiri.* (Some of my father's rocks have holes, some have not. Pennies. [Pennies in Southern Rhodesia coinage now have holes in the center; previous issues did not have holes.]) [Zezuru]

12.7. Many riddles have a close resemblance to proverbs, or in a particular language, can even be related to a particular proverb, which proverb constitutes either the answer or the question. Occasionally too, riddles can be related to folktales.

Q. *Bilanga nsambo, ngombe mafuta: Mokoba na mwasi wa mokonzi* [proverb]. A. *Ntina lokola: Oliaka okobanzaka.* (The fat cows last only seven years, the gardener will one day marry the wife of the chief [lit. Seven years, fat ox; the gardener with the wife of the chief]. The meaning is thus: Think when you eat.) [Lingala]

Q. *Ntangu ekoleka mikolo minso* [proverb]. A. *Lokola: Bana bakokoma bakolo.* (Time passes by every day. Answer: The children will become adults.) [Lingala]

Q. *Batu boni bakozalaka na mokili?* [proverb]. A. *Batu babale, mobali na mwasi* [proverb]. (How many people live in the country? Two, a man and a woman [i.e., All men are alike, when one knows one, one knows them all; all woman are alike, but a man is not like a woman.]) [Lingala]

Q. *Munsinwa mumukalo.* A. *Mbakantanta.* (The one who drinks not in the well. The sable bull.) [Lamba]. Compare the proverb: *Munsinwa mumukalo, amasengo alamutaβa.* (Mr. I-don't-drink-in-a-well, his horns get in the way [this is the name given to the sable antelope].)

Q. *Ndakabva kare ndichitswaka muti womwana, ndikamushayiwa.* A. *Pfupa reswoswe.* (I have long sought medicine for the child, but I could not find it. The bone of an ant. [Based on the fable in which a man was told by a doctor that the bone of an ant would save his sick child.]) [Karanga]

The Classification of Bantu Riddles

13. Doke, in his *Lamba Folklore*, classifies Lamba riddles in alphabetical order, the first word of the question serving as the basis for this classification. Smith and Dale do not seem to have any system of classification for the Ila riddles they have included in their book *The Ila-Speaking Peoples of Northern Rhodesia*.

H. A. Junod, in his short section on riddles in *The Life of a South African Tribe* classifies riddles according to whether the answer to the riddle is easily understandable and logical, or to whether the answer is obscure. This classification is inconsistent and arbitrary. He mentions that there are two main types of riddles in Tsonga-Ronga: those with an answer containing one word only, and those whose answer is a whole sentence. This last distinction was chosen by Junod and Jaques as the basis of classification for their riddles in *Vutlhari bya Vatonga*.[27]

13.1. The most generally adopted method of classification of Bantu riddles is according to the content of the answer. Schapera, for example, for the Kgatla riddles, adopts the following classification: (a) Natural phenomena, (b) The vegetable world, (c) The animal world (with further subdivisions),

---

[27] This book contains a collection of Tsonga and Ronga proverbs and riddles with their English translations.

(d) Crops and other foods, (e) The human body, (f) Domestic life, (g) Utensils and other objects, (h) The white man's culture. Fortune, Gray, Harries, and Comhaire-Sylvain adopt a similar method of classification, with minor variations. This is certainly the most satisfactory classification yet devised,[28] as it permits quick reference. Any large collection of riddles should be accompanied by an index.

The Song Riddle

14. The song riddles, as described by Harries in his article "Makua Song-riddles from the Initiation Rites," do not seem to differ very much from ordinary riddles, except for their use and function, i.e., (a) "they are action-songs accompanying a dance," and (b) "they have a didactic purpose" (p. 27).

The meanings of these riddles are usually obscure, and the children learn their significance during the rites. Some riddles, however, are not explained to them at all. The riddles are restricted to initiated persons, and must not be revealed to uninitiated persons or to women (or a woman must not reveal them to a man). "Some of these riddles contain the ritual name of the object indicated in the solution. This ritual name is really the child-name, the name assigned to the object as belonging to the state before the initiation...We must not understand from this that the child-name was actually used by the children before their initiation. They are told the ritual name for the first time in the rites, and told never to use it again..." (p. 27).

Q. *Akwile pirupelo, anotthatthua nikala.* A. *Woβa.* (It is the dead who lie, he starts at a piece of charcoal. Fear.) Explanation: *Mtu apacerie ulumia inoa, kankufya utthatthua kila nihuku. Cowopiha cinci cihokala βelaponi βa, mweteke wowoβetu.* (When a person has begun to be bitten [perhaps

---

[28] Not all folklorists would agree that classification by answer is the most satisfactory riddle scheme yet devised. For, as Miss Beuchat herself observes, there may be more than one traditional answer to the same riddle question. If, therefore, one were looking in a riddle collection classified by answers for a parallel to a riddle one had collected, one might be unable to locate the parallel simply because in this particular collection the identical riddle question had a different answer. Furthermore, since the question portion of the riddle is normally of greater interest than the answer, it is clear that the classification should be on the basis of the question, that is, upon the nature of the object that is allegedly described, rather than upon the answer, which is the object actually described. There could and should also be a supplementary index of answers. A riddle classification system based upon the nature of the question-comparison was proposed by Robert Lehmann-Nitsche in his *Folklore Argentino, I, Adivinanzas Rio-platenses* (Buenos Aires, 1911), pp. 23–69. [A few years later Lehmann-Nitsche published an account in German, "Zur Volkskunde Argentiniens," *Zeitschrift des Vereins für Volkskunde*, Vol. 24 (1914), 240–55.] The merits of the system attracted the attention of the eminent Swedish folklorist C. W. von Sydow, who tested it on a corpus of Swedish riddles, "Om Gåtor och Gåtsystematik," *Folkminnen och Folktankar*, Vol. 2 (1915), 65–80. It was this system that Archer Taylor modified for his superb collection of English riddles. Taylor thus groups his riddles under "Comparisons to a Living Creature," "Comparisons to an Animal," "Comparisons to Several Animals," "Comparisons to a Person," and seven other major classification headings. Taylor also provides an index of solutions. For this scheme and for a discussion of the problems of riddle classification, see Archer Taylor, *English Riddles from Oral Tradition*, pp. xiii-xxxi, 3–4.—Ed. Note

by] a snake, he doesn't fail to be startled every day. There are many dangerous things here on earth, walk with fear then.)

Q. *Ndrindima, ndrindima.* A. *Ukukuta.* (Rumble, rumble. The sound of thunder.) Explanation: *Kalai akala mwanati ncina nawe Nandrindima, winelia wawe panetania Ukukuta.* (Long ago there was an uninitiated girl whose name was Nandrindima, and her initiation rites were called *Ukukuta.* [They took place at the end of the dry season when the sound of thunder was in the air. It would be taboo for an uninitiated person to use the ideophone *ndrindima,* for it is the ritual name for thunder.])

The Problem or Conundrum

15. The question part of a riddle draws a comparison, or describes some part of nature or some object, and from the description given in the comparison, the solution must be found. The whole riddle, even if it has a fairly long "question" part, is usually relatively short. Another type of "riddle" exists, which is usually much longer in form than the riddles refered to so far, and in which no comparison between objects or situations is drawn. In these longer "riddles," a set of data is presented, and from these data the person must work out the solution to the problem. These have been called *problems* or *conundrums* by students of Bantu folklore.[29]

Few conundrums have been recorded up to the present day, but further investigation may prove that they are not as rare as they seem to be at present. According to Doke,[30] Duff Macdonald has referred to conundrums, although he has not given any for Yao or Nyanja;[31] Smith and Dale, in *The Ila-Speaking Peoples of Northern Rhodesia* quote three found among the Ila, and Weeks quotes two in *Congo Life and Folklore* (pp. 138 and 224). Two found in Yaunde are mentioned by Heepe in *Jaunde-Texte von Karl Atangana und Paul Messi.* Doke has recorded one found in Lamba in "Bantu Wisdom-Lore" (p. 119).

15.1. The following example is a conundrum quoted by Smith and Dale (pp. 332f.).

"A man and his wife went to visit their friends. On their return homewards they were accompanied by their respective mothers. On the road, the

[29] These conundrums can also be considered a type of tale rather than riddle. These so-called dilemma tales fall under the rubric of Motif Z16, Tales ending with a question. Some are found in India; many more are found in Africa. They are not common elsewhere and are not reported among the North and South American Indian peoples. In some instances, the tale is unfinished in that the perplexing question is left unanswered (cf., Motif H620, The unsolved problem: enigmatic ending of tale). One is tempted to speculate that the popularity of such tales in African cultures may be correlated with the penchant for palaver in these same cultures. Part of the pleasure for an audience that delights in verbal pyrotechnics is the debate that follows the statement of the dilemma. For a representative sampling of more than twenty dilemma tales, see Alta Jablow, *Yes and No: The Intimate Folklore of Africa* (New York, 1961), pp. 44–120. No doubt many more examples could be found in the surprisingly large number of African folklore collections. For an excellent survey of the principal collections, see William Bascom, "Folklore Research in Africa," *Journal of American Folklore,* Vol. 77 (1964), 12–31. —ED. NOTE

[30] Doke, *op. cit.,* p. 119.

[31] Duff Macdonald, "Yao and Nyanja Tales," *Bantu Studies,* Vol. 12, No. 4 (1938); and *Africana, or the Heart of Heathen Africa* (1882).

four were set upon by all manner of horrible creatures—lions, snakes, leopards, etc., etc. They managed to elude them and got to a river.

There they found a canoe, but to their horror it would only hold three people. Their enemies were pressing hard upon their trail. The river was full of crocodiles; they couldn't hope to swim, only three could escape. One must die! Who was it to be?

The man sacrificed his mother-in-law, you say. No! His wife would not allow him. She would not desert her mother, nor he his: the elders would not forsake their children. How did they get out of their difficulty? [The native answer is that they all sat down on the river bank and died together.]"

Bibliography

Comhaire-Sylvain, S., "Quelques devinettes des enfants noirs de Léopoldville," *Africa,* Vol. 19, No. 1 (1949), 40–52.

Doke, C. M., "Bantu Wisdom-Lore," *African Studies,* Vol. 6, No. 3 (1947), 101–20.

———, *Lamba Folklore.* New York: American Folklore Society, 1927.

———, *The Lambas of Northern Rhodesia.* London: G. G. Harrap.

Endemann, Charles, "Rätsel des Sotho," *Zeitschrift für Eingeborenen-Sprachen,* Vol. 18 (1927–1928), 55–74.

Fortune, G., "Some Zezuru and Kalanga Riddles," *NADA,* Vol. 28 (1951), 30–44.

Gray, E., "Some Riddles of the Nyanja People," *Bantu Studies,* Vol. 13, No. 4 (1939), 251–91.

Harries, L., "Makua Song-Riddles from the Initiation Rites," *African Studies,* Vol. 1, No. 1 (1942), 27–46.

———, "Some Riddles of the Makua People," *African Studies,* Vol. 1, No. 4 (1942), 275–91.

———, "Some Riddles of the Mwera People," *African Studies,* Vol. 6, No. 1 (1947), 21–34.

Heepe, M., *Jaunde-Texte von Karl Atangana and Paul Messi.* Hamburg: L. Friederichsen & Co., 1919.

Hunt, N. A., "Shona Riddles," *NADA,* Vol. 34 (1957), 66–74.

———, "Some Karanga Riddles," *NADA,* Vol. 29 (1952), 90–98.

Junod, H. A., *The Life of a South African Tribe,* Vol. 2, Neuchâtel: Attinger, 1913.

Junod, H. P., *Bantu Heritage.* Johannesburg: Horters, 1938.

———, and A. A. Jaques, *Vulhari bya Vatonga,* or *The Wisdom of the Tonga-Shangaan People.* Pretoria, 1936.

Krappe, A. H., *The Science of Folklore.* London: Methuen & Co., Ltd., 1930.

Lindblom, G., "Kamba Riddles, Proverbs and Songs," *Archives d'Études Orientales,* Vol. 20, Part III (1934), 1–58.

Macdonald, D., *Africana, or the Heart of Heathen Africa* (1882).

———, "Yao and Nyanja Tales," *Bantu Studies,* Vol. 12, No. 4 (1938), 251–85.

Nakene, G., "Tlokwa Riddles," *African Studies,* Vol. 2, No. 3 (1943), 125–38.

Norton, W. A., and H. Velaphe, "Some Sesuto Riddles with Their Translations" *South African Journal of Science,* Vol. 21 (1924), 569–72.

Nyembezi, C. L. S., *Zulu Proverbs.* Johannesburg: Witwatersrand University Press, 1954.

Schapera, I., "Kxatla Riddles and Their Significance," *Bantu Studies,* Vol. 6, No. 3 (1932), 215–31.

Segoete, E., *Raphepheng.* Morija, Basutoland: Morija Sesuto Book Depot, 1948.

Smith, E. W., and A. M. Dale, *The Ila-Speaking Peoples of Northern Rhodesia,* Vol. 2, London: Macmillan & Co., Ltd., 1920.

Weeks, J. H., *Congo Life and Folklore.* London: Religious Tract Society, 1911.

Structural Typology in North American Indian Folktales

Alan Dundes

In this article, folkloristic rather than linguistic form is analyzed. However, the point is made that the study of form per se is not an end in itself. The delineation of form is only a step that should be taken before investigating origin and function. It is through studies of form that one sees what folklore is. Once folklore can be accurately defined in terms of formal criteria, it will be much easier to search for origins, to comprehend the process of oral transmission, and to analyze the diverse functions.

For sources of the specific American Indian tales cited and for further discussion of structural analysis in folklore, see Alan Dundes, *The Morphology of North American Indian Folktales,* Folklore Fellows Communications No. 195 (Helsinki, 1964).

There can be no rigorous typology without prior morphology. In the case of North American Indian folktales, the lack of morphological units and analyses has precluded typological statements. The extent of the morphological void is illustrated by the fact that the casualist theory of American Indian folktale composition is still widely held. According to this view, American Indian folktales are composed of random unstable conglomerates of motifs. In 1894, the English folklorist Joseph Jacobs, in discussing primitive folktales generally, remarked,[1] "Those who have read these tales will agree with me, I think, that they are formless and void, and bear the same relation to good European fairy tales as the invertebrates do to the vertebrate kingdom in the animal world." In 1916, Franz Boas made a similar statement:[2] "European folklore creates the impression that the whole stories are units and that their cohesion

---

Reprinted from the *Southwestern Journal of Anthropology,* Vol. 19 (1963), 121–30, by permission of the publisher.

[1] Joseph Jacobs, "The Problem of Diffusion: Rejoiners," *Folklore,* Vol. 5 (1894), 137.

[2] Franz Boas, *Tsimshian Mythology,* Annual Report of the Bureau of American Ethnology, Vol. 31 (1916), 878.

is strong, the whole complex very old. The analysis of American material, on the other hand, demonstrates that complex stories are new, that there is little cohesion between the component elements, and that the really old parts of tales are the incidents and a few simple plots." Recently, Melville Jacobs[3] critized Boas for not carrying over a structural approach, which he used successfully in the study of language and plastic-graphic art, to the field of folklore.

It is true that while the structural or pattern approach was sweeping through linguistics, psychology, ethnomusicology, and anthropology proper in the 1920's and 30's, folklore as a discipline remained oriented to a narrowly historical approach and dedicated to atomistic studies. In 1934, there appeared Benedict's *Patterns of Culture;* in 1933 Helen Roberts published "The Pattern Phenomenon in Primitive Music," as well as her study *Form in Primitive Music.* In linguistics, Sapir's *Language* (1921) and "Sound Patterns in Language" (1925) were followed by Bloomfield's *Language* (1933) and Swadesh's "The Phonemic Principle" (1934). Köhler's *Gestalt Psychology* (1929) and Koffa's *Principles of Gestalt Psychology* (1935) reflected the same theoretical movement in psychology. In the thirties, the search for patterns was itself a pattern of culture. However, in the field of folklore, there was apparently no interest in a holistic synchronic approach. The major piece of folklore scholarship of the middle thirties was Stith Thompson's mammoth *Motif-Index of Folk Literature,* lexicon par excellence, epitome of the atomistic emphasis in folklore. The culture lag in folklore theory has unfortunately increased since the thirties and this is one reason why there have been so few notable theoretical advances in folklore.

One of the few exceptions is Vladimir Propp's *Morphology of the Folktale* published in 1928. By morphology Propp[4] meant "the description of the folktale according to its component parts and the relationship of these components to each other and to the whole." Propp, after defining and isolating a morphological unit which he termed "function," proceeded to analyze morphologically one hundred consecutive *Märchen,* a random corpus of tales, from the celebrated Afanasiev collection of Russian folktales. In analyzing the functions, that is, the units of plot narrative structure, of these hundred tales, Propp discovered that there was a limited number of functions, namely thirty-one, and that the sequence of these functions was fixed. This did not mean that all thirty-one possible functions necessarily occurred in any one given folktale, but rather that those which did occur did so in a predictable order. Having completed his morphology, Propp was able to proceed to

---

[3] Melville Jacobs, "Folklore," in *The Anthropology of Franz Boaz,* ed. Walter Goldschmidt, American Anthropological Association, Memoir 89 (San Francisco, 1959), p. 127.

[4] Vladmir Propp, *Morphology of the Folktale,* Indiana University Research Center in Anthropology, Folklore, and Linguistics, Publication 10 (Bloomington, 1958), p. 18.

typology, and he concluded[5] that all Russian fairy tales, on morphological grounds, belonged to one and the same structural type.[6]

In applying Propp's morphological framework to American Indian folktales, I have adopted some of the terminology and theory of Kenneth L. Pike, as expressed in the latter's *Language in Relation to a Unified Theory of the Structure of Human Behavior.*[7] Propp's function becomes thus a motifeme instead, which permits the associated notions of motif and allomotif. Folktales may thus be defined as sequences of motifemes. The motifemic slots may be filled with various motifs and the specific alternative motifs for any given motifemic slot may be labelled allomotifs. With the aid of this combined Proppian/Pike structural model, I was able to discern a number of clear-cut structural patterns in North American Indian folktales.

A large number of American Indian folktales consist of a move from disequilibrium to equilibrium. Disequilibrium, a state to be feared and avoided if possible, may be seen as a state of surplus or of lack, depending upon the point of view. The disequilibrium may be indicated by a statement that there is too much of one thing or too little of another. In the hoarded object tales, in which such objects as game, fish, food-plants, water, tides, seasons, sun, light, fire, and so forth are not available to the majority of mankind or to most of the members of a tribe, there is very often an initial statement of the socially or universally felt lack. An initial state of flood may be interpreted as either too much water or too little land, but in any case, there is the undesirable state of disequilibrium, which I will call "lack." *Folktales can consist simply of relating how abundance was lost or how a lack was liquidated.* In other words, something in excess may be lost or something lost or stolen may be found. Both of these situations fall under the rubric of moving from disequilibrium to equilibrium.

One structural type of American Indian folktale then consists of just two motifemes: Lack (L) and Lack Liquidated (LL). In the Malecite version of "The Release of Impounded Water," a monster keeps back all the water in the world (L). A culture hero slays the monster, which act releases water (LL). A Wishram tale based upon the same motifeme pattern is as follows: "A people on the Columbia had no eyes or mouths (L). They ate by smelling the sturgeon. Coyote opened their eyes and mouths (LL)." In an unpublished Upper Chehalis tale: "Once upon a time the world started going to pieces. A mint with lots of runners decided to sew it back together. It did so, and saved the world." There are not a great many tales which consist of only two motifemes, but there are some. The two motifeme sequence may be said to constitute a minimum definition of an American Indian folktale.

---

[5] *Ibid.,* p. 21.

[6] For an extensive review of Propp's study, see Claude Lévi-Strauss, "L'analyse morphologique des contes russes," *International Journal of Slavic Linguistics and Poetics,* Vol. 3 (1960), 122–49.—ED. NOTE

[7] Alan Dundes, "From Etic to Emic Units in the Structural Study of Folktales," *Journal of American Folklore,* Vol. 75 (1962), 95–105.

A much more common motifeme sequence is one with the following four motifemes: Interdiction, Violation, Consequence, and an Attempted Escape from the Consequence (abbreviated Int, Viol, Conseq, and AE). The Attempted Escape is an optional rather than obligatory structural slot. A tale may end with the Consequence. Furthermore, if there is an attempted escape, the attempt may be successful or it may be unsuccesful. The presence of the fourth motifeme, Attempted Escape, may depend upon the particular culture or particular informant within that culture. Similarly the success or failure of the attempt may also depend upon these factors.

A few examples may illustrate the nature of this folktale pattern. Notice the diversity of content within the identical structural form. In a Swampy Cree tale, a little boy is told by his sister not to shoot at a squirrel when it is near the water (Int). The boy shoots at a squirrel near water (Viol) and when he seeks to retrieve his arrow which had fallen in the water, he is swallowed by a fish (Conseq). Eventually, the fish is directed to swim to the sister, who cuts open the fish, thereby releasing her brother (AE). In a Lillooet tale, an old man warns some boys out fishing not to mockingly call for a whale to come (Int). The boys laugh and continue calling (Viol) whereupon a whale comes and swallows them (Conseq). The whale is directed to a certain beach where the people cut it open, permitting the boys to escape (AE). In an Onondaga tale with parallels among Eskimo, Plains and Woodlands peoples, a group of children is warned to stop dancing (Int). The children refuse (Viol) and are translated to the heavens (Conseq) where they become the Pleiades. The ending of a tale with an explanatory motif is common in American Indian folktales. The explanatory motif is not structurally obligatory; it functions rather as a stylistic terminal marker or literary coda. Sometimes the interdiction is implicit rather than explicit. In "The Rolling Rock," trickster offends a rock by taking back a present (e.g., a robe) which he has previously given it, or by defecating on the rock (Viol). The rock rolls after him in pursuit (Conseq). The protagonist usually escapes through the helpful intervention of friendly animals who destroy the rock (AE). In a Tlingit tale, some boys pull a piece of drifting seaweed out of the water on one side of their canoe and put it in again on the other (Viol). Permanent winter results (Conseq). In a Kathlamet cognate, the interdiction is explicit. The people of a town are forbidden to play with their excrements (Int). A bad boy does play with his (Viol) and the next night snow begins to fall. Winter comes permanently and people start to die of hunger (Conseq). The people escape these consequences by leaving the bad boy to die on the ice (AE). There is great variety of content in these tales; that is, there are a great number of allomotifs. This is what has led some anthropologists to believe that American Indian folktales lacked cohesion. However, the sequence of motifemes is exactly the same in these tales. Motifemically speaking, there is great cohesion between the component elements, contrary to what Boas thought.

Longer American Indian folktales may be composed of combinations of shorter motifeme patterns. A common six motifeme combination consists of Lack, Liquidation of Lack, Interdiction, Violation, Consequence, and Attempted Escape. In Orpheus, a man loses his wife (L), but regains her or can regain her (LL) if he does not violate a taboo (Int). Inevitably the man breaks the taboo (Viol) and loses his wife once again (Conseq). As an illustration of how diverse content can occur within a common structural frame, the Orpheus tale may be compared with the Zuni tale of "The Little Girl and the Cricket." A girl discovers a singing cricket and wants to take it home (L). The cricket goes home with her (LL), but warns her that she must not touch or tickle him (Int). The girl in playing with the cricket tickles him (Viol) and the cricket bursts his stomach and dies (Conseq). In tabular form, the two tales are as follows:

Motifemes	Orpheus	Girl and Cricket
Lack	Man wants to bring wife home from the dead	Girl wants to bring cricket home from fields
Lack Liquidated	Man does so	Girl does so
Interdiction	Man is warned not to look back at wife	Girl is warned not to touch cricket
Violation	Man looks back	Girl touches cricket
Consequence	Man's wife dies	Cricket dies
Attempted Escape	--------------------	--------------------

It should be noted that the consequence may be a form of lack, as it is in the Orpheus tale, for example. This suggests that in folktales where there is no initial lack given, there may occur a sequence of motifemes causing a state of lack. Usually the lack is the result of some unwise action or more specifically the result of a violation of an interdiction. Thus in some versions of earthdiver, the lack is stated initially: "Once there was no earth. Water was where the earth is now." On the other hand, the flood may be caused, as in the Upper Chehalis account, by foolishly flaunting a taboo. In the latter account Thrush is not allowed to wash his dirty face (Int), but he is induced to do so (Viol). After Thrush washes his face, it begins to rain heavily until the water rises and covers everything (Conseq). Then Muskrat dives four times for the necessary dirt in the usual earthdiver sequence (AE).

It is important to realize that these structural motifemic alternatives are not limited to any one historical tale; these alternatives may be found in many tales. In the widespread tale of Eye-Juggler, the trickster may simply lose his eyes (L) and regain them (LL). However, in many Plains versions, the two motifeme sequence is expanded. Trickster wishes to be able to imitate a man who is able to throw his eyes into the air and replace them (L). Trickster is given the power (LL), but he is warned that his eyes may only be thrown four times or that they may not be thrown too high or near trees (Int). Trickster disobeys (Viol) and loses his eyes (Conseq). On the basis of structural analysis, one might say that in *any* tale which begins with an initial lack, it is theoretically possible for *that* tale to begin with an inter-diction whose violation causes the lack. If this is so, then a knowledge of the alternative structural patterns might be of considerable use in constructing and evaluating historical-geographical hypotheses concerning individual folk-tales. What folklorists have previously considered to be subtypes of a par-ticular tale may be manifestations of much more general structural pattern alternation.

While it is clear that American Indian folktales are definitely structured inasmuch as they are composed of specific statable sequences of motifemes, it must be understood that all the existing motifeme patterns are not dis-cussed above. Another common pattern, for example, consists of Lack, Deceit, Deception, and Lack Liquidated.[8] Yet these few illustrative patterns should be sufficient to support the thesis that American Indian folktales are struc-tured. But structural analysis is not an end in itself and the question might be raised: what is the significance and use of the structural analyses of folktales?

First, typological statements can be made. As Roman Jakobson observed in commenting upon the Boasian approach to the study of American Indian languages, structural similarities should be pointed out. He noted, "Certain grammatical phonemic types have a wide continuous distribution without corresponding lexical similarities."[9] Voegelin and Harris[10] have made similar statements. They have said, for example, that "Structural comparability of languages may be stated independently of their genetic relationships." Just as Van Gennep noted that a common structural pattern characterized a variety of rites of vastly different content, that is, that the sequential pattern of separation, transition, and incorporation could be found in rites dealing with birth, puberty, marriage, death, and so forth, so common structural patterns in folktales of quite diverse content may be clearly delineated.

A second significant benefit accruing from structural analysis is a new technique of gaining insight into the cultural determination of content within transcultural forms. If a folklorist aligns all the tales with the same structure reported in a given culture, that is, aligns them motifeme by motifeme, he may then easily note whether or not a specific motifeme is manifested by a particular motif. For example, after aligning a number of Cheyenne tales based upon the Interdiction/Violation pattern, I discovered that invariably the interdiction forbade the use of a special power more than four times. In some cases, the content of the tale was considerably altered by Cheyenne informants to make it possible for this particular motif to occur. In a Cheyenne version of "Rolling Rock," one does not find the usual offense to

[8] Alan Dundes, *The Morphology of North American Indian Folktales* (Helsinki, 1964), pp. 72–75.

[9] Roman Jakobson, "Franz Boas' Approach to Language," *International Journal of American Linguistics,* Vol. 10 (1939), 192–93.

[10] C. F. Voegelin and Z. A. Harris, "The Scope of Linguistics," *American Anthro-pologist,* Vol. 49 (1947), 596.

the rock. Instead, trickster sees a man who can command stones to turn over without touching them and he desires this power (L). He is given the power (LL) on condition that he use it no more than four times (Int). He loses count, uses the power for a fifth time (Viol) and the stone pursues him (Conseq). A nighthawk saves trickster by breaking the stone into pieces (AE). Similarly, in an unusual version of "Bungling Host," trickster is given the power of scraping flesh from his back for food provided that he does not repeat the process more than four times. The cultural predilection for the "not more than four times" motif might have been noticed from the reading of one tale, but then again it might not have been. It is no longer necessary to employ so subjective an empirical approach. One need only align, or super-impose, all the tales in a culture based upon a particular motifeme pattern and then sight down the various motifs filling a particular motifemic slot.

Another benefit of structural analysis lies in the area of prediction in an acculturation situation. If one knows the structure of European folktales and the structure of American Indian folktales, one can predict with reasonable certainty what changes will occur when a European tale is borrowed by an American Indian group. For example, the Zuni version of Aarne-Thompson Tale Type 121, Wolves Climb on Top of One Another to Tree, is instructive. In the European tale, some wolves resort to climbing on top of one another to capture someone in a tree. When the lowest wolf runs away, the others all fall. In the Zuni version of this tale, Coyote wants to climb up a cliff to get some corn (L). Coyote gathers together his fellow coyotes and the group decides to ascend the cliff by holding on to one another's tail or by holding on to corn cobs inserted in their anuses (LL). The coyotes are all warned not to break wind (Int). However, the last coyote does so (Viol), causing the whole chain to tumble down. All the coyotes are killed (Conseq).

Whereas formerly folklorists were content merely to identify European tales among the North American Indians, it is now possible to show exactly how European tales have been cast in the mold of traditional American Indian folktale patterns, in this case, that of the Interdiction/Violation motifeme sequence. It is interesting to note that one of the most striking structural differences between European and American Indian folktales concerns the number of motifemes intervening between a pair of related motifemes, such as Lack and Lack Liquidated. The number of intervening motifemes may be considered as an indication of what may be termed the "motifemic depth" of folktales. American Indian tales have far less motifemic depth than European folktales. In the latter, Lack (Propp function 8a) and Lack Liquidated (Propp function 19) are widely separated, whereas in American Indian tales a lack is liquidated soon after it is stated. It is possible that the lesser motifemic depth of American Indian tales may account in part for the absence of either native or borrowed cumulative folktales among the American Indians, inasmuch as cumulative tales often consist of an extensive interconnected series of lacks to be liquidated within the frame of an initial lack and final liquidation of that lack. Such hypotheses might be tested by planting tales of a given structural pattern in a culture and re-eliciting them after a given period of time.

Perhaps the most exciting contribution of structural analysis lies in the uncharted area of cross-genre comparison. Rarely have folklorists attempted to compare the different genres of folklore. In fact, on the contrary, with respect to the genres of folktale and superstition, there has been within recent years an attempt to divide the field of folklore study into the two divisions of folk literature and folk custom. Herskovits, for instance, accepts this "dual mandate" as he terms it[11] and Bascom in an unequivocal statement[12] maintains that folklore to the anthropologist includes myths and tales but does not include folk custom or folk belief.

Yet, morphological analysis of the two genres reveals that a common structural pattern may underlie both. In a recently published structural study,[13] I proposed the following tentative generic definition of superstition: "Superstitions are traditional expressions of one or more conditions and one or more results with some of the conditions signs and others causes." The formula for superstitions may be stated simply as "If A, then B," with an optional "unless C." In a category of superstitions which I have termed "Magic," fulfillment of one or more conditions *causes* one or more results. The Chippewa believe, for example, that throwing dogs or cats into a lake will cause a storm. However, in "Conversion" superstitions, an undesirable result may be neutralized or even reversed so that a desirable result ensues. Thus in magic superstitions, there is a conditional action, which if fulfilled leads to a result. But there may be an accompanying conversion superstition which, employed as a counteractant, permits an individual to avoid or nullify the undesirable result of the magic superstition. Perhaps now the parallel between the structure of the Interdiction/Violation motifeme sequence in folktales and the structure of superstition may be seen. Consider the following Zuni folktale and superstition:

	Folktale		*Superstition*
Int:	A girl is warned not to hunt rabbits	Condition:	If a woman eats the wafer bread from the deer hunt
Viol:	She does		--------------------
Conseq:	A cannibalistic monster appears	Result:	she will have twins
AE:	The twin Ahaiyute save the girl	Counteractant:	unless the bread is passed around the rung of her house ladder four times

One must not be deceived by the apparent lack of an analogue to the Viola-

---

[11] Melville J. Herskovits, "Folklore After a Hundred Years: A Problem in Redefinition," *Journal of American Folklore,* Vol. 59 (1946), 93.

[12] William R. Bascom, "Folklore and Anthropology," *Journal of American Folklore,* Vol. 66 (1953), 285.

[13] Alan Dundes, "Brown County Superstitions," *Midwest Folklore,* Vol. 11 (1961), 28.

tion motifeme. In superstitions, it is always assumed that the condition will be fulfilled, or in other words, that the interdiction will be violated. It thus appears that it is possible to compare folktales and superstitions. Moreover, it would be interesting to know whether there is any significant correlation between the forms of folktales and superstitions of the same culture, especially with respect to the more or less optional Attempted Escape motifeme and the counteractant portion of superstitions. One would think that in cultures where there was a great preponderance of attempted escapes from the consequences of violating interdictions in folktales, there would be an analogous high incidence of counteractants or conversion superstitions. It should also be noted that this structural pattern may be found in other folkloristic genres. For example, in games, there are inevitably rules. If the rules are broken (and breaking the rules may be part of the game), there may be a penalty. Then depending upon the particular game or the particular version of the game, there may or may not be a means of nullifying or escaping the penalty.[14]

The importance of structural analysis should be obvious. Morphological analysis of American Indian folktales makes it possible for typological descriptive statements to be made. Such statements, in turn, make it possible for folklorists to examine the cultural determination of content, to predict culture change, and to attempt cross-genre comparison. It is to be hoped that structural analyses of the folklore of other geographical areas, e.g., Africa, will reveal whether or not certain structural patterns are universal.

Bibliography

Bascom, William R., "Folklore and Anthropology," *Journal of American Folklore*, Vol. 66 (1953), 283–90.

Boas, Franz, *Tsimshian Mythology*. Thirty-First Annual Report of the Bureau of American Ethnology. Washington: Government Printing Office, 1916.

Dundes, Alan, "Brown County Superstitions," *Midwest Folklore*, Vol. 11 (1961), 25–56.

——, "From Etic to Emic Units in the Structural Study of Folktales," *Journal of American Folklore*, Vol. 75 (1962), 95–105.

——, *The Morphology of North American Indian Folktales*. Folklore Fellows Communications No. 195. Helsinki: Suomalainen Tiedeakatemia, 1964.

Herskovits, Melville J., "Folklore After a Hundred Years: A Problem in Redefinition," *Journal of American Folklore*, Vol. 59 (1946), 89–100.

---

[14] The argument for cross-genre comparison via structural analysis is strengthened by a monographic article in which the same structural models are used for a variety of folklore genres. See Elli Kaija Köngäs (Maranda) and Pierre Maranda, "Structural Models in Folklore," *Midwest Folklore*, Vol. 12 (1962), 133–92. The application of structural analysis to folk dance, a form of folklore neglected by most folklorists, may also encourage cross-genre comparison. See György Martin and Ernö Pesovár, "A Structural Analysis of the Hungarian Folk Dance (A Methodological Sketch)," *Acta Ethnographica*, Vol. 10 (1961), 1–40. For a comparison of folktale and game structure, see Alan Dundes, "On Game Morphology: A Study of the Structure of Non-Verbal Folklore," *New York Folklore Quarterly*, Vol. 20 (1964), 276–88.—ED. NOTE

Jacobs, Joseph, "The Problem of Diffusion: Rejoinders," *Folklore* Vol. 5 (1894), 129–46.

Jacobs, Melville, "Folklore," in *The Anthropology of Franz Boas,* ed. Walter Goldschmidt. American Anthropological Association, Memoir 89, pp. 119–38. San Francisco, 1959.

Jakobson, Roman, " 'Franz Boas' Approach to Language," *International Journal of American Linguistics,* Vol. 10 (1939), 188–95.

Pike, Kenneth L., *Language in Relation to a Unified Theory of the Structure of Human Behavior,* 3 parts. Glendale, Cal.: Summer Institute of Linguistics, 1954–1960.

Propp, Vladimir, *Morphology of the Folktale.* Indiana University Research Center in Anthropology, Folklore, and Linguistics, Publication 10. Bloomington, 1958.

Voegelin, C. F., and Z. S. Harris, "The Scope of Linguistics," *American Anthropologist,* Vol. 49 (1947), 588–600.

The Transmission of Folklore

Because folklorists depend greatly upon the criterion of oral transmission in defining folklore, there have been a number of studies devoted to describing and analyzing this process. Here the concern is not what folklore is nor what its ultimate origin was, but rather the way in which folklore is passed from individual to individual, from culture to culture, from generation to generation.

Those who are dependent upon print, often to the extent of relying upon it instead of upon their memories, frequently assume that the existence of an item of folklore must be a most precarious one. Oral transmission is considered to be unreliable in contrast to the reliability of transmission by print. It is felt that folklore, to be preserved, must be orally communicated intact from a bearer of the tradition to a new bearer, and that this is extremely unlikely to occur consistently over long periods of time. If, for example, a superb raconteur of folklore dies without passing on his materials, it is feared that these materials may die with him. Or perhaps the person to whom he entrusts the task of perpetuating the traditions proves faithless to the trust. The infinite possibilities of the demise of a tradition because of a weak link in the human chain of transmission makes those unfamiliar with folklore suspicious and sceptical of the strength of oral tradition. It is imagined that only if the materials are written down or put in print can they be saved for posterity. Yet the amazing thing is that folklore, in the vast majority of cases, is saved for posterity without the aid of writing or print. One must remember that in most of the cultures of the world, *all* the information culturally defined as important is passed on orally. In some cultures, special individuals are selected, formally or informally, to be the repositories of oral tradition. In others, individuals simply assume the responsibility on their own.

For some kinds of folklore, it is conceptually useful to imagine a mass of traditions that each generation grows up into and through. For example, young girls learn many of the same jump-rope rhymes as the ones used by their grandmothers, and young boys learn the same marble games and terminology used by their grandfathers. Yet they do not learn these traditions from their grandparents. On the playgrounds, older children teach younger children folklore. Later when the older children have become adults and perhaps have forgotten they ever knew the materials, their former young imitators have become the older children who teach a new group of younger children. The traditions are on the playground, and it is almost impossible to avoid receiving and transmitting them. It is precisely this which constitutes the transmission of folklore. The investigation of this transmission process and the changes that occur when folklore, destined as it is to be forever in transit, is communicated from one person to another is an integral part of the study of folklore.

Folktale Studies and Philology:
Some Points of View

C. W. von Sydow

One of the greatest theoreticians in the history of folkloristics was Carl Wilhelm von Sydow of Sweden. Included among his chief interests were the mechanics of folklore transmission. Two of his related conceptual contributions are the distinction between active and passive bearers of tradition and the notion of oicotype.

Active bearers of tradition are those individuals who tell the tales and sing the songs. They may be contrasted with passive bearers of tradition who merely listen to the performances of active bearers. Acording to von Sydow, there are in any given community only a very few active bearers and yet these few individuals account for the continuity and dissemination of traditions. Von Sydow argues that folktales and other forms of folklore are not transmitted by some superorganic wave or stream moving in some mystical process of automigration. The *Märchen,* the most complex form of folktale, is transmitted, he contended, only if and when one active bearer communicates such a tale to another active bearer. If an active bearer migrates from a place before imparting his materials, the folklore may die out in that place. If in the new place, either because of language or culture, the active bearer fails to continue his active role, the folklore may not survive. Von Sydow admits that it is possible for passive bearers to become active bearers in the event of the death or departure of an active bearer in a community. But in any event, von Sydow believes that the number of active bearers is relatively small and that the transmission of folklore is carried out in irregular leaps and bounds, rather than by means of a smooth regular wave in the form of a concentric circle diffusing outward from a center point of origin.

Von Sydow borrowed the term *oicotype* from the science of botany where it denoted a genetic variety of plant that adapted to a certain environment (e.g., seashore, mountains) through natural selection and

Reprinted from C. W. von Sydow, *Selected Papers on Folklore,* ed. Laurits Bødker (Copenhagen: Rosenkilde og Baggers Forlag, 1948), pp. 189–219, by permission of Laurits Bødker and the publisher.

thus differed somewhat from other members of the same species. In folk-lore, the term refers to local forms of a tale type, folksong, or proverb, with "local" defined in either geographic or cultural terms. Oicotypes could be on the village, state, regional, or national level. The concept oicotype differs from the notion of subtype in that the oicotype is tied by definition to a very specific locale. A subtype of a riddle or folktale might be found in many different places with quite different cultural settings. What von Sydow calls oicotypification consists of the regular, almost predictable alteration that takes place when the content of a tale is changed to fit the culturally preferred pattern in a given locale.

Not all of von Sydow's many terminological proposals have been accepted by professional folklorists. His proliferation of terms for dif-ferent kinds of folktales have been used very little by other folklorists. He made categorical distinctions partly because he felt that the laws of transmission differed for the different categories. For example, what he terms chimera tales (*Schimäremärchen*), by which he says he means Aarne-Thompson Types 300–749 and 850–879 (which in English would be called fairy tales), are usually long, involved multi-episodic stories that demand special powers of memory and narration on the part of the taleteller. In contrast, single-episodic tales such as fables (animal or jocular) and *sagn* are transmitted much more easily. *Sagn* refers to short, sometimes believed, often local, single-episodic tales based upon events that did occur or could have occurred in objective reality, but which through the powers of the process von Sydow calls fabulation may be transformed into fiction with little regard for fact. *Memorates,* which are narratives of actual personal happenings, are usually not widely diffused, but some do pass into tradition. This type of *sagn* would be, in theory, based upon events that did occur. More common, however, are the other forms of *sagn,* which are fictional and which von Sydow labels *fabulates.* The types of fabulates include belief fabu-lates (*Glaubensfabulate*), which are stories associated with customs and beliefs (e.g., ghost stories), and person fabulates (*Personenfabulate*) which are stories told of definitely named individuals (e.g., Till Eulens-piegel).

Von Sydow was convinced that since there were laws governing the composition of folk forms, so there were also laws governing the trans-mission of these forms. His trenchant critique of the older theories of diffusion and his own stimulating theories are contained in this paper, which was originally published in 1945 in a *festschrift* (a group of essays honoring someone) for Danish folklorist Arthur Christensen.

Those interested in considering von Sydow's theories further should consult his *Selected Papers on Folklore,* ed. Laurits Bødker (Copen-hagen, 1948). For a discussion of active and passive bearers, see "On the Spread of Tradition," pp. 11–18; for the argument against auto-migration, see "Geography and Folktale Oicotypes," pp. 46–47; and for the elaborate scheme of categories and terms, see "Kategorien der Prosa-Volksdichtung," pp. 60–88, and "Popular Prose Traditions and Their Classification," pp. 127–45.

Folklore has figured in philology ever since the beginning of the last century when the Grimm brothers fixed the attention of philological scholarship on the popular tradition of tales and *sagns*. For it is obvious that every philologist working on old literature will often meet with some matter derived, more or less directly, from oral tradition. This is true of the myths, hero sagas, and family sagas that have come down to us from classical antiquity, from the East, and from early Scandinavian times, no less than of the tales, poems of chivalry, fabliaux, etc. of the Middle Ages and the Renaissance. Such poetry can only be fully understood when studied in the light of kindred matter derived from popular tradition. The scholar must not only be acquainted with popular motifs and acquire a thorough general view of the field; he must, of course, also know the laws that apply to such tradition.

The slow progress made in exploring popular tradition is bound up with the facts that a necessary general view has only been attainable by slow degrees, and that the explanation of the laws of tradition has too often and too long been replaced by ill-founded hypotheses, which have certainly been of some use, but have also led scholars astray and thus detained scientific research and prevented it from reaching the goal. It may be of some interest to review the errors of scholarship, the more so, as the demands to be made on future scholars also will thus stand out the more clearly.

The great and definitive discovery of the Grimm brothers was the international spread of folktales and the great antiquity that must often be ascribed to them. These two weighty facts, which have been thoroughly borne out by later discoveries, made a closer examination of them an important and significant task even by itself, apart from the bearing they may have on the study of old literature. When the Grimm brothers tried to account for these remarkable facts, they introduced the hypothesis that these folktales had been handed down from a remote Indo-European past, and that they were relics of a common mythology of the Indo-European peoples. Their hypothesis was natural at a time when the mutual relationships of the Indo-European languages had just been discovered, and some common features had been found in the myths of various peoples.

The first part of the hypothesis, the notion that the tales were relics of a common past, should be alive even yet, as a whole series of them can be shown to date back at least 3000 years, which fact proves it to be possible for tales from such a remote period to be handed down by oral tradition within one or several peoples. This must, however, be qualified by three important reservations. First, that new tales have been invented and may be invented at any time, and that accordingly a lot of folktales must be of a considerably later date. This is self-evident and was, of course, also realized by the Grimm brothers. Their Indo-European theory was certainly not conceived as applying to more than a certain number of tales, specifically the fantastic chimera tales, which bore a certain resemblance to myths. That the theory did not make a sufficiently clear distinction between the various categories of folktales, was due to the fact that terminology was as yet insufficiently developed.

The second reservation must be made in respect to loans of tradition from other peoples. The Grimm brothers were inclined to deny the possibility of loans, apart from purely exceptional cases. That a strong resistance to loans may be proved very often is sure enough. This may be seen from the Tale of the Two Brothers written down in ancient Egypt about 1300 B.C.[1] This remarkable tale was pieced together from an Indo-Persian tale and a kindred one from the Pontic countries with some particularly Egyptian additions, and did not in its totality belong to Egyptian folk tradition. The two stories here united exist as independent folktales even yet, one in Western Asia, the other in Slavic or Slavic-influenced countries; but although they have a very long time behind them, they have not spread beyond the area of Slavic culture, even if one or two records have been made which have clearly been brought by immigrants from the East. This tells strongly in favor of the view that loans from aliens by way of oral tradition is beset with considerable difficulties. There do exist, however, clear instances of loans from quite exotic peoples. Thus the tale of The Animal Sons-in-law and Their Magic Food (Aa552B) has been borrowed from the Eskimos into Danish and Norwegian popular tradition[2] and is thus certainly no ancient Indo-European heirloom.

The third reservation applies to the circumstance that the Indo-Europeans have absorbed part of the non-Indo-European peoples, who have thus become Indo-Europeanized, but may well have retained their own tradition of folktales, as indeed is most likely to be the case. All the Mediterranean peoples in Western and Southern Europe have from the start been superior to the Indo-European immigrants as regards peaceful civilization, and they must also be supposed to have made important contributions to the stores of folktales preserved by the Indo-Europeans of our day. There exist not a few tales which are hardly to be met with north of the Alps, but are among those in greatest favor in Southern Europe. An instance of this is the tale about the Three Oranges (Aa408) which was certainly taken down by Asbjørnsen in Oslo and must be supposed to have been brought there by some immigrant or

---

[1] Von Sydow himself studied this interesting tale, which was discovered in a papyrus manuscript in 1852. One of the prominent elements in the tale is the well-known Potiphar's wife motif K2111, in which a young man who resists the advances of an older married woman is later falsely accused by the same woman of trying to seduce her. Von Sydow's study, in Swedish, is "Den fornegyptiska Sagan om de två Bröderna," *Vetenskapssocietetens i Lund arsbok* (Lund, 1930), pp. 53–89. For a convenient summary of the tale and a list of its component motifs, see Stith Thompson, *The Folktale* (New York, 1946), pp. 275–76.—ED. NOTE

[2] Grundtvig-Ellekilde, *Eventyr* (1924), No. 5. [The relationship between Motif J2411.3, Unsuccessful imitation of magic production of food, in Tale Type 552B, found primarily in Norway and Sweden, and Motif J2425, The bungling host, one of the most widespread and popular American Indian tale types in which a trickster is unable to produce food magically when he imitates his host, is not completely clear. Von Sydow here suggests diffusion; Stith Thompson, in *The Folktale* (New York, 1946), p. 56, n. 11, suggests polygenesis.—ED. NOTE]

perhaps a book, but which is otherwise generally speaking not to be found north of the Alps. It is an important task for future folktale studies to mark out the border line in this respect between Indo-European folktale tradition proper on one hand, and Mediterranean and other tradition on the other. As yet no serious attempt to elucidate these facts has been made. I shall, however, point out an example which suggests most interesting problems.

The tale about the Magic Flight (Aa313)[3] is most singularly widespread. In fact, its occurrence seems to coincide with the extensive spread of megalithic culture, and it may therefore with great probability be characterized as a megalithic tale! Megalithic culture appears to have originated in the Middle East, presumably among a Mediterranean people, and it has been spread by colonization over the ocean to the islands and coastal districts in the Mediterranean and northward along the Atlantic coasts to the British Isles and to French, Northern German, and Scandinavian coastal districts, but also along the coast of the Indian Ocean to parts of India, to Japan, and to the islands in the Pacific as far as Samoa, perhaps even to America. The colonizing Megalithic people have everywhere been amalgamated with the original population of the countries colonized by them, and the strange tale of the Magic Flight has followed it persistently all over the wide area. This singular dissemination suggests that the tale in question was composed not later than about 2500 years B.C., which would give it an age of 4500 years at the least. We must not be too much amazed at this great antiquity, as the story enters into the composition of the early Greek (probably pre-Greek!) tale of the Argonauts[4] as an important part of it, which fact proves it to have existed in Europe at least for 3000 years. Somewhat similar must be the case of the tale of the Swan Maidens (Aa400),[5] which has much the same composition, many common motifs, and, broadly speaking, the same spread as has the tale of the Flight from the Ogre. When, in 1919, Helge Holmström published his work, *Studies on the Swan Maiden Motif,* he tried to account for the singularly wide circulation of the tale by the assumption that India,

---

[3] The most salient motif in Tale Type 313, The Magic Flight, is D672, Obstacle flight, in which fugitives throw objects behind them that magically become obstacles in their pursuer's path. The distribution of this motif is virtually worldwide.—Ed. Note

[4] Sven Liljeblad, "Argonauterne och sagan om flykten från trollet." in *Saga och Sed,* 1935. [For a brief consideration of some of the folklore elements in the tale of the Argonauts written in English, see Stith Thompson, *The Folktale,* p. 280.—Ed. Note]

[5] Motif D361.1, Swan maiden, is found as the introduction to a number of different tale types, for example, Type 400, The Man on a Quest for His Lost Wife, and Type 465, The Man Persecuted Because of His Beautiful Wife. The essence of the motif concerns a swan who transforms herself into a maiden. In many versions, a young man captures the maiden by stealing her swan clothes while she is bathing (Motif K1335). In a recent comprehensive monographic article, A. T. Hatto agrees with von Sydow in rejecting the doctrinaire Indianist theory of origin proposed by Holmström. However, Hatto proposes instead a possible origin in Arctic and sub-Arctic regions, a hypothesis based in part on the geographical distribution and migratory breeding patterns of swans, geese, and cranes. See "The Swan Maiden: A Folktale of North Eurasian Origin?" *Bulletin of the School of Oriental and African Studies,* Vol. 24, Part 2 (1961), 326–52.—Ed. Note

centrally situated in relation to the home countries of the widely spread variants, was the country of origin. The assumption was understandable, as at the time when the paper was written scholars did not, as a general rule, give a thought to inheritance, but saw every aspect of the dissemination of a tale as a result of migration, about the precise nature of which they had only very vague ideas. But as there is nothing else to bear out the assumption that India should be the original home of the tale, it is more reasonable to seek the explanation, not in the migration of the tale, but in the colonial formation brought about by the Megalithic people within an area of such immense extent.

The last part of the Grimm hypothesis, the derivation of the folktales from time-old myths, was very natural at a time when linguistic studies had suddenly given to the myths a novel interest and scholars had not yet come to understand the true nature of either the myth or the folktale. The mythological theory of the folktale must, however, be characterized as an absolute mistake, although useful in so far as it enhanced the interest in the folktales to a high degree and served as a strong lever to collecting activities. But for this strong incentive the stock of folktales taken down would certainly have been considerably more meager and scanty than it is now; and the possibilities of scholars arriving at good results would have been more limited.

If the mythological theory has thus done some good, we should not, however, be blind to the fact that, being false, it led the scholars of the nineteenth century most seriously astray. It had not been realized what a myth was precisely, among other reasons because popular beliefs and *sagns* associated therewith had not been studied, which is an indispensable condition for scientific mythological reasearch. Scholars were deceived by the apologetic interpretation of the myths as symbols of elements, natural phenomena, etc. made by the ancient Greek philosophers who endeavored thus to explain away what in many Greek myths was found objectionable from a religious or ethical point of view. These speculations of the ancient Greek philosophers were, however, in the nineteenth century understood as rendering the true meaning of the myth, and scholars therefore grafted this kind of allegorical interpretation onto folktales and myths instead of studying the common man's actual habits of thinking. When at length they became aware that the most dissimilar allegorical interpretations might with equal right be attached to one and the same mythological or folktale motif, it was realized that the procedure must be altogether wrong. Thus the whole study of mythology lost its former reputation and has not yet found its proper place in science. The failure led to the false inference that myths are without any scientific value, which is, indeed, an absurdity, because myths constitute an essential part of any religion. A properly planned study of mythology is therefore a natural ingredient of an adequate science of religion.

The next important achievement in the field of folktales was attained by the Indologist Theodor Benfey, who published, in 1859, his important discovery that the *Panchatantra,* the ancient Indian collection of tales, had reached Europe already in the Middle Ages through translations from Sanskrit into Medieval Persian, and further into Syrian, Hebrew, and ultimately into European vulgar tongues. He had thus established an important cultural influence from the East on Medieval Europe, which influence was not confined to the translation of the *Panchatantra,* but evinced itself also in the transfer of similar peoples' books into Latin and other European languages.

Starting from this fact, Benfey drew, however, an analogy equally bold and false: All our folktales, so he asserted, animal fables excepted, had been composed in India within historic times, in the centuries immediately following Buddha's appearance. Later on they had migrated to Europe, partly by way of literature, partly by oral tradition. He considered that the beginning of such a migration of tales might have been made through Alexander's Indian expedition, but that it was mainly through the intermediary of the Arabs and during the Age of Crusades, maybe also by the Mongolian conquest of Russia, that the great stream of Indian tales flooded Europe. Benfey himself realized, however, that all this was only a working hypothesis, and that the theory had to be proved by examination of every separate folktale. The faults in the theory were, however, very obvious.

As a matter of course, no analogy at all can be drawn from the migration of a literary collection of tales to Europe from India by way of literary translation to oral tradition. For the latter obeys its own laws which are altogether different from those governing written literature. The possibility that such an oral tradition may be spread by wandering mendicants, Buddhist or Christian, cannot be entirely ruled out in special cases; but there is here a very far cry from possibility to probability and actual fact, more especially if this is asserted to apply to all folktales. Mendicants will, e.g., as a rule, have no use for chimera tales and should accordingly not be credited with their dissemination. That Benfey did not realize immediately that his daring hypothesis was altogether mistaken was due, among other things, to the fact that at Benfey's time the folktales had not been collected to a sufficient extent, and that for this reason alone he could not have an approximately all-comprehensive view of the stock of folktales, in Europe or in India, apart from the literary collections known to him.

A sufficiently comprehensive view has not been possible till our own time, and then only thanks to the assiduous registration work done by such scholars as Reinhold Köhler, Johannes Bolte, Svend Grundtvig, H. F. Feilberg, Antti Aarne, Stith Thompson, and Albert Wesselski; in spite of this, however, only a few have allowed themselves the time to acquire such a comprehensive view.

If we study the *Panchatantra* and compare its contents with Aarne-Thompson's *Types of the Folktale,* it cannot escape us that there are here two quite different worlds. The index of tale types found in Aarne-Thompson is not complete, but its more than a thousand different numbers represent the European stock of folktales quite well. Very few of these, scarcely more than six, namely three animal fables and three jocular fables, are to be found among the ninety tales or so contained in the *Panchatantra,* and among these six some have so rarely been taken down in Europe that they are evidently borrowed articles that have slipped in accidentally from books and cannot be said really to have taken root in European tradition.

The chapbook, *The Seven Sages,* is of oriental origin insofar as the framework-story and four of the tales have actually been taken from the corresponding oriental collection held to be derived from an Indian source, which has not, however, come to our knowledge. The other eleven tales in our chapbook have been taken from European tradition but are missing in the oriental redactions of the same book.[6]

In Indian oral tradition there are likewise only a few tales that approximately correspond to, and may be identified with, European types. Thus it is shown already by comparing the type of folktale to be found in Asia and in Europe respectively, that a mass immigration of folktales from the East into Europe is out of the question; and the few cases of congruity do not in themselves prove India to be the donor and Europe to be the receiver, apart from just a few cases where it is a matter of loans taken exactly from written literature. That Benfey ventured to advance his theory about the Indian origin of all European folktales is thus in part a consequence of the fact that he neither had nor could have any comprehensive view of the European stores of oral tale tradition. Likewise he could not know that a whole series of European tales may now with certainty be attributed to a much earlier period than that of the rise of Buddhism, or the connections between India and Europe which he considered as decisive. That a folktale study built on so false an assumption as Benfey's Indian hypothesis could not forward research to any considerable extent is obvious. Other failings also added to the difficulties. At Benfey's time scholars had not learned to distinguish clearly between the sharply defined types of folktale. Benfey's just claim that his hypothesis should be tested in the case of every separate tale gave rise to scamped comparisons of the European tales with those of India, and if only *some* resemblance was found, the Indian origin was held to be established. When Benfey himself set out to examine some tales with strange helpers (Aa513), he grouped as variants of one and the same tale several altogether dissimilar tales without any mutual relationship and even belonging to quite different categories, merely because they contained characters with strange attributes, which were not, however, the same in the types compared. From the story in the *Panchatantra* about the lion and the bull who were intimate friends but

---

6 For a small sample of the scholarship on this important literary collection of folktales, see Domenico Comparetti, *Researches Respecting the Book of Sindibad* (London, 1882); William A. Clouston, *The Book of Sindibad* (Glasgow, 1884); and Killis Campbell, *The Seven Sages* (Boston, 1907).—ED. NOTE

were divided by a jackal who set them against each another by evil slander, various scholars of the Indian School have derived the tale of the Old Woman as Trouble Maker, in some Swedish variants called Kitta Grå, who could set a husband and wife at variance whom the Devil had not been able to divide (Aa1353).[7] The two tales are altogether different in respect of cast and details, but they build on the fact that it is possible to divide friends by slander. This method of picking a quarrel has been used innumerable times in real life without the mischief-maker having to learn it from one tale or another. And this kind of intrigue has everywhere been capable of creating such effects, so that entirely independent stories might be composed about it in different countries. The absurdity of deriving the tale of the Old Woman as Trouble Maker from the Indian tale about the Lion, the Bull, and the Jackal, of all tales, is shown, among other things, in the fact that the latter is obviously a *literary* tale, in which human matters have been deliberately remodeled into an animal fable, as has been done in various other tales in the *Panchatantra*. He who composed the tale of the Lion, the Bull, and the Jackal, is sure to have known stories with human actors such as Aa1353, for there are various types of such stories in India and in other countries, probably independent of one another. On the other hand, what is true in this case is that the tale was disseminated by preachers who had learned it from collections of homiletic examples, some of which were derived from the East, in part from India. We should not, however, in such cases overemphasize India as the country of origin. Jews and Arabs are at least as good composers of examples, and as the tale about the Old Woman as Trouble Maker in its European form does not appear to have been known farther East than among the Arabs, there is no occasion for seeking the country of its origin farther away.

The Indian School had thus from the start both an insufficient view of the material on which they theorized, and insufficient method. In spite of this, they have no doubt done some service to science. For they have contributed not a little to teaching scholars how to distinguish between myths and tales, and have thus been instrumental in putting an end to the thoroughly mistaken fantasies on myths prevalent at the time between Grimm and Benfey. Such a scholar as Reinhold Köhler, who had at first unreservedly approved Benfey's theory, was soon to become aware of the shortcomings of the school. He therefore changed right over into mere registration work, through which an important foundation of a more comprehensive view was laid. Average philologists, however, who have not gone in for folktale studies, have, precisely because of their ignorance of the European stock of types, dogmatically

---

[7] O. Gjerdman, "Hon som var värre än den onde," in *Saga och Sed,* 1941. [There is no apparent genetic connection between Motif K2131.2, Envious jackal makes lion suspicious of his friend the bull, and Motif K1085, Woman makes trouble between man and wife: the hair from his beard, in Tale Type 1353, The Old Woman as Trouble Maker. Once again, the question arises as to whether this kind of inexact parallel is to be attributed to polygenesis or to diffusion from a common source.—Ed. Note]

clung to the oriental origin of all tales. They have thus become confirmed in their view that a considerable part of the matter contained in the medieval collections of homiletic examples, probably the only folktale material in which they have taken interest, is actually oriental.

This does not, however, apply to all philologists. In his famous treatise on the fabliaux, so popular in the Middle Ages, Joseph Bédier,[8] the distinguished French philologist, established that the bulk of French fabliaux had no counterpart in the whole literature of oriental tales, and that those which had, were better in their French form than in the oriental. He was inclined, therefore, to maintain that this sort of jocular tale originated in France, admitting, however, that this could not be strictly proved, and that the same type of tale might well arise independently in any place.

This was a point of view which had also been urged by British anthropologists. It must be acknowledged as correct to a certain degree, inasmuch as one and the same idea, one and the same point, may give rise to narrative composition among various peoples. It is a possibility that must always be allowed for by the scholar. The notion that two stories with highly individual motifs should originate independently in different quarters, is however an absurdity. I can here refer to the above-mentioned example of the Bull, the Lion, and the Jackal on one hand, and the Old Woman as Trouble Maker on the other. The conformity between the two stories consists only of the universal human fact that friendship or love may be done away with by an artfully arranged campaign of slander. On the other hand, the very plot of the second tale, with a kind of contest between the Devil and the wicked woman to be able to sow dissension between husband and wife, is so individually devised that one would be apt to presume a traditional connection between all variants with that content. And this is further strengthened when the wife is enticed to cut some stubbles of beard from her husband's throat during his after-dinner nap in order to make sure of his love, while her husband has falsely been made to believe that the wife has promised to cut his throat that day. All variants with the whole of this content must have a common origin, and wherever in Europe they are found, they are almost certain to be derived, more or less directly, from the homiletic example.

The importance of Bédier's attack on the Indian theory consists not so much of the results of his examination. He did not arrive at a fixed, established result; and, with the better access to the material open to present-day scholars, a renewed scrutiny of the fabliaux might give quite different results. The important thing was, however, partly that he created justifiable doubts of an ill-founded hypothesis, and that he confined himself to a natural group governed by different laws from those that apply to other groups of tales. In the latter respect previous scholarship had been singularly careless. It could already be said of Grimm that he used the common appellation *Märchen* for

---

8 *Les Fabliaux* (Paris, 1895). [A more recent study is Per Nykrog, *Les Fabliaux* (Copenhagen, 1957).—ED. NOTE]

all popular tradition, even when thinking of the fantastic chimera tales only. Benfey had, at any rate, segregated animal fables as a distinct group which he found so different in kind from all other folktales that—for altogether insufficient reasons—he considered this group as originating in Greece and not in India, where, however, animal tales abounded. But when, on the other hand, he dealt with the rest of all the various groups indiscriminately, it must be called a serious mistake. Bédier spoke only of the jocular fables, even if he believed that the independent origin of the same tale among various peoples might apply to other groups of tales as well. His contribution was in any case a serious warning against founding thoughtless and one-sided hypotheses on a thing of so multifarious an aspect as the folktale. At the same time, however, his doubt of the possibility of attaining certain results deterred scholars from continuing studies of the folktale, and that may be the reason why, since his treatise, so little has been done in France in the field of folktale research.

The next step forward in folktale research was taken by Kaarle Krohn, the Finnish literary historian. From Julius Krohn, his father, he had learned the geographical method the latter had applied to the *Kalevala-cycle*, and he availed himself of it in his thesis, *Bär (Wolf) und Fuchs,* 1886, in which he examined the animal fable about the bear, or the wolf, fishing with his tail through a hole in the ice.[9] It was the first monograph on a folktale to be undertaken by careful scientific method. Krohn aimed at collating, as far as possible, all the variants of the tale, and furthermore each motif was made subject to close critical scrutiny. By a statistical and psychological examination of all the several variations in their geographical occurrence Krohn endeavored to reconstruct the original form of the tale and to determine its home, which he defined as Northern Europe. It could neither be India, nor Greece, as imagined by Benfey. Krohn also asserted that any people might produce folktales.

Kaarle Krohn's monograph marks an epoch in the history of folktale research, introducing for the first time a strict method. He thereby showed what thorough detailed work must be applied to the study of a folktale before it is possible to say anything with certainty about its original home, and that what was true of *one* tale could not be considered to apply as a matter of course to *all* folktales. His work was thus an urgent call for scientific sobriety. Originally he had thought of dealing with all fables about bears, wolves, and foxes. Having to give it up for reasons of time and scope, he had, however, thereby procured for himself a wider outlook on kindred matter, which was a great advantage in preparing the material scientifically.

What was wanting, however, in Kaarle Krohn's treatment of his animal fable, was the insight into the laws that govern the kind of material dealt with which is a prerequisite of any scientific investigation. Want of such insight was, however, most natural at his time. The work heretofore bestowed on the

---

9 This is Aarne-Thompson Tale Type 2, The Tail-Fisher.—ED. NOTE

folktales had not been thorough enough for scholars to have made, or to be able to make, the observations required by science concerning the origin, evolution, application, and spread of various tales. So it was self-evident that Krohn had to fill up the gaps in the knowledge of the tales then at hand with unchecked hypotheses.

Even in his thesis on the Bear (Wolf) and the Fox, such a hypothesis has led him to deny what actually appears from the material. When, in the title of the thesis, he brackets the wolf, it is because he considers the bear as belonging originally to the fable, and that the wolf has got into some variants probably by mistake instead of the bear. The fact is, however, that the whole of the medieval material always makes the wolf appear as the adversary of the fox who tricks him into fishing with his tail; and the same holds good of the whole of the Russian, German, British, and French material. It is only in Scandinavia and Finland that the bear has taken the place of the wolf. Krohn, however, considered this to be the original idea, because in that way an aetiological explanation is obtained, to account for the fact that the bear has no tail. This, he thought, must be the original reason why the tale has come to exist at all. He here neglected the fact that aetiological explanations of the shapes of animals are as a rule jocular, and that they have often been placed in a context where they must decidedly be secondary. Likewise, for an animal to lose his tail, in order that his utter failure may be made obvious, is not a very rare motif. There are, e.g., various fables about foxes, jackals, and wolves in which these animals lose their tails by some accident, but there is not the slightest occasion for assuming that the fable in question should originally have been made about a permanently tailless animal, in order to explain such a bodily structure. There is every reason for presuming a mutation of the fable, by which a facetious narrator intended to make the contrast between the strong animal and the sly more striking still than that between wolf and fox and at the same time to obtain a humorous explanation of the fact that the bear has no tail. This mutation of his of the wolf into bear got the ascendancy in the Scandinavian-Finnish area so as to become the sole prevailing oicotype of the fable there. Had the aetiological motif been the original one, the fact that it has not been maintained anywhere outside the Scandinavian area would have been incomprehensible.

Kaarle Krohn did not continue his work on folktale studies, but proceeded to devote himself exclusively to the continuation of his father's studies on the *Kalevala*. He set a fashion, however, through Antti Aarne, his pupil, who applied the same method to an array of profound, thorough monographs on folktales. His principal achievement, however, is his *Verzeichnis der Märchentypen*, later on adapted and enlarged in Aarne-Thompson, *The Types of the Folktales*, which is of supreme value for the registration and cataloguing of folktale types. This list of types is a systematic arrangement which makes it possible, in cataloguing a collection of tales, to quote only the systematic number of each tale; and it is a most helpful guide for the scholar.

The failings in the method of folktale studies instituted by Krohn and

Aarne consist, as has already been pointed out, in the circumstance that the life and laws of the folktale have not been sufficiently explored. The failing knowledge of these matters had to be replaced by working hypotheses which later on proved themselves to be false. The point of view of inheritance, which is indispensable, as the tales have indeed not only been spread abroad but also handed down through thousands of years, has been entirely lost from sight, while the concept of migration introduced by Benfey has been the sole prevailing point of view. This must be considered a serious instance of one-sidedness.

The very term "folk tradition" had in former times led to the false and romantic notion that this tradition belonged to the people in its totality, who were correspondingly imagined as consisting solely of composers of tales. This false idea must be supposed more or less to underlie Krohn's and Aarne's notion of how a tale migrates. They have availed themselves of two images to illustrate this view. One image is that the tale spreads like rings on the calm surface of water when a stone is thrown on it. The other, that the migration wells forth like a stream. Both are obviously wrong, founded on the false supposition that every one who hears a tale will carry it on to others. In fact the dissemination of a tale is desultory to a high degree. Only a very small number of active bearers of tradition equipped with a good memory, vivid imagination, and narrative powers do transmit the tales. It is only they who tell them. Among their audience it is only a small percentage who are able to recollect a tale so as to recount it, and a smaller percentage still who actually do so. Most of those who have heard a tale told and are able to remember it, remain passive carriers of tradition, whose importance for the continued life of the tale consists mainly in their interest in hearing it told again, wherefore they point out the active carrier of tradition, the *traditor,* as a good narrator, and call upon him to narrate. For a tale to be transferred from the place where the narrator has his home, some active carrier of tradition must not only come to the new place but also remain there long enough for a new *traditor* to be trained. That sort of transfer takes place in a most desultory manner, subject to no rule, and has not slightest resemblance to the rings that spread on water.

From that false hypothesis of his, that tales spread like rings on water, Kaarle Krohn inferred that if a tradition should be met with in two places A and B, it must exist also in the whole of the interjacent area. The inference is correctly drawn, but is nevertheless false, because all the premises are false. When Axel Olrik made the assertion that the Caucasian myth of the Fettered Giant was transmitted to the North from the realm of the Goths on the Black Sea by Goths visiting their old Northern homes, Krohn objected to this result as preposterous, because the myth about the Fettered Giant must then have occurred in the whole of the interjacent area of Russia. As it was not to be found there, a transfer from Caucasus to the North could not possibly have taken place.

Whoever knows anything about the actual life of tradition will easily be able to prove this inference to be false. The traveling Goth, going up the streams of Russia—indeed he was even to make the voyage through the Mediterranean and round Europe—need not on the whole journey make use of the traditions he bears in memory. Maybe he will not even get into touch with the people whose land he traverses, but whose language he does not know. And if a talk be brought about by means of an interpreter, or by gesture, it is done in order to get necessary information about the route, or of such things as he may need to acquire by barter. Certainly he will not take it into his head to serve up his stock of tales or *sagns* during these proceedings. And should it happen on a few occasions, it is almost certain that it will be a thing of so little actual interest to his audience, that it will not survive there. Whereas the traveler on his way will have no use for his stores of tradition, and no occasion to narrate, the more occasion will he have on reaching the North. He is the traveler from afar and will be the center of interest at feasts and other gatherings. He will be called upon to tell about all sorts of things. Opportunities for narration will crop up spontaneously, and the transfer of the myth about the Fettered Giant onto Loki, who belonged to the race of giants, but was on good terms with the gods until their rupture, is brought about without difficulty.

To folktale research, questions regarding the bearers of tradition and occasions to narrate must be problems of first rate importance, and if they are ignored, and scholars build instead on uncertain working hypotheses, the results must be false, more or less. Again, it is of vital importance to strike a right balance between the points of view of inheritance and dissemination, between the conservatism of tradition and its new formations.

These points of view should, I think, be self-evident, but when Aarne wrote his monographs, no one had opposed Krohn's comparison with the rings that spread on water, although Benfey had already realized the importance of the historic connections between the peoples. Krohn stressed his point by saying that, in his opinion, frontiers offered no resistance to the spread of folktales, because border populations are bilingual. Such border populations do not, however, play any important part in these matters, for the number of carriers or receivers of tradition is not greater among them than in other places. Denmark has, indeed, a common frontier with Germany, and on it a bilingual population, but the influence from German tradition that is to be met with in Denmark, is due less to a bilingual border population than to German immigrants, and to such Danes as have returned to the home country after a long stay in Germany. That Sweden, too, has German folktale traditions, can have nothing at all to do with a border population, but must be ascribed exclusively to German immigrants, or to Swedes that have returned home from Germany. In both cases German influence may naturally also be ascribed to tales that have been translated in children's books and chapbooks, a possibility which must be allowed for anywhere.

The other metaphor used by Kaarle Krohn to illustrate the way in which folktales are disseminated, was that of a stream welling forth in a certain direction. This metaphor, I think, he has most likely taken over from the Indian School. His first work was, indeed, directed against the one-sidedness of the Indian School. But it was an incontestable fact that traditions had been influenced by the East, and that France through her fabliaux had influenced the rest of Europe considerably. He therefore thought of these influences as streams springing partly from India, partly from France.

In this metaphor he was very literal. He pointed out, e.g., that in Finland two streams of folktale traditions had met, one from the East which had left a Russian stamp on the Karelian stock of tales, and one from the West which had marked the folk-tradition of Western Finland with a Swedish impress. He said to me that it seemed as if this fact suggested a law: "Where two streams of tradition meet they will check one another."

The whole of this reasoning, however, rests on a mistake. Eastern Finland had long been under Russian control, and it was not till 1809 that it was definitively united with Western Finland into a grand duchy. It was by no means the streams of tradition from the East and from the West, passing through bilingual border districts, that caused the formation of two such different areas of tradition. The part of Finland which had belonged to Sweden politically for so long a period, had been furnished at that time with a lot of Swedish officers and civil servants, who often brought with them servants of Swedish nationality. The part belonging politically to Russia received in like manner Russian garrisons and Russian civil servants. Among these Swedes and Russians, who had come into the country for political reasons, were many carriers of folktale tradition, and they implanted the folktale traditions of their home countries on Finland. The law of the streams that meet, is accordingly altogether mistaken and is based on a false hypothesis.

Another hypothesis, most natural for incipient folktale research, was that the original form of a folktale should be the most complete and the best, also the most logical; and likewise, that where the most original form is to be found, there will also be the original home of the tale. The better a folktale, the greater will be its popularity, and the more easily will it survive. Scholars will therefore be apt to presume that incomplete, or relatively poor, variants are products of degeneration. Such was my own view when I made my first efforts in the field of folktale research. It is, however, based not on experience, but on mere guesswork. However specious the argument, it must be characterized as a false hypothesis.

Not a few folktales have been composed with a *sagn* for a starting point, and then the original thing is, of course, the *sagn*. Such a *sagn* may be continued in the manner of a tale, and various tale composers may invent entirely different continuations. Striking instances of this are the various tales about the Grateful Dead (Aa505–508).[10] The nucleus of the tale is that a man

---

[10] Sven Liljeblad, *Die Tobiasgeschichte und andere Märchen mit toten Helfern* (Lund, 1927).

provides for the burial of an unburied corpse. To this nucleus there has been added, at the *sagn*-stage, even an event which is considered as a reward for the good turn, and with this addition the *sagn* is already to be found in Cicero (*De divinatione*, I, 27). But various tale composers have, starting from the *sagn,* gone on fabulating, making the grateful dead man enter into the service of the generous youth, however without giving himself away, and assist him on various occasions, so that he succeeds in winning a princess. We may imagine that the various tale composers had the *sagn* only at their disposal, but one or several of them may, of course, have heard a complete tale and composed another to the same opening. If so, the new tale may be considered as a mutation of the model; but such a thing will be difficult to decide with certainty in their case. There exists in the East a mutation of the opening about the Grateful Dead,[11] formed so that a prince severs a serpent from a frog, but in order not to bereave the serpent of its natural nourishment he gives it a piece of his own flesh. Later on both serpent and frog assume the human form, come to the prince as servants, and help him to win a princess much in the same way as in the tales about the dead helper. The resemblance between the two openings is so great that they cannot be altogether independent of each other. The last quoted form must be supposed to be a mutation of the opening about the dead helper, but fused onto other stories about severing serpent and frog (cf., e.g., *Gesta Romanorum,* 99).

Mutation is an important phenomenon in the tales, and it is not always easy to decide which of two or several mutations of one and the same folktale motif or composition is nearest to the original form. An original motif may be superseded by a new mutation, but a new mutation may also yield to the older form, being unable to assert itself at its expense. If a motif is particularly popular, this very fact may induce various narrators to mutate it in different ways.

As an example of such a motif, popular in its home country, where it exists in several mutations, take the motif *Hjaðningavíg,* well-known to Germanists. It was borrowed from Ireland by Norse poets, and during the viking age it was popular in the North, where it was mixed up with a German heroic saga, but has later on disappeared altogether from Northern popular tradition. In Irish tradition it is popular to this day and has been preferably attached to the *Finn-cycle.* It is about a contest which is ever renewed because a witch resuscitates the fallen warriors, who next day wage a new fight against their conquerors. The contest is brought to an end by a foreign hero, who does not go home to rest after the victory, but remains on the battlefield waiting for the witch. He withstands her lethargic sorcery and kills her. There exist, however, other mutations. One of them, for example, is about Finn's arrival in the country of the giants, where he is appointed court dwarf to the king of the giants. He becomes aware that the king is always tired, because he

---

[11] Georg Rosen, *Tuti-Nameh* (Leipzig, 1858), Vol. 2, 27.

has to wage a single combat every night with a redoubtable giant. Finn goes fighting in his place, defeats the giant, and the giant's father too, and in the end also the giant's mother, who was the worst of all. As to which of the various mutations is the principal form of the motif, there can, however, scarcely be any doubt in this case. The simplest and least specialized form is, I dare say, both the most common in Ireland and the most original.

Another instance is the Cinderella tale. *Strabo* has a tale of how Rhodopis, the beautiful hetaera in Egypt, when bathing, was bereft of one shoe by an eagle, who carried it away and let it fall into Pharaoh's lap. Pharaoh made up his mind to marry the one whom the shoe would fit. He made all women try it on, and thus found Rhodopis. This is one of the oldest records of the Cinderella tale, and we feel surprised at not finding the episode there about the prince's feast, at which she performed and enchanted him, and how she lost the shoe in her hurry to get home. We wonder if this is not a corrupt or a defective form. It is more logical to fall in love with one whom you see than with one whom you never saw.[12] As, however, the same episode is wanting in Further India too, where it is likewise an eagle that carries the shoe away to drop it into the lap of the king, we must consider the simple and less logical form to be the more original version. Later on, in some place or other, a tale composer improved on it by adding the episode of the prince's feast; and this additional episode came to prevail everywhere: It was only on the outskirts of the area, in Further India for example, or in a very ancient record taken down in Egypt, another marginal country, that the more simple version was maintained. The fact that the original version was preserved on the outskirts of the area over which the tale was spread, does not, however, imply that either of these countries should be its original home. On the fringes of the area, or in some other remote or isolated place, the more ancient and original form may have lingered, because the later and better version did not get so far. We cannot tell where the new episode about the prince's feast was composed, for every *narrator* of the older form will improve upon his version as soon as he hears the novel addition, exciting as it is, and more logical too. In this case, therefore, the original form does not give any indication as to where the original home was situated. The eagle that drops a shoe into pharaoh's lap is but a mutational variant of the bird that lets the golden hair of a woman fall into the lap of the king, with the

---

12 Aa510. [Anna Birgitta Rooth, a leading contemporary Swedish folklorist, has made a comprehensive study of this well-known tale. See *The Cinderella Cycle* (Lund, 1951). One must remember that the concept of "falling in love" is culturally relative. The notion is not found in all cultures. Moreover, marriages in many parts of the world were (and are) arranged marriages, arranged by the families of the principals, not by the principals themselves. In parts of Asia today, it is still not at all uncommon for newlyweds to marry without having seen much of one another prior to the wedding. Thus if a man does not have to see the girl he is destined to marry (and this would definitely be the case in infant betrothals), the motif in which the eagle carries the shoe to the pharoah or king need not be considered a corrupt or defective form. The eagle, like a professional marriage arranger, acts as a sanctioned intermediary.—ED. NOTE]

result that he sends the hero of the tale out to seek for its beautiful owner. The Cinderella tale must here be studied in connection with the various tales, the opening motifs of which, as to the hair, the lock, etc., have a mutational relationship to the eagle with the shoe. The various types of tale with several such mutations for their opening motifs may perhaps give a hint on this point.

A third example may be taken from the above-mentioned tale of the Magic Flight (Aa313). Among the laborious tasks assigned to the hero by the ogre, one has fallen out of many European variants. In Ireland and on the whole in Western Europe, i.e., in France and Spain as well, the hero is told to fetch an egg down from the top of a tree reaching to the clouds with a trunk as smooth as glass. The ogre's daughter, who has assisted the hero in his previous tasks, points out that there is nothing for it but to slaughter her and take all the bones out of her body. If he puts them against the trunk they will serve as a foothold enabling him to climb the tree. In getting down he must, however, take them with him and throw them into the sea. She will then come to life again; but he forgets a joint of her little finger at the top of the tree. That joint is missing from her body, which mishap turns out all for the best in one of his later tasks.[13]

This episode is not to be found at all in any of the variants taken down in more eastern regions, but in its artless ferocity it is very popular in the most westerly megalithic area of Europe. In Spain, however, another form of the same episode has been taken down: The hero has to fetch a ring from the bottom of the sea, and his helper points out that he must kill her and fill a vessel with her blood and another one with her flesh, and throw both vessels into the sea. She then is transformed into a fish, who fetches the ring out of the sea, and is restored later into her human form. It is obvious, in spite of dissimilarity in other respects, that both motifs are mutations of one and the same; for the episode has not only the same place in the composition of the tale; it also contains the killing of the girl and the feature that she is thrown into the sea. The episode with the ring is, however, less logical. Whereas slaughtering her is better accounted for by the circumstance that all the bones are required for steps, it seems incomprehensible why such procedure should be necessary for the sake of changing into a fish. The fact is, however, that the only Spanish record has one counterpart in Ireland, one in the Balkans, and one in Samoa, where it was taken down in the form of an ancient heroic ballad, which existed there before the arrival of the Europeans. I should be inclined, therefore, to see in this version a primeval form of the episode, ruled out, however, later on in the major part of the area, because it was found

---

[13] The task is picking out the helpful daughter from among her sisters who look exactly like her. This task (Motif H161, Recognition of transformed person among identical companions) is accomplished with comparative ease because of the missing joint (Motif H57.0.1, Recognition of resuscitated person by missing member). Other motifs mentioned by von Sydow include H1114, Task: climbing glass mountain, and F848.3, Ladder of bones.—ED. NOTE

illogical and unnecessarily brutal. In Western Europe, someone has brought about the mutation with the tree, possibly in connection with a motif about a glass mountain contained in a tale of Cupid and Psyche.[14] And this mutation has almost entirely supplanted the older motif. The latter has, however, as regards the ring on the bottom of the sea, many counterparts, more particularly in Mediterranean tradition, but with different solutions to the problem, the ring being found in a fish that has been caught, or fetched by some fish, frog, or natatorial bird, who was willing to help, etc.[15] If it be so, the original form does not indicate the country of origin. The tale must be supposed to have reached Samoa at the very end of its long wanderings, but it must have left the country of its origin before anyone had brought about the mutation with the tree, and certainly before the whole episode was discarded and replaced by something altogether different, as is the case in the bulk of variants taken down east of, say, the fifth meridian East of Greenwich.

Of a good many tales there exists a great number of mutations adapted, more or less, to the individual taste of the narrator, or invented with the intention of being able to offer something novel. The tale of The Ogre's (Devil's) Heart in the Egg (Aa302), e.g., has a great variety of mutational types, each with its own area of dissemination, but all of them obviously of the same type. There are also mutations intended for a definite social class. Of some tales, for example, there are special mutations for sailors, and for soldiers as well, adapted to the taste of the audience concerned by such attractive devices as making the hero a sailor or a soldier respectively.

In speaking of mutations I have confined myself to the more sweeping changes resulting from intentional remodeling. A good many changes are, however, brought about in a different way. Every receiver of a tale tradition will always make a few alterations in some motifs, partly on account of failing memory, partly in order to make the story conform better to his own views and tastes, or to kindred motifs in such other tales as he may know. More particularly, this is true of the side motifs of a tale. In a district with a good *narrator*, or where some book of tales has been read frequently, it may therefore occur that a good many persons recount by word of mouth, or write down on paper, one and the same tale with individual alterations accordingly. This does not prove that each of these people should have received his own tradition from his own separate *traditor*, as has been suggested in explanation of this fact.[16]

---

[14] This is Tale Type 425A, The Monster (Animal) as Bridegroom, which has been the subject of a number of monographs. See J. O. Swahn, *The Tale of Cupid and Psyche* (Lund, 1955). The ascent of the glass mountain does occur in the tale type, but is more commonly found as a suitor task (H331.1.1) in Tale Type 530, The Princess on the Glass Mountain, and it is this tale which could just as well have helped cause the changes in Tale Type 313.—Ed. Note

[15] See Motif B548.2.1, Fish recovers ring from sea, and Tale Type 736A, The Ring of Polycrates, for numerous references.—Ed. Note

[16] W. Liungman, *En traditionsstudie över sagan om prinsessan i jordkulan* (Göteborg, 1925).

Another alteration in the content of a tale is brought about by way of oicotypification, which consists of a certain unification of the variants within one and the same linguistic or cultural area on account of isolation from other areas. It may consist of the circumstance that one mutation has prevailed over the rest so as to become the oicotype of the tale within the area concerned. Oicotypification will, as a general rule, take a long time, and will therefore not evince itself in all folktales.[17] I shall quote but one or two examples.

The tale of Odysseus and Polyphemus (Aa1137), spread all over Europe, often contains an episode not to be found in the Odyssey. When the man has got out of the giant's den, the latter presents him with a gift of hospitality. Taking it, however, the man clings to the gift, which cries out and betrays his whereabouts so that the giant is on the point of catching him, and the man must cut off his finger, or hand, to get away. In Western European variants, more particularly in the Celtic ones, it is always a question of a golden ring; in the Eastern European variants it is a club, a stick, or an axe of gold. The oicotype appears thus in two different oicotypes, one with a ring, the other with a weapon. It is difficult to say which is the original, but they must be derived from a common source, the contents of which have been fixed in a somewhat different manner. We may ask at what time the common archetype may have existed, the method with a view to monographic investigation only. The necessary knowledge cannot be acquired by that kind of investigation, but only by all-round research into the stock of folktales in their natural context. A natural system which groups together such types as are closely related to each other, and which may illustrate each other as required, will be of great importance for this work. Continued registration work will also be necessary of course.

Krohn and Aarne saw in folktale monographs the immediate task to be performed by scholarship. By such monographs, however, it has not been possible to solve the most important problems of folktale research; and the interest these studies have attracted has been only slight. As a general rule scholars have confined themselves to using them for their first work; and in actual fact any student can, without previous knowledge, collect the material of variants needed for such a monograph from the handbooks now available. Once the material has been provided, he can of course arrange it geographically, find out special types, etc. Unless he is conversant with what is of particular interest to science, and with the life of the tales and the laws that govern them, the result will, however, be uninteresting, even if the grouping of the material will always give some new results.

---

[17] For an interesting application of the concept of oicotype to American materials, see the first appendix, "Toward the Discernment of Oicotype," in Roger Abrahams' important study of American Negro folklore, *Deep Down in the Jungle...Negro Narrative Folklore from the Streets of Philadelphia* (Hatboro, Penn., 1964), pp. 245–58.—ED. NOTE

Faced with the task of preparing a folktale monograph, even an able philologist who is not steeped in the problems of tradition will be almost as handicapped as a freshman, apart from the circumstance that his philological training may enable him to select more interesting subjects for examination. He will not take any type number at random from Aarne-Thompson, but will prefer a tale which has an obvious connection with one of the myths, legends of saints, fabliaux, or the like, in which he takes an interest because he knows that among scholars there is a desire for light to be thrown on them from traditional sources. He forgets, however, that oral tradition is governed by other than to which people it then belonged. Most often we are inclined to think of the remote period when Celts and Slavs lived side by side near the Carpathian Mountains.

We are struck by much the same idea when seeing how a mutation of the tale of The Ogre's (Devil's) Heart in the Egg (Aa302)[18] has been split up into two oicotypes, one Slavic, and the other Celtic. In the Slavic type a prince has won a princess, who gives him all the keys, warning him however not to open a certain door. He does so nevertheless, and then in the forbidden room he finds an ogre, or a giant, chained to the wall, or shut up in a barrel. The ogre asks for water, and the hero gives it to him. But then the chains, or the barrel, break, the ogre runs away with the princess and disappears. The corresponding episode in the Celtic oicotype of the same mutation makes the hero, on his way to fight three giants, pass a naked man hanging on a tree and asking to be set free. Twice the prince refuses his request, but the third time he sets him free. Then instantaneously the prince finds himself hanging naked on the tree; and the man he has set free runs away with the princess. It is obvious that there are here two different oicotypes of the same mutation. When the plot takes a different course, this is due to the circumstance that each of the two types has for a long period been developed independently, without any renewal of traditional connection.

All these questions about the bearers of tale tradition, of the cases in which a tradition is applied and can be transmitted, the changes that may be brought about by various kinds of mutation, and by oicotypification, are naturally of the greatest weight for a scientific study of the folktale; and the results of such study cannot, even by the best of methods, be correct unless they are based on a right knowledge of the life of the folktale, and the laws by which it is governed. When Krohn instituted his method, the necessary knowledge was not available, and he worked out laws other than those

---

[18] The tale as summarized by von Sydow appears to be Tale Type 502, The Wild Man, rather than Tale Type 302. His oicotypic distinctions still hold, of course. Incidentally, a version of Tale Type 502 has been elaborately analyzed by Carl Jung. See his essay, "The Phenomenology of the Spirit in Fairy Tales," in *Psyche and Symbol: A Selection from the Writings of C. G. Jung,* ed. Violet S. de Laszlo (Garden City, N.Y., 1958), pp. 61–112.—ED. NOTE

that apply to written literature. He is, e.g., accustomed to date a literary product from the oldest manuscript in which it is preserved, insofar as here is no reason for suspecting the oldest manuscript of being a copy of a lost manuscript of greater antiquity.

The tales and *sagns* of popular tradition are considerably more timeless than manuscripts, and a philologist who is not conversant with their true nature will easily draw the rash inference that the first allusion to be found in literature to a *sagn* or tale is derived almost directly from the archetype of the *sagn* concerned and accordingly considers it as dating back only one or two decades. He does not reckon with the possibility that the version given in his written source may be a faulty fragment, just as there are both faulty and good variants among the records taken down in the field by present-day scholars, as of course has always been the case. He has not a sufficient knowledge of the common people's habits of thinking and expressing themselves, nor the licenses taken by the popular taleteller as regards the development of side motifs of minor importance to the main plot. He therefore often attaches too great a weight to details which are altogether irrelevant for a critical examination of the subject.

To illustrate this I will give one or two examples. The earliest indication of the existence of the tale about The Magic Flight (Aa313) is, as mentioned above, to be found in the tale of the Argonauts. This cannot, however, be held to represent the original form of the tale to any higher degree than can the record of the Samoan heroic ballad of Siati[19] taken down in Samoa in the beginning of the nineteenth century. The Greek heroic tale consists of a fusion of at least three distinct tale types, the original episodes of which have partly supplanted each other, a fact which alone reduces their originality. Besides, artistic poetry has in many places remodeled it and alienated it from the original form and contents of the tale. Furthermore we are enabled to determine a few traits as being actually original, amongst other things they are in full conformity with the Samoan version as compared with all other variants. The marginal variant in Samoa gives us in more than one respect good criteria for determining the original form of the tale, although Samoa cannot possibly be the country of its origin.[20]

---

[19] G. Turner, *Samoa A Hundred Years Ago, and Long Before* (London, 1884), pp. 102ff.

[20] One of the most fascinating working hypotheses in folklore research is the concept of marginal survival or peripheral distribution. The idea is that versions from marginal regions or on the periphery of a region are more likely to be archaic forms. The older form may have died out or may have been greatly changed in its original locale. For example, French and Spanish settlers moved to the New World bringing their folklore with them. Some pockets of culture in the New World have been isolated and have remained ultraconservative so that it is possible to collect versions of Spanish tales in Central America and French tales in French Canada that are no longer told in Spain and France. Moreover, both the traits and language of the tales are often archaic, requiring, for example, the use of seventeenth-century dictionaries. Another instance of marginal survival is that several European tale types have been collected from the American Indians who borrowed them from early settlers. Some of these tales have not been collected from

Another example is the ancient Egyptian tale of The Two Brothers, which has been mentioned above. As it consists of two tale types that have been worked up in one, it helps the scholar to determine a good many of the features contained in both of them as original. By the very fusion, however, important traits have disappeared from each of them, being replaced by parts from the other. The ancient Egyptian record is accordingly not in its totality the original form of either of the tales from which it was drawn. If the tales of this group had been examined by a philologist without intimate knowledge of folktale research, prior to the discovery of the Egyptian scroll of papyrus, he would certainly have determined the date of the tale in some decade or other before the composition of the Russian chapbook containing the earliest European record of the tale, or he might simply have stated it to be Indian.

I point this out, on the particular occasion of a demand made on folklore research from philological quarters in Sweden, that it should be purely philological, which demand only proves that its maker does not understand at all how important it is for traditional matter to be studied according to its own laws. Still worse is a suggestion, no less singular, that folktale research should be purely Scandinavian, not comparative. Such national one-sidedness has indeed been attempted, but has been of no importance except as a warning.

On the other hand, it is evident that collaboration between philology and the study of folklore is of supreme importance. Philologists can produce much material of very great value to folklore research, as has from old literature been proved, I think, by the examples quoted. But the oral material is no less important for placing the contents of the ancient sources in the living whole to which they belong, and for supplementing their statements, which are often both fragmentary and otherwise corrupted.

It was an idea of Kaarle Krohn's that every separate type of tale should first be dealt with monographically. Later on "folktale research proper" was to be started. The very attempt has proved that folktale studies proper must be taken in hand long before all types of tales could be dealt with. These studies must be so directed as to undertake investigations that are of interest also to others than those belonging to the circle of professional folk-

---

descendants of the European settlers. See Alan Dundes "A Cheyenne Version of Tale Type 1176," *Western Folklore*, Vol. 23 (1964), 41–42, for an example.

The concept of marginal survival was included by Kaarle Krohn in his standard treatise on the Finnish (comparative) method as one of the criteria to be considered in trying to establish the oldest or basic form of an item of folklore. See *Die Folkloristische Arbeitsmethode* (Oslo, 1926), pp. 93, 115–16. The concept was restated by Warren Roberts in his comprehensive study of Tale Type 480, The Spinning-Women by the Spring, *The Tale of the Kind and Unkind Girls* (Berlin, 1958), pp. 8, 104. For an example in language in which Elizabethan idioms have been preserved in eastern Dutch Guiana Negro dialect, see A. G. Barnett, "Colonial Survivals in Bush-Negro Speech," *American Speech*, Vol. 7 (1932), 393–97; for an example in folk music, see Bruno Nettl, "The Hymns of the Amish: An Example of Marginal Survival," *Journal of American Folklore*, Vol. 70 (1957), 323–28.—Ed. Note

242   C. W. VON SYDOW

lorists, in the first place, of course, to the philologists, with whom as close a collaboration as possible must be established.

Here, e.g., the work of Axel Olrik and Moltke Moe[21] has been of exceptional importance by their inquiries into the fundamental laws of tradition, work based on a profound and comprehensive view of the stores of folktales and *sagns,* and on studies of their life in tradition. This work was carried out, of course, by methods altogether different from those applied to the monographs. Folktales must necessarily be studied not according to their types only, but above all by groups, so that the study of the individual type is connected with the study of all types belonging to the same natural group. This makes, however, considerably greater demands on the resources of the scholar than would suffice for a monograph of the old type. Here, first and last, the collaboration of as great a number of scholars as possible is required. In this connection, one important *desideratum* is a large-scale international research institute for the purpose.

Having emphasized the distinction between philological methods and that of folklore research, and the lack of understanding which has often made itself felt on the part of philologists in their attitude to folklore research, I want at the same time to express my thanks to Professor Arthur Christensen for his profound and sympathetic understanding of folklore studies and for the valuable work done by him on Iranian heroic epics as well as on oriental and occidental folktales. He is thus a living exemplification of what good results may be achieved by a synthesis of philology folktale research.[22]

---

[21] Von Sydow is probably referring to Moe's studies of epic laws, *Episke Grundlove* (Kristiania, 1914). Moltke Moe was the son of folklorist Jørgen Moe, whose collaboration with Peter Asbjørnsen resulted in a major collection of Norwegian folktales in 1843. Moltke Moe was a teacher of folklore rather than a collector, and among his students was Axel Olrik. For a moving tribute to Moe as one of the first university professors of folklore, see Axel Olrik's *Personal Impressions of Moltke Moe,* Folklore Fellows Communications No. 17 (Hamina, 1915).—ED. NOTE

[22] This paper was translated from "Några synspunkter på sagoforskning och filologi," in *Øst og Vest. Afhandlinger tilegnede Prof. Arthur Christensen* (København, 1945), pp. 140–66.

Some Experiments on the Reproduction
of Folk Stories

F. C. Bartlett

One of the most interesting aspects of the study of the transmission of folklore concerns the nature of the changes that occur in the process. A serious problem in studying change, however, is that the folklorist in the field usualy gets only half of the necessary data. When he collects a folksong or a nursery rhyme from an informant, he has no way of knowing the exact version or versions from which the informant originally learned the item. Although the folklorist can compare the collected version with versions from other cultures or even from other individuals in the same culture, it is difficult to study in minute detail the changes, if any, made by an individual as he relates the same item time after time.

Consequently, this study by psychologist F. C. Bartlett, one of the very few experiments ever made with folkloristic materials, is of great theoretical significance. In this famous experiment, Bartlett tried to discover what changes took place from the time an item was originally learned to when it was later iterated. By having both "before" and "after" data, Bartlett was able to formulate some "laws" of transmission based upon empirical experimental data.

Bartlett used essentially two different testing techniques, both of which had analogues in the oral transmission process. In one, which he called the method of repeated reproduction, each of 20 subjects, 7 female and 13 male undergraduates at the University of Cambridge, was given a folktale. The experimenter then asked each of the subjects to relate the tale and then, after varying periods of time, to relate it again. Subjects were asked to reproduce the tale a number of times after intervals of weeks, months, and even years. From these responses, Bartlett hypothesized some general principles of change to explain what happened when one individual told the same tale many times.

Bartlett termed the second testing technique the method of serial reproduction. In this technique, the first subject was given a tale, and 15 to 30 minutes later, asked to reproduce it. This reproduction, not the original version, was given to the second subject, who likewise after

Reprinted from *Folklore,* Vol. 31 (1920), 30–47, by permission of the publisher.

15 to 30 minutes was asked to reproduce the tale. The serial process continued until subject number 20 reproduced the story he had obtained from subject 19. From this process, Bartlett proposed several principles to explain what happened to material when it was transmitted from one person to another.

In theory, elements of Bartlett's experiment are closely related to critical factors in the process of folklore transmission. Active bearers of tradition do repeat their materials many times, and certainly in the case of free-phrase genres of folklore, changes do occur. By the same token, one active bearer may tell another active bearer, who in turn tells another, the same joke or the rules of a game, and once again changes may be introduced. Nevertheless, from the point of view of a folklorist rather than a psychologist interested in studying memory, the experiment had some serious methodological weaknesses.

In the first place, as Bartlett realized, the group was composed of isolated individuals. It was not a folk group with normal traditional channels of communication. However, if an English university traditional anecdote had been used, the group might have qualified as a folk group. Bartlett used as the material to be transmitted an American Indian (Kathlamet) folktale and an African cumulative tale. One cannot assume that the changes which occur when members of one culture borrow an item of folklore from members of another culture are necessarily the same as those which occur when an item of folklore belonging to the culture is transmitted solely within that culture. So the question arises: Was Bartlett testing the process of oral transmission of folklore generally or only the process as it occurs in an acculturation or culture-contact context?

Second, each subject *read* the tale twice. Here the question is whether or not visual and auditory memory are identical. In the transmission of folklore, materials are orally produced and aurally perceived (excluding for the moment such nonverbal forms as game and folk dance). In Bartlett's experiment, the subjects read the tales and *wrote* out the reproductions. Even non-folklorists know that there is a great difference between the conventions of writing and speaking. One does not write as one speaks, nor does one speak as one writes. Bartlett made quite a point of the amount of rationalization that was added to the test material, but this may be partially a result of the subjects' writing out their materials. Had the subjects reproduced the tale orally, there may or may not have been the same amount of rationalization. It is precisely because of the greater self-consciousness involved in writing rather than speaking (in writing one can see what one is saying and can "correct" or improve it) that folklorists almost never ask their informants to write out their materials. If the informants did this, the materials would undoubtedly be embellished and polished. The professional folklorist collects the oral versions and he, not the informant, writes it down so that the oral flavor and style may be preserved. (This, incidentally, is why many people are often repulsed when they attempt to read authentic field-recorded texts. Oral tales are meant to be heard, not read, and on the basis of the criteria for the written language, true oral tales do not usually read well.)

Another criticism was offered by folklorist Walter Anderson who reran Bartlett's experiment in an attempt to test his "law of self-correction." Anderson had earlier argued that a narrator does not hear a tale just one time from a single individual, but rather he hears the same tale from the same individual many times and perhaps the same tale from a number of different individuals. According to Anderson, the narrator draws from these various versions to construct his own version, and it is this exposure to many versions that diminishes the possibility of errors caused by faulty memories of individual raconteurs. Anderson pointed out that Bartlett's single chain of transmission was not comparable to the situation of the folk narrator. The folk narrator is on the receiving end of not just one but a number of series. In his modification of Bartlett's experiment, Anderson took a short obscure German legend, not known to 36 German students, and set up three parallel chains of serial reproduction. (Unfortunately, Anderson's subjects also wrote down their versions instead of having them collected by the experimenter.) The 3 chains of 12 partipants were run independently with no interaction. Anderson found that the three end products were similar to Bartlett's final versions in that they revealed degenerative change. Anderson concluded that even with a comparison of the final versions from each of the three chains, it was impossible to reconstruct the original version exactly. Note that Anderson's experiment did not really test his notion that a narrator receives his material from several sources. Had he run an experiment in which the members of one chain heard several versions from two or more other chains before reproducing the tale, he might have shed light upon his original hypothesis.

Perhaps the most important theoretical objection concerns the validity of the experimental model. The time element in particular is critical. Bartlett's subjects had a half-hour interval between receiving and transmitting; Anderson's interval was one day. To what extent are the changes that occur in these very short time intervals comparable to the changes that occur over the course of years rather than minutes and days?

There is some evidence that an artificial laboratory experiment can simulate the oral process to the extent that the changes recorded in the experiment parallel actual historical changes. In a fascinating experiment based upon Bartlett's serial reproduction technique, T. H. G. Ward took a historically related series of coins, starting from those of Philip II struck in Macedon between 359–336 B.C. and ending with coins struck in Yorkshire around 50 B.C. The experimenter selected a detail from each side of the coin: a laurel wreath on the head of Apollo and a chariot wheel. Oxford undergraduates were shown drawings of the figures for ten seconds and then asked to reproduce them serially. It was found that some of the changes in the details resulting from the serial reproduction experiment paralleled the actual changes that had occurred in the historical evolution of the coins. Although the conclusions were only tentative, they suggest that it might be interesting for a folklorist to run Bartlett's experiment using as the initial text the hypothetical archetype or original form of an item of folklore. It could then be seen if the changes introduced by the subjects of the experiment did or did not correspond to the changes suggested by the folklorist in his historic-geographic study of the development of the tale or song. One could also compare the end results of the serial chains with the later or even contemporary subtypes of the item. If this technique worked at all, it might even be possible on the basis of a laboratory experiment to predict the occurrence of possible changes in a particular item of folklore!

Bartlett's experiment should be rerun in a number of different field situations, using a genuine folk group and some of the group's less well-known folklore as the test material and having subjects speak and listen rather than read and write. The experiment could also be run with fixed-phrase folklore, where there would presumably be much greater stability and much less variation. Bartlett's contribution of attempting to bring folklore into a laboratory setting should be emphasized. For those who wish to make the study of folklore a social science, there must be concrete experimentation. Laws of transmission must not be simply postulated; they should be derived from the testing of hypotheses where it is possible to do so.

For a fuller account of Bartlett's experiments, see his book *Remembering* (Cambridge, Eng., 1932). Chapter V, pp. 63–94, treats the method of repeated reproduction, and a section of Chapter VIII, pp. 118–46, examines the serial reproduction of folktales. Another experiment was run by Albert Wesselski who arranged to have Sleeping Beauty (Tale Type 410) told to elementary school girls. The girls' retellings showed numerous changes, thereby confirming Wesselski's view that oral tradition was unreliable and that literary versions (like the Grimm collection) were the principal means by which *Märchen* were transmitted. See Wesselski's *Versuch einer Theorie des Märchens*, Prager Deutsche Studien (Reichenberg i.B., 1931), pp. 127–31. For a summary of Wesselski's views on transmission, see Emma Emily Kiefer, *Albert Wesselski and Recent Folktale Theories*, Indiana University Publications, Folklore Series No. 3 (Bloomington, 1947). For Anderson's research, see *Ein Volkskundliches Experiment*, Folklore Fellows Communications No. 141 (Helsinki, 1951). In 1955, a German doctoral dissertation by Kurt Schier modified and extended Anderson's experiment. Unfortunately, as Anderson points out, Schier, like Wesselski, used nine-year-old children as subjects, and such subjects are far from being von Sydow's active bearers of tradition. Most children are strictly passive bearers as far as *Märchen* are concerned. For a critical summary of Schier's findings, see Walter Anderson, *Eine Neue Arbeit zur Experimentellen Volkskunde*, Folklore Fellows Communications No. 168 (Helsinki, 1956). For the coin experiment, see T. H. G. Ward, "An Experiment on Serial Reproduction with Special Reference to the Changes in the Design of Early Coin Types," *British Journal of Psychol-*

ogy, Vol. 39 (1949), 142–47. Students interested in the experimental approach to the study of oral transmission will find it profitable to read Gordon W. Allport and Leo Postman, *The Psychology of Rumor* (New York, 1947). Three principles of change are delineated: leveling, sharpening, and assimilation. Rumor is similar to folklore but usually consists of nontraditional material. However, from Allport and Postman's point of view (p. 162), a legend is a solidified rumor. Those interested particularly in the changes that occur in the transmission of folk music may read the chapter on "Evolution," in Cecil J. Sharp's *English Folk Song: Some Conclusions,* 3rd ed. (London, 1954), pp. 16–31. In this study, which first appeared in 1906 at the same time that Olrik was working on his epic laws, Sharp discusses three principles: continuity, variation, and selection. For the laws of change in folk narrative (as opposed to Olrik's laws of form), see Antti Aarne, *Leitfaden der Vergleichenden Märchenforschung,* Folklore Fellows Communications No. 13 (Hamina, 1913), pp. 23–39 [briefly summarized in Stith Thompson, *The Folktale* (New York, 1946), p. 436]. Perhaps the best recent consideration of the transmission of folklore is by a leading Hungarian folklorist; see Gyula Ortutay, "Principles of Oral Transmission in Folk Culture," *Acta Ethnographica,* Vol. 8 (1959), 175–221.

Introduction

When a story is passed on from one person to another, each man repeating, as he imagines, what he has heard from the last narrator, it undergoes many successive changes before it at length arrives at that relatively fixed form in which it may become current throughout a whole community. To discover the principles according to which successive versions in such a process of change may be traced presents problems of considerable interest, both for psychology and for sociology. Moreover, precisely the same type of problems confront investigators who endeavor to study the diffusion of decorative and representative art forms, of music, of social customs, institutions, and beliefs, and in fact, of almost every element which enters into the varied and complex life of man in society.

One possible line of approach to the study of these problems is by way of psychological experiment. No doubt many of the most potent influences which help to determine the nature and direction of conventionalization in daily life are definitely social in origin. And such influences are not clearly brought out by the type of experiment the results of which I propose to discuss in the present paper. In these experiments subjects effected their reproduction of the presented material rather as isolated individuals than definitely as members of a group. Nevertheless, as the results show, the reproductions themselves illustrate the operation of principles which undoubtedly help to determine the direction and character of conventionalization as it occurs in everyday experience. And it cannot be forgotten that in none of his reactions is the individual wholly free from influences due immediately to his place in a community.

It often happens that a folk story which has been developed in a certain social group gets passed on to another which possesses different habits of life and thought, different social institutions, customs, beliefs, and belongs to a widely divergent level of development. Thereupon A, repeating the story to B, involuntarily introduces slight changes, perhaps replacing the name of an object which he has rarely or never seen by that of some other object with which he is familiar. B carries on the same process, and in this manner, by means of a number of alterations, many of them apparently trivial in nature, the material is gradually reduced to a relatively fixed form which, congenial to its new environment, bears only what may be called a "family likeness" to the story as found in the other community. It is then highly probable that, owing to the striking divergencies of the two versions, it will be denied that one could ever have been derived from the other, and a theory of their independent origin will be put forward.

In any attempt experimentally to investigate the problems thus arising, three ways in which change may be induced call for separate study. First, there are those changes which a single individual tends to reproduce by reason of repeated reproductions. Second, there are the results of the numerous successive changes introduced when a series of reproductions are obtained from different individuals, each person operating upon the reproduction of his immediate predecessor in the series. Third, there are the types of change which may be observed when these two ways of obtaining reproductions are mixed, and interchange of material under known conditions is effected. The present paper will deal briefly with results obtained from an application of the first two methods only.

The material chiefly employed in those experiments which are here to be described, consisted of folk stories developed in a community very different from that to which my subjects belonged, and containing striking, curious, and often unfamiliar incidents and names. Picture material was also given to be reproduced, care being taken that the mere drawing of the pictures employed presented no great difficulty. Subjects read the stories over twice to themselves at their own normal reading pace. The pictures were studied for a period of four minutes. First reproductions were in all instances begun fifteen minutes after the original study of the material. In cases where a subject gave repeated reproductions, no reference was allowed to the original, or to his own earlier renderings, in any of the tests following upon the first. Detailed analysis and discussion of the results are impossible within the limits of this paper, but will be published later.

Repeated Reproduction by the Same Individual

The results under this head will be very briefly summarized:

1. The repeated reproduction of stories by the same individual revealed definite widespread tendencies toward change. These were largely dependent

upon typical differences in the use of the various types of cue upon which reproductions may depend. Many subjects rely chiefly, for the details of their remembering, upon the use of words. In such cases the most important determining factors in the reproductions were the length and style of the original, together with the actual construction of the phrases. A subject of this class will often preserve some peculiar turn of phrase intact, even when incidents much more intrinsically important in a story are distorted. This preservation of the phrase is one illustration of a very common and important principle that may provisionally be called "the persistence of the trivial."

2. In repeated reproduction a subject's own earlier versions gain an increasingly important influence as time elapses. Upon its first presentation a story or picture is considered from a certain point of view, or under the influence of a certain attitude. This attitude not only persists, but usually plays a greater part with the lapse of time. To this, no doubt, is due the fact that inventions and transformations, once introduced, show great tenacity, and tend to be formed into related series. In a similar manner, an invention once introduced may easily bring about changes in material which has, up to this point, been correctly reported.

3. As a general rule, visual imagery tends to become more active the longer the interval preceding reproduction, and, at least in the case of stories containing the report of a number of incidents, increased visualization provides conditions which favor transformation.

4. Relations of opposition, similarity, subjection, and the like, occurring in the original, are very commonly intensified. This forms one illustration of a deep-rooted and widespread tendency to dramatization, and in particular, all those types of relation about the apprehension of which feeling tends to cluster are readily exaggerated or emphasized.

5. One of the most important of the general factors inducing transformation in repeated reproduction is the effort to rationalize. This is very prominent in serial reproduction, also, and will be defined and considered later.

Each of these factors might be further discussed and illustrated, but as I desire at present to lay chief emphasis upon the results obtained from serial reproduction, I shall proceed at once to discuss the latter.

Serial Reproduction

First, we will consider omissions, of which there were many in every series.

Each event, or incident, in a narration, possesses a certain potency of reproduction. To borrow terms used by Thorndike of words in a sentence, the incident, or event, may be under potent, or just normally potent, or over potent.[1] The under potent is omitted; the normally potent is reproduced; the over potent is not only reproduced, but may so dominate all the rest as to change the whole course of the narration.

Now so far as my observation goes, the under potent falls into one of three

---

[1] *Psychological Review*, Vol. 24 (1917), 220–34.

classes. First, there is omission of the irrelevant, then omission of the un-familiar, and then omission of the unpleasant.

Irrelevant is a term most often used in a certain kind of logic. Any con-stituent of a chain of argument which does not logically aid in establishing the validity of an argument is called irrelevant. But here the term must be used in a wider sense. Psychologically, everything is irrelevant which to the observer concerned does not appear fitting, or in place. And what does appear fitting, or in place, is determined by social environment and training, as well as by individual temperament and education. To most of the members of a modern civilized community, for example, the relevant and the irrelevant are almost wholly concerned with *connections* between facts, events, words, or arguments, and not merely with the character in itself of these elements. In a fantasy practically any sort of connection is enough to secure relevance, but clearly this is not so in the argument, or in the straightforward narrative. More and more, however, as we approach the primitive attitude, we cease to determine what is relevant by considering how the members of a series are related to a central aim or topic. We tend to arrive at that type of the relevant in which, apart from any elaboration whatever, material is merely accepted at once as being fitting or satisfactory. All of the stories used in these experiments were developed in relatively primitive communities. The type of connection between incident and incident was in the main merely temporal. It is not, of course, that the tales had no center of emphasis, but that the latter was, from the point of view of a modern reader, often obscured, and that events appeared to be strung to-gether haphazardly, just as they happened to suggest themselves to the mind of the narrator. These stories were reproduced by subjects who were either students or teachers at a university. Gradually the tales came to acquire some central character, which occupied the focus of attention, and everything not rationally leading up to this point was omitted. In a story entitled *The War of the Ghosts*,[2] for example, ghosts appear as a mere temporal incident in a somewhat inconsecutive original narration, and are beyond doubt meant to occupy a central position in the story. But the point of emphasis was by no means apparent to my readers. In every one of the series of reproductions all mention of ghosts drops out almost immediately, and this in spite of the fact that ghosts appear in the original title. To my subjects they afforded an illustration of an incident not capable of being regarded as explaining itself, and at the same time not explicitly connected by any assigned reason with the main thread of the story. Consequently they disappeared.

Clearly, it is a matter of no small importance to be able, taking any given level of social development, to state what are the main influences which determine the rejection of transmitted material as irrelevant, and how such influences work. But the study is of too great complexity to be entered upon here.

---

[2] This story was slightly adapted from a translation by Franz Boas, *Bureau of Amer-ican Ethnology,* Bulletin 26, pp. 182–84.

Omission of the unfamiliar is also frequent. It differs from omission of the irrelevant, in that it has nothing whatever to do, of necessity, with connections between parts of presented material. This becomes the more clear upon the consideration that when incidents, objects, or events unfamiliar in themselves are nevertheless related to anything that is familiar, what frequently occurs is not omission but transformation. A special case is where that which is unfamiliar in itself is rendered familiar by its content. It is then frequently preserved but transformed. Thus in my reproductions, "boats" invariably sooner or later replaced "canoes," and "rowing" replaced "paddling"; a "bush-cat" became an ordinary "cat," and "peanut" was transformed into "acorn." It is in this type of change that the direct influence of social and environmental factors is probably the strongest.

Omission of the unpleasant was very frequently illustrated. This needs little emphasis, as the principle is now well established. Several of the stories used were chosen purposely because they contained modes of speech, or reports of incidents somewhat opposed to modern conventions. Such modes of speech, and such relatively shocking incidents, always tended to disappear. This also was very marked when, in repeated reproduction, the intervals were extended. The material simply disappeared from the reproduction, leaving the subject entirely unaware that anything had dropped out. There is more than a little suggestion that material thus omitted may still have continued to exercise some influence in giving a new twist to the reproductions. Such functioning of factors from the unconscious is of particular interest in view of the development of contemporary psychology.

When we turn from omissions to transformations we find that here, also, the influence of three broad principles of change is evident. The first may be called the principle of familiarization, the second that of rationalization, and the third that of dominance.

It will be convenient to consider the first two together. Both familiarization and rationalization are, in fact, results of a common tendency to change all presented material into such a form that it may be accepted without uneasiness, and without question. The influence of this tendency is exerted upon absolutely all material which is received into and preserved within a mental system. Sometimes the effect is that specific reasons are evolved to account for the form of given material; sometimes, even when such reasons are lacking, the form of the material is changed into something which can be readily accepted simply because it is familiar. In both cases the result in terms of psychological attitude is the same, and a pleasant mood of unquestioning acceptance is evoked.

It is obvious that the operation of the principle of familiarization will give rise to strikingly different changes at different levels of social development, and in varying environments. For the most part, my stories, in their original form, consisted of reports of occurrences which could, within the community in which the tales were current, be accepted without explanation.

In *The War of the Ghosts*, for example, two young Indians are seal hunting, when they are accosted by warriors from a canoe, who ask them to help in a fight which is about to take place. One of the Indians agrees and goes with them. In the fight he hears somebody say: "That young Indian has been hit," but he feels no hurt. He merely remarks casually: "Oh, they are ghosts." He goes back home, tells his friends, lights a fire, and the next morning at sunrise falls down: "something black came from his mouth. He was dead."

Now in the original narration, although it is not put forward specifically as a reason, the casual "they are ghosts" serves as a rationalizing factor throughout the whole story. With this inserted, all the rest is satisfactory. But I have already shown how all mention of the ghosts dropped out of my reproductions. This leaves the two awkward and disconnected incidents of the painless wound and the strange death. It is interesting to pursue the adventures of these two incidents throughout the stories. I take one chain of reproductions only. In the original the painless wound incident is related thus:

"Presently the young man heard one of the warriors say: 'Quick, that young Indian has been hit.' Now he thought, 'Oh, they are ghosts.' He did not feel sick, but they said he had been shot.

"So the canoes went back to Egulac, and the young man went ashore to his house, and made a fire."

The first reproduction runs:

> Then one of the warriors called to the young Indian and said: "Go back to the canoe, for you are wounded by an arrow." But the Indian wondered, for he felt not sick.
>
> And when many had fallen on either side, they went back to the canoes, and down the river again, and so the young Indian came back to Egulac.

Next comes:

> Then one of the warriors called out to the young Indian: "Go back home now, for you are wounded."
> "No that is not so, for I feel no pain."
> But the warrior sent him back to the canoe, for he had been wounded by an arrow, though he could not be convinced of it, for he felt not sick.

Then:

> At last the warrior said to the young Indian: "Go home, for you are wounded." But the Indian replied: "Nay, that cannot be, for I feel no pain." Still the warrior urged him, and he returned to Egulac.

Then:

> And the young man fell, pierced through the heart by an arrow. And he said to the warrior: "Take me back to Malagua, for that is my home." So the warrior brought him back.

Then:

> Presently the young man fell wounded, with an arrow through his heart. "Take me to Malagua," he said to the warrior, "for my home is there." Then the warrior brought him to Malagua.

Then:

> During the fight the young man fell wounded, with an arrow through his heart. Then he said to the warrior: "Take me back to Momapan; that is where I live." So he took the young man back to his home.

Then:

> In the course of the battle the Indian was mortally wounded. "Take me home," he said, "to Momapan. That is where I come from. I am going to die." "Oh no," said the warrior, to whom he made his request, "you will live."

Then:

> In the course of the fight farther on the Indian was mortally wounded, and his spirit fled. "Take me to my home," he said, "at Momapan, for I am going to die." "No, you will not die," said a warrior.

Then:

> In the fight farther on he was mortally wounded, so that his spirit fled. "I am going to die," he said. "Take me back to Momapan." "You are not going to die," said the warrior.

Thus in a short series of nine reproductions the incident of the painless wound has been entirely transformed. The process of transformation may be readily traced. All reference to ghosts drops out of the very first reproduction, the title also disappearing, and this leaves the incident entirely "in the air," and unexplained. Together with this omission, and certainly connected with it, is the new statement that the Indian has been wounded by an arrow. That is to say, a real, flesh wound is implied. The arrow is, in fact, transferred to this incident from another part of the story—a type of change which very frequently occurs—but it serves the purpose of making the wound appear less mysterious. The next reproduction remains much the same, save that a more dramatic form is adopted, but the arrow then drops out, and the Indian is simply said to be "sore wounded." This immediately changes into the statement that the Indian was "pierced through the heart by an arrow," the weapon coming back in again just as before. Moreover, it appears natural for the wounded man himself to ask to be taken home. It is still odd, however, that the Indian should carry on a conversation after being shot through the heart, and soon he becomes merely "mortally wounded." In this form the narrative of the wound remains to the end—in a form, that is, denuded of all mysterious elements, and able to be accepted as satisfactory by my subjects. At the beginning of the series, every person said that the whole business of the wound bothered him very much. At the end the narrative was simply taken without question. At no point in the whole series of changes did any actual specification of reasons occur, but all the time a gradual process was going on in the direction of familiarization.

The death scene provides a yet more interesting series of changes. The original states: "When the sun rose, he (i.e., the Indian) fell down. Something black came out of his mouth. His face became contorted. The people jumped up and cried. He was dead."

Here are the series of reproductions:

I

It was near daybreak when he became weak, and when the sun rose he fell down. And he gave a cry, and as he opened his mouth a black thing rushed from it. Then they ran to pick him up, wondering. But when they spoke he answered not. He was dead.

There is considerable elaboration here, but the most interesting change is the transformation of the vague "something black" into the concrete "a black thing."

II

When the sun rose he suddenly felt faint, and when he would have risen he fell down, and a black thing rushed out of his mouth. And when the people went to him, and spoke to him, and would have raised him, he answered not, for he was dead.

This remains much the same, but the phrase telling that the people "would have raised him" had curious results. It must also be noticed that the death is now brought in definitely as a reason for the wounded man's silence at the end of the story.

III

He felt no pain until sunrise the next day, when, on trying to rise, a great black thing flew out of his mouth, and when his people approached him to raise him, they could not, for he was dead.

Here comes a very significant change, for the "something black" has become a "great black thing" which *flew* out of his mouth. The black thing gave to this subject a suggestion of a soul passing from a dead body, and it was due chiefly to this that "rushed out" was replaced by "flew out." An important step has been taken in a process of familiarization based upon the principle of assimilation to known beliefs. Here for the first time the people are said to be unable to raise the dead body *because* it was dead.

IV

At sunset his soul fled black from his mouth, and he grew stark and stiff. And when they came to lift him they could not, for he was dead.

Here the young man dies at sunset in conformity with a common convention. The subject was, in fact, vaguely reminded of certain familiar myths. He remembered that it is often considered fitting that a man should die as the sun goes down, while as regards the final transformation, he remarked: "I was thinking of the Greek myth, and visualized a picture in which the soul is flying from a dying man's mouth."

V

At sunset his soul fled black from his mouth, and his body grew cold and stiff. Then they came and tried to lift him, but could not, for he was dead.

This version is practically identical with the preceding one, but in the next a yet more commonplace record is produced.

VI

He died at sunset, and his soul passed out from his mouth. They tried to lift him up, but could not, for he was dead.

The "black thing" is now entirely superseded by the idea of the passage of the soul.

VII

Before the boat got clear of the conflict the Indian died, and his spirit fled. They stopped the boat and tried to lift him out, but could not, for he was dead.

Here a further troublesome element has disappeared. In spite of the desperate nature of his wound, the Indian has, up to this point, lived for a long time. But that he should do so had been a source of worry to all my subjects. In this version the wounded man at length, quite naturally, dies immediately. The very common and conventional phrase: "his spirit fled" is employed, and the idea of a material soul also disappears.

VIII

Before he could be carried back to the boat his spirit fled, and left this world.

An immediate death is now finally secured. Moreover, the incident of the corpse which could not be lifted is at last entirely transformed. The curiously long persistence of the latter incident affords a good illustration of what has already been provisionally referred to as "persistence of the trivial," or of the relatively novel, or meaningless. Sometimes a very unusual and out-of-the-way detail serves as an identification mark in a story, and as such it tends to reappear unchanged in many versions. In this particular case the omission is effected in a common and extremely interesting manner by a blending. Instead of being unable to lift the body, the people are merely balked in their attempt to get it to the boat before the man dies. The effect of the change is that both the death and the curious final incident are rendered more commonplace, and in that sense familiarized.

IX

He died, and his spirit left the world.

The transformation is now complete, and the result is a brief statement which my subjects accepted at once as not calling for any explanation.

Rationalization proper, in the sense of the definite provision of explicit reasons was constantly illustrated. Words such as "therefore," "for," and "because," were frequently inserted where they had been absent from the original. A particularly interesting type of rationalization was the tendency of the tales to acquire a moral. This occurred on several occasions, and is well illustrated by a comparison of the original with the final versions of another of the stories used. The story in question came from Central Africa, and may be called: *"The Son Who Tried to Outwit His Father."* The first version runs thus:[3]

> A son said to his father one day: "I will hide, and you will not be able to find me." The father replied: "Hide wherever you like," and he went into the house to rest. The son saw a three-kernel peanut, and changed himself into one of the kernels; a fowl coming along picked up the peanut, and swallowed it; a wild bush cat caught and ate the fowl; and a dog met and chased and ate the bush cat. After a little time the dog was swallowed by a python, that, having eaten its meal, went to the river, and was snared in a fish trap.
>
> The father searched for his son, and not seeing him, went to look at the fish trap. On pulling it to the river side, he found a large python in it. He opened it, and saw a dog inside, in which he found a bush cat, and on opening that he discovered a fowl, from which he took the peanut, and breaking the shell, he then revealed his son. The son was so dumbfounded that he never again tried to outwit his father.

In the course of twenty reproductions this quite straightforward narrative[4] became:

> A small boy, having got into some kind of mischief, wished to hide himself from his father. He happened to be standing under a tree when an acorn fell to the ground, and he immediately determined to hide himself within it. He accordingly concealed himself within the kernel. Now a cat chanced to be passing along that way, and when she saw the acorn she forthwith swallowed it. Not long afterwards a dog killed and ate the cat. Finally the dog himself was devoured by a python.
>
> The father of the boy was out hunting one day, when he met the python, and attacked and slew it. On cutting the beast open, he discovered the dog inside it, and inside the dog the cat, and inside the cat the acorn. Within the acorn he discovered his long-lost son. The son was overjoyed on seeing his father once more, and promised him that he would never again conceal anything from him. He said he would submit to the punishment he deserved, whatever his crime might be.

Thus the story of an ingenious youth has become that of a naughty little boy, deservedly punished, and with this change has gone a complete reversal

---

[3] J. H. Weeks, *Congo Life and Folklore* (London, 1911), p. 462.

[4] A close parallel for this cumulative tale, classified by Thompson as Motif Z43.5 (Boy changes self to nut; fowl eats nut; bush cat eats fowl; dog eats cat; dog swallowed by python), is cited by Kenneth W. Clarke in his unpublished doctoral dissertation, "A Motif-Index of the Folktales of Culture-Area V, West Africa," (Indiana University, 1958): Allan W. Cardinall, *Tales Told in Togoland* (London, 1931), p. 159. All twenty serial reproductions of the tale and discussion were published in Bartlett's *Remembering* (Cambridge, Eng., 1932), pp. 129–38.—ED. NOTE

of the son's attitude. Instead of being "dumbfounded" at his discovery, as he is to begin with, the boy is overjoyed and suitably penitent. The gradual process by which this end was secured cannot now be analyzed, but there is no doubt that the acquisition by the story of a moral flavor produced in my subjects a feeling of fitness and rightness which justifies its being treated as a case of transformation by rationalization. Other illustrations of the same tendency might readily be given.

The third principle of transformation noted was that of dominance. This occurs whenever some word, phrase, or event so stands out from the rest of the narrative as to exercise a definite and general transforming influence. A careful consideration and analysis of the conditions of dominance make it clear that among them affective factors are of prime importance. Moreover these affective factors are generally either of only slightly unpleasant, or else definitely of a pleasant character. The common dominance of "stock" words and phrases; of words and phrases evoking lively visual imagery; of words and phrases having a pleasant sound; of words and phrases recalling some personal experience; and of words which, in rhythmic writing, carry the stress, all come under this general head.

A very interesting case is where the dominant incident or character is extremely unusual, and even, apparently, relatively meaningless. The illustration already given of the transformation of the death scene from *The War of the Ghosts* has already shown how an inherently absurd element may yet persist unchanged for a long time. This would seem to occur most often in the reproduction of picture forms, and I have had several most striking illustrations of how some seemingly absurd detail may be faithfully reproduced, and may exercise a transforming influence that seems altogether out of proportion to its importance. At least one conclusion of practical value may be drawn from this. In any attempt to determine the affiliations of versions of stories, or of pictured representations, apparently trivial details may often deserve the greatest attention.

When, how, and why this should be so are questions with which I hope to deal in detail on some future occasion. But, in order to prevent misunderstanding, a few additional remarks must now be made. I have spoken provisionally of a principle of persistence of the trivial. Very often details which appear to be trivial to any persons not engaged in the reproductions are really far from trivial to those who have produced the versions in question. This gives a first broad distinction between what may be called the subjectively trivial and the objectively trivial. We then get three classes of cases: first, that of the persistence of detail which is objectively trivial, but subjectively significant, the significance being clear to the subject at the time at which he produces his reproduction; second, that which is objectively trivial, but subjectively significant, the significance being entirely hidden from the subject at the time at which he makes the reproduction; and third, that which is both objectively and subjectively trivial, but which nevertheless persists.

These three cases, and their conditions, have to be very carefully distinguished, and I shall hope to be able to show how particularly important each of the last two classes of cases may be.

Another extremely common type of change which does not appear to be capable of being brought under any of the general principles so far discussed is that of transposition. This takes many different forms. There may be duplication, in which case a detail is not only introduced into a wrong position but is also retained in its right position. More commonly it is omitted from its proper place, and then it may either be transferred bodily to some new position, or else it may itself suffer change, being mingled, by a process of condensation, with that part of the whole to which it is transferred. This is what occurred in the course of the transformation of the proper name Egulac to Mombapan[5] in *The War of the Ghosts,* and a further illustration has already been given in the fusion of the death and the body-lifting incidents from the same tale. Again, transposition may simply take the form of a reversal of the parts played by different persons. In *The War of the Ghosts* first the wounded man is *told* to go home and then later he himself *begs* to be taken home; first the young Indian declares his own conviction that he will live, but later he has the declaration taken from him by the warrior. There are many different modes and conditions of transposition, all of which may be illustrated clearly by means of experiments of the kind which I have here reported. It is highly desirable that this experimentation should be carried out, because changes by transposition very frequently indeed mark turning points in the history of the conventionalization of narrative material.

By a more extended discussion it would be possible to bring to light additional principles and modes of change. But enough has been said to show that, by the application of the methods here proposed, illuminating information may be obtained, with respect to the character and conditions of the changes undergone by material in process of conventionalization.

---

[5] In the original the two place-names are Egulac and Kalama. In the third reproduction these become Malagua and Komama. Malagua was thought to be "probably a compound of the two names," and in fact obviously contains constituents of both. Two reproductions later the dominant "o" of Komama is transferred, and with it the effect of the repetition of the "m." Malagua becomes Momapan, and Komama entirely disappears.

Some Cases of Repeated Reproduction

Robert H. Lowie

Bartlett's experiment had comparatively little influence upon anthropologists, but Robert H. Lowie, who had been greatly interested in folklore ever since writing his doctoral dissertation on North American Indian folklore under Franz Boas at Columbia Univesrity in 1908, was a notable exception. [Professor Lowie's dissertation was published as "The Test-Theme in North American Mythology," *Journal of American Folklore,* Vol. 21 (1908), 97–148.] In several very short studies, Lowie, who had re-elicited materials from his informants before coming upon Bartlett's research, presented these versions of the same item from the same informant. Like Bartlett, Lowie used American Indian folklore; unlike Bartlett, Lowie elicited it from American Indians in their native language.

One of the important discoveries made by Lowie in these studies was the distinction between form or frame and content. He remarked that although the substance remained essentially the same, there were choices or alternatives for the raconteur. If it can be shown that there are, as Lowie says, "alternative sequels for the same stage in a story," then this is a valuable contribution toward the understanding of transmission and change in folklore. For one thing, there would appear to be definite limits to variation. For another, it might be possible to correlate the particular choice of the raconteur with such factors as significant events in his life, his audience, the content of immediately preceding tales told by either himself or another taleteller, his rapport with the collector, and so on. In his analysis of the repeated reproductions of "A Battle with the Dakota," Professor Lowie tries to make this kind of correlation. Of course, explaining change is much more difficult than noticing change.

The fact that personal and cultural bias could cause changes in folk narrative was one of the reasons why Professor Lowie was so sceptical

Reprinted from Robert H. Lowie, *Studies in Plains Indian Folklore,* University of California Publications in American Archaeology and Ethnology, Vol. 40 (Berkeley, 1942), pp. 19–22, by permission of Luella Cole Lowie and the University of California Press.

of the reliability and historicity of oral tradition. Lowie's most provocative pronouncement on the subject was to the effect that he could not attach to oral traditions any historical value whatsoever under any conditions whatsoever. There has been a huge body of literature on both sides of the question. Some claim that oral tradition does contain historically accurate information; others like Raglan and Lowie say that in would-be oral history, there is always more fiction than fact. See Robert H. Lowie, "Oral Tradition and History," *American Anthropologist,* Vol. 17 (1915), 597–99. See also his presidential address to the American Folklore Society, "Oral Tradition and History," *Journal of American Folklore,* Vol. 30 (1917), 161–67. The representative scholarship includes David MacRitchie, "The Historical Aspect of Folklore," *Papers and Transactions. The International Folklore Congress 1891,* eds. Joseph Jacobs and Alfred Nutt (London, 1892), pp. 103–9; Martin P. Nilsson, "Ueber die Glaubwurdigkeit der Volksüberlieferung mit besonderem Bezug auf die alte Geschichte," *Scientia,* Vol. 48 (1930), 319–28 (for a translation into French of Nilsson's article, see the *Supplément* to that volume of *Scientia,* pp. 114–21); and David M. Pendergast and Clement W. Meighan, "Folk Traditions as Historical Fact: A Paiute Example," *Journal of American Folklore,* Vol. 72 (1959), 128–33. Two of the best general discussions are Knut Liestøl's *The Origin of the Icelandic Family Sagas* (Oslo, 1930), and Jan Vansina's valuable treatise, *The Oral Tradition: A Study in Historical Methodology* (Chicago, 1965).

The Water Fetcher's Communication

In 1910 and 1911 I witnessed initiations into the Tobacco Society of the Crow Indians. At one stage of the performance a man with a creditable war record was sent for water. After ceremonial preparations he dashed off, filled a vessel, and returned, thereupon reporting in a very low tone of voice to the owner of the initiation lodge.

Gray-bull, who had repeatedly served in this capacity, three times dictated to me the tenor of the water fetcher's (ak'i''cde) communication.[1] Unfortunately I am unable to give the intervals between successive recitations. Nevertheless the variants present some points of interest.

A

(1) du'xi-ra.u-m hε're bare''ky. (2) mirəxba''ke kuc basu''-m dapi''u-m icta'xia burutsi'ky. (3) kamba'ku'k. (4) o''pe awu'saru`əc ba''wi-m ahu'-m matsa''tsk a''xe ba''tsua ahu'-m matsa''tsk. (5) karako''m bo`k acε' ba''wi-m ma`-baku'pe' ha'm-nεtk. (6) i'tsikya`'ta o''pe da''kurutu`'k.

---

[1] R. H. Lowie, *The Tobacco Society of the Crow Indians,* Anthropological Papers of the American Museum of Natural History, Vol. 21 (1919), 153f., 185. I have corrected the orthography in the present paper and to some extent the translation.

TRANSLATION

(1) On a war party they went, among them I went. (2) The people [person?] toward [postposition] they ran, they killed, his gun I took. (3) Then I came back. (4) The tobacco you [plural] had planted when I reached, it was abundant extremely; round about the chokecherries were abundant extremely. (5) Then I came, the camp when I reached sick people there were none. (6) Peacefully the tobacco you were harvesting.

B

(1) ba꞉'tsuə o''ᵒce i'tsikya꞉ta bi''uk. (2) ba꞉isande'² ha'mnɛtk. (3) du'xi-warɛ-m ba꞉-rapi''ok da''ᵃkce wa''ritsky. (4) barasɛ' i'tsi-m kam-bo''k. (5) o''pe awu'saru꞉əc awa'kak o''pe ahu'k. (6) o''pe awa'ke wi'awak bo꞉m o''pe apa''re watsa''tsk. (7) apsa''roke i'tsikya꞉'te a''ra꞉ kuk ba''tsuə i'tsikya꞉ta diru'suk.

TRANSLATION

(1) Chokecherries ripening [i.e., the summer] safely we shall reach. (2) Sickness there is none. (3) I went on a war party, someone was killed, a coup I struck. (4) My heart being good [i.e., happy] I arrived. (5) The tobacco you planted I saw, the tobacco was plentiful. (6) The tobacco to see I wished, I came, the tobacco was growing excellently. (7) The Crow well were faring, chokecherries in safety you were eating.

C

(1) du'xi-ware꞉ky i'tsikya꞉ta ba꞉rapi'u icta'xia burutsi'ky. (2) karako''m bo''ia³ (?) aratci''-ruəc awa'ka-m ba''tsuə ahu'k. (3) a''ᵃxe bice'' ahu'k. (4) karako''m bo''ək bo''rə ace'' ahu'k. (5) bo''ra ace' ba''wi-m apsa''ruke i'tsikya꞉ta a''ra꞉kuk.

TRANSLATION

(1) I went on the warpath, in safety [i.e., without loss] they killed someone, his gun I took. (2) Then I came, your gardens when I saw, the chokecherries were plentiful. (3) Round about buffalo were plentiful. (4) Then I came, when I came (?) and the camp I reached, toward camp I signaled. (5) When I came and the camp I reached, the Crow well were faring.

Evidently the form of the report is not fixed, for the same informant's versions reveal variations. But the substance is identical, being composed of three themes: the speaker's war experience; his inspection of the tobacco garden and its environment as he returns; and his auspicious findings. The emphasis is throughout on the rosy side of life: a successful raid; a plentiful crop of the weed believed to ensure the tribal welfare; abundance of food generally; and the prosperity of the people as foreshadowed by the inspection. What, then, is the nature of the discrepancies?

Apart from purely verbal differences, the initial cue "war raid" would present a seasoned brave, such as Gray-bull, with a number of possibilities,

---

² As an alternative synonym word, ba꞉'kupe' was given by the informant.

³ This seems to me almost certainly a misreading of bo''ra; unfortunately I do not have access to my original transcription at the moment.

narrowed only by the need for eliminating untoward events. Of the four conventional feats of bravery recognized by the Crow, versions A and C introduce the capture of a gun, the other variant the striking of a coup. Since Graybull himself had in addition successfully led raids and cut horses from their pickets, the omission of these feats is not due to personal reasons. The failure to mention horses, however, may be due to archaizing, since some origin myths made the first tobacco planting pre-equestrian.[4] Quite naturally a lucky raid includes a killing, but characteristically without loss of a Crow. This concomitant is understood in the first two versions, made explicit by the term i'tsikya`ta in the last. The "signaling to the camp" would be out of place in the second version, but would be as appropriate in the first as in the third, since acis'-buxu'cuk seems to imply signaling that the homecomers are bringing booty.

Since wild vegetable fare was of subordinate importance, the mention of buffalo in a single variant contrasts sharply with the appearance of cherries in each version—twice in version B. However, this otherwise curious fact is readily explained: The season for the tobacco harvest is "when the cherries are ripe"; the phrase ba`'tsuəo'°ce is a cliché for designating the summertime; and like other standardized designations of seasons it appears prominently in prayers for long life and happiness.

The word i'tsikya`ta, already discussed in a special setting, is another cliché. Though requiring different translation according to the context, it invariably denotes a satisfactory situation, being simply the adjective i'tsi, good, with an adjectival suffix commonly denoting diminutiveness or affection. Thus, in a prayer the suppliant says, "i'tsikya`ta baku' wiawak," "In safety I want to return;" and elsewhere we find, "i'tsikya`'ta bawara'pbic bi'awuk," "Safely we'll take revenge" (compare above).

The three versions are of some interest as illustrating in miniature the type of changes to be expected when the same individual reproduces, untrammeled by the necessity of letter-perfect repetition, the essence of a traditional pattern. Evidently the informant clings to some stereotyped expressions, but he has the choice of explicitly stating or merely implying some circumstance; he may amplify by adding a specific image (such as the abundant buffalo, or the peaceful eating of cherries, or the signaling), he may choose between symbols (coup or gun-capture).

A Battle with the Dakota

The foregoing comparison was prompted by Dr. Lindgren's summary of Professor Bartlett's experiments on white subjects, each of whom reproduced after fifteen minutes, and subsequently at various intervals, a North American Indian tale he had read.[5] It has been recognized for some time that in-

---

[4] Lowie, *op. cit.*, pp. 186, 188.
[5] F. C. Bartlett, M. Ginsberg, E. J. Lindgren, R. H. Thouless, *The Study of Society, Methods and Problems* (London, 1939), pp. 363–66.

dividual storytellers within a tribe vary appreciably in their rendering of a tale; and this fact evidently affects intertribal comparison. But it seems equally important to ascertain how far the same individual departs from the norm as received by him. This would affect not only the evaluation of folktales, but of "historical" traditions as well.

A good illustration is available. In 1910 I bought a sacred shield belonging to Yellow-brow, then in the prime of life, and his father. Several years later Yellow-brow gave an account of its history, terminating in the description of a battle with the Dakota.[6] In 1931—without the slightest reference to this shield—the same informant launched into a long tradition, which similarly culminated in an account of hostilities, but with the Cheyenne. The native text, except for one prayer, has remained unpublished, but significant passages connected with the battle have been presented in English.[7]

Both times the narrator doubtless tried to picture the same occurrence. For one thing, the warriors prominent in both accounts almost entirely coincide in name; for example, Wants-to-die, Plays-with-his-face, Double-face, Young-white-buffalo, Passes-women. Second, both descriptions feature the nervousness of Double-face before battle, with some identical details, such as his desire to cry and to sing both sacred songs and those of the Big-dog society. Yet the enemy in the fuller report is the Cheyenne, not the Dakota tribe; the entire context differs; and along with amazing identities there are notable discrepancies not due to mere absence of items in the shorter narrative, which as a matter of fact embodies highly characteristic traits lacking in its rival.

I suggest the following explanation. Asked for the history of the shield he had sold me, Yellow-brow was primarily concerned with its validation as an object possessing supernatural power. Accordingly, he set out in characteristic Crow fashion, deriving it from a revelation in a vision. The visionary, after himself profiting from the shield, made replicas for his three sons and one nephew, bidding them above all to protect the women and children in camp rather than go on raids. Now, in his later version the battle follows the destruction of Dangling-foot and his small body of Crow by the Cheyenne, whence the thirst for revenge on the part of the survivors. Another good informant, Grandmother's-knife, also ascribed this massacre to the Cheyenne.[8] But in the earlier of the Yellow-brow accounts Dangling-foot is not mentioned; there is merely a generic reference to the enemy's having destroyed a detached company of Crow. Inasmuch as "enemy" was almost coterminous with "Dakota," the informant naturally glides from the generic term into this specific description, adhering to the identification throughout. Even his

---

6 R. H. Lowie, *The Religion of the Crow Indians,* Anthropological Papers of the American Museum of Natural History, Vol. 25 (New York, 1922), 415–18.

7 R. H. Lowie, *The Crow Indians* (New York, 1935), pp. 230–36, 332–34.

8 R. H. Lowie, *Myths and Traditions of the Crow Indians,* Anthropological Papers of the American Museum of Natural History, Vol. 25 (New York, 1918), 185.

conclusion, once more summing up the case for the value of his shield, is that ever since its acquisition the Dakota were repelled by the Crow.

This seems to explain very simply the shift from Cheyenne to Dakota, or vice versa.

Further, once launched on his glorification of the shield, Yellow-brow naturally enhanced its dignity by linking it with a stirring tradition of victory that probably had an original connection with quite different circumstances. However, when simply narrating what he regarded as the most striking events in the past of the Crow, he enlarged, indeed, on the battle; but the shield, however important to him, did not loom in his memory in that context, presumably because it did not really belong there.

This seems a factor to be reckoned with. A mind replete with the traditional lore often had alternative sequels for the same stage in a story. The lore, for example, may harbor two ways of escaping from a pursuing ogre; and a narrator conversant with both may choose one or the other according to individual preference or momentary caprice. That this is not pure guesswork is shown by an experience with Yellow-brow when he told the Old Woman's Grandson story. He actually told one episode in the briefer of two mutually contradictory forms current among his people, then corrected himself, retracing his steps so as to bring in a prerequisite element for the longer version.[9]

---

9 Lowie, *The Crow Indians,* p. 109.

Yugoslav Epic Folk Poetry

Albert B. Lord

One of the most elaborate studies in re-eliciting folklore has been undertaken, not with short ballad-length songs, but with sung folk epics some
of which contain as many as 13,000 lines. Albert B. Lord, Professor of
Slavic and Comparative Literature at Harvard University, has made
repeated field trips to Yugoslavia (in 1950, 1951, 1962, 1963, and
1964) to find out what has happened to the epic tradition he and
Milman Parry collected on their visits in the 1930's. To do this, Lord
attempted to collect the same epics from the same informants wherever
possible. Then by comparing the versions, he was able to see what was
remembered and what was not. His data provide an opportunity to
investigate the nature of variation and change through time within a
single tradition.

The interest in east European oral epics stems from the hope of
trying to shed light upon the techniques of epic composition that were
used in the Homeric epics. The assumption is that the techniques of epic
composition today are probably the same as those employed by epic
singers centuries ago. This is an instance of studying the present in
order to explain the past rather than vice versa. Lord found that the
epic singer remembers only the generalized plot frame, in which he
can place various formulas and conventional embroideries, rather than
the whole epic word for word. For a fascinating study of the art and
craft of epic composition, see Lord's *The Singer of Tales* (Cambridge,
Mass., 1960; paperback ed., New York, 1965). Another interesting
study, along somewhat similar lines, is Wolfram Eberhard's *Minstrel
Tales from Southeastern Turkey,* University of California Publications,
Folklore Studies, No. 5 (Berkeley and Los Angeles, 1955).

The purpose of this, my third, sojourn in Yugoslavia was twofold. First, I
was seeking out those singers of epic tales from whom Professor Milman
Parry of Harvard University had collected in the years 1933–35, in order to

Reprinted in slightly abridged and revised form from the *Journal of the International
Folk Music Council,* Vol. 3 (1951), 57–61, by permission of the author and the International Folk Music Council.

record versions of the same songs which he had collected.[1] Such material would enable us to determine with exactness the changes which take place, both on the musical and textual levels, in the singing of any given song by a given singer during a fifteen-year period. Second, I wished to observe the present state of the magnificent epic singing tradition of the Yugoslavs, not only in regard to the continued life of the older repertory but also to the vitality of the tradition in creating new songs from the stormy events of the past decade.[2]

Among the younger singers of epic tales from whom we collected in 1934 was Sulejman Fortić of Novi Pazar who was at that time a waiter in the hotel. An hour after arriving in Novi Pazar on May 13th, 1950, I found myself talking again with Sulejman, now 45 years of age. A great change had come over him. No longer a waiter, he was local president of the National Front and his chest was decorated with medals. I was glad to be able to record from his own lips the story of how his life had changed from one of poverty to one in which he felt that he was sharing in the development of his district. And his singing reflected this change in more confidence in himself and in his powers. This was especially apparent in the fewer instances of such "stalling" lines as "Then you should have seen him, my gray falcons!"

The best way to show the changes in lines is to place side by side brief passages from Fortić's 1934 and 1950 versions of the song of Bagdad.[3] After a formal introductory section (4 lines in two of the 1934 versions, 7 lines in one of the 1934 versions, and 12 lines in the 1950 version) the song begins:

1934	*1950*
Podranijo sultan Sulejmane,	Jedno jutro rano josvanulo,
Podranijo na bijelu dvoru,	Josvanulo, sunce jogrijalo;
Pa saziva paše ji vezire,	Podranijo sultan Sulejmane
Paše svoje ji vezire svoje	Ju Stambolu gradu bijelome,
Dok dođoše paše ji veziri,	Pa poziva paše i vezire,
Pa him care dugo besedijo:	Pokupijo paše i vezire,
	Pokupijo, pa him govorijo:

This is the English translation:

Sultan Sulejman arose early,	One morning dawn came early,
Arose early in his white castle,	Dawn came and the sun shone;

---

[1] For the field methods of Parry and Lord, see the introduction to *Serbo-Croatian Heroic Songs,* Vol. 1, "Novi Pazar," collected by Milman Parry, ed. and trans. Albert Bates Lord (Belgrade and Cambridge, 1954). For texts, transcriptions, and a morphology of lyric songs in the Parry Collection, which is located in the Harvard University library, see Béla Bartók and Albert B. Lord, *Serbo-Croatian Folk Songs* (New York, 1951). —ED. NOTE

[2] In the original article (p. 61), Lord gave one example of a contemporary song, which referred to the German invasion in 1941 and the fierce resistance "under the leadership of Tito and the Party."—ED. NOTE

[3] For further comment on the 1934 and 1950 versions of Fortić's song, see *The Singer of Tales,* pp. 117–18.—ED. NOTE

Then he summoned his pashas and
  viziers,
Even his pashas and viziers.
When the pashas and viziers came,
Then the sultan spoke to them at length:

Sultan Sulejman arose early
In Stambol, that white city,
Then he summoned his pashas and
  viziers,
He gathered his pashas and viziers,
He gathered them, and then said to
  them:

A comparison with two other versions of the same passage recorded in 1934
from the same singer immediately before the text in the left-hand column
above would seem to indicate that the differences over a period of fifteen
years are not much greater than those over a 10-minute interval:

1934 A

Jedno jutro rano josvanulo,
Podranijo sultan Sulejmane,
Pa saziva paše i vezire,
A dođoše paše i veziri
Na carevu bijelome dvoru
No što veli sultan Sulejmane:

1934 B

Podranijo sultan Sulejmane,
Podranijo na bijelu dvoru,
Pa saziva paše i vezire.
Dok dođoše paše i veziri,
Pa stadoše caru na divanu,
Ja sad care pa je besedijo:

This is the English translation:

One morning dawn came early,
Sultan Sulejman arose early,
Then he summoned his pashas and
  viziers,
And the pashas and viziers came
To the white castle of the sultan,
But what did sultan Sulejman say:

Sultan Sulejman arose early,
Arose early in his white castle,
Then he summoned his pashas and
  viziers.
When the pashas and viziers came,
Then they stood in council before the
  sultan,
And now the sultan spoke:

This example illustrates well the possibilities for investigation which this
new material offers.[4]

A comparison of the story as it is told in the 1934 and 1950 versions also
leads to tentative but important conclusions. The name of the heroine of
the song has been changed as well as the name of the city from which she
comes. Besides the expected expansion or contraction of themes, there are
some few changes in other details, as, for example, when a letter is sent by
the sultan to one of the Bosnian heroes it is not sent directly, as in the older
version, but through another hero. However, the main outline of the story
remains the same up to the very end. But the brief ending is radically
different in that in the older version the heroine abandons the hero and
refuses to marry him, whereas in 1950 the two are married and live happily
ever afterward. This latter ending agrees with the other versions of the
song which we have; the 1934 ending would seem to be a freak. This single
example indicates very well the essentially conservative character of the

[4] The above two sets of passages were published in *Serbo-Croatian Heroic Songs,*
Vol. 2 (Belgrade and Cambridge, 1953), 197, 198, 208.—ED. NOTE

tradition in so far as the major thematic material is concerned, and it will be interesting to see whether this is borne out by other analyses of other songs.

In 1935 we had collected from a singer near Bijelo Polje, Avdo Mededović,[5] two songs of over 12,000 lines in length, one on the phonograph records, the other by dictation. It was an especially moving experience to find Avdo still alive in his eightieth year. He was still able to sing for me, as a deeply appreciated favor, part of the same song which was recorded in 1935 and to recite the remainder of it and the other long song for the microphone. Here are the introductory lines to his song of Osman Delibegović and Pavičević Luka:

1935	*1950*
Riječ prva, Bože, ni pomozi!	Riječ prva, pomož', Bože jaki!
A druga je, amin, ako Bog da!	Evo druga, hoće, ako Bog da!
Amin, Bože, pomozi nam jaki	Samo da ga pominemo često,
Vazda na svaki čas i sahata!	Pa je kadar pomoći ne jaki,
Mirna sreća i veselje tvoje,	Da se Bogom krivo ne kunemo,
Da s gospodom rahat veselimo	Jer je stara boža poslovica,
Na ovome mestu e sedimo. . . .	Ko goj laže, Bog mu pomoć neće. . . .

This is the English translation:

The first word, O God, help us!	The first word, help us, Almighty God!
And the second, it shall be, if God grants!	Here is the second, it shall be, if God grants!
O Almighty God, be our help	If only we remember Him often,
Ever at every moment and hour!	Then can He help us in His might.
May Thy peace and happiness be ours,	Let us not swear falsely in God's name,
That we may have comfort and merriment with these sirs	Because there is an ancient divine proverb,
In this place where we sit. . . .	Whoever lies, God will not help. . . .

Because of age and illness Avdo's present version of this song is only some 8,000 lines in length, but it is still a fine song.

It was gratifying to discover that the fine old tradition which Avdo represents will continue for at least another generation. I found enough singers in their 20's or 30's, including Avdo's own son, who knew the old songs to ensure this. What will happen after these two generations have passed, however, is a great question. The enormous strides which the present Yugoslav government is making in blotting out illiteracy will, no doubt, have a deep effect on oral tradition.

---

5 For an account of this extraordinary singer whose repertoire included no less than 58 epics, see Albert Bates Lord, "Avdo Mededović, Guslar," *Journal of American Folklore,* Vol. 69 (1956), 320–30. In this interesting article, Lord reports an experiment made by Parry in 1935, in which it was arranged to have Avdo present while another singer sang an epic song that Parry had learned Avdo did not know. The other singer sang the 2,294-line song and when he had finished, Parry then asked Avdo if he could sing it. Avdo proceeded to sing a version of 6,313 lines. In 1951, Lord re-elicited this same song from Avdo who claimed that he had not sung the song since the one time he had sung it for Parry and that he had not even heard it during the years since 1935.—ED. NOTE

The Cock and the Mouse

Frank Hamilton Cushing

The study of the transmission of folklore includes both intracultural and intercultural transmission. Lowie and Lord studied repeated reproduction within one culture; this classic example of an American Indian borrowing of a European tale, collected by Cushing, is more an instance of serial reproduction involving two cultures. Although the "planting" of the European tale among the Zuni was unintentional, it turned out to be one of the first folklore experiments in the field.

In studying the borrowing of folklore by one culture from another, one finds something that decreases the possibility of discovering laws of transmission universally applicable to all cultures. What the borrowing culture does with the new folklore depends upon a great variety of factors, including such things as the similarity of the material to the already existing traditions and the over-all strength of the borrowing culture. A highly acculturated American Indian group, such as the Micmacs, tended to leave the European tales almost as they received them. In contrast, the Zuni drastically altered the European tales, as the present example, with its conspicuous four symbolism and its numerous terminal explanatory motifs, will demonstrate. In this sense, borrowed folklore can serve as an index of acculturation. The stronger the borrowing culture, the more likely it is that the new material will be shaped to fit indigenous oicotypal patterns.

Yet there are other very important factors that must be taken into account. For example, there is the matter of culturally relative attitudes and tendencies toward change. Bartlett was very much aware of these factors inasmuch as he reported that a serial reproduction experiment involving the same African cumulative tale employed in his Cambridge study had been carried out in India with Indian graduate students as subjects, and that a comparison of the Indian and English series revealed that the Indians showed a greater inclination to elaborate and to embroider. A similar distinction was found by S. F. Nadel in a very important research project in which he tried Bartlett's experiment in

Reprinted from Frank Hamilton Cushing, *Zuni Folk Tales* (New York and London, 1901), pp. 411–22.

a Nigerian school. Nadel composed a folktale modeled on tales common to the Nupe and Yoruba in Nigeria. The tale was then given to a group of 20 Nupe boys and another group of 20 Yoruba boys. In comparing the reproductions, Nadel found that the most obvious types of variation fell along cultural rather than individual lines. One of the most significant types of change concerned the addition of rational links and logical explanations by the Yoruba but not by the Nupe. The Nupe, on the other hand, were more interested in expanding upon such situational elements as details of time and place, which were of little importance for the logical development of the plot. The clear contrast between the tight logical retellings of the Yoruba and the loosely knit Nupe versions suggests that the laws of transmission and change are culturally relative, and in the final analysis, are probably "individually relative" as well.

For Bartlett's Indian experiment, see *Remembering* (Cambridge, Eng., 1932), pp. 138–46. Nadel's African experiment was published as "A Field Experiment in Racial Psychology," *British Journal of Psychology,* Vol. 28 (1937), 195–211. Those interested in the cultural relativity of change in folklore should also read May M. Edel's "Stability in Tillamook Folklore," *Journal of American Folklore,* Vol. 57 (1944), 116–27, in which she shows how variation is discouraged among the Tillamook Indians in the Pacific northwest in contrast to the Indians in the southwest (e.g., the Zuni), where variation is not only permitted but encouraged.

NOTE.—While on their pilgrimage to the "Ocean of Sunrise" in the summer of 1886, three Zunis—Pálowahtiwa, Waíhusiwa, and Héluta—with Mr. Cushing were entertaining their assembled friends at Manchester-by-the-Sea with folktales, those related by the Indians being interpreted by Mr. Cushing as they were uttered. When Mr. Cushing's turn came for a story he responded by relating the Italian tale of "The Cock and the Mouse" which appears in Thomas Frederick Crane's *Italian Popular Tales.* About a year later, at Zuni, but under somewhat similar circumstances, Waíhusiwa's time came to entertain the gathering, and great was Mr. Cushing's surprise when he presented a Zuni version of the Italian tale. Mr. Cushing translated the story as literally as possible, and it is here reproduced, together with Mr. Crane's translation from the Italian, in order that the reader may not only see what transformation the original underwent in such a brief period, and how well it has been adapted to Zuni environment and mode of thought, but also to give a glimpse of the Indian method of folktale making.—*Editor.*

Italian Version[1]

Once upon a time there were a cock and a mouse. One day the mouse said to the cock: "Friend Cock, shall we go and eat some nuts on yonder tree?" "As you like." So they both went under the tree and the mouse climbed up

[1] This is Aarne-Thompson Tale Type 2032, The Cock's Whiskers. The explanatory note immediately preceding this version was written by the editor of *Zuni Folk Tales,* not the present editor.—ED. NOTE

at once and began to eat. The poor cock began to fly, and flew and flew, but could not come where the mouse was. When it saw that there was no hope of getting there, it said: "Friend Mouse, do you know what I want you to do? Throw me a nut." The mouse went and threw one and hit the cock on the head. The poor cock, with its head all broken and covered with blood, went away to an old woman. "Old aunt, give me some rags to cure my head." "If you will give me two hairs I will give you the rags." The cock went away to a dog. "Dog, give me two hairs; the hairs I will give the old woman; the old woman will give me rags to cure my head." "If you will give me a little bread," said the dog," "I will give you the hairs." The cock went away to a baker. "Baker, give me bread; I will give bread to the dog; the dog will give hairs; the hairs I will carry to the old woman; the old woman will give me rags to cure my head." The baker answered: "I will not give you bread unless you give me some wood." The cock went away to the forest. "Forest, give me some wood; the wood I will carry to the baker; the baker will give me some bread; the bread I will give to the dog; the dog will give me hairs; the hairs I will carry to the old woman; the old woman will give me rags to cure my head." The forest answered: "If you will bring me a little water, I will give you some wood." The cock went away to a fountain. "Fountain, give me water; water I will carry to the forest; forest will give wood; wood I will carry to the baker; baker will give bread; bread I will give dog; dog will give hairs; hairs I will give old woman; old woman will give rags to cure my head." The fountain gave him water; the water he carried to the forest; the forest gave him wood; the wood he carried to the baker; the baker gave him bread; the bread he gave to the dog; the dog gave him the hairs; the hairs he carried to the old woman; the old woman gave him the rags; and the cock cured his head.

Zuni Version

Thus it was in the Town of the Floods Abounding,[2] long ago. There lived there an old woman, so they say, of the *Italia-kwe*,[3] who, in the land of their nativity, are the parental brothers of the Mexicans, it is said. Now, after the manner of that people, this old woman had a *Tâkâkâ* Cock which she kept alone so that he would not fight the others. He was very large, like a turkey, with a fine sleek head and a bristle-brush on his breast like a turkey cock's too, for the *Tâkâkâ*-kind were at first the younger brothers of the Turkeys, so it would seem.

Well, the old woman kept her Cock in a little corral of tall close-set stakes, sharp at the top and wattled together with rawhide thongs, like an eagle cage against a wall, only it had a little wicket also fastened with thongs. Now, try as he would, the old *Tâkâkâ* Cock could not fly out, for he had no chance to run and make a start as turkeys do in the wilds, yet he was ever

---

[2] Venice.
[3] "Italy-people."

trying and trying, because he was meat hungry—always anxious for worms;—
for, although the people of that village had abundant food, this old woman
was poor and lived mainly on grain foods, wherefore, perforce, she fed the
old *Tâkâkâ* Cock with the refuse of her own eatings. In the morning the old
woman would come and throw this refuse food into the corral cage.

Under the wall nearby there lived a Mouse. He had no old grandmother
to feed him, and he was particularly fond of grain food. When, having eaten
his fill, the old Cock would settle down, stiff of neck and not looking this side
nor that, but sitting in the sun *kâ-tâ-kâ-tok-ing* to himself, the little Mouse
would dodge out, steal a bit of tortilla or a crumb, and whisk into his hole
again. Being sleepy, the *Tâkâkâ* Cock never saw him, and so, day after day
the Mouse fared sumptuously and grew over-bold. But one day, when corn
was ripe and the Cock had been well fed and was settling down to his sitting
nap, the Mouse came out and stole a particularly large piece of bread, so that
in trying to push it into his hole he made some noise and, moreover, had to
stop and tunnel his doorway larger.

The Cock turned his head and looked just as the Mouse was working his
way slowly in, and espied the long, naked tail lying there on the ground and
wriggling as the Mouse moved to and fro at his digging.

"Hah! By the Grandmother of Substance, it is a worm!" cackled the
Cock, and he made one peck at the Mouse's tail and bit it so hard that he
cut it entirely off and swallowed it at one gulp.

The Mouse, squeaking "Murder!" scurried down into his sleeping place,
and fell to licking his tail until his chops were all pink and his mouth was
drawn down like a crying woman's; for he loved his long tail as a young
dancer loves the glory of his long hair, and he cried continually: *"Weh tsu
tsu, weh tsu tse, yam hok ti-i-i-!"* and thought: "Oh, that shameless great
beast! By the Demon of Slave-creatures, I'll have my payment of him! For
he is worse than an owl or a nighthawk. They eat us all up, but he has taken
away the very mark of my mousehood and left me to mourn it. I'll take
vengeance on him, will I!"

So, from that time the Mouse thought how he might compass it, and this
plan seemed best: He would creep out some day, all maimed of tail as he
was, and implore pity, and thus, perchance, make friends for a while with
the *Tâkâkâ* Cock. So he took seed down, and made a plaster of it with nut
resin, and applied it to the stump of his tail. Then, on a morning, holding his
tail up as a dog does his foot when maimed by a cactus, he crawled to the
edge of his hole and cried in a weak voice to the *Tâkâkâ:*

> *"Ani, yoa yoa! Itâ-ak'ya Mosa,*
> *Motcho wak'ya,*
> *Oshe wak'ya,*
> *Ethl hâ asha ni ha. Ha na, yoa, ha na!"*

> Look you, pity, pity! Master of Food Substance,
> Of my maiming,
> Of my hunger,
> I am all but dying. Ah me, pity, ah me!

Whereupon he held up his tail, which was a safe thing to do, you see, for it no longer looked like a worm or any other eatable.

Now, the *Tâkâkâ* was flattered to be called a master of plenty, so he said, quite haughtily (for he had eaten and could not bend his neck, and felt proud, withal), "Come in, you poor little thing, and eat all you want. As if I cared for what the like of you could eat!" So the Mouse went in and ate very little, as became a polite stranger, and thanking the Cock, bade him good-day and went back to his hole.

By-and-by he came again, and this time he brought part of a nutshell containing fine white meat. When he had shouted warning of his coming and entered the corral cage, he said: "Comrade father, let us eat together. Of this food I have plenty; gathered from yonder high nut tree which I climb every autumn when the corn is ripe and cut the nuts therefrom. But of all food yours I most relish, since I cannot store such in my cellar. Now, it may be you will equally relish mine; so let us eat, then, together."

"It is well, comrade child," replied the Cock; so they began to eat.

But the Cock had no sooner tasted the nut than he fairly chuckled for joy, and having speedily made an end of the kernel, fell to lamenting his hard lot. "Alas, ah me!" he said. "My grandmother brings me, on rare days, something like to this, but picked all too clean. There is nought eatable so nice. Comrade little one, do you have plenty of this kind, did you say?"

"Oh, yes," replied the Mouse; "but, you see, the season is near to an end now, and when I want more nuts I must go and gather them from the tree. Look, now! Why do you not go there also? That is the tree, close by."

"Ah me, I cannot escape, woe to me! Look at my wings," said the Cock, "they are worn to bristles—and as to the beard on my breast, my chief ornament, alas! it is all crumpled and uneven, so much have I tried to fly out and so hard have I pushed against the bars. As for the door, my grandmother claps that shut and fastens it tightly with thongs, be you sure, as soon as ever she finishes the feeding of me!"

"Ha! ha!" exclaimed the Mouse. "If that's all, there's nothing easier than to open that. Look at my teeth; I even crack the hard nuts with these scrapers of mine! Wait!" He ran nimbly up the wicket and soon gnawed through the holding-string. "There! comrade father; push open the door, you are bigger than I, and we will go nutting."

"Thanks this day," cried the Cock, and shoving the wicket open, he ran forth cackling and crowing for gladness.

Then the Mouse led the way to the tree. Up the trunk he ran, and climbed and climbed until he came to the topmost boughs. "Ha! the nuts are fine and ripe up here," he shouted.

But the *Tâkâkâ* fluttered and flew all in vain; his wings were so worn he could not win even to the lowermost branches. "Oh! have pity on me, comrade child! Cut off some of the nuts and throw them down to me, do! My wings are so worn I cannot fly any better than the grandmother's old dog, who is my neighbor over there."

"Be patient, be patient, father!" exclaimed the Mouse. "I am cracking a big one for you as fast as I can. There, catch it!" and he threw a fat nut close to the Cock, who gleefully devoured the kernel and, without so much as thanks, called for more.

"Wait, father," said the Mouse. "There! Stand right under me, so. Now, catch it; this is a big one!" Saying which the Mouse crawled out until he was straight over the Cock. "Now, then," said he, "watch in front!" and he let fall the nut. It hit the Cock on the head so hard that it bruised the skin off and stunned the old *Tâkâkâ* so that he fell over and died for a short time, utterly forgetting.

"*Té mi thlo kô thlo kwa!*" shouted the Mouse, as he hurried down the tree. "A little waiting, and lo! What my foe would do to me, I to him do, indeed!" Whereupon he ran across, before ever the Cock had opened an eye, and gnawed his bristles off so short that they never could grow again.[4] "There, now!" said the Mouse. "Lo! thus healed is my heart, and my enemy is even as he made me, bereft of distinction!" Then he ran back to his cellar, satisfied.

Finally the Cock opened his eyes. "Ah me, my head!" he exclaimed. Then, moaning, he staggered to his feet, and in doing so he espied the nut. It was smooth and round, like a brown egg. When the Cock saw it he fell to lamenting more loudly than ever: "Oh, my head! *Tâ-kâ-kâ-kâ-â-â!*" But the top of his head kept bleeding and swelling until it was all covered over with welts of gore, and it grew so heavy, withal, that the *Tâkâkâ* thought he would surely die. So off to his grandmother he went, lamenting all the way.

Hearing him, the grandmother opened the door, and cried: "What now?"

"Oh, my grandmother, ah me! I am murdered!" he answered. "A great, round, hard seed was dropped on my head by a little creature with a short, one-feathered tail, who came and told me that it was good to eat and—oh! my head is all bleeding and swollen! By the light of your favor, bind my wound for me lest, alas, I die!"

"Served you right! Why did you leave your place, knowing better?" cried

---

4 This detail of the mouse's gnawing off the cock's bristles is of some interest, as is the earlier detail in which the cock bit off the mouse's tail. Both these elements are in the Zuni tale, but *not* in Crane's version. From this an unwary reader might logically assume that these are Zuni embellishments on the European original. So thought Ruth Benedict, the foremost authority on Zuni folklore. In her extensive introduction to *Zuni Mythology,* Benedict claimed that the biting off of the mouse's tail was a Zuni literary addition, and she observed that the mouse's gnawing of the cock's neck bristles was an incident found elsewhere in Zuni lore. However, both these elements are common in other European versions of the tale type and are even mentioned in the tale type summary. One could argue that the talented Zuni narrator polygenetically invented these particular details, but what is obviously much more likely is that Cushing included these details when he told the tale to his Zuni friends. When the time came to publish the Zuni version, Cushing probably selected the Crane text because he considered it similar to the version he had related. For Benedict's comments, see *Zuni Mythology,* Vol. 1, Columbia University Contributions to Anthropology, No. 21 (New York, 1935), pp. xxxii-xxxiii. —Ed. Note

the old woman. "I will not bind your head unless you give me your very bristles of manhood, that you may remember your lesson!"

"Oh! take them, grandmother!" cried the Cock; but when he looked down, alas! the beard of his breast, the glory of his kind, was all gone. "Ah me! ah me! What shall I do?" he again cried. But the old woman told him that unless he brought her at least four bristles[5] she would not cure him, and forthwith she shut the door.

So the poor Cock slowly staggered back toward his corral, hoping to find some of the hairs that had been gnawed off. As he passed the little lodge of his neighbor, the Dog, he caught sight of old *Wahtsita's* fine muzzle beard. "Ha!" thought he. Then he told the Dog his tale, and begged of him four hairs—"only four!"

"You great, pampered noisemaker, give me some bread, then, fine bread, and I will give you the hairs." Whereupon the Cock thought, and went to the house of a Trader of Foodstuffs; and he told him also the tale.

"Well, then, bring me some wood with which I may heat the oven to bake the bread," said the Trader of Foodstuffs.

The Cock went to some Woods near by. "Oh, ye Beloved of the Trees, drop me dry branches!" And with this he told the Trees his tale; but the Trees shook their leaves and said: "No rain has fallen, and all our branches will soon be dry. Beseech the Waters that they give us drink, then we will gladly give you wood."

Then the Cock went to a Spring near by,—and when he saw in it how his head was swollen and he found that it was growing harder, he again began to lament.

"What matters?" murmured the Beloved of the Waters.

Then he told them the tale also.

"Listen!" said the Beings of Water. "Long have men neglected their duties, and the Beloved of the Clouds need payment of due no less than ourselves, the Trees, the Food-maker, the Dog, and the Old Woman. Behold! no plumes are set about our border! Now, therefore, pay to them of thy feathers—four floating plumes from under thy wings—and set them close over us, that, seen in our depths from the sky, they will lure the Beloved of the Clouds with their rain-laden breaths. Thus will our stream-way be replenished and the Trees watered, and their Winds in the Trees will drop thee dead branches wherewith thou mayest make payment and all will be well."

Forthwith the *Tâkâkâ* plucked four of his best plumes and set them, one on the northern, one on the western, one on the southern, and one on the eastern border of the Pool. Then the Winds of the Four Quarters began to breathe upon the four plumes, and with those Breaths of the Beloved came

[5] For numerous illustrations of the Zuni penchant for quadruplication, see Elsie Clews Parsons, "The Favorite Number of the Zuni," *The Scientific Monthly*, Vol. 3 (1916), 596–600.

Clouds, and from the Clouds fell Rain, and the Trees threw down dry branches, and the Wind placed among them Red-top Grass, which is light and therefore lightens the load it is among. And when the Cock returned and gathered a little bundle of fagots, lo! the Red-top made it so light that he easily carried it to the Food-maker, who gave him bread, for which the Dog gave him four bristles, and these he took to the old Grandmother.

"Ha!" exclaimed she. "Now, child, I will cure thee, but thou hast been so long that thy head will always be welted and covered with proud flesh, even though healed. Still, it must ever be so. Doing right keeps right; doing wrong makes wrong, which, to make right, one must even pay as the sick pay those who cure them. Go now, and bide whither I bid thee."

When, after a time, the Cock became well, lo! there were great, flabby, blood-red welts on his head and blue marks on his temples where they were bruised so sore. Now, listen:

It is for this reason that ever since that time the medicine masters of that people never give cure without pay; never, for there is no virtue in medicine of no value. Ever since then cocks have had no bristles on their breasts— only little humps where they ought to be;—and they always have blood-red crests of meat on their heads. And even when a hen lays an egg and a *tâkâkâ* cock sees it, he begins to *tâ-kâ-kâ-â* as the ancient of them all did when he saw the brown nut. And sometimes they even pick at and eat these seeds of their own children, especially when they are cracked.

As for mice, we know how they went into the meal bags in olden times and came out something else, and, getting smoked, became *tsothliko-ahâi,* with long, bare tails. But that was before the Cock cut the tail of the *tsothliko* Mouse off. Ever since he cried in agony: *"Weh tsu yii weh tsu!"* like a child with a burnt finger, his children have been called *Wehtsutsukwe,* and wander wild in the fields; hence field mice to this day have short tails, brown-stained and hairy; and their chops are all pink, and when you look them in the face they seem always to be crying.

Thus shortens my story.

The Functions of Folklore

The aspect of folklore of least concern to literary folklorists but perhaps of greatest concern to anthropological folklorists is function. The important question is not what is folklore, nor where does folklore originate, nor how is it transmitted? The important question is what does folklore do for the folk? Why do singers sing and audiences listen when and where they do?

There are many diverse functions of folklore. Some of the most common ones include aiding in the education of the young, promoting a group's feeling of solidarity, providing socially sanctioned ways for individuals to act superior to or to censure other individuals, serving as a vehicle for social protest, offering an enjoyable escape from reality, and converting dull work into play. (An example of the last function would be soldiers' marching songs and cadence counts or sailors' sea chanteys, which not only serve as time killers during tedious activities but also make the workers more efficient by coordinating their efforts.)

One of the most important single functions of folklore is permitting action that is usually not approved. There are in every culture words that should not be spoken and deeds that should not be done. However, the words and deeds appear in the folklore of these cultures, for example, in certain tongue-twisters. Wherever tongue-twisters have been recorded, there have been some in which the misarticulation results in the uttering of a taboo word. (In English: I slit a sheet; A sheet I slit; Upon the slitted sheet I sit.) Although it is decidedly improper for a child (or adult) to use the taboo word in normal conversation, the child is permitted to say the word if it is a natural "mistake" resulting from an unsuccessful attempt to master a tongue-twister. According to Freud, slips of the tongue are often meaningful on an individual basis—the "mistake" is what the individual really wanted to say. Such mistakes are, to use the phrase of children referring to a covert act of aggression committed under the guise of being a casual mistake, "accidental on purpose." Tongue-twisters permit socially sanctioned slips of the tongue with the added advantage that the responsibility for the slip is neatly shifted to an external force: tradition. Similarly in off-color jokes, the raconteur is permitted to refer to taboo topics, and should anyone object, the raconteur can reply, "That's the way the joke goes" to disclaim personal responsibility. Folklore thus *requires* the folk to do what they might want to do but which they are forbidden to do by the normal standards of cultural behavior. In adolescent party games, participants are required by the rules to kiss one another. Once again, the responsibility is shifted to a spinning bottle or to some other random agent.

If folklore can provide a means of either actually or vicariously doing what the folk would like to do, then clearly it provides a unique source of information for those interested in studying people. It can furnish answers to questions that if asked directly would probably not be answered. Folklore is much more effective because the folk are not completely aware of this function. Often folklore is easily collected while folk are telling tales and singing songs for entertainment or for education. The folklore is often undervalued and underestimated by most of the folk who, although they treasure and enjoy it, do not necessarily consider that telling it to inquiring ethnographers is unethical. In other words, the folk do not realize how much of themselves they are giving away when they allow a folklorist to collect their folklore.

For the folk, the functions of folklore are more important than form and origin. The folk care little about the definition of folklore or about origins of folklore. A woman singing a Child ballad in the southern mountains may not know or care that it is a Child ballad that diffused from England. However, the folk do care about function. They feel they know and like what folklore can do, whether it be for putting children to sleep at night or for passing the time on a job involving repetitious mechanical drudgery.

Four Functions of Folklore

William R. Bascom

There is no better introduction to the study of the various functions of folklore than this survey article by Bascom. The student may also wish to read Malinowski's pioneering essay on the function of myth, which first appeared in 1926. As Bascom notes, Malinowski emphasized that myth served as a charter for belief. It explained the present and made the unknowable future safe by reference to a knowable archetypal past. What Malinowski said about myth is also applicable to other folkloristic materials. For example, proverbs serve as both charters for belief and models for action (and so do superstitions). Proverbs, however, are secular charters, whereas myths are sacred.

Different types of folklore can share similar, if not identical, functions. In a verbal dueling situation, one can use catch tales (Aarne-Thompson Tale Types 2200–2249), riddles, and taunts, among other kinds of folklore. The function is the same; the form is different. It is equally important to realize that any one item of folklore may have several different functions. A work song that helps workers synchronize their efforts may also be sung as recreational entertainment by children at summer camp. The form is the same; the function is different. One cannot always tell from form alone what the associated contextual function is. Functional data must, therefore, be recorded when the item is collected. An item once removed from its social context and published in this way deprives the scientific folklorist of an opportunity to understand why the particular item was used in the particular situation to meet a particular need.

In a paper given at the El Paso meetings last year I expressed the opinion that the most effective way to bridge the gap between the anthropological and the humanist points of view towards folklore is through a common concern with common problems, rather than relying as in the past on a common interest in a common body of subject matter. I also attempted to explain the

Reprinted from the *Journal of American Folklore,* Vol. 67 (1954), 333–49, by permission of the author and the American Folklore Society.

anthropological approach to folklore, and extended the invitation for someone to present in a similar manner the viewpoint of the humanities.[1] I do not propose tonight[2] to reverse my role completely and take up my own challenge. I believe that this job can be done far more competently by a non-anthropologist, although I am still convinced that if this underlying disagreement can be brought out into the open and discussed moderately and rationally, in the same spirit in which I attempted to do it, it will be for the ultimate good of our Society.

This year, when we are meeting with the American Anthropological Association, I propose rather to expand on three of these common problems which are of especial concern to anthropologists, but which could only be mentioned in passing last year. These are: (1) the social context of folklore, (2) the relations of folklore to culture, which might be phrased as the cultural context of folklore, and (3) the functions of folklore. The most appropriate transition between what I said last year and what I have to say tonight is a quotation from Hallowell:

> So far as the anthropologists are concerned I believe it is fair to say that while it has been customary over a long period to collect a representative sample of the oral narratives of the people they happen to be studying, it is an open secret that, once recorded, very little subsequent use may be made of such material. Indeed, these archival collections, once published, often moulder on our shelves waiting for the professional folklorist, or someone else, to make use of them in a dim and uncertain future. . . .The consequence has been that, for many anthropologists, folklore becomes a floating segment of culture and the close study of the oral narratives of a people they investigate may remain of marginal interest to them, except for the obvious connections such as those between myth and religion.
>
> This marginal position which oral narratives have occupied in anthropological studies is not due to the inherent nature of the material but to a failure to exploit fully the potentialities of such data. Perhaps the major barrier has been the traditional emphasis upon problems of a literary-historical nature, almost to the exclusion of the investigation of other types of problems. Scholars, like the rest of folks, may become tradition-bound. Over a long period of time, at least, the major contributions to the study of oral narratives, both inside and outside of anthropology, seem to have remained within the literary-historical orbit. Consequently, anthropologists uninterested in the problem defined by this frame of reference have not bothered much with oral narratives, and those concerned with such problems have not made use of the material in any other way. . . .[3]

Despite the important contributions that have been made to the study of oral narratives from a literary-historical point of view and the further work that undoubtedly needs to be done, the fact remains that only a limited range of problems can be envisaged within this framework. Among other

---

[1] W. Bascom, "Folklore and Anthropology," *Journal of American Folklore,* Vol. 66 (1953), 283–90. [This essay is reprinted in this volume.—Ed. Note]

[2] Presidential address delivered at the Sixty-fifth Annual Meeting of the American Folklore Society, Tucson, December 27, 1953.

[3] A. I. Hallowell, "Myth, Culture, and Personality," *American Anthropologist,* Vol. 49 (1947), 544–45.

things, it seems pertinent to ask, for example, whether the study of oral narratives has by any means contributed its full share to our understanding of culture and its functioning in human societies, or whether the study of myth and tale has nothing whatsoever to do with investigation of human psychology and the adjustment of the individual to his culturally constituted world? If the use of oral narratives *is* relevant to such questions, then they should be one of the *primary* concerns of the anthropologist rather than an isolated subject matter that occupies a marginal position. In my opinion, such studies need to be put upon a much more comprehensive basis than that represented by the literary-historical approach alone. For this, two other frames of reference, which nicely supplement each other, are needed—the "functional" and the "psychological."[4]

The first point I wish to discuss is that of the social context of folklore, its place in the daily round of life of those who tell it. This is not a "problem" in the strict sense, but rather a series of related facts which must be recorded, along with the texts, if the problems of the relation between folklore and culture or the functions of folklore, or even the creative role of the narrator, are to be analyzed. These facts include: (1) when and where the various forms of folklore are told; (2) who tells them, whether or not they are privately owned, and who composes the audience; (3) dramatic devices employed by the narrator, such as gestures, facial expressions, pantomime, impersonation, or mimicry; (4) audience participation in the form of laughter, assent or other responses, running criticism or encouragement of the narrator, singing or dancing, or acting out parts in a tale; (5) categories of folklore recognized by the people themselves; and (6) attitudes of the people toward these categories. These factors have long been recorded, even if haphazardly and incompletely, by some folklorists, but the importance of understanding the "social context" of folklore, "its setting in actual life," was repeatedly emphasized by Malinowski in his *Myth in Primitive Psychology:*[5]

> The limitation of the study of myth to the mere examination of texts has been fatal to a proper understanding of its nature. The forms of myth which come to us from classical antiquity and from the ancient sacred books of the East and other similar sources have come down to us without the context of living faith, without the possibility of obtaining comments from true believers, without the concomitant knowledge of their social organization, their practised morals, and their popular customs—at least without the full information which the modern fieldworker can easily obtain. . . .[6]

> The anthropologist is not bound to the scanty remnants of culture, broken tablets, tarnished texts, or fragmentary inscriptions. He need not fill out immense gaps with voluminous, but conjectural, comments. The anthropologist has the myth maker at his elbow. Not only can he take down as full a text as exists, with all its variations, and control it over and over; he has also a host of authentic commentators to draw upon; still more he has the

---

[4] *Ibid.*, p. 546.

[5] B. Malinowski, *Myth in Primitive Psychology* (New York, 1926), p. 90. [This important essay by Malinowski is included in the Anchor paperback, *Magic, Science, and Religion* (Garden City, N.Y., 1954).—ED. NOTE]

[6] *Ibid.*, p. 18.

fulness of life itself from which the myth has been born. And as we shall
see, in this live context there is as much to be learned about the myth as in
the narrative itself.[7]

The text, of course, is extremely important, but without the context it
remains lifeless. As we have seen, the interest of the story is vastly enhanced
and it is given its proper character by the manner in which it is told. The
whole nature of the performance, the voice and the mimicry, the stimulus
and the response of the audience mean as much to the natives as the text;
and the sociologist should take his cue from the natives. The performance,
again, has to be placed in its proper time setting—the hour of the day, and
the season, with the background of the sprouting gardens awaiting future
work, and slightly influenced by the magic of the fairy tales. We must also
bear in mind the sociological context of private ownership, the sociable function and the cultural role of amusing fiction. All these elements are equally
relevant; all must be studied as well as the text. The stories live in native
life and not on paper, and when a scholar jots them down without being able
to evoke the atmosphere in which they flourish he has given us but a muti-
lated bit of reality.[8]

Malinowski's remarks touch upon the functions of folklore and upon the
relations of folklore to culture, as well as upon what I distinguish as the
social context of folklore. Moreover, the last quotation refers to some of the
specific features of what Malinowski calls the "fairy tale," which is only
one of three forms of narrative distinguished by the Trobriand Islanders
themselves:

1. Fairy tales (*kukwanebu*) are fictional, dramatically told, and privately owned.
   They are told in November, between the harvest and fishing seasons. There is
   a vague belief, not very seriously held, that their recital has a beneficial
   influence on the new crops which have been recently planted in the gardens,
   and they end with a formalized reference to a very fertile wild plant.
2. Legends (*libwogwo*) are believed to be true and to contain important factual
   information. They are not privately owned, told in any stereotyped way,
   or magical in their effect.
3. Myths (*liliu*) are regarded not merely as true, but as venerable and sacred.
   They are told when rituals to which they refer are to be performed, or when
   the validity of these rituals is questioned.[9]

Even this brief, familiar summary should show the importance of recording
the native categories of folklore. The times and places they are told, the
identity of the narrator and the composition of the audience, the factor of
private ownership, the style of recitation, the participation by the audience,
the attitudes of the people, and even the functions are to a considerable extent
unique or distinctive for the various categories which are recognized. Although
many studies of folklore still do not discuss the native categories, it is worth
noting that an excellent discussion of this important point is to be found in
Chatelain's comments on Mbundu folklore in the first volume of the *Memoirs*

---

[7] *Ibid.,* pp. 17–18.
[8] *Ibid.,* p. 24.
[9] *Ibid.,* pp. 20–30.

of this Society.[10] It is unfortunate that Chatelain's discussion cannot be quoted here in full, because it shows great insight into points which will be considered later.

Nevertheless, the literature is still surprisingly deficient on these "non-scientific" but extremely suggestive classifications, and also on the attitudes of the people towards their own folklore. It would seem that many folklorists neglect even to ask the simple question of whether or not the various tales, which they take great pains to record, are true. Nevertheless it is certainly significant that some groups, such as the Trobriand Islanders, the Marshall Islanders,[11] the Mbundu,[12] the Ibo and Yoruba,[13] the Ashanti,[14] the Mandan, Hidatsa, Arikara, and Dakota[15] distinguish between narratives which they regard as true and false, while the Ojibwa regard all their tales as true.[16] It is essential to the understanding and interpretation of folklore to know

---

[10] H. Chatelain, *Folktales of Angola,* Memoirs of the American Folklore Society, Vol. 1 (1894), 20–22.

[11] "The myths are generally accepted as true, though today parts, particularly those which tell of the old gods and demigods, may not be so regarded.... Modern myths...are the 'true' stories of today. Because their veracity is undisputed, they are very hard to get, for the people do not class them with the other forms of stories.... The fairy tale always begins with the word *kininwatne,* which without having specific meaning signifies 'this is a fairy tale; it may or may not have happened long ago; it is not to be taken seriously; it is not always supposed to be logical.' In ordinary discourse, a person exaggerating or telling an unbelievable story is accused of telling fairy tales." W. H. Davenport, "Marshallese Folklore Types," *Journal of American Folklore,* Vol. 66 (1953), 221, 223, 224.

[12] Three classes of narratives are distinguished in Kimbundu terminology. "The first class includes all traditional fictitious stories, or rather, those which strike the native mind as being fictitious.... The second class is that of true stories, or rather stories reputed true; what we call anecdotes.... Historical narratives...make a special class of history. They are the chronicles of the tribe and nation, carefully preserved and transmitted by the head men or elders of each political unit, whose origin, constitution, and vicissitudes they relate." Chatelain, *op. cit.,* pp. 20–21.

[13] W. Bascom, "The Relationship of Yoruba Folklore to Divining," *Journal of American Folklore,* Vol. 56 (1943), 129. According to an Ibo student in the United States, the Ibo also make this distinction.

[14] Despite the fact that folktales might refer to actual social situations and characters, the Ashanti storyteller stated before beginning "that what he was about to say was just make-believe" through the nominee "We do not really mean, we do not really mean (that what we are going to say is true)"; and he concluded, in one of their conventional endings, "This, my story, which I have related; if it be sweet, (or) if it be not sweet; some you may take as true, and the rest you may praise me (for the telling of it)." R. S. Rattray, *Akan-Ashanti Folktales* (Oxford, 1930) pp. xi, 49, 15, passim.

[15] "The Dakota Indians of the plains distinguish two classes of tales—the "true" and the "lying."...Other Indian tribes make somewhat similar distinctions. The Mandan, Hidatsa, and Arikara groups recognize three classes of storytelling which approximate very nearly to the myth, legend, and tale of Malinowski." M. W. Beckwith, *Folklore in America. Its Scope and Method,* Publications of the Folklore Foundation, No. 11 (Poughkeepsie, N.Y., 1931), 30.

[16] "The northern Ojibwa, for example, have no category of fiction at all; both their sacred stories and their tales are thought to be true. Consequently there is no art of imaginative fiction in this society, and no incentive to its creation." Hallowell, *op. cit.,* p. 547.

whether a given tale is regarded as historical fact or fiction. This bears directly upon the explanation of folklore as a form of amusement or as "literature," and on the troublesome, perennial problem of the nature of myth.

The problem of the "cultural context" or the relationship between folklore and other aspects of culture is in itself far more important. This problem has two distinct facets, the first of which concerns the extent to which folklore, like language, is a mirror of culture and incorporates descriptions of the details of ceremonies, institutions and technology, as well as the expression of beliefs and attitudes. Boas' classical analysis of Tsimshian myths[17] has demonstrated, in the words of Herskovits, that "a substantial body of folktales is more than the literary expression of a people. It is, in a very real sense, their ethnography which, if systematized by the student, gives a penetrating picture of their way of life."[18]

The recording of folklore, in itself, is a useful field technique for the anthropologist. It gives further leads for the investigation of the content of culture, insuring that important cultural details are not overlooked; it provides a nonethnocentric approach to the ways of life of a people, emphasizing, as Boas pointed out, the things which are important in their own minds;[19] it may offer clues to past events and to archaic customs no longer in actual practice, although not to the degree assumed by the Cultural Evolutionists;[20] it may provide a means of getting at esoteric features of culture which cannot be approached in any other way;[21] it reveals the affective elements of culture,

---

[17] F. Boas, *Tsimshian Mythology,* Annual Report of the Bureau of American Ethnology, Vol. 31 (Washington, 1916), 29–1037.

[18] M. J. Herskovits, *Man and His Works* (New York, 1948), p. 418.

[19] Speaking of his analysis of Tsimshian mythology, Boas states: "The underlying thought of this attempt was that the tales probably contain all that is interesting to the narrators and that in this way a picture of their way of thinking and feeling will appear that renders their ideas as free from the bias of the European observers as is possible. Matters that are self-evident to the Indian and that strike the foreign observer disappear while points of view will be expressed that may be entirely overlooked by the student." F. Boas, *Kwakiutl Culture as Reflected in Mythology,* Memoirs of the American Folklore Society, Vol. 28 (1935), v. "After all, what people choose to talk about is always important for our understanding of them, and the narratives they choose to transmit from generation to generation and to listen to over and over again can hardly be considered unimportant in a fully rounded study of their culture. When, in addition, we discover that all their narratives, or certain classes of them, may be viewed as *true* stories, their significance for actual behavior becomes apparent. For people *act* on the basis of what they believe to be true, not on what they think is mere fiction." Hallowell, "Myth, Culture, and Personality," p. 548.

[20] Benedict cites several instances which are preserved today only in Zuni folklore and ritual. R. Benedict, *Zuni Mythology,* Columbia University Contributions to Anthropology, No. 21 (New York, 1935), Vol. 1, xiv-xv.

[21] "Many years ago in recording tales at Zuni I learned the familiar fact that esoteric practices or terms are referred to or used freely in storytelling which would be withheld from a questioner." E. C. Parsons, *Taos Tales,* Memoirs of the American Folklore Society, Vol. 34 (1940)), 4.

such as attitudes, values, and cultural goals[22] and, moreover, may verbalize these in a form which needs only to be translated and quoted as evidence of a consensus of opinion.

Despite a general awareness of the importance of folklore as a part of culture and as a useful field technique, anthropologists, with a few outstanding exceptions, have neither fully explored the relations between folklore and culture, nor fully utilized the insights into culture which folklore can provide. As Hallowell has said:

> The relation between myth and ritual has been frequently discussed, to say nothing about the relations of myth to the prevailing world view and to religion. The relations of values expressed in narratives to actual conduct and sanctions is another large topic. I cannot help believing that the surface has hardly been scratched, and that much valuable material that would deepen our understanding of culture lies awaiting those who will systematically study oral narratives in relation to all aspects of a society.[23]

The extent to which folklore is a mirror of culture has been mainly the concern of anthropologists, but when stated conversely it becomes the concern of all folklorists: the folklore of a people can be fully understood only through a thorough knowledge of their culture. Malinowski, who emphasized this, points out how a typical Trobriand origin myth involving the simultaneous emergence of brother and sister might be misinterpreted as a mythological allusion to incest, which would be entirely erroneous. The sister is responsible for the transmission of the family line, and the brother, rather than the husband, is indispensable as the guardian. If, on the other hand, an attempt were made to determine the identity of the sister's husband, an outside observer "would soon find himself once more confronted by an entirely foreign set of ideas—the sociological irrelevance of the father, the absence of any ideas about physiological procreation, and the strange and complicated system of marriage, matrilineal and patrilocal at the same time." "Only a full knowledge of matrilineal ideas and institutions gives body and meaning to the bare mention of the two ancestral names, so significant to a native listener."[24] The full meaning of these origin myths becomes clear only when the kinship system, the legal concepts of local citizenship, and the hereditary rights to territory, fishing grounds and local pursuits are understood.

The second aspect of the problem of the relations between folklore and culture has to do with the fact that characters in folktales and myths may do things which are prohibited or regarded as shocking in daily life. Old Man Coyote, in numerous Plains tales, has intercourse with his mother-in-

---

22 "In addition to reflecting the life of a people as of the period when a given story of a living lore is told, folklore also reveals much about their aspirations, values, and goals." Herskovits, *op. cit.*, p. 419.

23 Hallowell, *op. cit.*, p. 548.

24 Malinowski, *op. cit.*, p. 41.

law, whereas the American Indian who finds humor and amusement in this situation must himself observe a strict mother-in-law avoidance. Whether it be the tales of violence or the tales of polygamy among the mild, monogamous Zuni, the unscrupulous and disrespectful behavior of the trickster in many bodies of folklore, or the mother-in-law jokes and obscene stories in our own puritanical society, the striking contrasts between folklore and actual conduct raise new problems of wider theoretical significance concerning the relations between folklore and culture. Over many centuries folklorists and other scholars have attempted to explain them, or to explain them away. Most of the earlier explanations are unacceptable today, but the problem itself remains with us as one of the most intriguing and basic of all the problems of folklore, raising significant questions about the nature of humor and the psychological implications and the sociological functions of folklore.

Long before the beginnings of folklore as a discipline, in the sixth century B.C., the Greek philosopher Xenophanes complained in a poem that the gods were credited with committing the worst crimes of mortals; somewhat later the Greek poet Pindar refused to repeat a story in which the gods were said to eat human flesh.[25] About 316 B.C., Euhemerus offered his theory that myths had their origin in actual historical characters and events, and that the gods were once men who were deified and worshipped after their death. Thus the gods had feet of clay, and the crimes of the gods were really crimes of men.

The Grimm brothers, with their theory of the spread of folklore through Aryan migrations and their etymological techniques, suggested that words in the tales had become mangled and misunderstood in the course of retelling, and that by reconstructing the original proto-Indo-European words the inconsistencies and absurdities in tales could be explained. Max Müller, who also used the etymological technique, but whose linguistic reconstructions reduced myths to allegories of nature, stated "to represent the supreme God as committing every kind of crime, as being deceived by men, as being angry with his wife and violent with his children, is surely proof of a disease [of language]."[26] The numerous scholars of the Nature Allegorical school who relied on the comparative method without even the verification of etymology, contended that what appeared to be shocking events were in reality beautiful allegories when their true meanings were understood, thus denying that there were any crimes or obscenities in myths and tales.

The British anthropologists and folklorists of the Cultural Evolutionary school contended that the discrepancies between folklore and conduct must be explained, not as derived from false etymologies from a common Aryan sun myth, but as survivals of an earlier, pre-Aryan state of savagery in Europe. In support of this they pointed out that the odd and inexplicable incidents in our nursery tales and the odd and superstitious beliefs and practices of country

25 Cited by A. Lang, *Myth, Ritual, and Religion* (London, 1887), Vol. 1, 3.
26 M. Müller, *Contributions to the Science of Mythology* (London, 1897), Vol. 1, 69.

people resembled the customs and beliefs of nonliterate peoples in various parts of the world. In the words of Lang,

> ...now, with regard to all these strange usages, what is the method of folklore? The method is, when an apparently irrational and anomalous custom is found in any country, to look for a country where a similar practice is found, and where the practice is no longer irrational and anomalous, but in harmony with manners and ideas of the people among whom it prevails.... Our method, then, is to compare the seemingly meaningless customs or manners of civilized races with the similar customs and manners which exist among the uncivilized and still retain their meaning.[27]

Of all the recognized "schools" of folklore, only the Diffusionists, the Functionalists, and the Finnish school have indicated little interest in this problem. The Diffusionists, such as Benfey and Cosquin, and the Finnish Historical-Geographical school have been preoccupied with the question of distribution of similar tales. While the contradictions between folklore and human conduct could be explained by the element of fantasy, or could develop through the operation of Aarne's laws or "principles" of folklore change,[28] the same laws or principles could as easily have operated to eliminate discrepancies between folklore and culture. Malinowski, despite his remarkable insights into folklore, makes no comment regarding the discrepancies between folklore and human conduct.[29]

The Psychoanalytic school provides well-known answers to what have been considered atrocities and obscenities, based largely on the identification of sex symbols and the Oedipus and Electra situation in myths. Some of the contradictions between folklore and culture are thus explained as wish fulfillment or escape from sexual taboos on a fantasy level by mechanisms comparable to those found in dreams or daydreams.

Finally, the American Anthropological "school" has been as eclectic in this respect as usual, refusing to accept any single explanation for the many different cultures and historical situations without first examining the specific facts bearing upon each case. Thus Benedict explains some of the discrepancies between Zuni folklore and custom in terms of cultural lag. The tales describe entering a house by a ladder through a hatchway in the roof, although doors have been common in Zuni since 1888. The use of stone knives, also, is retained only in folklore and in ritual. Benedict considers the possibility that accounts of polygamy in folklore may also be "survivals" from a period in which polygamy was actually practiced, but discards it because, first, "it is doubtful whether any folklore can be cited, from any part of the world that

---

[27] A. Lang, *Custom and Myth* (New York, 1885), p. 21.

[28] A. Aarne, *Leitfaden der vergleichenden Märchenforschung,* Folklore Fellows Communications, No. 13 (1913), 23–39.

[29] Radcliffe-Brown is concerned with the internal inconsistencies in mythology, such as the contradiction between the Andamanese view of lightning as a person who shakes his leg, and as a firebrand thrown by Biliku; but he is not concerned with the inconsistencies between the behavior of characters in folklore and members of a society. A. R. Radcliffe-Brown, *The Andaman Islanders* (Cambridge, Eng., 1933), pp. 396–97.

reflects cultural conditions as remote as those before pueblo culture took form."[30] Second, she rejects it on grounds that would also argue against borrowing this motif from neighboring polygamous cultures:

> In the second place, even if it were possible to interpret the Zuni folkloristic pattern of polygamy as a survival, we should still have to explain why the marriage with eight wives or with two husbands is prominent in Zuni mythology and not generally over North America. The simultaneous marriage with many wives was culturally allowed over most of the continent, but it does not figure in tales as it does in pueblo folklore. The presumption that is indicated by a study of the distribution of this folkloristic pattern in North America is that in the pueblo's polygamy is a grandiose folkloristic convention partaking on the one hand of usual mythological exaggeration and on the other of a compensatory daydream. Just as the hero of folktales kills a buck every day, or four in a single day, so he also is courted by eight maidens and marries them....Marriage with many wives is a Zuni fantasy of the same order as raising the dead or traveling with seven-league boots in other bodies of folklore. It plays a fairy-tale role in Zuni mythology which is automatically rendered impossible in those areas of North America where tales of polygamy and polyandry have bases in fact.[31]

Benedict cautiously concludes that it is hard to prove what compensatory elements are embodied in marriage with many wives, but that "other contrasts between custom and folkloristic conventions must be explained as fundamentally compensatory."[32] Thus, the abandonment of children at birth is a constantly recurring theme in Zuni folklore, but is alien to their culture. Seeking one's own death by summoning the Apache is another popular theme, but "suicide is unknown and even inconceivable to the Zuni mind, and violence is culturally taboo...."[33] "In each case the story is a daydream motivated by resentment, and maneuvers the daydreamer into the martyr's position," "without the necessity of any violent act save on the part of the Apache...."[34]

> Another theme, which also reflects Zuni culture but with a difference, is that of violent action based upon secret enmity. Grudges are cherished in Zuni. They are usually the rather generalized expression of slights and resentments in a small community. In actual life they give rise to malicious aspersions, but in folklore they are usually satisfied by nothing less than the death of the offender....In a culture in which homicide occurs with such extraordinary rarity that instances are not even remembered, the compensatory violence of these reprisals is the more striking.[35]
>
> Zuni folklore, therefore, in those cases where it does not mirror contemporary custom owes its distortions to various fanciful exaggerations and compensatory mechanisms. The role of daydreams, of wish fulfillment, is not limited to these cases of distortion. It is equally clear in the tales that most

---

[30] Benedict, *op. cit.*, p. xvi.
[31] *Ibid.*
[32] *Ibid.*
[33] *Ibid.*, p. xviii.
[34] *Ibid.*, p. xix.
[35] *Ibid.*, pp. xix-xx.

minutely reflect the contemporary scene....Their most popular theme is the triumph of the despised and weak and previously worsted. The poor orphan boy is victorious in hunting, in stick races, in gambling, and in courtship...; those who do not have witch power are triumphant over those who have...; the stunted ragamuffin Ahaiyute wins first place in everything.[36]

Certainly it can no longer be possible to regard folklore simply as a true and accurate mirror of culture, or to ignore the basic importance of investigating the actual behavior in any society, the ideal patterns of any culture, and the attitudes of any people whose folklore is to be interpreted. Even if there are societies in which contrasts between folklore and culture are completely absent, this fact in itself is important to know and to attempt to explain. Opler emphasizes

> ...the high correlation of the details of Jicarilla mythology with the actual conduct of the bearers of the culture and the forces which maintain it....[37]
>
> The compensations for satisfactions denied in reality by the culture, the elaborate daydreams, the exultant departures from the true culture ethic which are characteristic of many mythologies, are seldom encountered in Jicarilla legends. The culture heroes perform deeds that may be expected of no mortal, of course, but when a rite or observance is attributed to a supernatural or an animal, one may be sure that the Jicarilla carry out the details of that procedure in much the same way. And when feelings, attitudes, judgments, likes and dislikes are described for the protagonists in the myths, one may be fairly certain that the same responses belong to the normal reaction pattern of the average Jicarilla. In other words the myths provide a surprisingly accurate guide to Jicarilla culture....
>
> There is scarcely a story in this collection which does not reveal fidelity to the cultural round....
>
> It was in spite of initial scepticism that I came to recognize the degree to which Jicarilla mythology mirrored Jicarilla culture.[38]

Yet Opler's Jicarilla collection contains a typical tale of "Coyote and His Mother-in-law" and a tale of how "Coyote Marries His Own Daughter,"[39] and two years later Opler writes of the Lipan Apache:

> Of the four Athabaskan cultures which I have studied, the Lipan is the only one in which the mother-in-law avoidance is not required. Interestingly enough, Lipan Mythology does not include in the coyote cycle an episode in which the trickster violates his mother-in-law.[40]

As a final example of this point, Rattray, in his discussion of Ashanti folklore, refers to:

> ...the peculiarity presented by a people normally decorous in speech and conduct, whose Folktales nevertheless often contain the most Rabelaisian

---

36 *Ibid.*, pp. xx-xxi.

37 M. E. Opler, *Myths and Tales of the Jicarilla Apache Indians,* Memoirs of the American Folklore Society, Vol. 31 (1938), xi-xii.

38 *Ibid.*, pp. xii-xiv.

39 *Ibid.*, pp. 313–14, 280–82.

40 M. E. Opler, *Myths and Legends of the Lipan Apache Indians,* Memoirs of the American Folklore Society, Vol. 36 (1940), 7.

passages, who would yet consider it highly improper to relate these passages if divorced from the occasion and context in which they are nightly publicly paraded. . . .[41]

Subjects ordinarily regarded as sacred, e.g., the Sky-god, the lesser gods, fetishes, spirit ancestors, the sick, chiefs, sexual matters, appear to be treated as if profane, and sometimes even tend to become the subject of ridicule.[42]

In the middle of a story or between tales, actors may enter the circle and give extremely realistic and clever impersonations of various characters in the tale which call forth roars of laughter from all who witness them.

> On one occasion—it was in connection, I think, with a sketch depicting an old man covered with yaws—I asked someone seated beside me if people habitually laughed at persons inflicted by *Nyame* (the Sky-god) in this way, and I suggested it was unkind to ridicule such a subject. The person addressed replied that in everyday life no one might do so, however great the inclination to laugh might be. He went on to explain that it was so with many other things: the cheating and tricks of the priests, the rascality of a chief—things about which everyone knew, but concerning which one might not ordinarily speak in public. These occasions gave every one an opportunity of talking about and laughing at such things; it was "good" for everyone concerned, he said.[43]

From this, and from other evidence, Rattray concludes "that West Africans had discovered for themselves the truth of the psychoanalysts' theory of 'repressions,' and that in these ways they sought an outlet for what might otherwise become a dangerous complex."[44]

This has taken us already into our third problem and the consideration of what folklore does for the people who tell and listen to it. From what has been said it should be clear that folklore cannot be dismissed simply as a form of amusement. Amusement is, obviously, one of the functions of folklore, and an important one; but even this statement cannot be accepted today as a complete answer, for it is apparent that beneath a great deal of humor lies a deeper meaning. The same is true for the concepts of fantasy and creative imagination. The fact that the storyteller in some societies is expected to modify a familiar tale by introducing new elements or giving a novel twist to the plot is in itself of basic importance to the study of dynamics and the aesthetics of folklore, but one may ask why the teller chooses to introduce specific elements and twists.

Whatever one may think of the various applications of classical Freudian theory to folklore, one must admit that there are basic ideas here which go far beyond sexual symbolism and the Oedipus plot. Viewed in this light folklore reveals man's frustrations and attempts to escape in fantasy from repressions imposed upon him by society, whether these repressions be sexual or otherwise and whether they result from taboos on incest or polygamy, or from a taboo on laughing at a person afflicted by yaws. The concepts of compensation and the escape mechanism are fully as suggestive when applied to the familiar

---

[41] Rattray, *op. cit.*, p. xi.
[42] *Ibid.*, p. x.
[43] *Ibid.*, pp. x-xi.
[44] *Ibid.*, p. xii.

theme of rags to riches, or to the Cinderella and Frau Holle tales, as when they are applied to the Oedipus myth. But folklore also reveals man's attempts to escape in fantasy from the conditions of his geographical environment and from his own biological limitations as a member of the genus and species *Homo sapiens*. The same approach is also suggestive when applied to the Zuni hero who kills four bucks in a single day, to the Seven-League Boots, to the Magic Flight, to life after death, or to the psychological identification with a hero who conquers his enemies by magic, or with a trickster who overcomes his more powerful associates by shrewdness and cunning.

Classical Freudian theory has required considerable revision to make it applicable cross-culturally in a meaningful way. It has been necessary to reject Freud's hypothetical reconstruction of the primeval horde because it is based upon questionable sources and upon the premises of the Cultural Evolutionary school; to reject the interpretations of Abraham and Rank because their comparative method, as much as that of the Cultural Evolutionary school, tears superficially similar data out of their cultural contexts; and to reject Jung's "archetypes" and his ethnocentric application of European symbolism to all folklore because it disregards the influence of culture on both symbolism and folklore.[45] All of the classical Freudians seem to have relied upon a mystical racial or biological inheritance for the transmission of beliefs which are learned, and to ignore significant cultural differences. As Malinowski has shown, the Oedipus complex itself has its roots, not in the biological factor of sex as Freud assumed, but in the cultural factors of family structure and parental authority. Both the cultural context and the environmental setting must be known before the causes of repression or frustration can be identified, and their responses can be interpreted.[46]

---

[45] Karl Abraham was one of the first disciples of Freud. His study of mythology appeared in 1909, the same year that Otto Rank's *The Myth of the Birth of the Hero* was published. His consideration of the origin of masculine and feminine genders in Indo-European languages and his analysis of the Prometheus myth are stimulating. See "Dreams and Myths: A Study in Folk-Psychology," in Karl Abraham, *Clinical Papers and Essays on Psychoanalysis,* Vol. 2 (New York, 1955), 151–209.

Carl Jung's approach to folklore and mythology removes them from the province of the cultural anthropologist. Jung believes that the mind is not a *tabula rasa* at birth. There are, among other things, archetypes, which are living entities consisting of inherited forms of psychic behavior. Often the archetypes are manifested in myth. Archetypes are a priori and given, so that primitive mentality does not invent myths, it experiences them. Since archetypes are pre-cultural, they are essentially beyond the influence of cultural conditioning, and therefore Jung's theory eliminates the need for the study of cultural conditioning to understand mythic archetypes. This is why Jung's theory is so unpopular among anthropological folklorists. Jung was a prolific writer, but enough of a theoretical framework to understand his approach to folklore may be found in *Psyche and Symbol: A Selection from the Writings of C. G. Jung,* ed. Violet S. de Laszlo (New York, 1958.) For delineations of several of the archetypes that appear in myth, see C. G. Jung and C. Kerényi, *Essays on a Science of Mythology* (New York, 1963).—Ed. Note

[46] "The folklorist whose intent goes beyond the merely descriptive to the dynamic must be prepared to search out and listen to the cultural associations and contexts of his materials, just as the analyst must listen to the individual free associations of his patients. It is repeating the error of Frazer to accept descriptive similarities at their face value, and not to seek the local context of the symbol." W. La Barre, "Folklore and Psychology," *Journal of American Folklore,* Vol. 61 (1948), 388.

If Freud's biological determinism has been rejected, Freudian mechanisms have not; and when translated into cultural, rather than biological terms, Freudian mechanisms are meaningful and suggestive for the interpretation of folklore. Sex is a drive in all societies, but not the only drive; and even the blocking of learned secondary drives can produce frustration and escapes in fantasy. In this sense, as Kardiner has pointed out, folklore can be viewed as a projective system.[47]

However accurately folklore may mirror the familiar details of culture, and incorporate common situations from everyday life, as Benedict has shown, the unusual or even the impossible is an important ingredient of myths and folktales. Yet the unusual, and the impossible, are defined in terms of each individual culture and habitat, as well as in terms of the biological limitations of *Homo sapiens*. Any universals are to be sought in the common denominators of man's biological heritage, of his natural environmental settings, and of his sociocultural ways of life. But, knowing the range of both the factors of habitat and culture, it cannot be naively assumed that the European sex symbols are universal. As La Barre has said, "without a respect for cultural difference, one runs the risk of creating new etiological myths, rather than explaining the old ones."[48]

A second function of folklore is that which it plays in validating culture, in justifying its rituals and institutions to those who perform and observe them. Myth is not explanatory, Malinowski emphasized, but serves as "a warrant, a charter, and often even a practical guide"[49] to magic, ceremony, ritual and social structure.

> Myth fulfills in primitive culture an indispensable function: it expresses, enhances, and codifies belief; it safeguards and enforces morality; it vouches for the efficiency of ritual and contains practical rules for the guidance of man. Myth is thus a vital ingredient of human civilization; it is not an idle tale, but a hard-worked active force; it is not an intellectual explanation or an artistic imagery, but a pragmatic charter of primitive faith and moral wisdom. . . .[50]
> The function of myth, briefly, is to strengthen tradition and endow it with a greater value and prestige by tracing it back to a higher, better, more supernatural reality of initial events.[51]

When dissatisfaction with or skepticism of an accepted pattern is expressed or doubts about it arise, whether it be sacred or secular, there is usually a myth or legend to validate it; or a so-called "explanatory tale," a moral animal tale, or a proverb, to fulfill the same function. Malinowski's statement is so widely

---

[47] A. Kardiner and Associates, *The Psychological Frontiers of Society* (New York, 1945), p. 29.
[48] La Barre, *op. cit.*, p. 387.
[49] Malinowski, *Myth in Primitive Psychology*, p. 29.
[50] *Ibid.*, p. 19.
[51] *Ibid.*, pp. 91–92.

accepted today that it should not require further discussion, but it is interesting that as the founder of the "Functionalist school," this was the only function of folklore that he recognized, and that in his later works he devotes little attention to folklore.[52]

A third function of folklore is that which it plays in education, particularly, but not exclusively, in nonliterate societies. The importance of the many forms of folklore as pedagogic devices has been documented in many parts of the world, although perhaps most comprehensively in Raum's study of education among the Chaga of East Africa. Here ogre tales, like our bogey-man stories, are used in the discipline of very young children, and lullabies are sung to put them in a good humor. Somewhat later, fables or folktales incorporating morals are introduced "to inculcate general attitudes and principles, such as diligence and filial piety, and to ridicule laziness, rebelliousness, and snobbishness."[53] Proverbs are used to express a threat which the speaker may not later wish to carry out, to direct another's action where a blunt command might offend, or to incite a person to action through irony. Beginning at the age of about fourteen, "when a child flies into a rage, when he lies or steals, when he is recalcitrant or violates the code of etiquette, when he makes an ass out of himself, when he is cowardly, he hears his actions commented upon in the words of a proverb."[54] This is sometimes so effective that, as an adult, the Chaga can remember the situation in which they first heard a particular proverb. The formal instruction given to Chaga boys in the initiation ceremonies is often summarized or emphasized through the use of proverbs, and Raum feels that a number of these discussions or "lectures" are developed to support or justify the point made in a particular proverb. He also believes that the "examinations" or dialogues between teacher and student are related in form to the riddle. Some of the verbal instruction during the initiation ceremonies of boys and the preparation of girls for marriage is given in the form of songs; and throughout later life, songs of ridicule are important as a means of censuring misbehavior.

In many nonliterate societies the information embodied in folklore is highly regarded in its own right. To the extent to which it is regarded as historically true, its teaching is regarded as important; and to the extent to which it mirrors culture, it "contains practical rules for the guidance of man."[55]

> It is plain that the myth is of greatest functional importance to the Jicarilla in the guidance of his behavior, his beliefs, and his ceremonies....The mythology represents for him the summation of knowledge on the basis of which he must act....The mother or grandparent schools the child in ac-

[52] See B. Malinowski, *A Scientific Theory of Culture, and Other Essays* (Chapel Hill, N.C., 1944).

[53] O. F. Raum, *Chaga Childhood. A Description of Indigenous Education in an East African Tribe* (London, 1940), p. 214.

[54] *Ibid.*, p. 217.

[55] Malinowski, *Myth in Primitive Society*, p. 19.

cordance with its dictates. The ceremonial man conducts his rite in terms of directions found therein.[56]

The mythologic system of a people is often their educational system, and the children who sit listening to an evening's tale are imbibing traditional knowledge and attitudes no less than the row of sixth graders in our modern classrooms.[57]

Myths and legends may contain detailed descriptions of sacred ritual, the codified belief or dogma of the religious system, accounts of tribal or clan origins, movements and conflicts. Proverbs have often been characterized as the distilled wisdom of past generations and are unmistakably so regarded by many African peoples.[58]

Even African folktales, which are regarded as fictitious, are considered as important for the education of children, because many of them are animal fables or other moral tales. Riddles serve as a didactic device to sharpen the wits of young children, while dilemma tales, for which there is no "correct" answer, do the same for those who are more mature. Chatelain says of Mbundu anecdotes, "the didactic tendency of these stories is in no way technical, but essentially social. They do not teach how to make a thing, but how to act, how to live."[59] As opposed to practical instruction in productive techniques, folklore appears to be the principal feature in the general education of the child in nonliterate societies.

In the fourth place, folklore fulfills the important but often overlooked function of maintaining conformity to the accepted patterns of behavior. Although related to the last two functions, it deserves to be distinguished from them. More than simply serving to validate or justify institutions, beliefs and attitudes, some forms of folklore are important as means of applying social pressure and exercising social control. Although this clearly emerges in Raum's study of Chaga education, it is also to be distinguished from the function of education, not simply because it continues throughout adult life, but because it is employed against individuals who attempt to deviate from social conventions with which they are fully familiar. When this happens, a song of allusion, a proverb, a riddle, or a folktale may be used to express disapproval. Or, as among the Jicarilla Apache, it may be sufficient "to chide

[56] Opler, *op. cit.*, p. x.

[57] A. H. Gayton, "Perspectives in Folklore," *Journal of American Folklore*, Vol. 64 (1951), 149.

[58] The common notion of proverbs as distilled wisdom needs qualification. The wisdom is relative, not absolute. Wisdom is relative to specific situations in which one particular course of action may be better than another. The easiest way to disprove the idea that proverbs contain absolute wisdom is to match proverbs recommending opposite courses of action, for example, "Look before you leap" and "He who hesitates is lost." Another example is "A rolling stone gathers no moss" and "A tethered sheep soon starves." Biblical proverbs prove no exception. Solomon's advice "Answer not a fool according to his folly, lest thou also be like unto him" is immediately followed (Proverbs 26: 4–5) by "Answer a fool according to his folly, lest he be wise in his own conceit."—ED. NOTE

[59] Chatelain, *op. cit.*, p. 21.

aberrant conduct by inquiring scathingly of the transgressor, 'Did you have no grandparent to tell you the stories?' "[60] Among the Ashanti,

> It was also a recognized custom in olden times for anyone with a grievance against a fellow villager, a chief, or even the King of Ashanti to hold him up to thinly diguised ridicule, by exposing some undesirable trait in his character—greed, jealousy, deceit—introducing the affair as the setting to some tale. A slave would thus expose his bad master, a subject his wicked chief. Up to a point the storyteller was licensed. He took care, moreover, to protect himself by a public declaration to the effect that what he was about to say was just make-believe. He also, my informants stated, avoided the use of personal names.[61]

Folklore is also used to express social approval of those who conform, and certain forms such as "praise names" and songs of praise are specifically intended for this purpose. In many societies folklore is employed to control, influence, or direct the activities of others from the time the first lullaby is sung, or ogre tale is told them. Folklore may also become an internalized check on behavior, as shown by the previous quotations from Opler, or by Raum's statement about Chaga proverbs:

> Their intrinsic value to the Chaga lies in two qualities: they are an inheritance from their ancestors incorporating the experience of the tribe, and they serve as instruments both for self-control and for the control of others. Stefano Moshi said: "When a man is tempted by his own desire or by the suggestions of an evil friend and remembers a proverb he desists immediately. The youth of today treat many ancient things with contempt, but they never jest about proverbs. They respect the wisdom embodied in these sayings, for they strike like arrows into the heart."[62]

Because of the high regard in which they are held and because they are considered as especially appropriate to adult life, African proverbs are highly effective in exercising social control. Because they express the morals or ethics of the group, they are convenient standards for appraising behavior in terms of the approved norms. Because they are pungently, wittily and sententiously stated, they are ideally suited for commenting on the behavior of others. They are used to express social approval and disapproval; praise for those who conform to accepted social conventions and criticism or ridicule of those who deviate; warning, defiance, or derision of a rival or enemy and advice, counsel, or warning to a friend when either contemplates action which may lead to social friction, open hostilities, or direct punishment by society. Thus the Yoruba proverb "No matter how small the needle, a chicken cannot swallow it" conveys the lesson that an apparently weaker individual can cause unexpected difficulties for a more powerful rival. It can be used to warn or defy a more powerful enemy to treat the speaker more respectfully; to warn or advise a friend to change his behavior toward a rival who is weaker; or to

---

60 Opler, *op. cit.*, p. xii.
61 Rattray, *op. cit.*, p. xi.
62 Raum, *op. cit.*, p. 217.

ridicule and criticize someone whose behavior toward a weaker person has brought trouble on himself.

Examples of this type could be multiplied a hundredfold from the Kru, Jabo and Yoruba proverbs which have been analyzed in terms of the social situations to which they are appropriate.[63] It is more important to note the remarkably consistent emphasis on the conformity to the moral code, to the social conventions, and to the ideal forms of behavior. Dahomean proverbs are used "to give point to some well-meaning advice; to rebuke or praise a friend; to put an enemy in his place; to emphasize commendation or affection, or ridicule or blame."[64] Among the Jabo,

> Another important function of the proverb is to smooth the social friction and dissatisfaction, and to ease the individual in his efforts to adjust himself in his setting and fate. If people disagree, if they work at cross-purposes, if a man is dissatisfied with his position, if a person complains of injustice, an older, more experienced, or less concerned person is always at hand with a comforting, quieting, light-shedding proverb. The number of proverbs implying, "under the circumstances, what did you expect?" is impressive. The same proverb may be quoted for advice, instruction, or as a warning—always to prevent or lessen friction.[65]

Proverbs of this last type are especially interesting here, and are by no means confined to the Jabo. They warn the dissatisfied or the over-ambitious individual to be content with his lot, to accept the world as it is and his place in it, and thus to conform to the accepted patterns.

Although I have spoken loosely of the "functions of folklore," it is important to remember that the functions of the myth, legend, folktale, proverb, riddle, song, and each of the other forms of folklore are to some extent distinctive and must be analyzed separately. As their very names suggest, this is also true of the various types of song: lullabies, love songs, war songs, work songs, ballads, blues, religious songs, songs of praise, and songs of ridicule or allusion. To fully understand folklore and its role in man's life, we must have more knowledge of the specific functions of each of these forms in various societies, literate and nonliterate, and more of the tedious but extremely rewarding comparisons of the details of folklore texts with those of culture and actual behavior. It is only in this way, also, that we may hope to explain, rather than simply take for granted (somewhat thankfully) the fact that folklore *is* one of the human universals, and perhaps to understand why the importance of folklore has decreased as the written and printed word have spread and mechanical devices such as phonographs, radios, moving pictures, and television have been developed. Is it due to the competition of these forms of mass media in the field of amusement? Is it because of the loss of some

---

[63] M. J. Herskovits and S. Tagbwe, "Kru Proverbs," *Journal of American Folklore,* Vol. 43 (1930), 225–93; G. Herzog, *Jabo Proverbs from Liberia* (London, 1936); W. and B. Bascom, unpublished Yoruba proverbs.

[64] M. J. Herskovits, *Dahomey* (New York, 1938), Vol. 2, 323.

[65] Herzog, *op. cit.,* p. 2.

other function of folklore, such as education? Is it due to the inability of folk-lore to adapt itself to cultural change which is too rapid or too radical?

I have intentionally oversimplified the varied functions of folklore in order to stress certain important ones. To the four that have been discussed can be added the function of Trobriand Island "fairy tales" in garden magic, of Yoruba myths and tales in divination,[66] of Dahomean obscene stories at wakes,[67] of African proverbs in generalizing the specific[68] and in court trials,[69] or of folklore's function in integrating society and maintaining social cohesion as shown specifically in the analysis of Andamanese mythology.[70]

The four functions which I have discussed could be classified differently. They could be subdivided into various factors which have been distinguished,[71] or, as for the moment I prefer to do, they can be considered as grouped together under the single function of maintaining the stability of culture. Viewed thus, folklore operates within a society to insure conformity to the accepted cultural norms, and continuity from generation to generation through its role in education and the extent to which it mirrors culture. To the extent to which folklore contrasts with the accepted norms and offers socially acceptable forms of release through amusement or humor and through creative imagination and fantasy, it tends to preserve the institutions from direct attack and change. There is no difficulty, of course, in finding instances in folklore where laziness, complacency, or the lack of ambition and initiative are condemned, but are there any which suggest that the individual destroy or even disregard the institutions and conventions of his society?

---

66 Bascom, *op. cit.*, pp. 127–31.

67 "Similarly, at wakes or ceremonies for the dead, neither these (historical) tales nor the simple animal stories would be seemly, for the dead are held beyond the need for moralizing, and the obscene story is called to furnish entertainment." Herskovits, *Dahomey*, p. 325.

68 "Proverbs serve a specific and important intellectual function—that of subsuming the particular under the general." Herzog, *op. cit.*, p. 7. "The proverb is the product of the faculty of generalization, of getting at the principles, of inference and discrimination, combined with the gift of graphic and concise expression." Chatelain, *op. cit.*, p. 21.

69 "As in other parts of Africa, proverbs play an important part in the legal discussions of the Jabo. The chief aim of the legal machinery, after the facts of the case have been established, is to classify it. . . . In order to be dealt with it must cease to be a particular occurrence. In this light it is significant that this process of generalizing the particular case employs the body of formulas which performs that very function—the proverbs. . . . The more proverbs a man has at his command and the better he knows how to apply them, the better lawyer or spokesman he is considered to be. A proverb misquoted or applied badly may spoil the entire case." Herzog, *op. cit.* pp. 1–2. Herskovits and Tagbwe, *op. cit.*, pp. 254–55. "Proverbs are introduced. . .in pleas before courts of justice, in court testimony and court decisions, or in dissent from these decisions." Herskovits, *op. cit.*, p. 323.

70 Radcliffe-Brown, *op. cit.*, pp. 330–406.

71 Thus one might distinguish between amusement, creative fantasy, and psychological escape; between the mirroring of culture in folklore and the contrasts between them; between folklore as a validation of culture and as a guide to behavior and ritual; between its roles in embodying the content of education and as a didactic device; or between its roles as an internalized check on behavior, as a device for expressing social approval and disapproval, and as a means of suggesting that one be content with his lot.

Viewed in this light, folklore is an important mechanism for maintaining the stability of culture. It is used to inculcate the customs and ethical standards in the young, and as an adult to reward him with praise when he conforms, to punish him with ridicule or criticism when he deviates, to provide him with rationalizations when the institutions and conventions are challenged or questioned, to suggest that he be content with things as they are, and to provide him with a compensatory escape from "the hardships, the inequalities, the injustices"[72] of everyday life. Here, indeed, is the basic paradox of folklore, that while it plays a vital role in transmitting and maintaining the institutions of a culture and in forcing the individual to conform to them, at the same time it provides socially approved outlets for the repressions which these same institutions impose upon him.

---

[72] Herskovits, *op. cit.*, p. 421.

The Role of Proverbs
in a Nigerian Judicial System

John C. Messenger, Jr.

It is one thing to be told that proverbs are commonly used in African court trials, and quite another for the student to visualize just how proverbs are used in this context. In this interesting article, Professor Messenger of Indiana University gives some detailed examples. From these, one can see that proverbs among the Anang people of southeastern Nigeria are serious business and that competence in their use could be vitally important to an individual's welfare. It is not enough just to know the proverbs; one must also know how to apply them to specific situations.

As a simple exercise to show the necessity of recording context with text, read the appendix to this paper before reading the essay itself. After looking at the literal and free translations of the eleven Anang proverbs, the reader should see if he knows, for any given text, (1) precisely what the proverb means and (2) in what kind of situation it might be cited. It is sad to report that the majority of proverb collections consist of only the kind of information contained in Messenger's appendix. Such neglect of context and function make these collections of limited value.

The Anang, in common with other African peoples, possess a rich folklore tradition, comprising most importantly tales, proverbs, riddles, and song verses.[1] Proverbs are by far the most numerous and the most frequently employed of these forms of verbal art, and are used in all manner of situations— as a means of amusement, in educating the young, to sanction institutionalized behavior, as a method of gaining favor in court, in performing religious rituals and association ceremonies, and to give point and add color to ordinary conversation. Neighboring Ibo gave the Anang their name, the term denoting

Reprinted from the *Southwestern Journal of Anthropology,* Vol. 15 (1959), 64–73, by permission of the author and the publisher.

[1] This paper is a lengthened revision of one delivered in 1957 before the Central States Anthropological Society, and is based upon research conducted in Nigeria during 1951–1952.

299

"ability to speak wittily yet meaningfully upon any occasion," and not a little of Anang eloquence, admired by Africans and Europeans alike, stems from their skillful use of maxims. This paper recounts a number of proverbs collected during court hearings, places them within their cultural and juridical contexts, and assesses their use as rhetorical devices affecting the course of justice in Anang tribunals.

Second largest of the 6 Ibibio-speaking tribes of southeastern Nigeria, the Anang possess no centralized political organization but are divided into 28 subtribes, called *iman,* each of which is a group of villages ruled, to a limited degree, by a hereditary chief whose duties are mainly of a religious nature. The members of an *iman* share certain distinctive cultural traits and express a consciousness of unity; in addition, the meat of a particular animal is forbidden to them.

Politically preeminent is the community, or *obio,* rather than the subtribe, and a hereditary leader and a council of elders direct its affairs and perform important social and religious functions. The largest social grouping is the patrilineage, known as *ɛkpuk,* composed of both nuclear and extended families inhabiting a continuous tract of territory in the village. Each family lives in a compound surrounded by forest, bush, and land belonging to the head and farmed by his wives and children.

British rule over the Anang was established during the decade following the first contact of these two peoples in 1903. Native and Magistrates' Courts were gradually introduced which officially superseded the indigenous ones,[2] and continual action has been taken by the colonial government to eradicate the latter, an effort that has met with only partial success. Two of the five types of traditional courts, called *esop,* have been abolished, but the other three still flourish in many communities. This paper treats only the indigenous judiciary, and the maxims under discussion were transcribed during proceedings conducted by these illegal bodies.

With the breakdown of *iman* political forms as the result of acculturation, the highest Anang court no longer exists. This was an *esop* composed of the chief of the subtribe and the heads of the communities within the village group. It convened two or three times a year to try the most heinous crimes— murder, failure to observe the food taboo, and the theft of objects used for religious sacrifice. Market courts as well no longer exist, for Anang markets are not numerous and thus can be policed easily by the British authorities. At one time, the leaders of *obio* contiguous to a market made up the tribunal and conducted hearings involving traders from their own and other *iman.* The

---

[2] Most cases are tried in the Native Courts, the members of which are Anang elders, usually village and patrilineage heads, who have been assigned their position by the District Officer. They are sworn to uphold Native Law and Custom as delineated by the British—a body of statutes embracing both European and Anang concepts of morality— and their decisions are subject to review by the District Officer or appeal to the Magistrates' Courts.

crimes usually tried by this body were theft and usurping another's trading position.

The traditional courts still active are those serving the village, patrilineage, and family. Only a few *obio* tribunals continue to meet, and these sporadically, whereas patrilineage and family *esop* function in most communities as they did in the past. All try cases involving crimes not subsumed under Native Law and Custom, a state of affairs unofficially favored by some District Officers because they feel it allows the Anang to maintain a certain cultural equilibrium in a period of rapid change.

The head of the family and, if they reside in the compound, his adult brothers and sons form the family court, which convenes in the house of the compound leader at sunset on the day an offense is committed. The crimes most commonly tried are quarreling among wives, cruelty toward wives, disobedience of children, and petty stealing within the family group. The patrilineage *esop* meets weekly in a court building located in a small square central to the area inhabited by the kin-group. Presided over by the *εkpuk* head, this body consists of family leaders and sometimes old men who do not hold this position but who have high prestige. Most of the cases brought before the tribunal can be tried either here or in the village court, depending upon whether the principals are from the same or from different patrilineages. Chief among the offenses in this category are theft, assault with a deadly weapon, adultery, and causing an unmarried girl to become pregnant.

In the past, most Anang adjudication took place in the community *esop*. It was composed of *εkpuk* heads presided over by the village leader, and met once each week in the compound of the latter or in the court house serving his kin-group. Certain of the offenses which fell within its jurisdiction have just been mentioned: others of importance which could not be brought before other tribunals were: refusal to bear arms in inter-village warfare, striking parents or old people, performing sexual intercourse in the bush, practicing evil magic or witchcraft, and refusing to refund bride wealth following divorce. Today, in those communities where this *esop* continues to meet, the personnel of the court remains unchanged, and many of the crimes listed above still are tried, as well as some formerly falling within the province of the *imαn* tribunal.

Village court procedures are much the same as those of other judicial bodies. Usually only older men and women attend the sessions, the former far outnumbering the latter, and children are barred except when they are principals or serve as witnesses. Women seldom speak out except when asked to furnish evidence, although a very old woman of high social standing might act as a character witness or advise the judges as to a proper verdict. Once the presiding member has introduced the case under consideration, the plaintiff stands before the justices, termed *εkpε ikpε,* and pays a small "utterance fee," used to purchase palm wine for the court members following adjournment. He states his grievance, without benefit of a lawyer, in a speech that may last as long as an hour, following which he surrenders the floor to the defendant who proceeds in like manner. When the *esop* itself initiates a case, the chief justice speaks as the plaintiff. The *ɛkpɛ ikpɛ* and those in the audience pay rapt attention to the litigants as they deliver their talks, and outbursts of applause mark the course of a well-presented accusation or defense. Listeners are especially appreciative of an original or little known proverb that captures their imagination and is cleverly introduced at a crucial moment.

The presiding member maintains strict control over the hearing, preventing interruptions when the principals are addressing the tribunal and allowing neither to dwell upon irrelevant matters. Both are then questioned at great length, first by one another, next by the *ɛkpɛ ikpɛ,* and finally by elders in the room, and at this time each may call forth material and character witnesses to buttress his position. When the chief judge decides that sufficient evidence has been introduced, he seeks the opinions of important old men as to the innocence or guilt of the defendant and retires with his colleagues to ponder a decision, returning with them to announce the verdict they have agreed upon.

The court may call a diviner to uncover hidden facts if it lacks sufficient evidence for a conclusive decision, or it may consult an oath swearer if it is apparent that one of the litigants or witnesses is falsifying his testimony. Often confronting a person with one of these dreaded specialists is enough to induce him to present additional evidence or to alter his statement. If an oath is sworn, a trial must be postponed until the results of the oath can be ascertained. Periodically, *ɛkpɛ ikpɛ* are required to swear in public before a powerful oath administrator that they will neither accept bribes nor allow personal bias to influence their decisions.

The death penalty for a crime no longer can be exacted, but prior to the advent of the British those tried before the subtribal *esop* and found guilty were executed or, more commonly, sold into slavery. Lower tribunals were limited to levying fines and flogging convicted felons, this being the condition prevailing in the village court today. Fines are paid in cash or in domestic animals, both of which are shared by the justices. When a compensatory fine is ordered, there is usually a small accompanying punitive one that reverts to the members of the tribunal. As legal offenses are considered infractions of divine law, a guilty party, in addition to rendering a fine or being flogged, must perform a sacrifice before a particular shrine to placate the deity.

Now that we have examined in broadest outline the structural and procedural forms of the judiciary, let us discuss those factors which facilitate or hinder the administration of justice by the Anang courts. The strongest force acting to ensure equitable decisions is the belief of these people that their legal system is an instrument utilized by the deity, known as *abassi,* to punish those who have failed to conform to his divine moral code. It is held that a miscarriage of justice in the courts can result in an aroused *abassi* chastising not only the culprit, but also his relatives and even his fellow villagers. Thus, not only is the guilty one eventually forced to pay for his crime, but many innocent parties may suffer as well. Another supernatural sanction having great efficacy is the oath sworn by *εkpε ikpε,* for the oath spirit, at the behest of the deity, will quickly and ruthlessly attack any court member who engages in corrupt practices or who fails to act impartially during a hearing.

Democratic procedures certainly are evident in the conduct of a case. As we have noted, both plaintiff and defendant are given ample time to present their positions, and are forbidden to dwell upon extraneous issues that might unduly influence the justices. All aspects of the case are probed by the tribunal members, as well as by interested elders, through extensive questioning of the principals and witnesses. Pertinent evidence is examined with great care, the *εkpε ikpε* often traveling afar to view at first hand the site of a crime. Occasionally, an authoritarian chief justice fails to call for opinions on a verdict from the audience and dominates his colleagues when a decision is considered, but most often he seeks the judgments of at least a dozen elders, as well as agreement among the members of the *esop.*

Most apparent of the shortcomings of the Anang judiciary is the willingness of some judges to accept bribes and the tendency of others to express bias, especially when kin are involved. The people readily admit that the Native Courts are corrupt,[3] but they insistently hold that *εkpε ikpε* of the indigenous tribunals have always been inviolate. It became evident that there is some discrepancy between the ideal and the real in this area after several months were spent in the field during which numerous hearings were attended and informants queried. Bribery and partiality are occasionally manifested, and probably were in the past despite the spiritual sanctions against them. The reasons for this are threefold: first, a very few have unorthodox religious beliefs and doubt the avenging propensities of *abassi;* second, there are those whose pecuniary motives are so strong that they are willing to risk the consequences of immoral practices; and third, some possess charms procured at great expense from workers of evil magic which they believe can thwart supernatural retribution. Evidence also suggests that at times justices are prompted to declare the guilt of an individual when testimony fails to warrant it in order to share the fine, a condition that may have been more commonplace in the past when it was possible to sell convicted criminals into slavery for enormous profits. It is difficult to know how effective religious sanctions were half a century ago.

Anang justices of long standing were unconscious of and only slowly came to realize the influence of proverbs upon decision making in courts. As the Anang take every opportunity to display their eloquence and constantly

---

3 The Anang attribute corruption in these *esop* to the fact that oath swearing in them was discontinued in 1947, as the result of missionary pressures, and salaries paid sitting members are low.

employ adages, it appears that such verbal expression is taken for granted and its impact thus not evaluated. Proverbs were collected which seemed to affect verdicts in particular trials; it must be admitted, however, that *ɛkpɛ ikpɛ* did not always agree with the researcher as to whether they had been unduly influenced by maxims in these trials, therefore only those hearings in which at least one justice admitted being swayed are reported on in the following section.[4]

During a case in which a chronic thief was accused of robbery, the plaintiff aroused considerable antagonism toward the defendant early in the trial by employing the following proverb: "If a dog plucks palm fruits from a cluster, he does not fear a porcupine."[5] A cluster from the oil palm tree contains numerous sharp needles that make handling it extremely hazardous, therefore a dog known to pick palm fruits certainly would be unafraid to touch a porcupine. The maxim implies that the accused is the logical suspect since he was a known thief and lived close to the person who was robbed, and many in the audience regarded the trial as a mere formality. His guilt came to appear doubtful, however, in the light of evidence produced during the proceedings, and just before the *ɛkpɛ ikpɛ* were to retire he presented an adage that was instrumental in gaining his acquittal: "A single partridge flying through the bush leaves no path." Partridges usually travel close to the ground in coveys and can be followed by the trail of bent and broken grass they leave behind. In using this proverb the accused likened himself to a single bird, without sympathizers to lend him support, and called upon the tribunal to disregard the sentiments of those in attendance and to overlook his past misdemeanors and judge the case as objectively as possible.

In another case the precept "Something happened to the smoke which caused it to enter the bush and become mist" was employed by a person accusing a former friend of assault with a machete during a heated argument. The plaintiff wanted the court to know that he disliked bringing charges against the defendant in light of their former close association, but was compelled to do so because of the severity of the attack. He compared himself to smoke which rightfully belongs in the compound but which has been forced out into the bush by the wind to become mist. Witnesses were introduced to support the accusation, and later the defendant claimed that they had been bribed by his opponent to testify in the latter's behalf. The accused attempted to show the justices that, although posing as a friend, the plaintiff was in

---

4 Although it was certainly a good idea for Messenger to attempt to corroborate his own feeling that a judicial decision had been influenced by the citation of a particular proverb by consulting with the principals concerned, it does seem somewhat unlikely that many such informants would be willing to admit that they had been "unduly" influenced by proverbs. If, as Messenger states in the conclusion of his paper, the Anang do pride themselves on the objectivity of their judiciary, it is improbable that they would openly acknowledge that their decisions were based upon anything other than the objective facts of the case.—ED. NOTE

5 The linguistic data for this proverb and those to follow are found at the end of the paper, in the order of their citation.

reality a jealous enemy who had chosen this means to discredit him, ending his exposé with the adage "A leopard conceals his spots." Under ordinary circumstances a leopard resembles a large bush cat, but once angered it extends its limbs and arches its back revealing the distinguishing spots. The animal attempts to hide its identity by making itself as small as possible when stalking an intended victim. Thus the plaintiff was pictured as a dangerous foe hiding his true motives under the guise of friendship. The court was sufficiently impressed by this accusation in reverse to demand that the plaintiff and his supporting witnesses swear oaths as to the veracity of their claims, a demand they were afraid to comply with. When calling upon the specialist to administer the oaths, the presiding member appraised the case with the proverb "If an animal resembles a palm fruit cluster, how can it be butchered?" By this he meant that at this point in the hearing the evidence was so inconclusive that the $\varepsilon k p \varepsilon\ ikp\varepsilon$ would be unable to reach a verdict, just as an animal possessing the needles of a cluster would be difficult to handle. The chief judge admonished the plaintiff and his supporters with the maxim "If you visit the home of the toads, stoop" when they expressed their unwillingness to take oaths, thereby forfeiting the case. This adage is similar in meaning to our "When in Rome, do as the Romans do" and is frequently used by a presiding member when pronouncing a decision, by which he emphasizes the necessity of conforming to the divine moral code, in this instance not bearing false witness.

In still another case, a boy accused of impregnating an unmarried girl denied his guilt and accused a young man of having committed the act and boasting of it to other men in the *obio*. Not only did the girl contradict the defendant's plea, but the young man whom the latter had accused asserted his innocence. As the trial progressed, the case came to rest upon the girl's claim that the boy was guilty, especially after a number of witnesses admitted hearing the young man boast of his sexual exploits with her, exploits that she emphatically denied. The girl's relatives testified that her honesty was above reproach, and an oath might have been called for had not two witnesses spoken out using proverbs which influenced the judges to rule against the boy. The father of the boy, when called upon as a character witness, seemed reluctant to support his son, admitting that he often had punished the boy for sexual practices and telling lies. In light of this, he told the court, he considered his son capable of having committed the act for which he was accused and ended his testimony by using the precept, "The *nsasak* said she was ashamed of the small size of her offspring." Smallest of the birds in the region, the *nsasak is* thought by the Anang to be ashamed of its diminutive size. Naturally, they claim, the mother of the species is even more ashamed of its fledgling since it is far smaller than she. In employing this maxim, the father revealed his lack of faith in his son's claims and the great shame he felt at making the admission publicly. The proverb which finally persuaded the judges to declare the boy guilty was used by the girl's father when he was called upon as the last witness. He denounced the accused after telling the *ɛkpɛ ikpɛ* that her word was to be trusted absolutely, highlighting his speech with the proverb "The *ɛkɛnuk* tried to eat as much as the *ɔkɔnɔ* and his stomach burst." There are several types of rats in the area; one, the *ɛkɛnuk*, is only two or three inches in length, while another, the *ɔkɔnɔ*, is almost two feet long. The girl's parents likened the boy to the small variety and a married man to the large one; the youth is about to suffer for an act that only a married man is eligible to perform with his spouse.

Upon one occasion the misuse of a proverb by a defendant was instrumental in causing his conviction. A man accused of being an accessory in a theft became incensed at the manner in which evidence was turning against him as the trial proceeded. After a particularly damning piece of evidence was introduced by a witness with the precept "When the fire burned the dog, it also burned the hunter holding the rope attached to the neck of the dog," the accused pleaded his innocence with the maxim "The snail is bleeding." Since a snail, lacking blood, cannot bleed when wounded, the defendant was asserting that he could not be punished for a crime which he had not committed. He continued by berating his opponent, the witnesses who had testified against him, and finally the members of the tribunal, saying that if the latter convicted him they would be guilty of misconduct. He employed the proverb "Overeating destroys the soul" in condemning the justices, implying that they would be going beyond what the evidence indicated and would thus invite the punishment of *abassi* were they to rule against him. The *ɛkpɛ ikpɛ*, already disturbed by the inflammatory remarks directed at them, admitted that this precept consolidated their opinion as to his guilt. Once the verdict was announced, the accused in an emotional outburst admitted his involvement in the crime, claiming that he was not responsible for his conduct but was the unwilling victim of fate, and uttering the adage "The crayfish is bent because it is sick" to support his contention. In its natural condition a crayfish is elongated, but when trapped by fishermen and dried on a rack over the fire it curls up as a sick person might; the felon compared himself to the animal, compelled to do something against his wishes by a force over which he exerts little control.

These cases should suffice to illustrate the vital role played by proverbs in the dispensation of justice by Anang tribunals. In conclusion, it might be pointed out that adages play the same role in the Native Courts as they do in the indigenous ones, with like effect, and government officials appear as unaware of this obstruction to justice as the *ɛkpɛ ikpɛ* themselves. Before either judiciary can be considered equitable, Anang elders and colonial administrators must cope with this problem as well as with others, such as corruption, which are more obvious. It may be that the influence of proverbs is becoming less pervasive now that many justices in the tribe are aware of it. If this is so, it represents another example of the unpremeditated effect of anthropological research upon indigenous custom. There have been several instances of primitive peoples incorporating into their folklore tales related to them by anthropologists, and it is known that traditional theologies have been altered when inconsistencies in dogma were revealed by researchers. It may be that Anang judges will come to weigh more consciously the impact of maxims in arriving at their verdicts, for they pride themselves on the objectivity of their judiciary.

Texts of Proverbs[6]

If a dog plucks palm fruits from a cluster, he does not fear a porcupine.

εbuα	αmα	εbεk	oyop	kε	ifεrε	ibαkε	εdiɔŋ
dog	who	plucks	palm fruit	from	cluster	fears not	porcupine

A single partridge flying through the bush leaves no path.

ikpɔŋ	αsαsα	αmα	ɔfuɔrɔ	αfαŋ	εsidε
lonely	partridge	who	after flying	path	closes

Something happened to the smoke which caused it to enter the bush and become mist.

ŋkpo αkαnαm	nsuŋ	ikαŋ	εnye	oduk	ikɔt	αkαpα	otukubε
something happened	fly	fire	it	entered	bush	turned into	mist

A leopard conceals his spots.

εkpε	εdidip	nkεmε
leopard	conceals	spots

If an animal resembles a palm fruit cluster, how can it be butchered?

unαm	αmα	εtiε ntε	ifεrε	oyop	ebαk	diε
animal	who	resembles	cluster	palm fruit	butcher	how

If you visit the home of the toads, stoop.

εkpεdε αkα	iduŋ	ikwɔt	esɔsɔrɔ	kεnε	esɔsɔrɔ
if you go	village	toads	stoop	follow	stoop

The *nsαsαk* said she was ashamed of the small size of her offspring.

nsαsαk	εkεbo	kεbut	ntok	eyen	imum
nsαsαk	said	in shame	small	child	mute

The *εkεnuk* tried to eat as much as the *ɔkɔnɔ* and his stomach burst.

εkεnuk	εkεbo	idiα	ntε	ɔkɔnɔ	ekpα	obomo
εkεnuk	said	eat	as	ɔkɔnɔ	stomach	burst

When the fire burned the dog, it also burned the hunter holding the rope attached to the neck of the dog.

ikαŋ	αmαtα	εbuα	ɔfuɔrɔ	αtα	αkαmα	uduk	εbuα
fire	burned	dog	fly	burn	holder	rope	dog

Overeating destroys the soul.

ukαk	αdiα	εdε	uwot	ukpɔŋ
filled	eat	is	killing	soul

The crayfish is bent because it is sick.

ikifɔnɔfɔn	obu	εnye	ɔmukhɔ εkuŋ
ill	crayfish	it	bends

---

6 The Anang consonants are as follows: b, d, f, h, k, kp (labio-velar plosive with no Indo-European equivalent) ; m, n, ŋ (as ng in sing) ; ny (as gn in agneau) ; p, r, s, t, w, and v. Its vowels are as follows: α (as o in hot), ε (as e in met), e (as a in hate), i (as ee in meet), ɒ (as au in author), o (as oe in hoe), and u (as u in rule). There is no a (as a in hat) nor i (as i in hit). Long consonants and vowels are shown by doubling the letter (as in αbαssi). Anang (Ibibio) is a tonal language, and I have employed eight tonal designations; however, they are unnecessary in a paper such as this.

Folksongs as Regulators
of Politics

Betty Wang

One of the most important functions of folklore is its service as a vehicle for social protest. Wherever there is injustice and oppression, one can be sure that the victims will find some solace in folklore. Through jokes, songs, and proverbs, the anger of the folk is vent upon the often frighteningly unassailable individual or institution. If the folkloristic protest is permitted, it is perhaps because the blame for its composition usually cannot be affixed to any one person. It is a collective, not an individual, expression, and consequently the singer of a song of protest is not to be blamed for the content of his song. He is only reporting what the folk say.

Although folklore is commonly employed as a means of social protest, it is rarely officially acknowledged as such by political leaders. However, in this short, informative article, Betty Wang shows how Chinese political leaders used folk materials as a pulse of the people to discover how well or how poorly they were regarded. The need to be respected and revered is especially important in Chinese culture and may partially account for these unusual methods of gauging personal popularity.

One gets the impression that government was originally passive concerning folklore. It investigated folklore but did not mold it. However, in contemporary Communist countries, including China, the government reworks folklore for purposes of propaganda. The basic premise is that folklore is a reflection and weapon of class conflict. In fairy tales, the rich aristocratic kings are invariably defeated by poor deserving peasants who succeed in taking the king's land and riches for themselves. The moral is that feudal capitalistic society must be conquered by the poor but deserving common people (= folk). Y. M. Sokolov's textbook on Russian folklore repeatedly notes that folklore is an excellent source of material for agitation and propaganda. With this situation, one does not have folksongs as regulators of politics so much as politicians as regulators of folksongs.

Reprinted from *Sociology and Social Research,* Vol. 20 (1935), 161–66, by permission of the publisher.

The conscious manipulation of folklore does account for change, but the purist folklorist tends to reject the results of conscious as opposed to unconscious manipulation. He might consider them materials derived from folklore, but not folklore itself. It is interesting to contrast the conscious manipulation of folklore in Communist and in capitalist countries. Part of the ideological difference between them is reflected in the respective rationales for the recasting of folk materials. In the Soviet Union, folklore is molded for political ends; in the United States, folklore is molded for commercial ends. In the Soviet Union, the government sponsors changes in the folklore to sell communism; in the United States, individuals rewrite folklore to sell it for profit. Of course, these are goals put upon folklore, but true oral tradition, unlike written tradition, cannot really be squelched, censored, or stopped. In Russia no doubt there is genuine folklore that pokes fun at governmental controls just as in America there is folklore that ridicules the mercenary ethic and the millionaire.

For songs of social protest, see John Greenway's *American Folksongs of Protest* (Philadelphia, 1953). For samples of jokes, probably the most popular form of protest in American culture, see Donald C. Simmons, "Protest Humor: Folkloristic Reaction to Prejudice," *American Journal of Psychiatry*, Vol. 120 (1963), 567–70; or Arthur J. Prange, Jr., and M. M. Vitols, "Jokes Among Southern Negroes: The Revelation of Conflict," *Journal of Nervous and Mental Disease*, Vol. 136 (1963), 162–67. For the view that folklore can and should be an agent of social change, see Y. M. Sokolov, *Russian Folklore* (New York, 1950); and Gyula Ortutay, "The Science of Folklore in Hungary Between the Two World Wars and During the Period Subsequent to the Liberation," *Acta Ethnographica*, Vol. 4 (1955), 6–89. See also Richard M. Dorson, "Folklore and the National Defense Education Act," *Journal of American Folklore*, Vol. 75 (1962), 160–64; James Fernandez, "Folklore as an Agent of Nationalism," *African Studies Bulletin*, Vol. 5, No. 2 (May 1962), 3–8; Louis L. Snyder, "Nationalistic Aspects of the Grimm Brothers' Fairy Tales," *Journal of Social Psychology*, Vol. 33 (1951), 209–23. For a later look at the close relationship between politics and folklore in China, see Alsace C. Yen, "Red China's Use of Folklore," *Literature East & West*, Vol. 8 (1964), 72–87.

Perhaps the most remarkable testimony to the role of folksongs in the events of politics is to be found in a statement made to the *Tribune*, September 14, 1906, by Mr. Mitra, once proprietor and editor of the *Decan Post*, with regard to the agitation against the partition of Bengal into two provinces. Mr. Mitra deliberately states that the best test of finding out Hindu feeling toward the British Government is to see whether there are any ballads or nursery rhymes or folksongs in the Bengal language against the British.

"You can have it from me, and I challenge contradictions, there is no single ballad or nursery rhyme or folksong in the Bengali language which is against the British," he says.[1] This is where the soul of the people speaks out.

It is stated by Mr. G. L. Gomme,[2] that these facts, though frequently relating to minor events, often have reference to matters of the highest national importance, and perhaps nowhere more definitely is this the case than in the ballads or folksongs connected with particular localities.

Equally it has been true in China, when folksongs played a leading role in the administration of the empire. The Emperor Yui of Hsia Dynasty,[3] one of the three early dynasties in the history of China, in an effort to perform his role as the faithful and righteous son of heaven, whose duty it was to take the best care of his subjects, gave special assignments to a group of officers. The main line of duty of these officers was to go to the people and to find out people's opinion as it was commonly expressed in ballads and folksongs. When any improvement was to be made in the nation, or any rule was to be enforced, public opinion regarding the endeavor was sought. The expression used in ancient literature in this connection is *tsai Feng*, meaning to get the people's opinions and ideas expressed through folksongs.

Being a thoughtful and upright emperor, Yui took the happiness and suffering of his subjects as those of his own. When a big flood occurred throughout the heavily populated section along the Yellow River, he spent thirteen years away from home, refusing to see his family members, mainly for the purpose of conducting the flood waters into the sea. He was more than pleased when he received the following folksong:

> Hsia Yui Whang, Hsai Yui Whang,
> You are a friend as well as an emperor;
> You saved our chickens and saved us from flooding pond,
> A more prosperous year with more children we are nearer.

Another incident in connection with history is the construction of the Great Wall by Chin Shih Whang, known to be the most cruel and tyrannical king China has ever had. With the purpose of defending the country from foreign invasion, he ordered the erection of the wall within a short period of time. Thus many men deserted their families, and offenders were immediately executed. This wall, which runs just beyond the old capital of

---

[1] Mr. Mitra's premise was excellent, but one wonders whether there were not in fact some anti-English *blason populaire* traditions in India in 1906.—ED. NOTE

[2] *Folklore as An Historical Science* (London: Methuen and Co., Ltd.), p. 13.

[3] There is some doubt as to the historicity of Emperor Yui or Yü and his deeds. See James Legge, *The Chinese Classics,* Vol. 3 (London, 1939), 59; René Grousset, *The Rise and Splendour of the Chinese Empire* (Berkeley and Los Angeles, 1958), p. 11; Wolfram Eberhard, *A History of China* (Berkeley and Los Angeles, 1956), pp. 14–15. Whether Emperor Yü or the other figures mentioned are historical or not, the important point for folklore theory is that these leaders are believed to have used folksongs as an unimpeachable source of public sentiment.—ED. NOTE

China, Peiping,[4] is several thousand miles in length. It meanders its way over mountains, plateaus, river courses, and plains. While on one side it overlooks the magnificent Gobi Desert, on the other side there is the gorgeous and colorful Peiping with artificially built palaces and parks. Chinese like round numbers, therefore they call it "Van Lee Chang Cheng," meaning a great wall ten thousand miles long.

This emperor, who was powerful among friends and foes, was very much feared. In spite of the fact that people hated him, only wishing that the god of heaven would soon come to their rescue, they were not brave enough to stand against his will and order. Even the exhortation of his bosom councilors could not restrain him from building this wall. Thus, upon the completion of the gigantic endeavor, many people died as a result of hard work; many received capital punishment; and still many more lost their families. However, their soul spoke. They had folksongs among themselves. Through those songs they expressed their deep sorrow and lamented their misfortune. One of those songs was known to be the words of a young widow, whose husband only a few days after their marriage was called to enlist among the workers, to help build the wall. It runs as follows:

> With flowers blooming and birds singing,
> Spring is here calling us to visit friends far and near.
> Other women are accompanied by their husbands and sons,
> Poor me, I shall go to the wall where my husband's bones bear.
> Great Wall! Great Wall! If you can save us from enemies,
> Why not save first our dear ones?

This song, though from the mouth of a young widow, is only an expression of general feeling toward the merciless attempt of the emperor. Although their hatred toward the emperor was deep and fear of his tyranny was widespread, it was beyond their power to save themselves from the dungeon by openly protesting against the king. Their suppressed desire, however, found expression in folksongs, which were really channels through which their souls spoke.

Songs of similar import were numerous, almost as many as there were localities where the selfishness of the emperor was felt. Another song, on the contrary, eulogizes the greatness of the king and the magnitude of the Great Wall. It is the following:

> Great Wall, Great Wall, ten thousand miles long,
> Is situated at northern China and beyond.
> It is to keep the Middle Kingdom free from foreign invasion,
> And to make the Middle Kingdom free from emigration.
> If you ask me "Who built the wall?"
> I shall say "It was Chin Shih Whang, the greatest of all."

This song, which came into existence about two thousand years after the completion of the gigantic piece of work, carries with it an entirely different

---

[4] Before 1927, Peiping was called Peking, the capital of the late Ching Dynasty.

tone. The well-known explanation for this departure from the usual hateful attitude toward the emperor is that people who live after him do not experience his tyranny and naturally they can feel only the magnitude of the existing wall, and in turn the rare bravery of the emperor.

The extreme cruelty of the aforementioned emperor naturally leads us to think of Chow Wen Whang, the bighearted emperor of China. The magnanimity of his character, the generosity of his attitudes, his extreme consideration and thoughtfulness, and his belief in loving others more than he loved himself were praised throughout the history of China. Simultaneously, his wisdom is just as much spoken about as the wisdom of King Solomon. The wisdom of his administration was shown in the fact that he maintained an efficient staff primarily for the purpose of finding out popular ballads and folksongs in tea houses or along river banks where there were big congregations of people. Those folksongs were then classified and filed so as to ascertain the attitude of his subjects toward his administration and people's reaction toward his execution of public duties. "Wen Whang gathers folksongs in order to testify his failure or success," says the *Sze Chung,* one of the Chinese classics.

Throughout the following dynasties, emperors neglected the collection of folksongs and ballads until the revolution of 1911. This revolution overthrew the Manchu Dynasty, the ruling class which has been considered by Chinese as foreigners. On this occasion, folksongs came into play. While the whole nation was in topsy-turvy condition and overwhelmed with a revolutionary spirit, hatred against the Manchu rose to its highest pitch; in spite of the fact that many people did not have a sound knowledge of revolution or of democracy, they knew that one of the purposes for the nationwide agitation was to overthrow the foreigners who had ruled them for several hundred years. Thus, as the revolutionary forces gained victory from province to province and city to city, people accorded them warm welcome. Songs like the following were sung so as to show their approval of the heroic endeavor of the revolutionists:

> Manchu men, Manchu men, where is your face?[5]
> Who says you are big and who says you are strong?
> You find now all affairs in a maze,
> Soon you will leave this white mountain and royal town,
> Give back our water and land,
> We shall keep our own precious sand.

Scholars have been saying that this song was composed by one of the revolutionists as a piece of propaganda work, chiefly for the purpose of arousing interest and agitation on the part of the mass toward this dynasty of waning power, and for crystallizing public opinion in support of the revolu-

---

[5] "Face" to Chinese is like reputation.

tionists. The name of the author was thus withheld, but the song was popularly sung.

And later, in an effort to ridicule the practices of Manchus of keeping queues, revolutionists and their adherents again had a song which was sung at the time when the queue of every new revolutionary convert was cut. As ridicule is one of the means of protesting against certain disgusting practices and of getting rid of things undesirable, and as it is the means used in the matter of political cartoons, the song has proved expedient. Just as prohibitionists were once held up to public ridicule, those wearing queues were laughed at.

Thus, as a pair of scissors rested on the hair which was about to be cut, the following song was sung:

> Long queues, short queues,
> There will be no more queues.
> No more slaves to the Manchus,
> We shall keep our heads bald as members of the Han Tribe.

Still during a later stage, General Chiang Kai-shek, at present the president of the military affairs commission of the national government of China, then generalissimo of the country, made a northern expedition for the purpose of wiping out the corrupt politicians in the North and bringing the nation into a unified condition. While he started his war of unification, as it has been called, he suddenly made himself a hero and his biography was carefully studied in primary schools and his portraits were hung in public places. Carrying with him a mission to save China from political corruption and economic turmoil, General Chiang impressed every citizen, even peasants, as a unique personality. As soon as he accomplished his long-planned civil strife, folksongs with his name as their theme were on the lips of people including children who learned them as nursery rhymes.

> Dragon comes from the sky,
> And hero springs from the earth.
> Only he can save us and we do not deny.
> Chiang Kai-shek is a man of noble birth,
> No more li-king[6] and no more tax,
> Always we shall not vex.

---

6 *Li-king* was an intercity tax, which has been abolished.

Changing Agricultural Magic in Southern Illinois: A Systematic Analysis of Folk-Urban Transition

Herbert Passin and John W. Bennett

What happens to a group's folklore when the group's solidarity is weakened? In this article by Passin and Bennett, the superstitions of a group in southern Illinois are examined in terms of the group's becoming increasingly more urban. The hypothesis is that as a rural folk community becomes more urbanized, it also becomes less homogeneous and less well integrated. As the homogeneity of the group decreases, the authors argue, the magical system—in the form of agricultural superstitions—becomes likewise less coherent and less consistent.

The problem, in part, concerns the fate of folklore when function is changed or lost. If the folklore survives, it generally fulfills a function other than that which it originally fulfilled. One reason for the persistence of folklore is that old forms can be used to fit new functions. A sacred American Indian myth may be used as a bedtime story; a song sung by a dissident minority group engaged in a street demonstration can serve as entertainment at a teenage hootenanny, and so on.

In the case of the southern Illinois community examined by Passin and Bennett, it is clear that the superstitions will continue to be known for some time to come. However, knowing them is not the same as believing them, which in turn is not the same as practicing them. Some individuals may believe the superstitions to be true but may be too ashamed to practice them; others may both believe and practice. The present article provides an important contrast with most collections of superstitions in that the latter rarely give any information about belief and practice. The collector does not indicate whether the informant believes the superstition he relates or whether he practices it. Without this kind of informant contextual data, it is virtually impossible to discuss the function of superstitions in a given community, and further, it is equally difficult to see the changes in a folk's attitudes toward its folklore. Yet these attitudes and the historical changes in them can be equally as interesting as the folklore itself.

Reprinted from *Social Forces*, Vol. 22 (1943), 98–106, by permission of the authors and The University of North Carolina Press.

In order to generalize the folk-urban continuum it is necessary to conceive it as a transition from greater to lesser homogeneity.[1] With this conception the difference between such transitions in primitive and in modern societies becomes merely one of degree. In this article we propose to examine an hypothesis derived from the field of so-called "primitive" peoples.[2] It seems to us that if we can demonstrate the validity of the continuum in a modern setting we shall have made some contribution to any elaboration of the entire theory.

Although nowhere quite so explicitly stated as in the work of Redfield, it is generally acknowledged that in the transition of a community from a state of relative social homogeneity to heterogeneity, there are correlative changes in the ideological views of its members. This is, of course, an aspect of the historic development of rational and nonsacred attitudes, which is so well documented for the growth of modern industrial society.[3] One important phase of this change is in respect to the complex of beliefs and practices known as magic. This article is concerned with an empirical investigation of the kinds of changes in magic that seem to cohere, or go along with, a community in transition.

Within the conceptual framework of folk-urban theory, the following proposition is relevant to our inquiry: "The lesser the homogeneity of a culture (or the greater the heterogeneity), the lesser the organization (or the greater the disorganization)." From this may be derived the central contention of this study. In somewhat less compressed form, it may be stated that the system of magic prevailing in a homogeneous phase will tend to be more fragmentary, less internally coherent, and more disorganized as the community moves toward lesser homogeneity.

The research from which we have derived our central hypothesis has been done among so-called "primitive" societies. For our part, we shall examine magical changes in a modern rural community that has undergone change. It should be noted that the change from a folk to an urban type is essentially analogous to the change from a self-sufficient to a dependent rural community. The essential analogy lodges in the fact that both are changing from more to less homogeneity.[4] While the range we have studied does not cover the full length of the ideal-type continuum,[5] there is a demonstrable difference

---

[1] The reader will discover the basic ideas of this approach in the work of Robert Redfield, Ferdinand Tönnies, Émile Durkheim, Howard Becker, P. Sorokin.

[2] Cf. Redfield, *The Folk Society in Yucatan* (Chicago: University of Chicago Press, 1942).

[3] Cf. Richard H. Tawney, *Religion and the Rise of Capitalism.*

[4] Cf. the University of Chicago peasant study series, particularly H. Miner, *St. Denis, A French-Canadian Parish* (and Redfield's introduction); and E. H. Spicer, *Pascua, A Yaqui Village.*

[5] Becker formerly used "ideal type" but now prefers the term "constructed type." The difference, however, seems of little moment here, even though it is important in other contexts.

in respect to homogeneity between the two selected phases. For theoretical purposes this is the crucial factor.

As an incident to this study, the authors entertain the hope that the following purposes may be served: (1) a specific understanding of historical process in southern Illinois; (2) a contribution to folk-urban theory; (3) a concrete demonstration of the feasibility of general "law" in the field of society, whether primitive or modern; (4) a greater *rapprochement* between the disciplines of anthropology and sociology.

I

In the community of Stringtown, Illinois, and its immediately adjacent area,[6] the historic process of adaptation to expanding urbanism has involved a change from a folk-like homogeneous community to a heterogeneous "town-country" type.[7] The limits of this paper do not permit a detailed justification of this view, and the reader must be referred to existing available documentation.[8] The terminal points of this process, called respectively Old Stringtown and Stringtown 1939,[9] may be described for the purposes of our analysis as follows: Old Stringtown, the initial historic phase preceding the major onslaught of urbanism, was a (relatively) economically self-sufficient community, sacred in both outlook and social controls, highly integrated, with a marked dominance of primary-group controls, particularly familial. After the shattering historical impact of "moonshining," which served as midwife to the nascent urbanization, Stringtown 1939 became economically dependent upon the wider American economic scene. In association with this fundamental economic transition, the community came to rest more upon impersonal sanctions, the family declined in importance, the church virtually disappeared as an

6 The area of southern Illinois as a particularly tradition-rich region has recently been surveyed by folklorist Richard M. Dorson. A selection of its treasures appears as one of the seven regional repertoires of folklore contained in Dorson's excellent anthology of American folklore, *Buying the Wind* (Chicago, 1964). For this sampling of southern Illinois folklore as well as references to key collections, see *Buying the Wind*, pp. 289–414. —ED. NOTE

7 This term is taken from J. H. Kolb. Cf., "Family Life and Rural Organization," *Publications of the American Sociological Society*, Vol. 23 (1929), 147.

8 The following items are available: Passin, "Culture Change in Southern Illinois," *Rural Sociology* (September 1942); a somewhat more enlarged version in Passin, "Preliminary report of a field survey of culture change in the region of Unionville, Illinois, Summer 1939," SSRC [Social Science Research Council] (1941), mimeo'd; Bennett, Smith, and Passin, "Food and Culture in Southern Illinois," *American Sociological Review* (October 1942); Bennett, "Some Problems of Status and Social Solidarity in a Riverbottoms Community," *Rural Sociology* (forthcoming). [This was published as "Some Problems of Status and Solidarity in a Rural Society," *Rural Sociology*, Vol. 8 (1943), 396–408.—ED. NOTE]

9 These materials are based both upon Stringtown and the adjacent area, particularly the bottoms community studied by Mr. Bennett. The use of the name of Stringtown alone in the designation of phases must be understood merely as a literary convenience. It actually refers to the preindustrial phase of the rest of the area as well as of Stringtown.

effective agency of social control, and attitudes were progressively secularized. The verdict of heterogeneity is demonstrable in all phases of the communal life.

If we ignore the specific historic content and concentrate on form, it is apparent that Old Stringtown was similar to what is recognized as the folk, or primitive, society. In respect to content, the specific magical prescriptions are derived from what is evidently an Old English pattern, which was carried to most of the major settlements of this historic-ethnic group.[10] But while this is true even of the present-day remnants of magic, the organization of the items and their articulation in the general way of life of the community seem to depend upon nonhistorical factors. No one has convincingly demonstrated why it is that folk-type societies universally have magical systems. The present authors believe, however, that *given* the presence of magical items in the cultural *repertoire* of a people, under folk conditions they are effective because:[11] (1) no alternative beliefs are present to create conflict; (2) the system of beliefs is not subject to inner checks and alterations.[12]

The magical practices under consideration centered around the economic life of the people. These include the appropriate times for planting various crops, the significance of the Zodiac and other celestial phenomena, the determination of weather conditions, the time for the slaughter and care of livestock, and such industrial pursuits as making soap.

It was believed that successful crops required careful observation of traditional "signs." Lettuce and certain other garden crops must be planted on St. Valentine's day, February 14.[13] Failure to observe this prescription automatically results in a bad crop. Cucumbers must be planted in "dark moon" and by the Zodiacal "twin" sign. Potatoes and corn must be planted in the dark of the moon. Beans should be planted on Good Friday. In general, the principle seems to have been that plants that grow primarily above the

---

10 Compare some of the materials presented below with those found in Vance Randolph, *The Ozarks;* Mandel Sherman, *Hollow Folk;* and Harry M. Hyatt, *Folklore from Adams County, Illinois.* Memoirs Alma Egan Hyatt Foundation (New York, 1935).

11 There are several possible reasons why the folk consider magic to be effective. For a concise summary of Edward B. Tylor's discussion of some of these reasons, see Paul Bohannan, *Social Anthropology* (New York, 1963), p. 314.—ED. NOTE

12 Cf. Evans-Pritchard's classic account in *Witchcraft Among the Azande* (Oxford, 1937).

13 The ensuing description, although referring to a former period, is cast in the present tense for the sake of convenience of exposition. [Parallels for this superstition as well as the others cited in this paper may be found in Wayland Hand's superbly edited two volumes, *Popular Beliefs and Superstitions from North Carolina,* which constitute Volumes 6 and 7 of the *Frank C. Brown Collection of North Carolina Folklore* (Durham, 1961, 1964). For the general notion that certain vegetables should be planted on February 14th, see Item 8001. For corn and onions in particular, see Items 8127 and 8194. The reader may familiarize himself with this fine compendium of 8569 superstitions by looking up parallels for some of the other superstitions mentioned by Passin and Bennett. Professor Hand also provides an extensive bibliography of collections of American superstitions. —ED. NOTE]

ground should be seeded in "light moon," the others in "dark moon."[14] Things that grow along a vine should be planted when the signs are in the arms.

The signs are also significant in respect to the care of stock. Hogs should be slaughtered in the dark of the moon when the sign is between the thighs and the knees. Otherwise the meat swells up. To prevent hemorrhage and harmful aftereffects, castration should be performed by the same signs. The same sign determines the time of preserving meat. If it is not observed, the meat will "fry away into grease," the grease will unaccountably disappear, the meat will curl in the frying pan, and it will be difficult to make brown gravy. Stock should be weaned when the sign is in the head, or else "they go to hollerin'." (The same was suggested for human children.)

Soap must be made in the dark of the moon. Planking and house building must occur in the appropriate sign, or the roofing will curl upwards.

The coming weather, an item of extreme importance to farmers, can be predicted from a variety of signs, astral, floral, and faunal. These are sufficiently numerous to fill a small-sized volume and must be omitted here.

The magical prescriptions carry their own sanctions. Failure to comply results in unfortunate consequences, even disaster, for the skeptic or forgetful one. The potency of these underlying sanctions must be taken to indicate the urgent and immediate importance of the magical practices in the life of the people.

At the same time, the farmer carried on what from our vantage point may be designated as more rationalistic practices. What is of crucial significance, however, in determining the role of magic, is that magical and rationalistic agriculture were not practiced disjunctively, side by side as it were, but were both articulated in a consistent body of practice. The unitary practice of agriculture required the observation of both classes of activity, simultaneously and intertwined. To have a successful corn crop, the farmer selected his seed, plowed, planted by the sign, cultivated, and harvested. The sign was not a mere afterthought, even if one dictated by common-sense caution, but rather an integral part of the total agricultural process. In this we are able to observe a phenomenon common in the experience of the student of primitive society.[15]

Participation in this system of belief and practice was widespread, and in this fact we again see the mark of the folk society. Virtually everybody accepted the ideas and carried out the prescriptions. The following statements could be duplicated many times over:

> My father used the signs all the time. He wouldn't plant nothin' without 'em. He planted his potatoes in the dark of the moon every year of his life.

---

[14] The principle appears to be based upon sympathetic magic. The "light moon," waxing or increasing of the moon, is construed as a rising or upward movement; the "dark moon," waning or decreasing of the moon, is interpreted as a falling or downward movement. Hence, crops that grow above the ground and must grow *up* are planted in the light of the moon, whereas root crops that grow below the ground and must grow *down* are planted in the dark of the moon.—ED. NOTE

[15] Cf. Malinowski, *Coral Gardens and Their Magic* (London: George Allen & Unwin, 1935); Redfield, *op. cit.*

The reason they don't raise no crops worth nothin' now is because they don't use the signs.

It also seemed to be the case that the knowledge and practices of any one person were identical with those of others. There was a large overlapping area of magical knowledge among all members. Of course, some individuals had greater knowledge than others, and were accorded high esteem and consulted. But the central core of the concepts was shared in the minds of all the people and not carried exclusively by specialist practitioners.

The system generated no internal contradictions to plague the individual. Clearly understood, its major tenets of belief and practice interlocked to form a coherent fabric of compelling custom. The beliefs in respect to the properties of the lunar and Zodiacal phases, long hallowed by tradition and unchallenged by any corrosive agent of rationalism in the body politic, supported the practices. The sanction of fear of failure urged people to observe with little question.

Detailed prescriptions of the various elements by older informants are clear-cut and consistent. Their descriptions evince a high degree of detailed similarity with each other and point to the former wide diffusion and coherence of the pattern. Particularly noteworthy in this connection is the sharpness and clarity of the causal explanations.

> I tell you, if you take a board and lay it down on the ground in the dark of the moon, and lay another right next to it in the light of the moon, and wait a while, you'll find the grass under the one you put down in the light all long and green, while the grass under the one you put down in the dark will be dead. That's because the one you put down in the light don't press so tight to the ground. That's what's behind it.

The cause—that it doesn't press so tightly to the ground—is analogically applied to plants seeded in the light of the moon: ears of corn will remain upright on the stalk and not hang down towards the ground. This is undesirable since the ears are difficult to reach during shucking. Likewise, planks cut in the light of the moon will curl upwards; and hog meat slaughtered in light moon will curl upwards in the frying pan.

It is important to note that observance alone could not guarantee success, but transgression could assure failure. Thus failure, in despite of observance, could be explained by many factors within or without the system. Poor rational judgment could prejudice the outcome unfavorably; only abiding by all of the rules, rational *and* magical, could bring about success with the benevolent intervention of Nature. Once having accepted the system, it could not be destroyed from within, as Evans-Pritchard has shown so admirably for the Azande.[16] If, for example, a man planted his cabbage with due regard for the signs, and yet reaped failure, then perhaps some menstruating woman chanced in the vicinity of his cabbage patch (this would harm the cabbage), or he was not careful of some particular, or else Nature was simply capricious.

---

16 Evans-Pritchard, *op. cit.*

Neglect of the magical prescriptions automatically meant failure; observance did not eliminate all risk from the agricultural enterprise, it only reduced it.

What is relevant for the hypothesis under analysis, then, is that in the Old Stringtown phase, the system of interlocking belief, sanction, and practice was (1) total, not fragmentary; (2) internally consistent; (3) organized; (4) closely articulated within the wider system of agricultural and economic activity; (5) shared by all members of the culture alike; and (6) within the minds of the people constituted an identical content pattern. In short, it was a folk-type magical system.

II

With the post-World War I agricultural depression, Stringtown was drawn into the economic vortex of the wider American economy. How this happened in a concrete historical sense cannot be explained here for lack of space; some explanation is provided in earlier reports.[17] Since we are concerned with the consequences of the transition, it suffices our purpose merely to record the historical fact. The loss of economic self-sufficiency entailed far-reaching consequences for the society and a drift towards heterogeneity that goes on unabated today.

It is clear that the initial impact of urbanism involved the subsistence economic system; with the result that beliefs and attitudes accommodated to that system were among the first to break down and adapt to new conditions, or at least to show some perceptible effects of that widening of cultural horizon incident to the process of urbanization. Some of the specific factors instrumental in bringing about the new situation may be isolated for examination.

One of the most prominent consequences of the introduction of a cash crop economy was the concurrent need for more rational and efficient agriculture. Failures have immediate monetary consequences, and the rising money needs place a premium on success. The individual must pay attention to scientific practices and not let tradition interfere with sound practice. This imperious need makes the individual accessible to extrasystemic ideas. Thus people began to devote time to the study of catalogues, extension bulletins, and farm bureau publications, all of which provide an entering wedge for the differentiation of initially homogeneous beliefs and practices.

Furthermore, speed and precision in the planting of cash crops in order to make use of the limited farm labor supply became necessary, and individuals could not always observe the signs even if they wanted to. If the equipment (possibly borrowed) and the farm labor were available, the farmer had to put in his corn, whether the sign was traditionally propitious or not, or else court complete disaster. There is considerable evidence to show that this

---

[17] Passin, *op. cit.*

lack of accord between traditional prescription and utilitarian need caused great conflict and stress for individuals until they were able to rationalize it in some way.

With the general opening up of the community to urban influences and the increasing differentiation which followed, people began to accept secular and rational modes of thought from the urban models along with other urban values. On the one hand, the internal processes of heterogenization favored rational thought; on the other hand, acceptance of urban values supported the internal development.

The school occupies an interesting place in this course of events. Despite its rational curriculum, it was not the efficient cause of the change. Indeed, careful perusal of school records shows that there have been no major curricular innovations in perhaps fifty years. Rather the school was itself affected by the increasing secular and rational emphasis. For the school to be effective as a rational influence, the total state of the community had to change first.

The decline of the church contributed to the secularizing tendency by virtue of the elimination of sacred ways of thought from the minds of most inhabitants. Reciprocally, of course, its decline too was affected by the general change.

Finally, the appearance on the scene of alternate and competing systems of thought and behavior, fostered by urban values, hastened the destruction of the older system.

With this situation, what can be predicated of the character of the changes from our initial hypothesis? Verification of the hypothesis requires that the change be demonstrably in the direction of decrease of the degree of coherence, or integration of the beliefs. The concrete meaning of this idea will emerge in the course of the analysis.

All evidence goes to show that there has been a catastrophic decline in the total number of persons who believe in the magic. This is of fundamental importance, for now instead of a community of believers, we find a community in which full believers and unbelievers are sharply distinguished, and all the intermediate stages are discernible. Where formerly everybody, except a few perennial scoffers, accepted the beliefs implicitly, nowadays only a small band of oldsters or conservatives hold these ideas in their entirety, and they are subject to constant sniping and rational attack. They must now defend themselves for believing what was once taken for granted in the mental fabric of the culture. An oldster laments:

> Nowadays when you ask 'em if they plant by the signs, they git smart and say things. If you say, "Do you plant in the dark of the moon?" they will say, No, I plant in the ground!" all sech smart remarks ez that.[18]

---

[18] Even this witticism is traditional. See Alan Dundes, "Brown County Superstitions," *Midwest Folklore,* Vol. 11 (1961), 51.—Ed. Note

Most people reported that their parents observed the signs, although they themselves might not do so.

> No, I don't have no special signs for sowin'. My people did, the old folks.

Thus a survey of present practices would show that some people believe and some don't; that some practice and some don't.

The body of beliefs is not shared in common. By contrast with the former relatively even diffusion of the ideas throughout the general populace, at present there are wide differences among individuals with respect both to what they know and what they believe. Thus, as pointed out above, some frankly disbelieve. But of those who believe, different persons believe different things. The items of belief have become fragmentary and scattered irregularly among the people. Some persons understand gardening magic, or even the prescriptions about cucumbers as against beans; some believe only the live-stock injunctions. Since the evidence for this view would be excessively lengthy, the following comparison of some of the beliefs of two neighboring families will illustrate the drift of these remarks:

	SIGN	
Crop	*Family A*	*Family B*
carrots	dark moon	no sign
black-eyed peas	no sign	arms
crowder peas	no sign	head
turnips	head	no sign
pole beans	no sign	arms

A thoroughly documented comparison would be even more striking.

Actual knowledge varies considerably. Some persons know one set of signs, others another set. A person may know of the existence of a sign, but will not know what it is. He then may or may not refer for illumination to some better informed person, the Ladies Birthday Almanac, or some Zodiacal register. An old woman reported:

> I told my son when to plant his cucumbers. He said he didn't know when to plant 'em, so I looked it up in the Almanac and told him.

Our detailed analysis of what was believed currently in the community revealed a further striking phenomenon. The beliefs entertained are not only partial and fragmentary, but they are often actually contradictory and inconsistent. In this we can see the breakdown of the inner consistency and coherence of the system.

It will be recalled that in the older situation, beliefs were well integrated, that they did not contradict each other. At the present time, every fundamental element in the system is subject to conflicting interpretations. In the words of one perplexed farmer:

> The trouble with the signs is that no two fellers will say the same thing. My daddy-in-law says there's two weeks of dark of the moon to plant in,

but my own daddy says there's only two days. A couple fellers over here both said the dark of the moon come at different times, and both planted their potatoes by their own signs—and both of 'em raised good potatoes! That's the trouble with them signs.

Even persons who feel that lunar phases are important are not quite sure of their exact occurrence. In 1939 the confusion generated a serious community-wide controversy which was partially adjudicated by a letter to the *Prairie Farmer*! Some people believe that the lunar phases divide the month into equal periods of light and dark moon. Others hold with equal conviction that "dark moon is just when it's a little sliver, just beginnin' to full up. Now the light of the moon is when it's in its last quarter, full and bright." Still others hold to the conception of one or at most two days for the proper celestial conditions.

The same confusion is manifest in respect to the Zodiacal signs, although not to the same extreme degree. But there is much conflict over when the sign is in the arms, or the head, or the thighs.

Finally, the lack of coherence affects the very meaning of the signs. Compare the following prescriptions of three different individuals:

	Sign		
Crop	*A*	*B*	*C*
carrots	dark moon	head	none
potatoes	dark moon	arms	legs
garden peas	full moon	head	arms
beets	dark moon	head	none
cabbage	head	heart	head
lettuce	light moon	head	Feb. 14

It is also to be observed that the various practices still known or followed stand unsupported by the rich causal system of explanations which was so important in early days. People are no longer sure of the causes of the phenomena. While the explanation of the board is freely resorted to, it is significant that a directly opposite account is given as frequently as the one described.[19] Many will frankly admit that they are not sure whether the

---

[19] Sometimes there may be logical consistency behind apparent contradiction. For example, whereas there is agreement concerning the general effect of laying a fence in the dark of the moon, there is disagreement concerning the extent of the effect and consequently the practice to be followed. One of my informants in rural Indiana recommended setting fence posts in the *dark of the moon* so that they would stay in. On the other hand, there are superstitions reported elsewhere urging that fences be laid in the *light of the moon,* because if laid in the dark of the moon, the fences would sink into the ground and rot. The principle of downward movement associated with the dark of the moon is consistent, but the amount of movement is a critical variable. See Dundes, *ibid*. It is well to remember that the association of both good and bad luck with the same sign is not at all unusual as Ernest Jones explained. Moreover, the existence of alternate, variant forms of a superstition for the same act, e.g., planting a particular crop, is not necessarily a sign of the disintegration of a folk's belief system. Consistency is one of the analyst's favorite criteria; it is not often one of importance for the folk. However, the mixed emotions and attitudes of Passin and Bennett's informants toward the superstitions strongly support the disintegration hypothesis.—Ed. Note

grass is supposed to flourish or to die under the board in dark moon. Thus the individual who may be inclined to continue his observation of the signs will not know exactly why he anticipates certain results, nor, indeed, why he even bothers except for reasons of vague, traditional sentiment.

In current agricultural practice, the observation of sign and phase has become incidental to the main body of common-sense pursuits. The folk beliefs are no longer a necessary part of the procedure; magical and "rational" are disjunct. By this is meant the fact that in the minds of the people the two elements in the historic tradition that had once been fused in a dynamically unified pattern now form separate categories. The separation is continually indicated by doubters in the epithets of "old fogy ideas," "nigger ideas," and "superstitions"; by adherents, in the recognition that the special beliefs under consideration are singled out for scorn by others.

That most adult persons were reared in primary groups that inculcated these beliefs is a source of considerable conflict. Many feel uneasy in compliance; and many feel equally uneasy about noncompliance. People tend to be very defensive about the signs.

> Well, I'm sorta foolish about 'em myself...I think there's somethin' to 'em all right (very halting and embarrassed).

A middle-aged woman complained that her mother-in-law "makes fun of me because I can't tell the signs at my age." And yet this same mother-in-law said to one of the field staff, "I guess I'm jes' full of that sign foolishness. I don't know what good it is." A dialogue between husband and wife sets this off in fine relief:

> H: (to interviewer) It's mostly niggers have these superstitions. I don't plant by no signs. I plant when the ground's ready.
> W: Why, C., how can you say that? You fussin' aroun' here tryin' to get your potatoes in by the right sign! You know you always plant your potatoes in the sign.
> H: (very embarrassed) Oh quiet! I don't!
> W: (to interviewer) Now, don't you believe him.

The present state of affairs in regard to magic can be characterized further by the following considerations. Whereas formerly the system was maintained by its own internal sanctions and by traditional continuity from generation to generation, these are no longer accepted as adequate to still the pangs of doubt. All feel the desirability of submission to some rational, experimental test, however widely the anticipations of outcome may vary. This fact gives the current explanations about the board in dark moon a new significance: it is conceived as an experimental test. The following is an example of the current mood:

> You know, what a feller ought to do is to set down ever' time he went by the sign. It wouldn't cost him nothin' to do that. Then a feller could trace it up—'speriment like. You could try out the sign an' test it an' then you'd really know. If I was to git a farm again that's what I'd do. (He had lost

his farm during the 1937 flood.—*The Authors*.) Now, I got a good crop of potatoes one year, so I traced 'em up when I planted 'em an' it was in the new moon—that's the dark moon. I remembered that the year before I planted 'em in the light moon, an' I got just as good a crop.

Whatever the outcome of the particular experiment cited or proposed, it is clear that tradition is no longer enough; reason also must be satisfied.

Thus, in general contrast to the condition of magical belief in Old Stringtown, the present system is: (1) fragmentary; (2) internally contradictory; (3) relatively disorganized; (4) disassociated from other aspects of the culture; (5) unequally distributed among the people; and (6) forming no consistently accepted content pattern. It is a relatively secularized magical system.

III

The qualification "relatively" indicates the limitation suggested earlier in the paper. It would be very misleading to leave the impression of complete disintegration of magic in the community. The empirical case of Stringtown covers but a limited segment of the logically possible continuum. In its earlier phase it was only *relatively* homogeneous; at present it is only *relatively* heterogeneous. The course of subsequent historical development and the impact of the war in accelerating external contact and dependence may extend the process even further and present us with an even more heterogeneous picture.

But at present there are islands of homogeneity within the general disorganization. These result from the dual processes of (1) persistence of older elements for a variety of reasons, and (2) the adaptation of old elements to the new conditions—an important phase of cultural creativity. In respect to the latter, genuinely novel elements may develop in accommodation to the new cultural conditions.

These "foci of folkness" may be ranged in three categories: (1) the persistence of the old, (2) the conflict area, and (3) the new, emergent pattern.

1. It is not in magic alone that the older pattern has persistence-power, but rather in the whole social structure. Indeed, it is here proposed that the persistence of the earlier magic is associated with the partial carry-over of the earlier social categories into the urbanized stage. The point cannot be documented here at length,[20] but exhaustive analysis of the area has demonstrated a division, amounting to a dual status system, between those most affected by the economic changes and those least affected. Among the latter group, some of the older sanctions, motivations, and attitudes still form a system in terms of which people order their lives. They have been designated as conservative, well-to-do, religious farmers.[21] The others, by way of contrast, are

---

[20] The reader is here referred to the discussion of this subject in Passin, *op. cit.*, especially the SSRC version.

[21] Passin, *op. cit.*

irreligious sharecroppers. It is primarily among the conservative group, those participating in a semblance of the older system and who find their satisfactions therein, that most systematic belief in magic is found.

In the main the distinction, in a superficial statistical sense, is between the old and the young. The "old folks" in general are more folklike, more conservative; and the young are more eager for and accessible to urbanization, to the currents of change flowing in from the outside. But it is no simple function of chronological age that we are concerned with here, for underlying this perennial youth-age disagreement is a basic divergence in orientation between persons who direct their life course within the traditional confines and those who seek elsewhere for their satisfactions. This divergence runs like a red thread throughout the whole area. By way of confirmation of this judgment, we may point out that sons of the conservative families tend to accept much of the world-view of their parents, while older persons who have been dislocated by the impact of urbanism (usually economically) are much more urbanized in their outlook. The surest, most confident and competent assertions on magic come from the "conservative" group. It is often stated in the form that "my father did it; it's good enough for me." And conversely, the greatest doubt, uncertainty, and disbelief come from the urbanized sector.[22]

As long as there is still some basis for the old mode of life, we may expect the older system of magic to persist. It may be pointed out that this very phenomenon is a further confirmation of the hypothesis under consideration. It is found that even within the contemporaneous community, the areas of relative homogeneity (certainly less than in Old Stringtown) and of relative heterogeneity show the same systematic difference in regard to magic.

2. The area of conflict here concerns primarily what Frazer[23] and Malinowski[24] have called the "aleatory" element, the element of risk or luck which attends human endeavor. Many persons are torn between their rational doubt and the traditional impulsions which they acquired in their younger days. While they may feel the need for experimental evidence, they hesitate to accept a negative result as conclusive. They seem to fear to take the risk of noncompliance.

> I don't know whether plantin' by the sign makes any difference, but we think it might. Of course, sometimes when we plant by the sign it don't have no good luck either.

There is a residual apprehension, a fear of risking the possibility of a poor crop or some other disaster by not observing the sign.

> I dehorn cattle when the sign is in the thighs. I've heard of 'em bleedin' to death—hogs and cows both—if you don't do it by the signs. None of mine

---

[22] This is, of course, excluding such special cases as college graduates, whatever their origins.

[23] James Frazer, *The Golden Bough*.

[24] B. Malinowski, *The Myth in Primitive Psychology*.

> ever did that, but I watch it careful....Yes, I've done it out of the sign an'
> nothin' happened, but I like to watch it careful. I generally do it by the sign.

This fear of risk also tends to inhibit a complete secularization of agricultural practice.

There is one further aspect of the intermediate conflict area which seems to be achieving a satisfactory solution. The planting of gardens is still more subject to the observance of signs than is the planting of cash crops. Corn, bean, and hay crops are almost entirely free from magical control. The reason seems to be that the latter group is more dependent upon rational considerations—labor supply, rainfall, etc.—while garden crops do not require a precise schedule. The same holds true for the care of livestock. In both of these, the signs are more frequently followed than in the case of the large cash crops. In this way, both traditional motives and economic expediency are partially satisfied.

3. The adjustment to the rational atmosphere is, however, taking somewhat different lines. One is by way of using the signs "when possible."

> Yeah, I plant by the signs, but the season don't always let me.
> Well, I plant corn by the dark of the moon. That is, I try to do it, but sometimes the season interferes. The water might stay up late, or somethin' like that...I like to plant by the signs if I can. All of us aroun' here try to use 'em if the season don't interfere.

The most significant re-adaptation, however, is in the reduction of the importance of the sign so that it becomes only one among a number of other important elements. We have here virtually the basis for a new magical theory. The sign is important, but so are the rain, the condition of the soil, the season, the temperature, etc. The following is a characteristic explanation in these terms:

> Well...the way I think is that the season and the sign ain't got nothin' to do with each other. I guess the crop really depends more on the rain—that's what we call the season—it's really more important. I prefer to stay on that, anyway. What a feller ought to be able to do is plant by the sign and not have to worry about the season, but the rain won't let you do that. If you could plant just by the sign there wouldn't be no risk—just wait for the sign an' then put the crop in. But the rain interferes. See, if you had the same rain ever' year, you could fergit about it an' plant by the sign. You know that would work in these here countries where they got...giration (irrigation —The Authors). You could use nothin' but the sign 'cause you'd always have the same amount of water.

The final discernible mode of adaptation is a strictly individual one. Certain deviant personalities, "queer" in the conception of their neighbors, deliberately seek to cultivate past and exotic values, and by way of compensation for their present unadjustment, become extraordinary repositories of magical cult, even adding to the stock of traditional magical content by bringing in ideas from books and other sources. One such person—a descendant of one of the impoverished early settler families, who is feared by people because of his unpredictable "queerness," is reputed to know more about the signs than anybody else in the area. He is occasionally consulted when special magical information is required.

It is clear, then, that some of these magical attitudes never completely disappear. They constitute residues in the culture that are never completely eradicated as a result of urbanization. Resistant and reintegrating tendencies are fostered in part by rationalizations, pseudo-experimentalism, the persistence of earlier social configurations and their associated attitudes, and even by special individuals whose compensatory psychic needs drive them to keep in touch with the past.

Conclusions

1. The proposition that change from isolation and homogeneity to mobility and heterogeneity entails predictable consequences in terms of such processes as disorganization, secularization, and disintegration was tested. Magical beliefs and practices were specifically chosen for demonstration.

2. The hypothesis, although based upon results obtained among peoples outside of the Western culture-historical tradition, has reference not to concrete historic entities as such, but to type-situations. It is therefore applicable wherever the heuristic conditions which will satisfy its proposed variables may be found.

3. These may be found in three general types of situations: (a) in a comparison of two or more societies that come from discrete historical traditions, where differences in respect to isolation and homogeneity can be shown; (b) among two or more societies within an historically continuous culture-area, but where differentials in the historic process have brought about type-differences in the isolation-homogeneity range, as in Redfield's study; and (c) in the historic course of change in a given society, where the change has been in the direction of the mobile heterogeneous pole. Our study exemplifies this latter type.

4. The historic course of change in the Stringtown area has been from relative isolation and homogeneity to relative external contact and heterogeneity, as a consequence of economic changes.

5. Within this context, it was expected that detailed study of the system of magic, or of any other institution, would demonstrate a systematic change in the direction of secularization, rationalization, and disorganization.

6. The empirical course of magical change seems a fairly good fit to theoretical expectancy.

7. It was also found that reintegration occurred at precisely those points where some equilibrium was being achieved within the changing culture, whether as persistence or re-adaptation of entirely new elements.

The *It* Role
in Children's Games

Paul V. Gump and Brian Sutton-Smith

It has already been noted that experiments in folklore have been few in number, and it would appear that experiments dealing with the function of folklore would be especially difficult to engineer. For this reason, the following experiment designed by psychologists Gump and Sutton-Smith is of great interest.

Although the article was written for social workers to help them select appropriate games for particular individuals, the distinction between what the authors term the high-power *It* role and low-power *It* role has considerable theoretical value for folklorists. The distinction comes from *It* games, that is, games in which one person is selected, often by means of a counting-out rhyme, to operate as an individual in accordance with special rules not governing the behavior of the other players. A high-power *It* role is simply one in which the person who is *It* has a lot of power. He can control to a great extent the movements of the other players. By using the control potential of the high-power *It* role, it is possible for *It* to win or to be successful with a minimum of skill. On the other hand, a low-power *It* role is one in which the person who is *It* has comparatively little power to control the movements of others. Winning and success depend in large measure upon the skill and cleverness of the player who is *It*.

The relationship between the nature of the *It* role and the individual players who fill it is an important one. The *It* child's skill and personality can be tested or not depending upon whether the game is played with one set of rules or another. What a comparative folklorist might regard as a mere minor variation in the rules of a game, a sociological folklorist might see as a critical difference affecting the over-all function of the game for an individual and for a group.

Reproduced by permission of the authors and the National Association of Social Workers, successor to the American Association of Group Workers, from *The Group*, Vol. 17, No. 3 (February 1955), 3–8.

The present experiment was part of a larger research effort on the problem of how the ingredients of different children's activities and programs affect participants' individual and group behavior and experience.[1] The aim of the research is to develop concepts and findings which will assist the practitioner in selecting, inventing, and managing activities so that children's experiences in these activities will be beneficial.

Among the most prominent activities used in group work with children are games. Also, games are relatively coercive activities since they specify the roles persons shall take, the goals they shall seek, and other areas of behavior which many non-game activities leave to the choice of participants. Because games are coercive, they may be expected to determine behavior in a relatively predictable fashion. The prominence and the coerciveness of games suggested that they be given special study.

The ingredients of games differ widely and these differences may be expected to generate parallel variations in the experience and behavior of their participants. Such variations go beyond differences in game-required acts to differences in response to these acts. For example, the games of Tag and Beater-Goes-Around obviously differ in that one requires tagging and the other beating; however, the response to tagging (and being tagged) may be expected to be different from the response to beating (and being beaten).

Since a large proportion of all active games for children are *It* games, these games were selected for study. *It* games contain a central person who acts in opposition to the rest of the playing group or the "pack." One aspect of these games which seemed important in determining the experience of the *It*— and the reaction of the group or pack to him—was the *game-determined power* of the *It* role. This power is shaped by a number of game provisions: *It's* prerogatives in determining which pack member he will engage in competitive encounter and when this encounter will begin; his "trappings," for example, his game name *or* his power symbols; his protection against the combined efforts of pack members against him; and so forth. Power of this type resides entirely in the *It* role and is separate from the skill of the player occupying the *It* role.

The study investigated how behavior and experience of players in the *It* role were affected by the amount of power of the *It* role. One supposition was that a high-power *It* role would expose its occupants to *fewer* competitive failures in the game than would a low-power *It* role. A second related supposition was that relatively unskilled players could be protected from too frequent failure by enabling them to occupy a high-power, rather than a

[1] This investigation was supported by research grant M-550 from the National Institute of Mental Health, of the National Institutes of Health, Public Health Service. Its original title is "The Relationship of the Power of the *It* Role to Experience in the *It* Role."

low-power, *It* role. The problem of helping the unskilled participant in situations in which he can become the focal person is a real and a practical one. Readers are doubtless aware of the difficulties which arise when unskilled players are put into certain *It* positions. Their failure to find, catch, or tag skilled members of the pack leads to discouragement for themselves and boredom for the pack. The pack's derision of *It* for his failure intensifies his frustrations. Since a group worker can do nothing immediately to change skill, selecting or managing games so that lack of skill becomes less crucial is a potential solution. The study tested the supposition that lack of skill in *It* games can be partially compensated for by opportunity to occupy a high-power *It* role.

The experiment reported below, then, checked two basic suppositions which are closely related:

1. High-power *It* roles result in fewer game failures for *It* players in general than do low-power *It* roles.
2. High-power *It* roles result in fewer game failures for unskilled *It* players than do low-power *It* roles.

Since number of game failures might be expected to affect *It's* feeling about himself and the pack's feeling toward *It,* data relevant to these issues were also collected.

Experiment

GAMES PLAYED

Two games were employed which met the following criteria: the games significantly differed only with respect to the power of the *It;* they required the same basic skill—running speed; they permitted reliable measurement of amount of failure; and they were representative of a popular kind of children's game.

The games were Black Tom, and Dodge the Skunk; both are similar to Pom-Pom-Pullaway.[2] A field was lined with boundaries and with safe or "home" areas at either end. *It* was required to tag pack members as they ran from one home area to the other. Any player tagged was out; when *It* had tagged two of the three pack members, that game session was over and another *It* took over. Each *It* was given a handkerchief tail to wear as a symbol of *It*.

Black Tom, involving a high-power *It* role, differed from Dodge the Skunk, involving a low-power *It* role, in the following ways: The Black Tom *It* called a series of names the last one of which (Black Tom) was the signal that required the pack members to run to the opposite home. In actual play,

---

[2] J. H. Bancroft, *Games* (New York: The Macmillan Company, 1952), p. 184. [For a description of Pom-Pom Pullaway, see Paul G. Brewster's excellent annotated collection of American traditional games, *American Nonsinging Games* (Norman, Okla., 1953), pp. 76–77. See also his accounts of Wolf Over the Ridge, and Black Man, pp. 53, 56.—ED. NOTE]

Black Tom could come fairly close to players at home and then call the running signal when he thought he could tag a particular player. The Dodge the Skunk *It* called no signal and chased players as they ran, at will, from one home to the other. In actual play, *It* ranged about from the middle of the field in order to be able to choose runners from either home. In Black Tom, *It* had the opportunity to choose the time, place, and opponent for a competitive encounter; in Dodge the Skunk, *It* had no such choice; the pack members decided if and when they would attempt the dash across the unsafe field to the opposite home area.

POPULATION EMPLOYED

Forty boy campers,[3] 7 to 10 years old, were divided into 10 four-person playing groups. Boys of similar age but who differed in running speed[4] were put into each group. One skilled boy, i.e., a fast runner, two semi-skilled boys, and one unskilled boy were placed in each group. Data were collected on *It* role behavior for only the fast or skilled and the slow or unskilled boys. Boys of medium skill were included to enlarge the playing group and to screen the fact that the observers were focusing only on skilled and unskilled boys. These semi-skilled boys were *It* in games which observers considered practice sessions but which, to the playing groups, looked like the "real thing."

ADMINISTRATION

One experimenter taught the games using demonstrations and practice sessions so that the limitations and privileges of the *It* and pack roles were clarified. Ordinarily, each game session was over when *It* made two successful tags. However, in 8 of the 20 game sessions, unskilled *It* experienced such obvious and complete failure that further play would have been painfully discouraging. When both experimenters agreed that further play would not result in tagging success for the *It*, the game session was terminated and a new *It* assigned.

A total of 40 game sessions were included in the experiment: 10 skilled boys were *It* once in Black Tom and the same 10 were *It* once in Dodge the Skunk; the 10 unskilled boys went through this same regime.

DATA COLLECTION

The following data were collected: (1) the number of unsuccessful tag attempts made by each skilled or unskilled *It* before he tagged out two pack members, (2) the number and quality of verbal expressions made by *It* players, and (3) the general behavior of the pack toward the *Its*.

---

3 We wish to thank Mr. Bob Luby, Director of the Fresh Air Camp, Brighton, Michigan, for his help in the research. Counselors Al Camiener, Sherman Hesselman, Leonard Rachmiel and Jerry Wolberg contributed time, effort, and ideas to our research.
4 A series of foot races were held several days before the experiment in order to identify fast, medium, and slow runners.

Results

TAGGING SUCCESS

It players were eventually successful in tagging two other members in 32 of the 40 game sessions. The average numbers of tag attempt failures for these 32 games were as follows:

All players in high-power *It* roles: 1.7 tag failures;
All players in low-power *It* roles: 3.7 tag failures.

In general, then, boys endured markedly fewer tagging failures in high-power *It* roles than in low-power *It* roles. When these gross results were broken down to show differences for skilled and unskilled players, the following averages were obtained:

Skilled players in high-power *It* roles: 0.6 tag failures;
Skilled players in low-power *It* roles: 2.2 tag failures;
Unskilled players in high-power *It* role: 4.4 tag failures;
Unskilled players in low-power *It* roles: 6.7 tag failures.

The above numbers show two results: skilled players had fewer failures than unskilled ones, regardless of the power of the *It* role occupied; and both skilled and unskilled players had fewer failures when in the high-power role. The tendency of the high-power role to help unskilled boys is indicated by one further fact. In 8 of the 40 game sessions, unskilled *Its* completely failed to make the required two tags. However, only three unskilled *Its* so failed in the high-power *It* role, while these same three plus *two more* unskilled players failed completely in the low-power *It* role.

GAME ACTIONS AND ATTITUDES

The number of tag failures yields an objective picture of the intensity of the *Its* success-failure situation. The response of *It* to his role and the responses of others to him gives a psychological picture of this situation. Observations recorded of taunting and other expressive "side play" justified the following conclusions:

1. *The pack combined against "It" most frequently when he was in a low-power role.* In 6 of the 20 game sessions, pack members intrigued together against *It;* for example, "Same plan! When you put your hand down, all three of us run." These alliances occurred *only* in the game sessions of Dodge the Skunk (low-power *It*).

2. *The pack disparaged "It" most frequently when he was in the low-power "It" role.* Disparaging remarks were made before the game began to 6 unskilled *Its;* this happened equally frequently in Black Tom and in Dodge the Skunk. For example, before Dodge the Skunk, it was said of one unskilled boy about to be *It,* "Oh, Peter's easy to beat." Before Black Tom, one unskilled *It* was called "Spaghetti Balls." No skilled *It* received such pre-game disparagement.

Once the game began, however, it was the *game,* as well as the players' more abiding attitudes toward each other, which dictated the targets of taunts. There were 9 occasions of marked taunting of the low-power *It* in Dodge the Skunk—7 times to unskilled and twice to skilled *Its.* "C'mon you chicken. Lay an egg." "This skunk really smells" were typical disparagements of low-power *Its.* Unskilled boys in this low-power *It* role of Dodge the Skunk suffered other humiliations. Pack members began to *walk* past them, to run circles around them, to jeer in their faces, and to pull off their tails.

No comparable taunting was directed to either skilled or unskilled players in the high-power "It" role. Although it is the unskilled boy who suffers the most disparagement, this occurs mainly in the game role which offers him the least power.

3. *With unskilled players, a sense of failure occurred more often in the low-power "It" role than in the high-power "It" role.* In Dodge the Skunk, 3 of the 10 unskilled boys expressed their sense of failure and powerlessness by sighs and by complaints directed toward the experimenters; they wanted "out." The same boys did not make similar appeals in Black Tom. As it happened they were only slightly more successful in Black Tom, but apparently they *felt* less failure as a Black Tom *It.*

The tendency for *felt* power to be greater in a Black Tom *It* role was demonstrated also by results from post-game interviews. All of the unskilled boys (and all but one of the skilled boys) preferred to be *It* in Black Tom. Their reasons were that *It* has an easier job and that *It* has more power over players in Black Tom. Sample remarks were: "In Black Tom you can fool people," or "It's like a mystery. They don't know when you're going to say it."

Discussion

RELATION OF "IT" POWER TO EXPERIENCE IN THE "IT" ROLE

The above results demonstrate that the game-given power of a role is an important determiner of game experience. Power affects the amount of objective failure endured by the occupant of a game role, it affects the way this occupant is treated by the rest of the playing group, and it affects how he feels about himself and his situation.

The results also reveal that unskilled players are particularly likely to endure failure and derision in *It* roles. For most of the unskilled boys, failure and derision were less frequently encountered when they played a high-power, rather than a low-power, *It* role.

RELATION OF PERSONALITY TO EXPERIENCE IN AN "IT" ROLE

Although skill of participants and power of the role were two important factors determining success or failure in the *It* role, it appeared that a personality factor which might loosely be described as "drive" was also important to success. Unskilled boys who gained some success in a high-power *It* role differed from unskilled boys who failed in the following respects.

1. *Successful boys focused on a target pack member and they used strategy*. In contrast, the unsuccessful unskilled boys *let* things happen instead of *causing* things to happen. They would stand timidly in the middle of the field and call "Black Tom" and then chase one, then another fleeing player. Concentration of effort and exploitation of the high power of the *It* role were not employed by unsuccessful unskilled boys.

2. *Successful but unskilled boys sustained effort at climax points*. In contrast, there were those instances in which both observers were sure that an unskilled *It* was about to tag—only to watch a failure. The *It* would hesitate slightly at the crucial moment; he would slow down, or he would *drop* instead of raise his tagging hand. Whether these "climax failures" were due to simple fear of failing while extending oneself or to an emotional "tagging inhibition" could not be determined. It seemed possible that the aggression or assertion symbolized by the tagging act was sufficiently feared to create a momentary inhibition resulting in tagging failure.

The following game record is an example of a successful, yet unskilled boy using strategy, establishing focus, and maintaining effort at climax points.

Harry, a fat, awkward boy, is *It* in Black Tom. At first he has little success as he proceeds up and down the field after his fleet playmates. Then he begins to call "Black Tom" just as soon as the runners are safely home and so forces them to come out again immediately. A half-dozen such rapid calls fatigues the runners and they are now more in Harry's speed class. (Harry doesn't have to run as far as they do since they must go all the way home to be safe.) Harry then centers his efforts on one skilled boy: he chases him home calling, "Black Tom!" as he rushes up to the home line. The call forces the tired runner to leave home and Harry lunges and tags him as he comes out.[5]

RELATION OF "IT" ROTATION PROCEDURES TO EXPERIENCE IN THE "IT" ROLE

Another factor significantly affects the intensity of negative experience in the *It* role. The factor is time spent in the role. Amount of time spent in *It* roles is determined partly by the game-prescribed arrangement for rotation of *It* players. For example, in the game I Got It, the *It* is chased and when he fails—when he is tagged—he becomes a member of the chasing pack. Although the *It* role in I Got It is one of relatively low power, prolonged failure in the role is impossible. On the other hand, in Dodge the Skunk, the failure of *It* to tag leaves him in the *It* role and subject to an extended failure

---

[5] The possibilities inherent in *It* games for diagnoses of personality qualities—as opposed to qualities of sheer skill—seem worthy of systematic research. For example, observers also noticed that boys differed widely in terms of their desire to taunt the *It* and in their zest for the fleeing and anonymous pack role as contrasted to the more responsible and limelighted *It* role.

experience. Thus, although low-power *It* roles are likely to result in failure for the *It*, the *extent* of failure in the *It* role is significantly determined by the game-prescribed arrangements for rotation of occupants in the *It* role.

Summary

The ingredients of children's programs and activities were assumed to have important effects upon the behavior and experience of participants. One type of activity—*It* games—was selected for experimentation. One supposition tested was that high-power *It* roles—as contrasted to low-power *It* roles—lead to less failure for *Its*, to fewer negative reactions of the playing groups toward *It*, and to more positive feeling of *It* about himself and his situation. Results showed this supposition to be generally correct. A second and related supposition was that unskilled players could be helped to more frequent success and to a less negative experience if they were placed in high-power, rather than in low-power, *It* roles. Results generally favored this supposition; however, it was found that unskilled boys who also lacked the ability or the personal drive to exploit game advantage were not materially helped by such game role manipulation. The importance of game-prescribed *It rotation procedures* in determining the intensity of failure of unskilled players in the lower-power *It* role was also pointed out.

The present study investigated specifically the effect of the power of an *It* role upon the experience of game participants. However, this factor of *It* power is just one of many game factors which shape the experience of players. For example, the extent to which game arrangements sharpen and centralize competition may be expected to affect the intensity of hostile and other "combative" impulses felt and expressed by participants. The factor of chance, as opposed to skill, is also important in game structure. It is *probable* that the gratifications and frustrations accompanying appeals to chance differ from those accompanying appeals to skill; it is *certain* that the generally unskilled player will have more success in games of chance than in games of skill. Factors inherent in games—such as power of game roles, sharpness of competition, and chance determination of success—are deserving of serious attention from both the practitioner and the researcher. Once these factors are identified and their effects upon various types of participants are known, the way is open for the strategic use of games in work with children. Games then may be employed in a conscious and deliberate fashion so that participants enjoy the maximum of beneficial experience in game play.

Selected Studies of Folklore

The reader should now have realized that it is impossible to divide the study of folklore into neat subdivisions of origin, function, form, and transmission. The function of an item may affect its transmission, its transmission may affect its form, and so on. When a folklorist studies a particular ballad, folktale, or game, he may wish to take some or all of these aspects of folklore into account. Usually scholars investigate specific items of folklore rather than address themselves to such general problems as function or form. Accordingly, a sampling of some studies of individual specimens of folklore genres is presented.

There are literally thousands of studies of songs and tales—some are book length and some are short articles in professional journals. The examples contained in this volume represent only a fraction of the total range of such studies. From these considerations of a game, a lullaby, a barn symbol, a nursery rhyme, and a folktale, the student may see some of the special problems involved in doing research in folklore. There is the problem of assembling versions of an item that has international distribution. There is the difficulty in folksong of having two separate traditions to investigate: tune and text. (Different texts may use the same tune, and different tunes may have the same text.) The task in folk art of following a motif in its manifold appearances on a wide range of objects is an arduous one. The problems that arise from working with materials having both oral and literary tradition include the determination of the printing history of the latter. Finally, one of the basic problems, a problem of theory and method, is just what to do with the collected data. Precisely what does a folklorist do when he undertakes an exhaustive study of a tale or a game?

Each of the following studies deals with problems, general problems that are not limited to the specific data discussed. It is these problems that the student should seek to understand rather than the details of these particular studies. The issues are those faced by all folklorists, and it is appropriate that an introduction to any discipline end with some of the many questions rather than with some of the few answers.

Some Notes on the Guessing Game,
How Many Horns Has the Buck?

Paul G. Brewster

A student taking a course in folklore collects a rhyme or folktale, perhaps from a member of his or her family, and brings it to the instructor, who tells the student that the item has international distribution. From this, the student receives a vague impression that his bit of family folklore is known elsewhere, and he may tend to think that precisely his version of the rhyme or folktale is found in several different countries.

The true nature of the extraordinary multiple existence of folklore is clearly evident in this consideration of a traditional game that is widely distributed in Europe and Asia and goes back to the pre-Christian era. Paul G. Brewster, an American folklorist, who is one of the world's authorities on games, begins his article with a report of his own family fieldwork. He collected a version of How Many Horns Has the Buck? from his aunts in just the way that folklorists and folklore students anywhere might do. However, Brewster, recognizing from his knowledge of published collections of games that the game was an old traditional one, decided to try to discover just when and where it was played. This article is not a study of the game; it is rather the necessary *preparation* for a comparative study of the game, as Brewster indicates in his first footnote. (The reader can see the difference between the comparative and the functional approach to folklore by contrasting this article to the preceding experiment by Gump and Sutton-Smith.)

It may be profitable for the reader to see the preparation for a study rather than the study itself. It is sometimes easy to underestimate the work that goes into a piece of scholarly research if only the polished conclusions are read. In this article by Brewster the first step in undertaking a worldwide comparative study, the gathering of parallel texts, is begun. The reader can see for himself some of the problems involved in folklore research. First, there is the matter of finding versions of the game in the various printed collections. Whereas one can begin with the references in the *Motif-Index* in folk narrative, there is no comparable

Reprinted from *Béaloideas: Journal of the Folklore of Ireland Society,* Vol. 12 (1942), 40–78, by permission of the author and publisher.

index for games. Brewster had to look through the various standard collections of children's games—bear in mind that these collections are written in many different languages of the world. Whereas a scholar can get help in translating an item from one language into another, it is quite another matter to ask someone to look for parallels by reading through collections of games (assuming individuals with the appropriate linguistic competence can be found).

Besides the printed materials, there may be versions ensconced in many of the various archives of folklore located all over the world. Archives are repositories of unpublished collections of folklore, and there are often as many versions of an item in some of the larger archives as in all the printed collections put together. For example, in the parallels for Tale Type 302, The Ogre's (Devil's) Heart in the Egg, listed in the Aarne-Thompson Index, Thompson indicates that there are 92 versions in the Finnish folklore archive, 104 in the Danish archive, and 254 in the rich Irish archive, to take just one instance at random.

The comparative folklorist must know about these archives and must write to the archivists to enlist their aid. In the absence of archives in a particular country, there may be one or more professional folklorists who could be of assistance. In this article, Brewster acknowledges the assistance of the Swedish folklorist C. H. Tillhagen, Belgian folklorist Paul de Keyser, Argentinean folklorist Carlos Vega, Italian folklorist Raffaele Corso, and Turkish folklorist Pertev Boratav, among others. The study of folklore is international in scope, and it requires the co-operative efforts of folklorists all over the world. One or two versions from each of these individual scholars may be only one small piece in the puzzle, but without these pieces the life history of an item of folklore may never be traced.

The game of How Many Horns Has the Buck? is a particularly instructive example of an international form because it has a traditional verbal formula associated with it. Even if the student is unable to read all the languages, he can easily see the striking similarities, e.g., the word "buck" or its equivalent. In fact, a useful exercise might be to look for groupings (i.e., subtypes) of Brewster's texts that could be made on the basis of linguistic criteria or details of the rules for play or, ideally, both. In what areas, for instance, does one player sit astride another's back? In what areas does one put his face in the lap of another? Does this detail tend to be in complementary distribution with the detail of blindfolding?

From Brewster's compilation of versions, the reader should be able to see what the folklorist means when he says, apparently paradoxically, that an item of folklore may be everywhere the same and everywhere different.

For a convenient list of the names and addresses of twenty-five of the world's leading folklore archives, see Jan Harold Brunvand's "Sources of Texts for Comparative Studies of Tales," *The Folklore and Folk Music Archivist*, Vol. 3, No. 2 (Summer 1960). This journal, which is published jointly by the Indiana University Folklore Archives and the

Archives of Folk and Primitive Music, is primarily concerned with the problems of archiving folklore. In various issues, many of the American and European archives are described with some indication of the strength and nature of their principal collections. For a list of Latin American folklorists and folklore centers, see Felix Coluccio, *Folkloristas e instituciones folklóricas del mundo* (Buenos Aires, 1951); or Coluccio, *Guia de folkloristas* (Buenos Aires, 1962).

While collecting folklore of various kinds in the southern part of Indiana during the summer of 1938, I had the good fortune to recover, among other games, a text of How Many Horns Has the Buck? (How Many Fingers Do I Hold Up?).[1] According to the contributors, Miss Asenath Brewster, of Louisville, Kentucky, and Mrs. A. W. Corn, of Petersburg, Indiana, both aunts of mine, the game has been known and played in our family for at least three generations. Oddly enough, I had never known How Many Horns Has the Buck? except through printed versions, and little did I think then that it would turn up (almost literally) "in my own backyard."

The lines of the Indiana version run:

> Humpty dumpty hempty trot,
> Massa Bucky (Buck he?) ought to be shot;
> In come Buck with his long horns,
> How many horns do I hold up?

[While reciting the rhyme, the speaker pats the back of the other player, who is blindfolded, keeping time to the rhythm of the lines. When, on saying the last line, he holds up a finger or fingers behind the back of the blindfolded player, the latter must guess the number. If the guess is incorrect, the reciter cries, for example, *"Two,* you said, and *three* it was," and then continues as before. If the guess is correct, he says, "Two you said, and two it was," and the players exchange places.]

The great antiquity of the game is attested by the fact that a form of it was played by the Romans at least as early as the first century A.D.[2] Petronius

---

1 The number of texts in my possession is not sufficiently large to warrant the attempting of a comparative study just now. However, the amount of material is steadily growing, and I hope later to publish a thorough study of the game. The present paper is intended merely as a commentary on the variants which I have been able to obtain thus far.

2 Our game is not to be confused with the Roman *micare digitis* (*micare, micatio*), a "finger-flashing" game, in which each of two players suddenly extended a number of fingers on one hand, and a third player had to call the sum of all the fingers shown. Dr. Enäjärvi-Haavio falls into this error in her *The Game of Rich and Poor* (Folklore Fellows Communications No. 100) when she writes (p. 8): "We do not propose to discuss the parallels so often repeated in literature: how the game called in English Buck, Buck, How Many Horns Do I Hold Up? was known by the Egyptians; how the Romans called it *migare dicitis* (sic), its present Italian name being *Morra* and the Finnish name *Sarvisilla.*"

Arbiter, writing in the reign of Nero (54–68) mentions it as having been played by Trimalchio with a lad of his acquaintance.

Trimalchio, not to seem moved by the loss, kissed the boy and bade him get upon his back. Without delay the boy climbed on horseback on him, and slapped him on the shoulders with his hand, laughing and calling out "bucca, bucca, quot sunt hic?"[3]

To postulate the Latin form as the source of all subsequent versions would be an easy, but extremely rash, solution (?) to the problem of determining the provenience of the game. However, the question of origin is not to be so easily solved. In all probability the game goes back to an age much earlier than that of Petronius, and it may very well be that we have here merely another instance of Roman borrowing from the Greek, or, as has been suggested in the case of *Morra*, with which How Many Horns Has the Buck?

The Italian *Morra* (French *Mourre*) belongs with the Roman *micare digitis* rather than with How Many Horns Has the Buck? while the Finnish game bears a much stronger resemblance to our Feathers (Horns) than to any of those just mentioned, as the following text from Toivo Okkola, *Suomen kansan kilpa- ja kotileikkejä* (Helsinki, 1928) will show: "A s.c. sarvittaja (i.e., the leader of the game) is elected. The others are sitting in one group in front of him. The sarvittaja says: 'Sarvet, sarvet, sarvet,— pukin sarvet' ('Horns, horns, horns,—the horns of a buck'). At once everyone has to lift his forefingers stretched out from his fists beside his head as horns. If, again, he says for instance '...the horns of a dog,' everyone has to point down with his hands. Anybody who makes the mistage of lifting his fingers to horns when the animal mentioned by the sarvittaja does not have horns must give a forfeit; the same happens if he does not lift his fingers when he should or if he is too slow. To gather more forfeits the sarvittaja may lift his own fingers when you are not supposed to do it or the other way round, to mislead the rest with his 'example'" (p. 95).

Cf. the Latvian Horns, Horns, Who Has Horns? and All the Birds Fly and the Norwegian Horn Horn, Bukkehorn. A version of All the Birds Fly is found also among the Finns, who know it as Kaikki Linnut Lentävät. See Beckwith, *Jamaica Folklore*, Memoirs of the American Folklore Society, No. 21, 15, for a Jamaican form. [Professor Brewster has considered the Roman game elsewhere. See "A Roman Game and Its Survival on Four Continents," *Classical Philology*, Vol. 38 (1943), 134–37.—ED. NOTE]

[3] *Arbitri Satirae* (ed. Büchler), p. 84. Professor W. B. Sedgwick writes in "Notes on Petronius," *Classical Review*, Vol. 39, 118: "This game is played (or was recently) in Leicestershire, Yorkshire, and Cambridgeshire. Only in Cambridgeshire do they say 'Buck, buck, how many (fingers) do I hold up?' The identity with 'Bucca, bucca, quot sunt hic?" is to me inexplicable." Professor Sedgwick's second statement is incorrect; the formula quoted for Cambridgeshire is to be found in other parts of England as well, e.g., in Yorkshire (Gutch, *County Folklore*, Vol. 6, 139) and Northumberland (Balfour and Thomas, *County Folklore*, Vol. 4, 104).

In his inability to see the identity of "Bucca, bucca, quot sunt hic?" with the English formula, however, he is not alone. The original meaning of *bucca*, i.e., cheek (especially when puffed out), has been changed through metonymy. Thus, as Cesareo points out in his *De Petronii Sermone* (Rome, 1887), Juvenal uses it in *Satire* III, 35, as a synonym for *cornicen* or *praeco*, while in Petronius it is used for *domesticus*, the implication here apparently being that the cheeks are puffed out, not with blowing a trumpet or crying out a proclamation but with the gorging of food provided by the master. It is interesting to note, however, that a comment on this line in Michael Heseltine's English translation of Petronius (London, 1913) reads: "*Bucca* was a child's game...where one child was blindfolded and the others touched him on the cheek, and asked him how many fingers, or how many children had touched him." Georges (*Ausführliches Lat.-Deutsches Handwörterbuch*, 8 Aufl., 1913) equates *bucca* with *Schmarotzer, Parasit*.

is often confused,[4] a wholesale borrowing by Europe from China or Egypt.[5]
Whatever the origin of the game, there can be no doubt as to its popularity.
Friedländer speaks of its being known and played in Italy, Portugal, Béarn,
Andalusia, England, Germany, and Sweden.[6] To this list can now be added
with certainty the following: Ireland, Scotland, the Hebrides, France, Spain,
the Netherlands, Greece, Denmark, Estonia, the United States, Belgium,
Hercegovina, Turkey, Norway, Argentina, Japan, Switzerland, and India.[7]

---

[4] For descriptions of *micare,* the ancestor of *Morra,* see Marquadt, *Privatleben der
Römer,* 2d. ed. (1886), Vol. 1, 836; de Fouquières, *Les Jeux des Anciens* (1873), pp.
290–94; *Arch. Zeitung,* Vol. 29 (1871), 151–56; Gronovius, *Thes. Antiq.,* Vol. 7 (1699),
912, 1206–7; Smith, *Dict. of Greek and Roman Antiq.,* 3rd ed. (1891), Vol. 2, 171;
Annali dell' Instit., Vol. 38 (1866), 326–29 (particularly plates *U* and *V*); and Daremberg
and Saglio, *Dict. des Antiq.,* Vol. 3 (1889–1890), s.v. *micatio.* See also J. G. Wilkinson,
The Manners and Customs of the Ancient Egyptians, rev. ed. of Samuel Birch), Vol. 1,
32, and Vol. 2, 55. In this work is described a form of the game, the playing of which is
depicted on the tomb of Ibi at Thebes, dating to the reign of Psammetichos I (663–609
B.C.).
   That the game was one of chance rather than of skill is fully recognized by Cicero—
*Dicendum igitur putas de sortibus? Quid enim sors est? Idem prope modum quod micare,
quod talos iacere, quod tesseras, quibus in rebus temeritas et casus, non ratio nec
consilium valet* (*De Divin.,* Book 2, xli)...*nullum erit certamen, sed quasi sorte aut
micando victus alteri cedet alter* (*De Off.,* 3, 90). The fact that *micare* offered much
opportunity for cheating (e.g., through the failure of both players to throw out their
fingers simultaneously) gave rise to the proverbial expression *dignum esse, dicunt, quicum
in tenebris mices* (*De Off.,* 3, 77). See also *De Fin.,* 2, 52, and Otto, *Sprichwörter der
Römer* (1890), pp. 221–22.
[5] "So peculiar a game [i.e., *Morra*] would hardly have been invented twice over in
Europe and Asia, but it is hard to guess whether the Chinese learned it from the West,
or whether it belongs to the remarkable list of clever inventions which Europe has
borrowed from China. The ancient Egyptians, as their sculptures show, used to play at
some sort of finger game, and the Romans had their finger-flashing 'micare digitis,' at
which butchers used to gamble with their customers for bits of meat." (E. B. Tylor,
Primitive Culture, Vol. 1, 75).
   Corresponding to the Italian *Morra* are the Greek *daktulon epallaxis* (δακτυλων
επαλλαξις) and the Chinese *Mu chan* or "Thumb warfare" 手母 拇戲 The latter, known
also as *Hua-ch'üan* or "Waving the fists," can be traced back to the Five Dynasties
(A.D. 907–960). For information regarding the Chinese forms, I am indebted to the kindness of Dr. A. W. Hummel, of the Division of Orientalia, Library of Congress.
[6] Ludwig Friedländer, *Petronii Cena Trimalchionis,* p. 325.
[7] How Many Horns Has the Buck? is apparently unknown in Latvia, Poland,
Hungary, Mexico, Russia, China, and Finland; at any rate my inquiries among folklorists
of these countries would indicate that such is the case. Dr. Károly Viski, of Budapest,
writes me that he knows of no Hungarian form, and that the game does not appear in
the great collection of Kiss, *Magyar Gyermekjatek-gyüjtemeny* (Budapest, 1891). Mr.
Albert B. Lord, who has been kind enough to check through several Yugoslav and Russian
collections for me, informs me that he has been unable to locate it in Vuk Vrčevic,
Srpske narodne Igre; Vuk Karadžić, *Zivot i Obicaji Naroda Srpskoga;* or *Ljetopis*
(journal of the Matica Srpska); or in such Russian collections as P. Ivanov, "Igry
krest'anskih detei v kupanskom uêzdê" (published in *Sbornik Har'kovskago istoriko-
flologiceskoago obsestva,* 1886–1890); E. A. Pokrovskii, *Dêtskie igry* (Moskva, 1895);
and a recent Soviet publication, *Igry narodov USSR.* It is not in Dmitrij Zelenin,
Russische (Ostslavische) Volkskunde (Berlin u. Leipzig, 1927); the work of Kapica,
Dêtskij folk'lor (Leningrad, 1928), I have not been able to examine. [It is also found in
Africa and New Zealand. See Paul G. Brewster, "Some African Variants of 'Bucca,
Bucca,'" *Classical Journal,* Vol. 39 (1944), 293–96; Brian Sutton-Smith, "New Zealand
Variants of the Game 'Buck, Buck,'" *Folklore,* Vol. 62 (1951), 329–33.—ED. NOTE]

The names given the game are many and varied. In English-speaking countries it is known as Buck, How Many Horns Has the Buck? Buck-buck[8] or Buck Shee, Buck.[9] Italian children know it as Ad anca ed ancona,[10] A cancara e bella, Daino daino,[11] A cinquanta corna porta la crapa,[12] Al cavalletto,[13] Salincerbio (=*salire in cervo*), A Tinghe e Tingone, Maclena Celona, Biccicalla, or zóc del soc (=*giuoco del sotto*). The more usual German names are Wieviel Hörner hat der Bock? and Bock, Bock, wie viel Hörner hab ich?[14] In Sweden the game is called Bulta bockhorn or Bulleri bulleri bockhorn.[15] Gaelic names for it are Gearr a mhuchan[16] and Co miad adhairc air a' bhoc.[17] A Danish term is Gjaette fingre.[18] In the Netherlands the game is known as Bocken spelen, Bockhoren spelen, Bock over haghe spelen, etc.[19] The general name for it in Belgium is Bok-sta-vast,[20] a few of the local terms being Hamele-damele,[21] À drenner l'âgne,[22] Kiekela-kakel,[23] and Djower â fwêr tchuvau (=*jouer au fort cheval*).[24] The French term is Jouer au cheval-fondu.[25] In Estonia the game is called Sikka, pukka, mitu sarve? (Goatie, Buckie, How Many Horns?).[26] An Irish version printed by Lady Gomme bears the title Old Johnny Hairy, Crap In![27] The name in Turkey is Kač parmaq? (How Many Fingers?).[28] The Hercegovinan form of the game is known as Pogadalica.[29] Spanish terms for it are Recotín-

---

[8] M. C. Balfour and N. W. Thomas, *County Folklore*, Publications of the Folklore Society, Vol. 4 (London, 1904), 104.

[9] *Folklore Journal*, Vol. 5, 59.

[10] This and A cancara e bella seem to be the more common names.

[11] Cf. the English Buck-buck.

[12] Giuseppe Pitré, *Giuochi Fanciulleschi Siciliani, Biblioteca delle Tradizioni Popolari Siciliane*, Vol. 13, 174.

[13] This and the following Italian terms I owe to the kindness of Professor Raffaele Corso, of the Archivio delle Tradizioni Popolari Italiane.

[14] Böhme, *Deutsches Kinderlied u. Kinderspiel*, p. 633; Simrock, *Das deutsche Kinderbuch*, 3rd ed., p. 236; *Hessische Blätter*, Vol. 11 (1912), 139; Lewalter and Schläger, *Deutsches Kinderlied u. Kinderspiel*, pp. 24, 411; Rausch, *Das Spielzeichnis im 25 Kapitel von Fischarts "Geschichtklitterung" (Gargantua)*, p. 45.

[15] Pitré, *op. cit.*, p. xlvii.

[16] Maclagan, *The Games and Diversions of Argyleshire*, p. 42.

[17] This is the title of a Gaelic text sent me by Miss Anna Nic Iain, of the Isle of Barra.

[18] Kristensen, *Danske Börnerim, Remser og Lege*, p. 214.

[19] de Cock and Teierlinck, *Kinderspel & Kinderlust in Zuid-Nederland*, p. 294.

[20] So I am informed by Professor Paul de Keyser, of the Seminarie van Folklore, Rijksuniversiteit, Gent, in a letter of March 24, 1939.

[21] In Antwerp.

[22] In Liège and in the rest of the Walloon part of Belgium.

[23] In East Flanders.

[24] In Spa. Many other Flemish names are given in Junius, *Nomenclator*, and in Hoffmann von Fallersleben, *Horae Belgicae*, pp. 6, 181ff.

[25] Information furnished by Professor de Keyser. Cf. also de Cock and Teierlinck, *op. cit.*, p. 307.

[26] Information furnished by Dr. Oskar Loorits, of the Eesti Rahvaluule Arhiiv, Tartu (Dorpat), Estonia.

[27] *Traditional Games of England, Scotland, and Ireland*, Vol. 2, 449–50.

[28] Information furnished by Professor Tihomir Georgevic, of Belgrade, Yugoslavia.

[29] Information furnished by Mr. Albert B. Lord.

Recotán,[30] Pin, pam, cunillán,[31] Juego de los tres burros, and El garbancito.[32] In Greece the game is called πόσα,[33] ἀραὶ μπουραί, and πόσα φυλλα ἔχει το οενορί.[34] The children of India know the game as Kitte aṇḍe bōl (Tell Me How Many Eggs).[35] It is called in Japan Shika, shika tsuno nanbon? (Deer, Deer, How Many Horns?).

Ways of Playing[36]

ENGLAND

1. The game is played by two boys. The first stoops over so that his arms rest on a table; the other sits on his back. The latter holds up a number of fingers and calls upon the former to guess the number of "horns." If he fails, he continues in the role of guesser. When a correct guess is made, the two players exchange places.[37]

2. The game is played by two boys. One "makes a back"; the other jumps upon him. The rest of the action is like that in No. 1.[38]

3. The game is played by three boys. One stands with his back against a wall, the second bends over with his head against the stomach of the first, and a third player jumps upon the back of the second. From this point on, the action is identical with that of No. 1.[39]

---

30 Pitré, *op. cit.*, p. xlvi.

31 Maspons, *Jochs de la Infancia*, p. 45.

32 For the last two Spanish terms I am indebted to Dra. María Cadilla Martínez, of Arecibo, P. R.

33 *Folklore journal*, Vol. 2, 58.

34 For this information I am indebted to Professor Phédon Koukoulés, of Athens, who was kind enough to send me both a text and a description of the game. This is the name used in Syros; Loucopoulos, "Ποιά παιμνίοια παίζουν τα 'Ελληνόπουλα," p. 203.

35 For a consideration of this form of the game, see Paul G. Brewster, "The 'Kitte aṇḍe Bōl' Game of India," *Southern Folklore Quarterly*, Vol. 7 (1943), 149–52.—ED. NOTE

36 How Many Horns? should not be confused with (1) games in which the blindfolded player must identify another by feeling his clothing, or must guess with which finger or hand the other player has struck him (German: Blinde Kuh, Blinde Maus, Blinde Eule, Blinder Bock, Blinde Henne, Piep Maus, Blinde Katze, Narr mit der Kappe; Danish: Salte sure Ojne, Blinde-momme, fjaele Kuk, Mork-i-Haette, lege Mus i Morke; French: Mouche, Colin-maillard; Flemish: Blintspel, Het blindeken, Pieps; Italian: Mosca, Moscola, Mosca cieca; English: Hoodman Blind, Billy Blind, Blind Harie, Blind Hob, Blind Bucky Davy, Buck Hid, etc.; ancient Greek: *Myia chalke—μυία χαλκῆ*; (2) those in which the blindfolded player identifies another by his voice (Polish: Mruczek; Spanish: El pi; etc.); and (3) those in which the one blindfolded is required to guess the arrangement of the fingers with which he is struck (Puerto Rican and Cuban: Huevo o araña; Spanish: Pico, zorro y zaina; Flemish: Hamer-scheer-mes-lepel-forket-of-kuip, Hamer, scheer, kapmes of blok, Hamer, scheer, mes, kuip of eemer; French: Ciseaux, marteau, couteau; German: Stipti, Fausti, Grusti, Platti; Swedish: Pip, ram, tali, fusti; etc.). Pokrovskii describes a Russian game in which one player creeps up behind another, covers his eyes with his hands, and holds him prisoner until the blindfolded one guesses the other's identity by feeling his clothes and calls his name. In "Ajcajkyc," No. 1051 in *Igry narodov USSR* (1933), the players cover the eyes of one of their number, and each in turn strikes the palm of his hand. The blindfolded player must guess who hit him.

37 Gomme, *op. cit.*, Vol. 1, 46.

38 Balfour and Thomas, *op. cit.*, p. 104.

39 Gutch, *op. cit.*, p. 139.

WALES

1. The game is played by two boys. The guesser stands with his face toward a wall, keeping his eyes shut.[40]

2. The game is played by three boys. Identical with English No. 3.[41]

IRELAND

1. Players (no number specified) sit in a circle, with their right feet put out in front of them. The leader "counts out" by reciting to each in turn a verse, at the last line of which the player addressed draws in his foot. The last to draw his foot in kneels down and is blindfolded by the leader. The latter then puts his elbows on the back of the blindfolded player and strikes him with elbow or fist, reciting a rhyme. Then he holds up a number of fingers and calls upon the blindfolded boy to guess the number. If the latter guesses correctly the leader must exchange places with him. If the guess is incorrect, the guesser remains down, and another takes the leader's place.[42]

2. The game is identical with the Indiana version. An incorrect guess results in the guesser's receiving a particularly hefty thump.[43]

SCOTLAND

1. The guesser sits on a chair; the other player stands behind him. Suddenly releasing his thumbs from the pressure of the forefingers, the latter "flicks" the guesser on the cheeks with his thumbnails, at the same time repeating the accompanying rhyme.[44]

2. One player, the guesser, sits on a chair; the others stand behind him. One by one, they pinch him on the head with their thumbnails, keeping time to the reciting of a rhyme.[45]

GERMANY

1. Two boys play the game. The one who asks the number of fingers leaps upon the back of the other before saying the rhyme.[46]

2. The player asking the number of fingers held up mounts upon the back of the guesser, who is seated.[47]

3. One player sits; another puts his head in the first player's lap. Then one of the singing group holds up a number of fingers behind the back of the second player, calling upon him to guess the number. Should he miss, another rhyme is recited, and at the word "Bummeri" (see texts below) he is given a blow on the rear.[48]

40 *Folklore Journal,* Vol. 5, 59. Reported from Cornwall.

41 *Ibid.* Cf. Courtney, *Cornish Feasts and Folklore,* p. 186.

42 Gomme, *op. cit.,* Vol. 2, 449–50. Recovered in Kiltubbrid, County Leitrim. With the counting-out method employed, compare that described by Beckwith, *op. cit.,* p. 26.

43 Information furnished by Mr. Pádraig Mac Gréine, of Béal Atha na Laogh, Longford.

44 *Folklore,* Vol. 17, 228.

45 Maclagan, *op. cit.,* p. 42.

46 Rochholz, *Alemannisches Kinderlied u. Kinderspiel,* p. 434.

47 Böhme, *op. cit.,* p. 634.

48 *Ibid.*

4. The game is identical with the Indiana version.[49]

5. The game is identical with the Indiana version, except that the one who raises his fingers uses both fists on the guesser's back while reciting the rhyme.[50]

SWEDEN

1. The guesser sits on a chair or a stool, and another player strikes him on the back, while reciting a rhyme.[51]

2. One player, the guesser, sits on a stool; the other sits on the former's knee.[52]

3. One player, holding the head of the other between his knees, strikes him on the back to the rhythm of a rhyme that he recites.[53]

DENMARK

1. The players (no number specified) form a ring. One stands out with his back to another. The latter strikes the first player on the back with his hand, at the same time reciting a rhyme. Then he holds up a number of fingers, calling upon the first player to guess the number. If the guess is correct, the two players exchange places; if incorrect, the guesser must give a forfeit.[54]

NETHERLANDS

1. One player lies with his face in the lap of another. A third player strikes the back of the second, holds up a number of fingers, and challenges him to tell the number. If his guess is incorrect, all the other players strike him on the back, at the same time reciting a rhyme.[55]

2. One player stands bent over; another springs upon his back, holds up a number of fingers, and calls upon the first to guess the number.[56]

BELGIUM

1. One player stands with his back against a wall, holding his hands together and letting both arms hang down in front of him. A second player stands facing the first, bends forward, and lets his head (or both hands and head) rest in the clasped hands of the other. A third player, who mounts upon the back of the second, raises his hand in the air and extends a number of fingers. The first player then calls upon the second to guess the number. If the latter succeeds, the third player must change places with him. If he fails, he suffers a punishment of his own choosing.[57]

---

[49] *Ibid.,* p. 633.

[50] *Ibid.* Cf. Lewalter and Schläger, *op. cit.,* p. 24.

[51] For this information, and also for several Swedish texts from manuscript collections in the archives, I am indebted to Dr. J. Ejdestam, of the Landsmålsarkivet, Kungl. Universitets Bibliotek, Uppsala.

[52] Upl., Vittinge, 2254: 3, s. 2 (Landsmålsarkivet).

[53] Vgl., 25: 57, s. 102 (Landsmålsarkivet).

[54] Kristensen, *op. cit.,* p. 214.

[55] de Cock and Teierlinck, *op. cit.,* p. 299. From Maastricht.

[56] Information furnished by Professor Paul de Keyser.

[57] de Cock and Teierlinck, *op. cit.,* p. 303. From Antwerp. For a description of the way in which the game concludes, see the end of this section.

ESTONIA

1. The game is played by three boys. One is blindfolded, and leans over with hands on knees and his head against a tree or a wall. Another player gets upon the back of the first and strikes his neck in time with a verse which he recites. A third player acts as judge and decides whether the blindfolded player's guessing of the number of fingers held up by the rider is done fairly.[58]

HERCEGOVINA

1. A group of young men or boys (not more than ten in number) choose a leader. He, in turn, selects one of the other players to be the "baba" (old woman). The "baba" leans forward and covers his eyes. The leader then raises a number of fingers. When all except the "baba" have seen the number held up, one of the others strikes the "baba" from behind with the palm of the hand. The "baba" then attempts to guess the number, first having seized one of the other players by the arm. If the guess is correct, the player held by the arm becomes the next "baba." The entire game is played in silence.[59]

SERBIA

1. One boy mounts upon the back of another, and calls upon him to guess the number of fingers held up behind him. If he succeeds, the roles are reversed; if not, the other lad continues to ride on his back until he succeeds in making a correct guess.[60]

GREECE

1. Several players divide into sides and choose leaders. One of the leaders picks up a stone; the other leader guesses in which hand it is held. If he guesses incorrectly, all those on his side "make backs" and are mounted by those of the opposing side. The former are blindfolded by the hands of the riders. Each in turn is cuffed on the side of the head and commanded to guess the number of fingers held up by the rider. If the guess is correct, rider and ridden exchange places.[61]

2. One player mounts upon the back of another, and extending a number of fingers, challenges the former to guess the number held out. If the guess is correct, the players exchange positions. If it is incorrect, the game continues as before.[62]

---

[58] Liiv, *Laste Mängu-tuba*, p. 10. This information I owe to the kindness of Dr. Loorits, who tells me that there are no variants of the game in the Eesti Rahvaluule Arhiiv and that it seems to have been little known in Estonia.

[59] This description was given me by Mr. Albert B. Lord, of Harvard University, who obtained text and information regarding the game from Mr. Nikola Vujnovic, a native of the village of Burmazi. Mr. Vujnovic played the game in Hercegovina as a boy, and later played it in the army.

[60] For this information I am indebted to Professor Tihomir Georgevic, of Beograd, Yugoslavia, who played the game in Serbia as a boy. He points out that the name "Kač parmaq" is Turkish, and gives it as his opinion that the game was imported into Serbia from Turkey.

[61] *Folklore Journal*, Vol. 2, 58. From Samos. The player who is ridden is called ζῶον.

[62] Text and description communicated by Professor Phédon Koukoulés, of Athens, in a letter of October 9, 1939. From Syros.

3. One player closes his eyes. Another, standing behind him, puts the left hand over his eyes to make sure that he cannot see, and holding up a number of fingers of the right hand, calls upon him to guess the number. If the blindfolded one guesses correctly, the players exchange places; if not, the game is continued until a correct guess is made.[63]

UNITED STATES

1. One player hides his face in the lap of another and guesses the number of fingers which the latter raises.[64]

ITALY

1. One player is the master. He blindfolds the eyes of a second, who is to be the horse. A third player leaps upon the back of the second, who must guess how many fingers the former holds up.[65]

2. One player stands with his back to another, who strikes him with his fist in time to a rhyme that be recites.[66]

3. The game is played by three players. One, who is the master, is seated. Another, who is to be the horse, hides his face in the lap of the former. A third is the goat, who mounts upon the back of the second. The master makes sure that the second player cannot see the signs that the rider will make, and then both he and the rider recite a verse challenging the second to guess the number of fingers held up by the rider. If he succeeds, the second and third players exchange places; if not, he continues in his role.[67]

ARGENTINA

1. The first player, blindfolded, is struck repeatedly on the back with the fist of a second, the blows marking the rhythm of a quatrain which the latter sings. The last line, challenging the blindfolded player to guess the number of fingers extended, is spoken. If the guess is incorrect, a couplet giving the correct number is sung by the second player.[68]

---

63 Description communicated by Professor Koukoulés. See also Loucopoulos, *op. cit.*, p. 203.

64 Newell, *Games and Songs of American Children*, 3rd ed. (New York and London, 1911), p. 148. The author alludes to the form of the game in which one player mounts upon another's back, but writes: "We are not aware that the practice continues to exist in this country."

65 Pitré, *op. cit.*, p. xliv. Cf. *Archivio per lo Studio delle Tradizioni Popolari*, Vol. 1 (1882), 254.

66 *Ibid.*, p. 171. From Avola.

67 *Ibid.*, p. 169.

68 For this description and for an accompanying text I am indebted to the courtesy of Dr. Carlos Vega, of Buenos Aires. The text, writes Dr. Vega, was learned from his grandmother, who was born and reared in Málaga, Andalucía. He adds that the game is not common in Argentina.

The text of this variant is the only one for which I have a tune. It will have been noted, however, that singing is alluded to in German 2, and it seems quite probable that it may have been played a part in other variants as well. Certainly the strongly marked rhythm of the lines (not to mention that of the blows which accompanied the recitation of them) would have lent itself well to the making of a simple melody.

TURKEY

1. The players are divided into two groups, and form a circle. Those of the first group get down on their hands and knees; those of the second mount upon their backs. The leader of the game extends a number of fingers, and calls upon his "horse" to guess how many there are. If the guess is correct, the two groups exchange positions.[69]

INDIA

1. "It is played by two or more children—probably not more than four at a time. One of the children stands with body bent forward from the waist, resting his hands against a wall or a low window sill. Another child comes running from behind and hops onto the back of the first, holding his left hand over the eyes of the first in order to blindfold him. B then holds up a number of fingers of his right hand, away from the first child and at the back of his own body, which has to be guessed by the blindfolded child. If he guesses right, they change places. This is, of course, for two children. If there are more than two children willing to join the game, then the others stand grouped one behind the other, each additional child supporting his hands on the back of the one in front. And then the runner has to jump over the intervening heads onto the back of the first."[70]

2. "This game is played all over India and there are different rhymes. The game is generally played in the evening or in moonlight. Usually the number of players is from four to ten. The players divide themselves into two parties and then toss. The winning side ride on the losing side. Suppose in all there are eight boys, A, B, C, D (first party) and E, F, G, H (second party). Say the first party loses the toss, then they (A, B, C, D) have to become horses, by bending and keeping their hands on the knee, and have to stand in a circle. Then E rides on A, F on B, G on C, and H on D. He sits exactly as one sits on a horse. An exception is made in the case of a weak or little boy who can not stand the weight of a big or a heavy boy. In such a case the big boy stands by the side of the little boy and then catches one of his ears. For convenience, A, B, C, and D are called horses, and E, F, G, and H riders. One of the riders, who is generally the best singer, closes the eyes of his horse with one hand and raises the fingers of his other hand over his head, and recites a rhyme.

(1)

$$
\begin{array}{ccc}
 & A & \\
 & \uparrow & \\
 & E & \\
D \leftarrow H & & F \rightarrow B \\
 & G & \\
 & \downarrow & \\
 & C &
\end{array}
$$

---

[69] This description and a Turkish text I owe to the kindness of Mr. Pertev Boratav, of the Tarih Dil Coǧrafva Fakültesi, Ankara.

[70] Excerpt from a letter (December 22, 1939) written me by Dr. V. S. Sukthankar, of the Bhandarkar Oriental Research Institute, Poona.

If the guess is correct, then the riders *E, F, G,* and *H* become horses, and *A, B, C,* and *D* riders. But if the guess is incorrect, then each rider gets down and rides the next horse, as indicated below. The horses, *A, B, C,* and *D*, remain in their original positions.

(2)

$$A$$
$$\uparrow$$
$$H$$

$$D \leftarrow G \qquad\qquad E \to B$$

$$F$$
$$\downarrow$$
$$C$$

After every rhyme, just while getting down from his horse and riding a new one, the rhymer says humorously, "Ghoda hamara; Tattu Tumara" (Horse mine; pony yours).[71] This joke is repeated every time the guess is wrong.

The riders move in clockwise direction. When the rider closes the eyes of his horse, say *H* is closing *A's* eyes, the rest can see the fingers. Since *B, C,* and *D* belong to the party of *A,* they are always looking to the fingers and when the guess is correct, a clever fellow (horse) at once becomes erect and thus tries to throw off his rider. "All have a hearty laugh when a rider falls."[72]

3. "The children's guessing game alluded to by you has been played on this side of the country in almost exactly the same way as has been depicted by you. Only the variant in which the first player gets down on knees and the other mounts on his back is prevalent here."[73]

SPAIN

In four Spanish texts sent me recently by Professor Angel Gonzalez Palencia, of the University of Madrid, the game has been combined with Punpuñete, which is the Spanish equivalent of our Club Fist.

1. All the players arrange their fists as in the American Club Fist. Pointing at the bottom fist, the leader of the game asks, "¿Que hay aquí?" The rest reply, "Cajón." He then points to the next fist above and asks the same question. The answers are alternately "Cajón" and "Cajica." When the questioner has reached the top fist, the dialogue runs as follows:—

"¿Que hay aquí dentro?"
"Un sapico muerto"
"¿Quien lo ha muerto?"
"La gallina"
"¿Quien le llora?"
"La señora"

---

71 Only a warrior or a well-to-do man rides a horse; poor people and artisans use ponies.—CONTRIBUTOR'S NOTE.

72 Excerpt from a letter (March 26, 1940) written me by Mr. M. H. Shah, of the Rural Uplift Society, Indi, District of Bijapur, Bombay Presidency.

73 Excerpt from a letter (April 24, 1940) written me by Mr. Mam Chand Sandilya, Jhajjar, District of Rohtak, Panjab.

"¿Quien le canta?"
"La perdiz"

When the words "La perdiz" are uttered, the players cry out, "El que se ría pagará la moquita!" Then all move their fists about, one upon the other, until one of the players laughs.

The one who has laughed is forced to bend over and cover his face with his hands. The others then strike him on the shoulder, singing:

Recotín, recotán,
De la vera, vera van,
Por el cerro Ballubero
¿Cuantos dedos hay en medio?

At the last line, the players lay a certain number of fingers on his shoulder. If his guess as to the number is incorrect, they sing:

Si hubieras dicho *tantos,*
No llevarias tanto mal,
Recotín, recotán,
De la vera, vera van,
Por el cerro Ballubero
¿Cuantos dedos hay en medio?

The game continues until a correct guess is made.[74]

2. In this variant the leader asks, "¿Que es esto?" and the others reply, "Punpuñete." The dialogue at the close is:

"¿Que hay aquí dentro?"
"Un sapico muerto"
"¿Por donde sube?"
"Por las escalerillas"
"¿Por donde baja?"
"Por las soguillas"
"El que se ría pagará la moquita"

Then follows the same procedure as in the first variant, except that the players murmur "u-u-u-u" while moving their fists about. The rhyme accompanying the shoulder-striking shows a slight variation.

Recotín, recotán,
Las cabrillas por donde van
Del palacio a la cocina
¿Cuantos dedos hay encima?

3. In still another form of the game the players extend their open hands, and the leader pinches lightly each finger (or each hand, if the players are many in number), saying:

Al pizquillo—gorgorillo
Mi hermanica—la chiquitica

---

[74] From Zaragoza (Saragossa), northeast Spain. [For a description of Club Fist, see Paul G. Brewster, *American Nonsinging Games* (Norman, Okla., 1953), pp. 29–31.—Ed. Note]

Se encontró—una camisica
De que color—de pita y flor
Ha dicho mi madre
Que escondas—el quiquiriquí.

As the finger (or hand) of each player is pinched, he hides it. When all have been pinched, the owner of the last hand unhidden is "punished." He bends forward, covering his face, and the others strike him on the shoulder with hand and elbow alternately, to the accompaniment of the following rhyme:

Decodín, decodán
De la vera, vera van,
Por el cerro Gallubero
¿Cuantos dedos hay en medio?[75]

[The guessing of the number of fingers held up is a feature also of certain versions of the Dutch and Belgian Ezelke springen.[76] One boy stands with his back against a wall, holding his hands clasped loosely before him. A second player faces him and bends forward until his face rests in the hands of the first boy. Each of the other players in turn then leaps upon the back of the second. As soon as he has mounted, he must hold a number of fingers in the air and call upon the "ezel" to guess how many there are. If the latter succeeds, the first player becomes the next jumper, the former "ezel" takes his place at the wall, and the first jumper becomes the "ezel." Should the guess be incorrect, the one who began as "ezel" must retain his position.

In what appears to be a more common form of Ezelke springen the players divide themselves into two groups, the "ezels" and the jumpers; and several of the former, one directly behind another, assume a bent position at the same time. Here there is no element of guessing, since the game is one of agility rather than of cleverness.[77]

The unlucky guesser in a game of Hamele damele has at least one consolation, that of being allowed to choose the form of his punishment. Thus, if he chooses "daar hangt het spek," the other players seize him by the head, arms, and legs, lift him as high as they can, and then let him fall almost to the ground. This they do three times. Should he choose "vuistjes," all the others beat him on the back with their fists.[78]]

JAPAN

1. First, the order is decided by *janken*.[79] The one who has lost bends forward, resting both hands against a wall or some other stationary object. The winner rides on his back and holds out his fingers above the head of

---

[75] From Teruel, eastern Spain.
[76] See de Cock and Teierlinck, *op. cit.*, pp. 296 (Denderbelle and Herdersem) and 306.
[77] Cf. Gomme, *op. cit.*, Vol. 1, 52 (Bung the Bucket).
[78] de Cock and Teierlinck, *op. cit.*, pp. 303–4.
[79] With regard to *Jan Ken* (the name is probably a corrupted form of the Chinese 'ryan ken'—both fists), it seems to have been played originally with both hands, as its

the loser, calling "Deer, deer! how many horns?" The boy being ridden tries to guess the number. If he succeeds, they exchange places; if not, then he repeats.[80]

Texts[81]

ENGLISH

GE 1   Buck, buck, how many horns do I hold up?
           (Two) you say and three there be;
           Buck, buck, how many horns do I hold up?
           (Four) you say and (four) there be;
           Buck, buck, rise up!

GE 2   Buck-buck, hoo many fingers div aa had up?

GE 3   Buck, buck,
           Hoo mony fingers div I hod up?

GERMAN

GG 1   Himmel, Bimmel, Bindelstock,
           Wieviel Hörner hat der Bock?
           Wieviel Finger stehen?

           Hättest du die drei genommen,
           Wärst du glücklich vongekommen.

---

name suggests, although the *both* may refer to the hands of the two people playing. In its derived form *Ken,* it is still played with both hands.

"Jan Ken is played among children...generally to decide the order of choice or precedence, as in the case of drawing lots or 'heads or tails.' For instance, at cards, if we want to fix who shall play first, we play Jan Ken among the players. We say together 'jan-ken-pon!' ('pon' means nothing: an empty word to add another syllable), with a little pause after each syllable, at the same time holding up each our fists. At the word 'pon' each of us makes simultaneously his or her figure of a fist, e.g., *A* making *ishi*— stone (fist clenched), *B hasami*—scissors (index and second fingers separated), *C kami*— paper (palm flat, with all fingers separated), and *D hasami*. We can't make anything out of this, so we try again and if *B, D,* and *C* have *hasami,* then A is the loser.... There is also a regular game called Gū-choki-pā (Stone-Scissors-Paper); this is always played between two persons."—CONTRIBUTOR'S NOTE. [For a further consideration of this game, see Brewster, *op. cit.,* pp. 17–18. It is interesting that games, like folksongs, quilt patterns, and fiddle tunes, have several traditional names by which they are known. This often makes it difficult to collect folklore by simply asking for an item by name rather than by describing its content. The informant may know the item, but under a different though equally traditional name. In the area around San Francisco, Stone, Paper, Scissors, is called Rochambeau, and it is played as a game in itself rather than functioning as a pre-game counting-out rhyme. For the standard collection of counting-out rhymes, see Henry Carrington Bolton, *The Counting-Out Rhymes of Children* (London, 1888).—ED. NOTE]

[80] Description furnished by Professor Sanki Ichikawa, of the Imperial University of Tokyo. This version was recovered near Kyoto (province of Shiga) by Mr. Kunio Yanagita in 1940.

[81] I use here the Finnish method of classification of texts by linguistic groups; GE = Germanic—English; GG = Germanic—German; GD = Germanic—Danish; GV = Germanic —Flemish (Vlaamsch); CS = Celtic—Scottish; CW = Celtic—Welsh; RI = Romanic— Italian; RP = Romanic—Portuguese; etc.

GG 2
    Chnipis, Chnopis,
    Abermol e Dopis,
    Wie mängs (wieviel) Horn het uff der Bock?

    Hättisch du——errothe,
    Wärisch d'runger danne g'schnogge.
    Chnipis, Chnopis, etc.

GG 3
    Griwes, Grawes, Holberstock,
    Wie mant (wieviel) Hörner streckt der Bock?

    Hätsch s 'grotha,
    Hätsch a Horner mit verbrota.
    Griwes, Grawes, etc.

GG 4
    Es wollt ein Schmeid ein Rad beschlagen,
    Wieviel Nägel muss er haben?
    Fünfe oder sechse?

    Hättest du——gerathen,
    So wärst du nit gebraten.
    Bummeri, Zelleri,
    Schlägt den kleinen Fingeri!

GG 5
    Bommele, bommele, bommelstock,
    Wieviel Hörner hat der Bock?
    Wieviel Finger stehen?

GG 6
    Knibes, Knabes, röstige Rabes;
    Bockmann, wieviel Horn stohn op?
       (Eins, zwei, etc.)

    Hättstu besser gerode,
    Su wörste Künig worde.

GG 7
    Wieviel Hörner streckt der Bock?
    Eins, u.s.w.

    Hast du gut gerathen,
    Wirst du nicht gebraten.

GG 8
    Hopp die hopp, Kartoffelsopp,
    Wieviel Hörner hat der Bock?

GG 9
    Mingeldi, mingeldi, hopp, hurräh,
    Wieviel Finger sind in der Höh?

GG 10
    Rumpelti, pumpelti, Holderstock,
    Wieviel Hoerner streckt der Bock?

GG 11
    Tribeles, Trabeles,
    Nägelsstock,
    Wie viel Hörner
    Hat der Bock?
    Wie viel Finger
    Strecken aus?

Hast's errathen,
Schmeckt der Braten;
Birle, birle bump,
Der Kaiser ist ein Lump.

or

Hättest du die fünf gesprochen
Wärest du noch danne geloffen.
Birle, birle bump,
Der Kaiser ist ein Lump.

SWEDISH

GS   1

Bulleri, bulleri bock,
Hur många horn står opp?

Tre du sa', sju de' va,
Bulleri, bulleri, o.s.v.

GS   2

Buller i buller i bock,
Hur många horn står opp?

Fem du sa, fyra de va,
Buller i buller i bock,
Hur många horn står opp?

GS   3

Bulta, bulta bock
Sla pa rock
Hur många horn står det opp?

Tva,
Tva du sa
Fem det va,
Bulta, bulta bock, etc.

GS   4

Bulleri bock
Sla pa rock
Hur många horn sätter bocken opp?

Tva,
Tva du sa',
Fem de va', etc.

GS   5

Haka, faka,
Domla, knaka,
Hevelen, bevelen
Bavelen boff
Hur många horn
Vänder där opp?[82]

Tre,
Tre du sa',
Fem de va', 'c.

---

[82] It will be noted that this text has been influenced by a counting-out rhyme.

GS   6

> Bonka, bonka rögg!
> Ha 'mnoga ho'n stall' dä' opp?

GS   7

> Buller i buller i buller i bock
> Hur många horn sätter bocken opp?

GS   8

> Bullra, bullra bockhorn,
> Hur många horn står upp?
>
> Tva du sa, tre da va,
> Ligg du som du ligger
> Sa lustigt och bra.

GS   9

> Manka frull, manka frull, getahorn a bockahorn.
> Huru många femfingers streck star i värt?

DUTCH

GV   1

> Bok! Bok!
> Hoeveel vingers staan der op?
>
> Die (zegt het getal), die der staon,
> Die dich öm diin naas en oere gaon.

GV   2

> Kievela-kavel,
> A gat vol haver
> Stommeleren blok,
> Hoeveel horens staan der op?

GV   3

> Kiekela-kakel
> Mee a gat vol pestenakelen,
> Kiekeleren haan,
> Gruit hoeveel vingeren dat er staan?

GV   4

> Kievel de kaovel,
> Mij gat vol zaovel,
> Rijnke de tijnke,
> Hoeveel rijnkskes (ringjes) zijnder?

GV   5

> Kievela-kavelen,
> Pietje van den Broeck,
> Hoeveel horekes staan der op a 'n boek?

GV   6

> Hamele,
> Damele,
> Gat vol hamele(n)
> Op de doornlêere broek:
> Hoeveel vingeren steken er oep?

GV   7

> Kiewela, Kauwelen,
> A gat vol nagelen,
> Hoeveel horekes staander op de kop?

GV   8

> Kievela, kavel,
> Mee a gat vol zavel,
> Hoeveel horekens staander?

GV 9
> Sijmen de liever de laver de bock,
> Hoeveel horens staander op?

GV 10
> Die viif die sich
> Langs naas en oure gaon
> Raod de bok
> Raod de geit
> Raod wi mennig
> Hööre dat dao steit.

GV 11
> Kievela-kavel,
> Hoeveel horekes staan der op mijnen boek?

SWISS

GHel 1
> Pumedi, pumedi, Holderstock,
> Wie mange Finger streckt der Bock?
>
> Du hesch es rächt errate,
> Jetzt cha-n-i dir es schöns Tübeli brate
>
> Du hesch es nid errate,
> Jetz cha-n-i dir kes Tübeli brate.

or

> Hättisch drü errate,
> Su hätt dir es schöns Tübeli brate.

GHel 2
> Tipis, tapis, Eierlapis,
> Wi mängs Horn het der Bock
> Uf sinem Chopf?
> Zwöü Horn het der Bock
> Uf sinem Chopf,
> Zwöü stande-n-uf.

GHel 3
> Chnipis, chnopis,
> Abermal e Dopis,
> Wie mängs Horn het uf der Bock?
>
> Hättist du——errote,[83]
> Wärist drunger dänne gschnogge.[84]

GHel 4
> Knipis, knopis, Haberstock,
> Wie mängs Horn hed uf der Bock?
>
> Hest nid errate,
> Chast nid so dänne schnagge,
> Hedisch füfi grate,
> So hed i dir es Fischli brate.

GHel 5
> Gribis, grabis, Eiermues,
> Wi vil Hörner streckt der Bock
> Uf sim Chopf?

---

[83] Leichter Schlag.
[84] Darunter weg gekrochen.

DANISH

GD   1
        Vil du bind', vil du bik,
        Vil du Torngjaerde stik,
        Hvor mange holdes der nu i Vejret?

NORWEGIAN

GN   1
        No ska me pa ny baka brod
            ute i kampanne sky
        Ceitehonn, bukkehonn
        Cissa no kor mange fingrar
        Som striks stend i vere!

SPANISH

RE   1
        Recotín-Recotán
        De la vera vera van,
        Del palacio á la cocina
        Quántos deos tienes encima?

        Si *cinco* digeras
        No me mintieras,
        Los golpes que llevastes
        Tu me los dieras.

RE   2
        Trico, trico, tricotrán,
        La cabrita cordobán.
        El cuchillo ballestero
        Cuántos dedos hay en medio?

        Si hubieras dicho *tantoe,*
        Hubiertas acertao,
        Pero te has equivocao.
        Trico, trico, etc.

RE   3
            A la pe,
            A la me,
       A la corneta corné,
       Al xuaclu maduru:
       Adevina, Xuan cornudo,
       Cuantos deos tienes sobre el cu...?

       Si dijeras tantos,
       No pasarías tan mal;
       Como tienes que pasar.

RE   4
        María Andana la cuartana,
        Dónde vas tan de mañana?
        Del palacio a la cocina,
        Cuántos dedos tienes encima?

        Si tantos dijeres,
        No los perdieres;

Los golpes que llevastes,
Tú me los dieres.

RE   5

Recotin, recotan,
De la bera-bera-ban,
Der (del?) palacio a la cocina,
Cuantos deos tiene 'ncima?

RE   6

Recotin, recotan
Las campanas de San Juan
Unas piden bino
Y otras, piden pan.
Er pan esta 'n la cocina
Cuantos deos tiene 'ncima?

ARGENTINE

REArg 1

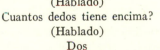

Re - co - tin   Re - co - tan   De la ve - ra

ve - ra van   De la Puer - ta'a la co - ci - na

(Hablado)
Cuantos dedos tiene encima?
(Hablado)
Dos

Si'hu - bie - ras   di - cho   tres

D.C.

te lo ha - bria per - do - na - do.

ITALIAN

RI   1

—Tringa e tringoda—
E si bella e si bona,
E si bella e maritata.
Quantu corna porta la crapa?

Si una dicia,
Mieglin facia.
E mo chi una m' ha' dittu,

Si bella e si bona,
Si bella e maritata.
Quantu corna porta la crapa?

RI   2

Cancara e bella,
Si' bona e si' bella,
Si' bedda maritata:
Quantu corna porta 'a crapa?
Tri avissi dittu,
Lu to nasu fora frittu,
Frittu e frittatu,
Lu to nasu fora cacatu.
Cancara e bella.
Si' bona e si' bella,
Si' bedda maritata:
Quantu corna porta la crapa?

RI   3

Venga, venga, Nicole!
E si' bella e si' bone,
E si' bona a mareta',
Quanta corne tiene 'ncape?

"Ne tenghe *treje*"
E si *quatte* avisse ritte,
'E cavalle fosse scritte,
'E cavalle re lu papa.
Quante corne tiene 'n cape?
"Ne tenghe *seje*"
E se *cinche* avisse ritte, etc.

RI   4   Cavallo dello Re, cavallo dello Papa
Quante corna ha la mi' capra?

RI   5

Biccicuccù Biccicuccù
Quante corna sta quassù?

E se cinque tu dicévi,
La cavalla tu vincevi.

RI   6

Anca e sincona
Sincona maritata
Quantu cucci porta 'na crapa?

RI   7

Tiribulli e tiriballi,
Quantu cucci di casicavalli?

RI   8

Quattru e quattr' ottu,
Scarrica di bottu,
Ciciri e favi;
Quantu corna porta la navi?

Tri tri avissi dittu,
Lu cavaddu di bonfittu,
La zitella maritata;
Quantu curniedda porta 'a me crapa?

RI   9
   So, so, so
   Quante corni ga il bobo
     or
   Mi son tu, ti te son so,
   Quanti corni mostrero. . . .

RI   10
   Tinghe e tingone,
   Si belle e si bone,
   Si belle a mareta,
   Quando corne tiene la crapa?

RI   11
   Pitte i pitte,
   I cavadd'a pare pitte,
   Pitte a lu meire,
   Quante corne tiene 'n cheipe?

Portuguese

RP   1
   Si dissesses que eram (*tantos*)
   Não perdias nem ganhavas,
   Nem levavas cutilada,
   Cutelinho, cutelão;
   Quantos dedos estao n'esta mão?

Béarnese

RF   1
   De coutin, de coutan,
   De las craben d'Aleman;
   De cisèl,
   De pourrèl,
   Quoant de cornes has darrè?

Irish

CI   1
   Hurley, burley, thump the trace,
   The cow ran through the market place.
   Simon Alley hunt the buck,
   How many horns stand up?

CI   2
   Hurley burley trump the case,
   The cow besmeared the market place.
   Simon Nally hunt the buck,
   How many horns stand up?

   (Two) you said and (one) it was,
   Hurley burley, etc.

Scottish

CS   1
   Aon phuicean da 'na phuican.
   Maide sul, cul an duirn,
   Tomhais romhad as do dheigh.
   Cia meud adhairc air a bhoc?

One pook of the pooks/Kiln beam, back of the fist./Guess before and afterwards./How many horns upon the buck?

CS   2
>   Aon mhuchain, da mhuchain,
>   Suim cul duin,
>   Tomhais romhad 's ad' dheigh
>   Cia mheud corag air am boc?

One squeeze, two squeezes/...?/Guess before and afterwards./How many fingers on the buck?

CS   3
>   Imprigan beag
>   Antrigan beag
>   Cul an duin,
>   Maide sula,
>   Tomhais romhad mar is urrain,
>   Cia meud adhairc th' air a bhoc?

Little Imprigan, little Antrigan,/Behind the Dun,/Kiln beam,/Guess before you as you can,/How many horns the buck has on?

CS   4
>   Lura-bocan, Lara-bocan,
>   Gaol an duine, maid' an doruisd,
>   Tomhais romhad mar is aithne,
>   Co meud adharc th' air a bhoc?

Pretty little buck/Dear to man, door stick,/Guess as you are able,/How many horns are on the buck?

> O briagach! cha teid am boc do'n gharadh chail,
> 's cha 'n fhaigh e shath an nochd.

"O liar! the buck will not come into the kail-yard, and will not get his fill tonight."

> Laochain bhochd! theid am boc do'n gharadh
> chail 's gheibh e 'shath 'nochd.

"Poor little hero! the buck will come to the kail-yard and get his fill tonight."

CS   5
>   Aon mhuchain, da mhuchain
>   Maide sur, cul an duirn,
>   Cearc bheag mhineach bhan
>   Rug aon ubh, air an spar,
>   'S thuit e sios air an lar.
>   Tomhais romhad 's do dheigh,
>   Cia mheud adhairc air a' bhoc?

One flick, two flicks,/Probing(?) stick, back of the hand/A small gentle white hen/Had an egg upon the spar/And it fell down to the ground./Guess before you and after/How many horns are upon the buck?

CS   6
>   Imricean beag, Emricean beag,
>   Maide suirn, cul an duirn,
>   Tomhais romhad mar a th' agad.
>   Co miad adhairc air a' bhoc?

Little traveller, little traveller,/Flue stick, back of the fist,/Guess on as well as you can/How many horns has the buck?

Is fírinneach am boc; gheibh e biadh is deoch an so an nochd.
"Truthful is the buck; he will get food and drink here tonight."
Is breugach am boc; cha 'n fhaigh e biadh no deoch an so an nochd.
"Untruthful is the buck; he will not get food and drink here tonight."

CS   7   Imricean beag, Emricean beag,
                     Buicean ciar, ciar am buicean,
                     Crag am buicean.
                     Tomhais romhad mar a th' agad.
                     Co miad adhairc air a' bhoc?

Little traveller, little traveller,/Dusky little buck, dusky little buck,/
Clumsy little buck./Guess on as well as you can/How many horns are
on the buck?

WELSH

CW   1   Buck shee, buck shee buck,
                     How many fingers do I hold up?

CW   2   Buck shee, buck, shee buck,
                     How many fingers do I hold up?

GREEK

Gre   1   Αραί, μπουραί ς' 'του τσομπανη την
                     αυλὴ φύτεψα μιὰ λεμονιά πορτοκαλιά,
                     πόσα ζύλα ς' τὰ βουνά.

UNITED STATES

GAm   1   Mingledy, mingledy, clap, clap, clap,
                     How many fingers do I hold up?
                                 Three
                     Three you said, and *two* it was, etc.

ESTONIAN

FE   1   Sikka, pukka, mitu sarve on sull?
                     Goatie, buckie, how many horns have you got?

TURKISH

Turk 1   Çatal matal kaç çatal?
                     How many prongs has the fork?

Turk 2   Bizim köyün imamı
                     Alttan alır samanı,
                     Üstten çıkar dumanı.
                     Çattı mattı kaç attı?

                     Le prêtre de notre village
                     Prend le foin par dessous,
                     Dont la fumée sort par dessus.
                     Combien a-t-il jeté?

INDIAN

Ind   1   Handol bandol chigari chandol
                Sehel gitti jan tere
                Kette, Kette Bol Teri Mekki Landi Kol.

     Buck has colored spots and horns. Tell me how many, how many.

Ind   2   Tum, Tum, Tariyo; Narasa Ghode Mariyo:
                Jamal ke zhad Neeche, Kitte ande Bol.

     The fine horse is mine. Say how many eggs are there under the jamal tree.

Ind   3   Handol Bandol charke ghodeke chandol
                Jamoonke zhad neeche ghode Kette Bol.

     The horse has spirits and different colors. Say how many horses there
     [grazing] under the jamoon tree.

Ind   4   Atak patak ka tattu
                    Gulal Shahi battu
                    Tu kai ghari ka narial
                    To bol ghunghun kai.

     O thou pony of a stumbling nature, colt of Gulal Shan [an imaginary
     name], for how long hast thou been an adept [in guessing] [if indeed
     thou art one], then guess, blockhead, how many fingers are there.

Ind   5   Tun tun tārā-ke
                    Nāc-ghōre nārā/
                    Jambul-ke jhād-pe
                    Kitte ande bōl//
            bōl kitte ande   jambul-ke jhād-pe

     Tell [me] how many eggs [there are] on the Jambul tree.[85]

List of Variants

GE   1   Gomme, *Traditional Games of England, Scotland, and Ireland,* Vol. 1, 46.
GE   2   Balfour and Thomas, *County Folklore* Vol. 4, 104 (Northumberland).

[85] "The jambul (from Sanskrit *jambu*) is a very common tree in India, with deep-violet, shining edible fruits. The name of the tree figures in one of the ancient names of India: *jambudvīpa.* Monier-Williams has the following note on *jambudvīpa* in his Sanskrit-English Dictionary (Oxford, 1899): '...the central one of the seven continents surrounding the mountain Meru (=India)... ; named so either from the Jambu trees abounding in it; or from an enormous Jambu tree on the (central) Mount Meru visible like a standard to the whole continent.' For *jambu,* M-W gives the meaning 'rose-apple tree' (*Eugenia Jambolana* or another species). The curious thing about the rhyme is that it is not in the local dialect (Marathī), but in a Northern dialect (Hindī), which is a sort of *lingua franca* of India."—CONTRIBUTOR'S NOTE.
"South of Mt. Meru grows the gigantic jambo tree Sudarsana, which, touches the skies, and bears fruit 1,115 cubits in circumference. When the fruits fall to the ground, they make a loud noise, and exude a silvery juice. The juice of the jambo becomes a river, and passes circuitously around Mt. Meru to the region of the Northern Kurus. 'If the juice of that fruit is quaffed, it conduces to peace of mind. No thirst is felt ever after; decrepitude never weakens them.' " (Wallis, *Religion in Primitive Society,* p. 49.)

GE   3   Gutch, *County Folklore,* Vol. 6, 139 (East Yorkshire).

GG   1   Lewalter-Schläger, *Deutsches Kinderlied u. Kinderspiel aus Kassel,* p. 24.

GG   2   Böhme, *Deutsches Kinderlied u. Kinderspiel,* p. 633, no. 523.

GG   3   *Ibid.,* no. 524 (Upper Alsace).

GG   4   *Ibid.,* p. 634, no. 525. (Kassel).

GG   5   *Hessische Blätter,* Vol. 11 (1912), 139.

GG   6   Böhme, *op. cit.,* p. 634, no. 526a.

GG   7   *Ibid.,* no. 526b.

GG   8   *Ibid.,* no. 526c.

GG   9   *Ibid.,* no. 526d.

GG   10   Rausch, *Das Spielzeichnis im 25 Kapitel von Fischarts "Geschichtklitterung" (Gargantua),* p. 45.

GG   11   Meier, *Schwäbische Kinderreime,* pp. 135, 424.

GS   1   Communicated by Dr. J. Ejdestam, of the Landsmålsarkivet, Uppsala.

GS   2   Same source.

GS   3   Communicated by Dr. C. H. Tillhagen, of the Nordiska Museet, Stockholm.

GS   4   Same source.

GS   5   Same source.

GS   6   Communicated by Dr. J. Ejdestam, of the Landsmålsarkivet, Uppsala.

GS   7   Same source.

GS   8   Same source.

GS   9   Same source.

GV   1   de Cock and Teierlinck, *Kinderspel & Kinderlust in Zuid-Nederland,* Vol. 1, 299 (Aalst-Mijlbeke).

GV   2   Communicated by Professor Paul de Keyser, of the Seminarie van Folklore, Rijksuniversiteit, Gent (East Flanders).

GV   3   Same source.

GV   4   *Oostvlaamsche Zanten,* Vol. 13 (November-December, 1938), 250.

GV   5   de Cock and Teierlinck, *op. cit.,* p. 298.

GV   6   *Ibid.,* p. 303.

GV   7   *Oostvlaamsche Zanten* Vol. 13, 250 (Aalst).

GV   8   *Ibid.*

GV   9   *Ibid.,* p. 251.

GV   10   de Cock and Teierlinck, *op. cit.,* p. 299.

GV   11   *Ibid.*

GHel 1   Züricher, *Kinderlieder der deutschen Schweiz,* p. 55, no. 878.

GHel 2   *Ibid.,* p. 56, no. 879 (Bern, Langental).

GHel 3   *Ibid.,* no. 880 (Solothurn).

GHel 4   *Ibid.,* no. 881 (Oberägeri).

GHel 5   *Ibid.,* no. 882 (Laupen).

GD   1   Kristensen, *Danske Börnerim, Remser og Lege,* p. 214.

GN   1   Stoylen, *Barnerim og Leikar,* p. 100.

GAm   1   Newell, *Games and Songs of American Children,* p. 148.

RE   1   Pitré, *Giuochi Fanciulleschi Siciliani,* p. xlvi.

RE   2   Sevilla, *Cancionero popular Murciano,* p. 51.

RE   3   Vigón, *Juegos y Rimas Infantiles,* p. 57 (Asturias).

RE   4   de Soto, *Biblioteca de las Tradiciones Populares Españolas,* Vol. 2, 150.

RE   5   Marín, *Cantos Populares Españolas*, Vol. 1, 51.

RE   6   Pitré, *op. cit.,* Vol. 1, 51.

REArg 1   Communicated by Sr. Carlos Vega, of Buenos Aires.

RI   1   *Archivio per le Tradizioni Popolari*, Vol. 1 (1882), 242 (Calabria).

RI   2   Pitré, *op. cit.,* p. 169.

RI   3   *Ibid.,* p. 173 (Pomigliano).

RI   4   *Ibid.,* p. 174 (Toscana).

RI   5   *Ibid.*

RI   6   *Ibid.,* p. 170 (Noto).

RI   7   *Ibid.,* p. 171 (Chiaramonte e Comiso).

RI   8   *Ibid.,* p. 172 (Acireale).

RI   9   Communicated by Professor Raffaele Corso of Naples.

RI 10   Same source.

RI 11   Same source

RP   1   Pitré, *op. cit.,* p. xlvi.

RF   1   *Ibid.,* p. xlv.

CI   1   Gomme, *op. cit.,* Vol. 2, 449 (County Leitrim).

CI   2   Communicated by Mr. Pádraig mac Gréine, of Béal atha na Laogh.

CS   1   Maclagan, *The Games and Diversions of Argyleshire*, p. 42.

CS   2   *Ibid.*

CS   3   *Ibid.,* pp. 42–43.

CS   4   *Ibid.,* p. 43.

CS   5   *Folklore,* Vol. 17, 228 (Lewis, Outer Hebrides).

CS   6   Communicated by Miss Anna Nic Iain, of the Isle of Barra.

CS   7   Same source.

CW   1   *Folklore Journal,* Vol. 5, 59 (Cornwall).

CW   2   Courtney, *Cornish Feasts and Folklore,* p. 186.

Gre   1   *Folklore Journal,* Vol. 2, 58 (Samos).

Gre   2   Communicated by Professor Phédon Koukoulés, of the University of Athens.

Gre   3   Loucopoulos, Ποιά παιμνίοια παίζουν τὰ ʿΕλληνόπουλα, p. 203.

FE   1   Liiv, *Laste Mängu-tuba,* p. 10.

SS   1   Communicated by Professor Tihomir Georgevic, of Belgrade, Yugoslavia.

SHerc 1   Communicated by Mr. Nikola Vujnovic, of Burmazi, Hercegovina.

Turk 1   Communicated by Mr. Pertev Boratav, of the Tarih Dil Coğrafya Fakültesi, Ankara.

Turk 2   Same source.

Ind   1   Communicated by Mr. M. H. Shah, of the Rural Uplift Society, Indi, District of Bijapur, Bombay Presidency.

Ind   2   Same source.

Ind   3   Same source.

Ind   4   Communicated by Mr. Mam Chand Sandilya, of Jhajjar, District of Rohtak, Panjab.

Ind   5   Communicated by Dr. V. S. Sukthankar, of the Bhandarkar Oriental Research Institute, Poona.

Jap   1   Communicated by Professor Sanki Ichikawa, of the Tokyo Imperial University.

List of References

Annali dell' Institut., Vol. 38 (1866), 326–29.

Archäologische Zeitung, Vol. 29 (1871), 151–56. Berlin, 1843–1885.

Archivio per lo studio delle tradizioni popolari, Vol. 1, 254. Palermo, Torino, 1882—.

Balfour, M. C., and N. W. Thomas, *County Folklore*, Publications of the Folklore Society, Vol. 4, 104. London, 1904.

Beckwith, Martha W., *Jamaican Folklore,* Memoirs of the American Folklore Society, No. 21, 15. New York, 1928.

Böhme, Franz Magnus, *Deutsches Kinderlied u. Kinderspiel,* pp. 526ff. Leipzig, 1924.

Classical Review, Vol. 39, 118. London, 1887—.

Collin, Carl S. R., " 'Bucca, bucca, quot sunt hic?': Beiträge zur Geschichte eines Kinderspieles," in *Studier tillegnade Esaias Tegnér,* pp. 369–79. Lund, 1918.

Courtney, M. A., *Cornish Feasts and Folklore,* p. 186. Penzance, 1890.

Daremberg and Saglio, *Dictionnaire des antiquités grecques et romaines d'après les textes et les monuments....*Paris, 1877–1918, Vol. 3 (1889–1890), *s.v. micatio.*

de Cock, A., and I. Teierlinck, *Kinderspel & Kinderlust in Zuid-Nederland.* Gent, 1902.

de Fouquières, Becq, *Les jeux des anciens,* pp. 290–94. Paris, 1873.

de Soto, Hernández, *Biblioteca de las tradiciones populares españolas,* Vol. 2, 150.

Enäjärvi-Haavio, Elsa, *The Game of Rich and Poor,* Folklore Fellows Communications No. 100. Helsinki, 1932.

Folklore. London, 1890—.

Folklore Journal, 8 vols. London, 1883–1889.

Friedländer, Ludwig, *Petronii Cena Trimalchionis,* p. 325. Leipzig, 1906.

Gomme, Alice B., *Traditional Games of England, Scotland, and Ireland,* 2 vols. London, 1894, 1898.

Gutch, Eliza, *County Folklore*, Publications of the Folklore Society, Vol. 6, 139. London, 1912.

Hessische Blätter für Volkskunde. Leipzig, 1902—.

Igry narodov SSSR. Akademia, Moskva-Leningrad, 1933.

Ivanov, P., "Igry krest'anskih dêtei v kupanskom uêzdê," in *Sbornik Har'kovskago istoriko-filologiceskoago obsestva* (1886–1890).

Kapica, O. I., *Detskij folk'lor.* Leningrad, 1928.

Karadžić, V., *Zivot i Običaji Naroda Srpskoga.* Belgrade, 1957.

Kiss, A., *Magyar Gyermekjatek-gyüjtemeny.* Budapest, 1891.

Kristensen, E. T., *Danske Börnerim, Remser og Lege.* Aarhus, 1896.

Lewalter, Johann, and Georg Schläger, *Deutsches Kinderlied u. Kinderspiel.* Kassel, 1911.

Liiv, J., *Laste Mängu-tuba.* Tartu (Dorpat), 1879.

Ljetopis (journal of the Matica Srpska). Novi Sad, 1827—.

Loucopoulos, D., *Ποιὰ παιγνιοια παίζουν τὰ 'Ελληνοπουλα.* Athens, 1926.

Maclagan, Robert Craig, *The Games and Diversions of Argyleshire,* Publications of the Folklore Society, Vol. 47. London, 1901.

Marín, F. R., *Cantos populares españolas,* Vol. 1. Sevilla, 1882.

Marquadt, Karl Joachim, *Das Privatleben der Römer, Handbuch der römischen Alterthümer*, Vol. 7. Leipzig, 1886.

Maspons y Labron, F., *Jochs de la Infancia*. Barcelona, 1874.

Meier, E., *Schwäbische Kinderreime*. Tübingen, 1851.

Meinsma, K. O., "Een merkwaardig drietal: koekoek, hoorndrager, hahnrey," in *Taal en Letteren*, Vol. 4 (1894), 177ff.

Newell, W. W., *Games and Songs of American Children*, 3rd ed. New York and London, 1911.

Okkola, Toivo, *Suomen kansan kilpa- ja kotileikkejä*. Helsinki, 1928.

Oostvlaamsche Zanten, Vol. 13 (November-December 1928), 245f.

Otto, August, *Die Sprichwörter u. sprichwörtlichen Redensarten der Römer*. Leipzig, 1890.

Pitré, Giuseppe, *Giuochi Fanciulleschi Siciliani, Biblioteca delle Tradizioni Popolari Siciliane*, Vol. 13. Palermo, 1883.

Pokrovskii, E. A., *Dêtskie igry*. Moskva, 1895.

Rausch, Heinrich A., *Das Spielzeichnis im 25 Kapitel von Fischarts "Geschichtklitterung" (Gargantua)*. Strassburg diss., 1908.

Rochholz, Ernst Ludwig, *Alemannisches Kinderlied u. Kinderspiel*. Leipzig, 1857.

Sevilla, Alberto, *Cancionero popular Murciano*. Murcia, 1921.

Simrock, Karl, *Das deutsche Kinderbuch*, 3rd ed. Basel, 1879.

Stoylen, Bernt, *Norske Barnerim og Leikar*. Kristiania, 1899.

Tylor, E. B., *Primitive Culture*, 3rd ed. [i.e., American] from 2nd English ed. New York, 1889.

Vrčevic, V., *Srpske narodne Igre*. Belgrade, 1868.

Wallis, W. D., *Religion in Primitive Society*. New York, 1939.

Wilkinson, J. Gardner, *The Manners and Customs of the Ancient Egyptians*, ed. Samuel Birch, 2 vols. London, 1878.

Zelenin, Dmitrij, *Russische (ostslavische) Volkskunde*. Berlin u. Leipzig, 1927.

Züricher, Gertrud, *Kinderlied u. Kinderspiel im Kanton Bern*. Zürich, 1902.

———, *Kinderlieder der deutschen Schweiz*. Basel, 1926.

Tina's Lullaby

Hugh Tracey

In this brief study, Hugh Tracey, an authority on African ethnomusicology, attempts to track down the origin of an American Negro lullaby. In order to hypothesize even an approximate location in Africa from which the lullaby may have been brought, Tracey had to take both tune and text into account. The complete study of folk music requires considerable knowledge of both music and language. The working back from the American Negro folksong to a possible East African child's song shows, in miniature, the problems, and some of the techniques employed in solving them, found in the historical study of folksong. Tracey's study also demonstrates the remarkable stability of oral tradition in that "meaningless" words were transmitted from one generation to another with surprising accuracy.

The Library was recently requested by Dr. Ruth L. Bartholomew of Paine College, Augusta, Georgia, U.S.A., to assist her in placing an old Negro lullaby which had been handed down by succeeding generations of an American family in that city who were keen to find out from which part of Africa the song might have come.

The first transcriptions of the song on paper which she sent us had proved baffling, and so we asked Dr. Bartholomew to send us a tape recording as she said that it was still remembered and could be sung by an old lady of over eighty years, Mrs. Johnson, who was a member of the family.

The tape duly arrived, together with a description of the circumstances surrounding the introduction of the lullaby into the States. The details were supplied by Mrs. Clifford Stephens, a direct descendant of Mr. Alexander Spencer. She wrote:

> Alexander Spencer felt that his daughter Isabella needed another nurse for her two children. When he heard that a slave boat had arrived in Charleston, he went there to purchase a suitable slave for his grandchildren. A tall,

Reprinted from *African Music*, Vol. 2, No. 4 (1961), 99–101, by permission of the author, who is also editor of *African Music*.

369

splendid-looking woman was offered and Alexander Spencer, being the highest bidder, got the woman and took her back to Augusta. The year was about 1854.

Before he left Charleston, he was told that this Tina was an African princess and had been captured with her eleven-year-old son. During the voyage from Africa to Charleston her son had died and was buried at sea. There was no substantiation for this story except the information given Mr. Spencer at the slave market.

Tina never learned to speak English, in fact made no effort to learn the language, but she managed to communicate with the other slaves in her own way. She was a wonderful nurse, took faithful care of the two children, and lived long enough to nurse a second generation of children without ever speaking a word of English.

All of the children and all of the slaves were devoted to Tina. The lullaby that she sang to the two generations of children has come down to the fourth, fifth, and sixth generations of children in the family. The soothing minor melody has been passed on from generation to generation, and the words as nearly as possible have been carried on without any knowledge of what the English translation would be. That the song is beloved is evidenced by the way it has been handed down from generation to generation to all branches of the family.

Several persons interested in this lullaby and its origin have tried in vain to locate the African dialect in which it is written. The meaning of its words will probably always remain a mystery to us but the song will never lose its charm.

The words of the lullaby as transcribed in America, read thus:

> A e yat ta rum bam bu wah ke dazee.
> Ae chik ah lu mi lun dah.
> Nick ah lu-u la me put awah.
> Nick ah lu-u la me wa-ah.

It is clear that this version contained several anglicisms in particular such vowel sounds as the long "a" which nowadays is more correctly written as the short "e" in African vernaculars. We, therefore, rewrote the text from the recorded voice of Mrs. Johnson and it then appeared to us in this form:

> E-e yat ta-rum-ba-mbo-o wa ki-de-zi
> Yei ni-ka-lu-mai la-nda.
> Ni-ka lu-u la-mi-i prr wa.
> Ni-ka lu-u la-a-mi wa-a.

This version clearly had a Bantu East Africa flavor about it rather than a Sudanic, West African, but the melody of the lullaby as sung by Mrs. Johnson in a western modality (as no African mode introduced by Tina could possibly have lasted) had clearly undergone a sea change and, in addition, the song was likely to have been antiphonal in its original African version.

The sounds of the lyric, conveyed aurally and without comprehension of their meaning through several generations of white American children, must surely have altered somewhat in the process; but not enough to prevent our guessing possible minor changes which would enable the sense of the original

to shine out. There were several clues, all of which indicated a Shona or
Manyika origin, possibly from the Zambezi valley where the "l" and "r"
sounds are freely interchangeable. Where a Shona-speaking person says "r"
a Nyanja or Ma'nganja from north of the river will change it to "l".

Tina, they said, while refusing to speak English, made herself well understood to other slaves, possibly those from her own region. It is therefore
perhaps not too much of a liberty to correct "l" sounds as sung by Mrs.
Johnson to the "r" sounds in this next version:

> Eya, tarumba mbambo wake tenzi.
> Yei, ndikatumai muranda
> Ndikarurami pari wo?
> Ndikarurami wo-ye.

Here, at last, is a typical child's song from the eastern Shona-speaking
people. The word *tenzi* is still in everyday use in the Sabi valley, the southerly
region of the Manyika people and, if the other corrections are allowed, it
would place Tina's origin as being somewhere within Manyika-speaking
country. If she had come from the more northerly districts of her language
group, either from the borders of Mtoko, or from down below the Inyanga
hills in Moçambique towards the ancient trading center of Sena on the
Zambezi, Tina would no doubt have been familiar with the "l" sound in
place of the "r". The construction of the sentences, however, suggests
Manyika rather than Ma'nganja from just across the river.

It is known that nearly a hundred shiploads of slaves from the Zambezi
basin were taken round the Cape to join in the convoys of slave ships from
the Ivory, Gold, and Slave Coasts, although this relatively small East African
contribution to the total slave market has frequently been overlooked.

We feel justified therefore in placing Tina's origin somewhere within the
Eastern Shona or Manyika regions, between the Manyikaland highlands and
the coast or, roughly, somewhere between the towns of Umtali and Beira.

The English translation of the song as it now stands is a little obscure and
with the help of a Southern Rhodesian Manyika and Ndau speaker from
Chipinga, we offer the following:

> Yes, I ran quickly to his father, the Chief.
> Indeed, I have sent a messenger.
> Where shall I go to straightaway?
> Then I will go straightaway.

A small child has been sent by his *Tenzi*, the headman of the village, and,
no doubt, a senior relative or *Bambo,* to take a message to some nearby
village and the child who conveyed the Tenzi's instructions now asks for
another mission. As a child's verse this would be in keeping with many a
folksong of the region, reflecting a very local incident.

We suggest, therefore, that we have located Tina's home country within
a reasonable margin of possible error and there is little doubt that the old

Georgian or South Carolina lullaby is a product of Zambezia. The question now remains whether any African from this region can identify the tune or provide an equivalent song which could be as nearly related to Tina's lullaby as her words. Songs of a hundred years ago have had time to change considerably in an African village, and we are not hopeful that any further detective work would bring added results. In the meanwhile the descendants of Alexander Spencer of Augusta, Georgia, can be fairly certain that their nanny was an East African Tina.

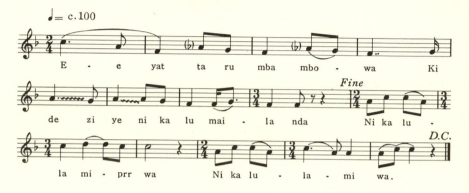

Tina's Lullaby, as sung by Mrs. Johnson, Augusta, Georgia. Transcribed by A.T.N.T.

Origin and Significance of
Pennsylvania Dutch Barn Symbols

August C. Mahr

Folk art has not received as much attention from folklorists as has folk music. For example, in American folklore journals the articles on folk music far outnumber those on folk art, probably because more European folk music survived in the New World than did European folk art. Nonetheless, some folk art, such as quiltwork, embroidery, Easter egg coloring, and costume design, continues to thrive in many areas of this country. In this essay, August Mahr, Professor Emeritus of German at Ohio State University, examines the Pennsylvania Dutch Barn symbol, which is one of the most striking examples of American folk art.

The difficulties in tracing a particular folk design are perhaps greater than for other types of folklore. In no other form does one find the incredible variety of objects to investigate in searching for one specific motif. As Mahr's study illustrates, the same motif can occur on objects as diverse as a harness ornament, the back of a chair, a piece of linen lace, and the side of a barn.

Noteworthy in this essay are the skillful use of barn typology and the historical records of immigration into Ohio to illuminate the possible historical origin of barn symbols. Also of interest is Mahr's distinction between the objective and the subjective significance of folk material. The folk may not be aware of the historical origin of their material, but they do have strong emotional ties to this material. Mahr's consideration of what the barn symbols mean to the Pennsylvania Dutch people is one of the most valuable parts of his article. His account of his fieldwork, in which he received information in the "native" language but not in English, provides a marvelous insight into the nature of the relationship between folk and folklore. As their language belongs to them, so also does their folklore. The collector using another language is by definition an outsider and is normally not permitted to share the in-group material, particularly if it is secret rather than public folklore.

Those interested in learning more about Pennsylvania Dutch folklore, one of the richest bodies of tradition in the United States, may consult

Reprinted from *The Ohio Archaeological and Historical Quarterly*, Vol. 54 (1945), 1–32, by permission of the author and the Ohio Historical Society.

Richard Dorson's description of this unique regional culture in *American Folklore* (Chicago, 1959), pp. 76–90, 291–92; and his sampling of their folklore in *Buying the Wind* (Chicago, 1964), pp. 107–61.

On a great number of Pennsylvania Dutch barns,[1] there are geometrical ornaments painted on the outside walls; ornaments which, as a rule, show some sort of star within a circular disk (Figs. 1, 2, 8, 10b). They occur most frequently in Berks and the neighboring counties; less frequently, in other parts of Pennsylvania; and, locally, even in Ohio and other states of the Union where Pennsylvania Dutch farmers have settled.

Due to Ohio's close proximity to Pennsylvania, as well as to its importance, in early frontier days, as both a temporary and permanent place of settlement for eastern farmers venturing westward, it is in Ohio that not only barns of

FIGURE 1. Barn near Circleville, Pickaway County, Ohio. Courtesy of the Ohio Historical Society Library.

[1] This study grew out of a paper read before the Anthropology Section of the Ohio Academy of Science, at its annual meeting, in May 1943, at Columbus, Ohio. The writer is glad to express his gratitude to Professor Edgar N. Transeau of Ohio State University for the photographs taken in Pennsylvania, of barns shown in these pages; to Dean Carl F. Wittke, and Professor Clarence Ward, both of Oberlin College, for photographs and scholarly aid; to Professors John W. Price, and Wilmer G. Stover, both of Ohio State University, and to Dr. James H. Rodabaugh and Mrs. Margaret Stutsman, of the Ohio State Archaeological and Historical Society, and Mrs. Mary Jane Meyer, of the Ohio War History Commission, for helpful fieldwork; to Dr. Jean Weltfish, of Columbia University, for valuable bibliographical advice; to the Graduate School of Ohio State University for generous help in securing the illustrative material; and last but not least, to the publishing houses, in London, of A. Zwemmer, Macmillan & Co., Ltd., and Methuen & Co., Ltd., for their permission to reproduce pictures, from works, published under their imprint, as illustrations of this article.

Pennsylvania Dutch structure are more frequently found than anywhere else outside of Pennsylvania, but here one may also see the barn symbols that are so striking a characteristic of the Pennsylvania Dutch counties mentioned above.

The Pennsylvania Dutch barn in question is of the so-called Swiss bank-barn type. It means that it is erected along an embankment in such a way that its main entrance door leads to the heavily planked floor of its wooden upper story. This floor is at the same time the ceiling of the lower story formed by the stone base structure which contains the stables for the livestock and is accessible through doors on the lower level of the slanting terrain. As a rule, the barn, in its full length, carries a wooden fore-bay which projects from the upper story and overhangs the outside wall of the stables to the extent of about six to eight feet. Frequently, however, the barn is built on level ground with a ramp leading to the upper story. In Pennsylvania as well as Ohio, these barns are usually red, often with white arches over the white-framed fore-bay openings. Wherever barn symbols are found, they are painted in various colors on the fore-bay, or the back, or the gable sides, or on all four walls of the wooden superstructure.

The one or other barn with such star-shaped symbols on its outer board walls is found in practically every region of Ohio where Pennsylvania Dutch from Berks County or its neighborhood have settled. The writer has selected at random a few locations where they are in evidence today:

Route 188, 1 mile east of Circleville, Pickaway County; farm of Mr. S. Paul Valentine (red barn with two black-and-yellow eight-pointed stars in white disks on fore-bay). This is, without a question, one of the finest Berks County barns in Ohio. It was erected, c. 1840, by a man of the name of Berger, from Pennsylvania. With each repainting, the symbols, that are as old as the barn, were retouched in black-and-yellow in order to retain the original appearance of the building (Fig. 1).

Route 23, between Columbus and Delaware, a mile north of Stratford, Delaware County (red barn with three six-pointed stars on fore-bay).

Route 203, between Delaware and Radnor, Delaware County (red barn with three six-pointed stars on fore-bay, and one eight-pointed star in each gable). The barn is known as "the old Sharadin barn."

Route 33, between Logan and Rock Bridge, Hocking County, 2–3 miles south of Rock Bridge (red barn with a star in each gable).

Route 73, between Waynesville and Franklin, Warren County (barn with three sky-blue five-pointed stars on each gable side).

Route 18, 2 miles north of Republic, Seneca County; farm of Mr. L. J. Neikirk (red barn with white curved club-armed swastika[2]).

Route 53, 7 miles north of Upper Sandusky, Wyandot County; farm of Mr. R. R. Everhart (red barn with white five-pointed star in white ring). Date on barn: 1916.

Despite the considerable number of additional places where such barn symbols occur in Ohio, it is an undeniable fact that they are gradually passing

---

[2] Cf. *infra*, p. 391.

FIGURE 2. Barn at Kempton, Berks County, Pennsylvania. Courtesy of the Ohio Historical Society Library.

out of existence, the main reason being that their magic symbolism is rapidly dropping into oblivion under the leveling effect of the changed environment. Although to a much lesser degree, the same holds true for the Pennsylvania Dutch countryside proper: about fifty years ago practically no barn in Berks County was without such symbols; today they have become much rarer.

By far the majority of Germans that settled in Ohio up to 1820 did not come from Germany directly but from Pennsylvania[3] and, in particular, from Berks County. The organized Moravian (and other sectarian) colonies excepted, settlers from Berks County are frequently listed in early Ohio local records. Trepte mentions several German families from that county who, in 1796, founded and named "Miamisburg" (Montgomery County).[4] About 1810, the settlers of Germantown (Montgomery County, Ohio), almost without an exception, were Germans from Berks and Center Counties.[5] Other Pennsylvania counties in the neighborhood of Berks that appear in the records, especially of Montgomery County, Ohio, as having contributed German settlers, are Lancaster County,[6] York County,[7] and Lebanon County.[8]

Pennsylvania Dutch immigration into Ohio after 1820—this being approximately the last year covered by Trepte's excellent study—has not yet been

[3] H. Trepte, *Deutschtum in Ohio* (Doctoral dissertation, Leipzig, 1931) [in *Deutsch-Amerikanische Geschichtsblätter*] (*German-American Review*), Vol. 32 (Chicago, 1932), 174ff.

[4] *Ibid.*, p. 308; see also note (a): "This [Berks] was one of the counties that gave Ohio most of her Pennsylvania Dutch" (trans. A. C. M.).

[5] *Ibid.*, pp. 312 and 313, n. (a), (c), and (g).

[6] *Ibid.*, pp. 309 and 322.

[7] *Ibid.*, pp. 308 and 323.

[8] *Ibid.*, p. 313, n. (e).

sufficiently explored to furnish reliable data. Yet, it is definitely certain that within the next few decades after 1820, a great number of Germans from Pennsylvania and, particularly, from Berks and the neighboring counties established themselves in various parts of Ohio.[9]

It is an outstanding characteristic of the Pennsylvania Dutch that they have emigrated from Pennsylvania in groups rather than individually and that, thereby, they have preserved a great many of their traditions and general habits of life in the new environment. What, therefore, in the subsequent pages is said about the Pennsylvania Dutch and their barn symbols in Pennsylvania basically applies also to those in Ohio or other locations where they have settled. This study, however, is concerned with the fundamental facts about these symbols rather than with their present-day application.

The barn symbols are popularly called "Hex Signs," that is, protective magic against witchcraft. The "Dutch" in Pennsylvania and, in particular, the owners of barns that bear such marks assure the inquisitive stranger, however, that the object of these designs is exclusively decorative. Obviously, they are sensitive about their "Hex Signs," especially so if that term is used, and even the most tactful of investigators soon finds out that he has been handling a "hot potato."

A similar guardedness in this matter prevails among some authors of books on Pennsylvania Dutch life and customs, especially among those of native stock who are sensitive of the feelings of their relatives and friends. It is not often that one finds a writer, himself of Pennsylvania Dutch extraction, expressing himself with the refreshing frankness of Mr. Weygandt who writes: "The symbols are supposed to keep lightning from striking the barn that has them painted on its wooden sides, and to prevent the animals housed in the barn from being bewitched, or 'ferhexed' as we say in the vernacular."[10] Some of the native authors touch upon the subject lightly in smiling embarrassment. Others beat about the bush with vague phrases of apology for what might look like superstition unbecoming an otherwise quite sober-minded group of Americans. One of the authors has even tried to remove the stigma of superstition by proving that, far from being "Hex Signs," all the various barn symbols are "the Lilies of Ephrata" in disguise.[11] The beautifully illustrated book provides edifying reading to the fancier of local sentimental literature, but it helps in no way to solve the question about the origin and meaning of the barn symbols.

---

9 For instance, the writer knows, from family records, that a group of families which almost might be called a "colony," about the middle of the last century, moved from Berks and Dauphin Counties, Pennsylvania, to Delaware County, Ohio, where they are still in evidence.

10 C. Weygandt, *The Red Hills*, ... (Philadelphia, 1929), p. 126; similar statements, *ibid.*, pp. 10f., 65f.

11 J. J. Stoudt, *Consider the Lilies How They Grow. An Interpretation of the Symbolism of Pennsylvania German Art* (Allentown, Penn., 1937).

What is needed here, is an unbiased and unemotional approach. The key point is that the Pennsylvania Dutch farmers, particularly in Berks County and its neighborhood, always have been, and in many respects still are, not merely farmers but peasants in the best European sense. Not everyone who tills the soil and raises livestock is a peasant. Whereas the mere farmer's activities are based on cold empiric facts that may be learned in agricultural schools, the peasant's life is governed by fixed customs, if not ritual, peculiar to his particular group and origin. These customs attend all his chores in the fields, in the cattle barn, in the house, and rule his domestic relations, his dealings with his fellows, his dress, his habits of eating and drinking, his recreations, in short, every step of his earthly pilgrimage from the cradle to the grave. Most of these rules and customs reach down into times immemorial. They contain many taboos that today are no longer obvious, and they include innumerable symbolic actions and signs traceable to prehistoric magic as well as to pagan mythology and ritual.

The Pennsylvania Dutch are quite unique in this country, in that they have tenaciously clung to a great many of the peasant traditions which their ancestors had brought with them from the Old Country. Again and again, they migrated in larger and smaller groups from the same parts, mostly the Upper Rhine, the Rhenish Palatinate (*Rheinpfalz*) and Switzerland, but also from other West and South German states. They are further unique in that they maintained their communal form of life in the New World, both to their own benefit and that of William Penn and his Quaker associates. The greater number of these so-called "Palatines" (*Pfälzer*) landed, mostly in the harbor of Philadelphia, between 1710 and 1775.[12]

This adherence of the Pennsylvania Dutch, for more than two centuries, to the native peasant customs of their German forefathers can only be explained by the fact that they did not lose their original group consciousness after they had settled in America. Instead of being readily absorbed by the new environment, as were the countless individual settlers from other German, and non-German, peasant communities of Europe, the Pennsylvania Dutch possessed in the peasant traditions of their old homeland a cultural force that was sufficiently strong to shape their new environment into a peasant community of distinctive character. In achieving this, they were substantially aided by a very happy coincidence: the amazing similarity between their old homeland and Pennsylvania. This similarity not only extends to the physiognomy of the landscape but also to climate and soil conditions. There is hardly a region in the Keystone State which has not an almost exact counterpart somewhere in southwestern Germany. Such exceptionally good fortune allowed them to continue in their new home, with a minimum of adjustments, where they had left

12 Cf. R. B. Strassburger, *Pennsylvania German Pioneers,* 3 vols. (Norristown, Penn., 1934). This is a publication of the original lists of arrivals in the port of Philadelphia from 1727 to 1808.

off in the Old Country. Nothing, in the new environment, was so essentially different as to estrange them from their native peasant views and practices.[13]

Strangely enough, this important basic fact has been ignored by a recent writer about "the Dutch country."[14] He has the feeling that there is a derogatory connotation implied in the term "peasant" since to him "peasant" and "serf" are synonymous. His definition of "peasantry" makes no allowance for its most distinguishing, *cultural* feature: namely, the age-old devotion of the peasant, steadfastly carried from generation to generation, to fixed customs that govern every phase of his life. On the grounds of this omission, Mr. Weygandt denies the peasant character of the rural Pennsylvania Dutch community. Indeed, his particular notion of what constitutes "peasantry" leaves him no other choice.

One may grant some of his prerequisites "for the development of a peasantry," such as "a long-established civilization," "stability in social conditions," and "a very slowly changing order down the years." But peasantry certainly does *not* include "a rigid caste system, recognized and unchallenged privilege, a frank and ungrudging acknowledgment on the part of the many that a chosen few are set above the crowd." It does not agree with the facts of history that "there must be all these conditions or a peasantry cannot be."

The free peasants of Switzerland, for example, have maintained for more than six hundred years their model democratic republic, with its rural citizenry adhering, as staunchly as ever, to their magnificent old peasant culture. For another example, there is the free peasantry of Dithmarschen who, in 1500, victoriously defended, in the battle of Hemmingstedt, their liberty against the combined nobles of Denmark and Holstein. True, there are regions where the peasants used to live in a condition of thraldom; but there are surely as many where, for ages, they have been living as their own masters on their own soil. These well-known facts certainly do not bear out the statement: "Above all there must be laborers on land of which they do not themselves own a foot for peasantry to be. A peasantry presupposes an agricultural society, in which the laborer works not for himself, but for a landowner. A peasantry cannot exist in a country in which a landlord class does not exist, in which authority and position and money do not persist in a family generation after generation."

Of course, a peasantry of Mr. Weygandt's definition could not exist in the United States, but that does not alter the fact that the Pennsylvania Dutch deserve credit for having preserved, right in our midst, what according to all

---

[13] That is exactly the reverse of what happened to the Holland Dutch immigrants, who eventually became the "Boers" in South Africa. Citing S. Cloete's *The Turning Wheel,* R. Peattie (*Geography in Human Destiny* [New York: Stewart, 1940], pp. 34f.) demonstrates how the totally different environment transformed these stolid Dutch peasants into impassioned, adventuring pioneers, an entirely novel type that retained next to none of its ancestral peasant features.

[14] C. Weygandt, *The Dutch Country* (New York, 1939), pp. 109f.

accepted standards is a true German peasant culture. The majority of those immigrants from the Palatinate and Switzerland, who came to Pennsylvania by the shipload throughout most of the eighteenth century, were peasants in the best possible sense. Indeed, a great many of them brought to this country more than enough money for the purchase, and subsequent cultivation, of large tracts of fertile farmlands. Had they been, in their German homeland, down-trodden day laborers or serfs, they would never have been the model farmers that they are still today, nor would they have possessed the moral dignity and cultural vigor prerequisite to maintaining themselves, in the New World, as a close-knit and unique peasant community.

The barn symbols here discussed occur in America exclusively with the Pennsylvania Dutch peasantry. Hence one may expect some light on their origin and significance from analogous occurrences in German peasant art which, like the peasant art of any part of Europe, is a depository of prehistoric and pagan values otherwise long obliterated.

Of the unlimited number of different ornamental patterns that exist on earth, only a very few have been designed as vessels for symbolic concepts. Most of the symbolic ornaments encountered in Pennsylvania Dutch peasant art and, in particular, as barn signs, are stars with five, six, eight, or more, points (Figs. 1, 2, 8, 10b), but there also occurs the one or other design that is not a star, as, for instance, the Swastika (Fig. 10a).

As one examines the general distribution of these symbolic patterns one easily sees that their use by the Pennsylvania Dutch is just one instance among many others. Up to the present day, and regardless of period styles and local tendencies in the decorative arts, they occur in the peasant art and craft, not of Germany alone, but of all European countries without an exception.

Naturally, the question arises: where and why have they originated? And next: why and how have they spread the way they did?

There is ample evidence[15] that these various symbols that occur in European peasant art, inclusive of the Pennsylvania Dutch area, have their origin in a Cult of the Sun that during the Bronze Age was practiced "in Ireland on the west and throughout the greater part of Europe."[16]

It is more than probable that the cultic initiative came from the Mediterranean, and that the symbols, along with the Sun Cult, were carried over well-established trade routes all throughout Europe. Some of these routes, the earliest in fact, were the sea lanes by which the Cretans and Mycenaeans transported their finished products, mainly bronze objects and pottery, not only along the entire Mediterranean coast but also "to Great Britain for copper and tin; to Ireland for gold; they also visited the coasts of the English

---

[15] Cf. *infra*, pp. 385ff.

[16] H. F. Cleland, *Our Prehistoric Ancestors* (New York: Coward-McCann, Inc., 1928), pp. 254ff.

Channel, and the North Sea; and traded for amber with the inhabitants of Denmark."[17]

By far the greater exchange of goods took place, however, over cross-continental trade routes. Two of them led to the amber deposits of the North: one ran from the Adriatic over the Brenner Pass, down the river Inn to the Danube, and from there, across the Bohemian Forest, down the valley of the Moldau and along the river Elbe to its mouth. Another started at the Gulf of Trieste, ran northeast to Laibach and Graz and descended to the Danube. "The tributary March was then ascended and, after crossing Moravia, the route passed through Silesia and followed the Oder to the [Baltic] coast." A branch route "diverged from this one at Posen and followed the Vistula to Danzig."

"A third less important route led to the North Sea from the Mediterranean, by way of the Rhone and the Rhine."

"Besides these main 'Amber Routes' there were routes across Alpine passes to France and Germany which followed the Rhone, Loire, Seine and Rhine, and routes to and along the broad Danube Valley by way of the Inn, Save, and other tributaries."[18]

Considering the indubitable existence of the Sun Cult among the people who utilized these trade routes both by land and sea for over a thousand years previous to the dawn of history, one is not surprised to find the symbolic emblems of that Cult spread, even today, among the folk of the entire area that was once traversed by these trade channels. The most significant of all was the Danube Valley route, not only because of its importance as a direct connection between Southeastern and West Central Europe but also because it was traversed on a great number of points by the "Amber Routes." The most careful and methodical exploration of Bronze Age sites, throughout the entire European continent, over many decades, has proved that "the Sun Cult must have been in honor throughout Europe for at least 1500 years, and was consequently one of the most enduring religions the world has known."[19]

Beyond being graphic representations of the powers venerated, the symbolic signs in practically every known religion that possesses such, are widely used for magic purposes. The people carry them on their bodies as protective amulets, they apply them to their houses, stables, and barns, furniture and household utensils, either to ward off evil influences or to enlist the aid of beneficent powers in securing fertility and good health for themselves, their livestock and their crops. This being true today, in Christian countries, it must have been even more so in prehistoric times when religion and magic were one and the same.

---

[17] *Ibid.*, pp. 261f.

[18] The above survey of the Bronze Age trade routes of Europe has been condensed, and partly quoted, from Cleland's *Our Prehistoric Ancestors*, pp. 256ff., where also a good map is found (p. 258).

[19] *Ibid.*, p. 255.

It has been argued that designs of this nature may have originated independently in various parts of the earth. That may be true for a very few and
very primitive ornamental patterns, such as straight and curved lines, both
single and parallel; zigzag and wavy bands; crosshatch; triangles, quad-
rangles and circles. It *cannot* apply, however, wherever a symbolic significance
attaches to the ornament. Once a design has acquired the quality of symbol,
this quality inevitably functions as the vehicle by which the design as such is
carried from place to place. This elemental interrelation remains constant,
regardless of modifications that both the symbolic meaning and the design
itself may have undergone during their wanderings throughout the ages. It
also explains why today these designs are promiscuously and interchangeably
applied as propitious symbols, while their original function, magic or ritual,
has long been obliterated or, at best, can be but vaguely discerned through
the veil of time.

No matter what amount of migration and political regrouping has taken
place on the continent, during the Early European Iron (Hallstadt) Age and
the subsequent eras of history, the ancient symbols have continued in use
among the European peasantry, up to this day. This proves indirectly that all
participants in such migrations and political reshufflings, invaders and invaded
alike, possessed the identical substratum of magic concepts and were
unaffected by subsequent religious creeds of a higher spirituality successively
superimposed upon them. It is still in this magic substratum, unchanged

FIGURE 3. Cretan terracotta sarcophagus with symbols. From H. Th.
Bossert, *The Art of Ancient Crete*, Fig. 362. Courtesy of A. Zwemmer,
London.

FIGURE 4. Mycenaean gold pendant. From C. Schuchhardt, *Schliemann's Excavations*, Fig. 152. Courtesy of Macmillan & Co., Ltd., London.

FIGURE 5. Mycenaean gold foil disk. From H. Th. Bossert, *The Art of Ancient Crete,* Fig. 193k. Courtesy of A. Zwemmer, London.

throughout the ages and apparently unchangeable, that even today all popular credences are rooted. For the validity of this statement it matters not *what* magic is used, but *that* magic is used.

The first dating of the application of such symbolic designs in the European Bronze Age becomes possible through their occurrence in the Aegean Culture of the Eastern Mediterranean.[20] They are found on the Island of Crete, and at Mycenae, and some even in pre-Aegean cultures of Western Asia. Figure 3 shows a star-shaped symbol on a Cretan terracotta sarcophagus (of c. 1300 B.C.); Figure 4 represents a gold pendant with many-pointed stars, probably used as an amulet. It was found, by Schliemann, at Mycenae, and it is to be dated at c. 1550 B.C. Of the same provenience date and magic function, is the gold foil ornament shown in Figure 5, whose design is the "six-petaled flower-star"[21] so familiar to all students of folk art.

---

[20] For the dating of the Bronze Age, cf. O. Montelius, "Bronzezeit," in *Reallexikon der Vorgeschichte,* ed. M. Ebert, Vol. 2, 925; quoted Cleland, *op. cit.,* p. 208.

[21] The writer has adopted this term for the sake of convenient description although the design surely was never meant to represent a flower.

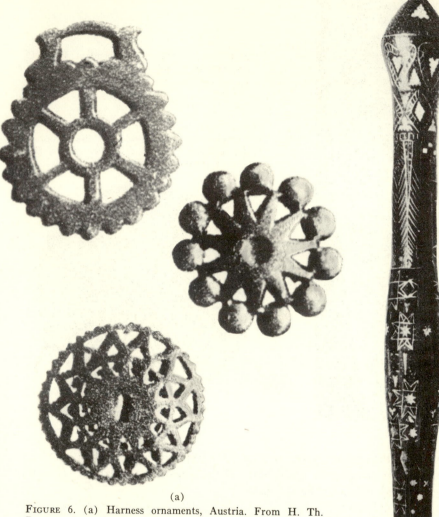

(a)

FIGURE 6. (a) Harness ornaments, Austria. From H. Th.
Bossert, *Peasant Art in Europe,* Plate XXXIV, 7, 13, 15.
(b) Whip handle, Slovakia. From *Peasant Art in Europe,*
Plate CIII, 18. Courtesy of Ernst Wasmuth, Berlin.

(b)

Evidently all three of these starlike designs are symbols of the sun. It
appears that all of them, especially the latter, secondarily and much later,
acquired some bearing on fertility, for they are almost universally found,
alone or in combinations, on peasant utensils pertaining to the care of livestock, in particular, of horses (Figs. 6 and 7).[22]

[22] Further illustrations: from Sweden, in Charles Holme, *Peasant Art of Sweden,
Lapland, and Iceland* (London: The Studio, 1910), Figs. 189, 192, 196; from Tyrol, in
Charles Holme, *Peasant Art of Austria and Hungary* (London, The Studio, 1911),
Figs. 138–40; from Northern Italy, in Charles Holme, *Peasant Art of Italy* (London,
The Studio, 1913), Figs. 341–43, 366–68, 373–74.

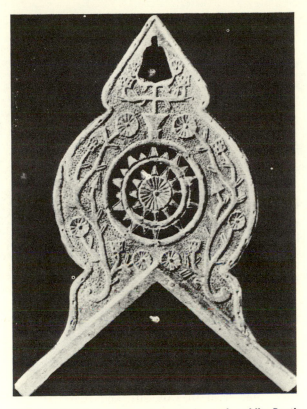

FIGURE 7. Painted wooden ornament for pack saddle, South Tyrol. From H. Th. Bossert, *Peasant Art in Europe,* Plate 36, 17. Courtesy of Ernst Wasmuth, Berlin.

The connection of the sun symbol with the horse is primary, that with other livestock, secondary and by analogy, as it were. Danish and Irish Bronze Age findings prove that the horse itself figured as a symbol in this early Sun Cult. In Denmark there was discovered "an engraved bronze disk six inches in diameter, covered with gold foil, mounted on a wheeled carriage drawn by a horse." Similar disks found in Ireland show a design almost identical with that on the Danish disk. "The date of this sun chariot is about 1300 B.C. The Irish disks have lugs on the margin exactly as in the Danish specimen, the lower one for fastening it to the axle and the upper one for holding the reins."[23] The discovery of two more horses, fragments of a ceremonial carriage, and of another sun disk prove beyond a doubt the age-old connection of the horse with sun worship, later fixed in the familiar Graeco-Italic myth of the sun god traveling across the sky in a chariot drawn by horses. Although in northern and central Europe no such later formulation seems to have originated (or, if originated, was superseded by other religious notions), yet the persist-

23 Cleland, *op. cit.,* p. 254.

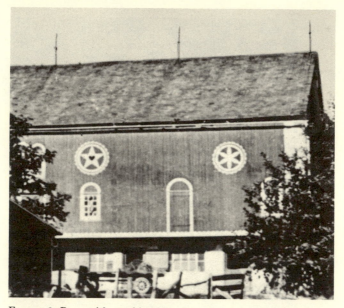

FIGURE 8. Barn with combination of symbols, south of Longswamp, Berks County. Courtesy of the Ohio Historical Society Library.

ent occurrence, in European peasant art, of sun symbols in connection with horses shows the enormous surviving power of the primeval concept.

As stated above, it appears that the initiative toward this widespread Sun Cult came from the Aegeans, and that the Cult itself, together with its symbols, traveled along the various cross-continental trade routes, from the coastal trading posts of the Aegeans, to practically all parts of Europe. Indirect evidence for this comes from the fact that symbolic objects pertaining to other Aegean cults were likewise found at various inland points of Europe while the cults themselves have left no traces. Several copper specimens of the typically Cretan symbolic Double-Ax, found in France and Germany, "with a perforation too small to take an actual shaft, seem to mark an early trade route," for "it is likely, too, that this sacred symbol was invested with an exchange value."[24]

Moreover, from the Copper Age until far into the Early Iron (Hallstadt) Age, there occur, especially in Ireland, but also elsewhere, crescent-shaped personal ornaments very similar to those luniform necklaces of embossed gold foil found in Mycenaean tombs. It matters little whether they are to be interpreted as moon symbols or as horns of the Sacred Bull whose worship was linked, on the Island of Crete, with that of the Double-Ax. Doubtless they were cultic symbols, and their occurrence in central and western Europe is surely due to Aegean influences having filtered in from the coastal trading

[24] V. G. Childe, *The Dawn of European Civilization* (London and New York, 1927), pp. 34, 258, 313 (Map IV); see also *supra*, Fig. 3, left half.

(a)

(b)

(c)

FIGURE 9. (a) Mangling board, Westphalia, Germany.
From O.v. Zaborsky-Wahlstätten, *Urvätererbe in
deutscher Volkskunst,* Fig. 29. (b) Weaver's thread
guide, Poland. From H. Th. Bossert, *Peasant Art in
Europe,* Plate CXIII, 13. Courtesy of Ernst Wasmuth,
Berlin. (c) Linen lace, Island of Crete (modern). From
Peasant Art in Europe, Plate LXXII, 1 & 4.

posts. A probable reason for the universal acceptance of the Sun Cult may have been its singular appeal to the inhabitants of the northern moderate zone. Its symbolic "astral representations, especially the solar disk or forms derived from it"[25] have been continually used for magical purposes from the earliest times to the present day.

The frequent combination of the "six-petaled flower-star" with some other solar symbol on European peasant utensils pertaining to horses and cattle[26] is also found on a number of Pennsylvania Dutch barns, as is shown in Figures 8 and 10b.

Similar combinations also occur, all over Europe, on various kinds of objects used by the peasantry in the processing of flax and wool, in the spinning and weaving of linen, in the making and laundering of linen goods, particularly on distaffs, weaver's tools, mangling boards, laundry beetles, etc., and they are even found in the patterns of lace (Figs. 9a, b, c).[27]

Evidence for the prehistoric connection of magic sun symbols with spinning is found in the occurrence of the swastika, both angular and curved, on a great many spinning whorls unearthed by Schliemann on the site of ancient Troy (3rd and 4th city).[28]

Besides, the above-mentioned combination of symbols is frequently used on cradles, beds, salt containers, spoons, spoon racks, and other implements of the peasant household.[29]

The heart-shaped figures, occasionally combined with any of these symbols, may belong to a later stratum of symbolism, although certain heart-shaped ornaments do occur on ancient Cretan pottery.

The "six-petaled flower-star," evidently as a pre-Christian sign of immortality, appears as the predominant symbol on graveposts in Bosnia.[30]

In some parts of the Old Saxon region (*Niedersachsen,* Germany), stars, in combination with other symbols, are frequently painted on, or carved into, the frames of barn doors (Fig. 11a; Zabarsky-Wahlstätten, *Urvätererbe in deutscher Volkskunst,* Fig. 22).

Also with the Pennsylvania Dutch, these symbols, apart from their use as barn signs, are applied to all kinds of utensils of the rural household.

Another symbol used by the Pennsylvania Dutch, both on barns and otherwise, is the swastika; not, however, the familiar, angular form but the

---

[25] Cleland, *op. cit.,* p. 298.

[26] *Supra,* p. 383ff.

[27] Further illustrations: from Sweden, Lapland, and Iceland, in Holme, *Peasant Art of Sweden, Lapland, and Iceland,* Figs. 143–47, 149, 152, 155, 158, 159, 173–75, 177, 179, 180; from Russia, in Charles Holme, *Peasant Art of Russia* (London: The Studio, 1912), Figs. 188–202; from Lithuania, in *ibid.,* Figs. 527–31; from Italy (Abruzzi), in Holme, *Peasant Art of Italy,* Fig. 362a.

[28] Numerous illustrations in Schliemann's *Ilios,* some of which are reproduced in Thomas Wilson, "The Swastika, . . ." in *Reports, Smithsonian Institution; U. S. National Museum, 1893–1894* (Washington, D.C., 1896), Figs. 64, 69, 78, 101.

[29] For illustrations see the standard works on peasant art, as previously cited.

[30] Holme, *Peasant Art of Austria and Hungary,* Fig. 506.

(a)

(b)

FIGURE 10. (a) Barn at Wescoesville, Lehigh County, Pennsylvania, with club-armed swastika. (b) Barn, south of Wescoesville, with modified swastika. Courtesy of the Ohio Historical Society Library.

(a and b) Carvings in frames of barn doors, Herford, Westphalia.

(c) Relief sculpture on Tombstone, Herford.

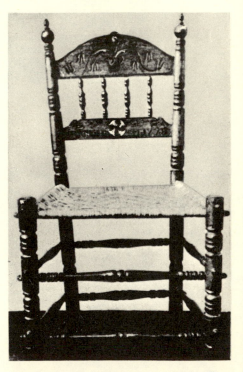

(d) Carving on chair, Lower Vistula. From O.v. Zaborsky-Wahlstätten, *Urväterbe in deutscher Volkskunst,* Figs. 45–47.

FIGURE 11. Club-armed swastika.

swastika with curved club-shaped arms such as found on a barn at Wescoes-ville (Lehigh County) (Fig. 10a). Another barn, about one mile south of Wescoesville, on the road to Macungie, shows a variant: instead of all four arms bending in the same direction, here both the upper and the lower pair of arms are curved towards each other (Fig. 10b). Although this modification of the symbol is likewise of great antiquity (cf. note 28), it may be regarded, in the present case, as merely a local variant. That is all the more likely since other variations which are purposely fanciful also occur as barn symbols in southeastern Pennsylvania.

The pure form of the curved club-armed swastika is likewise found in other parts of the Pennsylvania Dutch area, both as a barn symbol[31] and applied to other objects. An elaborate piece of needlework "made in 1826 by an emigrant from the Palatinate"[32] shows two of them below a third, which is a variant of the pure form.

As a barn symbol it also occurs in Ohio where it can be seen painted on the barn of Mr. L. J. Neikirk, Route 18, two miles north of Republic, in Seneca County (cf. *supra*).

In Germany it is not at all frequent, except in a clearly defined area in Westphalia: the District of Herford; secondarily, it occurs in the flat lands at the mouth of the Vistula (*Weichselniederung*), near Danzig, a region colo-nized, centuries ago, by settlers from the Old Saxon country, presumably Westphalians from the Herford area.

This swastika with curved club-shaped arms is merely a variant of the more familiar, angular design. As a symbol, most probably also of the sun, the swastika presumably originated in India, in prehistoric Dravidian times. From there it traveled both west and east, possibly even, by way of northeastern Asia, into the western hemisphere.[33] Wherever it occurs later on, be it the East or the West, it conveys some propitious meaning of good luck, happiness, long life, or magic protection against evil influences. In a few cases, it was secondarily adopted into later religions and local cults.

An attempt to trace the swastika, and in particular its curved variant, into western Europe again leads to the Aegean culture of the Island of Crete. On a clay vessel (Middle Minoan I, c. 2100 B.C.) there occurs the curved swastika, probably an importation from an earlier, Anatolian culture (Fig. 12).

It evidently spread, together with the other symbols of the Sun Cult, from the sea inland by way of the continental trade routes of the Bronze Age, for it occurs, for instance, on a modern wooden stamp, from Brittany (France), used for the marking of consecrated bread (Fig. 13). The design, far from being Christian, is a swastika-like symbol found, in basically the same form, on a Cretan vessel (Middle Minoan II, c. 1800 B.C.) (Fig. 14).

---

[31] *American Architect,* Vol. 151 (1937), 74.
[32] *American-German Review,* Vol. 7, No. 5 (June 1941), 2.
[33] About the history of the swastika, see especially Wilson, *op. cit., passim.*

FIGURE 12. Cretan vessel with swastika. From J. D. Pendlebury, *The Archaeology of Crete,* Plate XIX, 1. Courtesy of Associated Book Publishers, Ltd. (Methuen), London.

FIGURE 13. Bread stamp from Brittany, France (modern). From H. Th. Bossert, *Peasant Art in Europe,* Plate L, 6. Courtesy of Ernst Wasmuth, Berlin.

FIGURE 14. Cretan vessel (Middle Minoan II). From H. Th. Bossert, *The Art of Ancient Crete,* Fig. 340. Courtesy of A. Zwemmer, London.

A striking similarity, that can hardly be called accidental, prevails between two swastika designs, both on sword pommels, the one from Mycenae (Fig. 15a), the other from a Bronze Age deposit in Denmark (Fig. 15b).[34]

The very same tendency in design appears in a symbolic rock sculpture of

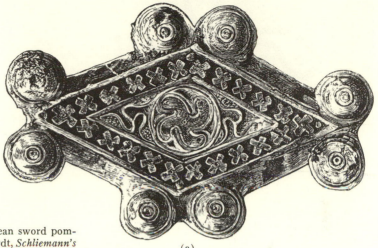

(a)

FIGURE 15. (a) Mycenaean sword pommel. From C. Schuchhardt, *Schliemann's Excavations,* Fig. 232. Courtesy of Macmillan & Co., Ltd., London.

(b) Danish sword pommel (Bronze Age). From J. R. Allen, *Celtic Art in Pagan and Christian Times,* plate opposite p. 58.

(b)

---

[34] It may prove of some archaeological importance that a design of very much the same character has been found on a piece of Moundbuilder potteryware, at Clendora Plantation, Louisiana ("Lower Mississippi Area"); cf. H. C. Shetrone, *The Mound-Builders* (New York and London: Appleton-Century-Crofts, 1941), Fig. 82 (p. 142), pp. 145f., 371ff.

FIGURE 16. Rock sculpture, Ilkley, Yorkshire. From J. R. Allen, *Celtic Art in Pagan and Christian Times,* p. 58.

FIGURE 17. Handle of Celtic bronze tankard. From J. R. Allen, *Celtic Art in Pagan and Christian Times,* plate opposite p. 150.

the British Bronze Age, near Ilkley, in Yorkshire (Fig. 16). Its "winding band" character reveals its connection with the ornamental style demonstrated in Figures 15a and 15b.[35]

There are strong indications that people who made this rock sculpture were Celts of the Goidelic dialect type. Moreover, it was in Celtic-speaking Brittany that the bread stamp with that swastika-like symbol was found which has been discussed previously. Further, the region about Herford, in Westphalia, where the curved club-armed swastika prevails, represents, in its peasant houses, a much older, almost purely Celtic, type than those of the surrounding Saxons.[36] There is other evidence that this region about Herford is to be regarded as an enclave with a Celtic past in the otherwise Saxon area.[37] This permits the inference that the curved club-armed swastika symbol was especially cultivated by Celtic people. Such an assumption is strengthened by the fact that Celtic ornamentation, as a whole, from the late Bronze Age onward, for centuries favored the swastika and related patterns, and, in their delineation, showed a tendency toward curved, bulging designs with clubshaped terminations (Fig. 17).[38]

The universal occurrence of these age-old designs as propitious or magic symbols among the European and, in particular, the German peasantry naturally makes it impossible to determine by which of the various German groups that constitute the Pennsylvania Dutch any given symbol was introduced. The very fact that, even in the German homeland, they all had been familiar with all those symbols and their miraculous powers, renders the whole question immaterial.

In this connection the writer wishes to mention Mr. Weygandt's statement that "some of the shapes of these [barn] symbols undoubtedly have their origin in Rosicrucian symbols, which were a matter of moment to several groups among the German Pietists, etc., etc."[39] It is unfortunate that Mr. Weygandt is not more explicit about the symbols he had in mind, as he wrote these lines. Among the symbolic signs of the Rosicrucians, such as presented by Jennings,[40] the writer has found only three symbols that are used as Pennsylvania Dutch barn signs: the familiar pentagram (*Trudenfuss*);[41] a six-pointed star;[42] and an eight-pointed star,[43] the two latter, moreover, expressly and unmistakably designated as sun symbols. Should Mr. Weygandt

---

[35] Cf. J. R. Allen, *Celtic Art in Pagan and Christian Times* (Philadelphia: Jacobs, n.d.), pp. 57ff.

[36] A. Meitzen, *Siedlung und Agrarwesen der Westgermanen,...* (Berlin: Hertz, 1895), pp. 315ff.

[37] A. v. Hofmann, *Das deutsche Land und die deutsche Geschichte* (Berlin and Leipzig: Deutche Verlagsanstalt, 1923), pp. 30ff.

[38] Cf. Allen, *op. cit.*, pp. 150f., where this style of design is appropriately termed "flamboyant."

[39] C. Weygandt, *The Red Hills,* ... (Philadelphia, 1929), p. 126.

[40] H. Jennings, *The Rosicrucians,...*, 6th ed. (London, n.d.).

[41] *Ibid.*, p. 299 (Fig. 235).

[42] *Ibid.*, plate I, bottom.

[43] *Ibid.*, plate I, top.

have referred to these star symbols as being of Rosicrucian origin, then he would have to explain how the identical symbols also occur on Pennsylvania Dutch household articles in exactly the same application as on analogous peasant utensils all over Germany and the rest of Europe. It is obvious that the Rosicrucians came by these symbols the same way as did the Pennsylvania Dutch: by way of age-old heritage.

In none of the German lands from which the mixed population of Pennsylvania's barn sign area had recruited itself, does one find such symbols painted on the front of barns as in Berks and the adjacent counties. In fact, with the exception of certain districts in Lower Saxony where they occur on the frames of barn doors,[44] one finds them painted on houses only in Switzerland, mainly in the Canton of Bern. While the contribution of the North German plains of Lower Saxony to the population of the Pennsylvania Dutch country side is negligible, Swiss peasants from the Canton of Bern have not only settled in great numbers in Berks County and the neighboring region, but they have also made their Alemannian type of barn the generally accepted form in these counties and beyond. In their applying the star symbols to all kinds of household utensils they do not differ from the Palatines and other settlers from Upper Germany that moved into Pennsylvania. But they *do* differ *in their tendency* of applying stars and related ornamented disk patterns to human habitations, frontally and otherwise, although not to barns.[45]

The fact that the homes in the New Country were not built of wood, as they had been in the Swiss homeland, while the barns continued to be wooden structures, may have been the reason why the symbols were applied, not to the residence with its limited wall space of stone masonry, but to the front of the barn, for this provided the familiar expanse of board wall for symbolic ornamentation.

Once *the tendency to paint symbols on the barns* had been introduced by the Swiss, the other German immigrant groups readily adopted it as they had similarly adopted the Swiss type of barn. The only districts in the Pennsylvania Dutch area where barn symbols have never been applied are the communities of the Mennonites (in particular, the Amish) who have always regarded their use as sinful.

Swiss initiative has left its traces in still another item of Pennsylvania Dutch farm architecture: the carved gable posts found on barns in Dauphin County, especially near Linglestown (Fig. 18). In mentioning this, the writer is not even digressing since these posts, basically, share with the barn symbols an ancient cultic significance and protective magic function. Their probable provenience from the worship of Donar (Thor), the highest god of the Ger-

---

44 *Supra*, Fig. 11.

45 Cf. E. Gladbach, *Charakteristische Holzbauten der Schweiz* (Berlin and New York: Hessling, 1906), plate IX, 3: Door with Stars; plate XXVI, 1 and 5: Chairs with Stars; plate XXIX: Ornamented Disks (A.D. 1828). See also *The Brochure Series of Architectural Illustration* (Boston: Bates & Guild, 1901), Vol. 7, 79: Six-pointed Star on eave console of residence, in a street at Adelboden, Canton of Bern.

FIGURE 18. Barn with gable post, Linglestown, Dauphin County, Pennsylvania. Courtesy of the Ohio Historical Society Library.

mans south of the Wodan-worshipping plains region of Old Saxony, makes it appear that their presumable functions were the protection of the barn against lightning, and the securing of fertility for the cattle kept therein. It is certain that they were introduced into Dauphin County from the Alemannian region, the very heart of the ancient Donar Cult, as is evident from the names of early settlers listed in assessment and taxation records of Paxtang Township, 1777 and 1780. They are almost all German-Swiss.[46]

The author cannot consider this study in the origin and significance of the barn symbols completed without also touching upon their *subjective* significance. In other words, it is not sufficient for a comprehensive treatment of this topic to have discussed their objective significance on the basis of historical and archaeological evidence. The much more important side of their significance is covered by the question: what do they mean to the people who apply them even today in the Pennsylvania Dutch country?

The unquestionable credence these magic symbols have been receiving, both in Europe and Pennsylvania,[47] can only be explained on the basis of peasant psychology, which is group psychology. The *individual* peasant may be entirely honest in telling the stranger that he does not believe in "such things." Just the same, as a *member of his peasant community* he cannot extricate himself from the *group belief* which is super-individual. He applies symbols to his barn or household utensils, not because he, as a person, feels that he must have them, but because "one has to have them." The group spirit commands it so.

With outsiders he does not even touch upon such matters; it is taboo. A feeling akin to chastity keeps his lips sealed in the presence of the "gentile" from "abroad," who "does not speak his language." This is not merely a figure of speech but is to be taken literally. That was brought home to the writer by an unforgettable experience:

---

[46] W. E. Egle, *History of the Counties of Dauphin and Lebanon, ...* (Philadelphia, 1883), pp. 101 and 289.

[47] For literary evidence, cf. Mr. Weygandt's statements, *supra*, p. 377.

A few years ago, I spent a few days in Berks County as a guest in the home of an old lady, now dead. She was of old Pennsylvania Dutch stock and loved to tell stories about the days of the past and about the people she had known. I would not tire listening to her, nor would she, answering my questions.

In the beginning of my stay, she spoke to me in English, as she would to all visitors not of the native kin. Some fine day, however, she discovered that I did not only understand her Pennsylvania Dutch but that I even could talk "her own language." This I accomplished by simply speaking my Rhine-Hessian home dialect with a few concessions to Berks County vocabulary and phonology. No matter how well or how badly I did it, I distinctly felt that I now was "accepted": *I spoke her language,* I was no longer an "outsider." Every word, every gesture from her intimated that she trusted me with "understanding."

A day or two later, as usual, I was helping her in the kitchen with the washing of the breakfast dishes. Although she appreciated the little service, it always embarrassed her a bit that a man, moreover a guest, should be doing housework as long as she, a woman, was around to do it. The point was that her "group" does not approve of men doing kitchen chores. This embarrassment always drove her into her shell, as it were, and made her speak English.

That particular morning, our talk somehow drifted toward the delicate topic of *Hexerei* (witchcraft) and protection against it by means of barn symbols and other magic. Quite casually, I asked her whether the people in the neighborhood really believed in it. She said that she did not think so although she was not quite sure. Maybe, there were still a few that did. Never was I to think that she and her family had ever believed in things of that sort.

All this had been said in English, mind you. It was obvious that she had conveyed to me what the "group" expected her to answer the "outsider" who asked such questions. Thereafter, she was silent, so pointedly silent that no request to drop the subject could have been more eloquent.

Then came the psychological climax. After a pensive pause, her face quite unexpectedly brightened, and she broke into storytelling. *This time in Pennsylvania Dutch.* She told me stories about her father, her mother, her sisters, and other members of her *Freundschaft* (kith and kin): what each of them had done, on this and that occasion, to ward off evil influences that threatened them from certain people reputed to practice witchcraft. Some such person had come to the house, under a flimsy pretext, or had been observed loitering near the cattle barn. Then, of course, the preventive measures had to be taken which "everybody" takes in such a case. Although there were *Hex Signs* on the barn, certain objects were shoved under the doorstill of the cow stable; certain chalk marks were written on door posts; certain herbs were hung near the cattle stands. Otherwise the cows might have dried up, or given bloody milk.

All this and more she told me, revelling in memories. How was that to be explained? Was she aware of contradicting herself? No, she was not.

What had happened, was this: All the time that we had been speaking English, under the cloud of her embarrassment, I had been to her the "outsider" who "did not speak her language," that is, the language of the "group." Furthermore, in conformity with her "group" ethics, she had told the "outsider" what, under the circumstances, "one says" to the "outsider" in the outsider's language. He need not, in fact he *must* not, know what the "group" knows and believes.

Of a sudden, however, it must have occurred to her that, after all, I *did* "speak her language" and, therefore, really was an "insider." So she dropped into Pennsylvania Dutch, and as she was "speaking her language," she was speaking "within the group," where alone it is spoken and understood, and where secretiveness is not in order. She felt that there was no harm done by my being "in the know," and so she told me all she remembered.

Time will show how long the Pennsylania Dutch will be able to maintain themselves as a group. Advancing radially from the big cities, the standardizing and mechanizing forces of today's steel-and-concrete civilization are steamrolling over the peasant minority of the countryside. At the rate of this deadly onslaught, group consciousness is being wiped out and, along with it, the barn symbols, the beliefs for which they stand, and all other values of this old peasant culture.

Bibliography

Allen, J. R., *Celtic Art in Pagan and Christian Times*. Philadelphia: Jacobs, n.d.

Bossert, H. Th., *The Art of Ancient Crete*. London: Zwemmer, 1937.

————, *Peasant Art in Europe*. Berlin: Wasmuth, 1926.

Childe, V. G., *The Dawn of European Civilization*. London and New York, 1927.

Cleland, H. F., *Our Prehistoric Ancestors*. New York: Coward-McCann, Inc., 1928.

Hofmann, A. v., *Das deutsche Land und die deutsche Geschichte*. Berlin and Leipzig: Deutsche Verlagsanstalt, 1923.

Holme, Chas., *Peasant Art of Austria and Hungary*. London: The Studio, 1911.

————, *Peasant Art of Italy*. London: The Studio, 1913.

————, *Peasant Art of Russia*. London: The Studio, 1912.

————, *Peasant Art of Sweden, Lapland, and Iceland*. London: The Studio, 1910.

Meitzen, A., *Siedlung und Agrarwesen der Westgermanen,....* Berlin: Hertz, 1895.

Pendlebury, J. D., *The Archaeology of Crete*. London: Methuen & Co., Ltd., 1939.

Schuchhardt, C., *Schliemann's Excavations*. London: Macmillan & Co., Ltd., 1891.

Trepte, H., *Deutschtum in Ohio*. Doctoral dissertation, Leipzig, 1931 [in *Deutsch-Amerikanische Geschichtsblätter (German-American Review)*, Vol. 32 (Chicago, 1932), 155–409].

Wilson, Thos., "The Swastika, . . ." [In *Reports, Smithsonian Institution; U. S. National Museum, 1893–1894* (Washington, D. C., 1896), pp. 757–1011].

Zaborsky-Wahlstätten, O.v., *Urvätererbe in deutscher Volkskunst*. Leipzig: Koehler & Amelang, 1936.

Something About Simple Simon

Harry B. Weiss

The fool is one of the most popular of all folk characters. In European folklore, he is often associated with a particular place (the association of *blason populaire* is made by citizens of another place). In English folklore, it is the men from Gotham; in German, it is the people from Schilda; in Danish, it is the people from Molbo; in Yiddish, the people from Chelm; and so on. Frequently the same international tale types are found localized in very different cultures.

Sometimes the folk character is a paradoxical combination of wisdom and stupidity. One of the best known of these wise fools is the Turkish Hodja who has a counterpart in almost every culture in the Middle East and Arabic North Africa. The American Indian fool is usually a trickster figure, one who tricks his victims just a little more often than he is tricked by them.

The fool, like the clown, has a great appeal for children who can easily identify with an individual who is not quite able to function intelligently as an adult, though he tries very hard to do so. Simple Simon is this kind of fool, and in his nursery rhyme adventures, he continues to have considerable appeal.

In this survey of Simple Simon, there is a particular problem in folklore research, namely, the tracing of the history of publication. In the folklore of literate as opposed to nonliterate peoples, print is an important agent of transmission and cannot be safely ignored in studying the development of a rhyme, ballad, or tale. The difficulty stems from the fact that so often folkloristic materials are published in very ephemeral form. The form might be a single sheet of paper, a broadside, upon which the words of the ballad are printed with a notation that they are to be sung to the tune of so and so. Such broadside ballads, as folklorists term them, can account for the persistence or popularity of one form of a ballad rather than another. Since these ephemeral forms were not made to be preserved, they are sometimes hard to locate even a few years after their initial appearance. It would be something like

Reprinted from *Bulletin of the New York Public Library,* Vol. 44 (1940), 461–70, by permission of the publisher.

trying to collect all the printed proverbs put into Chinese fortune cookies. No doubt these printed versions have some influence in transmitting certain proverbs, but where would one go to find a collection of them? In part, this is a literary problem. Students of literature are frequently faced with the task of tracing the publishing history of an author's work through many different editions. However, in folklore, the problem is much more complicated in that the oral tradition goes on at the same time. A man who published broadside ballads might have copied some from earlier broadsides or he might have set down some versions he heard in oral tradition. As Archer Taylor pointed out, the two traditions, the literary and the oral, have mutually reciprocal influence. To trace the publishing life history of an item of folklore, be it folksong or nursery rhyme, one must be both folklorist and bibliographical sleuth.

For other nursery rhymes, see Iona and Peter Opie, *The Oxford Dictionary of Nursery Rhymes* (Oxford, Eng., 1951). In this definitive collection which contains 550 rhymes, Simple Simon is number 476. For discussion of fools and numskulls, see Stith Thompson, *The Folktale* (New York, 1946), pp. 190–96; or browse through Motifs J1700–J2751 for an inventory of the world's traditional foolishness. Besides W. A. Clouston's standard survey, *The Book of Noodles* (London, 1888), there is Danish folklorist Arthur Christensen's study of the fools of Molbo, *Molboernes vise Gerninger* (Copenhagen, 1939). Christensen, in another work, discusses the international distribution of nine Danish noodle tales, *Dumme Folk*, Danmarks Folkeminder nr. 50 (Copenhagen, 1941). The principal study of the Hodja is Albert Wesselski's *Der Hodscha Nasreddin*, 2 vols. (Weimar, 1911). [For a collection in English, see Henry D. Barnham, *Tales of Nasr-ed-Din Khoja* (London, 1923).] For a fine comparative essay on the Hodja's Algerian counterpart, see René Basset's "Recherches sur Si Djoh'a et les anecdotes qui lui sont attribuées," in Auguste Mouliéras, *Les Fourberies de Si Djeh'a: Contes Kabyles* (Paris, 1892), pp. 1–79. For a study of the American Indian trickster, see Paul Radin's *The Trickster: A Study in American Indian Mythology* (New York, 1956), which includes an essay "On the Psychology of the Trickster Figure," by C. G. Jung.

For studies of the broadside ballad, see George Malcolm Laws, *American Balladry from British Broadsides* (Philadelphia, 1957); and Leslie Shepard, *The Broadside Ballad: A Study in Origins and Meaning* (Hatboro, Penn., 1962). If the reader wishes to gain some appreciation of the enormity of the task of following publishing histories of folkloristic works, he may look at a study by T. F. Crane, one of the first American folklore scholars, who traced the history of individual tales as they appeared and disappeared in the various editions of the Grimm collections. See "The External History of the *Kinder- und Hausmärchen* of the Brothers Grimm," *Modern Philology*, Vol. 14 (1917), 577–610; Vol. 15 (1917), 65–77, 355–83. [There has been considerable study of the Grimm collection since Crane's article. For references, see Wilhelm Schoof, *Zur Entstehungsgeschichte der Grimmschen Märchen* (Hamburg, 1959).]

Another excellent example of publication research is contained in
N. M. Penzer's *The Ocean of Story,* 10 vols. (London, 1924–1928),
which, incidentally, is an immense and outstanding literary collection of
Indic folktales. Included in the *Ocean of Story* is the *Panchatantra,*
a smaller collection of tales which appears to have reached Europe by
the eleventh century and which exists in over 200 versions in more than
50 languages. For some of the bibliographical biography of this classic
folktale collection, see "Appendix I, The Panchatantra," in N. M.
Penzer, *The Ocean of Story,* Vol. 5 (London, 1926), pp. 207–42. Penzer
did another incredible piece of research in his study of Basile's
Pentamerone, an important seventeenth-century collection of Neapolitan
tales that were written in dialect and first published in 1634–1636.
See "Appendix A, The Bibliography of the Book," in N. M. Penzer,
The Pentamerone of Giambattista Basile, Vol. 2 (London, 1932), pp.
165–271.

Simple Simon is one of those autochthonous characters that most persons
take for granted and on which the last word cannot be written, and in this
respect he is something like Mother Goose. His relatives, such as noodles.
simpletons, chuckleheads, addleheads, rattlepates, nincompoops, dunderpates
and various silly persons of both sexes had been circulating among different
peoples of the world long before anyone thought of putting records of them
down in writing. And for this reason their origins are lost in antiquity. Simple
Simon belongs to the "silly son" jests, which are found in the folklore of all
countries, and what is herewith presented has been mined from various
sources in The New York Public Library.

To most people, the name Simple Simon recalls the nursery rhyme beginning "Simple Simon met a pieman," but there apparently was another Simple
Simon, a married one, with a cruel wife, and his misfortunes were greater than
those of the one who met the pieman. Perhaps the married Simple Simon was
the nursery one grown up, but not any the wiser. Again, there may have been
two distinct Simple Simons, with two distinct sets of misfortunes. This, however, is all speculation, but for the sake of convenience, I shall consider them
as separate personages. Nevertheless, it is my private opinion that there was
really only one Simple Simon, and that he masqueraded under different names
in different countries and had different misfortunes. At all times he was the
"silly son," and in the present account we shall follow only the misadventures
he had while known as Simple Simon.

As early as the seventeenth century, according to Fraser, a prose history of
Simple Simon was common in England. This appeared as a popular chapbook,
entitled *Simple Simon's Misfortunes and his Wife Margery's Cruelty, which
began the very next Morning after their Marriage,* or some variation of this
title. It was published in different places, including Aldermary Churchyard,
and Bow Churchyard, as well as in other parts of London, from 1710 on; in

Coventry by John Turner; in Warrington, Newcastle, Leicester, Birmingham, Manchester, etc., at various times from 1760 to 1835 and later. The 1710 London edition appeared as a broadside ballad. The Aldermary Churchyard edition is a twenty-four page illustrated chapbook, in prose except for "a pleasant Song of many more of the miserable Misfortunes of Simple Simon; shewing his neglect in keeping Sheep; his drinking a Bottle of Sack, in order to poison himself, being quite weary of his life," which appears at the end and which was sung to the tune of *Delights of the Bottle*.

The account opens with Simple Simon and his wife having a terrible battle because on the morning after his marriage he put on his roast-meat (holiday) clothes, intending to walk abroad with her. Margery, however, who had more of her mother's fury than her father's meekness, packed him off to work, but on the way he was delayed by stopping at an alehouse where he and some cronies decided to drink to Margery's health. This little party was interrupted by Margery, who dispersed the happy gathering with her sharp tongue and a club. When Simon reached home that night, he was punished by being bound hand and foot, placed in a basket and hung in the chimney over a small, smoky fire. In the morning he resembled a red herring, and upon his plea—

> In love release me from this horrid smoke
> I will never more my wife provoke;
> She strait did yield to let him down from thence,
> And said, "Be careful of the next offence."

However, not long after, Simon lost a sack of wheat that he was carrying to the mill, because he trusted a stranger on horseback, who told him he might lay the sack on his spare horse. Of course, the stranger rode past the mill and that was the last of the sack. For some reason his wife did not punish him for this, but she spoke about it for several days.

Another time he was sent to the market with a basket of eggs and upon getting there he stopped to watch a fight between two butter women. Upon trying to part them, one of the women pulled him down and broke his eggs. This so angered him that he pitched into the fray in order to be revenged, and a constable arrested them all, supposing that they were drunk, and put them in the stocks. When he reached home, after being released, his wife fell upon him with such fury that he jumped out of the parlor window and spent the night sleeping in the pigsty. In the morning he asked forgiveness on his knees and it was granted.

Still another time, while his wife went visiting, he was supposed to make a fire and put on the kettle. This he did, but while on his way to the well for water, he chased an ox that was running away from a butcher, and after the excitement was over he returned to find the bottom of his kettle burned out. When his wife returned and saw what had happened, she cuffed him about the kitchen in such a horrid manner that the neighbors came in and pleaded with her to stop.

Simple Simon's last misfortune involved the loss of some money, which his

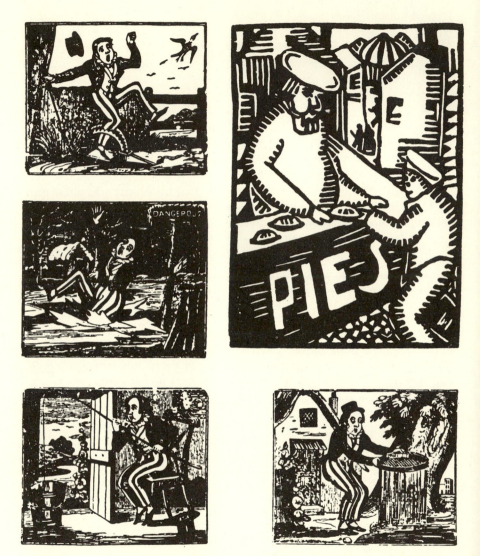

<small>UPPER RIGHT: Reproduction of the block print by Dorothy Eiffert from *Four and Twenty Block Prints for Four and Twenty Rhymes*, Number Three of the University of Washington Chapbooks. Reproduced by permission of the University of Washington Press. REMAINDER: Reproductions of some of the woodcuts used by James Catnach to illustrate *The History of Simple Simon*.</small>

wife had given him for the purchase of soap. While crossing a bridge a flock of crows overhead so frightened Simon that he dropped his money in the water. Then he pulled off his clothes and jumped in to search for it. While he was thus engaged, a ragman came by and gathered up Simon's clothes and he was forced to return home minus both clothing and money. Upon seeing him, his wife fell into a "horrid sweat" and taking the dog whip she made poor Simon dance the "canaries" for two hours.

The "pleasant song" found at the end of this prose account starts off by telling how Simon's wife was fond of tippling and how she kept a bottle of sack hanging behind the door, giving Simon to understand that it was poison. Then follow more misadventures of Simon, his failure as a shepherd, his stupidity in the dairy, his difficulties with the pigs and his consumption of the whole bottle of sack in an effort to end his life, and finally another beating administered by his irate wife after which he was supposed to lead a happy life.

This is the tale, of the married Simple Simon, that is no longer popular, although it has been reprinted in collections of chapbook tales. Another chapbook account, that had some degree of popularity was *The comical history of Simple John, and his twelve misfortunes; which happened all in twelve days after the unhappy day of his marriage. Giving a particular account of his courtship and marriage to a scolding wife; which has been a mortifying misery to many a poor man.* This tale, which has been attributed to the authorship of Dougal Graham, appeared in chapbooks published in Glasgow, 1780, 1796, 1805, 1817, 1828; Edinburgh, 1821, 1823; Sterling, 1823, 1828; Kilmarnock, 1820; Paisley, 1839; and at other places in undated issues. John Fraser believed that Dougal Graham wrote only the racy introduction to Simple John and that he stole the balance of the account from one of the many earlier editions of Simple Simon published at Newcastle, changing the name of the hero from Simon to John. MacGregor, who edited two volumes on the *Complete Works of Dougal Graham*, believed that Graham wrote the whole thing. A comparison of the texts of *The misfortunes of Simple Simon* and *The comical history of Simple John* reveals only very slight similarities in the two accounts, and certainly Simple John seems to be in the style of Dougal Graham, who, if he really wrote it, may have gotten the idea from reading Simple Simon. Sometimes the first part of Simple John, up to "Misfortune 1" was published as *The miseries of poor, simple, innocent silly Tam.*

Although many English chapbooks were exported to America and others were reprinted here after the Revolution and during the first part of the nineteenth century, I have been unable to find any record of the publication or circulation in America of either the married Simple Simon or Simple John. Of course, the absence of such records is not conclusive, nevertheless it seems safe to assume that neither was popular in America.

As for the other Simple Simon of "pieman" fame, this came to us from

England and strange to say, I could not locate its appearance in print in this country earlier than 1869, when four verses of Simple Simon appeared in *Mother Goose's Melodies* published by Hurd and Houghton of Boston. It does not seem possible that this is its first appearance in print in America, and I am sure that earlier records will come to light when the present article is in print. This is usually what happens. Early English editions are also difficult to locate. About 1838, Ryle and Paul of 2 & 3 Monmouth Court, Seven Dials, London, published *The Royal Book of Nursery Rhymes,* and included therein are fifteen rhymes devoted to the misfortunes of Simple Simon, together with eight illustrations. Previous to this time James Catnach of London brought out a little paperbound book entitled *The History of Simple Simon,* in seventeen verses and with nine illustrations. The Catnach Press was founded by John Catnach about 1790 at Alnwick. In 1813, following his death, the business was conducted by his son James in London, to which city his father had moved. James retired in 1838 and the business went to Ryle and Paul. Ryle was Catnach's brother-in-law and Paul had been a boy in the office. This information indicates the approximate time of the appearance of *The Royal Book of Nursery Rhymes* and *The History of Simple Simon* referred to above.

About 1810, James Kendrew of York published a 32mo sixteen-page *History of Simple Simon* containing fifteen verses and fifteen illustrations. I am sure that there were English editions published previous to 1800 because some of the rhymes were common knowledge long before that time.

It may be noted, from the accompanying check list, that separate editions of *Simple Simon* are scarce in America, although from 1869 to the present time two or three verses have been included more or less persistently in books of nursery rhymes. Sometimes fourteen verses are included, but more often only the two or three devoted to Simple Simon meeting the pieman, and fishing in his mother's pail. In many cases the absence of the other verses is perhaps made up by the full-page colored illustration which often accompanies the brief account. It was thought at first that Simple Simon would be found in John Newbery's *Mother Goose* presumably published in London about 1760 and reprinted in America about 1785 by Isaiah Thomas of Worcester, Massachusetts, but he is strangely missing from these melodies. And he does not appear either in the *Mother Goose* edition published in Boston in 1833 by Munroe & Francis. Although I have always had the greatest respect for Mother Goose's age, wisdom, outlook, and charm, as reflected by her writings, I was amazed and disappointed at her neglect of Simple Simon.

Because *Simple Simon* is so frequently abbreviated in modern collections of nursery rhymes, the complete text of fifteen verses from the Ryle and Paul edition of *The Royal Book of Nursery Rhymes* is herewith reproduced. This version of *Simple Simon* was illustrated by eight woodcut illustrations depicting Simon in as many unfortunate situations.

Simple Simon

Simple Simon met a pieman
  Going to the fair!
Says Simple Simon to the pieman,
  Let me taste your ware.

Says the pieman unto Simon
  First give me a penny;
Says Simple Simon to the pieman,
  I have not got any.

He went to catch a dicky bird
  And thought he could not fail
Because he had a bit of salt
  To put upon his tail.

He went to see if cherries ripe
  Did grow upon a thistle,
He pricked his finger very much
  Which made poor Simon whistle.

Once Simon made a great snowball
  And brought it in to roast,
He laid it down before the fire,
  And soon the ball was lost.

He went to ride a spotted cow
  That had a little calf,
She threw him down upon the ground
  And made all the people laugh.

Now Simple Simon went a-fishing
  For to catch a whale,
But all the water he had got
  Was in his mother's pail.

He went to shoot a wild duck,
  But the duck flew away,
Says Simon I can't hit him,
  Because he would not stay.

Then Simple Simon went a-hunting
  For to catch a hare,
He rode an ass about the street,
  But could not find one there.

He went to take a bird's nest,
  'Twas built upon a bough,
A branch gave way, down Simon fell
  Into a dirty slough.

Simon was sent to market,
  To buy a joint of meat,
He tied it to his horse's tail
  To keep it clean and sweet.

He went to slide upon the ice,
  Before the ice would bear,
Then he plunged in above his knees,
  Which made poor Simon stare.

He went for water in a sieve,
  But soon it all run through,
And went all o'er his clothes
  Which made poor Simon rue.

He washed himself with blacking ball,
  Because he had no soap,
And then said to his mother
  I'm a beauty now I hope.

He went to eat some honey,
    Out of the mustard pot,
It bit his tongue until he cried,
    That was all the good he got.

The following additional verses, differing from the preceding, were found among the seventeen that were published in James Catnach's *History of Simple Simon*.

He bought a ship to see it float,
    He stood upon the shore,
It floated down with the tide,
    How Simon he did roar.

Simple Simon went to bathe,
    To try if he could swim,
He jumped into a dirty ditch
    Which made poor Simon grin.

Simple Simon went a-poaching,
    For to shoot some game,
A man trap caught him by the leg,
    Which gave poor Simon pain.

He went for water in a sieve,
    But soon it all run through,
And now poor Simple Simon
    Bids you all adieu.

When one considers most present-day accounts, it is apparent that *Simple Simon* has been reduced to a tabloid state, a picture, and a verse or two. Perhaps even nursery reading matter has grown to such a volume that the children cannot cope with the situation except by reading excerpts and digests.

Although nursery jingles appear to be nonsense for the amusement of children, through many of them run veins of folklore, and traces of local history, and many of them have phantom kinsfolk in foreign countries. In 1930 there was published *The Real Personages of Mother Goose,* by Katherine Elwes Thomas, in which a political interpretation is advanced in explanation of the origin of many of our Mother Goose rhymes. According to this critical and scholarly study, which is interesting as well, "the nursery rhymes, largely of Jacobite origin, are political diatribes, religious philippics, and popular street songs, embodying comedies, tragedies, and love episodes of many great historical personages, lavishly interspersed with English and Scotch folklore flung out with dramatic abandon." This thesis, of course, removes, for some persons, the glitter and capriciousness associated with such trivialities as are expressed in nursery rhymes.

So far as *Simple Simon* is concerned, Miss Thomas considers the common three verses wherein Simon has an experience with a pieman, and where he goes fishing for a whale in his mother's pail. Miss Thomas calls attention to the fact that immediately upon the death of Queen Elizabeth in 1603, Sir Robert Carey dashed to Holyrood Palace and was the first to salute James VI of Scotland as King James I of England. James I then proceeded to fill up his empty treasury. He is identified as the pieman of the pasquinade and England as the Fair to which he went. The pieman's wares were titles of nobility, the increase of Star Chamber fines, and his right to exact maintenance from his subjects for himself and court wherever he traveled in any part of the kingdom. Many Simple Simons did not get their requests granted until they showed their "pennies." In the fishing verse, Parliament is identified as the Simple Simon who went fishing. This body, outraged at the behavior of the king, demanded that his illegal taxation stop. However, James dissolved Parliament and sent four of its leading members to the Tower, and so all the water they got was in their mother's pail.

The phrase "Let me taste your ware," was, according to Miss Thomas, the same as one directed previously at the king's mother. The English ambassador at Holyrood, during Mary's reign, writing October 27, 1561, complained that trade was cut off from him, that merchants knew the value of their wares and prices, and "whatsoever craft, falsehood, or deceit is in all the subtle brains of Scotland, is either fresh in this woman's memory (Mary, Queen of Scots) or she can bring it out with a wet finger."

On the other hand, Dwight Edwards Marvin in his *Historic Child Rhymes* mentions that the piemen of old London wandered about the city, summer and winter, and attended fairs and markets, crying

> Pies, all hot! hot! hot!
> Penny pies, all hot! hot!
> Fruit, eel, beef, veal or kidney pies!
> Pies, all hot! hot! hot!

As for Simple Simon in the abstract, the adventures and drolleries of the simple or silly son are found among the jests of all peoples. This son always jumbles up everything he tries to do and is the despair of his mother who tries to set him straight, and his activities and misadventures have been related in the chapbooks and nursery tales of many countries.

W. A. Clouston in his *Book of Noodles* brought together in his chapter on "The Silly Son," many examples, from widely scattered sources, of the doings of Simple Simons. In Norwegian folk tales there is a Silly Matt who is intellectually the counterpart of our English Simple Simon, and in Russia, Matt has a brother who engages in various stupidities. There are also silly sons in the popular tales of Italy, Arabia, India, Turkey, Japan, etc., and frequently there are resemblances between the different accounts. There is no doubt that Simple Simon has traveled from one country to another, and that even yet, regardless of his origin, he is an internationally known blunderhead.

Bibliography

Ashton, John, *Chapbooks of the Eighteenth Century.* London: Chatto and Windus, 1882, xvi, 486 pp. 12°. *KF[1]

British Museum, Department of Printed Books. *Catalogue of Printed Books and Supplement.* London: W. Clowes & Sons, 1880– . f°.

Catalogue of English and American Chapbooks and Broadside Ballads in Harvard College Library. Cambridge, Mass., 1905. 8°. (Harvard College Library. Bibliographical contributions. No. 56.) *GB (Harvard)

Clouston, William Alexander, *The Book of Noodles: Stories of Simpletons; or Fools and Their Follies.* London: Elliot Stock, 1888, xx, 278 pp. 16°. ZBL

Cunningham, Robert Hayes, ed., *Amusing Prose Chapbooks, Chiefly of the Last Century.* London: Hamilton, Adams & Co., 1889, 350 pp. 8°.

Fairley, John Alexander, *Dougal Graham and the Chapbooks by and Attributed to Him.* Glasgow: J. Maclehose & Sons, 1914, 91 pp. 4°. NCC (Graham)

Fraser, John, *The Humorous Chapbooks of Scotland.* New York: H. L. Hinton, 1873–[74], 2 vols. 12°. NDP

Graham, Dougal. *The Collected Writings of Dougal Graham...*, ed., with notes... by George MacGregor. Glasgow: T. D. Morrison, 1883, 2 vols. 8°. NFC

Halliwell-Phillipps, James Orchard, *The Nursery Rhymes of England.* London and New York: Frederick Warne and Co., 1886, 333 pp. 8°. NAS

Hindley, Charles, *The Catnach Press.* A collection of the books and woodcuts of James Catnach, late of Seven Dials, printer. London: Reeves and Turner [1869]. 48 pp., plates, facsims. 12°. MDON

———, *The History of the Catnach Press.* London: C. Hindley [the younger], 1886, 308 pp., plates, facsims. 8°. *KAG (Catnach)

Thomas, Katherine Elwes, *The Real Personages of Mother Goose.* Boston: Lothrop, Lee & Shepard Co., [c. 1930], 352 pp., illus. 8°. ZBW

Preliminary Check List, by Titles, of Publications Containing Simple Simon, Mostly in the New York Public Library[2]

Ancient Illuminated Rhymes. Simple Simon. New York: McLoughlin Bros., n.d., 8 l., col'd illus. 24°. American Antiquarian Society
Cover carries col'd illus. of Simple Simon and the pieman. Title page. 1 p. music. 1 p. of 3 verses (2 about pieman and 1 about fishing in his mother's pail). 1 p. blank. 1 p. illus. entitled "Simple Simon meets the pieman." 2 blank pp. 1 p. illus. of "Simple Simon goes a fishing." 1 p. Simple Simon and the dickie bird. 2 blank pp. "Simple Simon goes a hunting." 1 p. blank; 1 p. with 3 more verses about catching dickie bird; hunting a hare and looking to see if plums grew upon thistle; 1 p. music; 1 p. blank. Advt. of books sold by McLoughlin Bros. on last cover page. (4 full-page col'd illus., all very good.)

[1] This and the other similar alphabetical abbreviations refer to various collections housed in the New York Public Library. The abbreviations are explained in Karl Brown's *A Guide to the Reference Collections of the New York Public Library* (New York, 1941). —ED. NOTE

[2] For help in the preparation of this list, I am gratefully indebted to Miss Helen A. Masten, Mr. Wilbur Macey Stone, and Mr. W. N. H. Harding. And I am especially indebted to Mr. Robert J. Sim, who drew the text figures.

The Big Book of Nursery Rhymes, ed. Walter Jerrold, illus. Charles Robinson. London: Blackie & Sons, Ltd. (190– ?), 320 pp., 17 col'd pl. sq. 8°.　　　Children's Room
Three verses.

A Book of Nursery Rhymes; Being Mother Goose's Melodies Arranged in the Order of Attractiveness and Interest by Charles Welsh, illus. Clara E. Atwood. Boston: D. C. Heath & Co., cop. 1901, 169 pp., illus. 12°.　　　Children's Room
Six verses.

The Boyd Smith Mother Goose; with numerous illustrations in color and in black and white from original drawings by E. Boyd Smith; the text carefully collated and verified by Lawrence Elmendorf. New York and London: G. P. Putnam's Sons, cop. 1919, xx, 223 pp., illus., col'd plates. 4°.　　　Children's Room
Five verses.

The Complete Mother Goose; with illustrations in color and in black and white by Ethel Franklin Betts. New York: Frederick A. Stokes Co. (cop. 1909), 227 pp., col'd front., illus., col'd pl. 8°.　　　Children's Room

Four and Twenty Block-Prints for Four and Twenty Rhymes; old nursery rhymes illustrated by students in art structure under the direction of Helen Rhodes.... Seattle: University of Washington Book Store, 1927, 17 l. illus. 4°. (University of Washington Chapbooks, No. 3.)　　　3-MAR p.v.130
Two verses, 1 illus.

Gems from Mother Goose. Little Boy Blue. New York: McLoughlin Bros., 1898, 6 l. illus., part col'd. 4°. Cover title.　　　NAS p.v. 16
One page—nearly all occupied by colored illus. of Simple Simon meeting pieman; two verses only at bottom of page.

Historic Child Rhymes, a monograph...by Dwight Edwards Marvin. Norwell, Mass.: The Ross Bookmakers, 1930, 9 p.l., 21–266 pp. 16°.　　　ZBW
Five verses.

A History of Nursery Rhymes, by Percy B. Green. London: Greening & Co., 1899, xvi, 196 pp . 12°.
Three verses.

Little Songs of Long Ago; "More Old Nursery Rhymes." The original tunes harmonized by Alfred Moffat, illus. H. Willebeek LeMair. London: Augener, Ltd.; Philadelphia: David McKay (1913– ?), 63 pp., col'd illus., obl. 4°.　　　Children's Room
One verse and music.

Lois Lenski's Mother Goose. New York and London: Harper & Bros. (cop. 1927), 84 pp., illus., some col'd, sq. 12°.　　　Children's Room
Also published under title: *Jack Horner's Pie.* Fourteen verses. 1 page of illus.

Mother Goose; a comprehensive collection of the rhymes made by William Rose Benet; arranged and illus. Roger Duvoisin. New York: Heritage Press (cop. 1936), 144 pp., col'd front., illus., some col'd. f°.　　　Children's Room
Eight verses.

Mother Goose Dramatized, by Someple (pseud.). Lebanon, O.: March Bros. (1923), 125 pp., illus. 12°. (Written by Gladys Lloyd.)　　　NAC p.v. 99
Simple Simon is one of the characters, and Baa, Baa, Black Sheep points to Simple Simon and recites three verses.

Mother Goose Garden; a fantasy for a garden in one act, by Constance Wilcox.... New York: S. French (cop. 1920), 172–214 pp. 12°.　　　NAC p.v. 143
Dedicated to "All Simple Simons who are wiser than they know." One of the characters in this play is Simple Simon. No reference to antics of Simple Simon.

Mother Goose for Grown-ups, by Guy Wetmore Carryl, illus. Peter Newell and Gustave Verbeek. New York and London: Harper & Bros., 1900, 7 p. l., 3–115 (1) pp., front., plates. 8°.　　　NBI
Pages 39-42—"The Gastronomic Guile of Simple Simon." Humorous account at a county fair where he eats—2 cakes, 6 buns, lady fingers, an eclair, 10 assorted pies, etc., costing $1.22. After putting a curb on his appetite, he took to flight—the moral being the pieman should have known from his actions that Simple Simon had no cents.

Mother Goose; or, National Nursery Rhymes and Nursery Songs. Set to original music by J. W. Elliott. With illus., engraved by the brothers Dalziel. New York: G. Routledge and Sons, 1872, 110 pp., front., illus. 4°.　　　Children's Room
One-half page music of Simple Simon. Words refer to Simon meeting pieman. Illus. accompanying it is by G. J. Pinwell and shows Simon dickering with the pieman at the fair.

Mother Goose Nursery Rhymes, complete ed., 240 illus. by Gordon Browne, R. Marriott Watson, L. Weedon, and others.... New York: A. L. Burt (190–), xix, 379 pp., col'd front., illus., col'd plates. 12°.   ZBW
Four verses.

Mother Goose, the old nursery rhymes, illus. Arthur Rackham. London: William Heinemann; New York: Century Co., 1913, 3 p.l., ix–xxiii, 262 pp., 1 pl. illus. 8°.   MEM
Three verses.

Mother Goose Rhymes. (New York): The P(latt) & M(unk) Co., Inc., n.d. No. 861.
Two verses. 1 col'd illus.

Mother Goose Rhymes, ed. Watty Piper. New York: Platt & Munk Co., Inc., 1937–1938.
Two verses. 1 illus.

Mother Goose in Silhouettes, cut by Katharine G. Buffum. Boston: Houghton Mifflin Company (1907), 3 p.l., 78 pp., 1 pl. illus., sq. 24°.   Children's Room
One verse.

Mother Goose's Chimes, Rhymes & Melodies. Philadelphia: H. B. Ashmead (18— ?), 96 pp., sq. 16°.   ZBW
Four verses. This book profusely illustrated with pen-and-ink sketches.

Mother Goose's Melodies. Boston: Hurd & Houghton, 1869. Collection of W. M. Stone.
Contains four verses.

Mother Goose's Melodies; or, Songs for the Nursery; illus. in color by Alfred Kappes. ...Boston: Houghton Mifflin Company, 1884, xix, 186 pp., col'd front., illus., plates (part col'd). 4°.   NAS
Four verses.

Mother Goose's Melodies for Children; or, Songs for the Nursery; with notes, music, and an account of the Goose or Vergoose family; illus. Henry L. Stephens and Gaston Fay.... New York: Hurd & Houghton, 1872, xix, 186 pp., plates. 8°.   ZBW
Four verses.

Mother Goose's Nursery Rhymes, ed. L. Edna Walter, illus. Charles Folkard. New York: The Macmillan Company, 1924, 216 pp., illus., col'd pl. 12°.   Children's Room
Eleven verses.

Mother Goose's Nursery Rhymes, a collection of alphabets, rhymes, tales, and jingles; 220 illus. by Sir John Gilbert...John Tenniel, Harrison Weir, Walter Crane, and others. New York: Williams Co. (cop. 1886), vi, 8–162, 14–271 pp., illus. 8°.   ZBW
Four verses.

Mother Goose's Nursery Rhymes and...Songs, set to music by J. W. Elliott. New York: McLoughlin Bros., n.d., 111 pp. 8°.   Children's Room
Music and 4 lines about pieman.

The New Adventures of Simple Simon. London: J. L. Marks (c. 1830), 7 hand-colored woodcuts. 8°.   (Gumuchian cat.)

Nurse Lovechild's Legacy: Being a Mighty Fine Collection of the Most Noble, Memorable and Veracious Nursery Rhymes, embellished by C. Lovat Fraser. New York: Henry Holt and Co., 1924, 60 pp., 1 l. illus. 12°.   *KP (Curwen)
Printed in Great Britain at the Curwen Press. Three verses.

The Nursery Rhyme Book, ed. Andrew Lang, illus. L. Leslie Brooke. London and New York: Frederick Warne & Co., Ltd. (cop. 1897), 288 pp., illus. 12°.

Children's Room
Three verses.

Nursery Rhymes, with drawings (some col'd) by L. Leslie Brooke. London and New York: Frederick Warne & Co., Ltd. (1914), (30) pp., illus., col'd plates. 4°.

Children's Room
Three verses.

Nursery Rhymes, with pictures by C. Lovat Fraser. London: T. C. & E. C. Jack, Ltd. (1922?), 46 pp., illus. (some col'd). 4°.   Children's Room
Three verses.

Old King Cole and Other Medieval Plays, by Josephine Elliott Krohn; with an introduction by Constance D'Arcy Mackay and general notes on production by Cora Mel Patten. New York: George H. Doran Company (cop. 1925), xiv pp., 1 l. (17)–208 pp. 12°. (Lettered on cover: The Drama League junior play series.)   NASH
Contains incidental music for Old King Cole, Sing a Song of Sixpence, and Simple Simon. Contents: Old King Cole, The Queen of Hearts, Sing a Song of Sixpence, Simple Simon.

Ring O' Roses: A Nursery Rhyme Picture Book, with numerous drawings in color and black and white by L. Leslie Brooke. London and New York: Frederick Warne & Co., Ltd., n.d. (56) pp., illus., col'd plates. 8°. Children's Room
Contains Simple Simon.

Simple Simon. York, Eng.: J. Kendrew (ca. 1820). 32°. (Gumuchian cat.)

Simple Simon. Simon cutting his mother's bellows open, to see where the wind lies. Printed and sold by T. Batchelar, 14 Hackney Road Crescent. (London, n.d.), 16 pp., blue paper covers, illus. 48°. Boston Public Library

Simple Simon and Other Rhymes. New York: Saml. Gabriel Sons & Company. "Linenette book," one of a series in a "Mother Goose Library."
One verse.

Simple Simon Simple: a Domestic Comedy in Three Acts, by Henry Rowland. Boston, Mass., and Los Angeles, Cal.: Walter H. Baker Company (c. 1936), 112 pp., diagr. 12°. (On cover: Baker's edition of plays.) NBL p.v. 416
Simple Simon lives in small town with wife, who runs a boarding house. Simon is always in cellar tinkering with things he has invented. Town people call him Simple Simon. Invents a water heater and interests town miser, and gets a loan. He signs a paper and miser hopes to get his property, should heater fail to work. However, Simple Simon is not simple and he outwits miser. Includes romance around Simple Simon's son, daughter, etc.

Sing-A-Song-O'-Sixpence, five plays by Eleanor Denton, illus. Elizabeth Montgomery.... Oxford: B. Blackwell, 1927, 56 pp., illus., music, pp. 32–33. 4°. NASH
Includes Simple Simon among contents. Play built around Simple Simon and his experience with pieman, his fishing, etc.

Six Comedies for Girls, by Freda Isobel Noble. Glasgow: Brown & Son & Ferguson, Ltd. (1934), 107 pp., incl. front., music. 12°. NAFH p.v. 117
Simple Simon included, but not the nursery character.

Willy Pogany's Mother Goose. New York: Thomas Nelson & Sons (cop. 1928), unpaged, col'd front., illus., some col'd., sq. 8°. Children's Room
Six verses.

The Star Husband Tale

Stith Thompson

In this important study by one of the world's greatest folklorists, the techniques employed in the Finnish or historic-geographic method are applied to American Indian rather than to European materials. The method consists of a series of specific steps. First, as many versions as possible of the item to be studied must be located, assembled, and arranged in some convenient form of organization. In studies of European folklore, the literary versions are listed first, in chronological order; then the oral versions are listed in geographic order. Thompson groups the American Indian materials by culture area, moving from west to east.

The next step is one of the most critical. By empirical inspection of the corpus of texts, the folklorist breaks the tales into principal traits, traits that demonstrate some variation. The variation of a trait's content is a potential means of distinguishing smaller groups of versions that share a particular subtrait. For example, if one of the traits, say Trait A, is the number of women in the tale, then versions may be distinguished on the basis of whether they have one woman, two women, or some other number of women. Eventually, if one finds that a whole group of versions share a number of identical subtraits, one may have isolated a subtype of the basic tale type. A way of facilitating the identification of similar tales is to write each version of the tale in abstract form using the abbreviations for the subtraits. If, for example, the first trait, Trait A, has such forms as A1 (one woman), A2 (two women), etc., then the abstract of a tale having two women would begin with A2. In similar fashion, one would write the tale in symbol shorthand such that the formula might look like A2, B1, C1, D2, E3, and so on. The formula could be easily compared with the formulas of other versions. For example, of the following three versions, it is obvious which two are more similar to one another:

A2, C1, B1, D2, E3, F5, F10, K3a, I1, L1, M3c, M3b, N2
A1, C2a, B3b, F2, E2, G1, H1a, I2, J2, K3b, L3, N1
A2, C1, B1, D2, E3, I3, J2, K2, L1, N2

Reprinted from *Studia Septentrionalia*, Vol. 4 (1953), 93–163, by permission of the author and the Universitetsforlaget, Oslo, Norway.

Of these tales (versions 4, 43, and 78 in Thompson's study), the first and third have more in common than do either with the second. This method may appear to be unnecessarily complicated, but one must remember that if a folklorist is trying to compare as many as a thousand versions of a tale, it is almost impossible to do so by reading the full narrative accounts and keeping them all in mind. By comparing the trait sequences, one can much more readily note similarities and differences. No doubt some enterprising folklorist will one day use an electronic computer to help him separate groups of similar tales from an unwieldy corpus of texts.

The hypothetical archetype is established by looking at each trait individually to determine what was the probable archetypal form of the trait. Such factors as early recordings or literary versions (in the case of Indo-European materials) and widespread or peripheral distribution are taken into account. (It is the combination of chronological criteria [historic] and of geographical spread [geographic] that has led to the name "historic-geographic method.") After the archetype for each individual trait is hypothesized, the projected list of archetypal traits is put together as a possible basic type or archetype of the whole tale. (In the case of complex tales, archetypes for the traits of each subtype may be postulated in order to arrive at subtype archetypes. Then from these, the folklorist may reconstruct a projected archetype of the parent form of the tale from which the subtypes might have evolved.) The hypothetical archetype is in part a statistical abstraction that may or may not correspond to even one actual recorded version of the tale in the initial corpus. That is why Thompson in this study of the Star Husband is careful, upon having delineated the archetype, to ascertain whether or not there are versions that correspond to his suggested basic type. His finding several of the eighty-six versions that did provides some support for his hypothetical reconstruction.

One of the chief criticisms of the historic-geographic method is that it is the study of folklore for its own sake, that the study of variation and stability is not meaningfully related to human factors. Tales spread and traits drop off with superorganic ease, and it is for this reason that some anthropological folklorists eschew this type of study. On the other hand, there is in theory no reason why the comparative method could not and should not be the preliminary basis for other kinds of analyses of folklore. The folklorist who collects one version of the Star Husband from an American Indian informant may be interested in knowing if and how his particular informant has varied the tale. For the determination of such facts, the historic-geographic method is of great value. However, the conclusions of most historic-geographic studies leave some significant questions unanswered. Why did the archetype, assuming the reconstruction is valid, arise in the first place? Why did subtypes evolve and why did they evolve precisely where they did? Why does the tale in its multiple forms continue to be told (or not to be told)? For these kinds of questions, a synthesis of approaches to folklore is needed. The study of historical origins and of paths of diffusion are a part, an important part, of the whole. But the study of psychological origins and of function is also a part of the whole. The combination of these approaches can lead to a fuller understanding of the nature of folklore.

The standard reference for the historic-geographic method is Kaarle Krohn, *Die Folkloristische Arbeitsmethode* (Oslo, 1926). [A Spanish summary, "Metodologia Folklorica," was published by Ralph Steele Boggs in *Folklore Americas,* Vol. 5, No. 1 (June 1945), 1–13.] For an excellent description of the method, see Walter Anderson, "Geographische-historische Methode," in Lutz Mackensen, ed., *Handwörterbuch des deutschen Märchens,* Vol. 2 (Berlin and Leipzig, 1934–1940), 508–22. For discussions in English, see Archer Taylor, "Precursors of the Finnish Method," *Modern Philology,* Vol. 25 (1928), 481–91; or Taylor's model study, *The Black Ox,* Folklore Fellows Communications No. 70 (Helsinki, 1927). For one of the best illustrations of the method as applied to a complex European *Märchen,* see Warren E. Roberts, *The Tale of the Kind and the Unkind Girls* (Berlin, 1958).

Although the method has been primarily used in studying folktales, it has also been applied to many other forms of folklore. For a study of a ballad, "Lady Isabel and the Elf-Knight," Child No. 4, see Holger Olof Nygard, *The Ballad of Heer Halewijn, Its Forms and Variations in Western Europe: A Study of the History and Nature of a Ballad Tradition,* Folklore Fellows Communications No. 169 (Helsinki, 1958); for a superlative study of a traditional circumlocution, namely, "the devil is beating his wife" as a folk expression referring to the sun's shining while it is raining, see Matti Kuusi's comprehensive 420-page monograph, *Regen bei Sonnenschein; zur Weltgeschichte einer Redensart,* Folklore Fellows Communications No. 171 (Helsinki, 1957). For a study of a riddle, see Antti Aarne's essay on the riddle of the year as a tree with twelve branches in his *Vergleichende Rätselforschungen,* Vol. 1, Folklore Fellows Communications No. 26 (Helsinki, 1918), 74–178; summarized in Archer Taylor's *English Riddles from Oral Tradition* (Berkeley and Los Angeles, Cal., 1951), pp. 413–16. For a game, see Elsa Enäjärvi Haavio's 343-page study, *The Game of Rich and Poor: A Comparative Study in Traditional Singing Games,* Folklore Fellows Communications No. 100 (Helsinki, 1932).

Introduction

The serious study of the folktale goes back little more than a century. When the Grimm Brothers began to speculate about the nature of their famous collection around 1820, it appeared clear that the historical and comparative study of tales handed down by word of mouth would call for methods and techniques quite different from those customarily employed in the investigation of literary texts. With manuscripts or printed documents the scholar is attempting to establish a direct chain of association binding one of these immediately to another. Version A of a manuscript was written, let us say, in Italy in the fifth century by a known author. Version B was a reworking of A by a French monk in Paris in the eleventh century. We see the monk at work on the old manuscript and our investigation is concerned with establishing the fact of his access to the manuscript and with seeing what changes he made in it. But the fact that A is from Italy and B from France and that six centuries separate them is of minor importance. Once written and safely preserved the manuscript could be used at any time and place. And no one need concern himself with the historical events of the centuries while it lay in the library or of the rivers and mountains and political boundaries it crossed when it was eventually carried to Paris and to the monk's cell.

With the oral tale, however, all these things become important. We find ourselves confronted with five hundred versions of a well-knit story coming from all parts of Europe and much of Asia and showing significant or insignificant resemblances to other tales, not only in this region but in remote parts of the world. At first view these hundreds of variants may seem to be filled with chance divergences—a mere kaleidoscopic shifting about of motifs and episodes. But as we look at them more closely we become aware that men and women have been telling the tale through the centuries and in many lands and that the life of the tale is a part of their lives and can be understood only when we know these tellers and hearers. We are not surprised therefore that the seeming lawlessness is only apparent and comes only because so many men in so many places have left their marks on the tale. The study of such a story, the attempt to find order in the seeming confusion, involves the use of elaborate analysis which will show that all these variations are obeying laws or combinations of laws, however complicated or baffling. If one is to determine the direction the tradition has traveled he must try to reconstruct a theoretical original and at least attempt to trace the historical and geographical conditions under which the tradition has been kept alive in the memories and in the interests of the intervening generations. For such an investigation of an oral tale, the ordinary techniques of literary history are useless.

But the scholars of the nineteenth century did not immediately approach the problem just stated. They had but few versions of folktales before them and did not realize the difficulties of the study of a single tale. Instead, they at once and prematurely tried to solve two leading questions: (1) Where do folktales come from? and (2) What do folktales mean? This is not the place to follow these discussions, or to trace the activities of the various schools— Grimm, Benfey, Andrew Lang, and their contemporaries.

By the end of the nineteenth century it was becoming increasingly clear that the only way to arrive at any valid statements about folktales in general is to study folktales in particular. After many of these come to be known then we shall be ready for larger syntheses and the statement of tentative laws. The leading spirit in the promotion of these monographic investigations was Kaarle Krohn of Finland, so that the historic-geographic method evolved by him and his disciples for these studies is sometimes called the Finnish method.

Since the present study is an example of this method, it is sufficient to say here that its successful use depends on the thorough analysis of a large number of versions—enough to give the findings some statistical validity. The analysis attempts to establish an archetype and subtypes and to arrive at a probable life history of the tale. Thirty or forty monographs on European-Asiatic tales have appeared, and Krohn, as his last work, made a synthesis of the results.[1]

Two major criticisms of this way of studying tales have secured a considerable hearing and have raised doubts in the minds of many as to the validity of the method as a whole. First, it is contended that literary versions of the tale are so influential as to make studies of the oral tradition worthless. Another school is impressed with the importance of linguistic and national boundaries and opposes the idea of slow and gradual wavelike traveling of a tale.[2]

No one can doubt the important bearing of these points, and the better scholars who have used the historic-geographic method have always given attention to these. But the fact remains that we do not know just what influence the literary tradition has had, nor just what may be the role of linguistic or other boundaries in promoting or retarding the dissemination of a tale.

More could certainly be discovered about these matters if we could find a story with no possible or likely literary influences. We could then see whether this purely oral tradition behaves in the same way as the European tales already studied. We could say with some confidence what happens when there is no writing.

For such purpose the tales of the North American Indians are eminently suitable. There are available at least fifty well-integrated tales which show no likelihood of influence (1) from other continents or (2) from written or printed tales. The purpose of this paper is to present a historic-geographic study of one of the best known of these tales.

Many collectors of folklore from the North American Indians have recorded a story which they generally call "The Star Husband."[3] It is found scattered

[1] Thompson is referring to Kaarle Krohn's *Übersicht über einige Resultate der Märchenforschung,* Folklore Fellows Communications No. 96 (Helsinki, 1931).—ED. NOTE
[2] The first criticism was made by Albert Wesselski, the second by C. W. von Sydow. See Stith Thompson, *The Folktale* (New York, 1946), pp. 440–42.—ED. NOTE
[3] I am greatly indebted to the late Mrs. Gore Campbell, whose study of this tale, made twenty years ago as a Master of Arts thesis at Indiana University, served as a starting point for the present investigation. After Mrs. Campbell's untimely death a number of students in my seminar on the folktale, at Indiana University, helped to review all of the material and to bring it down to date. Most helpful in this respect was Mrs. Mildred

over a good part of North America north of Mexico, but not in all areas. Thus far 86 versions have been reported.

In its simplest form (Type A) the story is as follows: Two girls are sleeping in the open at night and see two stars. They make wishes that they may be married to these stars. In the morning they find themselves in the upper world, each married to a star—one of them a young man and the other an old man. The women are usually warned against digging but eventually disobey and make a hole in the sky through which they see their old home below. They are seized with longing to return and secure help in making a long rope. On this they eventually succeed in reaching home.

The tale in the simple form is found on the Pacific coast from Southern Alaska to Central California, in the Western Plateau and Plains from the Arizona and New Mexico border north far into Canada; then in the Great Lakes area and east to Nova Scotia. Some versions are found in Oklahoma, Texas, and Louisiana. It has not been reported in the Southwest among the Pueblos or the Navaho or Apache.

By breaking the tale down into its parts one sees that the versions show variations at some fourteen different points. Analysis of the versions in respect to all these traits has been made essentially in the manner familiar to all those who use the historic-geographic method. The listing is geographical by culture areas. By close comparison of the variations and especially by observation of the exceptional treatment of certain items it is possible to establish without room for reasonable doubt the affinities of nearly all the versions.

They are examined in a strictly determined geographical order for each plot element and a table is prepared to show the results. Every variation in treatment is thus noted and brought into easy comparison with all other variations. Totals are kept for each of the possible treatments, so that it is possible at a glance to see (1) how general or how exceptional it is in the light of the whole tradition and (2) just what is its geographic distribution. After the tables are prepared they are used for the construction of maps which will permit more immediate and easier geographic interpretation.

B. Mitcham who devoted a great deal of time and used excellent judgment in bringing together much new material. To all of these I owe a debt of gratitude for invaluable aid.

This tale was included among those studied by Dr. Gladys Reichard in her investigation of literary types and dissemination (*Journal of American Folklore,* Vol. 34, 269ff.). She proceeded by a somewhat different method from that here employed.

It might seem that after all this assistance has been received there would be little left to do. But aside from a careful recheck and rereading of all the versions, I have constructed many tables and maps, not only those used here but a number of others which were useful at various stages of the study, and I have then tried to interpret the material without regard to anyone else's findings. In general lines my conclusions agree with Mrs. Campbell's and Dr. Reichard's careful studies, but disagree with those of some of my seminar students.

Abstracts of Variants[4]

ABBREVIATIONS OF WORKS REFERRED TO

BBAE—Bulletin of the Bureau of American Ethnology.
CI—Publications of the Carnegie Institution.
CNAE—Contributions to North American Ethnology (Smithsonian Institution).
CU—Columbia University Contributions to Anthropology.
Curtis—E. S. Curtis, *The North American Indian,* 20 vols., Cambridge, Mass., 1908—.
FM—Field Museum of Natural History, Anthropological Series.
GSCan—Geological Survey of Canada, Anthropological Series.
JAFL—Journal of American Folklore.
JE—Publications of the Jesup North Pacific Expedition.
MAFLS—Memoirs of the American Folklore Society.
Nat. Mus. Can.—Publications of the National Museum of Canada.
PAES—Publications of the American Ethnological Society.
PaAM—Anthropological Papers of American Museum of Natural History.
RBAE—Report of the Bureau of American Ethnology.
UCal.—University of California Publications in American Archeology and Ethnology.
UWash—Anthropological Publications of the University of Washington.

TRAITS OF THE TALE

Numbers in parentheses refer to the traits of the tale studied in the next section. These principal traits are: A. Number of women; B. Introductory action; C. Circumstances of introductory action; D. Method of ascent; E. Identity of husband; F. Distinctive qualities of husband; G. Birth of son; H. Tabu broken in upper world; I. Discovery of skyhole; J. Assistance in descent; K. Means of descent; L. Results of descent; M. Explanatory elements; N. Sequel.

ESKIMO AREA

1. Smith Sound: Kroeber, *JAFL,* Vol. 12, 180. Collected 1897–98 in New York City. Probably does not belong to Star Husband cycle.

A woman (A1) is carried to upper world (D3a) by a supernatural being (B3a), the moon (?) (E1). She disobeys injunction against looking (H2, I1) into another house and has the side of her face burned as punishment. She sees her son on earth but cannot go to him.

2. Kodiak 1: Golder, *JAFL,* Vol. 16, 28, no. 5. Collected in Russian, Unga Island, Alaska, c. 1901.—Fragmentary.

Two girls (A3) sleeping on the beach (C1) make wishes to marry the moon (B1, E1). He carries them through the air by their hair (D3). One

---

[4] Thompson, like many folklorists (including Brewster in his study), uses the terms *variant* and *version* interchangeably. See Stith Thompson, "variant," in Maria Leach, ed., *The Standard Dictionary of Folklore, Mythology, and Legend,* Vol. 2 (New York, 1950), 1154–55. The editor's feeling is that the section should be entitled "Abstracts of Versions," with the term *variant* being reserved for those versions that diverge appreciably from standard forms. For example, the first version abstracted, an Eskimo tale collected by A. L. Kroeber, which differs markedly from the usual Star Husband tale, could properly be termed a variant.—ED. NOTE

girl opens her eyes and falls. Other goes to the upper world and marries moon. She is forbidden to look around the sky world (H2), especially behind a curtain in a house where pieces of moon are kept. Moon sticks to her face but her husband removes it.

3. Kodiak 2: Golder, *JAFL,* Vol. 16, 21, no. 3. Collected in Russian, Unga Island, Alaska, c. 1901.—Fragmentary.

A chief's daughter (A1) is rescued from a murderous husband (C3) by a supernatural old woman, who carries her in a basket (D5) to the sky (B3a). She marries the woman's son, Star (E3), a one-sided man (F8). They have a son (G1). She discovers a hole in the sky (I1). The old woman (J2) lets her down to earth in a basket (K2) with warning against opening her eyes (K7a). She reaches home safely (L1), but later returns to the sky world (N6). Introduction is irrelevant.

Mackenzie Area

4. Kaska: Teit, *JAFL,* Vol. 30, 457, no. 13. "The Sisters Who Married Stars." Collected 1915, foot of Dease Lake.—Type III.

Two sisters (A2) sleeping out (C1) wish that they may be married to red and white stars (B1). They find themselves (D2) next morning in the upper world married to stars (E3), one with a red and the other with a white blanket (F5). The husbands are hunters (F10). Eventually they long to return home and make a skin rope (K3a) and let themselves down (I1) through a hole in the sky. They lodge in the top of a tree (L1). Explanation of marks on wolverine (M3c) and of origin of beavers (M3b). Sequel: trickster animals under tree: wolverene duped (N2).

5. Carrier: Jenness, *JAFL,* Vol. 57, 200. "The Girls Who Were Carried into the Sky." Collected 1924–25, Fort Fraser.—Type III.

Two girls (A2) are carried to the sky (B3a) along with their whole village when a supernatural man dances and raises a whirlwind (D6). They have been sleeping outside (C1) and find themselves lying on an open plain in upper world. An old woman (J2) helps them to find a skyhole (I3) and to make a wool rope (K3c). They are lowered in a box. They reach the earth safely (L1). Sequel: trickster animals under tree: wolverene duped (N2).

North Pacific Area

6. Tahltan: Teit, *JAFL,* Vol. 34, 247. "The Girls Who Married Stars." Collected 1915, Telegraph Creek.—Type III.

Two girls (A2) sleeping out (C1) wish to be married to two stars (B1). They find themselves in the upper world (D2) married to the starmen (E3), who are hunters (F10). They discover the skyhole (I1) and become homesick. They make a skin rope (K3a) and descend to a treetop (L1). Explanation of wolverene's habits (M7). Sequel: trickster animals under tree: wolverene duped (N2).

7. Ts'ets'aut: Boas, *JAFL,* Vol. 10, 39, no. 12. 'The Stars." Collected winter 1894–95, Portland Inlet.—Type III.

Two sisters (A2) sleeping out (C1) wish to be married to two stars (B1). They find themselves next morning (D2) in the upper world married to two stars (E3), one with a white blanket (white star) and one with a red (red star) (F5). The husbands are hunters (F10). The girls eventually become homesick and through a hole in the sky which they find (I1) they descend on a skin rope (K3a). They lodge in a treetop (L1). Sequel: trickster animals under tree: fisher duped (N2).

8. Bella Bella: Boas, *MAFLS,* Vol. 25, 107. "The Sun Husband." Collected 1925 by George Hunt. Type I**.

Chief's two daughters (A2) sleeping out (C1) with four others wish for sun, moon, and stars (B1). They find themselves in the upper world (D2). One of the girls marries the Sun (E2) and after ten months bears him a son (G1). The Sun Husband shows her a skyhole (I3) and sends her, the son, and her sister home in a basket (J4, K2). She brings good fortune to her family (L1). The son becomes a transformer (N1a).

9. Chilcotin 1: Farrand, JE, Vol. 2, 31, no. 16. "The Sisters and the Stars." Collected 1897.—Fragmentary.

Two sisters (A2) sleeping out (C1) wish to be married to two stars (B1). Next morning they find two starmen (E3) with them (in the upper world?) (D2), an old man (big star) and a young (small star) (F4). They try to escape and kick open a hole (I1), through which the old man falls to his death. Explanation: treatment of wounds (M6a).

10. Chilcotin 2: Farrand, JE, Vol. 2, 28, no. 12. "The Adventures of the Two Sisters." Collected 1897.—Fragmentary.

After various adventures (C3), two sisters (A2) run away to the sky world (B3c). They are kept by an old woman who warns them against opening a certain box (H2). They disobey and discover a skyhole (I1). The old woman helps them (J2) descend on a rope of vines (K3e) in a basket (K2), and, one after the other, they reach home safely (L1).

11. Songish: Boas, *Indianische Sagen von der nordpacifischen Küste Amerikas* (Berlin, 1895), p. 62. Collected c. 1893. Type I.

Two girls (A2) sleeping out (C1) after digging roots (C2a) wish to be married to two stars (B1). They awake in upper world (D2) married to starmen (E3). They are cautioned against digging (H1) but disobey and discover a skyhole (I1). They make a rope (K3) and descend safely (L1).

12. Klallam: Gunther, UWash, Vol. 1, 135, no. 4. Collected c. 1924, Port Angeles, Washington.—Type I**.

Two girls (A2) wish for stars as husbands (B1, E3), a bright one and a dim one. The stars steal them and take them to the sky, where they see strange sights. They come to a skyhole (I1) and make a ladder of cedar boughs (K4) on which they safely descend (L1). Ladder is still to be seen on Vancouver Island (M2).

13. Quileute 1: Farrand-Mayer, *JAFL,* Vol. 32, 264, no. 10. "The Star Husbands." Collected 1898.—Type V.

Two girls (A2) sleeping out (C1) wish for two stars as husbands (B1, E3). They are taken by two starmen to sky (apparently translated in sleep) (D2) and find themselves married to an old man (red star) and a young man (blue star) (F4). The girls want to get back home and are permitted to do so (but means is not specified) (K1, L1). Origin of constellations explained (M1b). Sequel: war of sky and earth people (N3).

14. Quileute 2: Andrade, CU, Vol. 12, 71. "The Star Husband."

Two girls (A2) sleeping out (C1) after digging roots (C2a) wish for two stars as husbands (B1). They find themselves in the sky (D2) married to the stars (E3), a small one and a large one. One of the girls is helped down from the sky by Spider-woman (J1a) but the rope (K3) is too short and the girl is left suspended (L1) until she turns into a star (M1b). Sequel: war of sky and earth people (N3).

15. Quinault: Farrand, JE, Vol. 2, 107, no. 5, "The Ascent to the Sky." Collected 1898.—Type V.

Two sisters (A2) sleeping out (C1) after digging roots (C2a) wish for two stars as husbands (B1). They awake in the upper world (D2) married to stars (E3), an old man (bright star) and a young one (dim star) (F4). The younger girl gets the help of Spider-woman (J1a) in making a rope (K3) to descend to earth, but it is too short and she hangs on it until she dies (L2). Sequel: war of sky and earth people (N3). Explanations: Stars (M1b), animal markings and other characteristics (M3) (all in the sequel).

16. Chehalis 1: Adamson, *MAFLS,* Vol. 27, 95. "Star Husband." Collected 1926. —Fragmentary.

Two girls (A2) sleeping out (C1) wish for two stars as husbands (B1, E3). They find two men—an old (bright star) and a young (dim star) (F4) sleeping with them.

17. Chehalis 2: Adamson, *MAFLS,* Vol. 27, 95. "Star Husband." Collected 1927. —Type I.

Two girls (A2) sleeping out (C1) wish for two stars as husbands (B1). They find themselves in the upper world (D2) married to stars (E3), an old man (dim star) and one even older (bright star) (F4), but soon tire of them. Spider helps them (J1) descend on a spider-web rope (K3d) so that they reach home safely (L1).

18. Snuqualmi 1: Haeberlin, *JAFL,* Vol. 37, 373, no. 2. "Star Husband." Collected c. 1920.—Type IV.

Two sisters (A2), out digging fern roots (C2a) wish for two stars as husbands (B1). They find themselves in the upper world (D2) married to stars (E3), an old man (red star) and a young one (white star) (F4). The husbands are hunters (F10). The youngest sister bears a son (G1). The girls are warned against digging (H1) but disobey and open a skyhole (I1), through which a gust of wind blows (I4). They make a cedar-twig ladder (K4) on which they successfully descend (L1). Explanation: geographical features (M2) and animal characteristics (M3). Sequel: boy becomes transformer (N1a).

19. Snuqualmi 2: Haeberlin, *JAFL,* Vol. 37, 375, no. 2a. "Star Husband." Copied by the author from *Tacoma Evening News,* no date.—Type IV.

Two sisters (A2), out digging fern roots (C2a) wish for two stars as husbands (B1). They find themselves in the upper world (D2) married to stars (red and white) (E3). One of the women bears a son (G1). (The father is white star and the boy is called Moon. See F6). The girls are warned against digging (H1) but disobey and open a skyhole (I1), through which a gust of wind blows (I4). They are helped by an old woman (J2) and make a cedar-twig ladder (K4) on which they successfully descend (L1). Explanation: Moon (M1a), geographical features (M2) and animal characteristics (M3). Sequel: Boy becomes transformer (N1a). This is a close parallel to Snuqualmi 1. Variations seem incidental.

20. Snuqualmi 3: Ballard, UWash, Vol. 3, 69. Collected 1916 from Snuqualmi Charlie (born c. 1850), Tolt, Washington.—Type IV.

Two sisters (A2) out digging fern roots (C2a) wish for two stars as husbands (B1). They find themselves in the upper world (D2) married to stars (E3), an old man (white star) and a young one (red star) (F4). The husbands are hunters (F10). One of the women bears a son (G1). The girls are warned against digging (H1) but disobey and open a skyhole (I1), through which a gust of wind blows (I4). They make a cedar-bark ladder (K4) on which they successfully descend (L1). Explanation: moon (M1a). Sequel: boy becomes transformer (N1a).

21. Puyallup 1: Curtis, *The North American Indian,* Vol. 9, 117. "Star Husbands." Collected c. 1905. "The same myth is told by the Twana."—Type IV.

Two girls (A2) are taken to the sky world as wives of two stars (E3), one young and one old (F4). One woman bears a son (G1). They are warned not to dig (H1) but disobey and open a skyhole (I1). They make a vine rope (K3e) on which they successfully descend (L1). Explanation: Shape of Bluejay's head (M3d). Sequel: boy becomes transformer (N1a).

22. Puyallup 2: Adamson, *MAFLS,* Vol. 27, 356. "Star Husband." Collected 1926.—Type I.

Five sisters (A5) digging roots sleep out (C1, C2a) and wish for stars as husbands (B1). They find themselves in the upper world (D2) living with the stars (E3), old (bright star) and young (dim star) men (F4). They dig and discover a sky hole (I1), through which a gust of wind blows (I4). They make a vine rope (K3e) on which they successfully descend (L1).

23. Cowlitz: Adamson, *MAFLS,* Vol. 27, 269. "Sun and Moon." Collected c. 1926.—Type IV.

Two sisters (A2) digging roots sleep out (C1, C2a) and wish for stars as husbands (B1). They find themselves in the upper world (D2) living with the stars (E3), an old (small star) and a young man (big star) (F4). One of the girls bears a son (G1). They are warned against digging (H1), but do so and open a skyhole (I1), through which a gust of wind blows (I4). They make a rope of roots (K3f) on which they successfully descend (L1). Sequel: boy becomes transformer (N1a).

24. Coos 1: Frachtenberg, CU, Vol. 1, 51. "The Girls and the Stars." Collected before 1913, from Jim Buchanan (d. 1939).—Fragmentary.

Two girls (A2) sleeping out (C1) wish for stars as husbands (B1). They find themselves married to stars (E3) an old man (small star) and a young one (big star) (F4).

25. Coos 2: Jacobs, UWash, Vol. 8, 241. "Star Husband." Collected 1932 at Florence, Oregon (a garbled rendering of a tale heard from Jim Buchanan).—Fragmentary.

Two girls (A2) sleeping out (C1) wish for stars as husbands (B1). They find themselves married to stars (E3), an old man (bright star) and a young one (dim star) (F4).

26. Coos 3: Jacobs, UWash, Vol. 8, 169f. "Star Husband." Collected 1933 from Mrs. Annie M. Peterson. Learned by her from a woman in South Slough, Oregon.—Fragmentary.

Three girls (A4) sleeping out (C1) wish for stars as husbands (B1). They find themselves married to stars (E3) an old (dim star) and two young men (bright stars) (F4).

CALIFORNIA AREA

27. Maidu: Dixon, PAES, Vol. 4, 183, no. 10. Collected 1902–3.—Type I**.

Two girls (A2) sleeping out (C1) wish for stars as husbands (B1). They find themselves in the upper world (D2) married to red and blue stars (E3). They each have a child (G1). They make a sinew rope (K3b) and climb down. The husbands discover their flight, cut the rope and drop them to their death, but they are later revived (L2a).

28. Patwin: Kroeber, UCal, Vol. 29, 306. "Ascent to the Sky." Collected 1923.

A girl (A1) is carried to the sky by whirlwind (B3a, D6, E6). She is cautioned against digging (H1) but disobeys and discovers a skyhole (I1). The husband helps her descend (J4, K1, L1). Later she dies and returns to the sky (N6).

29. Washo 1: Lowie, UCal, Vol. 36, 350. "The Star Husbands." Collected 1926, Coleville, Calif.—Type I**.

Two women (A2) sleeping out (C1) wish for stars as husbands (B1). They find themselves in the upper world (D2) married to bright and dim stars (E3). One has a child (G1). They dig (H1a) and open a skyhole (I1). They make a sinew rope (K3b) and are descending. The child goes back and tells his father the women are escaping. The husband cuts the rope and they fall and are killed (L3).

30. Washo 2: Curtis, *The North American Indian,* Vol. 15, 154. "The Women Who Married Stars." Collected c. 1910.—Type I**.

Two girls (A2) wish for stars as husbands (B1). They find themselves in the upper world (D2) married to Moon and Sun (E1a). The white star is Moon, the red star is Sun (F6). The older woman bears a son (G1). They discover a skyhole (I1) and make a sinew rope (K3b) and are descending. The child tells his father the women are escaping. The husband cuts the rope and they fall and are killed (L2). Explanation: backward state of the Indian (M4b).

PLATEAU AREA

31. Shoshone 1: Liljeblad manuscript, collected at Ft. Hall, Idaho, April 30, 1943, by Sven Liljeblad.—Type I.

Two sisters (A2) sleeping out (C1) wish for two stars as husbands (B1). They find themselves in the upper world (D2) married to stars (E3), an old man (dim star) and a young (bright star) (F4). They find a skyhole with the help of an old woman (I3) and with her help (J2) make a rope of roots (K3f) on which they reach the earth safely (L1), since they obeyed her warning not to look about during the descent (K7a).

32. Shoshone 2: St. Clair-Lowie, *JAFL,* Vol. 22, 268, no. 6. "The Star Husband." Collected before 1909 from Wind River Shoshone of Wyoming. The tale said not to be found among Lemhi Shoshone of Idaho.—Type I**.

Two girls (A3) sleeping out (C1) wish for two stars (B1). Two stars (E3), young men (F2), come and take them to the upper world. One of the girls bears a son (G1). She is warned against digging roots (H1a) but disobeys and open up a skyhole (I1). With the help of her husband (J4) she escapes on a skin rope (K3a) and reaches the earth with her child (L1). Later she returns to the sky (N6).

33. Wasco: Curtin, PAES, Vol. 2, 302, no. 6. "Five Stars Visit the Earth." Collected before 1909.—Type I*.

Five girls (A5) sleeping out (C1) wish for five stars as husbands (B1). They are visited by starmen (E3). One of them, an old man (dimmest star) (F1) disgusts the girl. Hence young girls always dislike old husbands (M5b). Explanation of cliffs (M2). Origin myth sequel (N4).

34. Wishram: Spier and Sapir, UWash, Vol. 3, 276. "Star Husband." Collected 1905 in Yakima Reservation, from Mrs. Mabel Teio. Original home of tribe opposite the Dalles on Columbia River. (Note: "The Wishram have the spider-rope incident but Mrs. Teio did not know it.")—Type I*.

Two girls (A2) sleeping out (C1) wish for two stars, big and little, as husbands (B1). A star (E3), a meteor-like man (F9), comes and sleeps by the younger girl.

35. Kutenai: Boas, BBAE, Vol. 59, 247, no. 70. "The Star Husband." Collected 1914 among Upper Kutenai.—Type I.

Two girls (A3) sleeping out (C1) wish for two stars as husbands (B1). One of the girls finds herself in the upper world (D2) married to a star (E3), an old man (small star) (F1). She is warned against digging roots (H1a) but does so and discovers a skyhole (I1). She lets herself down on a rope (K3) and arrives safely, but is later killed by the husband (L1a).

36. Shuswap: Teit, JE, Vol. 2, 687. Collected 1900.—Fragmentary.

Two girls (A2), sleeping out (C1) wish for a star as husband (B1). Next morning an old man with sore eyes (F1) (bright star) (E6) is in bed with them. They escape.

PLAINS AREA

37. Sarsi: Curtis, *The North American Indian,* Vol. 18, 140. "The Girl Who Married a Star."

Two sisters (A3) sitting out at night (C1) wish for stars as husbands (B1). One of them is carried to the upper world with her eyes closed (D3) and is married to the star (E3), a young man (F2). She bears a son (G1). Though warned against digging parsnips (H1a) she does so and discovers a skyhole (I1). With the assistance of her husband (J4) she descends safely (L1) on a skin rope (K3a).

38. Blackfoot 1: Wissler and Duvall, PaAM, Vol. 2, 58, no. 3. "The Fixed Star." Collected 1903–7 in Montana.—Type IIa.

Two girls (A3) are sleeping out (C1). One wishes for a star as husband (B1, E3). Later while gathering wood (C2b) she is met by a young man (F2), who takes her to the upper world by means of a feather while her eyes are closed (D3, D7). The Star's father and mother are Sun and Moon. She bears a son (G1). She is warned against digging turnips (H1a) but disobeys and opens a skyhole with assistance of crane (I3). They are let down on a spider-web rope (K3d) by help of Spider-man (J1b) and reach home safely (L1). Origin explanations (M1b, M3a, M7b, N4).

39. Blackfoot 2: McClintock, *The Old North Trail* (London, 1910), p. 491. "Poia." Collected 1905 in Montana.—Type IIa.

Two sisters (A3) are sleeping out (C1). One wishes for a star as husband (B1). Later while she is gathering wood (C2b) she is met by a young man (F2), the Star (E3) who takes her to the upper world by means of a feather (D7), with her foot on a spider web and a juniper branch in her hand. She must keep her eyes closed (D3). Star's father and mother are Sun and Moon. She bears a son (G1). She is warned against digging turnips (H1a) but disobeys and opens a skyhole with assistance of crane (I3). She and her son are let down on a spider-web rope (K3d) with the help of Spider-man (J1b) and reach home safely (L1). Sequel: Star Boy (N1).

40. Gros Ventre 1: Kroeber PaAM, Vol. 1, 101, no. 25. "The Women Who Married a Star and a Buffalo." Collected 1901, see nos. 41, 42.

Two girls (A3) sleeping out (C1) wish for two stars as husbands (B1). One of them is taken to upper world by a star (E3). Sequel: Second girl marries a buffalo and is rescued (N5).

41. Gros Ventre 2: Kroeber, PaAM, Vol. 1, 100, no. 24. "The Women Who Married the Moon and a Buffalo." Collected 1901, Ft. Belknap Reservation, Northern Montana.

Two women (A3) sleeping out (C1) wish for moon and star as husbands (B1). The one who had wished for the moon (E1) sees a porcupine (B2) and follows it up a tree to the upper world (D1), though warned by her friend (D1a). The porcupine turns into Moon who spends his days hunting (F10). She bears Moon a son (G1). She is warned against digging roots (H1a) but does so and discovers a skyhole (I1). With the help of her husband (J4) she descends on a sinew rope (K3b) and reaches home safely (L1). Sequel: Second girl marries a buffalo and is rescued (N5).

42. Gros Ventre 3: Kroeber, PaAM, Vol. 1, 90, no. 21. "Moon Child." (See no. 41.)

Sun and Moon dispute about women (B2a) and Moon (E1) agrees to bring an earth-woman to the sky. He turns himself into a porcupine (B2) and lures a woman (A1) after him up a tree (D1) to the sky world, where he becomes a young man (F2) and marries her. She wins a chewing contest from the wife of Sun. She bears Moon a son (G1). She accidentally finds a skyhole (I1). With help of her husband (J4) she descends by means of a sinew rope (K3b). But he sends down a rock which kills her and spares the son (L3). Explanations: moon's spots (M1a). Sequel: Moon Boy (N1).

43. Cree 1: Bloomfield, Nat. Mus. Can., Vol. 60, 177, no. 21. "Sun Child." Collected 1925, Battleford Agency, Saskatchewan.—Type II.

A woman (A1) digging turnips (C2a) is enticed away (B3b) by a young man (F2), the Sun (E2), and they go to the upper world. She bears him a son (G1). She is warned against digging for wild turnips (H1a). She finds a skyhole with the help of an old woman (I2), who lets her down (J2) on a sinew rope (K3b). The husband sends down a rock which kills her but spares the son (L3). Sequel: Sun Boy (N1).

44. Cree 2: Bloomfield, Nat. Mus. Can., Vol. 60, 314, no. 34. "The Foolish Maidens and One-Leg." Collected 1925, Battleford Agency, Saskatchewan.—Type III.

Two sisters (A2) wish for two stars as husbands (B1). They find themselves in the upper world (D2) married to stars (E3) a young man (dim star) and an old one (bright star) (F4). With the help of an old woman (I2) they find a skyhole and (J2) descend on a skin rope (K3a). They break the prohibition against looking (K7a) and land in the top of a tree (L1). Explanations: wolverene's marks (M3c). Sequel: trickster animals under tree: wolverene duped (N2).

45. Cree 3: Skinner, PaAM, Vol. 9, 113. Collected c. 1908 from Rupert House Cree (Southeast shore James Bay).—Type I*.

Two girls (A2) marry two stars (E3), but are unhappy because they see their husbands only at night. Fragmentary.

46. Assiniboine: Lowie, PaAM, Vol. 4, 171, no. 18. Collected 1907, Morley, Alberta.—Type III.

Two women (A2) see stars through the roof (C1b) and wish for them as husbands (B1). They are taken to the upper world by the stars (E3), a young (small star) and an old man (big star) (F4). They are warned against digging (H1) but disobey and find a skyhole (I1). Spider (J1) lets them down on a spider-web rope (K3d) with injunctions against looking (K7a). They look and lodge in the top of a tree (L1). Sequel: trickster animals under tree: wolverene duped (N2).

47. Arikara 1: Dorsey, CI, Vol. 17, 45, no. 14. "The Girl Who Married a Star." Collected 1903, Ft. Berthold Reservation, North Dakota.—Type II.

Two girls (A3) are sleeping out on an arbor (C1a). One of them wishes for a star as husband (B1). Next day she follows a porcupine (B2) up a tree (D1) to the upper world. He is the star (E3), a middle-aged man (F3). She bears a son (G1). She is warned against digging in valleys (H1c) but she disobeys and discovers a skyhole (I1). An old woman (J2) helps her make a sinew rope (K3b) but it is too short, so that she and the boy do not reach the ground. The husband sends down a rock which kills the woman but spares the son (L3). Sequel: Star Boy (N1).

48. Arikara 2: Dorsey, CI, Vol. 17, 56, no. 15. "The Girl Who Married a Star." Collected 1903, Ft. Berthold Reservation, North Dakota.—Type IIa.

Two girls (A3) are sleeping out (C1a). One of them wishes a star for her husband (B1). She finds herself in the upper world (D2) married to the star (E3). She bears a son (G1). She is warned against digging turnips (H1a), but she disobeys and discovers a skyhole (I1). With help of an old woman (J2) she makes a sinew rope (K3b), but it is too short and she and the boy do not reach the ground. The husband sends down a rock which kills the woman but spares the son (L3). Sequel: Star Boy (N1).

49. Hidatsa 1: Lowie, UCal, Vol. 40, 2. Collected 1910–11 at Ft. Berthold Reservation, North Dakota.—Type II.

Sun and Moon dispute about women (B2a). Moon (E1) turns himself into a porcupine (B2) and lures a woman away from her companion (A3) up a tree (D1) to the sky world. The woman bears a son (G1). She wins a chewing contest with Sun's wife. She is warned against digging (H1a) or shooting a meadow lark (H3). She discovers a skyhole (I1). She and the boy descend on a sinew rope (K3b) but it is too short. The husband sends down a rock which kills her but spares the son (L3). Explanation: Moon's spots (M1a). Sequel: Moon Boy (N1). (This is practically identical with Gros Ventre 3.)

50. Hidatsa 2: Beckwith, MAFLS, Vol. 32, 117. Collected 1931.—Type II.

Sun and Moon dispute about women (B2a). Moon (E1) turns himself into a porcupine (B2) and lures a woman away from her companion (A3) up a tree (D1) to the sky world. She wins a chewing contest with Sun's wife. The woman bears a son (G1). She is warned against digging (H1a) or shooting a meadow lark (H3). They disobey and discover a skyhole (I1). With the help of spider (J1) they descend on a sinew rope (K3b), but it is too short. The husband sends down a rock which kills her but spares the son (L3). Explanation: Moon's spots (M1a). Sequel: Moon Boy (N1).

51. Crow 1: Lowie, PaAM, Vol. 25, 52. Collected c. 1914, Crow Reservation, Montana.—Type II.

Sun and moon dispute about women (B2a). A girl (A1) gathering wood (C2b) follows a porcupine (B2) up a tree which stretches to the upper world (D1). She finds that she is married to the Sun (porcupine) (E2). She wins a chewing contest with Moon's wife. She bears Sun a son (G1). She is warned against digging (H1a) or shooting a meadow lark (H3). She disobeys and discovers a skyhole (I1). With the help of Spider (J1) they descend on a sinew rope (K3b) but it is too short. The husband sends down a rock which kills her but spares the son (L3). Explanation: Moon's spots (M1a). Sequel: Sun Boy (N1).

52. Crow 2: Lowie, PaAM, Vol. 25, 57, Collected c. 1914, Crow Reservation, Montana.—Type II.

Two girls (A3) making moccasins (C2c) see a marvelous porcupine. One of them follows it (B2) up a tree which stretches to the upper world (D1). She finds herself married to a man (E6). She bears a son (G1). She is warned against digging (H1a) or shooting a meadow lark (H3). She disobeys and discovers a skyhole (I1). With help of the husband (J4) she and the son are lowered in a bucket (K5) on a sinew rope (K3b) but the rope is too short. The husband sends down a rock which kills the woman but spares the son (L3). Sequel: Star Boy (N1).

53. Crow 3: Lowie, PaAM, Vol. 25, 69. Collected c. 1914, Crow Reservation, Montana.—Type II.

A girl (A3) gathering wood (C2b) is lured up a tree by a porcupine (B2). Her friend warns her (D1a) but the tree stretches to the upper world (D1). She finds herself married to a man (E6). She bears a son (G1). She is warned against digging for turnips (H1a) and shooting a meadow lark (H3). She disobeys and discovers a skyhole (I1). With help of the husband (J4) she and the son are lowered on a sinew rope (K3b), but it is too short. The husband sends down a rock which kills the woman but spares the son (L3). Explanation: stars (M1b). Sequel: Star Boy (N1).

54. Crow 4: Simms, FM, Vol. 2, 299, no. 17. Collected 1902 from an old man.—Type II.

Sun and Moon dispute about women (B2a). A woman (A1) gathering wood (C2b) is lured up a tree by a porcupine (B2). The tree stretches to the upper world (D1), where she marries Sun (E2). She bears him a son (G1). She is warned against digging (H1) and shooting a meadow lark (H3). She disobeys and discovers a skyhole (I1). With help of the husband (J4) she and the son are lowered on a sinew rope (K3b) but it is too short. The husband sends down a rock which kills the woman but spares the son (L3). Sequel: Sun Boy (N1).

55. Cheyenne: Grinnell, JAFL, Vol. 34, 308. "Falling Star." Collected "many years" before 1921 from White Bull, a Northern Cheyenne.—Type II.

Two girls (A3) are sleeping out (C1). One of them wishes for a star as husband (B1). In spite of warning from her friend (D1a) she follows a porcupine up a tree (B2) which stretches to the upper world (D1). She marries the Star (E3), a middle-aged man (F3). She is pregnant (G1). She is warned against digging (H1a) but disobeys and discovers a skyhole (I1). She descends on a grass rope (K3g) but it is too short. She falls and is killed but her unborn son is saved (L3). Sequel: Star Boy (N1).

56. Dakota 1: Riggs, CNAE, Vol. 9, 90. Date of collection unknown. Author's association with the tribe (Santee Dakota) 1837–1883.—Type IIa.

Two girls (A3) sleeping out (C1) wish for two stars as husbands (B1). They find themselves in the upper world (D2) married to two stars (E3), an old man (bright star) and a young (dim star) (F4). One girl becomes pregnant (G1). She is warned against digging roots (H1a) but disobeys and discovers a skyhole (I1). She falls through it (K6) and is killed, but bursts open and the son is born (L3). Sequel: Star Boy (N1).

57. Dakota 2: Wallis, JAFL, Vol. 36, 85, no. 19. "Spider and Thunder Boy." Collected 1914 at Griswold, Manitoba.—Type IIa.

Two girls (A3) are taken to the sky and married to Thunders (E4). Both become pregnant (G1). They are warned about digging for carrots (H1a). The youngest girl falls (K6) through the skyhole (I1) and is killed but her son is thus born (L3). Sequel: Thunder Boy (N1).

58. Arapaho 1: Dorsey and Kroeber, FM, Vol. 5, 330, no. 135. "The Girl Enticed to the Sky." Collected before 1903.—Type II.

Women are (A3) gathering wood (C2b). One is lured by a porcupine (B2) and in spite of warning from her friend (D1a) follows him up a tree (D1), which stretches to the upper world. There she marries Porcupine (E5). She is warned against digging for roots (H1a) but she disobeys and discovers a skyhole (I1). She lets herself down on a sinew rope (K3b) but it is too short. The husband sends down a rock to kill her but she survives (L1).

59. Arapaho 2: Dorsey, FM, Vol. 4, 212. "Little Star." Collected before 1903.—Type II.

Sun and Moon dispute about women (B2a) and Moon agrees to bring an earth-woman to the sky. Two girls (A3) are gathering wood (C2b) and see a porcupine which, in spite of warning from her friend (D1a), lures one of them (B2) into a tree (D1) which stretches to the upper world. Here the porcupine becomes Moon (E1), a handsome young man (F2). She wins a chewing contest with the wife of Sun. She bears a son (G1). She is warned against digging for roots (H1a) but she disobeys and discovers a skyhole (I1). She lets herself down on her lariat (K3b) but it is too short. The husband sends down a rock which kills her but saves the son (L3). Explanations: moon's spots (M1a), Sun-dance ceremonies (M4a), time of human gestation (M5a). Sequel: Moon Boy (N1).

60. Arapaho 3: Dorsey and Kroeber, FM, Vol. 5, 321, no. 134. Collected before 1903.—Type II.

Sun and Moon dispute about women (B2a) and moon agrees to bring an earth-woman to the sky. Girls sleeping out (C1) wish for stars as husbands (B1). Later four of them are gathering wood (C2b) and one (A3) follows a porcupine up a tree (B2) in spite of warning from her friends (D1a). The tree stretches to the upper world (D1). Here the porcupine becomes Moon (E1), a handsome young man (F2). She wins a chewing contest with the wife of Sun. She bears a son (G1). She is warned against digging for roots (H1a) but she disobeys and discovers a skyhole (I1). She lets herself down on a sinew rope (K3b) but it is too short. The husband sends down a rock which kills her but spares the son (L3). Explanation: moon's spots (M1a). Sequel: Moon Boy (N1).

61. Arapaho 4: Dorsey and Kroeber, FM, Vol. 5, 332, no. 136. Collected before 1903.—Type II.

Sun and moon dispute about women (B2a) and Moon agrees to bring an earth-woman to the sky. Two women (A3) see a porcupine and one follows it (B2) up a tree in spite of warning from her friend (D1a). The tree stretches to the upper world (D1). Here the porcupine becomes Moon (E1). The woman has a chewing contest with the wife of Sun. She bears a son (G1). She is warned against digging for roots (H1a) but she disobeys and discovers a skyhole (I1). She lets herself down on a sinew rope (K3b) but it is too short. The husband sends down a rock which kills her but spares the son (L3). Explanation: moon's spots (M1a). Sequel: Moon Boy (N1).

62. Arapaho 5: Dorsey and Kroeber, FM, Vol. 5, 339, no. 137. Collected before 1903.—Type II.

Moon comes to earth to get an earth-woman. A woman (A1) sees him in the form of a porcupine (B2) and follows him up a tree which stretches to the upper world (D1), where porcupine becomes Moon (E1), a handsome man (F2). She has a chewing contest with Moon's other wife. She bears a son (G1). With the help of an old woman she finds a skyhole (I3). The old woman (J2) lets her down on a sinew rope (K3b) and she reaches home safely (L1). Explanation: moon's spots (M1a). Sequel: Moon Boy (N1).

63. Arapaho 6: Dorsey and Kroeber, FM, Vol. 5, 339, note 3. Collected before 1903.—Type II.

Two women (A3) going for water (C2c) see a porcupine. One follows it (B2) up a tree which stretches to the upper world (D1). Here the porcupine becomes Moon (E1). She becomes pregnant (G1). She escapes (I1) on a sinew rope (K3b), but it is too short. The husband drops a stone on her head and kills her but the unborn boy is saved (L3). Sequel: Moon Boy (N1).

64. Arapaho 7: Dorsey and Kroeber, FM, Vol. 5, 340, no. 138. Collected before 1903—Type II.

Sun and Moon dispute about women (B2a). Women (A3) gathering wood (C2b) see a porcupine and one follows it (B2) up a tree which stretches to the upper world (D1). Here the porcupine becomes Sun (E2), a young man (F2), and marries her. She bears a son (G1). She is warned against digging roots (H1a) but she disobeys and discovers a skyhole (I1). She lets herself down on a sinew rope (K3b) but it is too short. The husband sends down a rock which kills her but spares the son (L3). Sequel: Sun Boy (N1).

65. Arapaho 8: Salzmann manuscript.[5] Collected July 1949 from John B. Goggles, aged 63 in Ethete, Wyoming, by Zdenek Salzmann.—Type II.

Two sisters (A3) are sleeping out (C1). One wishes for a star as husband (B1). Her sister warns her against such a wish (D1a). Next day they are gathering wood (C2b) and one girl sees a porcupine and in spite of warning from her sister (D1a) follows it (B2) up a tree which stretches to the upper world (D1). The porcupine becomes Star (E3) and marries her. He is a hunter (F10). She bears a son (G1). She is warned against digging for a certain plant (H1a) but disobeys and discovers a skyhole (I1). With the help of an old woman (J2) she descends on a sinew rope (K3b), but must not look around (K7a). The rope is too short. The husband sends down a rock which kills the wife but spares the boy (L3). Sequel: Star Boy (N1).

66. Pawnee 1: Dorsey, CI, Vol. 59, 56, no. 13. "The Girl Who Married a Star." Collected c. 1902 in Oklahoma.—Type IIa.

Two girls (A3) are sleeping out on an arbor (C1a). One of them wishes for a star as husband (B1). She finds herself in the upper world (D2) married to the Star (E3). She bears a son (G1). She is warned against digging deep (H1), but she disobeys and discovers a skyhole (I1). She lets herself down on a sinew rope (K3b), but it is too short. The husband sends down a rock which kills her but spares the son (L3). Sequel: Star Boy (N1).

67. Pawnee 2: Dorsey, *MAFLS,* Vol. 8, 60, no. 16. "The Girl Who Married a Star." Collected before 1904.—Type IIa.

Two girls (A3) are sleeping out on an arbor (C1a). One of them wishes for a star as husband (B1). She finds herself in the upper world (D2) married to the Star (E3), an old man (F1). She bears a son (G1). She is warned

---

[5] This version was published. See Zdenek Salzmann, "An Arapaho Version of the Star Husband Tale," *Hoosier Folklore,* Vol. 9 (1950), 50–58.—ED. NOTE

against digging deep (H1), but she disobeys and discovers a skyhole (I1). She lets herself down on a sinew rope (K3b), but it is too short. The husband sends down a bolt of lightning and kills her, but the son survives (L3). Sequel: Star Boy (N1).

68. Pawnee 3: Grinnell, *JAFL,* Vol. 7, 197. "Pawnee Star Myth." Collected "several years" before 1894.—Type IIa.

Two girls (A3) are sleeping out on an arbor (C1a). One of them wishes for a star as husband (B1). She finds herself in the upper world (D2) married to the Star (E3). She bears a son (G1). She is warned against digging deep (H1), but she disobeys and discovers a skyhole (I1). She lets herself and son down on a sinew rope (K3b) but it is too short. The husband sends down a rock which kills her but spares the son (L3). Sequel: Sun Boy (N1).

69. Oto: Kercheval, *JAFL,* Vol. 6, 199. "The Chief's Daughters." Collected before 1893 in Nebraska.—Type I.

Two sisters (A2) sleeping out (C1) wish for stars as husbands (B1). They find themselves in the upper world (D2) married to the stars (E3), a chief (dim star) and his servant (bright star) (F7). They are warned against digging (H1), but disobey and open a skyhole (I1). With the help of an old man (J3) they make a skin rope (K3a) on which they successfully descend (L1).

70. Kiowa: Mooney, RBAE, Vol. 17, 238. "Star Husband." Collected 1892 in Oklahoma.—Type II.

A girl (A1) is lured up a tree by a porcupine (B2). The tree stretches to the upper world (D1) where the porcupine turns into the son of the Sun (E2) and marries her. She bears a son (G1). She is warned against digging for roots (H1a), but she disobeys and discovers a skyhole (I1). She lets herself and son down on a rope (K3) but it is too short. The husband sends down a rock which kills her but spares the son (L3). Sequel: Sun boy (N1). —An interesting native drawing accompanies the text. This colored drawing is in two parts: (1) the girl following the porcupine up a tree and (2) the husband with three other people above sending down the stone which has almost reached the woman and child hanging on the rope.

71. Wichita 1: Dorsey, CI, Vol. 21, 298, no. 57. "The Woman Who Married a Star." Collected 1900–3 in Oklahoma.—Type VI.

A woman (A1) wishes for a star as husband (B1). She finds herself in the upper world (D2) married to the Star (E3), an old man (F1). She is warned against digging up a large rock (H1b), but she disobeys and discovers a skyhole (I1). She lets herself down by a weed rope (K3h) but it is too short. She is rescued (L1) by buzzard (J6a). Explanation: origin of certain taboos (M7a).

72. Wichita 2: Curtis, *The North American Indian,* Vol. 19, 102. "The Woman Who Married a Star."

A woman (A1) seeing stars through a hole in the roof (C1b) wishes for a star as husband (B1). She find herself in the upper world (D2) married to the Star (E3), an old man (F1). She lets herself down by a rope of soapweed (K3h), but it is too short. She is rescued (L1) by buzzard (J6a). Explanation: origin of certain taboos (M7a).

SOUTHWEST AREA

73. Seama: Espinosa, *JAFL,* Vol. 49, 88. "Yellow Corn Elopes with Sun." Collected 1931. Probably does not belong to the Star Husband cycle.

Sun (E2) elopes (B3b) with a woman (A1) and takes her to the sky. She bears a son (G1). Spider-woman (J1a) helps her come back home (L1). Sequel: son returns to sky (N6).

SOUTHEAST AREA

74. Caddo 1: Dorsey, CI, Vol. 41, 27, no. 14, "The Girl Who Married a Star." Collected 1903–5 in Oklahoma.—Type VI.

A girl (A1) sleeping out on an arbor (C1a) wishes for a star as husband (B1). She finds herself in the upper world (D2) married to the Star (E3), an old man (F1). She finds a star hole at the suggestion of her sister-in-law (I2), who helps her (J5) make a bark rope (K3i) and lets her down. The rope is too short, but she is rescued (L1) by buzzard (J6a) and later hawk (J6b). Explanation: origin of certain taboos (M7a).

75. Caddo 2: Dorsey, CI, Vol. 41, 29, no. 15. "The Girl Who Married a Star." Collected 1903–5 in Oklahoma.—Type VI.

A girl (A1) wishes for a star as husband (B1). She finds herself in the upper world (D2) married to the star (E3), an old man (F1). She is warned against digging up a large rock (H1b) but she disobeys and discovers a sky-hole (I1). She lets herself down on a soapweed rope (K3h), but it is too short. She is rescued by black eagle (J6c) and brought home (L1).

76. Koasati: Swanton, BBAE, Vol. 88, 166, no. 4. "The Star Husbands." Collected 1908–14 at Kinder, Louisiana.—Type I*.

Two girls (A2) sleeping out (C1) make wishes for stars as husbands (B1). They find themselves in the upper world (D2) married to stars (E3), an old man (bright star) and a young one (dim star) (F4). They return home (L1) in their sleep. Ending fragmentary.

WOODLAND AREA

77. Ojibwa 1: Speck, GSCan, Vol. 9, 47. "The Wish to Marry a Star." Collected 1913, Bear Island, Lake Timazami.—Type III.

Two girls (A2) sleeping out (C1) wish for stars as husbands (B1). They find themselves in the upper world (D2) married to stars (E3), an old man (white star) and a young (red star) (F4). An old woman lets them see through a skyhole (I3). She (J2) helps them make a root rope (K3f) and lets them down in a basket (K2) but they lodge in a treetop (L1). Sequel: trickster animals, wolverene duped (N2).

78. Ojibwa 2: Jones, JAFL, Vol. 29, 371, no. 15, "The Girls Who Married Stars." (Only a Summary. May be the same as No. 79.) Collected before 1915 at Bois Fort, north of Lake Superior.—Type III.

Two girls (A2) sleeping out (C1) wish for stars as husbands (B1). They find themselves in the upper world (D2) married to stars (E3). An old woman shows them a skyhole (I3) and lets them down (J2) in a basket (K2) but they lodge in a tree (L1). Sequel: trickster animals: wolverene duped (N2).

79. Ojibwa 3: Jones-Michelson, PAES, Vol. 7 (II), 151, no. 13. "The Foolish Maidens and the Diver." Collected before 1919.—Type III.

Two girls (A2) sleeping out (C1) wish for stars as husbands (B1). They find themselves in the upper world (D2) married to stars (E3), an old man (red star) and a young (white star) (F4). An old woman shows them a skyhole (I3). She lets them down (J2) in a basket (K2) with injunction against looking (K7a) but they lodge in a tree (L1). Sequel: trickster animals: wolverene duped (N2).

80. Ojibwa 4: Jones-Michelson, PAES, Vol. 7 (II), 455, no. 55. "The Foolish Maiden and her Younger Sister." Collected before 1919.—Type III.

Two girls (A2) sleeping out (C1) wish for stars as husbands (B1). They find themselves in the upper world (D2) married to stars (E3), an old man and a young one (F4).—Fragmentary. This is *preceded* by: Trickster animals under tree: wolverene duped (N2). Explanation: animal markings (M3c).

81. Ojibwa 5: Radin and Reagan, *JAFL*, Vol. 41, 116, no. 22. "The Two Sisters." Collected 1911–14 at Sarnia, Ontario.—Type I.

Two girls (A2) sleeping out (C1) wish for stars as husbands (B1). They find themselves in the upper world (D2) married to stars (E3), a bright and a faint one (F4). An old woman shows them a skyhole (I3) and helps them back to the earth again (J2), but they must not look about on the way down (K7a). Though one of them (L4) breaks the taboo, the other helps her home (L1).

82. Micmac 1: Rand, *Legends of the Micmacs* (New York, 1894), p. 160, no. 20. "The Two Weasels." Collected c. 1870 in Falmouth, Nova Scotia.—Type III.

Two girls (A2) sleeping out (C1) wish for stars as husbands (B1). They find themselves in the upper world (D2) married to stars (E3), an old one (small star) with eye-water cup and a young one (large star) with war paint (F4a). The husbands (J4) warn the girls to keep quiet until squirrel and chipmunk sing (H4, K7b) and then they find themselves in the top of a tree (L1). Sequel: Trickster animals under tree: badger duped (N2).

83. Micmac 2: Rand, *Legends of the Micmacs* (New York, 1894), p. 306, no. 55. "Badger and the Star Wives." Collected September 7, 1870 from Susan Christmas. "She professes to have learned this story...when she was a small child, from an old blind woman in Cape Breton."—Type III.

Introduction: Swan Maiden Story.—Two women (A2) sleeping out (C1) wish for stars as husbands (B1). They find themselves in the upper world (D2) married to stars (E3), an old man (small star) with eye-water cup and a young one (large star) with war paint (F4a). The husbands are hunters (F10). The women are warned not to move a flat stone (H1b), but they disobey and discover a skyhole (I1). The husbands warn the girls not to move until ground squirrel and chickadee sing (H4, K7b). One breaks the taboo and therefore they lodge in a tree instead of reaching the ground (L1). Sequel: Trickster animals under tree: badger duped (N2).

84. Micmac 3: Parsons, *JAFL*, Vol. 38, 65. "Star Husbands: Sucker Man." Collected 1923 at Whycocomagh, Cape Breton Island. Learned from a woman who died in 1895. People report hearing stories from her in 1870.—Type I*.

Two girls (A2) sleeping out (C1) wish for stars as husbands (B1). They find themselves in the upper world (D2) married to stars (E3), an old man (small star) with eye-water cup and a young one (large star) (F4a). The husbands are hunters (F10). The girls attempt to escape and are chased by a blood-sucking spirit.

85. Passamaquoddy 1: Prince, PAES, Vol. 10, 61, no. 12. (Tale of Lox, the Indian Devil or Mischief Maker." Collected c. 1912 near Eastport, Maine.

Introduction: Swan Maiden story.—Two girls (A2) sleeping out (C1) wish for stars as husbands (B1). They find themselves in the upper world (D2) married to stars (E3), an old man (red star) with eye-water cup and a young one (yellow star) with war paint (F4a). They are warned against lifting a certain rock (H1b) but disobey and discover a skyhole (I1). The husbands (J4) warn them not to move until ground squirrel and chickadee sing (H4, K7b). One of them breaks the taboo and therefore they lodge in a tree instead of reaching the ground (L1). Sequel: Trickster animals under tree: wolverene duped (N2).

86. Passamaquoddy 2: Leland, *Algonquin Legends of New England* (Boston, 1885), p. 140. "The Surprising Adventures of two Water Fairies." Collected 1882 at Campobello, New Brunswick.—Type III.

Introduction: Swan Maiden story.—Two women (A2) sleeping out (C1) wish for stars as husbands (B1). They find themselves in the upper world (D2) married to stars (E3), an old man (red twinkling star) with eye-water cup and a young one (yellow star) with war paint (F4a). They are warned against lifting a certain rock (H1b), but they disobey and discover a skyhole (I1). The husbands warn them not to move until chickadee and squirrels begin to sing (H4, K7b). One of them breaks the taboo and therefore they find themselves in the top of a tree instead of reaching the ground (L1). Sequel: Trickster animals under tree: wolverene duped (N2).

Analysis of the Principal Traits

TRAIT A. NUMBER OF WOMEN

1. ONE.—*Eskimo:* Smith Sound; Kodiak 2.—*California:* Patwin.—*Plains:* Gros Ventre 3; Cree 1; Crow 1, 4; Arapaho 5; Kiowa; Wichita 1, 2.—*Southwest:* Seama.—*Southeast:* Caddo 1, 2.—Total: 14.

2. TWO.—*Mackenzie:* Kaska; Carrier.—*North Pacific:* Tahltan; Ts'ets'aut; Bella Bella; Chilcotin 1, 2; Songish; Klallam; Quileute 1, 2; Quinault; Chehalis 1, 2; Snuqualmi 1, 2, 3; Puyallup 1; Cowlitz; Coos 1, 2.—*California:* Maidu; Washo 1, 2.—*Plateau:* Shoshone 1; Wishram; Shuswap.—*Plains:* Cree 2, 3; Assiniboine; Oto.—*Southeast:* Koasati.—*Woodland:* Ojibwa 1, 2, 3, 4, 5; Micmac 1, 2, 3; Passamaquoddy 1, 2.—Total: 42.

3. TWO AT BEGINNING, THEN ONE.—*Eskimo:* Kodiak 1.—*Plateau:* Shoshone 2; Kutenai.—*Plains:* Sarsi; Blackfoot 1, 2; Gros Ventre 1, 2; Arikara 1, 2; Hidatsa 1, 2; Crow 2, 3; Cheyenne; Dakota 1, 2; Arapaho 1, 2, 3, 4, 6, 7, 8; Pawnee 1, 2, 3.—Total: 27.

4. THREE.—*North Pacific:* Coos 3.—Total: 1.

5. FIVE.—*North Pacific:* Puyallup 2.—*Plateau:* Wasco.—Total: 2.

When we come to a study of the distribution of the various traits of the tale, it becomes clear that the inclusion of the Smith Sound and the Seama variants (Nos. 1 and 73) will only bring confusion. It is doubtful whether these two stories belong in the cycle at all, and for that reason they will be considered separately.

As for the number of women concerned in our story, the table and map give a clear indication. Either throughout the whole story or just at the beginning we find two women in 69 of the 86 versions. These are spread over the whole area of distribution.

In the Plains, from the Cree in the north to the Caddo in the south are found 10 versions in which only one girl appears. Except for the Wichita and Caddo at the southern boundary, these are associated with Trait B2 in which we have one girl enticed into the upper world by a porcupine, and in which there is no room for a second girl in the main action.

Aside from these versions with one woman in the Plains area there are a number which seem to be transitional between two women and one. The story begins with two women but when one of them follows the porcupine husband or goes alone to the upper world the second drops out and is not heard from again. There are 27 of such transitional versions. Of these, 14 are associated with the porcupine-husband type in the central Plains (B2) and the other 13 not so associated, but belong, sometimes illogically to other forms of our tale.

It would seem reasonable, therefore, to suppose (1) that the original tale had two girls (69 versions) and their adventures in the sky world; that (2) the porcupine husband concerned one woman's adventures and sometimes mentions only one (5 versions); (3) that the influence of the two forms just mentioned brought about transitional forms starting with two girls and ending with one. This happens by uselessly adding one girl in the porcupine versions (14) or by losing sight of the second girl in the other forms of the tale (13). This theory of the transitional nature of A3 is borne out by its geographical distribution: the versions associated with the porcupine husband are in the center with other tales of that group, while the other examples of A3 are on the periphery separating that group from other Star Husband tales.

The presence of three (A4) or five (A5) girls sporadically in three tales would seem to be a mere matter of confusion and not to indicate a real tradition.[6]

TRAIT B. INTRODUCTORY ACTION

0. TRAIT NOT PRESENT.—*North Pacific.*—Puyallup 1.—*Plains:* Cree 3; Dakota 2.—Total: 3.

1. WISH FOR STAR HUSBAND.—*Eskimo:* Kodiak 1.—*Mackenzie:* Kaska.— *North Pacific:* Tahltan; Ts'ets'aut; Bella Bella; Chilcotin 1; Songish; Klallam; Quileute 1, 2; Quinault; Chehalis 1, 2; Snuqualmi 1, 2, 3; Puyallup 2; Cowlitz; Coos 1, 2, 3.—*California:* Maidu; Washo 1, 2.—*Plateau:* Shoshone 1, 2; Wasco; Wishram; Kutenai; Shuswap.—*Plains:* Sarsi; Blackfoot 1, 2; Gros Ventre 1, 2; Cree 2; Assiniboine; Arikara 1, 2; Cheyenne; Dakota 1; Arapaho 3, 8; Pawnee 1, 2, 3; Oto; Wichita 1, 2.—*Southeast:* Caddo 1, 2; Koasati.—*Woodland:* Ojibwa 1, 2, 3, 4, 5; Micmac 1, 2, 3; Passamaquoddy 1, 2.—Total: 62.

2. PURSUIT OF PORCUPINE.—*Plains:* Gros Ventre 2; Arikara 1; Crow 2, 3; Cheyenne; Arapaho 1, 5, 6, 8; Kiowa.—Total: 10.

[Gros Ventre 2, Arikara 1, Arapaho 3, 8 and Cheyenne combine traits 1 and 2 and appear in both lists. To Trait 2 should be added the 9 versions of Trait 2a below, making a total for Trait 2 of 19.]

---

6 The presence of five girls is no mere matter of confusion inasmuch as five is the pattern number of several American Indian groups in western North America (e.g., in the Pacific Northwest and in northern California). The quintupling is as much a part of their oral literary tradition as trebling is in ours. For a discussion of five as a pattern number in Clackamas Chinook folklore, see Melville Jacobs, *The Content and Style of an Oral Literature* (Chicago, 1959), pp. 224–28. The antiquity of five as a symbolic number is suggested by its occurrence in South America and in China. See Robert H. Lowie, "Five as a Mystic Number," *American Anthropologist,* Vol. 27 (1925), 578; William Edgar Geil, *The Sacred 5 of China* (Boston and New York, 1926).

2a. Sun and moon dispute about women and decide to get earth and water wives: Pursuit of porcupine.—*Plains:* Gros Ventre 3; Hidatsa 1, 2; Crow 1, 4; Arapaho 2, 3, 4, 7.—Total: 9.

3. Miscellaneous.

3a. Girls carried to sky world by supernatural being.—*Eskimo:* Smith Sound; Kodiak 2.—*Mackenzie:* Carrier.—*California:* Patwin.—Total: 4. [In both Carrier and Patwin the abductor is Whirlwind.]

3b. Elopement.—*Plains:* Cree 1.—*Southwest:* Seama.—Total 2. [Little resemblance in these versions.]

3c. Girls run away to sky world.—*North Pacific:* Chilcotin 2.—Total: 1.

It is in the introductory action that the development of the tale is most clearly seen. The beginning with the girl (or girls) wishing for stars (B1) occurs 62 times and over the complete area of distribution. In the central Plains, however, are found 19 versions in which a girl pursues a porcupine into the upper world (B2). These tales are all concentrated in a relatively small area completely surrounded by the more usual wish for the stars—an area generally corresponding to that in which one girl appears. In five versions we have both the wish for the stars and the porcupine husband (B1 and B2) and all of these have two girls at the beginning and only one later (A3). The 4 Wichita and Caddo tales at the southern end of the area have the unusual combination of one girl (A1) and the wishing for stars (B1).

As a part of the porcupine story (B2) there are found 9 versions which begin with a dispute by the sun and moon about the value of earth and water wives. These are scattered almost at random among the porcupine versions and are so logical a plot element that they probably represent a real part of the porcupine tale.

When we observe the whole area we seem to have before us a story of two girls (A2) and their dreams about star husbands (B1). Then within the territory from the Gros Ventre south to the Kiowa we find a special development, the porcupine husband (B2), sometimes retaining the more usual introduction of the wishes for the stars. All of the miscellaneous forms (B3) are sporadic.

Trait C. Circumstances of Introductory Action

[What the girls are doing when action begins.]

0. Not mentioned.—*Eskimo:* Smith Sound.—*North Pacific:* Klallam; Puyallup 1.—*Plains:* Gros Ventre 3; Cree 3; Dakota 2; Arapaho 4, 5; Wichita 1.—*Southwest:* Seama.—*Southeast:* Caddo 2.—Total 11.

1. Sleeping (lying) in open at night.—*Eskimo:* Kodiak 1.— *Mackenzie:* Kaska; Carrier.—*North Pacific:* Tahltan; Ts'ets'aut; Bella Bella; Chilcotin 1; Songish; Quileute 1, 2; Quinault; Chehalis 1, 2; Puyallup 2; Cowlitz; Coos 1, 2, 3.—*California:* Maidu; Washo 1, 2.—*Plateau:* Shoshone 1, 2; Wasco; Wishram; Kutenai; Shuswap.—*Plains:* Sarsi; Blackfoot 1, 2; Gros Ventre 1, 2; Cree 2; Cheyenne; Dakota 1; Arapaho 3, 8; Oto.—*Southeast:* Koasati.—*Woodland:* Ojibwa 1, 2, 3, 4, 5; Micmac 1, 2, 3; Passamaquoddy 1, 2.—Total: 49.

1a. Sleeping on an arbor.—*Plains:* Arikara 1, 2; Pawnee 1, 2, 3.—*Southeast:* Caddo 1.—Total: 6.

1b. STARS SEEN THROUGH ROOF.—*Plains:* Assiniboine; Wichita 2.—Total 2.
2. PERFORMING TASK.
2a. DIGGING ROOTS.—*North Pacific:* Songish; Quileute 2; Quinault; Snuqualmi 1, 2, 3; Puyallup 2; Cowlitz.—*Plains:* Cree 1.—Total: 9. [Of these Songish, Quileute 2, Quinault, Puyallup 2, and Cowlitz have both digging roots and sleeping in open.]
2b. GATHERING WOOD.—*Plains:* Blackfoot 1, 2; Hidatsa 1, 2; Crow 1, 3, 4; Arapaho 1, 2, 3, 7, 8.—Total: 12.
2c. MISCELLANEOUS TASKS.—*Plains:* Crow 2; Arapaho 6.—Total: 2.
3. MISCELLANEOUS CIRCUMSTANCES.—*Eskimo:* Kodiak 2.—*North Pacific:* Chilcotin 2.—*California:* Patwin.—*Plains:* Kiowa.—Total: 4.

Because of its frequency (57 versions) and wide occurrence it would seem that the wish for a star husband (B1) is usually made when the girls are sleeping out. But as a part of the porcupine story in the Plains the girls are gathering wood (10) or attending to another task (2). Among five tribes of the state of Washington the girls are digging roots, though usually they also sleep out. This would seem to represent a single locally developed tradition. The Cree version with the root digging probably does not belong with this group.

The general relation of the versions already discussed under Traits A and B are confirmed by Trait C. But the specially close connection between Quileute, Quinault, Puyallup, and Cowlitz tribes around Puget Sound begins to appear.

TRAIT D. METHOD OF ASCENT

[Versions marked with an asterisk indicate that the element is lacking.]

0. NOT INDICATED—*Eskimo:* Smith Sound.—*North Pacific:* Chilcotin 2; Klallam; Chehalis 1; Puyallup 1; Coos 1, 2, 3.—*Plateau:* Shoshone 2; Wasco*; Wishram*; Shuswap*.—*Plains:* Gros Ventre 1; Cree 1, 3; Assiniboine; Dakota 2.—*Southwest:* Seama.—Total: 18.
1. STRETCHING TREE.—*Plains:* Gros Ventre 3; Arikara 1; Hidatsa 1; Crow 1, 2, 4; Arapaho 5, 6, 7; Kiowa. (Also all of 1a, below.)—Total: 10, (including 1a: 19).
1a. WARNING FROM FRIEND.—*Plains:* Gros Ventre 2; Hidatsa 2; Crow 3; Cheyenne; Arapaho 1, 2, 3, 4, 8.—Total: 9.
2. TRANSLATION DURING SLEEP.—*Mackenzie:* Kaska.—*North Pacific:* Tahltan; Ts'ets'aut; Bella Bella; Chilcotin 1; Songish; Quileute 1, 2; Quinault; Chehalis 2; Snuqualmi 1, 2, 3; Puyallup 2; Cowlitz.—*California:* Maidu; Washo 1, 2.—*Plateau:* Shoshone 1; Kutenai.—*Plains:* Cree 2; Arikara 2; Dakota 1; Pawnee 1, 2, 3; Oto; Wichita 1, 2.—*Southeast:* Caddo 1, 2; Koasati.—*Woodland:* Ojibwa 1, 2, 3, 4, 5; Micmac 1, 2, 3; Passamaquoddy 1, 2.—Total: 42.
3. CARRIED THROUGH AIR WITH CLOSED EYES.—*Eskimo:* Kodiak 1.—*Plains:* Sarsi; Blackfoot 1, 2.—Total: 4.
4. CARRIED THROUGH AIR BY HAIR.—*Eskimo:* Kodiak 1.—Total: 1.
5. CARRIED IN BASKET.—*Eskimo:* Kodiak 2.—Total: 1.
6. TRANSPORTATION IN WHIRLWIND.—*Mackenzie:* Carrier.—*California:* Patwin.—Total: 2.
7. TRANSPORTATION BY FEATHER.—*Plains:* Blackfoot 1, 2.—Total: 2.

The versions which indicate how the ascent to the sky is made show the same general division already apparent in the traits just studied. One group has the ascent on a tree which stretches magically to the sky. This occurs in 19 versions—exactly those having the pursuit of the porcupine (B2 and B2a) and nowhere else. In nearly half of these (9) we have warning from a friend (B2a).

Most of the remaining variants of the tale tell of the wishes for the star husband and indicate that the girls found themselves in the upper world when they awoke (42 versions) or they are taken up in some magic fashion (10). Almost a fourth of the tales fail to indicate any method of ascent.

It seems clear from its frequency and distribution that except for the porcupine group of tales, the translation to the upper world during sleep is the normal form. The stretching tree belongs to the porcupine group of tales—a special Plains development. Probably this group usually contained the warning from the friend against following the porcupine. It is a reasonable way of getting rid of the second girl, who is useless for the development of the plot, but its appearance in the versions is quite at random, as if the tellers of the tale sometimes forgot to include it.

TRAIT E. IDENTITY OF HUSBAND

0. NOT INDICATED.—*Mackenzie:* Carrier.—*North Pacific:* Chilcotin 2.—Total: 2.

1. MOON.—*Eskimo:* Smith Sound; Kodiak 1.—*Plains:* Gros Ventre 2, 3; Hidatsa 1, 2; Arapaho 2, 3, 4, 5, 6.—Total: 11.

1a. MOON AND SUN.—*California:* Washo 2.—Total: 1.

2. SUN.—*North Pacific:* Bella Bella.—*Plains:* Cree 1; Crow 1, 4; Arapaho 7; Kiowa.—*Southwest:* Seama 1.—Total: 7.

3. STAR.—*Eskimo:* Kodiak 2.—*Mackenzie:* Kaska.—*North Pacific:* Tahltan; Ts'ets'aut; Chilcotin 1; Songish; Klallam; Quileute 1, 2; Quinault; Chehalis 1, 2; Snuqualmi 1, 2, 3; Puyallup 1, 2; Cowlitz; Coos 1, 2, 3.—*California:* Maidu; Washo 1.—*Plateau:* Shoshone 1, 2; Wasco; Wishram; Kutenai; Shuswap.—*Plains:* Sarsi; Blackfoot 1, 2; Gros Ventre 1; Cree 2, 3; Assiniboine; Arikara 1, 2; Cheyenne; Dakota 1; Arapaho 8; Pawnee 1, 2, 3; Oto; Wichita 1, 2.—*Southeast:* Caddo 1, 2; Koasati.—*Woodland:* Ojibwa 1, 2, 3, 4, 5; Micmac 1, 2, 3; Passamaquoddy 1, 2.—Total: 60.

4. THUNDER.—*Plains:* Dakota 2.—Total: 1.

5. PORCUPINE.—*Plains:* Arapaho 1.—Total: 1.

6. MAN.—*Plateau:* Shuswap.—*Plains:* Crow 2, 3.—Total: 3.

7. WHIRLWIND.—*California:* Patwin.—Total: 1.

It is clear that the story is rightly called the Star Husband not only because of the number of versions in which we deal with a star (60) but because of their distribution over the whole area. The appearance of the moon (11) or the sun (7) does not seem to correspond, except very roughly, to the porcupine group noticed in the traits just studied. They naturally occur in those tales introduced by a dispute between sun and moon about women (B2a) which may well be a special development within the porcupine group of tales in the Plains. But star husbands occur all over the Plains as well as elsewhere.

TRAIT F. DISTINCTIVE QUALITIES OF HUSBAND

0. NONE GIVEN.—*Eskimo:* Smith Sound, Kodiak 1.—*Mackenzie:* Carrier. —*North Pacific:* Bella Bella; Chilcotin 2; Songish; Klallam; Quileute 2.— *California:* Maidu; Patwin; Washo 1.—*Plains:* Gros Ventre 1; Cree 3; Arikara 2; Hidatsa 1, 2; Crow 1, 2, 3, 4; Dakota 2; Arapaho 1, 4, 6; Pawnee 1, 3; Kiowa.—*Southwest:* Seama.—*Woodland:* Ojibwa 2.—Total: 29.

1. OLD MAN.—*Plateau:* Wasco; Kutenai; Shuswap.—*Plains:* Wichita 1, 2. —*Southeast:* Caddo 1, 2.—Total: 7.

2. YOUNG MAN.—*Plateau:* Shoshone 2.—*Plains:* Sarsi 1; Blackfoot 1, 2; Gros Ventre 3; Cree 1; Arapaho 2, 3, 5, 7; Pawnee 2.—Total: 11.

3. MIDDLE-AGED MAN.—*Plains:* Arikara 1; Cheyenne 1.—Total: 2.

4. OLD MAN AND YOUNG MAN in accordance with size (brilliance, color) of stars wished for.—*North Pacific:* Chilcotin 1; Quileute 1; Quinault; Snuqualmi 1, 3; Chehalis 1, 2; Puyallup 1, 2; Cowlitz; Coos 1, 2, 3.— *Plateau:* Shoshone 1;—*Plains:* Cree 2; Assiniboine; Dakota 1.—*Southeast:* Koasati.—*Woodland:* Ojibwa 1, 3, 4, 5; Micmac 1, 2, 3; Passamaquoddy 1, 2. With Puyallup 1 and Ojibwa 4 and 5 the correspondence is not explicitly stated.—Total: 27.

4a. OLD MAN'S EYE WATER AND YOUNG MAN'S WAR PAINT.—*Woodland:* Micmac 1, 2, 3; Passamaquoddy 1, 2.—Total: 5.

5. TWO MEN WITH DIFFERENT COLORED BLANKETS.—*Mackenzie:* Kaska.— *North Pacific:* Ts'ets'aut.—Total: 2.

6. RED STAR SUN AND WHITE STAR MOON.—*North Pacific:* Snuqualmi 2.— *California:* Washo 2.—Total: 2.

7. DIM STAR CHIEF, BRIGHT STAR HIS SERVANT.—*Plains:* Oto 1.—Total: 1.

8. ONE-SIDED MAN.—*Eskimo:* Kodiak 2.—Total: 1.

9. METEOR-LIKE MAN.—*Plateau:* Wishram 1.—Total: 1.

10. HUNTERS.—*Mackenzie:* Kaska.—*North Pacific:* Tahltan; Ts'ets'aut; Snuqualmi 1, 3.—*Plateau:* Shoshone 1.—*Plains:* Gros Ventre 2, Arapaho 8. —*Woodland:* Micmac 2, 3.—Total: 10. (Not included on map.)

Only F4 and F4a show distinctiveness and wide dissemination (27 versions). The young man and old man in the upper world, corresponding (often inversely) to the size or brilliance of the stars wished for, naturally occur only when there are at least two girls (A2) and do not belong in the porcupine versions of the tale. In the 5 variants from the Micmacs and Passamaquoddies of the extreme Northeast the old and young men are further characterized by the old man's having an eye-water cup and the young one his war paint.

In addition to the 27 versions specifically described as F4 and F4a we note that F5, F6, and F7 all have the contrasting husbands and may well be variants of F4. The Wasco version of F1 implies the presence of younger men along with the old and therefore probably should be labeled F4 also. The young and old husbands would then appear as the standard form for most versions which indicate any qualities (32). For the porcupine group we sometimes have a young man (10) or middle-aged man (3), but with no clear-cut distribution, and the difference between them does not seem important. It is necessary in these versions that the husband be vigorous enough to beget a son.

The Wichita and Caddo tales, which deal exclusively with an old man, form a little group to themselves.

In some versions it is mentioned that the husbands are hunters, but the appearance of this item seems to be quite at random and to depend on the interest of the teller of the tale in supplying realistic details. In other versions it was to be assumed that the husbands hunted.

TRAIT G. BIRTH OF SON

0. No.—*Eskimo:* Smith Sound; Kodiak 1.—*Mackenzie:* Kaska; Carrier.—*North Pacific:* Tahltan; Ts'ets'aut; Chilcotin 1, 2; Songish; Klallam; Quileute 1, 2; Quinault; Chehalis 1, 2; Puyallup 2; Coos 1, 2, 3.—*California:* Patwin.—*Plateau:* Shoshone 1; Wasco; Wishram; Kutenai; Shuswap.—*Plains:* Gros Ventre 1; Cree 2, 3; Assiniboine; Arapaho 1; Oto; Wichita 1, 2.—*Southeast:* Caddo 1, 2; Koasati.—*Woodland:* Ojibwa 1, 2, 3, 4, 5; Micmac 1, 2, 3; Passamaquoddy 1, 2.—Total: 46.

1. YES.—*Eskimo:* Kodiak 2.—*North Pacific:* Bella Bella; Snuqualmi 1, 2, 3; Puyallup 1; Cowlitz.—*California:* Maidu; Washo 1, 2.—*Plateau:* Shoshone 2.—*Plains:* Sarsi; Blackfoot 1, 2; Gros Ventre 2, 3; Cree 1; Arikara 1, 2; Hidatsa 1, 2; Crow 1, 2, 3, 4; Cheyenne; Dakota 1, 2; Arapaho 2, 3, 4, 5, 6, 7, 8; Pawnee 1, 2 3; Kiowa.—*Southwest:* Seama.—Total: 40.

In the simple plot of the two girls and their escape from the star husband there is no place for the birth of a son in the upper world, and the large number (46) and geographic spread of the variants lacking this item is to be expected. Practically none of the tales on the periphery of the area Nova Scotia to California and Alaska have the son, and it may be assumed that the basic tale said nothing of a child.

But several groups of versions do have the birth of a son:

1. Most important is in the Plains from the Sarsi south to the Kiowa, in which the son is necessary to prepare for the story of Star Boy (N1), which appears as a sequel. This is usually, though not always, a part of the porcupine group.

2. The three Pawnee tales, Arikara 2, and Dakota 1 and 2 are exactly like this group except that the second girl goes to the sky as a result of her wish for a star husband, instead of following a porcupine.

3. On the North Pacific coast among the Bella Bella, Snuqualmi, Puyallup, and Cowlitz the story leads into a characteristic cycle of that area, the tale of the transformer. In all of these versions we have two or more girls marrying star husbands but only one bearing a son.

4. In California the birth of a son or sons has no relation to a sequel, but seems quite incidental.

Trait H. Taboo Broken in Upper World

0. No taboo broken.—*Eskimo:* Kodiak 2.—*Mackenzie:* Kaska; Carrier. —*North Pacific:* Tahltan; Ts'ets'aut; Bella Bella; Chilcotin 1; Klallam; Quileute 1, 2; Quinault; Chehalis 1, 2; Puyallup 2; Coos 1, 2, 3.—*California:* Maidu; Washo 2.—*Plateau:* Shoshone 1; Wasco; Wishram; Shuswap.— *Plains:* Gros Ventre 1, 3; Cree 2, 3; Arapaho 5, 6; Wichita 2.—*Southwest:* Seama.—*Southeast:* Caddo 1; Koasati.—*Woodland:* Ojibwa 1, 2, 3, 4, 5; Micmac 3.—Total: 39.

1. Digging (or disturbing ground).—*North Pacific:* Songish; Snuqualmi 1, 2, 3; Puyallup 1; Cowlitz.—*California:* Patwin.—*Plains:* Assiniboine; Crow 4; Pawnee 1, 2, 3; Oto.—Total: 13.

1a. Digging roots (of various kinds).—California: Washo 1.—*Plateau:* Shoshone 2; Kutenai.—*Plains:* Sarsi; Blackfoot 1, 2; Gros Ventre 2; Cree 1; Arikara 2; Hidatsa 1, 2; Cheyenne; Crow 1, 2, 3; Dakota 1, 2; Arapaho 1, 2, 3, 4, 7, 8; Kiowa.—Total: 24.

1b. Moving large rock.—*Plains:* Wichita 1.—*Southeast:* Caddo 2.— *Woodland:* Micmac 2; Passamaquoddy 1, 2.—Total: 5.

1c. Digging in valleys.—*Plains:* Arikara 1.—Total: 1.

2. Looking.—*Eskimo:* Smith Sound (part of house); Kodiak 1 (behind curtain).—*North Pacific:* Chilcotin 2 (into box).—Total: 3.

3. Shooting at meadow lark.—*Plains:* Hidatsa 1, 2; Crow 1, 2, 3, 4.— Total: 6.

4. Making noise before squirrel (chickadee, etc.) sings.—*Woodland:* Micmac 1, 2; Passamaquoddy 1, 2.—Total: 4. (Not included on the map.)

The warning against digging in the upper world, whether as a general prohibition (H1) or digging for specific things (H1a, H1b, H1c), is certainly an original feature in the Star Husband tale. It is found in 43 versions in all parts of the area, in that characterized by the porcupine husband as well as elsewhere.

The taboo against looking in the Kodiak 1 and Chilcotin 2 versions fulfills the same function as the digging prohibition in the rest of the tradition. In all there are 47 versions with explicit taboo.

The frequent failure of this taboo to appear seems generally to be a mere oversight, since no motivation remains for the opening of a skyhole.

1. Several tales are confused or fragmentary in this part of the story and may be disregarded: Carrier; Chehalis 1; Coos 1, 2, and 3; Wasco; Wishram; Shuswap; Gros Ventre 1; Cree 1; Koasati; Ojibwa 4–12 versions.

2. Several are so closely knit in all other particulars to tales having this trait that its presence in the tradition to the tribe may be safely assumed This is certainly true of the group around Puget Sound: Klallam; Quileute 1 and 2; Quinault; Chehalis; Puyallup 2. It also certainly belongs in such Gros Ventre and Arapaho versions as lack it. Its presence in the Maidu and the remaining Washo tale may be assumed on the strength of Patwin and Washo 1, which show that the tradition is in California. All the Wichita and Caddo variants probably had it and all the Micmac. This group contains 15 versions. The absence of the taboo is thus accounted for in 27 versions.

There remain the Kaska, Tahltan, Ts'ets'aut, Cree 2, 3 and Ojibwa 1, 2,

3 and 5 in which we have otherwise well-told stories lacking the taboo—9 versions. Eight of these are tales having as sequel the tricksters under the tree (N2), which, as we shall see later, are generally much alike in all their details from the Kaska all the way to the Micmacs. That the digging taboo belongs to this group we see from the Micmac and Passamaquoddy versions which preserve it.

If the reasoning here is cogent we can conclude that the prohibition against digging is an original feature of the tale which for various reasons has frequently dropped out.

The taboo against shooting at a meadow lark is always associated with a digging taboo. It is confined to the Hidatsa and neighboring Crow, and indicates a very close relation between the tales of these two tribes.

Likewise the warning not to move until the squirrel and chickadee sing belongs in the Micmac and Passamaquoddy tribes along with the digging taboo. The incident shows considerable age in these tales and indicates the closeness of the traditions of these northeastern peoples.

Trait I. Discovery of Skyhole

0. Trait not present.—*Eskimo:* Kodiak 1.—*North Pacific:* Quileute 1, 2; Quinault; Chehalis 1, 2; Coos 1, 2, 3.—*California:* Maidu.—*Plateau:* Wasco; Wishram; Shuswap.—*Plains:* Gros Ventre 1; Cree 3; Wichita 2.—*Southwest:* Seama.—*Southeast:* Koasati.—*Woodland:* Ojibwa 4; Micmac 1, 3.— Total: 21.

1. By own efforts.—*Eskimo:* Smith Sound; Kodiak 2.—*Mackenzie:* Kaska.—*North Pacific:* Tahltan; Ts'ets'aut; Chilcotin 1, 2; Songish; Klallam; Snuqualmi 1, 2, 3; Puyallup 1, 2; Cowlitz.—*California:* Patwin; Washo 1, 2.—*Plateau:* Shoshone 2; Kutenai.—*Plains:* Sarsi; Gros Ventre 2, 3; Assiniboine; Arikara 1, 2; Hidatsa 1, 2; Crow 1, 2, 3, 4; Cheyenne; Dakota 1, 2; Arapaho 1, 2, 3, 4, 6, 7, 8; Pawnee 1, 2, 3; Oto; Kiowa; Wichita 1.—*Southeast:* Caddo 2.—*Woodland:* Micmac 2; Passamaquoddy 1, 2.— Total: 52.

2. At another's suggestion.—*Plains:* Cree 1, 2.—*Southeast:* Caddo 1.— Total: 3.

3. With another's assistance.—*Mackenzie:* Carrier.—*North Pacific:* Bella Bella.—*Plateau:* Shoshone 1.—*Plains:* Blackfoot 1, 2; Arapaho 5.— *Woodland:* Ojibwa 1, 2, 3, 5:—Total: 10.

4. Gust of wind through skyhole.—*North Pacific:* Snuqualmi 1, 2, 3; Puyallup 2; Cowlitz.—Total: 5. (Not included on map.)

The failure of some versions to have the motif of the hole in the sky through which the escape is made can usually be explained as mere omissions from the tale. In the following the skyhole is implied, since there is a descent from the sky on a rope or (Micmac 1) by magic: Quileute 2, Quinault, Chehalis 2, Maidu, Arapaho 6, Wichita 2 and Ojibwa 4. All of these 7 may be considered to have the trait, so that in all there are 72 with it.

The question as to whether the hole is found by the girls' or girl's own efforts does not seem to be important in the study of the tale. Everywhere most of the versions have the discovery made without outside help.

A special detail showing the close relation of the tales from the Puget Sound area is that of the gust of wind through the skyhole. The Snuqualmi, Puyallup, and Cowlitz tales here again are linked together.

TRAIT J. ASSISTANCE IN DESCENT

0. LACKING.—*Eskimo:* Smith Sound; Kodiak 1.—*Mackenzie:* Kaska.— *North Pacific:* Tahltan; Ts'ets'aut; Chilcotin 1; Songish; Klallam; Quileute 1; Chehalis 1; Snuqualmi 1, 3; Puyallup 1, 2; Cowlitz; Coos 1, 2, 3.—*California:* Maidu; Washo 1, 2.—*Plateau:* Wasco; Wishram; Kutenai; Shuswap. —*Plains:* Gros Ventre 1; Cree 3; Hidatsa 1; Cheyenne; Dakota 1, 2; Arapaho 1, 2, 3, 4, 6, 7; Pawnee 1, 2, 3; Kiowa 1.—*Southeast:* Koasati.— *Woodland:* Ojibwa 4; Micmac 3.—Total: 44.

1. SPIDER.—*North Pacific:* Chehalis 2.—*Plains:* Assiniboine; Hidatsa 2; Crow 1.—Total: 4.

1a. SPIDER-WOMAN.—*North Pacific:* Quileute 2; Quinault.—*Southwest:* Seama.—Total: 3.

1b. SPIDER-MAN.—*Plains:* Blackfoot 1, 2.—Total: 2.

2. OLD WOMAN.—*Eskimo:* Kodiak 2.—*Mackenzie:* Carrier.—*North Pacific:* Chilcotin 2; Snuqualmi 2.—*Plateau:* Shoshone 1.—*Plains:* Cree 1, 2; Arikara 1, 2; Arapaho 5, 8.—*Woodland:* Ojibwa 1, 2, 3, 5.—Total: 15.

3. OLD MAN.—*Plains:* Oto.—Total: 1.

4. HUSBAND.—*North Pacific:* Bella Bella.—*California:* Patwin.—*Plateau:* Shoshone 2.—*Plains:* Sarsi; Gros Ventre 2, 3; Crow 2, 3, 4.—*Woodland:* Micmac 1, 2; Passamaquoddy 1, 2.—Total: 13.

5. SISTER OF STAR.—*Southeast:* Caddo 1.—Total: 1.

6. BIRD.

6a. BUZZARD.—*Plains:* Wichita 1, 2.—*Southeast:* Caddo 1.—Total: 3.

6b. HAWK.—*Southeast:* Caddo 1.—Total: 1.

6c. EAGLE.—*Southeast:* Caddo 2.—Total: 1.

In more than half of the 86 versions the descent from the sky is made without outside help. Such versions are scattered over the entire area, and might seem to indicate that this absence of outside aid is an essential part of the plot. Yet the evidence presented by the distribution of this item is extremely difficult if not impossible to interpret clearly.

1. The variants without help sometimes occur in tribes which have other versions containing a helper. This indicates that at least sometimes the failure to name a helper may be an oversight (Hidatsa 1 and Arapaho 1, 2, 3, 4, 6, 7). In Quileute 1 and Ojibwa 4 the details of the descent are left vague, and in Smith Sound, Kodiak 1, Chilcotin 1, Coos 1, 2, and 3, Wasco, Wishram, Shuswap, Gros Ventre 1, and Cree 1 this part of the tale is entirely missing. With all these subtractions, however, there still remain 24 versions, well scattered, that lack the helper. Of these several will be found on other evidence to constitute a unified tradition: (a) Kaska-Tahltan-Ts'ets'aut, (b) Songish-Klallam-Snuqualmi-Puyallup-Chehalis (all Puget Sound tribes), (c) Maidu-Washo in California.

2. The help of the Spider (man or woman) occurs in 9 versions, but except for the Quinault and Chehalis and the two Blackfoot tales, there seems to be no relation between them.

3. The help of the old woman is probably more widespread than the actual figures (15) show. There should probably be added the 6 Arapaho versions and the one Hidatsa which do not mention the helper. Sometimes also the Spider is spoken of as an old woman. It probably represents the normal form of the tale in several tribes and serves to confirm the close relation between the Ojibwa and Cree in Canada and the Arikara and Arapaho in the Plains. But the lack of continuity is still not easy to explain.

4. The husband himself helps with the descent in 13 versions, well scattered over the area. Except for the Micmac-Passamaquoddy group in the extreme northeast and the Gros Ventre-Crow-Shoshone in the Plains no significant groupings appear.

5. The bird as helper is characteristic of the four Wichita-Caddo tales, which in other ways form a small group to themselves.

TRAIT K. MEANS OF DESCENT

0. NO DESCENT.—*Eskimo:* Smith Sound; Kodiak 1.—*North Pacific:* Chilcotin 1; Chehalis 1; Coos 1, 2, 3.—*Plateau:* Wasco; Wishram; Shuswap. —*Plains:* Gros Ventre 1; Cree 3.—*Woodland:* Ojibwa 4; Micmac 3.— Total: 14.

1. DESCENT BUT MEANS NOT SPECIFIED.—*North Pacific:* Quileute 1.— *California:* Patwin.—*Southwest:* Seama.—*Southeast:* Koasati.—*Woodland:* Ojibwa 5; Micmac 1, 2; Passamaquoddy 1, 2.—Total: 9.

2. BASKET.—*Eskimo:* Kodiak 2.—*North Pacific:* Bella Bella; Chilcotin 2. —*Woodland:* Ojibwa 1, 2, 3.—Total: 6.

3. ROPE.—*North Pacific:* Songish; Quileute 2; Quinault.—*Plateau:* Kutenai.—*Plains:* Kiowa.—*Woodland:* Ojibwa 3.—Total: 6.

3a. SKIN ROPE.—*Mackenzie:* Kaska.—*North Pacific:* Tahltan; Ts'ets'aut. —*Plateau:* Shoshone 2.—*Plains:* Sarsi; Cree 2; Oto (lariats).—Total: 7.

3b. SINEW ROPE.—*California:* Maidu; Washo 1, 2.—*Plains:* Gros Ventre 2, 3; Cree 1; Arikara 1, 2; Hidatsa 1, 2; Crow 1, 2, 3, 4; Arapaho 1, 2, 3, 4, 5, 6, 7, 8; Pawnee 1, 2, 3.—Total: 25.

3c. WOOL ROPE.—*Mackenzie:* Carrier.—Total: 1.

3d. SPIDER ROPE (STRING).—*North Pacific:* Chehalis 2.—*Plains:* Blackfoot 1, 2; Assiniboine.—Total: 4.

3e. VINE ROPE.—*North Pacific:* Chilcotin 2; Puyallup 1 (withe), 2 (brush). —Total: 3.

3f. ROOT ROPE.—*North Pacific:* Cowlitz.—*Plateau:* Shoshone 1.—*Woodland:* Ojibwa 1.—Total: 3.

3g. GRASS ROPE.—*Plains:* Cheyenne.—Total: 1.

3h. WEED ROPE.—*Plains:* Wichita 1, 2.—*Southeast:* Caddo 2.—*Woodland:* Ojibwa 1.—Total: 4.

3i. BARK ROPE.—*Southeast:* Caddo 1.—Total: 1.

4. LADDER.—*North Pacific:* Klallam (bough); Snuqualmi 1 (twigs), 2 (roots), 3 (bark).—Total: 4.

5. BUCKET.—*Plains:* Crow 2.— Total: 1.

6. FALLING.—*Plains:* Dakota 1, 2.—Total: 2.

7. DESCENT WITH TABOO.

7a. LOOKING TABOO.—*Eskimo:* Kodiak 2.—*North Pacific:* Chilcotin 2.— *Plateau:* Shoshone 1.—*Plains:* Cree 2; Assiniboine; Arapaho 8.—*Woodland:* Ojibwa 3, 5; Micmac 2; Passamaquoddy 1, 2.—Total: 11.

7b. STIRRING (MOVING) TABOO.—*Woodland:* Micmac 1; Passamaquoddy 1, 2.—Total: 3.

Disregarding the 14 more or less fragmentary versions which have no descent from the sky and the 9 which merely state that the women reached the earth, but do not specify the means, there are left 63 versions with descent described. Of these, 55 are said to be by rope, and 4 by a ladder, which may well be thought of as a kind of rope. In 6 we have descent in a basket, with a rope to hold it implied. This makes a total of 65 out of a possible 67, or very nearly all.

Several ways of reaching the earth seem to indicate special traditions within limited areas. Thus the descent entirely through observing a taboo against moving until certain animals sing is peculiar to the Micmac-Passamaquoddy group. The basket descent shows the close interrelationship of three Ojibwa versions, as does the falling from the sky for the two Dakota tales. On the other hand, no significant groupings appear when we examine in detail the particular kinds of rope used. The primary place of the rope descent in all forms of the story is clear, though it is worthy of note that it does not occur in any of the Micmac-Passamaquoddy tales of the extreme northeast.

TRAIT L. RESULTS OF DESCENT

0. LACKING.—*Eskimo:* Smith Sound; Kodiak 1.—*North Pacific:* Chilcotin 1; Chehalis 1; Coos 1, 2, 3.—*Plateau:* Wasco; Wishram; Shuswap.—*Plains:* Gros Ventre 1; Cree 3.—*Woodland:* Ojibwa 4; Micmac 3.—Total: 14.

1. SAFE DESCENT.—*Eskimo:* Kodiak 2.—*Mackenzie:* Kaska; Carrier.—*North Pacific:* Tahltan; Ts'ets'aut; Bella Bella; Chilcotin 2; Songish; Klallam; Quileute 1, 2; Chehalis 2; Snuqualmi 1, 2, 3; Puyallup 1, 2; Cowlitz. —*California:* Patwin.—*Plateau:* Shoshone 1, 2.—*Plains:* Sarsi; Blackfoot 1, 2; Gros Ventre 2; Cree 2; Assiniboine; Arapaho, 1, 5; Oto; Wichita 1, 2. —*Southwest:* Seama.—*Southeast:* Caddo 1, 2; Koasati.—*Woodland:* Ojibwa 1, 2, 3, 5; Micmac 1, 2; Passamaquoddy 1, 2.—Total: 44.

1a. LATER KILLED.—*Plateau:* Kutenai 1.—Total: 1.

2. WOMAN (WOMEN) KILLED.—*North Pacific:* Quinault.—*California:* Washo 2.—Total: 2.

2a. WOMAN KILLED, LATER REVIVED.—*California:* Maidu.—Total: 1.

3. WOMAN KILLED, SON SAVED.—*California:* Washo 1 (boy, not son).— *Plains:* Gros Ventre 3; Cree 1; Arikara 1, 2; Hidatsa 1, 2; Crow 1, 2, 3, 4; Cheyenne; Dakota 1, 2; Arapaho 2, 3, 4, 6, 7, 8; Pawnee 1, 2, 3; Kiowa.— Total: 24.

4. ONE WOMAN FALLS.—*Woodland:* Ojibwa 5.—Total: 1.

The general pattern of our story, as indicated by 44 versions from every part of the area, demands that the woman return home safely. But a glance at the map will show that there is a large area in the Plains in which the wife is killed but the son saved. This usually occurs in versions we have already noted as having (1) one active girl, (2) the pursuit of a porcupine, and (3) the birth of a son in the upper world, and it normally leads on to the sequel we shall call Star Boy. The details of this incident are so exactly repeated as to make certain a common tradition. The husband in the sky sends down a rock to kill the wife and spare the son.

In spite of this impressive tradition in the Plains it is clear from the large number of versions (44) and the wide dissemination that the tale, except for this area, demands that the women return safely.

TRAIT M. EXPLANATORY ELEMENTS

(Explanations marked with an asterisk are organic to the tale; others seem to be mere afterthoughts or at most incidental.)

0. NO EXPLANATIONS GIVEN.—*Eskimo:* Smith Sound; Kodiak 1, 2.—*Mackenzie:* Carrier.—*North Pacific:* Ts'ets'aut; Bella Bella; Chilcotin 2; Songish; Chehalis 1, 2; Puyallup 2; Cowlitz; Coos 1, 2, 3.—*California:* Maidu; Patwin; Washo 1.—*Plateau:* Shoshone 1, 2; Wishram; Kutenai; Shuswap.—*Plains:* Sarsi; Blackfoot 2; Gros Ventre 1, 2; Cree 1, 2, 3; Assiniboine; Arikara 1, 2; Crow 2, 4; Cheyenne; Dakota 1, 2; Arapaho 1, 6, 7, 8; Pawnee 1, 2, 3; Oto; Kiowa.—*Southwest:* Seama.—*Southeast:* Caddo 2; Koasati.—*Woodland:* Ojibwa 1, 2, 3, 5; Micmac 1, 2, 3; Passamaquoddy 1, 2.—Total: 59.

1. HEAVENLY BODIES.

1a. MOON.—*North Pacific:* Snuqualmi 2, 3.—*Plains:* Gros Ventre 3*; Hidatsa 1*, 2*; Crow 1; Arapaho 2*, 3*, 4*, 5*.—Total: 10.

1b. STARS.—*North Pacific:* Quileute 1, 2; Quinault.—*Plains:* Blackfoot 1; Crow 3.—Total: 5.

2. GEOGRAPHICAL FEATURES.—*North Pacific:* Snuqualmi 1, 2; Klallam.—*Plateau:* Wasco.—Total: 4.

3. VEGETABLE AND ANIMAL FEATURES.

3a. ORIGIN OF TURNIPS.—*Plains:* Blackfoot 1*.—Total: 1.

3b. ORIGIN OF ANIMAL.—*Mackenzie:* Kaska (beaver).—Total: 1.

3c. ANIMAL MARKINGS.—*Mackenzie:* Kaska.—*North Pacific:* Quinault.—*Plains:* Cree 2.—*Woodland:* Ojibwa 4.—Total: 4.

3d. BODILY SHAPE OF ANIMAL.—*North Pacific:* Snuqualmi 1*, 2*; Puyallup 1.—Total: 3.

3e. BLINDNESS IN ANIMAL.—*North Pacific:* Quinault.—Total: 1.

4. HUMAN SOCIETY.

4a. SUN DANCE CEREMONY.—*Plains:* Arapaho 2*.—Total: 1.

4b. BACKWARD STATE OF THE INDIAN.—*California:* Washo 2*.—Total: 1.

5. PERSONAL CHARACTERISTICS.

5a. TIME OF HUMAN GESTATION.—*Plains:* Arapaho 2*.—Total: 1.

5b. WHY YOUNG WOMEN DISLIKE OLD HUSBANDS—*Plateau:* Wasco*.—Total: 1.

6. MEDICINE.

6a. TREATMENT OF WOUND.—*North Pacific:* Chilcotin 1*.—Total: 1.

7. MISCELLANEOUS EXPLANATIONS.

7a. ORIGIN OF TABOOS.—*North Pacific:* Tahltan.—*Plains:* Wichita 1, 2.—*Southeast:* Caddo 1.—Total: 4.

7b. PAINTING ON LODGES.—*Plains:* Blackfoot 1*.—Total: 1.

In view of the general belief that most American Indian tales are myths and that myths are constructed primarily to explain natural phenomena, it has seemed worthwhile to make note of all such explanations. The results are negative.

The only explanation, which seems to have established a tradition, is that of the spots on the moon (M1a) resulting from a contest in the upper world between the wives of Moon and Sun. Sun's wife in anger throws herself at

Moon's face. This is found in practically all the tales beginning with B2a and is probably a basic part of the porcupine group of tales.

TRAIT N. SEQUEL

0. NO SEQUEL.—*Eskimo:* Smith Sound; Kodiak 1.—*North Pacific:* Chilcotin 1, 2; Songish; Klallam; Chehalis 1, 2; Puyallup 2; Coos 1, 2, 3.—*California:* Maidu; Washo 1, 2.—*Plateau:* Shoshone 1; Wishram; Kutenai; Shuswap.—*Plains:* Sarsi; Cree 3; Arapaho 1; Oto; Wichita 1, 2.—*Southeast:* Caddo 1, 2; Koasati.—*Woodland:* Ojibwa 5; Micmac 3.—Total: 30.

1. PLAINS STAR BOY SEQUEL (MOON BOY, SUN BOY).—*Plains:* Blackfoot 2; Gros Ventre 3; Cree 1; Arikara 1, 2; Hidatsa 1, 2; Crow 1, 2, 3, 4; Cheyenne; Dakota 1, 2; Arapaho 2, 3, 4, 5, 6, 7, 8; Pawnee 1, 2, 3; Kiowa.—Total: 25.

1a. BOY BECOMES TRANSFORMER.—*North Pacific:* Bella Bella; Snuqualmi 1, 2, 3; Puyallup 1; Cowlitz.—Total: 6.

2. TRICKSTER ANIMALS UNDER TREE.—*Mackenzie:* Kaska; Carrier.—*North Pacific:* Tahltan; Ts'ets'aut.—*Plains:* Cree 2; Assiniboine.—*Woodland:* Ojibwa 1, 2, 3, 4; Micmac 1, 2; Passamaquoddy 1, 2.—Total: 14.

3. SKY WAR SEQUEL.—*North Pacific:* Quileute 1, 2; Quinault.—Total: 3.

4. ORIGIN MYTH SEQUEL.—*Plateau:* Wasco (cliff).—*Plains:* Blackfoot 1 (star, lodge decorations, implements, ceremonies).—Total: 2.

5. BUFFALO HUSBAND SEQUEL.—*Plains:* Gros Ventre 1, 2.—Total: 2.

6. RETURN TO SKY AS SEQUEL.—*Eskimo:* Kodiak 2.—*California:* Patwin.—*Plateau:* Shoshone 2.—*Southwest:* Seama.—Total: 4.

It is by the sequel to the main action that the interrelation of the various groups of Star Husband tales can best be seen.

1. The Plains Star Boy sequel (1) is the usual manner of closing the tale in which one girl follows the porcupine (B2), bears a son in the upper world (G1) and is killed by the husband who sends down a rock with instructions to spare the boy (L3). The boy is cared for and eventually becomes a tribal hero who kills monsters and helps his people. There are 25 versions having this sequel, all of them in the Plains.

Of these all have the porcupine introduction except for eight (Blackfoot 2; Cree 2; Arikara 2; Dakota 1, 2; Pawnee 1, 2, 3) which are all combinations of the wish for the star husband (B1) with much of the usual porcupine tale. In other words the group is transitional between the B1 and B2 introductions. Most of these versions are also at the edge of the porcupine-husband area of dissemination.

2. In a small group of North Pacific tribes this tale has been used as an introduction to their usual stories of the culture hero who goes about transforming things (N1a). This is quite a different cycle from the Plains Star Boy. It confirms the close relationships of the tales of these tribes of Puget Sound and the British Columbia coast.

3. The widely spread group of versions with the trickster animals under the tree as a sequel (N2) will be discussed in some detail later (p. 453).

4. The sky war (N3) as a sequel shows the close relationship of the Quinault tale to those of their neighbors, the Quileute.

Construction of Basic Type and Subtypes

TYPE I. THE BASIC TALE (ARCHETYPE)

As one after another of the traits of the Star Husband tale have been examined a very clear picture has emerged. (1) We have a basic story with little variation over the whole area, (2) a special and practically uniform variation in the Plains area (not, however, entirely replacing the basic story), and (3) several different sequels, each in a clear-cut geographic area.

If we are to examine the basic form of the tale we shall have (1) to disregard the sequels, each of which has developed in its own area and has not affected the tale itself, and (2) to set aside for later consideration the special Plains redaction characterized by the pursuit of a porcupine.

When these eliminations have been made we find a common tale with the following traits: *Two girls (65%) sleeping out (85%) make wishes for stars as husbands (90%). They are taken to the sky in their sleep (82%) and find themselves married to stars (87%), a young man and an old, corresponding to the brilliance or size of the stars (55%). The women disregard the warning not to dig (90%) and accidentally open up a hole in the sky (76%). Unaided (52%) they descend on a rope (88%) and arrive home safely (76%).* The formula can be stated as: A2, B1, C1, D2, E3, F4, G0, H1, I1, J0, K3, L1.

About this description there can be reasonable doubt only in connection with Trait J, where the evidence is somewhat conflicting.

When we have constructed this basic tale we cannot say immediately that we have the original form of the story. We must study the general geographic situation to see whether a tale of this form actually exists in such numbers or in such places as could have produced all the extant versions.

Is this basic form actually represented in any of the 86 versions we have? Yes, the following are completely typical: Songish; Chehalis 2; Puyallup 2; Shoshone 2; Kutenai; Oto; Ojibwa 5. The following fragmentary versions are typical *so far as they go:*[7] Coos 1, 2, 3; Wasco; Wishram; Cree 3; Koasati; Micmac 3. This form of the tale also appears with only a single difference in detail in the following:[8] Bella Bella; Klallam; Maidu; Washo 1, 2; Shoshone 2; and in the whole group of versions ending with the trickster animals under the tree. Disregarding that group, however, since it is certainly a special development in the tale, we can say that in 15 versions we have the basic form of the tale without any changes and a number of others with only a single modification. Tales of this form are found over the entire area of distribution, even among the Plains tribes which for the most part use the porcupine type.

For the purposes of this study we are, therefore, assuming that this form is the archetype from which all other versions were produced by some individual or group changes. How reasonable is this hypothesis?[9]

---

[7] Indicated as Type I*.

[8] Indicated as Type I**.

[9] One possible objection to the hypothesis concerns the supposedly fragmentary texts. Given Thompson's hypothetical archetype, then it does follow that such texts as Coos

As we proceed to show the various modifications of this archetype we shall see that they consist in either (1) the simple addition of an item or (2) a single change which necessitates several other changes to bring about consistency. The first type of modification occurs in several groups of tales on the periphery of the main area—California, Puget Sound, Oklahoma, Texas, and Canada. It seems inconceivable that any one of these should have originated the story, for it is beyond all probability that any one trait should be consistently forgotten, and never recur elsewhere. The other group in which

---

1, 2, 3, and Chehalis 1 are fragments that have degenerated from the original fuller form. However, as von Sydow pointed out in "Folktale Studies and Philology," the assumption that the original form of a folktale should be the most complete and most logical may be a false one. Many of the versions considered by Thompson to be fragments may not necessarily be incomplete tales. Some were, after all, told as complete stories by informants. Also the fact that there are several very similar fragments (e.g., Chehalis 1 and Wishram) suggests a traditional form rather than an idiosyncratic narrator's faulty version. Calling these versions fragments is somewhat like throwing away the data that doesn't fit the theory.

It is significant that 39 of the 86 versions do not have a taboo broken in the upper world (Trait H). Thompson, who includes this as an archetypal trait, remarks that the frequent failure of the taboo to appear seems to be a mere *oversight* on the part of the narrator. He also states that several tales are *confused* or *fragmentary* in this part of the story and may be *disregarded* (my italics). The point is that if the taboo was *not* an original feature of the tale, then what Thompson terms fragmentary versions (although he labels some of them Type I*) may be closer to the older form of the tale. The innovation of adding a taboo, once the girls were in the sky world, may have come later. It is just as logical to assume that tales evolve as to assume that tales devolve or decay.

The following version of Star Husband was collected by the editor on June 4, 1963, near Mayetta, Kansas, from Henry Shohn, age 43, a Winnebago, who said he had learned the tale from his step-father George Rice Hill from Winnebago, Nebraska, around the year 1927. The tale is presented to show that a "fragmentary version" can be told as a complete tale and at the same time to demonstrate to the reader the nature of a virtually unedited oral version of a folktale.

"This is a story of a stars husband. I don't mean is a movie star, but regular star, in the sky. There was a two, couple, girls; they chum around together. And one evening, at night, they was out in the country; they was layin' down, looking up in the sky, and they seen stars. Then a one of 'em said, 'I hear them stars are persons.' And she picked out one star that—it was shiny bright and 'I wished I would have that one for my husband.' So the other one said, she looked up and there was one star that was dim, you can hardly see it, 'And I wish I would have that one for my husband,' she said. Then, they went sleep. In the morning when they woke up, the first one here, that picked out that bright star, she had a old man laying along side of her and he said, 'This is what you been wishin' for. So it's established, you want to marry me,' he said. So the other one spoke up an' he said, 'Well this is what you wish.' This was a young man, that little dim star. Then he told them, 'You gonna be on this earth and when you die, passed away, your spirit gonna come up in the sky where we at and we gonna be together.'"

When the informant was asked if there were any more to the tale, he said no. When he was asked specifically if the girls went to the sky and escaped, he said he hadn't heard it that way. Although the tale, from an esthetic point of view, our Western esthetic point of view, is not as entertaining as one in which the girls are confronted with a taboo in the sky world, it nevertheless might be the original form of the tale. For a structure-oriented discussion of the relative merits of the two possibilities of evolution and devolution, see Alan Dundes, *The Morphology of North American Indian Folktales,* Folklore Fellows Communications No. 195 (Helsinki, 1964), pp. 87–91. If the fragmentary version or Type I* is the archetype, the trait formula might be A2, B1, C1, D2, E3, and F4.—Ed. Note

several differences from the archetype occur, the porcupine-husband type, is found without exception in the center of the main area. It has characteristic traits: A1, B2, C2, D1, L3, N1. That these should all completely drop off and produce the same archetype to the north, south, east, and west in even less likely.

This archetype must have existed over all or most of its present area of distribution anterior to the special developments which we shall later notice.

Can we go further back in the history of the tale than the existence of this archetype over its present area? Not with any certainty. We have excellent examples of the archetype on the Pacific Coast (Songish), in the middle (Oto) and in the East (Ojibwa 5) but have no way of knowing where the tale originated or just what movements in tradition may have spread this archetype over the continent. Nor does an analysis of the tale into the motifs out of which it is composed help us know anything of its origin. Comparisons with tales of marriages to celestial beings in tales of other continents or to the magic fulfillment of wishes or the basket from the sky—interesting as they may be—avail us nothing in the quest for the actual origin of this tale.

Taking the archetype as we find it, we may now examine the special developments which our analysis has revealed.

TYPE II. THE PORCUPINE REDACTION

Repeatedly in the analysis of the traits of the tale we have noticed one group of versions which differ from the basic type in a characteristic fashion. These twenty versions are Gros Ventre 2, 3; Cree 1; Arikara 1; Hidatsa 1, 2; Crow 1, 2, 3, 4; Cheyenne; Arapaho 1, 2, 3, 4, 5, 6, 7, 8; Kiowa.

When we take these versions and examine them we find that it is easy to construct a subtype which we may call the Porcupine redaction: *A girl (100%) while performing a task (84%) follows a porcupine (95%) up a tree which stretches to the upper world (95%). The porcupine becomes the moon (45%), the sun (25%), or a star (15%) in the form of a young man (30%). The girl marries him and bears a son (95%). She is warned not to dig (80%) but disobeys and discovers a skyhole (85%). By her own efforts (45%) or with the help of her husband (25%) she descends on a sinew rope (85%) but it is too short. The husband sends down a rock with instructions to kill the wife and spare the son (85%). Sequel: The adventures of Star Boy (Moon Boy or Sun Boy) (90%).*

The formula for this subtype is therefore A1, B2, C2, D1, E1 (or 2), F2, G1, H1, I1, J4, K3b, L3, N1. The special characteristics of the group are A1 (one girl), B2 (pursuit of porcupine), C2 (adventure while performing task), D1 (ascent on tree), G1 (birth of son), L3 (woman killed and son saved), N1 (Star Boy sequel).

All the versions in the group follow this formula, with the slightest exceptions. The Cree variant at the north end of the area omits or obscures the crucial theme of the pursuit of the porcupine, but otherwise remains true to form. Gros Ventre 2 substitutes another sequel for Star Boy. This is taken from Gros Ventre 1, which does not belong to this subtype.

The area covered by this subtype is small in relation to the distribution of the basic type. The tribes concerned stretch continuously from the Kiowa in Oklahoma to the Cree in southern Canada and never far to the east or west.

The mutual relations of these versions are not easy to clarify. The basic subtype is told by all the tribes and thus indicates a unified tradition throughout. But in addition there are certain elaborations shared by several of them and showing a specially close relation:

1. *Sun and moon dispute.* The first of these begins the story of a dispute between the sun and moon as to the value of earth women or water women as wives (B2a). The Moon (E1) chooses the earth woman and comes to earth as a porcupine. Later in the upper world Moon's wife has a contest with Sun's wife, a frog, in chewing charcoal, and in the course of the contest frog flies on to Moon's face. This is the cause of the spots on the moon (M1a). This elaboration serves to introduce the porcupine incident and has a certain artistic value, though the chewing contest in the upper world hardly helps the story. This elaboration appears in tales of four different tribes (Gros Ventre 3; Hidatsa 1, 2; Crow 1; Arapaho 2, 3, 4, 5); that is in eight of the 20 versions. It looks like an addition which has been widely adopted in part of the versions, but without a clear-cut geographical pattern. Apparently the tale may be told either with or without it in a single tribe such as the Crow, the Gros Ventre, or the Arapaho.

2. *Warning against shooting meadow larks.* A special feature reinforcing the closeness of the Crow and Hidatsa tradition occurs in the part of the story where the wife is warned against digging. In all the Hidatsa and Crow tales the son is warned not to shoot meadow larks. Nothing is made of this point later in the tale and it seems to be put in merely to take care of the son in an appropriate way.

It is impossible to tell where within this small group of tribes the porcupine husband redaction may have developed. But it is certainly somewhere within the area, for there is nothing even suggesting it elsewhere.

Within the porcupine husband redaction are a number of versions where a certain connection with the basic type is retained, even though it is useless for this redaction. The basic type concerns the adventures of two women; the porcupine subtype, those of only one. The basic type also contains the wish for a star husband by girls who are sleeping out. These elements may be worked into the story by beginning with two girls sleeping out and wishing for star husbands. Later while performing a task one of the girls follows a porcupine in spite of the warning of her friend. This is true of Gros Ventre 2, Arikara 1, Cheyenne, Arapaho 1, 2, 3, 4, and 8. Besides these several begin with two or more women, but have nothing about the sleeping out or the wishing. All the women but one merely disappear from the tale. Such is true of Crow 2, Arapaho 6, 7.

Besides these transitional forms within the porcupine group there are several others on the edge of that area. At the northwest the Sarsi and Black-foot 1 and 2 are like the basic type, but in the middle change to one girl and her adventures. At the northeast of the area in Dakota 1, 2 and Arikara 2 and in the three Pawnee versions at the southeast border, we find the same situation, but always leading to the Star Boy sequel, otherwise confined to the porcupine group.

TYPE III. ANIMAL TRICKSTERS UNDER THE TREE

An examination of the map for Trait N will reveal a group of round dots, standing out like a brilliant constellation in the northern sky. These represent the versions of the Star Husband tale which end with a well-defined episode concerning a series of animal tricksters (N2). The story begins with *the complete basic type*. When the two girls escape from the upper world, however, instead of reaching the ground safely they lodge in the top of a tree. Various animals, e.g., the wolf, the lynx, and the wolverene, pass under the tree. The girls appeal to each to rescue them and agree to marry the animal in return. The first two animals refuse, but the wolverene agrees and takes the girls down. They usually deceive the wolverene and escape.

This rather complex subtype of the tale is remarkably uniform in its whole distribution, from the Kaska in the far Northwest through the Ojibwa north of Lake Superior to the Micmac in Nova Scotia (Kaska; Carrier; Tahltan; Ts'ets'aut; Cree 2; Assiniboine; Ojibwa 1, 2, 3, 4; Micmac 1, 2; Passama-quoddy 1, 2.) This area forms an enormous crescent, never coming south of the international border. How unvaried this tradition is we may illustrate by the fact that in the 13 versions in which the trickster animals are indicated, ten name the wolverene as the dupe.

The near identity in detail makes it certain that this Canadian group of versions, extending as it does over thousands of miles, constitutes a single development of the basic tale. This must have originated at one time and place and then have traveled over the whole area. Where is this invention likely to have occurred? Two of the most northwesterly tribes, Kaska and Ts'ets'aut differ in one respect from the others of the group. Instead of being married to an old and a young man, the girls find themselves with two men having different colored blankets. This shows a local modification which has not been carried elsewhere, and would make it likely that these tribes at the northwest extreme were receivers rather than originators of this story of the tricksters under the tree. The same situation is found with the Micmac and Passamaquoddy tribes at the northeastern horn of the crescent. These four variants agree with each other in warning the girls not to move until they hear the squirrel or chickadee sing and in having a magic descent from the upper world. This replaces the skyrope descent.

Since both extremes have developed characteristic, even if slight, variations, it would seem reasonable to suppose that this subtype developed somewhere near the middle of this large crescent, where that area comes in contact with the general field of distribution of the basic type. This could have happened among the western Cree or the Ojibwa around Lake Superior or even in some group not represented by our versions. It is to be noticed that the western Cree have both this subtype and a slightly incomplete form of the porcupine husband story—and is the only place where these two special developments come together geographically.

Regardless of in what part of this central area—Western Ontario to Saskatchewan—the trickster tale may have started, it could very well have spread out within that area through frequent and long continued contacts of large numbers of people. But for dissemination to such far-off tribes as those at the northwest and the northeast limits, it would be more reasonable to expect that the tales were carried immediately by individuals who for one reason or other traveled long distances. Whether this was facilitated by the activities of the Cree on their east-west trade route or by the moving about in connection with early European exploration, or otherwise, we may be sure that it was not necessary either (1) that whole tribal migrations should be involved or (2) that the tale should have spread gradually through all the intervening territory.

Origin and primary development at the center of the area, then, followed by long-distance dissemination and subsequent development at the extremes would best explain the trickster subtype as we now find it.

TYPE IV. ORIGIN OF THE TRANSFORMER

Five versions from tribes on or very close to Puget Sound (Snuqualmi 1, 2, 3, Puyallup 1, and Cowlitz) form a unified group. They have two distinguishing characteristics. (1) The surviving boy becomes the transformer, a culture hero who goes about changing things into their present shape. This is an independent cycle among these peoples and has been amalgamated with the basic type of the Star Husband tale by having only one of the two girls who marry the star husbands bear a son. The second unifying motif is the mention in all but one of them of the gust of wind which comes up through the skyhole.

They also begin the story with the girls out digging roots. Sometimes it is also stated that the girls are sleeping out (Puyallup 2, Cowlitz) and that may be implied in the rest. This opening of the story with the root digging is also found in three versions outside this group but in close proximity to it (Quileute 2, Quinault, and Songish). The appearance of this incident in these contiguous tribes is good evidence of the unity of their tradition.

TYPE V. THE SKY WAR

On the Pacific Coast of the Olympic Peninsula of Washington, the Quileute and Quinault tribes have used the Star Husband to introduce their tale of the

War of the Sky and Earth People. Generally speaking these versions (Quileute 1, 2, Quinault) resemble the Puget Sound group, as indicated in the preceding paragraph. They have not had to modify the basic type in order to accommodate their sequel.

TYPE VI. THE BIRD RESCUER

In the Wichita (1 and 2) and Caddo (1 and 2) versions certain characteristic changes have been made. We have all the usual action of the basic type but there is only one girl and she is always rescued when the sky rope is too short, by a bird (buzzard or eagle). No influence of this form is found outside this restricted area.

FRAGMENTARY VERSIONS

The following fragmentary versions have the earlier part of the basic type but are not typical for the later part: Kodiak 1, Chilcotin 1.

The following contain only the earlier part: Chehalis 1, Shuswap, Gros Ventre 1.

The following are not typical in the earlier part of the story but have retained the later part well: Kodiak 2, Chilcotin 2, Patwin.

DOUBTFUL VERSIONS

Although the tales cited from the Smith Sound Eskimo and the Seama of New Mexico have sometimes been referred to as versions of the Star Husband, it seems clear from our analysis that neither of them has more than a remote suggestion of the main action of the tale. They have been retained here only for purposes of comparison.

Conclusion

HYPOTHETICAL DEVELOPMENT

From previous analyses the following hypothesis seems reasonable:

1. A simple story of the marriage of two girls to the stars, followed by a successful escape spread over a good part of the present United States and southern Canada, except for New Mexico and Arizona and perhaps the whole Southeast. Where this simple form originated cannot now be determined with any exactness, but it must have been from near the center of the area of present distribution. The Pacific Coast forms show a good deal of variation as if they represent traditions received from outside at sundry times from a common original. The central versions on the other hand show little variation. The Central Plains would seem the most reasonable place of origin for the simple tale or basic type.

2. A special development, retaining all of Type A but adding the incident of the tricksters passing under the tree, developed on Canadian soil. It appears, as we have said, in a vast crescent, the horns of which are southern

Alaska and Nova Scotia and the lowest point of which lies north of the Great Lakes. Though there is remarkable uniformity in the tales throughout this enormous stretch of country, a close examination of the details indicates that development of the subtype at either the eastern or western extreme is very unlikely, and that a more central point, perhaps north of Lake Superior or even among the Plains Cree, would best explain the present distribution. This redaction is found nearly altogether on a great east-west trade route of the Indians and may have been carried in both directions from the center by wandering groups such as the Cree. Because of its great expanse of territory covered by this form of the tale, it would seem to have been spread primarily by traders or travelers rather than through gradual mile by mile, wavelike dissemination.

3. In the Central Plains the story of the girl and the porcupine-star husband developed over a relatively small area, with its center in the present state of Wyoming. Slight variations occur as we move in different directions, but the links between next door neighbors are always clear. Here there is little evidence of the trader or traveler, but indication of slow and slight spread through daily association at close range.

A special feature of this subtype is that it sometimes serves to introduce "Star Boy," a hero tale of a number of the Plains tribes. In this way it comes to have a certain ceremonial or religious significance. But in spite of this, there seems to be little or no correlation between the presence of this tale and any particular religious or ceremonial patterns.

4. Around Puget Sound the basic type was modified to fit into the tale of the Transformer current among those tribes, and on the coast of Washington into the story of the Sky War. These both seem to be adaptations of a borrowed story to material with which they were already familiar. The Caddoan tribes of Oklahoma, on the southern edge of the general area, developed the tale of the girl rescued by the bird.

5. Especially on the periphery of the general area of distribution appear a number of fragmentary versions, though these are often found side by side with well-preserved tales. They, therefore, represent individual cases of disintegration of tradition.

Age

It is, of course, quite impossible to tell just when this tale began to be told. From its point of origin, the basic type (I) spread all over the Plains, to the Pacific Coast, and as far south as Louisiana. The earliest recordings of this basic type are from the Oto of Nebraska (1892) and the Songish of Vancouver Island (before 1895). There are also early fragmentary collections indicating the presence of this type among the Maidu (1902), the Wishram (1905) the Cree of James Bay (1908), the Shoshone of Wyoming (1909) and the Koasati of Louisiana (1910). These dates are of little importance except as indications of a time when it is certain the tale was in a particular tribe.

Somewhere in the Central Plains the porcupine redaction was constructed by a skillful change of several details. We know that this had taken place completely by 1892 among the Kiowa, who not only had the tale at that time but had made a very good drawing to illustrate it. The other collections of Type II were mostly made from 1900 to 1910 but one made as late as 1949 shows no appreciable change.

The Transitional form we have designated as Type IIa had developed in the Plains as early as about 1870 (Dakota). Other relatively early records are Pawnee (1892, 1902), Arikara (1903), and Blackfoot (1905).

The best indication of age for our tale comes from the Micmac versions of Type III. They were recorded in 1870 but from a woman who heard them when she was a child, perhaps about 1840. If this tale developed from the basic type somewhere about the Great Lakes it must have done so as early as perhaps 1820 or 1830, since it had produced the specific Micmac-Passamaquoddy form by about 1840. It had reached the southern borders of Alaska at least by 1894 (Ts'ets'aut). The central versions of this type were collected later (Assiniboine, 1907).

The Puget Sound Transformer tale, Type IV, was apparently current at least by about 1880, since one of the Snuqualmi versions was learned from a man born about 1850.

The Sky War type (V) was first taken down on the Pacific Coast in 1898.

The Wichita-Caddo type (VI) in Oklahoma was recorded in 1900 and 1903.

An examination of versions in a single tribe or group taken down a half century apart shows practically no change. Examples are Arapaho 1–7 (before 1903) and Arapaho 8 (1949), or Micmac 2 (c. 1840), Passamaquoddy 2 (1882) and Passamaquoddy 1 (c. 1910).

It would seem from these facts that this tale in its basic form must go back at least to the eighteenth century. But that is as close as we can come to an estimate of its age.[10]

---

10 There has been an attempt to locate an earlier version of the tale. In 1962, C. E. Schorer published from a manuscript collection a version of what he claimed was a Star Husband tale. The tale had been collected sometime before 1825 and was therefore several years older than any version cited by Thompson. Unfortunately, the tale is clearly not a version of the Star Husband but is rather a variant of the North American Indian form of Swan Maiden (Motif D361.1). See C. E. Schorer, "Indian Tales of C. C. Trowbridge: The Star Woman," *Midwest Folklore*, Vol. 12 (1962), 17–24.

One possible piece of evidence that the tale did exist well before the eighteenth century is the great likelihood that the North American Indian tale of star husband is cognate with the South American Indian tale of star wife. This is suggested in part by Thompson's listing of the relevant motifs as C15.1, Wish for star husband realized, and C15.1.1, Wish for star wife realized. In the South American tale type, it is a man on earth who wishes for a star wife. She takes him to the sky and, in some versions, warns him not to touch the fire. He does so and is burned. Then either he dies or returns to earth.

OTHER CONSIDERATIONS

The various folktale studies of the past, and especially the criticisms directed toward the historic-geographic method, suggest several questions to the student of this tale. If one makes no attempt to generalize about tales as a whole but confines himself to this story alone, he can come to some very safe conclusions.

(1) Language frontiers or even the boundaries of linguistic families have played little or no role in retarding or facilitating the spread of this tale. (2) There is no perceptible connection with tales outside the American Indian tradition—only a few parallels, showing no truly genetic relationship. (3) No correlation appears between the presence of this tale (or any of its forms) and any basic mythological or religious concepts. Its popularity, for example, does not indicate the presence or absence of any particular interest in stars. (4) The versions we have are in all stages of structural development from a bare outline or a bald account by an unskillful teller to an elaborate performance by a master of the narrative art. Yet the plot outline usually shows itself clearly and seems little influenced by the activities of the individual racon-

---

In at least two South American tales, it is a girl who marries a star husband. This might indicate that star husband is the older form, which has been largely replaced in South America by the star wife tale. In any event, the case for cognation is strengthened by a number of interesting parallel details. For instance, the Smith Sound Eskimo version, which Thompson included reluctantly, saying that it probably did not belong to the Star Husband cycle, has as punishment for the looking taboo the burning of the side of the girl's face. As noted above, the burning is a common consequence in the South American tale type, and in one Chamacoco version collected by Alfred Métraux, an authority on South American Indian folklore, Star Woman is said specifically to be "half-burned." The connection between a star spouse and being burned could be part of a tradition common to both continents.

Another curious detail is concerned with Trait F, Distinctive Qualities of Husband. Thompson includes in his basic tale the trait of the two stars being an old man and a young man corresponding, sometimes inversely, to the size or brilliance of the stars. In the two Brazilian Indian tales in which the protagonist is a woman, there is a curious alternation of the star husband's appearance in terms of age and youth. (Since there is only one girl and not two, the parallel could obviously not be exact.) It is related that star husband is young at night, but that by day he appeared decrepit and old. This apparent similarity to the North American Indian tradition could be explained by polygenesis, in that it is a natural phenomenon that even the brightest stars at night are invariably dim and feeble during the day, but then again the similarity might be part of a common tradition.

If Star Husband and Star Wife are related tales, then both tales would have to be considered in attempting to reconstruct the hypothetical archetype. Moreover, if the texts from the two Brazilian Indian peoples are part of the Star Husband cycle, the age of the tale would have to be greater than several hundred years, inasmuch as during that time interval there has been no contact between North and South American Indians. For the Brazilian Indian texts, see Charles Wagley, "World View of the Tapirape Indians," *Journal of American Folklore,* Vol. 53 (1940), 256; Fritz Krause, *In den Wildnissen Brasiliens* (Leipzig, 1911), pp. 346–47. This last Carajá text is summarized by Alfred Métraux in his extended discussion of the Star Wife tale. See his *Myths of the Toba and Pilagá Indians of the Gran Chaco,* Memoirs of the American Folklore Society 40 (Philadelphia, 1946).—ED. NOTE

teurs. The best of them preserve the tradition most faithfully and seem merely to elaborate certain details but not to change anything basically.

The study of this purely oral tale displays the operation of the same general laws of change as those worked out by many students of Old World narratives. We find that in the end we are confronted with facts almost completely geographic in nature. The dissemination has occurred from centers—sometimes slowly in waves, sometimes with great mobility through the influence of far travelers.

Though our study has been unable to penetrate into the mysteries of ultimate origin or to fix exact dates, it has by means of its analytical method shown how a tale like the Star Husband when once invented adapts itself to new conditions and takes on new forms, but in spite of time and distance maintains its basic pattern.

Trait A. NUMBER OF WOMEN

★ 1. One
● 2. Two
◤ 3. Two at beginning, then one
◉ 4. Three
▬ 5. Five

---

[11] As a basis for the following maps, I have been granted the courteous permission to use the unpublished "Map of Indian Tribes of North America" by Harold Driver, John Cooper, Paul Kirchoff, William Massey, Dorothy Rainier, Leslie Spier.

Trait B. INTRODUCTORY ACTION

○ 0. Trait not present
● 1. Wish for star husband (without 2)
☆ 2. Pursuit of porcupine
✪ 2a. 2 + sun and moon dispute
◖ 3. Miscellaneous

Trait C. CIRCUMSTANCES OF INTRODUCTORY ACTION

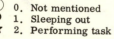 0. Not mentioned
● 1. Sleeping out
★ 2. Performing task

Trait **D**. METHOD OF ASCENT

○ 0. Not indicated
☆ 1. Stretching tree
★ 1a. Warning from friend
● 2. Translation during sleep
■ 3-7. Miscellaneous

Trait E. IDENTITY OF HUSBAND

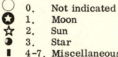

0.   Not indicated
1.   Moon
2.   Sun
3.   Star
4-7. Miscellaneous

Trait **F.** DISTINCTIVE QUALITIES OF HUSBAND

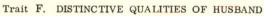

○　0.　None indicated
✪　1.　Old man
☆　2.　Young man
▲　3.　Middle-aged man
●　4.　Old man and young man
★　4a.　Old man's eye water and·young man's war paint
◗　5.　Two men with different colored blankets
■　6-9.　Miscellaneous

Trait **G.** BIRTH OF SON

○ 0. No

⭐ 1. Yes

466

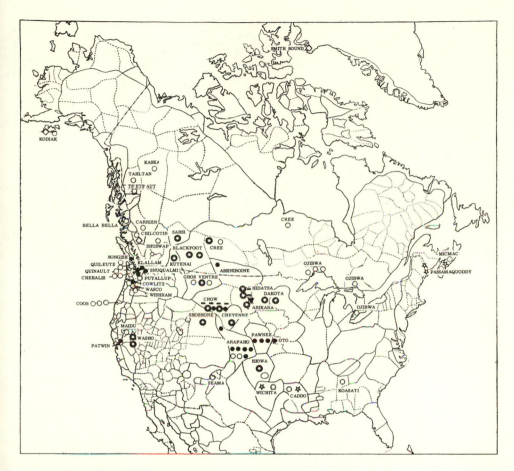

Trait **H.** TABOO BROKEN IN UPPER WORLD

○ 0. No taboo broken
● 1. Digging (or disturbing ground)
✪ a. Roots (of various kinds)
☆ b. Large rock
▼ c. Not dig in valleys
◇ 2. Looking
▬ 3. Shooting at meadow lark

Trait I. DISCOVERY OF SKY-HOLE

0. Trait not present
1. By own efforts
2. At another's suggestion
3. With another's assistance

468

Trait **J**. ASSISTANCE IN DESCENT

- ○ 0. Lacking
- ● 1. Spider
- ✪ 2. Old women
- ▼ 3. Old man
- ☆ 4. Husband
- ◣ 5. Sister of star
- ◇ 6. Bird

469

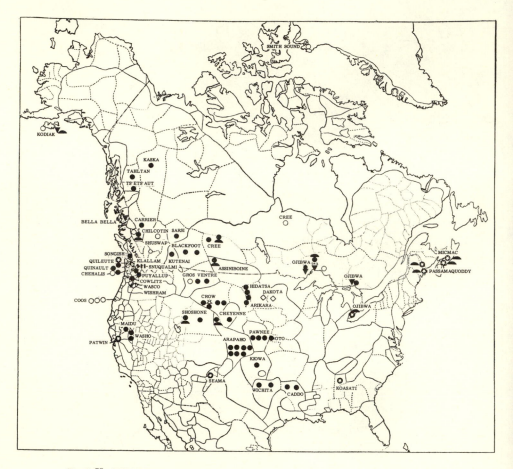

Trait **K.** MEANS OF DESCENT

○   0.   No descent
◉   1.   Descent - but means not specified
▼   2.   Basket
●   3.   Rope
▮   4.   Ladder
☆   5.   Bucket
◇   6.   Falling
◣   7.   Descent with taboo

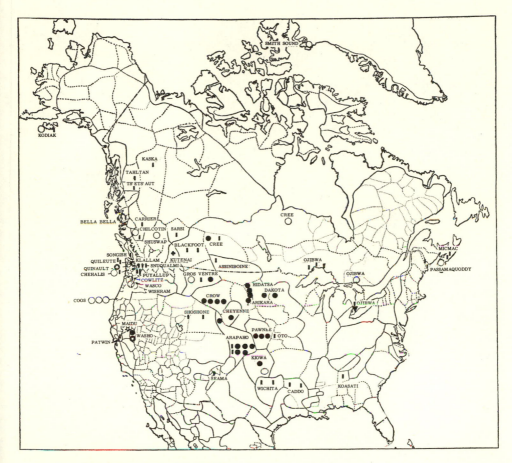

Trait L. RESULTS OF DESCENT

○ 0. Trait lacking
⍩ 1. Safe descent
+ a. Later killed
⊛ 2. Woman (women), not killed
☆ a. Woman killed, later revived
● 3. Woman killed, son saved
▼ 4. One woman falls

Trait **M.** EXPLANATORY ELEMENTS

- ○ 0. No explanations given
- ● 1. Heavenly bodies
- ✪ 2. Geographical features
- ★ 3. Vegetable and animal features
- ☆ 4. Human society
- ◆ 5. Personal characteristics
- ▲ 6. Medicine
- ✚ 7. Miscellaneous

472

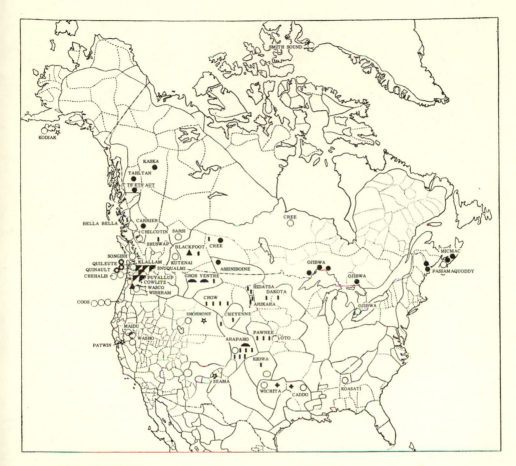

Trait N. SEQUEL

○	0.	No sequel
▮	1.	Plains Star-Boy sequel
◣	1a.	Boy becomes transformer
◉	2.	Trickster (girls in tree)
◆	3.	Sky war
▲	4.	Origin myth
⬟	5.	Buffalo husband tale
☆	6.	Return to sky
✚	7.	Miscellaneous

TYPES OF THE STAR HUSBAND

- ● Type I. The Basic Tale (complete and incomplete)
- ▲ Type II. The Porcupine redaction
- ■ Type IIa. Intermediate Versions
- ☆ Type III. Trickster Animals Under the Tree
- ✛ Type IV. Origin of the Transformer
- ✪ Type V. The Sky War
- ◗ Type VI. The Bird Rescuer
- ○ Fragmentary Versions

Suggestions for Further Reading in Folklore

There are thousands of books and articles on folklore. The titles mentioned here represent only a small sample of the total folklore literature. However, these selected items may lead the student into the particular phase of folklore scholarship in which he is most interested.

Two surveys of the discipline, written in English, that provide a useful introduction are Martha Warren Beckwith, *Folklore in America: Its Scope and Method* (Poughkeepsie, N. Y., 1931); and E. J. Lindgren, "The Collection and Analysis of Folklore," in *The Study of Society,* ed. F. C. Bartlett et al. (London, 1939), pp. 328–78. A more recent survey is Richard M. Dorson's "Current Folklore Theories," *Current Anthropology,* Vol. 4 (1963), 93–112. Those especially interested in learning how and what to collect may wish to consult Seán Ó Súilleabháin, *Handbook of Irish Folklore,* a guide, that appeared in 1942 but has been recently reprinted (Hatboro, Penn., 1963); Charlotte Sophia Burne, *The Handbook of Folklore,* which appeared in 1913 as a revision of George Laurence Gomme's 1890 guide and which has also been reprinted (London, 1957); and the modern aid, Kenneth S. Goldstein, *A Guide for Field Workers in Folklore* (Hatboro, Penn., 1964).

Some of the more recent general introductory works on folklore are listed below. Items written in languages other than English have been included for several reasons: (1) to assist a student interested in the folklore scholarship of a particular area, e.g., Spain, in finding relevant references; (2) to remind all students of the international nature of folklore materials and folklore studies. Most of the following books contain extensive bibliographical notes.

General Works on Folklore

Bach, Adolf, *Deutsche Volkskunde,* 3rd ed. Heidelberg, 1960.

Bhagwat, Durga, *An Outline of Indian Folklore.* Bombay, 1958.

Boberg, Inger M., *Folkemindeforskningens Historie i Mellem- Og Nordeuropa.* [*The History of Folklore Research in Central and Northern Europe*]. Copenhagen, 1953.

Carvalho Neto, Paulo de, *Concepto de Folklore.* Montevideo, 1956.

Cocchiara, Giuseppe, *Storia del folklore in Europa,* 2nd ed. Turin, 1954.

Corso, Raffaele, *Folklore: Storia-Obbietto-Metodo-Bibliografia,* 4th ed. Naples, 1953.

Dorson, Richard M., *American Folklore.* Chicago, 1959.

————, ed., *Folklore Research Around the World,* Indiana University Folklore Series No. 16 (Bloomington, 1961). This group of survey articles on folklore scholarship in various parts of the world was also published in the *Journal of American Folklore,* Vol. 74 (1961), 287–468.

Gennep, Arnold van, *Le Folklore.* Paris, 1924.

Guichot y Sierra, Alejandro, *Noticia Histórica del Folklore.* Seville, 1922.

Hautala, Jouko, *Johdatus kansanrunoustieteen peruskäsitteisiin* [*Introduction to the Basic Concepts of the Science of Folklore*]. Helsinki, 1957.

Hoyos Sáinz, Luis de, and Nieves de Hoyos Sancho, *Manual de Folklore: La Vida Popular Tradicional.* Madrid, 1947.

Hultkrantz, Åke, *General Ethnological Concepts: International Dictionary of Regional European Ethnology and Folklore,* Vol. 1. Copenhagen, 1961.

Krappe, Alexander H., *The Science of Folklore.* London, 1930. This historico-literary survey of the different genres of folklore has been reprinted in a paperback edition (New York, 1964).

Leach, Maria, ed., *Standard Dictionary of Folklore, Mythology, and Legend.* New York, 1949, 1950, 2 vols.

Lutz, Gerhard, ed., *Volkskunde: Ein Handbuch zur Geschichte ihrer Probleme.* Berlin, 1958.

Morote Best, Efraín, *Elementos de Folklore (Definicion, Contenido, Procedimiento).* Cuzco, Peru, 1950.

Moya, Ismael, *Didactica del Folklore.* Buenos Aires, 1948.

Ramos, Arthur, *Estudos de Folklore: Definiçao e limites, Teorias de interpretaçao,* 2nd ed. Rio de Janeiro, 1958.

Sokolov, Y. M., *Russian Folklore.* New York, 1950.

Thompson, Stith, ed., *Four Symposia on Folklore,* Indiana University Publications Folklore Series No. 8 (Bloomington, 1953).

Toschi, Paolo, *Guida allo Studio delle Tradizioni Popolari,* 3rd ed. Turin, 1962.

Varagnac, André, *Definition du Folklore.* Paris, 1938.

Vega, Carlos, *La Ciencia del Folklore.* Buenos Aires, 1960.

There are, of course, works of a less general nature, works devoted to just one form of folklore. For folk music, the beginning student might refer to Bruno Nettl's excellent *Introduction to Folk Music in the United States,* rev. ed. (Detroit, 1962); and his *Folk and Traditional Music of the Western Continents* (Englewood Cliffs, N. J., 1965). In these fine surveys, the student will find selected references to the vast folk music literature. Those especially interested in the ballad may want to read M. J. C. Hodgart's *The Ballads* (London, 1950), or G. H. Gerould's classic, *The Ballad of Tradition,* now available in paperback (New York, 1957). For a representative sampling of ballad scholarship, the student should see MacEdward Leach and Tristram P. Coffin's selection of important essays by leading ballad specialists, *The Critics and the Ballad* (Carbondale, Ill., 1961). For surveys of ballad scholarship, one could consult Sigurd B. Hustvedt, *Ballad Books and Ballad Men* (Cambridge, Mass., 1930); and D. K. Wilgus, *Anglo-American Folksong Scholarship Since 1898* (New Brunswick, N. J., 1959). A useful bibliographical aid is Jaap Kunst's *Ethnomusicology,* 3rd ed. (The Hague, 1959).

A student wishing to learn more about the folktale should read Stith Thompson's *The Folktale* (New York, 1946). Although it needs to be brought up to date, it remains the best introduction to the folktale in English. References to some of the more recent European scholarship may be found in Roger Pinon, *Le Conte Merveilleux Comme Sujet d'Etudes* (Liège, 1955); and Max Lüthi's paperback, *Das Europäische Volksmärchen,* 2nd ed. (Bern and Munich, 1960). For a survey of the anthropological as opposed to the literary approach to the folktale, one should read J. L. Fischer, "The Sociopsychological Analysis of Folktales," *Current Anthropology,* Vol. 4 (1963), 235–95. Also recommended: the section on folklore (pp. 397–524) in Franz Boas, *Race, Language, and Culture* (New York, 1940); Bronislaw Malinowski's essay "Myth in Primitive Psychology," which is contained in his paperback *Magic, Science, and Religion* (Garden City, N.Y., 1954); and Melville Jacobs, *The Content and Style of an Oral Literature* (Chicago, 1959).

If the student wishes to examine the materials of folklore rather than folklore scholarship, he should read anthologies made by folklorists rather than by popularizers. For the ballad, he might look at Mac-Edward Leach, *The Ballad Book* (New York, 1955). For children's games, there is the 1963 Dover paperback edition of William Wells Newell, *Games and Songs of American Children,* first published in 1883; and the 1964 Dover paperback edition of Lady Alice B. Gomme's *Traditional Games of England, Scotland, and Ireland,* a standard collection whose two volumes appeared in 1894 and 1898 respectively. For specimens of children's folklore, one should browse through Peter and Iona Opie, *The Lore and Language of Schoolchildren* (Oxford, 1959). An excellent collection of texts is Richard M. Dorson, *Buying the Wind* (Chicago, 1964), which gives authentic examples of most of the major genres of folklore from seven American regional repertoires. Another excellent source of examples of American folklore is the *Frank C. Brown Collection of North Carolina Folklore,* 7 vols. (Durham, 1952–1964). A convenient, inexpensive, paperback anthology of African folk narratives is Susan Feldmann's *African Myths and Tales* (New York, 1963). A fine collection of narratives from one African culture is Melville J. and Frances S. Herskovits, *Dahomean Narrative* (Evanston, Ill., 1958), which incidentally contains an important introductory essay, "A Cross-Cultural Approach to Myth" (pp. 81–122). For recommended collections from other areas, the student should check standard bibliographies and the book-review sections of leading folklore journals.

Bibliography

Even the professional folklorist has difficulty in keeping track of folklore scholarship around the world. To try to keep abreast of the latest trends in folklore theory and research, the folklorist utilizes a number of standard bibliographical tools, tools that can save many hours of labor. From 1917 on, there has been an international folklore bibliography, and this is one of the most valuable of the folklorist's aids. This *Internationale Volkskundliche Bibliographie* is a cooperative enterprise that depends upon the contributions of folklorists all over the world. Naturally, since it takes some time to coordinate all the items, the bibliography is always several years behind. For current scholarship, one should consult the various annual bibliographies. For example, the spring issue of the *Southern Folklore Quarterly* each year is devoted to a bibliography of the preceding year's folklore studies. There is also an "Annual Bibliography of Folklore" published in the *Journal of American Folklore Supplement* since 1955 but more recently (1964) issued as a separate number of *Abstracts of Folklore Studies,* a new publication of the American Folklore Society initiated in 1963. Another source is the folklore section of the annual bibliography contained in the April supplement of the *Publications of the Modern Language Association* (*PMLA*). These listings of folklore studies are obviously more extensive than the comparatively few folklore entries in such aids as the *Readers' Guide to Periodical Literature* and the *International Index to Periodicals.*

The student should realize that there are many specialized bibliographies that list books and articles dealing with the folklore of one region or one people. For example, there is Charles Haywood's *A Bibliography of North American Folklore and Folksong,* 2nd ed., 2 vols. (New York, 1961); and there is Ralph Steele Boggs, *Bibliography of Latin American Folklore* (New York, 1940). There are also bibliographies for particular genres of folklore. For the riddle, one has Archer Taylor, *A Bibliography of Riddles,* Folklore Fellows Communications No. 126 (Helsinki, 1939); and Aldo Santi, *Bibliografia delle Enigmistica* (Florence, 1952). For the proverb, there are such guides as Wilfred Bonser and T. A. Stephens, *Proverb Literature: A Bibliography of Works Relating to Proverbs* (London, 1930); and Otto E Moll, *Sprichwörter-bibliographie* (Frankfurt, 1958). A number of useful bibliographical aids in folklore is surveyed in the third chapter (pp. 109–50) of Katharine Smith Diehl's *Religions, Mythologies, Folklores: An Annotated Bibliography,* 2nd ed. (New York, 1962). Another valuable bibliographical source consists of catalogs of special library collections of books on folklore. For example, there is the *Catalogus van Folklore in de Koninklijke Bibliotheek,* 3 vols. (The Hague, 1919–1922); and a list of the folklore holdings contained in the John G. White Collection of Folklore, Orientalia, and Chess, which is located in the Cleveland Public Library, *Catalog of Folklore and Folksongs,* John G. White Department, Cleveland Public Library, 2 vols. (Boston, 1965).

PERIODICALS

One of the very best ways of discovering what a discipline consists of is to look at the professional journals in that discipline. Accordingly, someone interested in the study of folklore could learn a great deal by reading extensively in the various folklore journals. However, since there are several hundred folklore journals published in different parts of the world, one is forced to be selective. For a listing of these journals as well as the literary and anthropological journals in which important folklore articles frequently appear, one should consult volumes of the *Internationale Volkskundliche Bibliographie,* each of which provides a list of the journals abstracted. Of course, in doing this, one should bear in mind that several important journals are no longer published and would thus not be listed in current volumes. Examples of such journals include the *Archivio per lo studio delle tradizioni popolari* (1882–1906), *Mélusine* (1878–1912), *La Tradition* (1887–1907), and the *Zeitschrift für deutsche mythologie und sittenkunde* (1853–1859).

The leading American folklore journals are *Journal of American Folklore* (1888); *Western Folklore* (1947), formerly *California Folklore Quarterly* (1942); *Southern Folklore Quarterly* (1937); *Journal of the Folklore Institute* (1964), formerly *Midwest Folklore* (1951), which was formerly *Hoosier Folklore Bulletin* (1942); and *New York Folklore Quarterly* (1945). Other American folklore journals include *Folklore Americas* (1941), *Kentucky Folklore Record* (1955), *Keystone Folklore Quarterly* (1956), *North Carolina Folklore* (1954), *Northeast Folklore* (1958), *Publications of the Texas Folklore Society* (1911), *Tennessee Folklore Society Bulletin* (1935), and *West Virginia Folklore* (1950). For a more complete listing of American folklore periodicals, see William J. Griffin, "The *TFS Bulletin* and Other Folklore Serials in the United States: A Preliminary Survey," *Tennessee Folklore Society Bulletin,* Vol. 25 (1959), 91–96.

When one realizes that there are just as many folklore journals in Germany as there are in the United States, one begins to grasp the immensity of the problem of keeping track of the contents of the world's folklore journals. A small but representative sample of these journals follows:

AUSTRIA
> *Österreichische Zeitschrift für Volkskunde* (1947), formerly *Wiener Zeitschrift für Volkskunde* (1919), which was formerly *Zeitschrift für österreichische Volkskunde* (1895).

BELGIUM
> *Le Folklore Branbançon* (1921).

BRAZIL
> *Revista Brasileira de Folclore* (1961).

CHINA
> *Folklore Studies* (1942).

ENGLAND
> *Folklore* (1890), formerly *Folklore Journal* (1883), which was formerly *Folklore Record* (1878).
> *Journal of the English Folk Dance and Song Society* (1932), formerly *Journal of the Folksong Society* (1899).

FRANCE
> *Arts et Traditions Populaires* (1953).
> *Bulletin Folklorique d'Ile-de-France* (1938).

GERMANY
  Hessische Blätter für Volkskunde (1902), formerly *Blätter für Hessische Volkskunde* (1899).
  Zeitschrift für Volkskunde (1929), formerly *Zeitschrift des Vereins für Volkskunde* (1891).

GREECE
  Laographia (1909).

HOLLAND
  Volkskunde (1888).

INDIA
   Folklore (1959), formerly *Indian Folklore* (1956).

IRELAND
  Béaloideas: Journal of the Folklore of Ireland Society (1927).

ISRAEL
  Yeda-'am: Journal of the Israel Folklore Society (1952).

ITALY
  Lares (1930).
  Tradizioni (1961).

PERU
  Folklore Americano (1953).

POLAND
  Lud (1895).

RUMANIA
  Revista de Etnografie și Folchor (1964), formerly *Revista de Folclor* (1956).

SPAIN
  Revista de dialectologia y tradiciones populares (1944).

SWEDEN
  Arv (1945), formerly *Folkminnen och folktankar* (1914).
  Folk-Liv (1937).

SWITZERLAND
  Schweizerisches Archiv für Volkskunde (1897).
  Schweizer Volkskunde (1911).

UNION OF SOUTH AFRICA
  Tydskrif vir volkskunde en volkstaal (1944).

The student should also know that among the many journals not listed above there are some devoted to the folklore of special groups, such as gypsies or persons displaced for political reasons (e.g., those who have fled from East Germany): *Journal of the Gypsy Lore Society* (1888), *Jahrbuch für Volkskunde der Heimatvertriebenen* (1955). Still other journals are devoted to particular problems, such as archiving: *The Folklore and Folk Music Archivist* (1958); or to a particular genre, such as the folktale: *Fabula* (1958). Two journals that dealt with obscene folklore are *Anthropophyteia* (1904–1913) and *Kryptadia* (1883–1911). In many instances, the content of folklore journals is made more accessible by the existence of comprehensive indexes. For example, there are indexes to the *Journal of American Folklore* and the English journal *Folklore:* Tristram P. Coffin, *An Analytical Index to the Journal of American Folklore,* Publications of the American Folklore Society, Bibliographical and Special Series, Vol. 7 (Philadelphia, 1958); Wilfrid Bonser, *A Bibliography of Folklore as Contained in the First Eighty Years of the Publications of the Folklore Society* (London, 1961). There is also a useful index to Finland's important FFC monograph series: *FF Communications Nos. 1–195* (Helsinki, 1964).

DISCOGRAPHY

Within recent years, there has been a flood of phonograph recordings of folklore, especially folk music. Some folklore journals, e.g., the *Journal of American Folklore* and *Western Folklore* have instituted record reviews similar to book reviews. Perhaps the best way for the beginner to discover the vast range of these recordings is to read through several record catalogs. Interested students may send for the current catalog of *Folkways Records,* one of the best of the commercial companies, by writing to Folkways Records & Service Corp., 117 West 46th Street, New York 36, New York, and the current catalog of phonograph records issued by the Library of Congress. This catalog is available at a cost of twenty-five cents from the Recording Laboratory, Music Division, Library of Congress, Washington 25, D.C. To determine what folk music records are available at a given time, one may consult such guides as the Folk Music section of the *Schwann Long Playing Record Catalog,* published monthly by W. Schwann, Inc., of 137 Newbury Street, Boston, Massachusetts, and found in most record shops. Some records are very instructive. For example, Kenneth S. Goldstein's *The Unfortunate Rake,* Folkways Records FS 3805 (1960), designed for classroom demonstration, puts together on one record twenty versions of a ballad (one version of which is "The Streets of Laredo"); this provides an excellent example of the paradoxical combination of stability and change in oral tradition. Other useful records include Charles Seeger's *Versions and Variants of Barbara Allen,* Library of Congress record AAFS L 54; and the two Library of Congress records of Anglo-American folktales from North Carolina: Duncan Emrich's *Jack Tales,* AAFS L 47 and L 48.

Opportunities for Graduate Study

In the United States, there are several graduate programs in folklore where individuals may study toward M.A. and Ph.D. degrees *in folklore.* Information about graduate work in folklore may be obtained by writing to (1) The Folklore Institute, Indiana University, Bloomington, Indiana; (2) The Graduate Folklore Program, University of Pennsylvania, Philadelphia, Pennsylvania; (3) Center for the Study of Comparative Folklore and Mythology, University of California, Los Angeles, California; (4) Folklore Committee, Department of Anthropology, University of California, Berkeley, California; (5) Curriculum in Folklore, University of North Carolina, Chapel Hill, North Carolina; (6) American Folk Culture Program, c/o New York State Historical Association, Cooperstown, New York.